On Jordan's Banks

Ohio River Valley Series

Rita Kohn, Series Editor

On Jordan's Banks

Emancipation and Its Aftermath in the Ohio River Valley

DARREL E. BIGHAM

THE UNIVERSITY PRESS OF KENTUCKY

Publication of this volume was made possible in part by a grant
from the National Endowment for the Humanities.

Editorial and Sales Offices: The University Press of Kentucky
663 South Limestone Street, Lexington, Kentucky 40508–4008
www.kentuckypress.com

Cover photograph: Courtesy of Bernie Spencer at
http://www.nkyviews.com/bracken/augusta08.htm

Map on pages 2–3: By Dick Gilbreath

09 08 07 06 05   5 4 3 2 1

Library of Congress Cataloging-in-Publication Data

Bigham, Darrel E.
  On Jordan's banks : emancipation and its aftermath in the Ohio
River Valley / Darrel E. Bigham.
      p. cm. — (Ohio River Valley series)
  Includes bibliographical references and index.
  ISBN 0-8131-2366-6 (hardcover : alk. paper)
  1. African Americans—Ohio River Valley—History—19th century. 2. Slaves—
Emancipation—Ohio River Valley. 3. Ohio River Valley—History—19th century. I.
Title. II. Series.
  F520.6.N4B54 2005
  977'.00496073—dc22   2005018312

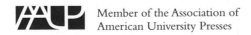 Member of the Association of
American University Presses

Contents

Illustrations follow page 214

Series Foreword

The Ohio River Valley Series, conceived and published by the University Press of Kentucky, is an ongoing series of books that examine and illuminate the Ohio River and its tributaries, the lands drained by these streams, and the peoples who made this fertile and desirable area their place of residence, of refuge, of commerce and industry, of cultural development, and, ultimately, of engagement with American democracy. In doing this, the series builds upon an earlier project, "Always a River: the Ohio River and the American Experience," a multifaceted project sponsored by the National Endowment for the Humanities and the humanities councils of Illinois, Indiana, Kentucky, Ohio, Pennsylvania, and West Virginia, with a mix of private and public organizations.

Each book's story is told through the men and women acting within their particular time and place. Each directs attention to the place of the Ohio River in the context of the larger American story and reveals the rich resources for the history of the Ohio River and of the nation afforded by records, papers, artifacts, works of art, and oral stories preserved by families and institutions. Each traces the impact the river and the land have had on individuals and cultures and, conversely, the changes these individuals and cultures have wrought on the valley with the passage of years.

With *On Jordan's Banks: Emancipation and Its Aftermath in the Ohio River Valley,* Darrel Bigham brings forward a story that has been a sleeping giant for more than a century. Through meticulous scholarship, Bigham utilizes primary and secondary sources not only to interpret the rural and small-town past previously disregarded by historians; but equally, he illustrates how the strengths of the formerly enslaved persons became the fuel of the civil rights movement. He shows how the power of the Reverend Martin Luther King's pulpit descended directly from the leadership of preachers whose churches were the locus of free blacks as they built coherent support systems and grassroots empowerment in new hamlets, neighborhoods, and communities.

On Jordan's Banks is must reading for today's black youth so they can grow through the grace, dignity, and determination of people who refused merely to overcome. They triumphed and became the emancipated builders of the economy: artists, teachers, inventors, thinkers, entrepreneurs. They stood on Jordan's banks, crossed the Jordan, and never forgot the visionaries who preceded them. Those who now squander this bequest will be reminded of their latent legacy through a thorough reading of this long-awaited volume. Each generation must remember and thrive through diligence and faith in their own ability to make and leave a footprint of valor. Bigham illuminates the emergent black experience just before, during, and immediately following the Civil War by contrasting and comparing settlements in counties along the southern and northern banks of the Ohio River. He shows how geography shapes these experiences, eventually spreading them into the northern interior as railroads and later buses carry rural dwellers to industrial jobs. Their collective experience in turn shapes that of the larger nation.

On Jordan's Banks is a book to be read, not summarized. Bigham's epilogue is especially noteworthy as a challenge to us all to pay attention to neglected sources. While he concludes that "virulent racism," now as before, constrains options for African Americans, the book itself challenges the reader to do no less than what is possible even in the least hospitable of worlds. Built on the interpretation and synthesis of past activities, *On Jordan's Banks* is a call to present and future action.

Rita Kohn
Series Editor

Preface

This study resulted from two separate but related research and writing projects. One was the work begun in the early 1970s that led to the 1987 publication of *We Ask Only a Fair Trial: A History of the Black Community of Evansville, Indiana* by Indiana University Press. The other was the scholarship generated by the "Always a River" project, a collaborative effort of the state humanities councils in the six states touched by the Ohio River. For that endeavor, I wrote a chapter on economic development in the anthology *Always a River.* The project created a series of works on the Ohio Valley as well, of which Rita Kohn of Indianapolis remains the editor, that have been published by the University Press of Kentucky. In preparation for my *Towns and Villages of the Lower Ohio,* a 1998 volume in that series, I expanded my ongoing research on African Americans well beyond the Evansville region. I then proposed another volume that would focus on race relations and black community-building in the corridor stretching from Catlettsburg, Kentucky, and cross-river Ironton, Ohio, downstream to the mouth of the Ohio at Cairo, Illinois.

Fortunately, historical resources aplenty are to be found on the Internet as well as in the repositories of libraries in the region. As with earlier efforts, I have benefited enormously from the wealth of material available at Evansville's Willard Library, which possesses an extensive collection of primary and secondary sources on state and local history. To Willard's staff, I express my gratitude for years of generous and thoughtful assistance. I also appreciate the support provided by the rich regional history collection in the Special Collections Department of the Rice Library at the University of Southern Indiana.

My interest in the history of African Americans of this region began in 1972 in the living room of John and Josephine Elliott of New Harmony, Indiana. The Elliotts introduced me to the late Solomon and Alberta Stevenson of Evansville, both active in Evansville civil rights activities. There emerged an extensive oral history program on black Evansville that I directed, and

that project prompted me to begin researching and writing about blacks in Evansville and the surrounding area. Josephine and John, both deceased, became good friends of my wife and me. These two remarkable people contributed enormously to the development of their beloved town and of the University of Southern Indiana. To their memory I dedicate this book.

On Jordan's Banks

Lower Ohio River Valley, 1880

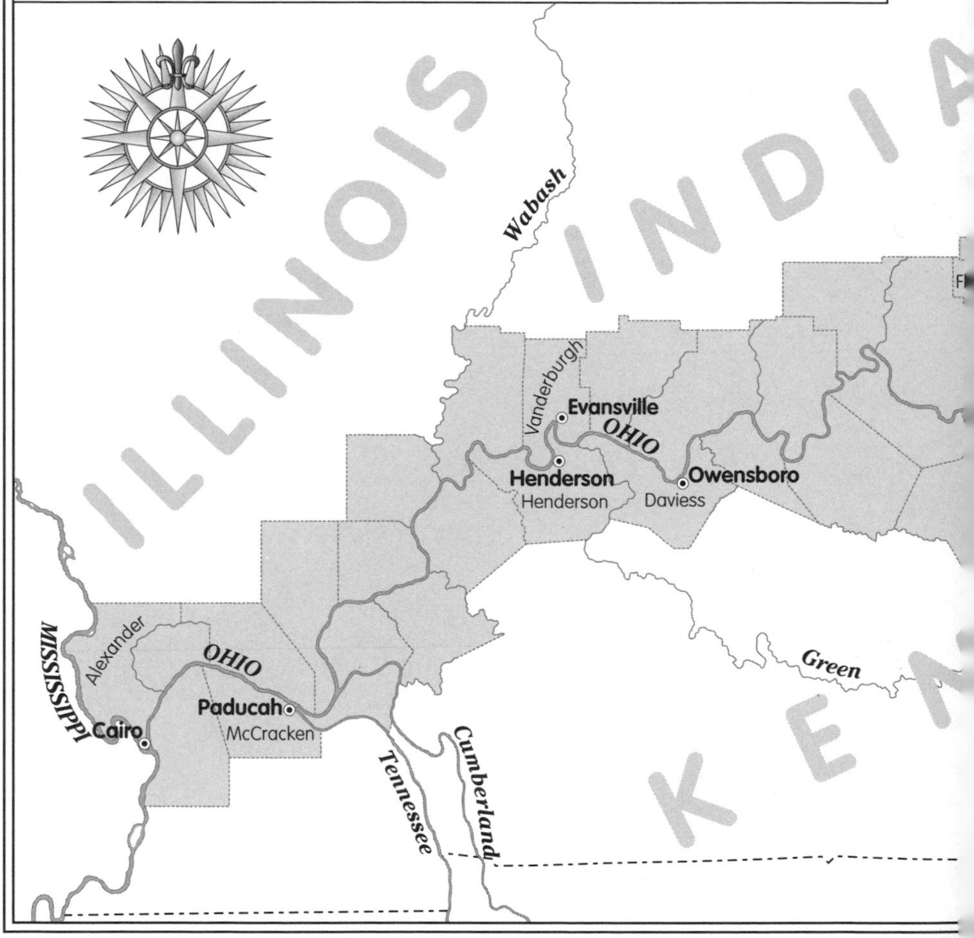

ILLINOIS

INDIA

Wabash

Vanderburgh • Evansville
OHIO

Henderson
Henderson

Owensboro
Daviess

OHIO

MISSISSIPPI

Alexander

Paducah
McCracken

Cairo

Tennessee

Cumberland

Green

KEN

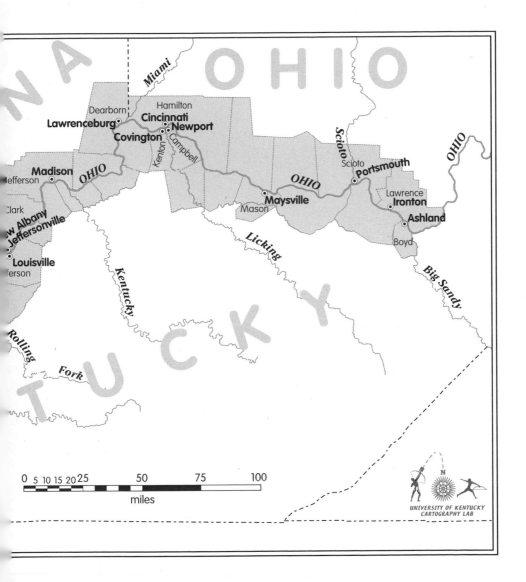

INDIANA

OHIO

Miami

Dearborn
Hamilton
Lawrenceburg
Cincinnati
Newport
Covington
Kenton
Campbell

Scioto

OHIO

Scioto
Portsmouth

Jefferson
Madison
OHIO

OHIO

Lawrence
Ironton

Clark
Mason
Maysville

Ashland

w Albany
Jeffersonville
Boyd

Louisville
erson

Kentucky
Licking

Big Sandy

Rolling

KENTUCKY

Fork

0 5 10 15 20 25   50   75   100
miles

UNIVERSITY OF KENTUCKY
CARTOGRAPHY LAB

Prologue

The Ohio River Valley
as a Region

Much has been written about the history of settlement along the Ohio River and the economic consequence of the river, but that literature is limited in scope. We know a great deal about the largest places—Cincinnati, Louisville, and Pittsburgh—and little about the others, such as Ashland, Cairo, Evansville, New Albany, and Metropolis. Moreover, historians have generally ignored the region between the Falls of the Ohio at Louisville and the mouth of the Ohio at Cairo.[1]

If histories of the Ohio Valley have been uneven in their range, they have been virtually silent regarding African Americans who lived on the Ohio's banks. Histories of Kentucky, Ohio, Indiana, and Illinois are in varying degrees asymmetrical in their exploration of Ohio River counties and towns, and that imbalance is especially evident in their treatment of African Americans. There are studies of blacks in Cincinnati, Louisville, Evansville, and a few communities in Illinois, but most scholars have ignored African Americans in this part of the nation. This is an egregious historical gap, given the significant presence of African Americans in the region from the late eighteenth century onward.[2]

The Ohio's importance for Kentucky was paramount beginning with statehood in 1792. As of 1860 the commonwealth, from Catlettsburg to Ballard County, fronted on well over two-thirds of the waterway—665 of its 981 miles between Pittsburgh and Cairo. Kentucky's black population was also considerably larger than that of the states across the river. On the eve of the

Civil War, 52,397 African Americans lived in Kentucky's Ohio River counties. They represented slightly more than 22 percent of the state's total. By contrast, a total of 12,479 resided in the river counties of Illinois, Indiana, and Ohio. Blacks in those counties accounted for 11, 34, and 21 percent, respectively, of the African American population of their states.[3]

Little historical study has been done of the contrasts and continuities that existed along this shared waterway, America's first interstate highway and arguably the most vital tributary of the Mississippi. On the south bank was a labor system, slavery, that shaped not only Kentucky's economy, but also its society, culture, and government both before and after the Civil War. The demographic roots of most of the people on the north bank also lay to the south, and those origins were reflected in (among other things) a culture that was virulently racist. From the outset the economies of settlements on the two banks were intertwined as well, and the linkages remained strong even after the coming of railroads.[4] However, the Ordinance of 1785 and the Northwest Ordinance of 1787 created systems of land development and ownership and of labor, education, and government on the north bank that were vastly different from those to the south. Immigrants and migrants from the Middle Atlantic States and New England settled as a rule on the free-labor north bank. In terms of government, a notable difference lay in the township focus to the north and the county emphasis to the south.

The differences were enhanced by the absence of bridges. When bridges were built, they signified the desire of capitalists on both shores to enhance their economic ties. The first was not opened until 1867—John Roebling's suspension railroad bridge linking Cincinnati and Covington. The second, connecting Louisville and New Albany, Indiana, was completed four years later. Below the Falls, it was not until 1885 and 1889 that railroad bridges were erected at Evansville and Cairo, respectively. Vehicular bridges were not constructed before the late 1920s.[5]

Cultural and economic differences between settlements on the north and south banks were readily apparent to visitors to the region. Typically people contrasted the industriousness of the people on the north shore with the slothfulness of those to the south. Usually cited as evidence was the presence of towns and factories on one side and undeveloped, almost wild expanses on the other.[6] These observers attributed the differences to slavery, which had been present in Kentucky's river counties since the late eighteenth century. Slavery was eliminated from the upper valley in 1863, when West Virginia was formed out of the slave state of Virginia. It was not legally abolished in Kentucky until December 1865, when the Thirteenth Amendment was ratified, despite

Kentucky's opposition. Much of the north bank, though, resembled the south—rural, sparsely populated, and agrarian.

A most intriguing aspect of Ohio River history is how and why places on both shores were shaped by the presence or the absence of slavery, and what happened when slavery was abolished and free labor became the rule on both sides of the waterway. This work focuses on a critical time in the region's development—between the time when the system of labor that was fundamental to the peoples of the south bank was eliminated and the time when another system, ostensibly like that of the peoples of the north bank, replaced it. There were accompanying changes as well as continuities in the relationships between former slaves and former owners and among whites who had supported slave labor. Thousands of former slaves, moreover, moved across the river to northern counties, where blacks had generally not been welcome before the Civil War. White-black relations were changing there as well. And on both sides of the river, African Americans built new lives as free persons. The fact that this new start occurred generally in cities and towns intensified the challenges facing the once rural, agricultural laborers who now had to adapt to city life.

The locus of this study is Kentucky's 25 Ohio River counties, between Boyd and Ballard, and the 25 cross-river counties of Illinois, Indiana, and Ohio—6 in Illinois, 13 in Indiana, and 6 in Ohio. Studies of African Americans in this part of America have, like explorations of other topics, utilized the political unit as the framework for analysis. As a consequence almost all of them lack comparative perspectives—overlooking, for example, regional variations created by geography and culture. This omission is especially ironic, given the centrality of the Ohio in the development of these states. The only comparative study focuses on the largest cities, overlooks experiences in smaller communities and rural areas, and does little with social and cultural history.[7]

Using the Ohio River rather than state boundaries as the basis for comparison, one is struck by the varieties as well as the similarities in experiences and outcomes for African Americans who resided along its banks in the era of the Civil War and its aftermath. Slavery or the absence of it created an obvious difference between north- and south-shore communities before 1865; and even after the abolition of slavery in December 1865, traditional ways of doing things did not disappear, especially in predominantly rural counties. In urban settings—notably Louisville, as compared with Cincinnati or Evansville—more changes were evident.

Geography also mattered. From east to west the Ohio flowed past counties of Kentucky situated in distinctive regions—the Appalachians, the Blue-

grass region, western Kentucky or the Pennyroyal, and the Jackson Purchase. Each area had unique topographic, economic, and settlement patterns.[8] Many of these landforms extended across the river into Ohio, Indiana, and Kentucky. Southeastern Ohio counties, for example, were Appalachian in character; the dramatic limestone outcroppings known as "the Knobs" that separated the Bluegrass from western Kentucky crossed over from Kentucky, just west of Louisville, into southern Indiana; floodplain dominated both sides of the river from Hancock County, Kentucky, and its Perry County, Indiana, neighbor westward to the mouth of the river; and the sparsely settled bottomlands of Kentucky's Purchase region extended across the river to a narrow strip of land in Illinois. One should also consider that the distance between the Tennessee-Kentucky border and the Ohio declined considerably between Ashland and Cairo. Slaves who sought to escape to the North had a considerably longer journey through eastern Kentucky, as compared with the Purchase region. Accordingly, southern Illinois had a much larger population of African Americans from Tennessee and the lower South than did southern Ohio and most of southern Indiana.

Such demographic patterns persisted after the Civil War. Many counties on either side of the river were rural and sparsely populated to begin with and remained so into the 1880s. In 1860 African Americans on the Kentucky side resided in the country rather than in towns (see table 5, in the appendix), except for Louisville. On the north shore, relatively few lived outside of cities and towns. After the war, blacks on both banks gravitated to urban areas. Generally, though, their numbers and proportions did not make them a sizable part of river counties' populations. Notable exceptions were Jefferson, Henderson, McCracken, and Union counties in Kentucky and Alexander and Pulaski counties in Illinois. Where blacks' numbers or share of the population was substantial, their ability to influence the ways in which whites shaped their lives was much greater than where their numbers were small.

A related factor was culture. In most settlements, virtually all whites traced their roots to Kentucky and the upper South. In some cities, though—chiefly Cincinnati, Evansville, and Louisville—there were also many immigrants, especially Germans and Irish, who, like whites in the upper South, looked unfavorably on black settlement and did their best to thwart blacks' ambitions. Migrants from New York and Pennsylvania and especially those from New England also clustered in some north-bank cities and, being more sympathetic to black newcomers, ameliorated their lives.

One also needs to consider patterns of economic development, and especially transportation. With the exception of Louisville and possibly Paducah,

Kentucky's business and civic leaders before the Civil War were committed to traditional ways of making money and dealing with public improvements. There were virtually no urban areas, few factories, and only a handful of modern transportation connections to the Ohio River. Louisville's rail connection to Nashville, Paducah's to the new Mobile and Ohio Railroad, and Henderson's plans for a railroad that would connect it to Evansville on the north and Nashville on the south were anomalies. To the north, although most counties were also agricultural and rural, factories flourished in a number of towns, and vital north-south canal and rail connections dominated the landscape.

The lay of the land and its resources, the patterns of population growth and development, the impact of settlement and culture, and the ways in which people made money, in short, help to account for variety as well as continuity.

This work is divided into three eras—the years immediately before the Civil War, the period of Civil War and the abolition of slavery in 1865, and the postwar years to the mid-1880s, when Jim Crow or de jure segregation was becoming well entrenched in Kentucky and also evident across the river. Most of the text is allocated to 1865–85, though the moment of emancipation for many blacks occurred earlier than the ratification of the Thirteenth Amendment. Within each period, I have sought to offer representative examples from each region of Kentucky and its counterpart across the river. One cannot fully understand the dynamics of this period without dealing with the linkages that existed then and persist to this day—for example, Ashland and Ironton, Covington-Newport and Cincinnati, Louisville and Clarksville–Jeffersonville–New Albany, Henderson-Owensboro and Evansville, and Paducah and Brookport-Metropolis.

The book is intended for laypeople as well as academics. Although it refers to many primary sources, its emphasis is on synthesis of secondary accounts, written as early as the 1860s, in order to provide comparative analysis of the development of black communities and black-white relationships along a 665-mile-long corridor. In many respects the experiences of blacks on the north shore of the river differed only by degree from those on the south shore. But differences could also be more significant, especially in matters relating to formal separation of the races and the incidence of racial violence. I hope the reader shares my belief that during this time of vast social, economic, and political change, when African Americans on either side of the Ohio were generally given little wherewithal to make a meaningful new start, the most remarkable advancement was the creation of communities that provided shelter and advanced the causes of the race. During a time in which whites in the North rapidly forgot that the Civil War was about race and liberation as well as

the Union and peacemaking and sought to make peace with their former white enemies, blacks on either side of the Ohio, like their brothers and sisters elsewhere, not only endured. They persisted.[9]

PART ONE

BEFORE THE WAR

1

Uneasy Slavery in Kentucky along the Ohio

Antebellum Kentucky was rural and agrarian, heavily dependent on the growing of corn and tobacco and the raising of horses and mules. Along the Ohio River, only two counties—Jefferson (Louisville) and Kenton (Covington)—had a large manufacturing base. Jefferson County had 436 factories that employed 7,400. Kenton had 144 employing 1,100.[1] Only five river towns had more than 2,500 residents. Louisville, with 68,000, was by far the largest (see appendix, table 3).

Slavery was Kentucky's curse. With little or no cotton production, a mountainous east where slavery was rare, and few crops compatible with slavery, Kentucky shared its extensive, porous northern border with free territory. Opponents of slavery were close by, and opportunities for slaves to run away were plentiful. Slavery in Kentucky was also moving in a different direction, compared to most of the South. Although there were 225,483 slaves in the state in 1860, or 19.5 percent of the population, the number of slaves was lower in Kentucky than in eight other slave states. Only three states had a smaller proportion, and the percentage had been dropping since 1830. This decline was the result of many factors, including the low level of cotton, sugar, and rice production and the demand for slaves in the lower Mississippi valley.[2] Slave trading became vital to Kentucky's society and economy. Slave dealers were listed alongside respectable businessmen in Louisville's city directories

and newspaper advertisements. But slave trading was loathsome to many. In 1841 Kentucky-born Abraham Lincoln described manacled slaves being taken south by a slave trader: "They were chained six and six together. A small iron clevis was around the left wrist of each, and this fastened to the main chain by a shorter one at a convenient distance from the others; so that the negroes were strung together like so many fish upon a trot-line."[3] Especially gruesome were the "work houses" of Louisville, where bondmen were kept in vile conditions before being transported downriver. There were also those who would kidnap either free blacks or alleged runaways. Louisville's blacks, though, were not passive observers. On a number of occasions they organized themselves to thwart such kidnapping efforts.[4]

It was little wonder that the Lower South was apprehensive about Kentucky: it was the first of a series of dominoes that could trigger a wholesale collapse of slavery. Kentucky and Arkansas, for example, were the only states that did not prohibit slaves from being taught to read. Kentucky required that blacks charged with a crime be given a trial by jury. Public discussion of slavery was freer than in any state to the south. Before 1849 Kentucky law prohibited the importation of slaves by purchase. And the state had hundreds of miles of borderland with the free-labor Northwest.[5]

But efforts were undertaken by midcentury to reinforce the institution of slavery. Having successfully sought the aid of the Ohio legislature to assist the commonwealth in returning fugitive slaves (Illinois and Indiana were not thought to be as susceptible to eastern antislavery views), Kentucky's leaders tarnished their state's image as a moderating force between North and South. Kentucky "managed to live with itself under an invented myth of republicanism. This obscured the fact of near oligarchic rule." Through the influence of planters like Senator Archibald Dixon of Henderson, the ban on slave importation was lifted in 1849, and the 1850 constitution made manumission much more difficult. Slaves freed by their owners had to leave the state, and their owners had to provide funds for their transportation and a year's subsistence.[6]

Accordingly, Kentucky resembled its counterparts to the south in many ways. More white people left than entered the commonwealth, because of slavery's threat to free labor, and slavery stunted the growth of the fine arts and of reform, especially public school reform. Capital tied up in human labor limited economic development. The effects on those enslaved, in turn, were devastating. It is little wonder that the election of Abraham Lincoln in 1860 created profound fear among slavery's defenders, as he threatened to create a constituency through patronage in the border states that would begin peeling

off slave states from the Deep South's borders and expose it to eventual loss of its distinctive way of life.[7]

The proportion of blacks in all Ohio River counties except Henderson declined steadily after 1830. Only Daviess, Henderson, Mason, Meade, Oldham, and Union counties exceeded 20 percent in 1860. Most blacks resided in rural areas, and their portion of town populations was relatively insignificant. Exceptions to the rule were the town of Henderson, where nearly 50 percent of the residents were African Americans, and Owensboro, with about 33 percent. Louisville and Paducah were, respectively, 10 and 14.6 percent black (table 2).[8]

Slavery's presence, moreover, was uneven. There were relatively few slaves in the two large counties opposite Cincinnati, apparently reflecting the economic and cultural reach of the Ohio city. In the eastern, Appalachian part of Kentucky, slavery never gained a strong foothold. In some counties downriver from Louisville, like Hardin and Meade, a significant number of Baptists opposed the institution. By contrast, two of five people in the entire Henderson County population were slaves. A tobacco-growing and exporting county, Henderson signified an effort to transplant Tidewater Virginia values and institutions to western Kentucky. Henderson County's customs spilled over into neighboring counties, notably Union.[9]

Louisville was more like its upriver rival, Cincinnati, and also St. Louis. Jefferson County had more than 10,000 slaves in 1860—the highest number in the state. Slightly over half—the highest proportion of any south-bank county—lived in Louisville. All but 90 of the county's 2,000 free blacks resided in the city. Jefferson County accounted for almost one-fifth of the state's free blacks (table 2). African Americans lived in all of Louisville's eight wards, but distribution was uneven. By number Ward 7 had the most (1,238), but by percentage Ward 4, with 1,175 blacks, was first (nearly 21%). Three-fourths of the slaves lived in Wards 1, 4, 5, 6, and 7.[10]

Louisville's free blacks—about 3 percent of the total population—accounted for the same proportion of the populace as did African Americans in Cincinnati. One study of the two cities has noted other similarities: the ratio of females to males (about 0.9), the percentage of children (slightly over 22, below the national average of 24.4), and the proportion of people owning their own homes (about 4%). The average value of homes owned by Cincinnati blacks was higher than the average in Louisville—$2,693 as compared to $1,518—but a slightly higher percentage of free blacks in Louisville owned their own homes. Louisville's African Americans compared favorably with their upriver counterparts in the ratio of people employed as artisans. The "index of

occupational opportunity" for them was fourth-highest in the nation and above Cincinnati's.[11]

The growth of Louisville, a manufacturer of hemp, tobacco, and foundry products and a major river port, was accelerated by the chartering of the Louisville and Nashville Railroad in 1850. The city attracted immigrants, especially from Germany and Ireland. Many of its citizens disliked slavery. In the election of delegates to the constitutional convention in 1849, voters divided evenly between proslavery and antislavery delegates.[12]

Louisville was unusual in another respect. Rather than living in slave quarters, slaves in Louisville resided with their owners, often in an outbuilding behind the owner's home. Many were concentrated in the more affluent parts of the city, north of Walnut Street between Second and Eighth streets. Generally those living with owners or those who hired themselves out ate well and did not experience the weekly rationing of food characteristic of slavery in rural areas. Free blacks, along with those hiring their time and "living out," resided in the same wards (3, 4, and 5) but farther south, closer to the southern city limit. There was also a growing free black presence west of Sixth Street. Socialization occurred in public streets, at the homes of free blacks, or in "grog shops."[13]

Most slave-owners were merchants, who used slaves primarily as domestic workers. Perhaps that fact explained why women consistently outnumbered men. In light of manumission laws, owners had two options—selling slaves downriver or hiring them out to local manufacturers. Yearly contracts were signed in December, and newspapers were filled with job advertisements. About one in seven slaves were employed as servants. Many worked in factories, while others were employed as skilled workers such as carpenters, plasterers, bricklayers, and blacksmiths. Free and slave blacks who were draymen, hackmen, and teamsters traveled to and fro across the river via ferries. On riverboats, slaves were musicians, roustabouts, waiters, stewards, and firemen. A number of boys were hired as jockeys. Slaves also hired themselves out. "Those who hire their own time," observed one white Louisville man, "not only act without restraint themselves, but their example induces others to believe that they can take the same liberties . . . that they can work or play as they please."[14]

Such slaves were developing the habits of wage-earners, and thereby contributing to the creation of a distinctive black community. Blacks' self-awareness and relative lack of subservience precipitated conflicts with white workers, who resented their competition for low-paying jobs. This psychological and social climate also produced the generation of blacks that would lead Louisville from slavery to freedom in the 1860s.[15]

Free blacks' occupations generally resembled those of slaves who hired themselves out. Most were servants. Some had small businesses, such as barbershops, but opportunities to purchase land and to establish businesses were limited. An exception was Washington Spradling Sr. (1805–1868). Son of an overseer and a slave, he was freed at an early age and after moving to Louisville established a barbershop. Spradling was a shrewd businessman and acquired $30,000 worth of property, mostly by buying, selling, and leasing land, chiefly in the Russell neighborhood. After the war his son Washington junior established Smoketown on property inherited from his father. The elder Spradling offered legal advice to many people and purchased the freedom of approximately thirty-three slaves. He also helped to found Methodist churches on Centre and Green streets.[16]

Federal slave schedules and state and local tax records from 1860 provide valuable insight into patterns of slave distribution and ownership. The river counties with the highest average number of slaves per owner were generally in western Kentucky (table 2). Henderson County's 943 owners had on average 6 slaves. Jefferson County had the most owners, 2,226, but less than 10 percent of them owned 10 or more slaves. Most of the latter lived in rural Jefferson County. Thirteen owned more than 20 slaves each.[17]

In Louisville, by contrast, the 1,432 slave-owners possessed on average 3 slaves each. Only 41 had more than 10. Samuel Breals, who owned 26, was the city's leading slave-owner. The Sisters of Charity possessed a young woman, age seventeen. Cedar Grove Academy owned 5 slaves. Quite a few men, for example Silas Miller, who employed 51, and Michael Kean, who employed or hired out 29, benefited from the hiring-out process. The National Hotel and the United States Hotel, between them, hired 36. According to tax records, Jefferson County's slaves were worth $4.9 million, or about $499 each. As a percentage of total assessed property, this was considerably less than the ratio in the rest of the state's river counties, since the total value of all Jefferson County property was $54.6 million.[18]

Somewhat similar patterns prevailed upriver in the two counties opposite Cincinnati. In Campbell County, just one in three slaves lived in Newport. The city had only 39 slaves and 17 slave-owners. In rural environs there were 32 owners. Most free people of color lived in the city. There were significantly more slaves in neighboring Kenton County (567), but they accounted for only 2.2 percent of the county's population. Of them, 198 lived in the city of Covington, and well over half resided in Wards 3 and 4. The number of free blacks was about the same as in Campbell County.[19]

Quite a bit of variety existed outside of these three urbanized counties. In Boyd County, for instance, there were only 156 slaves. There were also 17 free people of color. Unlike his counterpart in other river counties, the Boyd County census enumerator identified a considerable number of slaves by their first names. In at least eight cases it appears that these could have been families. G.W. Brown, for instance, possessed Matilda, who was 38 years old; Annie, 21; Elizabeth, 16; James, 12; Mary, 4; Theodora, 2; and Martha, 1—possibly a widowed mother and her six children.[20]

In Mason County nearly 21 percent of the population—about 3,700 people—was enslaved. There were just 382 free blacks. Most of the slaves resided in the rural environs of Maysville, which itself had only 230 slaves and 89 owners, or just below 3 slaves per owner. Outside Maysville, the typical owner had 5 slaves.[21] In early summer 1860, the tax assessor indicated the county's slaves were valued at $1,064,400, or about $399 each. Slave property accounted for one-eighth of all of the assessed value of real and personal property.[22] Mason County's production of tobacco was immense—about 1.8 million pounds. It also harvested a half million bushels of corn, much of it produced by the slaves of 549 white men and women. Of them, 7 were planters.[23]

Downstream Trimble County, across from Madison, Indiana, had much less fertile land, a fact reflected in its slave population—only 14 percent of its inhabitants. The 175 owners claimed on average between 4 and 5 African Americans each. One man, Martin N. Roberts, owned 66 slaves. Thirteen others owned 10 or more.[24]

Western Kentucky and Jackson Purchase counties generally had higher numbers and proportions of slaves and planters. Slaves represented from 11 to 41 percent of the population in the counties below the Falls of the Ohio. The number of free black people in these counties was minimal—24 at most in one of them.[25] Hardin County, just downstream from Jefferson, had 2,539 slaves, evenly distributed among its three census districts. They accounted for about 17 percent of the total population. Just 5 of the 513 slaveholders held more than 20. By contrast, slaves represented 41 percent of the residents of Henderson County, where nearly 1,000 white people, about one of fourteen residents, owned black people. Of these, 169 whites held 10 or more, and 67 possessed 20 or more. Alexander B. Barrett, whose personal and real property was worth $1.9 million (of the county's total $14.6 million), held 140 slaves. Archibald Dixon, prominent Whig politician and U.S. senator, owned 124. Lazarus Powell, a former governor, had 56. Henderson's planters owned three-fourths of the county's slaves.[26] According to Henderson County tax records, two of five taxpayers owned slaves.[27] The average value of each slave was $412.

The eight Barretts on the tax rolls held 264. They also produced 477,000 pounds of tobacco. William and Jackson McClain, with 190 slaves, grew 609,000 pounds of tobacco. Two Dixons, Archibald and Robert, his son, possessed 153 slaves and raised 488,000 pounds of tobacco. (The county's total tobacco production was 6.1 million pounds.)[28]

In neighboring Union County, also a major producer of tobacco, approximately one in four people were enslaved. Of them, 266 lived in the Ohio River village of Uniontown, and another 171 resided in Caseyville, downriver on the Ohio. Four-fifths lived in rural sections of the county. Of the 96 persons who owned 10 or more, 79 lived in the countryside. One of the owners was Archibald Dixon of Henderson, who had 20.[29]

Daviess County, just upriver from Henderson, had slightly fewer slaves. Nonetheless, slavery—tied to tobacco—was an integral part of the county's economy and culture. As elsewhere, most African Americans resided in the country. Owensboro had less than one-tenth of the county's slaves. Outside of the town, the most prominent owner was Alexander B. Barrett of Henderson, owner of 74 slaves.[30] Downstream from Henderson, rural Crittenden County had 181 slave-owners and 867 slaves, assessed at $354 per slave. Most whites owned 5 or fewer.[31]

The most populous and economically developed county in this region was McCracken, which had more factories and wage-earners than any other lower-Ohio town except Evansville. But it also had 1,738 slaves, of whom 670 lived in Paducah. Like those in the town of Henderson, a significant number of Paducah's slaves stemmed and packed tobacco for export. But just 178 whites in the town owned blacks. Two-thirds of those owning 10 or more slaves resided outside the city. Slaves' total value was assessed at $350,200, or $536 per person. The county's total real and personal property was listed at almost ten times that amount—$3.4 million—a pattern resembling Louisville and Jefferson County. And as in Louisville, a majority of slaves were above age sixteen. That was an exception to the rule, since most counties exported adult slaves downriver. Slavery was inefficient for a small-farm economy that grew mostly cereals, hemp, and tobacco, but farther south the demand for slaves was insatiable.[32]

What do we know about Kentucky's slaves, other than how many there were and how they were distributed? The typical bondman worked on a small farm, not a plantation. The master possessed on average five slaves. The only slave state whose owners had fewer was Missouri. Over time, black slavery became "'ingrained and convenient' among small landholding white farmers, and with

the passage of time and increased profits from farms where bondsmen worked the fields, the institution became almost sacred."[33]

Most slaves worked side-by-side with their owners. They were engaged in tasks that "were, for the most part, routine and could be learned easily and checked without difficulty." Those who worked as field hands performed the hardest, most monotonous jobs, but some preferred field work because it "provided them with opportunities to express opinions to fellow bondsmen away from their masters' watchful eyes." Field work varied according to owners, seasons, and crops. Tobacco, the mainstay of most river counties, required virtually year-round employment, from soil preparation and planting in late winter to curing and stripping and tying leaves into bundles for shipment to market in late fall.[34]

Slaves toiled in many other capacities: among others, as personal or domestic servant, tanner, spinner, weaver, carpenter, or barber. Many slaves working on the docks and rivers were hired out, but others "worked with or for their masters" moving cargoes in river towns. Slaves also "built roads, canals, and bridges, and tourists frequently commented on the number of bondsmen working in hotels and restaurants where they were waiters, maids, and cooks." They also "worked as butchers, midwives, jockeys, groomsmen, and stablemen."[35] Children also worked—as houseboys or nurses, or more frequently in the garden or in the field. At age ten, for instance, Allen Allensworth was sent by his Louisville owners to work on a Henderson County tobacco farm. Apprenticing children was a convenient, inexpensive means for masters to get skilled laborers. Slaves' living conditions varied in quality with the status and the goodwill of owners. Housing generally consisted of modestly furnished, small log cabins. In towns, alleys were lined with "live-out" quarters of slaves.[36]

Slaves' families had a tenuous existence. Slaves were property, and their marriages were not legally recognized. Children of female slaves remained chattel even if their fathers were free. Parent-child relationships, love, courtship, and marriage depended on owners' caprice. Owners moved their slaves with them when they relocated from one region to another, though sometimes slaves persuaded their owners to sell them locally instead. Hiring out also weakened family unity. Marriages were easiest when slaves lived on the same farm. The threat of sale and the brutalizing effects of labor on black males meant that slave families were often headed by women. In 1846, for instance, an Owensboro slaveholder sold Mary Stowers and her young daughter but kept her four-year-old son Willis, who was eventually bought by an Alabama cotton farmer. Nevertheless, sometimes slaves were able to persuade their

owners—occasionally with contributions from meager savings—to keep families together.[37]

Regulation of movement was strict. Blacks could not be away from their residences for more than four hours without a pass. Thus they were restricted to an area eight to ten miles from their homes. Clandestine "unlawful assemblies" resulted in arrest and severe penalties. Town regulations supplemented state laws. In Henderson slaves could assemble or preach only on Sunday and only before 10:00 p.m. Up to twenty stripes could be administered to violators. Similar regulations existed in Louisville, though they were somewhat more liberal: church services were also permitted before 10:00 p.m. on Wednesdays. In all towns and cities, night watchmen enforced such regulations, and nighttime slave patrols operated in most counties. The Ohio shore was carefully monitored.[38]

Masters also restricted slave mobility by visiting the slave quarters and by issuing passes to perform specific duties. Some, however, gave general, open-ended passes that permitted travel inside and outside Kentucky for extended periods of time. Although small numbers of slaves, with passes in their pockets, "constantly traveled along Kentucky's highways and railroads," their mobility was always subject to the whims of patrols. Hunting, catching, watching, and whipping blacks was a favorite sport of young whites. Slaves detested most being rousted at night by whites allegedly searching their cabins for weapons or runaways.[39]

Slaves were "more mobile than has generally been believed," though, because the slave codes were applied loosely and unevenly and because it was difficult to patrol an overwhelmingly rural state that had poor roads. Most slaves knew the rural roads and footpaths well enough to get around freely with or without their masters' approval. Kentucky's slaves enjoyed varied forms of recreation, from playing games, storytelling, and music in the cabins to Saturday night dances, Sunday worship and social gatherings afterward, and celebrations of holidays, especially Christmas and New Year's Day.[40]

Some slaves, perhaps not surprisingly, expressed no desire to become free by running away. One Ohio River ferryboat captain objected to Elisha Green's boarding his vessel because his open-ended pass led the white to think Green would run away, but Green chided the captain, saying, "I do not want freedom in that way." Nonetheless, few slaves did not detest the system that controlled virtually every aspect of their lives. Declared one Trimble County slave, "Nothing exceeds [slavery] for its wickedness."[41]

Emancipation by the owner was the most common means of acquiring freedom. Kentucky had 176 manumissions in 1860, about one in nine of those

in all border states. Emancipation could be a grueling experience, however, if one's children or spouse remained in bondage. Some freed slaves stayed in the commonwealth, while others crossed the Ohio. Departures accelerated in the 1850s. A handful of former slaves—perhaps 660 at most—migrated to Liberia thanks to the support of the Kentucky Colonization Society, which ceased operation in 1859. Slaves could also purchase their freedom, but the process was quite difficult and slaves' sources of funds to do so limited. Males usually purchased themselves before purchasing other family members.[42]

Those who could not look forward to emancipation expressed opposition in many ways, mostly nonviolent—ranging from humor and music to work slowdowns or temporarily running away. Whites were sometimes murdered. "The most famous case occurred in Henderson County in 1862," declares Marion Lucas, "when a slave or group of bondsmen seized their overseer, who had repeatedly flogged them, and strangled him with his own suspenders." All six were tried, and one was executed. Farmers in the region "publicized [his] execution, and in similar cases, owners took slaves to hangings, hoping to make an impression on them."[43] The fear of slave uprisings was omnipresent. Though no such insurrection occurred in Kentucky, occasional scares struck white settlements, and usually the scapegoats were abolitionists.[44]

Since twenty-five of Kentucky's counties bordered free-soil states, and seven of the commonwealth's largest towns were river ports, running away was the most convenient route to freedom. The largest population centers of the state were less than one hundred miles from the Ohio, and several lay on it. Covington was directly across the river from Cincinnati, the largest city on the north shore. The farther one traveled downstream from the Falls, the closer the Ohio was to the Kentucky-Tennessee border and to the Deep South. Only one county lay between McCracken and Tennessee.[45]

Conventional wisdom may be erroneous when it describes "slaves' counterculture back at the slave quarters as their most successful resistance." The error is not in celebrating their counterculture, but rather in failing to appreciate that only running away allowed blacks to "outplay whites in the divide-and-conquer game." This form of resistance, moreover, gave "no cause for panicky whites to mass for slaughters in the slave quarters. Better still, some northern whites aided unarmed runaways." At the top of the Border South, "potential fugitives saw better chances, in precisely the region of the Slave South where white heretics enjoyed better opportunities." If the number of slaves declined, "already slack borderland commitments to the institution could grow slacker still." Then opponents of slavery like Cassius Clay of Kentucky

could "better sell their proposal that border legislatures quicken the slave drain and thus produce a totally white population." In reality, the number of reported fugitives was quite small—119 in 1860—but that was an increase from the 23 reported in 1850, and whites' perception of the fugitive slave threat mattered a great deal more than the numbers.[46]

The decision to leave for good was extremely difficult. In order to do so, slaves needed to have knowledge and intelligence, to be sure, but courage, opportunity, and opposition to slavery combined to make that judgment for many. Sometimes slaves ran away during uncertain times, such as a change in the owner's status. Others fled after having visited free territory. Still others deserted when threatened by harsh punishment or when they, or relatives or friends, were faced with sale southward. A slave mother with eight children who often sold produce in Cincinnati packed her belongings in a wagon, covered them with vegetables, met her husband and children just south of Covington, and crossed the river. She had just learned that her owner planned to sell some of her children. She unloaded her family, with the aid of Cincinnati blacks, and hired a man to drive the wagon back to Kentucky. She and her family eventually reached Canada.[47]

Running away involved almost insurmountable obstacles. Those who regularly ran errands for their owners across or on the river and returned faithfully "stood the best chance of crossing without suspicion." Dick Daily, a Carroll County slave, traveled often to Madison, Indiana, carrying his master's produce. Because of his faithfulness, he was allowed to go to Madison whenever he desired. "One Saturday night in 1857 he gathered his four children from a nearby farm, crossed the river in a skiff, and fled northward." Planning was critical for successful escapes. Levi Coffin told of a slave in Boone County "who adopted the ploy used by Cassie and Emeline in *Uncle Tom's Cabin*. Realizing that she would be hotly pursued if she tried to cross the Ohio River immediately, the slave prepared a hiding place in a haystack." There she hid, fed by friends for six weeks, before paddling a skiff across the river.[48]

Despite historians' descriptions of a well-organized network of stops on the Underground Railroad, the reality for most runaways was a hard, self-made flight to freedom. Traveling for weeks, usually at night, with little food or rest, and lacking certainty about which direction to go toward free soil and Canada, some managed to travel farther south and become re-enslaved. Slaves were fed stories that whites in the north were hostile. Many of the latter did assist in apprehending runaways. And there were black spies "who operated along the Ohio River, waiting to betray them for a price."[49]

Yet many slaves escaped, usually because they knew that most blacks whom

they approached would assist them. Black neighborhoods and churches, or places where blacks worked—like the Washington Hotel at Third and Main streets in Evansville—were known safe havens. African Americans, often nameless but described by their age or occupation, were by word of mouth allies. Particularly helpful were former slaves living on the north shore. That the process of escape was commenced by blacks and that the Underground Railroad depended heavily on black agents are not well-known aspects of the story.[50]

"Knowing or meeting someone who had contact with free soil was very important for slaves who contemplated obtaining their freedom." This was especially crucial for slaves who lived in towns and villages near the Ohio, and particularly in larger communities like Louisville, where slaves helped their comrades escape, and where runaways could blend into the crowd. One of the city's wealthiest black freemen, Washington Spradling, is credited with aiding many runaways.[51]

Agents of the Underground Railroad were occasionally active on the south side of the river. Most preferred not to become directly involved in liberating slaves. A Louisville white man, whom Levi Coffin identified only as Jones, was frequently approached by local blacks for aid because they knew he was "kindly disposed toward their race." Jones would go to the wharf, engage a stateroom on the Cincinnati and Louisville packet in his own or some other name, and get the key to the room. Just before the boat departed Louisville, "while there was a great bustle on the wharf and along the gangway, he would have the fugitives come on board with their bundles—as if they were servants bringing the baggage of their master or mistress"—and would smuggle them out of slave territory in his stateroom. Sometimes he accompanied them. The year before his arrest and conviction and sentencing to two years' imprisonment, he helped twenty-seven slaves escape. That sort of activity by whites— the "special forces" of the Underground Railroad—was uncommon. More typical was the role played by John Van Zandt, a white abolitionist in Hamilton County, Ohio, who conspired to help nine slaves escape from Kenton County. They fled unassisted and met him after crossing the river. He then conducted them to their next stop.[52]

Some whites risked their freedom and their lives by crossing the Ohio into Kentucky. Thomas Brown, who moved to Henderson, peddled millinery from his wagon between Hancock and Union counties, using a compartment in the cart to carry slaves to freedom. He was eventually arrested by the Democratic sheriff in Evansville and imprisoned for three years in Union County. He was fortunate enough to survive and to write about his experiences, but one of his fellow prisoners, an Evansville black man, died in prison. The most

famous and perhaps most reckless of the whites who helped slaves escape was Calvin Fairbank, a native New Yorker and Oberlin College graduate who rescued his first slave in 1837. Subsequent forays into Kentucky led to his being arrested at least three times. He was eventually pardoned in 1864. Two white men, Peter and John Manny, ages 30 and 24, were listed by the Meade County census-taker in 1860 as residents of the county jail in Brandenburg. Possibly brothers, they were identified as natives of "Canada East." They were in prison for enticing a slave to leave his owner.[53]

Although Canada was not exactly "the promised land," it did offer blacks the chance to start over. Memories of home remained strong, however, especially if family members had been left behind. Henry Bibb was one of a number of escaped slaves who returned to Kentucky to liberate loved ones. He made two attempts to rescue his wife and daughter. Both had been sold, and he never saw them again.[54]

As Levi Coffin reminisced, "the Ohio River . . . was the principal barrier between [the fugitives] and freedom, but they generally found some means to cross it." Returning and risking recapture "indicated just how much they wanted others to experience that new condition—freedom."[55]

For those who did not run away, freedom could come in stages because slave hiring or leasing "provided flexibility for an archaic institution and typically worked to the benefit of owners." Renting slaves took three forms: informally sharing slaves who had particular skills, a formal written agreement, and placing slaves with commission agents and traders for leasing.[56]

Rented slaves were important to the owners of hotels, restaurants, taverns, steamboats, and factories. Despite state laws, many owners permitted their slaves, "including entire families, to engage in whatever business they desired, provided they paid them a specified weekly or monthly sum." In Livingston County, for instance, an owner "allowed his slave, Allen, to 'bargain and trade for himself' and to travel at his pleasure from Smithland to Morgantown, Virginia."[57]

Rented slaves had "a slight degree of freedom" only when they were permitted to hire their own time and purchase their freedom. It took many years to do so. Free blacks, moreover, had few of the constitutional or legal guarantees that whites had. Nevertheless, "free blacks, who tended to reside in urban areas where numbers provided a feeling of security and a sense of independence, joined with slaves to create a black community." Such achievements, notes Marion Lucas, were "truly amazing."[58]

The number of free blacks in Kentucky in 1860 was 10,684, or 4.52 percent of the population. About one-third lived in Ohio River counties (table

1), mostly in Jefferson County. Only 313 lived in western Kentucky counties and just 92 in the Purchase. Census records for 1860 provide valuable insight into their lives. Some gained a modest amount of wealth, and many were able to establish their own households—in many cases extended (including relatives like siblings, parents, grandchildren, or nephews or nieces of the head of the household) or augmented (by boarders or lodgers), and sometimes both extended and augmented. Such organization provided shelter, protection, nurture, and additional family income and was a means of coping with the vagaries of life in a slave state.

Examples from several counties will suffice. Thirteen of the free blacks in Breckinridge County resided in families and lived close to each other. Adam Smith, age 53 and a farmer, had personal property worth $500. He had a wife, Lucinda, age 55. Milton, age 26, and Jemima, age 22, were probably their son and daughter or daughter-in-law. The four lived in the household of, and presumably were employed by, Rhoda Sheets, a white woman identified as a farmer. Two residences away was the family of Pleasant Morman, a black farmer who headed his own household. A native of Virginia, he had real property worth $1,250 and personal property valued at $694. He was 72. His wife, Jemima, also a Virginian, was 70. City, age 26, who also lived in the household, was almost certainly their daughter. She was a native of Kentucky, a fact suggesting that her parents had migrated to the state at least 26 years before. A third household, four houses away from Adam Smith, was headed by Lizzie Wolfolk, age 63 and a Virginian by birth. She was probably a widow. Five men and women, ages 33 to 21, presumably her children, also resided in the home. Lizzie's personal property was valued at $300.[59]

Similar patterns existed in Daviess County. Most free blacks lived in rural areas. A few were born outside of Kentucky, chiefly in Virginia. Eight people lived in the extended household of Milford Shaw, a black man who was 35: his wife, Eliza; five children between ages 11 and 2; and Nancy Shaw, a 20-year-old domestic servant who was possibly his sister. The residence of Isom McFarland, who was 60, included his wife, Mollie, also 60, and three others with the same surname. Jane, who was 27, probably was the mother of Eliza and Isom, ages 5 and ten months. The most unusual arrangement was the household of Jim Stout, a 52-year-old Virginian. It included Hanna Stout, age 80, probably his mother, and Patsy Talbott, also 80 and possibly a relative. Both were also Virginians. The home likewise sheltered Henry Parlin, a 25-year-old native of New York, and William Squires, a 21-year-old from Ohio. Both were laborers.[60]

Crittenden County had nineteen free blacks, most of whom lived in rural

white households. Pape Love, 54 and a native of North Carolina, was evidently a widower. Listed with him in the household of Andrew Love, a white farmer and possibly his former owner, were four other blacks named Love: Sarah, 16; Flora, 13; Agnus, 11; and Nancy, 9. All four were natives of Kentucky and probably his children. Ester Yeaky, perhaps a widow, was 50, a native of Kentucky, and a resident of the household of J.C. Henson, a white hotel keeper. Four other Yeakys were enumerated under her name: Malvina, 23, and Alonsa, Will, and Sarah, ages 7, 4, and three months, probably her daughter and grandchildren.[61]

Free blacks encountered a variety of daily threats. They always had to be ready to prove their status through freedom certificates. Mobility was limited—for example, railroad authorities often denied passage to freemen, even though they had free papers, unless a respectable white person verified their status. Poor blacks were especially vulnerable if they were "found in a town with no visible employment." There were other threats. In theory, free blacks could purchase slaves, "provided they were members of their own family, but very few freemen possessed enough capital to buy their relatives." Another danger was kidnapping. A third was whites' "unwillingness to respect their legal rights." The home of Samuel L. White, a black Louisville photographer, musician, and composer, was regularly threatened by white hooligans. J.C. Brown, a black Louisville mason who worked as far away as Bardstown and Shelbyville, angered "white masons, who threatened to 'break every bone in his body' if he did not leave Louisville."[62]

Although free blacks were found in all of the sections of towns along the Ohio, most resided in predominantly black enclaves. This was particularly evident in Louisville, where those who were relatively well off rented or owned dwellings in a four-block area bounded by Ninth, Chestnut, Eleventh, and Walnut streets. More than half of the city's free black residences contained two parents, and most fathers were employed.[63]

Since they had to compete with slave as well as white labor, freemen's wages were less than those of their counterparts across the river, except in some occupations shunned by whites. At the top of the professional ladder was the ministry. Because their income was usually limited, preachers like Samuel L. White of Louisville taught music to whites as well as blacks. Others taught school. Barbering was another respected occupation. The most successful barbers held a great deal of clout in black communities, because most of their patrons were whites, and access to whites was a measure of one's worth. The same can be said of blacks who succeeded as tailors or entertainers.[64]

Free Louisville blacks were also important players in food services and

commerce. Some ran grocery stores, sold vegetables, ran confectionery or butcher shops, or operated ice cream parlors. Whites as well as blacks were patrons. "One catering operation built such a reputation in Louisville that it was the gathering spot for well-known citizens and Northern officers after the outbreak of the Civil War." Black men were hostlers and stable keepers; black women served as cooks in homes, hotels, and restaurants. Black men were stevedores, pilots, and stewards aboard steamboats and worked in the building trades. Madison Smith manufactured stoves that he marketed in the Louisville region. Still others owned and operated saloons or sold used furniture, carpets, and clothing to customers of both races. Peter Lewis was possibly the only black in Louisville who was a paint contractor, keeping "a crew busy painting Louisville's buildings."[65]

Free and enslaved Kentucky blacks had by 1860 developed distinctive patterns of worship. Black preachers who ministered to slaves as well as freemen "demonstrated unusual qualities of character and leadership long before they entered the ministry." They were "frequently conservative and cautious in their relations with whites . . . [but] stubbornly opposed compromise with white authorities on religious matters." Black preachers—especially if they were slaves—had a difficult time gaining acceptance from whites. They had to secure formal recognition from white ministers who were present at their ordination services. But black preachers were more likely to gain emancipation, were more mobile than most, and gained a rudimentary education. Weekday duties included helping "members in economic distress or mending hostile relationships between slaves and their masters." In instances of the kidnapping of freemen, they called their flock "to prayer and fasting before consoling the distressed or organizing demonstrations against unfair treatment, always being careful not to push too hard."[66]

Many African Americans formed their own congregations, typically with the guidance of white committees whose members provided organizational and financial advice. These churches were second in importance only to the family, as they nurtured the soul, promoted self-respect, developed lay leadership, and served as cultural and social havens.

By 1860 Louisville's blacks had eight churches. The earliest was the "Colored" or "African"—later Fifth Street—Baptist Church, formed out of the white First Baptist Church in 1842 with 475 charter members. Its founding pastor, Henry Adams (1803–1872), was a Georgia-born slave. His influence in the black community before his death in 1872 was immeasurable, as was his strong relationship with white leaders—perhaps too cozy, as Thomas James

observed (see chapter 3). He was credited with 10,000 conversions and 1,300 baptisms. Despite meager earnings of slave or free members, the congregation raised funds via weekly offerings and from assessments and solicitation by agents. Adams regularly received one-quarter of the money he solicited, for the congregation was usually unable to pay him his full salary. In 1858 members also erected a new building on Fifth Street, between Walnut and Chestnut, that was "one of the finest church buildings owned by blacks in America."[67]

The second Baptist congregation, initially named Second African or Colored Baptist and renamed Green Street Baptist in 1860, was initially a mission of the white First Baptist Church. A Virginia-born former slave, Richard Sneethen, was its pastor. Highly regarded for his preaching skills and his spiritual guidance, he built up the membership to 725 before his death in 1872. Sneethen brought financial stability to the congregation, and during his tenure a new brick structure worth six thousand dollars was erected on Green (now Liberty) Street.[68]

Black Methodists were also numerous and active. Center Street Methodist Church, formed in the early 1830s, secured a building erected on a lot owned by Washington Spradling in 1835. During the Civil War, whites' preoccupations allowed its members to secede from the Methodist Episcopal Church, South, and to join the African Methodist Episcopal Zion Church. Called Quinn Chapel African Methodist Episcopal Church, it began worship services in a stable in 1840, moving to the basement of a partially finished brick structure in 1854 and finishing the edifice four years later. Its pastor, Willis R. Revels, raised a great deal of money in northern states. That fact, along with the church's many free black members and its educational program, gave it the sobriquet "abolition church." Fourth Street Methodist Church, later known as Asbury Chapel, worshipped in a building purchased from white Methodists by a free black Methodist minister, James Harper, in 1845. Harper requested, and the judge handling the sale approved, the unusual practice of giving control to five black trustees. Later a court upheld their decision to join the African Methodist Episcopal Church and take title to the property with them.[69]

In other parts of the mostly rural commonwealth, separate churches were less common, and different congregational forms existed. The experience of the African Baptist Church of Henderson illustrated one—a gathering of slaves and freemen in log cabins that was eventually brought under whites' supervision. A slave, Willis Walker, became the pastor of the congregation, which worshipped separately in the basement of the white church. A second form was the union meeting house, resorted to when congregations could not afford separate structures. A third appeared in larger towns, where blacks could

afford to form autonomous, separate churches. One such church was First African Baptist Church of Maysville. Elisha W. Green, a black member of the white church, was recognized as the group's pastor in the 1850s.[70]

When it came to religious practices among African Americans in Kentucky, it is likely that religious concepts inherited from Africa played an important part, although they varied in practice. "African religions became flexible, realistic, and pragmatic. Traditionally, Africans viewed God as the creator and sustainer of life in a man-centered universe." What emerged was "a highly moral religion, much concerned with both personal and social conduct." Unique African superstitions "apparently played only a small role in the religion of black Kentuckians. . . . [and] they never identified their religion as African." They "sought regularity—orthodox acceptability—in their relationships with white congregations while simultaneously demanding independence." But African "religious ideology contained much that enabled slaves to adapt readily to the Christianity of their enslavers. . . . The belief in a supreme God who gave comfort in time of trouble, the emphasis on social conduct, and the emotional message of both black and white ministers made the transition [to Christianity] easy."[71]

Worship and church programs differed in levels of refinement. Some themes, however, were pervasive. The Old Testament allowed African Americans to identify with the children of Israel—their loving but stern Jehovah, their suffering in slavery in a foreign land, and their eventual liberation. From the New Testament they learned of Jesus, who through his suffering atoned for their sins and was the supreme example of mercy. Some blacks translated messages about faithfulness into a belief in a better life after death, but others could turn images like that of crossing over the River Jordan into a set of plans to cross the Ohio into freedom. However the messages were interpreted, many slaves believed that their religion gave them a victory over their masters.[72]

Black churches were like white churches in many ways. They offered the usual services beyond the immediate spiritual needs of the congregations. Larger churches created committees to visit members who were ill. Individual deacons of First Colored Baptist in Louisville were assigned to each of the city's wards in order to supervise visitation. A standing committee at the same church was responsible for handling applications and disbursing funds for the burial of indigent members. Sometimes controversies arose over what was appropriate. At First Colored Baptist, some members objected to the use of a fair to raise money. Older members at Fourth Street Baptist objected strongly to the introduction of a violin in a church service. Quinn Chapel's members disagreed over the purchase of an organ. Church members also squabbled among them-

selves and sometimes with their pastors over doctrinal or organizational matters. Although there was much cooperation between churches—ministers exchanging pulpits, participating in ordination services, or supporting each other in difficult times—hostilities sometimes arose between pastors and members of their congregations and resulted in church splits. George Wells, for example, formed Second Colored Baptist, taking about one hundred members from First Baptist with him. Church leaders were especially careful to keep whites from learning of such disagreements.[73]

The greatest threat to the black church came from whites. This took many forms—harassment of pastors by newspaper editors or white ministers, for one, and curfews, for another. In Louisville, an ordinance required that a white be present at services that blacks conducted, but it "was only loosely applied." Night watchmen were "required . . . to guard closely against noisy disturbances." Hostility to blacks' religious practices usually "involved churches located near white residential areas." Black ministers were sometimes harassed during church services, either by organized bodies or by angry individuals. The situation deteriorated during 1860–61.[74]

Nevertheless, black churches played a variety of roles in their communities, from hosting picnics on holidays for Sunday school scholars to offering Sunday afternoon concerts by church choirs. Louisville's Mozart Society developed from a series of concerts led by William H. Gibson Sr., a prominent church layman and a talented musician. Churches were also "the center of intellectual development" by increasingly "opening their doors for informational speeches, exhibitions, and lectures in the two decades before the Civil War."[75]

Education, too, was a major activity of churches. Some white churches supported black ones in this endeavor because of a sense of Christian duty. Many slaves as well as free people wanted to read and write in order to advance themselves. Learning took place through the master's guidance or that of his family members. By 1860 Henry Adams's school on Woods Alley between Ninth and Tenth streets in Louisville employed four teachers. Green Street Baptist, Asbury Chapel, Jackson Street Methodist, Center Street Methodist, Ninth Street Methodist, and St. Mark's Episcopal churches also had schools.[76]

Louisville's most noted educator was William H. Gibson Sr., a native of Maryland who was recruited by the pastor of Asbury Chapel. By 1860 about one hundred slaves and freemen regularly attended day and night classes in the basement of the church. The school offered algebra, geometry, and Latin in addition to its basic "three R's" and music instruction. Gibson also opened branch schools at Quinn Chapel and in Frankfort and Lexington.[77]

Mediating between the realities of racial oppression and the hopes for fairness and a better life beyond this world, African American churches and other social organizations represented blacks' desire for racial autonomy and self-expression. They were "the nucleus around which blacks organized their own social, educational, and cultural activities." A sign of the emerging black community was the New Year's Eve ball organized by free and slave blacks on the eve of the Civil War at the Falls Cities Hotel. The event was praised for "the gentilities of the dance, the promenade, and supper table . . . with commendable ease and grace."[78]

2

Incomplete Freedom
on the North Shore

The lives of blacks on the free side of the Ohio River were severely restricted, since most whites in the lower Midwest shared the cultural values of Negrophobes across the river.[1] Blacks resided in inferior housing and
occupied the lowest rung on the occupational ladder. They could not vote,
testify against whites in court, or serve on juries or in the militia. In Illinois and
Indiana they could not send their children to public schools, and in Ohio
access to public education was limited. Blacks who were not residents of Illinois or Indiana as of midcentury were forbidden by law to settle there. Passage
of the federal Fugitive Slave Law in 1850 made life for all blacks tenuous, as
slave-catchers became omnipresent. Some whites favored emancipation because it would eliminate blacks' desire to escape northward, while others preferred to send the freemen already residing in their state somewhere else. Whites
were not so much antislavery as they were antiblack.[2]

Labor on the north shore was free, however, and parents could hope for a
better life for their children. Not all whites, moreover, were hostile.[3] Abraham
Lincoln, arguably the most prominent son of the Ohio Valley, "a white world
with strong racial antipathies," was from his youth onward "generous to blacks."[4]
Even whites who were antiblack might realize that harassment of free blacks
strengthened the blacks' ties with each other and their enslaved brothers and
sisters. Despite the "shadow of the dream," demands for fair treatment would
eventually yield some positive results.[5]

The number and the proportion of blacks in north-shore counties was generally much lower than on the south shore. Largely because of constitutional and statutory restrictions and a tradition of harassment and violence, blacks represented a minuscule portion of the total population (see appendix, table 5). Only in Ohio was the proportion for the entire state above 1 percent. The Buckeye State had by far the largest number of blacks—36,673, as compared with 11,719 in Indiana and 7,660 in Illinois.

In Indiana about one in three blacks resided in river counties. In Ohio, about one in five did, and in Illinois it was about one in nine. These ratios reflect economic opportunity in northerly counties, shelter provided by sympathetic whites in the interior, and capricious living conditions along the Ohio. In Indiana, for example, the largest number of blacks lived in and around Indianapolis, and many others resided in the Whitewater River Valley, where Quakers were numerous. Illinois's Ohio River counties possessed limited natural and mineral resources and were the most culturally Southern among north-bank counties.[6]

In Ohio, Hamilton County had by far the largest number of blacks, with 4,608, and Brown County had the highest percentage, 3.7. Four of the six river counties opposite Kentucky exceeded the state's average of 1.6 percent. The counties with the lowest proportion were Appalachian, like their Kentucky counterparts. In Indiana, blacks were most numerous in Clark, Floyd, and Harrison counties, directly across the river from Louisville. These and upriver Jefferson and Dearborn counties had a higher percentage of blacks than the state's average. Counties downstream from the Falls of the Ohio were lower, except for Gallatin County in Illinois, which had the highest proportion of blacks of any north-bank county, slightly over 5 percent. Congress had permitted slavery in that region, which was rich in salines. The counties with the lowest proportion of blacks, Alexander and Pulaski, lay opposite the Jackson Purchase. Massac County, across the river from Paducah, also in the Purchase, had an African American population of only 1.8 percent.[7]

One of the most striking facts is that the Indiana counties of Warrick, Posey, and Vanderburgh had less than 300 blacks in all, while thousands of slaves lived directly across the Ohio in Daviess, Henderson, and Union counties. Indiana's restriction on migration, by itself, did not explain this. Upriver Jefferson County, Kentucky, had more than 10,000 blacks, but many were either hired slaves or free, and controls were looser. Not surprisingly, many blacks lived in the two Indiana counties across the river from Louisville. By contrast, Daviess, Henderson, and Union counties, overwhelmingly rural, had a large cohort of planters, whose ability to control blacks' lives was substantial.

Most African Americans on the north shore of the river in 1860 were natives of the upper South. Well over half in Cincinnati had been born in Kentucky or Virginia. In Vanderburgh County, Indiana, of those not listing Indiana as their state of birth, almost all were from Kentucky, Tennessee, or Virginia. The same was the case in Gallatin County, Illinois.[8]

Studies of mulattoes and female-male ratios reveal that in Cincinnati, mulattoes constituted 54 percent of the African American population, a much higher proportion than in any other north-shore city. This "reflected the dynamics of interracial sex, particularly between white men and black women." By the 1850s, a mulatto elite had emerged. In Vanderburgh County only one in eight blacks were mulattoes. The ratio of females to males was somewhat higher in Cincinnati (1.07) than it was in Evansville (.97).[9]

In five of the seven urban north bank counties (those with towns of 2,500 or more people) at least six in ten blacks lived in these towns, not in the countryside (see table 4). One-quarter of the 883 in Illinois's six river counties were in Shawneetown. African Americans, though, represented a relatively small share of cities' total population (see table 3). New Albany, with a 7.5 percent black population, had the highest proportion. Cincinnati, Ironton, and Portsmouth in Ohio ranged from 2.3 to 3.4 percent. Evansville's percentage was less than 1.

Each town had distinctly black neighborhoods. Half of Evansville's tiny black population, for example, resided on or near Lower Water Street, near Pigeon Creek. The first black church structure, erected in 1843, was located there. Most blacks in New Albany resided in West Union. The largest number of Madison's blacks lived in "Georgetown," in the Third Ward, north of Fourth Street, between Walnut and Main streets. The city's three black churches and schools were in the vicinity of Fifth and Walnut streets.[10]

Blacks in Cincinnati first settled in Little Africa, near the waterfront, but by the 1850s many had moved to Bucktown, an area on the east side of the city beyond Fifth and Sycamore streets. In 1850 Cincinnati blacks inhabited 106 clusters, which consisted of "two or more families living in the same dwelling with another African American family, next door to another black family, or a few doors away from other black households."[11] These clusters averaged five households and twenty-seven people. As elsewhere, blacks resided in the most broken-down, low-rent sections of the city. One in fourteen lived in alley structures. Landlords made a great deal of money from free blacks, because whites restricted the choices available to them. The 1860 census of Cincinnati disclosed increased concentration of blacks' residences. Almost half

lived in Wards 4 and 13. The percentage of blacks in the city was just 2.3, but in Ward 13 it was 13 percent and in Ward 4 it was 7.3.[12]

African American neighborhoods generally bore names pejoratively created by whites, but these regions allowed blacks to create and to sustain institutions that gave the people a sense of who they were and what they could achieve. Created was a "commons," a place where blacks interacted. Despite racism, blacks were not consumed with white machinations. They had a social universe of their own, with its distinctive sights, smells, and sounds.[13]

Residential discrimination was one of many constraints facing African Americans. Illinois had only 7,600 blacks. Only eight towns had 100 or more black residents, and Shawneetown, with about 200 in 1860, was the only southern Illinois town in that group. Beginning with the constitution of 1818, Illinois created a plethora of "black codes." Blacks could not vote or serve in the militia. Lifetime indentured servitude became commonplace in Gallatin and Pope counties.[14] A law passed in 1845 required blacks to produce a certificate of freedom and to post a $1,000 bond, and the law permitted whites to turn in blacks—slaves or servants—for even the slightest infractions. The revised constitution of 1848 forbade free blacks to settle in the state and whites to bring slaves into the state in order to free them. The General Assembly in 1853 imposed a fine of up to $500 on whites who violated that portion of the constitution. Blacks were deemed to be runaways if after ten days in the state they could not document their freedom, and they were fined. If they did not pay their fine, sheriffs could take them into custody and sell their services to cover the fine and court costs. The person then had to leave Illinois in ten days or face a larger fine. The 1853 law also allowed slave-owners "passing through" the state to retain their slaves, a provision that produced a great deal of chicanery.[15]

Indiana had similar restrictions. Racial bigotry prevailed in the constitutional convention of 1850–51, dominated by Democrats and rural interests. As in Illinois, a separate vote was held on the portion of the revised constitution (Article XIII) that forbade blacks to settle in Indiana after the end of 1851 and stipulated that fines collected from whites who violated the constitution by employing blacks be used for colonization. This provision was supported by more voters than the rest of the constitution was. Blacks living in the state on November 1, 1851, were required to register with their county clerk.[16] In 1852 the General Assembly created a state fund from fines to support the Indiana Colonization Society's efforts to relocate free blacks in Africa. Although this law remained on the books until 1865, few blacks chose to leave for Liberia.[17]

Ohio also imposed a number of restrictions on African Americans, but they were somewhat less harsh. One reason was Ohio's proximity to New England and the Middle States, which supplied a higher proportion of its population than that of Illinois and Indiana. In the most recent history of Ohio, Andrew Cayton points to another factor: that African Americans in the Buckeye State "were disproportionately involved in public conversations about the meanings of citizenship." Calling public meetings, writing petitions, publishing newspaper articles, and holding conventions nearly every year prior to 1860, black men such as John Parker and John Mercer Langston called on whites to provide access to education, the ballot box, and public places. Black Ohioans could thus "strengthen, not threaten, the emerging middle-class status quo."[18]

Although Ohio's proscriptions against blacks resembled those of Illinois and Indiana, the laws were unevenly enforced, and over time some moderation occurred. The legislature of 1849 repealed most of the black codes. Free blacks could attend public schools and testify in court but could not vote; ride inside public stage coaches; attend white colleges, academies, or seminaries; or be housed in state institutions for the deaf and dumb, the mentally ill, or the poor.[19]

A new constitution was created at the same time as Indiana's (1851), but the outcome for blacks was different. Regarding the ill-fated proposal that black children be allowed to attend school with whites, one delegate to the convention in Cincinnati declared. "I will not encourage the emigration of blacks into this state, nor will I make it so much the interest of that class to remain here. . . . I want them separate from the whites . . . [but] those who prefer companionship with Africans might go where they are."[20] The new constitution did not forbid free blacks to settle in the state, but it defined them as second-class citizens. They could not serve in the state militia, attend white public schools, or vote.[21]

The color line was rigid on the entire north bank of the river. Blacks were routinely excluded from hotels, restaurants, theaters, and other public accommodations.[22] Of all the proscriptions that blacks faced, though, "none seems to have weighed so heavily . . . as the fact that they were barred from the schools." Averred a black Hoosier, this was "an outrage upon the SOUL; *a war upon* THE IMMORTAL PART." Since most blacks were in Indiana to stay, "the question arises, would you rather have us among you in an educated and enlightened condition, or would you rather have us in an ignorant and degraded condition?"[23]

Indiana's first school law (1852) specifically excluded black pupils. Another law (1855) prevented blacks and mulattoes from paying school taxes. In

1860 about two-thirds of white children attended a public school. At most one-quarter of its black youth received a rudimentary education, through the assistance of black churches and sympathetic white organizations. In Madison the 1859 city directory listed the "Georgetown School," along with its teacher, Ellen P. Siddall. She may also have been an agent of the American Missionary Association. The annual conference of the African Methodist Episcopal (AME) Church in Indiana reported a church-run day school in New Albany, but nothing is now known about its location and length of operation. Undoubtedly it was like the others. Terms were irregular and short, usually two or three months. Most such schools offered only spelling, reading, writing, and arithmetic.[24]

An attempt to improve black schooling, the Eleutherian Institute in Lancaster, ten miles northwest of Madison, was an academy designed to train teachers. Opened in 1848, it was the brainchild of Rev. Thomas Craven, an antislavery Baptist minister from Oxford, Ohio. Craven obtained the land and secured funding for the erection of the dormitory and classroom buildings. The school flourished between 1855 and 1861. On the eve of the Civil War it had a staff of eight and about 100 students. Forty blacks, many of them former slaves, attended the school. The school's catalog stated that "the God of the Bible is practically recognized as the Father of the Human Race, its advantages being open to all." The school was necessary because blacks were excluded from public schools and "therefore doomed to hopeless ignorance, unless extraordinary efforts are put forth by themselves and their friends."[25]

This humble effort to educate blacks faced strong resistance from local whites. The property of school sympathizers was routinely savaged, and some staff members at the school were indicted for allegedly violating Article XIII of the new constitution. The charges were dropped after Stephen C. Stevens, a former member of the Indiana Supreme Court and an ardent antislavery attorney and judge in Madison, aided the staff members. Beset with continual financial problems and hampered by the death of Reverend Craven in 1860, the school closed shortly after the beginning of the war.[26]

Downstream, the census of 1860 disclosed that thirteen black youth between ages 6 and 14 had attended school in Evansville the previous year. In 1856 two black men appealed to the City Council for funds to support a black school run by a Mr. Green. Though their appeal was supported by several prominent white businessmen, action was tabled indefinitely. In the fall of 1859, Eleanor E. Johnson, a native of Massachusetts, arrived in the city to teach at the AME Church. She was supported by the American Missionary Association of New York City. At least one black student, a servant of German Catho-

lic entrepreneur John A. Reitz, attended parochial school at Holy Trinity Church.[27]

In Ohio, by contrast, a law passed in 1849 permitted blacks to send their children to public schools, but only if the races were segregated. Black taxpayers were to fund and govern their public schools. The state's top court subsequently ruled that separate schools were required if a district had more than twenty pupils. It also supported the exclusion of children from white schools if their blood was deemed three-fifths or more black. Implementation of the new legislation was slow, especially along the Ohio. Cincinnati officials did not comply with the law until the state's top court forced them to in 1858. The Colored Education Society ran three schools—two completely funded by African Americans. In 1860 about three in four white children attended public schools in Cincinnati, as compared with about two in five blacks.[28]

The architect of black schools in Cincinnati was native son John Isom Gaines (1821–1859). Educated by a student from Lane Theological Seminary, he graduated from Gilmore High School, established by white opponents of slavery in 1844. Gaines made his living selling groceries to black river travelers from his humble shop on the riverfront. He was one of six men elected to the first black school board and served as clerk of the school board and chief administrator until his death. Gaines led a successful but protracted legal battle to force whites to release tax moneys. Gaines was also elected president of the 1856 State Convention of Colored Men and chaired the State Central Committee. His reports as clerk reflected "verbal eloquence and dedication to the education of the black youth." His was "the seminal voice in an increasing crescendo of black self-prise [sic]."[29]

By 1860 Cincinnati had about a thousand black pupils, distributed among schools in the eastern and western districts. Walnut Street divided them. The growing western district had twice as many pupils as the eastern. Graded by three levels, schools served youth between the ages of six and seventeen. The schools were overcrowded and dilapidated, partly because of the low number of taxpayers: only 123 of 3,000 blacks were listed in the first school enumeration. District divisions also reflected class lines, since wealthier blacks resided in the eastern region bounded by Sixth, Seventh, Sycamore, Broadway, and McAllister streets. The "Black 400" dominated the fashionable block between Fifth and Sixth streets east of Broadway.[30]

The colored school board was controlled by black clergymen. Rev. Phillip B. Ferguson served the longest, from 1856 to 1870. The most influential teacher was Peter H. Clark, teacher-administrator in the western district beginning about 1850. Clark was an outspoken advocate of emigration to Africa, a posi-

tion strongly opposed by Gaines. Clark and Gaines worked together, though—
unsuccessfully—for a statewide black school system headed by a black man.
The two also sought the creation of the Ohio Colored Teachers Association,
formed shortly after Gaines's death. Clark vigorously opposed integration,
because he feared loss of quality as well as of teaching positions, income, and
community self-determination.[31]

By the early 1860s, with school expenditures a modest $12,274, the col-
ored public schools were the second-most-important institution, after churches,
in black Cincinnati. Most black leaders, including Clark, insisted that all teachers be African American, though that was not always possible because there
were not enough trained black teachers. Black schools were the pride of black
Cincinnatians, and black scholars symbolized the hope of the community. Black
schools provided training for business, professional, and civic affairs in Cincinnati and the nation.[32]

As destructive as exclusion, black codes, and limited access to education were,
harassment by whites was wanton and sometimes deadly. Few supposedly
friendly whites, moreover, rose above paternalism. The Whig and later Republican *Evansville Daily Journal,* for instance, frequently published stories about
rowdy behavior by "big and little buck negroes" on High Street, where they
intermingled "entertainments" with fisticuffs. The demeaning use of dialect
was common. "How to Get a Hat," for instance, described how Pomp had
secured a hat: "at a shop, ob course," he insisted. When asked the price of the
hat, Pomp explained, "I don't know nigger . . . de shopkeeper wasn't dar."[33]

In many counties along the river, blacks' numbers were quite small, and
most worked as farm laborers. Hence whites had little social intercourse with
them. When they encountered blacks, many whites assumed that they were
runaways. "Strange negroes" in places like the river counties of Illinois were
likely to attract slave-catchers, who whisked them off to Paducah and re-
enslavement.[34] Undoubtedly whites' previous lack of contact with blacks or
their fear of blacks' settling and taking away their jobs triggered antiblack
outbursts. The uneven application of black codes and exclusion laws led some
whites to take the law into their own hands. Violence was always near the
surface. The widespread presence of regulators, coercive bands of white men
committed to white supremacy, encouraged extralegal activities. In 1857 white
men in Mound City, Illinois, attempted to expel every African American there.[35]

Vigilantism and antiblack violence were pervasive and in some communities aided and abetted by local newspapers, such as the *New Albany Ledger.*
There was apparently no widespread violence against blacks in New Albany

until the summer of 1860. Some black leaders at a picnic had denounced the indignities inflicted by ignorant Irish and German workers and urged blacks to stand up for their rights. As a consequence a mob of young white men descended on black men and women at a dance and chased them to the small black district north of the railroad station. The *Ledger* denounced the actions of the black leaders and enlisted George Washington Carter, a barber who was the wealthiest black man in the city, to write a letter distancing himself from the remarks made at the picnic. Passions remained high. City officials intervened and established order—by rounding up and expelling blacks suspected of violating Article XIII. Whites in neighboring Jeffersonville made it clear that they did not want these men either, and drove them away.[36]

In Evansville a racially charged conflict occurred in late July and early August of 1857. The locus of the problem was a small black settlement just west of city limits. This cluster of rural farm dwellings due north of Henderson had existed since the late 1830s and was large enough to support a church. Sparked by a dispute over ownership of a pig, a fracas between blacks and whites and the subsequent arrest of five black men led hundreds of whites to march on the settlement and to attempt to expel the blacks who lived there. The Republican editor blamed the Democratic editor for inciting the riot by printing antiblack handbills and singled out the Democratic sheriff-elect as ringleader of the vigilantes. On August 19 the *Evansville Daily Journal* reported that all of the blacks had departed, having sold or leased their land.[37]

The situation in Ohio was as perilous. One factor was blacks' isolation in rural areas, where they were farmers or farm laborers. In urban areas there was relatively little conflict because blacks did menial labor, and custom and law kept African Americans "in their place." The slow growth of the state's black population was also an ingredient. But justice could be capricious, as in the case of one man accused and jailed in Manchester (Adams County) for allegedly raping a white woman. In late November 1856 he was taken to Kentucky and hanged. And entire populations could be threatened, as mobs occasionally savaged black communities. The most serious conflicts occurred in Cincinnati, where a number of race riots transpired between 1829 and 1843. Perceived threats to whites' jobs by a growing black population and alleged violation of the black laws were the causes.[38]

Leonard Curry's study of antebellum riots describes the 1841 crisis in Cincinnati as one of the most violent and disgraceful, one that ranked with the Philadelphia riot of 1834. In Cincinnati, as in the other cities, blacks were "isolated by prejudice, suppressed, restricted, emotionally traumatized, and the object of casual insult and assault by any drunken, irritated, or arrogant white

of however low degree."[39] In the long run, though, "the black community regrouped and took a stand for its rights in the Queen City." A young newcomer, John Mercer Langston, who had arrived the year before to join his two brothers, declared that this event "failed to hush the voices of the eloquent colored men themselves who through such experience were learning what their rights were and how to advocate and defend them."[40]

The Fugitive Slave Law of 1850 encouraged slave catching and kidnapping. The law provided active federal support for those seeking to apprehend runaways. U.S. commissioners were empowered to issue warrants for the arrest of fugitives and their return to slavery. An affidavit from a person claiming to be the owner or his or her representative sufficed as evidence of ownership, and fugitives were denied the right to testify in their own behalf. Commissioners earned a ten-dollar fee if they found for the claimant but only half that if they released the fugitive. Commissioners could deputize any citizen as a member of a posse to assist in enforcement of law, and heavy fines or jail times faced those who resisted the posse.[41]

Many northerners found the law distasteful, especially because it created a class of people who pursued fugitives for a living.[42] Frontline towns from Portsmouth to Cairo became dangerous places for all blacks, whatever their legal status. Nearly half of the cases in which owners manumitted their slaves in Floyd County, Indiana, for example, occurred in the 1850s. But even freed slaves had little security. Hattie McLain of Evansville recalled how she—the daughter of a slave and her white master—was brought by her father to Evansville, where mother and daughter were freed. Despite having certificates of freedom, slave-catchers kidnapped them and took them to Henderson County, where they were re-enslaved.[43]

Officers of the law and persons posing as allies often turned out to be accomplices of slave-catchers. Douglass Polly of Ironton, Ohio, was freed by his owner. He subsequently purchased the freedom of his brother and his wife, as well as their seven children, and brought them to the Ohio town. But the relatives of the former owner, now deceased, disputed his bequest and hired slave-catchers, who stole the children and a grandchild born in Ironton and took them to Kentucky. The mother was able, after long and arduous litigation, to recover three children and the grandchild. The other four were sold into slavery in Virginia. Another fugitive reached what he thought was safe haven in Ripley, Ohio. After feeding him a meal, the perfidious innkeeper threw a rope over his head from behind, put him on a steamer to Cincinnati, and took him to his master in Covington, where the innkeeper received a reward.[44]

The maladies created by the Fugitive Slave Law were numerous. In one case, nine women and children escaped from Covington and were hidden in a Cincinnati stable by a free mulatto who had promised to aid their flight to Canada. Instead, the mulatto claimed the one-thousand-dollar reward for their capture and led the owners to their hiding place. In another case, a federal marshal captured an alleged runaway named Lewis and escorted him back to Cincinnati. The federal commissioner was troubled by the claims of the marshal, who had produced an affidavit allegedly signed by the Kentuckian who claimed Lewis was his slave. The defense argued that Lewis had come into Ohio with his master's consent and was thus free. Lewis made the federal commissioner's decision-making moot by fleeing the city. Most troublesome was the status of slaves legally emancipated by owners in Cincinnati, as they were immediately subject to kidnapping.[45]

Arguably the most difficult case involved the Simon Garner family, Simon and his wife, their son and daughter-in-law, and their four grandchildren. They escaped on January 27, 1856, from plantations sixteen miles from Covington. The elder Garners and their son were claimed by one owner, and the son's wife, Margaret, and the four children by another. All were sheltered in a home near Cincinnati, where they were confronted by marshals and local officials. The son fired on them, wounding one. Margaret took the life of a three-year-old child and wounded another rather than have them returned to slavery. In the trial that followed, the defense claimed that the Garners had been in Ohio before, with the consent of their masters, and were free. The court upheld the claims of the two owners. Black Cincinnatians were incensed over the Garners' treatment, especially that of Margaret, and raised money for their defense. Antislavery Democratic governor Salmon P. Chase intervened, asking the governor of Kentucky to return "escaped" prisoners in a murder case. The latter complied, seeing an opportunity to establish a precedent for similar claims by his state. Unfortunately, by then the owner had sent Margaret and her family southward, and they could not be located.[46]

Blacks' security was even more tenuous downstream, especially in Illinois. In Cairo a gang of fifty whites from Missouri terrorized blacks' homes looking for runaways and, finding none, departed with several free blacks. Because rural sections of that part of the state were not safe places for "strange Negroes," it is not surprising that black newcomers to Illinois tended to bypass the southern part of the state and settle in and around Chicago, where they could avoid federal marshals and find employment.[47]

Federal officials generally enforced the Fugitive Slave Law, the successful operation of which remains debatable. Instead of settling the slave controversy,

it intensified it. The law devastated blacks, but it also strengthened community coherence among them. Blacks in "frontline" towns like Cincinnati assisted those fleeing from slavery. Blacks' flight from slavery did not diminish, and sympathetic whites' interest in protecting fugitives as well as in providing them legal assistance accelerated. The proximity of large, free settlements intensified south-shore whites' fears and emboldened free blacks on the north shore to risk life and limb to aid runaways.[48] The publication of *Uncle Tom's Cabin* in 1852, the passage of the Kansas-Nebraska Act, and the Dred Scott decision exacerbated this climate.

Madison, Indiana, was the one place along the Ohio where the contest between the forces of freedom and slavery was most heated. A number of antislavery operatives across the river were supported by black agents of the "liberty line" in Madison, of whom William Anderson, who arrived in 1836, was the chief. Conversely, a number of proslavery elements were active in the Indiana town. Almost as dangerous was Ripley, a deeply divided town on the river in Brown County, Ohio. The chief operative on the line there was John Parker, who had been attracted to the region by the white abolitionist Presbyterian minister, John Rankin. Both Anderson and Parker had brushes with death. While most white abolitionists, like Levi Coffin, scorned slave-stealing south of the river, ex-slaves did not, and they had substantial networks of allies southward. These "special forces" members were respectable men in their communities. Others in the "special forces" were shadowy, mysterious characters who also worked the Kentucky side of the river to assist runaways.[49]

Most whites on the north shore opposed any efforts that violated the law. The Whig and later Republican *Evansville Weekly Journal,* for instance, deplored the fact that slaves being transported on a steamboat docked at the wharf for repairs had to be taken into the city for safe keeping because bystanders had encouraged them to run away. A correspondent reported that in Newburgh a black man being taken to jail by a slave-catcher resisted and was aided by "meddlesome" and "dangerous" local abolitionists, who helped him escape and were charged with kidnapping. Advertisements describing runaways and promising rewards were frequent in that paper and its Democratic counterpart throughout the 1850s. The *Journal* tied the timing of slaves' running away to their fondness for roasting ears, in season in late summer.[50]

There were whites as well as blacks in most towns and villages who were allies of free and runaway blacks. Probably the most renowned was Levi Coffin (1798–1877), a Quaker who had moved to Cincinnati in the 1840s.[51] One of the many lesser-known heroes was Evansville's Andrew L. Robinson (1808–1883), a native of Vermont who tried his hand at running a dry goods store

and then moved to Delphi, Indiana, where he practiced law for twelve years. While there he served two terms in the state House of Representatives and was Speaker of the House. An ardent Baptist and a free-soil Democrat, he came to Evansville in 1848 and was elected prosecuting attorney for the Evansville region. His law partner for many years was another Vermonter, Horatio Q. Wheeler, an abolitionist who was father of the Evansville public schools.[52] Robinson refused to detain alleged runaways in court when the owner was not present. In the summer of 1853, for example, he rescued a five-year-old girl who had been taken from the local orphan asylum by a Southern woman, who was on a steamer bound for Bowling Green, Kentucky. The Whig newspaper described him as a "philanthropist, an avowed friend of the colored race."[53]

Much of what we have been told about the Underground Railroad reflects romantic interpretations based on oral tradition that feature benevolent white abolitionists actively assisting runaways. Behind these impressions are efforts by Wilbur Siebert, a historian who began to collect and record stories that were published in 1898 as *The Underground Railroad*. His book fed "the apparently infinite need in American society to believe in an organized, secretive crusade by whites and blacks together to free slaves in the antebellum era." Siebert "cultivated Northerners' desires to participate in the reminiscence industry" and developed the themes of filial piety and "alternative veteranhood," a means by which women and civilian men demonstrated that they had also served the cause of freedom before and during the Civil War. "Living martyrs" studded Siebert's work, such as a white woman in Adams County, Ohio, "who was remembered for resisting slave hunters with 'a kettle of boiling water on the stove as her only means of defense.'" Blacks were rarely named in these reminiscences. By the 1890s slavery, like the war, was "the subject of nostalgia, of self-congratulatory adventure tales. Masked in this comforting haze was a real history of Underground Railroad heroism, as well as the deteriorating condition of American race relations."[54]

All escapes were dangerous, and there were few people whom fugitives could trust. Ingenious means of running away were hatched over lengthy periods of time. Runaways had to be self-reliant and courageous. Success in escaping depended on being able to travel independently and on possessing forged passes or certificates of freedom. When fugitives identified those who aided them, they usually named free colored people.[55]

Early postwar county histories illustrated the perspective promoted by writers like Siebert. The first history of Adams County, Ohio, published in

1880, boasted that the county had had one of the earliest antislavery societies in the nation but otherwise said very little about the presence of African Americans in the county. The Halliday House in Cairo, Illinois, portrayed itself after the war as a station on the Underground Railroad. The most comprehensive study of the Underground Railroad in Indiana was published in 1915 by an aged man who described the antislavery work of his father more than six decades earlier. His heroes were whites, and African Americans were rarely visible.[56]

By contrast, Emma Lou Thornbrough's pioneering history of Indiana blacks not only identified several major escape routes northward (through Vanderburgh County, Leavenworth, New Albany, Madison, and Lawrenceburg), but also stressed the importance of blacks as agents on the liberty line. Recent scholarship has confirmed the identity of those African Americans she named—for instance, five Madison men: Chapman Harris, Elijah Anderson, Henry Thornton, Griffin Booth, and George Baptiste.[57]

The record in Evansville, a frontline town on the Underground Railroad, is problematic. The Lyles settlement west of the city was doubtless a haven, as was perhaps the basement of the Washington Hotel in the city. From there those seeking freedom would travel north either on the roadbed of the Evansville and Crawfordsville Railroad or on the Wabash and Erie Canal towpath to safe havens in central Indiana and then to Canada.[58] According to oral-history records gathered by Works Progress Administration workers in the mid-1930s, ferrymen posing as fishermen who were agents of the "Antislavery League" kept all-night watches for light signals from the Kentucky side of the river that indicated there were fugitives wishing to cross to Evansville. Robinson, the attorney mentioned above, defended these "fishermen." One of the most plausible accounts identified George Stuges, an African American, as a guide who frequently brought runaways to the riverbank and lit signals for the ferrymen.[59]

Recent studies of the Underground Railroad in southeastern Indiana provide more certainty about the operations of the liberty line there. The Bell family, Virginia-born whites who owned land in southern Harrison County, across the river from Brandenburg, Kentucky, was suspected by locals of being abolitionists. The Mauckport Road northward from that point in Harrison County was frequently used by runaways and their pursuers. Most locals considered it disreputable and dishonorable to aid fugitives, and capturing runaways was lucrative. In September 1857 Charles Bell and one of his sons and Oswald Wright, a former slave, aided a runaway but were captured and jailed in Brandenburg. Two Bell brothers freed their father and brother the following

summer, but Wright, moved to another jail, spent five years in prison before returning to Corydon in 1864.[60]

Blacks residing in Floyd County, especially in the West Union part of New Albany, actively assisted runaways from Louisville. The frequency with which the *New Albany Daily Ledger* maligned and berated the residents of that neighborhood supplies indirect evidence of such efforts. It is also likely that several white men who belonged to the Second Presbyterian Church aided fugitives, and that congregation had some black members who were possible allies. Several other New Albany blacks were identified as agents—notably Henson McIntosh, who was arrested by Louisville authorities in 1861, and a woman named Sarah Lucas, who allegedly shared her free papers with a runaway woman from Louisville.[61]

The great-niece of a slave named Lewis Barnett recounted in 1936 a story repeated often by her parents, who were former slaves. About to be sold, her great-uncle escaped with twelve others traveling through New Albany. A black family sheltered them for two days, but they were recaptured and returned to Louisville. Barnett was sold for fifteen hundred dollars and taken to New Orleans. After the war he returned to New Albany three times to visit his relatives. The children heard the story many times, and each time he pointed out his escape route down Cherry Street.[62]

The region from neighboring Clark County upstream to Dearborn County had several escape routes that were largely manned by free blacks. Some were opened as early as 1820 and operated as late as 1861. Madison, the state's largest city until the mid-1840s, was the catalyst for Underground Railroad activity "stretching from Skylight to Carrolton, Kentucky and from Bethlehem to Brooksburg on the Indiana side of the Ohio River."[63]

After free blacks from Virginia (William Anderson, mentioned earlier as a chief antislavery operative, and the five identified by Thornbrough) arrived in Madison in the middle to late 1830s, a more aggressive, better-organized approach to signaling and establishing routes and operations was created. These skilled workers settled in the new Woodburn Addition to Madison, an area that came to be named "Georgetown," after George Hopkins. Chapman Harris helped establish St. Paul's Baptist Church on Fifth Street in 1849. At night he transported slaves from skiffs at the riverfront to Lancaster in the interior. Baptiste, a barber, was credited with bringing 187 slaves to freedom through the help of whites who lived on the corner of Second and Jefferson, close to his shop and home. Coordination between free blacks and white abolitionists also improved in this period. The momentum was stopped by a series of mob attacks on the homes of free blacks. Elijah Anderson fled to Lawrenceburg.

Griffin Booth moved to Canada, and Baptiste to Detroit. Harris relocated outside of town, where he recruited and trained a cell of free blacks and Kentucky slaves that was active into the 1850s.[64]

Thanks to the arrival of William Anderson and also to proximity to Cincinnati, Underground Railroad activity in Dearborn County became substantial. Anderson, who passed for a white man, was the most prominent agent in southeastern Indiana. A blacksmith who made fine wrought-iron fences and fancy ironwork, he helped to establish the AME Church in Lawrenceburg. As elsewhere, whites in the Anti-Slavery League were important allies. These whites posed as fishermen and peddlers, helping inform slaves of escape times and places and providing them with clothing likely to be worn by whites and free blacks, as opposed to distinctive slave garb.[65]

Losses of slaves in Boone and other northern Kentucky counties were substantial. Consequently, Kentuckians increased the use of slave-catchers and detectives in Indiana. Lawrenceburg's mayor turned over one alleged runaway to a slave-catcher. The fact that Lawrenceburg's tiny black population—about one hundred—was compressed into a small area near the courthouse, and that most whites were unsympathetic to the presence of blacks also worked against William Anderson and his compatriots. In November 1856 he was captured and sentenced to the Kentucky State Penitentiary in Frankfort. On the day he was to have been released in February 1861, he was found murdered in his cell.[66]

In Ohio, black churches near the river—for example, the Macedonia Missionary Baptist Church in Lawrence County, Ohio, and Union and Zion Baptist churches in Cincinnati—were major centers of opposition to the enforcement of the Fugitive Slave Act, which threatened the life of free black communities. Cincinnati became the leading training ground for those seeking to undermine slavery. John Parker, who had settled in Ripley, Ohio, after purchasing his freedom for eighteen hundred dollars, received his training in Cincinnati. So did Gabriel Johnson, who set up a safe house for fugitives near the river in Ironton. By 1860 many runaways lived in western Canada, opposite Detroit. Henry Bibb, a fugitive who fled to Canada and unsuccessfully attempted to free his wife and child in Kentucky on several returns to the state, published the *Voice of Freedom* in Cincinnati. He boasted that in 1855 thirteen slaves arrived from Covington by way of Cincinnati—five of them the property of the mayor.[67]

Enforcement of the Fugitive Slave Act proved to be problematic in Ohio's river towns, especially Cincinnati, owing to strong opposition from African Americans and some whites. Blacks in those towns were in a good position to

help runaways because many slaves came and went as workers on steamboats or as servants of white travelers. The north-bank blacks actively encouraged the slaves to run away, partly because they believed the end of slavery would improve their own living conditions. By assisting runaways, however, they also jeopardized their own security and safety, because the city had many proslavery whites.[68] Nonetheless, blacks' homes along the river allowed fugitives to "enter an organized community. . . . 'There can be no doubt about the fact that Cincinnati's politically astute African-American population was well aware of its own strategic significance in the fight against slavery.' Slaveholders also made this observation, and it is reasonable to assume that blacks in Cincinnati were troublesome to slavemasters."[69]

As in the quest for public education, the struggle for freedom enlisted a number of white allies: merchant Levi Coffin and his wife; educators Theodore Dwight Weld and Augustus Wattles at the city's Lane Theological Seminary; and attorneys such as Salmon P. Chase. Many Cincinnatians loathed the Fugitive Slave Law because it compelled federal officials to enforce slavery in a state whose constitution forbade slavery. Opponents attempted to stymie the enforcement of the hated law by legal means—for example, by insisting that "judges could not appoint commissioners to exercise judicial authority."[70]

In his *Reminiscences,* Coffin described Cincinnati as both a real and a symbolic line between slavery and freedom where slave-catchers were omnipresent. In one case, a hunter, dressed as a woman, appeared in the basement of a black church in Cincinnati where fugitives often stopped. The wife of the sexton was suspicious and sent for Coffin, whose interrogation revealed the visitor's true identity. Members of the church inflicted severe punishment on him. Coffin's numerous examples of blacks playing an active part in assisting fugitives passing through the city and turning to whites when trouble was imminent strengthens the conclusions of a recent study that places African Americans in the frontline of the struggle for freedom.[71]

Underground Railroad activity in southern Illinois was relatively insignificant in comparison, mostly because of the paucity of black residents, the overwhelming number of whites with upper South roots, and the region's lack of towns. The chief trail to freedom in the state stretched northward from St. Louis, but a feeder branch originated at Cairo and followed the Illinois Central Railroad, which connected that town with Chicago in the mid-1850s.[72]

Whites who attempted to aid blacks in southern Illinois faced enormous risks. Newspapers like the *Golconda Herald* attacked any hint of opposition to slavery or racial discrimination. One Methodist minister in Metropolis permitted blacks to worship in a separate section in his church, but when two

white women refused to condone such discrimination by sitting in that section, they were threatened with tarring and feathering. Agents of the American Missionary Association began to settle in the region in 1856. Within four
years there were salaried agents in Golconda, Metropolis, and Shawneetown.
They held a variety of occupations, but their real purpose was agitation against
slavery. James West, for instance, peddled Bibles and tracts and sought to educate illiterate blacks. His work was especially dangerous because Democrats
controlled most post offices, where it took great courage to receive antislavery
literature sent in the mail. By 1860 the organization had about seventy adherents in the region. One of the most audacious was George Luchan, an Oberlin
graduate, who preached at the Shawneetown AME Church in January 1859
and made friends in the small black community. West reported that he was
threatened with tarring and feathering if he set foot in Massac County and
was accosted and nearly lynched while traveling in Pope County. Mobs jeopardized Luchan's life several times.[73]

Blacks on the north shore had a modicum of protection in the communities
they had erected. Most were tiny. Cincinnati's, the largest in the Old Northwest, was able to create churches, fraternal and benevolent organizations, schools,
professions, and businesses. Blacks also played an active part in conventions
that attempted to guarantee constitutional and legal equality and in efforts to
assist fugitives from slavery across the river. Cincinnati's blacks, for example,
established an AME congregation on February 4, 1824. Less than a decade
later, Mound Street Union Baptist Church was organized. By 1860 the city's
blacks boasted five churches. They also had eleven fraternal and benevolent
societies that provided benefits during sickness and at death, as well as fellow-
ship and recreational opportunities. Women's societies promoted moral uplift
and temperance. Leaders of these organizations came from the black elite, the
"Black 400."[74]

Though of minuscule value by whites' standards, the property amassed by
Cincinnati's blacks was worth more than blacks' property in any other Ohio
River city, including Louisville and Pittsburgh. Eighty-eight held property
valued at $1,000 or more. The top two were hucksters—Joseph J. Fowler and
Richard Phillips, who between them owned property worth $31,000. The
upper ranks were also filled with such occupations as stevedores and barbers,
the latter job providing "black men their most promising opportunities to
earn a living, purchase real estate, and increase their standing." A resident recalled that if there was "anything like an aristocratic class of such persons it was
found in Cincinnati." The whole black community "gave evidences in every

way . . . of its intelligence, industry, thrift, and progress; and in matters of education and moral and religious culture, furnished an example worthy of the imitation of their whole people."[75]

The black elite, among which were businessman John Isom Gaines, clergyman Philip B. Ferguson, and teacher Peter H. Clark, also provided leadership in civic affairs. Although most were light-skinned, or mulattoes, they fought against constitutional and legal proscriptions of the rights of all African Americans. They helped to organize and participated in the state conventions of colored citizens in the decade of the 1850s. These leaders confronted two challenges, though. On the one hand, the black elite, many of whom depended on whites for their income, could not avoid being influenced by whites' portrayal of the black masses as profligate and shiftless. On the other, their livelihoods were also linked to dark-skinned black laborers and poor people. As the latter secured a small but tenuous foothold in the economy, their progress generated resistance and hatred from many whites.[76]

Color, gender, and ideology produced some tensions within black Cincinnati. Skin pigmentation mattered, because light skin connoted higher status and influence. Color lines were reinforced by law and politics. For example, the Ohio Supreme Court ruled that males with more than 50 percent white ancestry could vote. Gender mattered. Black women were active in churches, antislavery societies, temperance unions, and sewing circles. They raised money for fraternal, religious, social, and political organizations that men dominated. Women attended political and civil rights conventions, but they were often denied the right to vote. Black Cincinnatians also had ideological divisions. Some leaders thought that organized protest would diminish the standing that blacks had in whites' eyes, while others confronted the evils of slavery and racism directly. Although most favored interracial efforts, a few, like Clark, advocated black nationalism and emigration to Africa.[77]

Other black communities on the north shore resembled Cincinnati's in many respects, though on a much smaller scale. In Indiana, African Americans were disadvantaged economically because they had limited resources and faced strong racial prejudice. The vast majority, whether in towns or on farms, were laborers or servants. Some, such as Fountain Thurman in Jefferson County, Indiana, became relatively wealthy. But less than 6 percent of the black population of Indiana owned real estate, the average value of which was $628. More than half of those who owned property lived in just nine Indiana counties, three of which were on the Ohio: Clark had 24, and Floyd and Jefferson had 46 each. The total value of real estate in these three counties was about $75,000, one-quarter of the blacks' total in the state.[78]

In Vanderburgh County, by 1860 blacks had acquired real estate valued by census-takers at $11,760 and personal property worth another $4,500. Only nine heads of household owned any property, and one person—Sina (or Lena) McDaniel, a widow who had three children and an extended household totaling ten persons—accounted for one-third of the total value of realty. Another person of note was James Carter, a fifty-year-old native of Kentucky who had arrived in Evansville about 1840. He ran the National Hotel, on Water between Pine and Leet streets. Probably the most influential blacks were the pastors of the county's two churches, but they possessed little property of value. Like those in other towns, Evansville's blacks were also distinctive because of the substantial number of black women who worked, mostly as domestics and washerwomen. A fairly typical family was that of Aaron Flowers, a twenty-eight-year-old steamboat hand, and his wife, Charlotte, who took in washing.[79]

African Americans took seriously the American dream of not only striving for material advancement, but also forming families and organizations to support each other. Getting started was a challenge. Three men arrived in Evansville from Cincinnati in early April 1854 to open a barber shop on Water Street. Two days after their arrival, a German American barber insisted that the men were violating Article XIII of the new state constitution. Although the county recorder ruled there was no conclusive proof to sustain the charge, so that the three were released from custody, they left town.[80]

Census records for Vanderburgh County in 1860 reveal that of the 128 black persons enumerated, all but 16 resided in the 24 households that blacks headed. Of these, 14 were nuclear—father, mother, and children—and the remainder were either extended or augmented. Females headed a relatively high number of black families (10) because of the short life expectancy of black males and the exigencies of life, including slave-catching along the Ohio. Desertion and divorce may also have been factors.[81]

Blacks also formed religious institutions, fraternal societies, and benevolent organizations. Churches were by far the most numerous and influential, particularly the AME. A powerful force in religious life as well as in education, social hygiene, race pride, and racial unity, the church was "a symbol of the ability of members of their race to elevate themselves through their own efforts."[82] Initially north-bank African Americans joined white denominations, especially the Methodist Episcopal Church, but whites' discrimination and blacks' desire for autonomy brought about the shift to black churches. An interesting case was that of Walnut Street Methodist Church in Madison, where all of the members were black. When some members and their pastor, William

J. Anderson, withdrew to form a branch of the AME Church, membership dropped dramatically, and the church lacked a regularly assigned minister thereafter.[83]

The AME denomination offered blacks an opportunity to improve by their own efforts. A dark-skinned native of India and a former Quaker, William Paul Quinn, began his work with the AME Church as circuit rider. He created nearly fifty churches in Indiana and Ohio and became a bishop of the denomination.[84] One of the first AME congregations in Indiana was Bethel, formed in about 1841 on a farm west of Mount Vernon. The Evansville African Methodist Church was organized sometime before June 5, 1843, when its four trustees leased land and subsequently built a church on Leet Street. A Bayou Society purchased land in the summer of 1850 for a second church in the county, located near the Lyles settlement in Perry Township.[85]

Second to the AME in membership was the Baptist Church. Most black Baptists before 1865 were members of white churches, but thereafter they formed their own congregations. Liberty Baptist Church of Evansville, organized in March 1865, was illustrative of that pattern. Exceptions were black churches formed in New Albany (1846) and in Madison (1849). An Indiana association of black Baptists, founded in 1858, claimed eight churches and 306 members in 1864. Three of the largest ones were in Ohio River communities—Charlestown, Madison, and New Albany.[86]

Fraternal and benevolent organizations also appeared. Only one of Indiana's fifteen black Masonic lodges in 1860 was located in an Ohio River town—New Albany. Black benevolent societies and temperance groups were closely linked to churches. The Indiana AME Conference reported that there were seven black temperance societies in the state, two in Ohio River counties—Clark and Floyd. Church leaders were also tied to community development. Some towns annually celebrated the emancipation of slaves in the West Indies on August 1. Parades, picnics, and speeches focused on education and self-improvement. In these gatherings the participation of clergymen was prominent.[87]

But Indiana blacks' advancements along the Ohio remained tenuous. Racist assumptions, always present, often led to calamity. In February 1859, for instance, a mob of white men descended on an old frame tenement house on the corner of Leet Street and the Wabash and Erie Canal in Evansville that they alleged to be a house of ill fame inhabited by whites as well as blacks. Willard Carpenter owned the dwelling. The men burned the place, "silently tolerated long enough." It turned out that this was the dwelling of a law-abiding mulatto woman whose husband was away, working on a steamboat.[88]

Relatively little has been recorded and written about antebellum African

Americans in the tiny Ohio River communities of Illinois. Blacks in Shawneetown, like those in neighboring Golconda and Metropolis, had their own church. They had worshipped in either their homes or white churches before 1842, when Presbyterians—who had admitted blacks, albeit to the balcony—gave blacks their old church building. Five years later, members purchased a lot for a new structure, but they split over whether to affiliate with the Baptists or the AME Church. Hence no new church (or school) was built until the 1850s.[89]

Illinois river county blacks' economic and social state resembled that of those upriver. In 1860, for instance, 54 percent of southern Illinois black heads of household owned no real estate, and only 6 percent had real property worth more than one thousand dollars. Census records also reveal similarities in household organization. The state census of Pope County in 1855 indicated that all of its 183 African Americans lived in the thirty-two households that blacks headed—twenty-five by males and seven by females. The largest household contained 11 residents and the smallest 2, and the average size was 6.[90]

The federal census of 1860 identified 54 African American residents in Alexander County. All but 12 lived in Cairo, the county seat. Forty-two resided in the eleven black-headed households in the county and 12 in white households. The largest black household contained 6 persons, and the average one 4. Most, one can infer, were made up of extended families. Blacks in Alexander County who headed households were mainly employed in service occupations, like all but one of the blacks living in white households. Not surprisingly, few had much property. Of the eight family heads who declared they had real or personal property or both, the wealthiest, David Griffey, owned land worth $400. He also claimed personal property valued at $150.[91]

In Gallatin County in 1860, the vast majority of African Americans lived in black-headed households. About four in five families were nuclear or extended. Most households contained five to six people. Single-parent families constituted one in six, and most were female-headed. Perhaps typical was Jeremiah Smith, a fifty-five-year-old free black preacher from North Carolina, who after his wife's death had moved to Gallatin County from Alabama with two of their children and a son-in-law. Smith's son, Bryant, born in 1820, eventually set up a separate household, and he, too, became a preacher. It appeared to be commonplace for blacks to move into the area in extended families, seeking safety in numbers. Pressures against newly freed blacks in the South combined with cheap land and the promise of a better life in the North to prompt the migration. Almost all of the blacks aged twenty or less were natives of Illinois, while the largest share of those who were older had been

born in Kentucky and Tennessee. About half had been freed before settling in Gallatin County. Others had been brought there by their masters to be manumitted or had received certificates of freedom after completing their indentures.[92]

Quite a few Gallatin County blacks owned animals and tools—for example, for blacksmithing. As noted by John Mack Faragher, black-white interaction was a necessity for personal as well as business matters. Black blacksmith John Smothers, for instance, traded at a white-owned store in Shawneetown. Probate records reveal that most attained only humble fortunes. William "Billy" Ewing left an estate worth $18 and was buried in a shroud that cost $1.69 and a coffin valued at $5.60.[93]

By occupation, eight in ten black household heads in 1860 were common laborers, farmhands, or farmers. A few were skilled workers. The county had one black preacher—AME—indicating which group had won the battle over the affiliation of the new church structure. Nearly all blacks with real property were farmers, the wealthiest of whom were Moses Barker, Cornelius Elliott, and Zachariah Wilson. The value of their farms, which totaled 1,021 acres, ranged from $4,000 to $4,600. Elizabeth Ward, whose property was valued at $5,400, was the wealthiest black in the county.[94]

As the moderate successes of African Americans in Gallatin County demonstrate, life on the north shore of the Ohio on the eve of the Civil War was promising, though restricted. In 1860, however, the bulk of the black population along the Ohio lived on the south shore, in slavery, and in the country. The war would change not only where people lived, but also the conditions under which they lived.

PART TWO

THE IMPACT
OF THE
CIVIL WAR
ON
BLACKS

3

Conflict and Remnants
of Slavery on the South Shore

Civil war brought mostly unintended change, but the initial goal of preserving the Union was achieved. Although many feared that the Ohio might become the dividing line between the antagonists, Kentucky remained in the Union. Native son Lincoln observed that that achievement outweighed even a divine blessing. The commonwealth contributed between 90,000 and 100,000 men to the Union Army. But Kentucky was a slave state, and 25,000 to 40,000 men served in the rebel army. Most significantly, Kentucky's slave-owners were ultimately forced to emancipate any slaves who had not already freed themselves. About one-quarter of the state's men in Union blue were ex-slaves.[1]

Until recently, though, blacks did not figure in histories of Civil War Kentucky. The emphasis was on battles, military contributions, guerrilla warfare, and socioeconomic change. Even the most recent history of the state contains relatively little on the topic. The chapter on the war stresses the financial losses experienced by slave-owners and ends with a discussion of the deleterious effects of slavery on whites: the state was "retarded economically by the presence of slavery."[2]

The war's imprint on the commonwealth was enormous, since it was a slave state with economic, social, and cultural ties both to other slave states and to the Old Northwest. Its river border was a porous boundary between divergent labor systems. Some of the most important early engagements of the war

occurred in or near western Kentucky. U.S. Grant's occupation of Paducah early in the war proved to be one of the most critical events in the war in the west. Confederate raids into Kentucky in late summer 1862 briefly threatened Union forces at Louisville. Incursions into the state continued, however, and guerrilla warfare persisted through early 1865.[3]

Union troops occupied much of the state beginning in September 1861. Relations with civilian authorities were strained—on matters relating to loyalty and especially to emancipation and black troops. Consequently, Kentuckians increasingly turned against the president. In the presidential election of 1864, the commonwealth was one of just three Union states to vote for his opponent.[4]

Possibly the most notorious Union commander was General E.A. Paine, in charge of the western part of the state beginning July 19, 1864. Paine imposed from his headquarters in Paducah what even recent historians of the state have called a seven-week-long "reign of terror." Prominent citizens were fined arbitrarily but could purchase exemptions from the charges. Several were executed without "even a pretense of a trial." Hundreds of men were conscripted to work on a fort but excused if they paid up to three hundred dollars. Paine fled across the river; when he was tried by military authorities, he received only a reprimand.[5]

Kentucky's economic and social fabric was also significantly altered. Assessment of slaves in 1860 was $107.5 million; at the end of the war it was $7.2 million. The number of farm workers, black and white, plunged, devastating agricultural production and leading to a decrease in acreage under production. Armies caused huge property losses, such as those inflicted by Confederate raiders on the Louisville and Nashville Railroad. In the meantime, prices for consumer goods and realty soared. River trade on the Mississippi and the Ohio and the latter's main tributaries was disrupted and subject to restrictions from Union officials until early 1864. The towns of Henderson, Owensboro, and Paducah were especially hard hit. Louisville, though, prospered as a commercial and manufacturing center.[6]

Kentuckians could not avoid the social consequences of the war: families, churches, and communities were divided over the war. With many men off to war and laborers scarce and costly, women entered the workforce as farmers or as factory workers. They raised funds, made clothing and bandages, served as nurses, and educated their children. The war cut school attendance almost in half, as teachers either went off to war or took better-paying jobs, and as young men enlisted or dropped out of school to work.[7]

The imprint of war varied by region. Kentucky's Ohio River tributaries

and its Mississippi border on the west invited military activity by both sides throughout the war.[8] Many raids and skirmishes occurred throughout 1862–65 between Brandenburg and Paducah on the Ohio. Hawesville's trade with cross-river Cannelton was shut down by Union blockade, and Confederate guerrillas damaged riverboats and coal mines around Hawesville that produced fuel for Union gunboats and merchant steamboats. A Union gunboat bombarded the town June 24, 1864, after receiving reports that guerrillas were present.[9]

Counties on the south shore of the river were not united in their views. Sympathy with the Confederacy was strongest in the Purchase and the Pennyroyal, a region that included Breckinridge, Crittenden, and Livingston counties. Ballard County, for instance, contributed 400 men to the Confederate Army and only 100 to the Union Army. Similar patterns existed at Smithland and Brandenburg. Profound bitterness resulted from alleged and real damage to property. Smithland's citizens resented Union soldiers' use of churches and homes as stables and hospitals, and Brandenburgers claimed that Union troops severely damaged their courthouse. West Point, just downriver from Louisville in Hardin County, was also a pro-Confederate bastion, and anti-Union views increased when the town was occupied by Michigan troops in September 1861.[10]

By contrast, some counties, especially Campbell and Kenton, across from Cincinnati, had few slaves, like their Appalachian counterparts upriver, and relatively few supporters of the Confederacy. Covington had a large percentage of German immigrants and a large Unionist majority. Its economic ties to Cincinnati grew with the building of a pontoon bridge in late summer 1862 that expedited the erection of fortifications and the sending of men and supplies to ward off Confederate troops under Edmund Kirby Smith. (War had stalled construction of John Roebling's suspension bridge, begun in 1856.) Because of the county's strategic position, two Union forts were constructed there. Unionism was also intense in neighboring Newport, whose breweries, meat processing plants, and iron factories prospered.[11]

In the three Appalachian counties—Boyd, Greenup, and Lewis—Union feeling was strong, and therefore the Republican Party became the dominant force in wartime and postwar political culture. Nine thousand Union troops, for instance, were moved from the Cumberland Gap to Greenup County, providing a stronghold on that section of the Ohio River. The economies of these counties did not suffer during the war.[12]

Divisions also occurred within counties. In Hancock, farmers along the top of the ridge that lay inland from the Ohio had few slaves and little need for

them. Hawesville, a rowdy coal mining town of 1,128, was largely Confederate in sympathy. Old slave-owning families around Lewisport, by contrast, tended to be pro-Union. On Sunday, June 19, 1864, a steamer bound for Owensboro landed at Hawesville to take on coal. Robert Beauchamp, a prominent planter and merchant, joined other townspeople to observe, because a recruiter of Negro troops was present. A number of passengers were black men en route to service in the Union Army. One of Beauchamp's slaves broke free and fled toward the vessel. Beauchamp's men attempted to stop him, and an exchange of gunfire ensued. When the craft eventually arrived in Owensboro, a defiant. state guard commander placed the recruits in the city jail. But Union authorities enrolled them—including the fugitive—the next day.[13]

Confederate sympathies were strong in Breckinridge County, and guerrillas, mostly horse thieves, were a continual threat. Yet the county's loyalties were divided by Sinking Creek, with pro-Union sentiment strong below it and pro-Confederate feeling strong above it. Similar observations can be made about Union County, strategically located downriver from Evansville and a major source of coal and tobacco. Pro-Confederate sentiment was strongest in the southern part of the county. In the fall of 1864, members of the Indiana Home Guard from Posey County occupied Uniontown, purportedly a haven for Confederate raiders.[14]

Henderson and Daviess counties, both having large numbers of slaves and planters, furnished many men to the Union Army, but anti-Unionist sentiment was aggravated by the presence of Union troops. The towns of Henderson and Owensboro also suffered financially from the disruption of river trade and the capturing of much of that business by merchants in Evansville and Louisville. Raids by Confederate guerrillas also hurt them.[15]

Pro-Unionists in Henderson County were led by Senator Archibald Dixon, a wealthy planter. His sons, however, were Confederate sympathizers. When the 32nd Indiana, led by James M. Shackelford from Evansville, occupied Henderson in October 1861, pro-Union opinion declined sharply. Support for Henderson native Adam Johnson, leader of Confederate forces in the region, was strong. The war postponed a number of capital projects, chiefly the rail line southward to Nashville that had been launched in 1859. The town emerged from the war, however, with its tobacco stemmeries and other businesses intact.[16]

A similar pattern existed in Owensboro and Daviess County. One of the first companies of Confederate troops from Kentucky was formed in Owensboro in the summer of 1861. A regiment of Union troops arrived there in the fall of 1861, and hundreds remained in and around the town for the remainder of the

war. As in most of the commonwealth, opposition to President Lincoln mounted after the issuance of the Emancipation Proclamation and the introduction of black troops. Former Whig leaders generally shifted to the Democratic Party. Owensboro's commerce suffered from the Union embargo and from guerrilla forays. The town was raided twice in 1864, and the courthouse was severely damaged by guerrilla-inflicted fire in January 1865.[17]

Matters were similar in downriver Paducah. When Confederates occupied nearby Columbus, Kentucky, in early September 1861, Ulysses Grant moved his Illinois troops upriver to the mouth of the Tennessee, creating immediate resentment toward the alleged intruders. That view persisted during the war. Union trade regulations, which continued into early 1864, disrupted commerce, as did Confederate efforts to prevent cotton, tobacco, rice, molasses, and other goods from being shipped northward. Emancipation and black troops offended many and enhanced the appeal of the Democratic Party. Such views were exacerbated by the arrival of the 8th Colored Heavy Artillery in March 1864, and its use of Paducah as a recruiting station. The town was sacked twice by Nathan Bedford Forrest. The more serious attack occurred on March 25, 1864, when 1,800 Confederate troops drove Union forces back into Fort Anderson on the Ohio. Four Union regiments held fast, forcing Forrest, who suffered more than 300 casualties, to withdraw. Part of his force then descended on Fort Pillow down the Mississippi River and brutalized black troops there. One of the four Union regiments in Paducah—the black one—might have received the same treatment, had the fort surrendered.[18]

Events in the counties just below and above Louisville also demonstrated division of opinion. Trimble County, across from Madison, Indiana, was Unionist. Several skirmishes between Union and Confederate troops occurred in upriver Boone and Gallatin counties. In each, troops were actively recruited for the Confederacy. Military arrests of allegedly disloyal citizens occurred there, notably in midsummer 1864. Maysville, in Mason County, had strong economic ties to the state of Ohio, and two Union Army camps were constructed nearby. Yet Mason County produced the core of the 4th Kentucky (CSA), and Maysville was briefly occupied by Confederate cavalry troops in June 1864.[19]

When the Civil War erupted, Louisville was a thriving industrial and mercantile center second in rank, in the region, only to Cincinnati. Trade southward in wholesale groceries, dry goods, and drugs was highly profitable. Pork and farm implements were major products. The city boasted the largest cast iron foundry in the West. But the war disrupted trade, and not until the fall of Vicksburg and Port Hudson in July 1863 was commerce with New Orleans resumed. Until January 1864, moreover, merchants were required to have fed-

erally issued licenses to trade. The war made it impossible for them to collect debts owed by Southerners, who had been middlemen in antebellum commerce. Not surprisingly, Louisville's wholesale merchants strongly sympathized with the Confederacy.[20]

More than 100,000 Union soldiers, mostly in the Army of the Cumberland, passed through the city during the war. The headquarters of the Union Army in Kentucky was Louisville, and about 80,000 Union troops were stationed in or near the city. General Jeremiah T. Boyle was commander from May 1862 through January 1864, and three other men succeeded him. Louisville was also a major supply base for Union troops and had nineteen hospitals for Union wounded. And the L&N Railroad prospered as a carrier of men and supplies. Louisville's manufacturers, small retailers, and blue-collar workers generally were Unionist.[21]

At war's end the city possessed a strong manufacturing economy. The valuation of real and personal property had risen sharply. Trade now depended on an army of salesmen—drummers, often Confederate veterans—who sold Louisville products via small independent merchants in crossroads stores from Louisiana to South Carolina. Rail connections and a railroad bridge across the Ohio, completed shortly after the war ended, gave the city distinct advantages and lessened dependence on river commerce.[22]

As significant as these events were, however, the ending of slavery mattered most. Despite public pronouncements that Confederate leaders made, saying that the war was about self-determination and the "rights" of states, slavery's protection was paramount. The slavery-based revolt by a minority of Southern whites against the Union not only united most Northern whites but also opened fissures among whites in the border South that led to that slave region's remaining in the Union. As the war progressed, problems of slave management—"rascality" and runaways—grew exponentially. Ties between African American workers and their masters became increasingly shaky. The collaboration that emerged between Lincoln and his army and slaves who ran away was a major cause of the defeat of the Confederacy.[23]

Slavery's demise in Kentucky was ragged. The constitutional elimination of slavery in December 1865 was a symbolic act, because few slaves were left. Even so, it was ironic that Kentucky, a state that claimed that slavery was less burdensome to African Americans and more so to its white masters, was the last to free its slaves. The last battle over slavery occurred in Kentucky, "as violence erupted between black soldiers, returning to get their families, and slave owners."[24] After 1865, moreover, former Confederate officers dominated

Kentucky state government. Former slaves found their behavior proscribed and evocative of slavery.[25]

The crisis of the late 1850s had prompted some African Americans, free and slave, to flee across the Ohio to protect themselves from what they feared that conflict between whites might do to them. Others, believing Abraham Lincoln's campaign was linked to emancipation, decided to wait for their imminent liberation. When he was elected, rumors of emancipation spread. Some slaves were convinced they were going to be freed on March 1, 1861.[26]

News of the war reached most slaves in the months that followed, but it was often contradictory. Masters assured slaves that their status would be unchanged. Contacts with Union troops and assistance from educated blacks helped to alter that view. But in the early days of the conflict, life was "more complicated and uncertain" for most because of harassment from Negrophobes and local authorities. For instance, freedmen who left the state and returned faced prison sentences, and false arrests took months to correct. Louisville blacks claimed they had "no redress" against authorities like "Home Guards" who invaded their homes at night, allegedly searching for weapons, or who tormented them on the street. Blacks gathering in churches were suspected of encouraging abolitionism. Vagrancy laws impeded blacks' mobility, and fugitive slave laws were not relaxed. "Meanwhile, bondsmanship, including hiring out and the slave trade, continued."[27]

But hostilities "created new opportunities for a few bondsmen." Skilled workers secured higher wages, and some black capitalists grew rich. Some blacks perceived that whites were more willing to work with them and were less hostile to black mechanics. Cruelty became less frequent. And many blacks took advantage of circumstances to violate the slave code and became "less inclined to obey orders."[28]

Probably most Kentucky slave-owners subscribed to the notion that blacks had smaller brains than whites and, like wild animals, better ability to see, hear, and smell. Blacks were deemed sensual and imitative and deficient in discipline and intellectual ability, genetically prone to run away and to engage in acts of rascality. Rumors of uprisings increased after the war began. Fears intensified as men went off to war and women and children were left to handle the slaves. The arrival of Union troops took the lid off a pot that had been boiling for years and made control of slaves virtually impossible.[29]

The arrival of federal troops meant that "the legendary North Star that had once illuminated the road out of bondage lost its strategic importance. Freedom was as close as the nearest Union camp." As one Kentucky runaway exclaimed, "It used to be five hundred miles to git to Canada from Lexington,

but it's now only eighteen miles."[30] Many slaves struck out on their own, either accompanying Union soldiers or flocking into Union camps, but "the habits and dependency learned as slaves, as well as the need to survive, prompted many to refrain from any premature or hasty assertion of their freedom. If doubts persisted, both reason and fear sustained those doubts."[31]

Kentucky's drama was shaped by Kentucky's slaves and whites as well as by Union officials and soldiers. News of the war got through to slaves in many forms, and the progress of Union forces increased slaves' restiveness. Their actions indicated little acceptance of warnings by whites that Union soldiers were to be feared. Said one slave to a soldier, "I thought you must be down-right heathen, but you are real good-looking people and don't seem to do nobody no harm."[32]

Slaves who thought the Ohio was a thousand miles away and ten miles wide soon learned otherwise. An observer at Owensboro declared that more fugitives crossed over to Indiana there in 1861 than in the previous sixty years. The chief attraction was army camps, where protection and jobs were to be had. Each company of the regiment stationed at Paducah employed five or six slaves. They were more readily received if they declared they were freemen or that their masters were Confederates.[33]

Growing antislavery sentiment in the Union and the impossibility of banning fugitives from Union military lines gradually altered soldiers' views. By the end of 1862, soldiers from the Northwest commonly described Kentucky slaves as not only "intelligent, true, and loyal to the Union," but also "alert and 'very anxious to know every step' that was taken by the Union Government in reference to slavery." Union troops "undermined the exclusive authority of the master over the slave" when masters left for the army or loyal owners and slaves sought the troops' protection.[34]

Troops had been instructed not to tamper with slavery, but blacks deluged Union camps. The Confederate invasion of the commonwealth in late summer 1862 put even more slaves in motion. There were, nonetheless, practical considerations such as the presence of more fugitives than jobs and political ones such as the need to maintain relations with Kentucky's white leaders. Union Army officers were ordered by General Ambrose Burnside of the Department of the Ohio neither to impede efforts of civil authorities to return slaves to their owners nor to encourage slaves to escape. The regions around Henderson and Owensboro, as reported by the *New York Tribune* in September 1863, were the worst, as blacks entering Union lines there were arrested, jailed, and sold in southern Kentucky. Around Louisville, however, contraband slaves were retained as agricultural laborers or as soldiers.[35]

Generals varied in their reactions. William Tecumseh Sherman insisted that runaways be returned to their owners and refused fugitives shelter in his camps. Others sheltered refugees from Confederate states but not those from Kentucky. In 1862 officers still had no instructions on handling the growing number of runaways, and conflicting orders persisted. Some officers harbored slave women; others did not. Some refused to accommodate any slaves. Some permitted owners to enter their camps to remove slaves; others refused to do so. Federal troops' attitudes complicated matters. Few were abolitionists, but midwestern soldiers were increasingly hostile to slave-owners and willing to use force to prevent re-enslavement.[36]

Three factors—impressment of blacks, emancipation, and enrollment of black soldiers—"transform[ed] this growing migration into a serious problem." Impressment for military labor of large numbers of blacks, free and slave, by Confederate and Union armies disrupted families and created refugees. The threat of a Confederate invasion of northern Kentucky in the late summer of 1862 prompted Cincinnati authorities to impress more than 1,000 free and black men, including blacks found on the streets and in jails as well as black ministers, to build fortifications. There were not enough men south of Cincinnati, however, and hence more than 1,100 freemen in that city were rounded up, caged like animals, and unable to let their families know of their whereabouts. They were required to dig entrenchments in Kenton County.[37]

When slaves learned of the Emancipation Proclamation, many were emboldened to enter Union lines, and officers grew less sensitive to whether the fugitive's owner was loyal or rebellious. Whites, in turn, became increasingly bitter toward the Lincoln government.[38]

The Union officer who was most aggressive against slavery was Kentucky native General John M. Palmer, an abolitionist ex-Democrat who had helped to organize the Republican Party in Illinois and was a friend of Abraham Lincoln. Assuming command of the Union Army in Kentucky in early 1865, he recalled what he felt on arriving in Louisville. He had decided that "all that was left of slavery was its mischiefs, and that I would encourage a system of gradual emancipation, a thing that had been desired so long, and which the colored people had pretty well established for themselves." One of his first acts was to ask Rev. Thomas James, an African American agent of the American Missionary Association, to tour local prisons to determine whether local officials and military recruiters had conspired to jail black men for refusing to join the army. James discovered hundreds chained and barred in slave pens and freed them. Palmer responded to threats on James's life by warning the mayor and councilmen that he would hang anyone who killed James.[39]

Palmer subsequently informed black soldiers that an act of Congress in March had freed both them and members of their families. Fugitives came to Louisville by the hundreds, including many not related to soldiers, because they believed the law applied to them. Palmer did nothing to discourage that belief. An average of 200 were arriving weekly by April. In early May Palmer annulled the slave code that limited mobility of slaves and free blacks. He also gave free passes for travel anywhere fugitives desired—1,900 of them in the last two weeks of May, 671 in the first three weeks of June, and 2,230 in September. About 10,000 fugitives had left Kentucky by the end of October 1865.[40]

Palmer's actions came at the end of a four-year process by which Kentucky's slaves were unchained. African Americans liberated themselves by running away, by purchasing their freedom, or by being helped by men like Palmer. The Thirteenth Amendment liberated the remainder. Communities' postwar memories disclosed divergent views of the official date of liberation.

Regional divisions in Kentucky contributed to the varied forms and times of liberation. Significant differences existed in the level of slave labor along the Ohio. In Louisville, many free blacks lived among thousands of slaves, of whom a large number lived autonomously. Slavery was a major presence in Daviess, Henderson, Mason, and Union counties, but not in Campbell, Kenton, and the Appalachian counties. The nature of the topography and the level of urbanization on the north shore of the river—as manifested, for example, in the location of slaves' escape routes—also contributed to the dynamics of emancipation.

The war dramatically altered black Kentuckians' lives. At its end thousands had left the state, but many thousands who were free remained. Henderson County, for example, had had 5,767 slaves in a total population of 14,262 in 1860. Five years later all of these men, women, and children were free. The annual ritual of slave trading during December and January, which persisted into the early years of the war, was ended. On August 4, 1864, black men wearing Union blue arrived in Henderson for garrison duty. By 1870 there were 14,000 fewer African Americans in the state than ten years earlier. Many of those who remained in the state had moved to cities and towns, especially Louisville. By mid-1863 approximately 100 black men were registering daily for service in the Union Army. All told, Kentucky furnished more black men to the Union Army—nearly 24,000—than any other slave state except Louisiana. This number represented 56.5 percent of eligible slaves and freemen between ages 18 and 45 and 13 percent of all the black troops in the Union Army.[41]

The end of the war, wrote William Wells Brown in 1867 in the first Afri-

can American history of the Civil War, produced "no negro [*sic*] saturnalia, no violent outbreak of social disorder, no attempt to invade those barriers of social distinction that must forever exist between the African and Anglo-Saxon." Slavery had been "the cancer of the Southern social system. . . . It rooted itself into the body of Southern society, attacking the glands, terminating in an ill-conditioned and deep disease, and causing the republic excruciating pain." It "brought disaster and grief upon them, and the sorest of evils upon us. It brought us blood and civil war, ruined commerce and desolated fields, blocked ports, and rivers that swarm with gunboats."[42]

Louisville, despite its modernity, its strong northern commercial ties, and its relatively lax form of slavery, was nonetheless a slave city. A Union Army officer from Ohio, John Beatty, vividly recalled his first visit in the spring of 1862. "My attention was directed to a sign bearing the inscription, in large black letters, NEGROES BOUGHT AND SOLD."[43] But such matters would change dramatically. The decision of the United States in March 1864 to recruit black men in Kentucky for the Union Army was the coup de grâce, for black soldiers were automatically freed and their owners compensated at the rate of three hundred dollars for each. An average of one hundred men enlisted daily at Taylor Barracks, located at Third and Oak streets. Owners coming to Louisville to apprehend the ever-growing stream of runaways were bewildered by the scale of their enlistment in Union blue and their total rejection of their owners' worldview. The presence of Union troops also heartened other African Americans to run away. But that "would have come to nothing if large numbers of slaves in Kentucky had not taken the initiative by passively refusing to act the part of slaves any longer." Slaves' departure for the north shore of the Ohio and for cities and towns and their enlistment in military service combined to "create an acute labor shortage in Kentucky by 1865. . . . [but] few slaves who had broken with their former masters were willing to return to them. Returning to the supervision of the old masters seemed too much like a voluntary return to the life of a slave."[44]

African Americans' military service strengthened white Kentuckians' opposition to Lincoln. "Peace Democrats" were elected mayor of Louisville in 1863 and 1865. Louisville strongly supported McClellan for president in 1864. His 4,986 votes far exceeded Lincoln's 1,942 (but the latter was an amazing increase, as he had received just 91 in 1860). Attracted by the city's prosperity as a commercial and manufacturing center that was not under military government, these men—many of them Confederate veterans—went into law, insurance, real estate, sales, and related professions.[45]

Most of the labor supporting the Union Army in Kentucky was provided by impressed blacks and refugees. It was only a matter of time before the recruitment of black troops began, bringing even more slaves to Union lines. President Lincoln had authorized the use of black troops in the fall of 1862 but exempted Kentucky for fear of adverse reaction from loyal whites. Hence Kentucky blacks initially served in units formed to the north.[46]

The issuance of the Emancipation Proclamation was followed by active recruitment of blacks in the North. Within six months more than thirty regiments had been formed and camps established to register and train them, and recruitment was occurring virtually everywhere in the North. Eventually more than 186,000 enlisted. Lincoln sought to limit enlistment to slaves of disloyal masters, but army recruiters generally overlooked these distinctions. "The promise of freedom to enlistees and their families went far, in fact, to undermine the entire institution of slavery in those regions excluded from the Emancipation Proclamation." Declared Lincoln for a Kentucky newspaper, "I claim not to have controlled events, but confess plainly that events have controlled me."[47]

Between the middle of 1863 and the spring of 1864, when recruitment of Kentucky blacks began in earnest, recruiters were especially active in the gateway cities of Evansville and Cincinnati. In the latter part of 1863, Lincoln moved toward the formation of Kentucky units by authorizing a census of black men. In addition, the War Department permitted the formation of a black artillery regiment in the Western Tennessee District, which included Paducah. Agents from Illinois to Massachusetts came to the commonwealth to recruit, beginning in January 1864. Governor Thomas E. Bramlette was outraged and wrote a lengthy letter of protest to the president on February 1, 1864, securing an audience with him. Although Lincoln assured Bramlette as late as the fall of 1863 that no Kentucky blacks would be recruited, the federal manpower shortage and the presence of more than forty thousand draft-age slaves led the president to seek the enlistment of slaves in Kentucky units. Impressment, moreover, had softened local resistance to blacks' presence, as had the erosion of slavery. The time was right for Lincoln's request.[48]

In March 1864 the governor, visiting Lincoln with the state's attorney general and U.S. senator Archibald Dixon, agreed to support the enlistment of blacks, but only when deficits were created by whites' failing to meet draft quotas. Marion Lucas has described this as "an obvious face-saving gesture" since recruitment had begun west of the Cumberland two months earlier.[49]

The provost marshal of Kentucky soon complained that his state was not receiving credit for blacks recruited across the river in Cincinnati, and eventually recruiting offices in Campbell and Kenton counties, which had few slaves,

were permitted to enlist men from nearby counties that had large numbers of slaves. Kentucky was credited with these men, thus lowering the number of whites who had to be drafted. The repeal of the Fugitive Slave Law on June 28, 1864, facilitated blacks' recruitment. The second draft call of July 1864 made Kentucky liable for almost 17,000 men, but only 4,000 white men enlisted. During the summer of 1864, Adjutant General Lorenzo Thomas, assigned the task of raising black troops for the Union Army, began recruiting all available, able-bodied slaves, without regard to their owners' wishes. Military camps were garrisoned to receive and protect these men in a number of Kentucky towns, including Covington, Owensboro, Paducah, and Louisville.[50]

This represented the first unfettered chance for slaves to flee, and men came by the thousands to Louisville to claim their freedom by enlisting in the army. This was also the opportunity to assert their manhood, to engage in a great crusade, and to lay the basis for a better life after the war. Brisk enlistment also occurred at Henderson and Owensboro, and by July 1 about 200 had joined at Paducah and 600 at Smithland and Columbus. Kentucky was credited with 1,000 who had signed up in Evansville. About 14,000 had enrolled by the end of September. Most of the men who served in Kentucky units enlisted between April 1, 1864, and March 31, 1865.[51]

The experience of George Washington Buckner—later an Evansville teacher and subsequently a physician and minister in Liberia—may have been typical. Born in Green County, he was barely ten when his mother awoke him one night and instructed him to say good-bye to his uncles. This was his most vivid memory from his youth—the departure of his mother's four brothers for the Union Army.[52] Many other slaves also slipped quietly away from their cabins when they had the chance. Others found the experience not so easy— such as one man whose owner caught him after federal troops had helped him escape. (He succeeded the second time, walking all the way from Elizabethtown to Louisville.) Some slaves enlisted only after a lengthy time of soul-searching. Such was the case of one slave, Elijah Marrs, who persuaded twenty-seven others to join him. Marrs, whom the others had elected "captain," organized a rendezvous at the black church, where Sandy Bullitt, a recently drafted black preacher, gave them a farewell sermon. They departed that night, marching without food, and arrived tired and hungry at the Louisville recruiting office the next morning, September 26, 1864, having chosen to fight for "the principle of freedom."[53]

For many black enlistees, their first experience of violence came not from Confederate troops but from whites who attacked them as they traveled to Union camps or when they arrived at recruiting stations. Owners arrived at

recruiting offices and military camps to reclaim their property, sometimes threatening retaliation on the families that the recruits had left behind.[54] For these and other reasons, the number of men seeking to enlist dropped markedly in the fall of 1864. General Thomas met the resulting deficiency by ordering impressment of slaves into the army. The Evansville correspondent of a Louisville newspaper reported that Union troops were nightly raiding slave cabins for recruits. The 120th U.S. Colored Infantry, a Kentucky unit, descended on Henderson County in June and zealously rounded up every black male they could find. A similar raid occurred in Union County. Units of Kentucky black troops scoured the countryside in September, and bloodshed resulted as these men clashed with whites. The forcible induction of blacks did not end until the end of the war. Most slaves saw this as liberation, but some did not. When one Henderson-area slave demurred, a white lieutenant in the 120th threatened him with jail, and he, like most faced with that choice, decided to enlist.[55]

Whites, especially at Henderson, complained about the actions of overzealous Union recruiters. They also grumbled that recruiters, especially from Indiana, were disrupting the slave system in order to hire substitutes or to fill draft quotas. They lamented the loss of laborers, for which they were not compensated. But mostly they hated seeing former slaves in blue uniforms. Troops were portrayed as indolent and imprudent and were attacked with insults and stones. For the slave, though, army service represented many things— an opportunity to destroy slavery, but also freedom, revenge, food, clothing, shelter, excitement, and a sense of worth.[56]

Kentucky remained a "special case," because the federal authorities had promised in March 1864 to enroll only free blacks and slaves who applied to serve in the army. Loyal owners were assured that they would be paid up to three hundred dollars for each recruit and that "property taken by enlistees would be returned when slaves joined the army." Slave recruits were to be assembled at Louisville and taken to camps outside the commonwealth for training.[57]

These policies produced mixed results, especially after Thomas's active recruiting of slaves, regardless of their circumstances. Some owners cut their losses by enrolling their slaves and pocketing the bounties due slaves who enlisted. (After July 1864 bounties were promised only to the slaves.) Other whites used slaves to escape the draft. They enlisted their slaves, who received little or no money, or promised "slave substitutes cash they never received." Some whites, however, paid slaves a great deal of money to serve as substitutes. In the last year of the war, "buying and selling blacks as substitutes for whites was common. Since Federal policy loosely defined 'runaways' and 'refugees' as eligible for induction, making it difficult for them to escape military service,

black Kentuckians sometimes concluded that they had no choice but to become substitutes." Some also signed up as substitutes for wealthy Northerners. The state legislature sought to eliminate outside recruiters by making their activities a misdemeanor offense, and troops and gunboats were stationed along the Ohio to be on watch. The legislature also forbade removal of substitutes from the state. Many "'substitute brokers' were really 'bounty scalpers' who took most of the money, leaving them with a pittance."[58]

White hostility to the recruitment of blacks remained strong. Recruiting agents for the Union Army often found themselves endangered. Many whites considered them incendiary, for the agents proposed to arm black men. Without army protection, agents and recruits could not travel to the nearest Union camp without fear of harassment. That danger was especially evident west of the Cumberland, where guerrillas prevented blacks from going to Paducah to enlist. The provost marshal of the state recorded cases of slaves being "whipped, mutilated, and murdered for trying to enlist and recruiting agents had been 'caught, stripped, tied to a tree and cowhided' before being driven out of town." What made this more exasperating was the agents' "frequent lack of success in obtaining many enlistments." Recruiters also encountered opposition from many white Kentucky army officers.[59]

When slaves and freemen entered the army, they completed an enlistment form that indicated occupation, physical condition, and company assignment. All but a handful indicated that they had an occupation, and of these more than 97 percent were farmers or laborers. Medical examinations disclosed that black men were markedly robust. The physician at Paducah who examined slaves from fifteen western counties was struck by their upper body strength, as was his counterpart at Owensboro. E.P. Buckner, the army's physician at Covington, gave sixteen hundred physicals and left the most comprehensive record. Buckner attributed slaves' good condition to nutrition and exercise. His examinations concluded that they had fewer disabilities than other racial groups. Only the Louisville examiner asserted that men in his district were physically inferior to whites.[60]

Blacks served in all-black units of the U.S. Colored Troops and were commanded by white officers and a few black noncommissioned officers. Most were mustered in at Louisville and some at Covington, Henderson, Owensboro, and Paducah. The first colored Kentucky infantry regiment was the 100th, assembled in May and June 1864. The 5th U.S.C. Cavalry, organized in September, was the first unit of horsemen from the Bluegrass State. The 8th Colored Artillery, formed in Paducah in April 1864, was the first regiment of its kind. In addition to troops supplied to other states, Kentucky created two

cavalry, fourteen infantry, and three artillery regiments. Kentucky's black troops served in eastern and western campaigns, although some—like the 8th U.S.C. Heavy Artillery and the 108th U.S.C. Infantry, mustered in at Owensboro in August 1864—spent most of their time in the region where they were formed.[61]

Entering the military proved to be frightful for many blacks: there were accidental shootings of comrades in barracks and, more commonly, housing and food were poor. But being called by name by an officer, and receiving a uniform and rations, made one realize how different and how much better freedom was. The work of the U.S. Sanitary Commission in improving camp conditions also mattered a great deal. Preachers seemed to be omnipresent, offering religious services nightly and all day Sunday. Letter writing was a favorite activity; and for those who were illiterate, chaplains and Sanitary Commission members were willing helpers. Camp life also provided men the chance to form new friendships or to meet old chums. Camps also provided classes in reading and writing, music and religion—many of them through the American Missionary Association—and offered men many different forms of recreation, from games and wrestling matches to picnics. Men used their weekend passes to visit women in nearby towns, and some earned extra money through a variety of enterprises.[62]

Voluntary societies, primarily in Louisville, supplemented the inferior medical care provided black troops and helped the Sanitary Commission. Louisville's Green Street Baptist Church had a Soldiers' Aid Society led by three black women who cared for sick and wounded soldiers in Louisville and New Albany. Fifth Street Baptist Church had a similar group. The Colored Ladies' Soldiers' Aid Society, which met mostly in African Methodist Episcopal churches, raised money to help sick soldiers and their families. Several other societies also assisted the sick and disabled. Fairs, concerts, and lectures were used to raise funds for these activities.[63]

By contrast, most white officers and troops initially treated black troops as laborers, not fighting men. Most of those who served in the field were guards or pickets. But there were notable exceptions. Shortly after Smithland was occupied by Union troops, many blacks came into Union lines there and began drilling on their own. Joining white troops at Smithland was the 13th Colored Heavy Artillery Regiment, organized in Louisville. Black men were actively recruited into the Union Army there, and the 8th U.S. Colored Heavy Artillery Regiment included many Livingston County men.[64]

More emblematic were those black troops recruited in Henderson and Owensboro who served garrison duty. Henderson furnished 194 black men to the Union Army. Whites generally found the practice distasteful. The first postwar

history of the city, written by the son of a former planter, asserted that white federal troops as well as Henderson residents were offended when 160 black troops occupied the courthouse in August 1864, using it as a barracks. The same historian found Colonel John Glenn's recruitment of black troops in the county, aided by a Louisville detective, to be shameless and disgraceful. Farmer George W. Smith, visiting Evansville in May 1864 from Henderson in search of a runaway slave, visited the recruiting office for black troops: "an office established upon our borders for the purpose of stealing from us our property." Smith said Evansville appeared to "be in a prosperous condition and one would hardly think [war was] devastating the country."[65]

On March 12, 1865, according to the first historian of Henderson County, "one of the most willful and horrible murders ever perpetrated in the state" occurred, the shooting of a loyal white man by colored troops. This was allegedly a retaliatory act for the hanging of black troops earlier in the year. This, to the historian, was part of a sad story: the palace of justice, the courthouse, was used as a barracks for black troops and a prison for rebel prisoners, and the black occupiers were not even punished for the wanton murder of an innocent white man.[66]

In Owensboro, a recent history reveals much when it declares that the town was "deluged" by black troops in August 1864. Nearly two hundred men recruited in Henderson County were sent there. Colonel John Moon used them to form the nucleus of the 118th U.S. Colored Infantry. The men, writes the historian, were noted for their disrespectfulness and sullenness. That these troops used the courthouse as their quarters—as in Henderson and Hawesville— was deemed terrible. This recent account overlooks the fact that in early November 1864, after the arrival of three companies of colored troops, two of the soldiers were murdered, one by a guerrilla raider.[67] Similarly, residents of Paducah—although a black regiment helped save it from the clutches of Confederate general Nathan Bedford Forrest—seemed mostly interested in complaining after the war about the damages that Union troops, and especially blacks, inflicted on local property.[68]

Generally black troops in Kentucky "encountered hostility from whites, both civilians and soldiers." That situation remained unchanged for many at war's end. But some whites came to respect blacks' willingness to fight and their gallantry in the field; furthermore, "the rate of volunteering among blacks of military age . . . testifies to both their desire for freedom and their courage."[69]

The flood of slaves coming into Union lines by the fall of 1862 often contained multiple members of families. Slaves were increasingly likely to flee in

family groups. Their experiences were often harrowing, and many were recaptured. The number of slave families entering Union camps grew dramatically after March 3, 1865, when federal legislation enabled the wives and children of black troops to gain their freedom. Some slaves' wives learned of their freedom through letters from their husbands stationed in Union camps. Such was the case with Lucinda, wife of Henry, stationed at Camp Nelson. Her husband advised her to hire herself out or to join him, and she signed an agreement with her owner to work three days a week for two dollars. Two weeks later the owner awoke to find Lucinda gone—though the kitchen was cleaned, bread was ready for baking, and kindling was there to start a fire.[70]

Those slaves who stayed were more independent and, according to most owners, insubordinate. "In 1864 a Louisville newspaper lamented that slaves in many Ohio River counties could no longer 'be controlled by their masters.' . . . [Owners] who offered slaves financial incentives usually fared better than those who tried to maintain the status quo."[71] Thoughtful whites realized that slavery was destined for ruin and made peace with their slaves, freeing them and sometimes giving them land in addition.

By the end of the war federal officials estimated that nearly three in four of the state's slaves were legally freed. General Palmer reported to President Andrew Johnson in July 1865 that he was "straining at the leash to destroy this last remnant."[72] The demise of slavery produced other effects: among others, a massive decline in tobacco, hemp, and wheat production. The state's black population dropped sharply, while the number of blacks across the river increased dramatically: by 72 percent increase in Ohio, 115 percent in Indiana, and 277 percent in Illinois. Louisville's black population grew by 120 percent in the decade.[73]

Unfortunately, until late in the war many refugees encountered "hunger, poor housing, unsanitary conditions, and hatefulness" behind Union lines. At Camp Nelson, south of Louisville, General Speed S. Fry demanded that anyone "unfit for military service—women, children, the elderly, the ill"—be returned to their masters. Despite the threat of the lash for those who disobeyed his orders, many continued to come. Fortunately, sympathetic soldiers came to their aid. A U.S. Sanitary Commission worker declared that nowhere had he "seen any cases which appealed so strongly to the sympathies of the benevolent as those congregated in the contraband camp at Camp Nelson." Fry "periodically swept the camp with troops, harassing refugees out of his lines, only to see them return." In late November 1864 he decided to solve this by expelling those living in the camp and by destroying the shantytown "to prevent their return." Four hundred women and children, poorly clothed in

subfreezing weather and many of them sick, were driven "from their huts into 'the wintry blast.'"[74] Of them, 102 died from exposure.

Religious organizations like the American Missionary Association and the Sanitary Commission helped to mitigate these practices. Especially noteworthy was the work of John G. Fee of the AMA. Acting on his own, Fee served as preacher, teacher, protector, and defender of those at Camp Nelson, advocating social equality and seeking rations, reading materials, and other supplies. His pleas for a change in government policy did not succeed until reports of the November expulsion reached General Lorenzo Thomas, who in mid-December announced that families of recruits would be provided food and shelter in all rendezvous camps. Thereafter harsh conditions were eased but not eliminated.[75]

Louisville had a large refugee camp by the fall of 1864, a ten-acre site at Eighteenth and Broadway, then just outside city limits. In the preceding two years, fugitives had endured unimaginable conditions, receiving aid mostly from Northern freedmen's aid societies and from free blacks in Louisville. By the fall of 1864 the federal government began to assume more responsibility for refugees. In early 1865 General Palmer appointed Thomas James to supervise the refugee camp. James established a temporary refugee home, sought to address the need for more permanent housing, created strict rules governing conduct, and opened the first school for refugees' children.[76] James recalled:

> I was ordered by General Palmer to marry every colored woman that
> came into camp to a soldier unless she objected to such a proceeding.
> The ceremony was a mere form to secure the freedom of the female
> colored refugees; for Congress had passed a law [in March 1865] giving
> freedom to the wives and children of all colored soldiers and sailors in
> the service of the government. The emancipation proclamation,
> applying as it did only to states in rebellion, failed to meet the case of
> slaves in Kentucky, and we were obliged to resort to this ruse to escape
> the necessity of giving up to their masters many of the runaway slave
> women and children who flocked to our camp.[77]

After Congress passed the law freeing soldiers' families, Palmer addressed an enthusiastic, overflow crowd at Center Street Church on March 20, declaring that slavery was for all intents and purposes dead in the state. James recalled what Palmer did on the Independence Day that followed: "The colored people of Kentucky were called upon for the first time to celebrate the Fourth of July. I spoke to General Palmer about it, and he, approving the idea, issued a proc-

lamation for the purpose. There was but a single voice raised against it, and that, strange as it may seem, was the voice of a colored Baptist preacher named Adams. But the slave holders had always pursued the policy of buying over to their interest a few unworthy colored ministers."[78]

Thousands of blacks, thinking that they would be set free on that day, flocked to Johnson's Woods, near the city. Black soldiers were recruited to protect the assembly, estimated at about 10,000. Thousands paraded through city streets, led by 800 soldiers and a band. Organizations participated—members of mutual aid societies like the United Brothers of Friendship and the Colored Ladies' Soldier's and Freedman's Aid Society, government employees, and members of various skilled trades. Another 600 soldiers brought up the train. Prominent whites and blacks spoke to the huge throng. Palmer had not planned to address the multitude but did so when he was told that they would not disperse unless they heard from him.[79]

In his memoirs Palmer remembered saying that "human slavery had ceased to exist." A black newspaper correspondent heard him insist that "henceforth and forever, *you are free,* you, and your children, and your broken families." He spoke glowingly of the black soldier in the war but returned to the family theme: "If any one has your children, go and get them. If they will not give them to you, steal them out at night. I do not think you will be committing any crime, nor do I believe the Almighty Ruler of the Universe will think you have committed any." The general urged the blacks to work only for wages, to quit employers unwilling to pay them, and in general, to "help yourselves."[80]

The Civil War at once simplified and complicated the lives of Kentucky's African Americans. It ended slavery, as blacks contributed their labor and their lives for the Union cause. But the terms of liberty were left unclear—especially whether blacks were citizens. Many battles remained to be fought before the promise of freedom would be fully achieved.[81]

Signs of advancement were evident, though. The formation of separate churches, for example, accelerated. In Louisville, members of the Center Street Methodist Church left the Methodist Episcopal Church, South, and affiliated themselves with the African Methodist Episcopal Zion Church. Insecurities created early in the war forced church socials and youth singing groups in Louisville to temporarily cease operations, and for a time in 1862 churches suspended their services. Green Street Baptist Church had to hire a watchman to guard the congregation during night services. Yet pastors and lay leaders remained vocal supporters of freedom and of blacks' enlistment in the army, and churches provided meals, shelter, and aid in camps for black soldiers. The

Baptist Church in Paducah became a hospital for Union soldiers. The foundation was laid for the formation of the General Association of Colored Baptists. Churches also helped to teach former bondmen to read and write, and by the end of the war eight churches in Louisville sponsored day schools for black youth.[82]

Most significantly, the war would demonstrate how deeply blacks valued family life and opportunities to improve themselves. The Civil War would bring self-selection of names, legal formation of marriages and families, establishment of more churches and schools, and creation of a free workforce. The war also emboldened leaders to insist on civil rights and the vote.[83]

The war set vast numbers of people in motion, and many left the state for good, crossing the river for what they assumed would be a better life in Illinois, Indiana, and Ohio. It is to those states during the war that we now turn our attention.

4

Blacks and Whites
Together and Apart
on the North Shore

The Civil War's consequences for the north shore are not as well known to readers of history as are those for the south. By war's end, a huge number of black newcomers resided in many counties on the north bank. Leaving agricultural labor behind them, most moved into towns and cities. They created their own institutions and began speaking openly about their place in the American arena. Moreover, blacks and whites got to know each other, often for the first time, and as equals—at least on paper.

On the eve of the war few counties had appreciable numbers of blacks (see appendix, table 5). In 15 counties there were less than 250 African Americans, and in only 8 were there more than 500. Over half of the 12,513 residing in these 25 counties lived in Hamilton County, Ohio. Blacks accounted for less than 3 percent of the population in 20 counties and for less than 2 percent in 14. Cincinnati, the city with the largest number of African Americans, was only 2.3 percent black. More typical was Vanderburgh County, Indiana, with 128 blacks, less than 1 percent of the county's population. North-bank blacks were also clustered opposite the largest Kentucky towns—Maysville, Newport, Covington, Louisville, Owensboro, Henderson, and Paducah. Few blacks resided across the river from such heavily rural counties as Breckinridge, Crittenden, Livingston, and Ballard.

With the notable exception of Cincinnati, black settlements had hardly any churches, fraternal societies, mutual aid organizations, schools, and businesses. Because of such legal proscriptions as Article XIII of the Indiana Constitution of 1851 and the denial of the right to vote, these small black settlements were as a rule voiceless and powerless. The racial values of whites on the north shore of the river resembled those of their Kentucky counterparts. Potent racism, sometimes leading to wanton acts of violence, was widespread.

The story of the war's economic and social impact is well known. Initially the conflict disrupted river trade on the Mississippi and the Ohio and its tributaries, and federal licenses were required of those engaging in commerce. Commerce flourished after the opening of the Mississippi in July 1863. So did factory production, because of the demand for goods to supply the Union Army and the formation of new markets in Southern territory. Cincinnati was most notable in this regard as a producer of shoes, clothing, wagons, harnesses, rifled muskets and cannons, pontoon bridges, gunboats, and rams, as well as beef, pork, and lard.[1]

Southern Illinois, though demographically and commercially linked to the upper South, was generally Unionist. A significant reason was the strong support given by the prominent Democrat John A. Logan, who formed the Illinois 31st and eventually became an eminent Union general. Attorney Green Raum was a major force in persuading Metropolis men to support the Union. The 131st Illinois was organized and encamped at the rebuilt Fort Massac, and Massac County provided five-sixths of its army-age male voters to the Union Army. Company B of the 18th Illinois was almost exclusively Shawneetown men.[2]

The most dramatic changes in Illinois's Ohio River country occurred at Cairo and Mound City. A Union Navy shipyard at Mound City became the chief depot of the inland fleet, employing more than one thousand. Cairo became a vital western army base and supply center. At the southern terminus of the Illinois Central Railroad, it shipped huge amounts of freight to the western theater of war. Hundreds of thousands of troops moved southward through the town. In 1862, moreover, the railroad established an office to handle refugees from the South. Prosperity continued after the war, thanks to the railroad gateway. Cairo's population nearly tripled in size during the 1860s.[3]

The war's effects were also felt along Indiana's Ohio River corridor. Larger towns organized whole regiments in the summer of 1861. (Of the original 1,046 officers and men of Evansville's 25th Indiana, though, just 26 officers and 460 men were mustered out four years later.) The economies of the larger

towns burgeoned after July 1863. Coal mining and the manufacturing of iron goods, wagons, foodstuffs, and textiles in Evansville expanded dramatically. By contrast, Cannelton, site of one of the largest cotton mills in the United States, experienced grievous losses, as supplies of cotton were cut off; the mill was forced to close in 1863. Cannelton's trade with Hawesville was also blocked. Yet Perry County supplied 3,558 men to the Union Army, by percentage near the top among Indiana counties. Even in the smallest towns and villages, women organized relief societies to aid refugees and wounded soldiers.[4]

The size of the black population in Ohio, Indiana, and Illinois counties in 1870 attests to sensational demographic changes in the Civil War era (table 6). In fifteen of the twenty-five counties, there were now at least 500 African Americans. Eleven had more than 1,000, and five exceeded 2,000. Only one north-bank county—Dearborn County in Indiana, adjoining Hamilton in Ohio—experienced a numerical decline. Another, Crawford in Indiana, had no black residents in 1860. A third, Gallatin in Illinois, grew by less than 50 percent, but it, like Hamilton County, had had a relatively high base to begin with. Counties on the lower Ohio, from Spencer County, Indiana, to the mouth of the Ohio, experienced the most impressive growth rates. Most newcomers settled in towns and villages. Approximately four out of five African Americans in Hamilton County lived in Cincinnati, for example, and two of three in Vanderburgh County resided in Evansville. Similar patterns existed in Alexander, Gallatin, Massac, and Pulaski counties in Illinois and in Clark, Floyd, Jefferson, Posey, and Spencer counties in Indiana.[5]

Quite a few black newcomers arrived before or just after the end of the war. The Illinois census in the summer of 1865 in Pulaski County reveals that about fifteen hundred African Americans had arrived during the war. They accounted for five-eighths of the number in the federal enumeration five years later. Examination of families listed in the federal population schedules of 1870 allows one to make similar conclusions about other places. Two examples will suffice. In Evansville's First Ward, census-takers registered Henry Trandman, a 54-year-old laborer, and his wife, Dallas, age 50. Both were natives of Kentucky. So were three males with the surname Trandman between ages 16 and 34, all laborers and possibly their sons. There was also a 4-year-old member of the family, William, who had been born in Indiana—their son or grandson. The census was taken in late June. Assuming that William was as old as a month shy of his fifth birthday, and that his gestation period was normal, the earliest he could have been conceived was November 1864. (If he had just turned four, that would have been September 1865.) It is unclear whether

conception occurred in Indiana or Kentucky, but this family was in Evansville by the summer of 1865. Joseph Green, another Kentucky-born laborer who was 40, lived in the same ward, with his wife, Emile, who was 30. Maria, 16, and Edwin, 14, presumably their daughter and son, were also Kentuckians. But Nelson, 6, was Indiana-born. His age indicates that he was in the state at the latest in late June 1864 and possibly as early as July 1863. Conception occurred either in Kentucky or Indiana between November 1862 and October 1863. These records also disclose that large numbers of blacks—as in other towns—moved across the river in family groups, not as individuals. The war, in a word, had accelerated the work of the Underground Railroad—what W.E.B. Du Bois called a "Great Strike." It set thousands of slaves in motion, making preservation of prewar labor conditions south of the river impossible.[6]

If Cairo, Mound City, Evansville, and Cincinnati were representative, fugitives began crossing the river in a trickle in 1862 that became a torrent by 1864–65. The most dramatic change occurred in Cairo, where the African American population grew by 3,834 percent in the 1860s. The character of the war was changing. One study portrays the war as the beginning of occupational change and rather generally asserts "the emergence of a free black proletariat."[7] Many, however, were not new to nonfarm work, as they had been employed in tobacco factories and in transportation on the south bank.

Another aspect of wartime change is indisputable. Early in the Civil War William Parham, a black teacher in Cincinnati, declared this would be a war against prejudice. That prediction seemed naive at first. When the war began, few whites in the region even thought the war was a struggle to free slaves. The war—as illustrated by Ohio governor David Tod's rejection of a petition to raise a black regiment—was not to eliminate slavery or alter the status quo for free blacks. Cincinnati authorities prohibited public demonstrations by blacks in support of the war effort. There and in Evansville white workers attacked black workers on the docks and destroyed their property in neighboring districts. Largely because of African Americans' initiative—in volunteering their service to the Union Army and in voting for freedom with their feet—the war ultimately became a war for black liberation. The huge numbers of blacks living in the largest towns on the river attested to that certainty.[8]

In Cairo, for instance, migration northward occurred in waves that reflected Union military successes to the south as well as increased boldness of bondmen. Numbers also reflected the breakdown of owners' control of slave-rich counties to the south. The first wave included families—penniless and ragged. The second, also desperately poor, was more likely to be single men, recruited by the War Department in an experiment to use contraband labor.

One historian of Illinois described Cairo as an "Ellis Island for this immigration."[9] Under martial law and "legally amenable to such a policy," the town was a haven for runaways, beginning with the passage of the Confiscation Act of July 1861. Although the Illinois Central Railroad transported one to four cars of migrants daily to northern communities of the state, the levees of Cairo remained, in the same historian's words, literally "dark with Negroes."[10]

Substantial increases occurred in Cairo during August and September 1862, following the passage of the Confiscation Act of July 1862 and the announcement of the Preliminary Emancipation Proclamation. Agents of the American Missionary Association (AMA) reported that contraband camps were overcrowded, filthy, and disease-ridden. A smallpox epidemic broke out in September, killing forty in two weeks. The employment of black newcomers was an economic necessity for the town as well as for the African Americans. It also provoked wanton attacks by whites on these workers, since many of the whites were also newcomers, German and Irish as well as American white workers.[11]

The U.S. government was the primary supporter of these unfortunates, providing food, shelter, clothing, blankets, and other necessities. The commanding officer was ordered to take care of all who arrived and to put all able-bodied men to work building fortifications and levees. Housed in temporary barracks on the west side of town, these laborers did not want to return to slavery, but they were not wanted by communities to the north. Life in Cairo was especially difficult during the winter of 1862–63. Most fugitives were women and children. In April 1863 Adjutant General Lorenzo Thomas reported that there were 1,583 wards of the government in Cairo, of whom 281 were adult males. Initially owners and their agents from Kentucky and Missouri visited these camps to reclaim their human property, but that practice slowed dramatically by 1863. Agents of the U.S. Sanitary Commission and the AMA, as well as black societies, especially those in Chicago, helped to raise funds and to provide for relief of those in the camps, whose numbers were swelled by expatriates from Canada, Northern free blacks, and fugitives from slave states unaffected by the Emancipation Proclamation—especially Kentucky and Missouri. Examining the condition of contrabands in Cairo, Levi Coffin noted something else besides their desperation and suffering. "What struck Coffin more forcefully than their misery was the exuberance of their rejoicing.... He experienced singing like nothing he had ever heard before."[12]

Ohio's African American population also increased sensationally, rising 72 percent in the 1860s. By 1870 the state was second only to Pennsylvania in the number of black residents and to New Jersey in the proportion of them. Most settled in southern and central portions of the state, and most counties west of

the Scioto River experienced increases of 50 to 100 percent. Ironton and Portsmouth grew by 150 percent.[13]

As in Illinois, the growing number of fugitives crossing the river fanned whites' fears. Tensions rose over where blacks settled and whether they would undercut white laborers' living conditions. But whites' level of stress diminished somewhat as the projected tidal wave of black migration proved unfounded and as Copperhead influence in the state, led by Clement Vallandigham, waned. Blacks continued to come, especially from Kentucky, though numbers were relatively small during the war owing to the existence of slavery and the blacks' lack of opportunity to leave bondage. The use of black fugitives in Kentucky as laborers on roads and fortifications and in camps, as well as Kentucky's exclusion from provisions of the Emancipation Proclamation, helped also to limit northward migration before early 1865. So did the fact that along this stretch of the Ohio, slaves to the south did not live as close to the river as those directly across from Indiana and Illinois.[14]

David Gerber has observed that the character of the migrants, their destinations in Ohio, and the forces aiding their settlement helped to explain why neither economic catastrophe nor race wars occurred. The state census of 1862–63 revealed, for one thing, that 62 percent of the blacks coming into south and central Ohio had arrived in family groups. Half settled in the countryside, and the remainder was split among villages, small towns, and cities. The need for farm workers during the war contributed to settlement patterns. Finally, those living in towns and cities were aided by whites' and blacks' philanthropic activities.[15]

Indiana's experiences resembled Illinois's more than Ohio's. Apprehensiveness about the war's liberating slaves and producing a flood of blacks into Indiana was omnipresent. As hundreds poured into the larger towns, where proslavery and antiblack sentiment was intense, tensions mounted, especially in working-class neighborhoods. Capture of runaways did not cease, therefore, when the war began: in May 1862, for instance, a fugitive from Louisville was taken near New Albany and his captors were rewarded seventy-five dollars. But fugitives continued to come, and many found shelter in the small black neighborhoods of the river towns and cities.[16]

After the Preliminary Emancipation Proclamation, even though it did not apply to Kentucky, the number of fugitives from the Bluegrass State greatly increased. Some were furnished passes by Union soldiers. Authorities at New Albany, where many attempted to cross the river, set up a guard at ferry docks on either side of the river to block blacks without legitimate passes and to return them to their masters. Fifteen slaves, freed by members of a Michigan

regiment in 1862, crossed the Ohio, expecting to follow the Underground Railroad northward, only to be arrested and returned. The following year, fugitives who believed the Emancipation Proclamation applied to them found themselves subject to the clutches of slave-catchers. Hoosiers and Kentuckians engaged in this thriving business, and even free blacks were not safe. Although some whites were arrested in New Albany in April 1863 for having sold several free blacks in Kentucky, the practice continued into 1864. Most whites assumed that all blacks were runaways. This even applied to the slaves whose owners, during the latter stages of the war, brought them across the river, freed them, and gave them certificates of freedom. At least six of the slaves receiving manumissions and freedom certificates in New Albany beginning in 1827 were freed during the war or just after it. On August 4, 1865, for example, Thomas B. Hanley freed his slave John Christopher in that city.[17]

Numbers of immigrants rose sharply from the summer of 1863 onward, as large numbers of black Kentucky men sought to enlist and their families followed them. Hundreds were recruited in Ohio River towns for the first northern unit, the 54th Massachusetts.[18] The success of Massachusetts and subsequently other states in attracting black recruits, combined with the difficulty of filling draft quotas with white men, led local and state officials to reconsider their opposition to recruiting black men. The performance of black troops in the field also helped change minds.[19] Accordingly, Governor Oliver P. Morton of Indiana applied for permission to create a black regiment in November 1863. Recruiting agents were sent not only to Indianapolis but also to Evansville and New Albany. Everywhere black men registered enthusiastically. Officials in Evansville and other places complained that their black men were being credited to Marion County, but that was because the central Indiana county gave bounties. River towns responded with their own incentives. Floyd County paid its recruits $50, and the city of New Albany another $50. A federal bounty of $300 was instituted in June 1864. When New Albany found it difficult to fill its quota with local black men, officials began recruiting in Kentucky, especially slave-rich Henderson County. About 300 black men were reported on one boat headed upriver to New Albany in early June 1864. Many slaves underwent great difficulties and risked their lives in attempting to enlist in Indiana. Eight Owensboro slaves, for instance, fled northward in March 1864 to do so. One was captured in Vincennes, but the others made it to camp in Indianapolis, where their owners confronted Union officers. These officers and angry black troops blocked their efforts to return with the seven.[20]

One can appreciate the resentment created when rival New Albany re-

cruited black men in Evansville's backyard. But by August 1864 Evansville was credited for having enlisted 200 and sent them to Indianapolis, where most were enrolled in the 28th Regiment of Colored Volunteers. Many came from Henderson. The business of hiring black substitutes was brisk, and as much as $550 was being paid. "A liberal proportion are substitutes for gentlemen of the Copperhead persuasion who have a great horror of 'niggers,'" chortled the Evansville editor about the lively trade in black substitutes, "except on particular occasions."[21] Hoosier blacks also served in the 8th, 13th, 14th, 17th, 23rd, and 65th infantry regiments and the 4th Heavy Artillery Regiment. Some also joined Michigan and Rhode Island units.[22]

In late August 1864 a recruitment station was opened in Henderson to permit Kentucky to get credit for the huge pool of black men in that region. Between 150 and 200 enlisted within a few days. On August 23 the *Evansville Daily Journal* reported that 160 "Ethiopians" had arrived the previous night, en route from Henderson to Owensboro for assignment. The unit, the 46th Infantry, encamped on the waterfront and departed two days later. The orderliness of its members impressed many white observers. Similar stories appeared over the following eight months. The editor urged the local marshal to fill Evansville's draft quotas with the scores of fugitives arriving in the city by early 1865 and proposed appointment of a special recruiting officer "to gather in the Ethiopians" as their numbers and the demand for substitutes grew.[23]

The number of blacks recruited in Evansville and credited to the city is difficult to document—possibly 800 of 1,537 recruits. Many of the remainder were credited to Kentucky.[24] A few recruits died in the city. The city's public cemetery, Oak Hill, recorded the interment of its first black soldier, John Rudell, in July 1863. Two more men—a soldier and a sailor—were buried there the following year.[25]

In Illinois, as in Indiana, acceptance of blacks' service in uniform came slowly. The *Cairo Gazette* opposed forming a black regiment, declaring that "the aid of the low, grovelling, ignorant African is not needed to quell this rebellion" and portraying blacks as "nearly savage." During much of the Civil War the Illinois General Assembly was controlled by Democrats, who attempted to revise the state's constitution and create greater proscriptions on African Americans' freedom. The federal government's enlistment of black men, along with emancipation, alienated many white southern Illinoisans. The most dramatic evidence thereof was the fate of the Illinois 107th, whose members mutinied because of Lincoln's racial policies. The unit was disbanded.[26]

Recruiters from other states found Illinois's Ohio River towns rich sources of volunteers. Recruitment speeded up in the summer of 1863, when Adju-

tant General Lorenzo Thomas was sent west to recruit black men in the Mississippi Valley. Later that summer Illinois governor Richard Yates decided black men would be valuable means of meeting the state's draft quotas. Secretary of War Edwin Stanton authorized the formation of what became the 29th Illinois Regiment, U.S. Colored Troops. A number of blacks recruited in Cairo, Mound City, and Shawneetown belonged to companies C, D, and E. Eleven volunteered in Gallatin County. Averaging 24.6 years of age, all were farmers or laborers; most were former slaves. James M. Bell, for instance, was a 27-year-old farmer who owned property worth fifty dollars. He became an engineer in the army. Three of these eleven men died in service.[27]

The 29th became part of the 9th Corps. Along with the Indiana 28th, it was involved in the siege of Petersburg. Like other black regiments, its men endured low pay and whites' hostility. By the time it was mustered out at Brownsville, Texas, in November 1865, it had lost 158 men. Illinois's African Americans would also serve in twenty-two other infantry and six artillery regiments in the Union Army. About 450 of them came from the extreme southern portion of the state.[28]

The situation in Ohio was somewhat similar. Democratic Representative William Allen charged in the House of Representatives on February 2, 1863, that the nation "was organized on the basis of the negro, has lived and grown into power upon the negro, and it will go down with the negro, if the country goes with it." Black troops would be "potent in the hands of tyrants in crushing out our own liberties." By contrast, an Ohio lieutenant, Jacob Bruner, wrote matter-of-factly to his wife from Milliken's Bend, Louisiana, on April 28, 1863, informing her that he had chosen to go into a colored regiment—the 9th Louisiana—as an officer. He added that "some may laugh (at my expense) but I don't regard them and don't ask their friendship or favor."[29]

Blacks' offers to enlist initially met stern resistance. Governor William Dennison, like many Republicans, had opposed the extension of slavery on racist rather than moral grounds. However, his successor, David Tod, encouraged John Langston's recruitment of blacks for the 54th Massachusetts. Two southern Ohio black recruits became prominent officers—James Monroe Trotter of Cincinnati, a teacher, who became a lieutenant, and Martin Delaney of Wilberforce, who attained the rank of major, the highest reached by any African American in the war. In June 1863 Tod informed the War Department of his intention to form a black regiment. The 5th and the 27th, the first two Ohio black regiments, were organized between January and August 1864. Ohio contributed five black infantry regiments and one artillery regiment, and 5,092

recruits were credited to Ohio in the Union Army and Navy, making Ohio the fourth-highest state in the number of blacks in service.[30]

An early history written by an African American about the recruitment of blacks in Cincinnati contrasted the "bright, interesting faces" of Northern blacks with those from Southern plantations: "stolid-appearing, their faces with but little more expression than those of animals." Living in shedlike barracks erected in front of a local government building, they would sing plantation songs each night after supper. "The voices of this immense multitude went up in a grand orchestra of sound. The tunes were plaintive, weird-like, and the whole exhibition one that could not but affect the thoughtful mind." This African American declared that it was "singularly appealing to one's best interests to look upon these poor children of nature."[31]

Whites' responses to the arrival of black newcomers were not universally hostile. In 1865 Indiana Presbyterians pledged financial support to the Freedmen's Aid Society. In the same year, the Indiana Methodist Conference offered continued support for colonization, while also endorsing emancipation and pledging funds for freedmen's aid. Members of the Society of Friends were especially solicitous. The Indiana Yearly Meeting of 1863 adopted a resolution authorizing the creation of a Committee on the Concerns of the People of Color to relieve physical needs, to promote spiritual and educational welfare, to support establishment of schools and hospitals, and to help in establishing farms. The United Brethren of the Whitewater Valley even endorsed granting black men the vote. Some whites also helped blacks establish churches and schools.[32] These were exceptions to the rule, however, and in the end, blacks would generally have to rely on their own resources.

A number of factors shaped whites' reactions. Most had had little experience with African Americans before the war unless they frequented riverfronts or encountered servants on steamboats and in hotels and restaurants. Black newcomers tended to settle in the towns and cities because jobs were available there. Buying a farm presented a huge financial obstacle for them. Whites' images of them, inherited via reading or word of mouth, stressed their propensities to either brutal or childlike behavior. Now whites encountered blacks directly, and many of the whites responded out of fear—whether for their safety or for the security of their jobs.

The number of prewar free blacks and their proportion of the total citizenry in an area also made a difference. When the war began, few towns and cities had appreciable black communities like the one in Cincinnati, where there were enough blacks to support an economic and social infrastructure

but not so many that they threatened whites' control. Black newcomers there did not have to build a community from scratch. The newness of the town was also important. The notable illustration of that fact was Cairo, whose white and black populations were minuscule before the war but substantially higher by 1865. Both whites and blacks, residing in a very small space, hemmed in by two rivers and marshy environs, had to create a community from virtually nothing and learn to coexist.[33]

Location along the Ohio River also shaped white-black relations. On the upper reaches of the Ohio there continued to be comparatively few African Americans in Kentucky, and hence few on the northern side. Resistance of whites was correspondingly modest. In contrast, Cincinnati was located opposite the Bluegrass region, a rich source of migrants. So were New Albany, Jeffersonville, and Madison. Cincinnati, despite its reputation for racism, also was home to a significant number of Quaker and Yankee opponents of slavery. Smaller numbers of these opponents resided in Evansville, Madison, and New Albany. Few were found downstream in Metropolis, Brookport, Cairo, and Mound City, which lay across from the slave-rich Purchase region. These places were also closer to Tennessee and the Deep South than any others along the north bank of the river. Whites' resistance to black newcomers was especially vigorous in these parts of Illinois.

Finally, the war itself shaped white-black relations. On the one hand, it produced racial tension and violence by increasing the numbers of blacks on the north shore and diminishing antebellum racial disabilities. On the other, it steeled "efforts of Negrophobes to resist the consequences of the war and to maintain the *status quo.*"[34]

Racial stereotyping was commonplace. Even whites who were considered friendly, like the Republican editor in Evansville, referred to "able-bodied sons of Africa" and to the local provost marshal's "trotting 'smoked Yankees' through the examination preliminary to admission to the dignity of soldier of the Republic."[35] Slaves across the river in Henderson were commonly identified as "darkies" or "Ethiopians" who, when unsupervised, tended to have "jolly times."[36]

Hostility and violence were much in evidence. Anxiety about the influx of blacks was certainly behind the holding of a special census in Ohio in 1862–63. Not all whites who believed that the war could not transform blacks into citizens were Southerners. The *Cincinnati Enquirer,* for instance, declared in late May 1865 that although "slavery is dead, the negro is not, there is the misfortune. For the sake of all parties, would that he were." Kentucky's William Wells Brown, the first African American to write a novel (1853) and to publish

a play (1858), wrote that "hatred to the negro is characteristic of the people of Cincinnati; more so, probably, than any other city in the West."[37]

Hatred of the Negro was certainly obvious in September 1862. The arrival of large numbers of fugitives and free blacks led military and government officials to coerce blacks to work on defense projects. Less than two months after riots against black newcomers in the summer of 1862, city leaders forced black men to work on fortifications in Kenton County because of their fear that Braxton Bragg's invasion force in Kentucky would reach the Ohio. Brown described the "special police" employed to round them up as "composed of a class too cowardly or traitorous to aid, honestly and manfully, in defence of the city. They went from house to house, followed by a gang of rude, foul-mouthed boys." Their captain "exhibited the brutal malignity of his nature in a continued series of petty tyrannies."[38]

According to a report to the governor, about 400 men were treated rudely and violently and penned up on Plum Street before being taken across the river. When Union general Lew Wallace heard of this, he ordered the camp demolished and established headquarters for voluntary enlistment in a Black Brigade. To gain the confidence of the men, he permitted those who had been forcibly enlisted to return home.[39]

The next morning about 700 volunteered to serve. Members of the Black Brigade proved to be highly interested in their work and were never compelled to work or disciplined. For three weeks, they built miles of roads, rifle pits, and magazines and cleared many acres of forest. Although most were poor, they presented their white officer with a sword as a token of appreciation for his leadership. Their spokesman added his hope that when unsheathed the sword would be an instrument of freedom. Some sympathetic whites still did not consider these men soldiers—only laborers gathered together in an emergency to build fortifications. A notable exception was the editor of the *Cincinnati Gazette,* whom prominent Cincinnati educator Peter Clark considered a strong ally. Clark insisted that the brigade was Ohio's and the Union's first black military unit.[40]

Downstream in Indiana, reports that river towns were "filling up with strange Africans" prompted Democrats—like one New Albany editor—to demand that Article XIII of the state constitution be enforced. Otherwise, "the result would be a migration of Negroes which existing laws would be powerless to check."[41] The *New Albany Daily Ledger* expressed gratitude that there were no freedmen's aid societies in New Albany, since they encouraged misdeeds by blacks, creating "lazy, trifling, good-for nothing negroes" who did not know their "proper position."[42] The same newspaper increased its support of

colonization, saying of whites and blacks, "the further apart the better." Its Republican counterpart in Evansville also believed Africa was the best place for ex-slaves.[43]

Not surprisingly, Indiana Democrats were hostile to blacks' being recruited for the Union Army. The Democratic editor in New Albany saw the use of black troops as a sign of weakness in Northern society. Some whites even championed permanent exclusion from the state of those who had enlisted elsewhere. The editor also believed that the Freedmen's Bureau that was created in March 1865 would encourage violation of laws and insults against whites and promote shiftlessness.[44]

The increased number of African Americans living on the north shore of the river and the coming of emancipation fanned Illinois whites' fear of an onslaught of African Americans. Secretary of War Edwin Stanton hurt Illinois Republicans politically in the summer of 1862 by ordering the dispersion of contrabands at Cairo throughout the state. His decision was prompted by poor camp conditions, the economic depression caused by the temporary closing of the Mississippi, and high freight rates. The Copperhead element in the Democratic Party had a field day and did well in the fall elections, gaining control of the state legislature. Similar results occurred in the fall elections in Indiana and Ohio. Illinois Democrats attempted to revise the state constitution by including a number of antiblack provisions. Although the main body of the proposed constitution did not pass, hence destroying the antiblack amendments, these racially charged proposals had been submitted separately to the voters and overwhelmingly approved. Had they been implemented, ex-slaves would have been forbidden to settle in the state and denied the right to vote and to hold office.[45]

Democratic editors and legislators brazenly played the race card by warning workers of a bombardment of blacks from the South who would threaten their wage levels. In 1863 Indiana Democrats, like their counterparts in Illinois, introduced numerous antiblack resolutions, all of which failed to pass. One of those provided that all African Americans in Indiana must show proof that they had a right to reside in the state under the state constitution. Those who could not would have had to leave within ninety days; and if they did not leave, they would have been assessed a huge fine—five hundred dollars for the first conviction. Continued disobedience would have led to prison terms of two to ten years. The state Democratic platform in 1864 preserved the hope for an even more stringent exclusion law.[46]

Democrats also persisted in charging Republicans with intentions of race-mixing. This was a major issue in Evansville, as in other towns. Horatio Q.

Wheeler and Andrew L. Robinson were charged with, among other things, plotting to admit black youngsters to the relatively new public schools, the creation of which most Democrats still resented. This was a central theme in city elections from April 1863 onward. Democrats also asserted that Republicans wanted to have only abolitionists hired as teachers. F.M. Thayer, editor of the Republican daily, responded by asserting that Republicans desired neither. "The unfortunate people have a school of their own [with the aid of the American Missionary Association], and it is honorable to our city that it is so."[47] Similar accusations in the fall election campaign led him to insist that "the cry of 'nigger equality' . . . has lost its magical influence."[48]

Although whites' sympathy for blacks grew, especially after January 1863, hostility and random acts of violence persisted. In Evansville, the most serious assault occurred on January 3, 1864, when a number of "fast young men on a splurge" stabbed to death the pastor of the African Methodist Episcopal (AME) Church, a Reverend Jackson, described by the *Evansville Daily Journal* as quiet and inoffensive. A soldier apprehended one of the culprits, who was taken to the provost marshal. The latter instructed the soldier to take the man to a civilian judge for arraignment. However, the soldier released the man, who disappeared. "Nobody feels an interest in the case," wrote the editor, "because he [the pastor] is colored."[49]

Following Governor Yates's decision to raise a black regiment in Illinois, members of the Sons of Liberty and Knights of the Golden Circle intensified their attacks on blacks. They targeted men attempting to enlist at Shawneetown, for example, and attacked seventy-four men en route to Quincy to enlist. Nevertheless, Silas Rhodes wrote the Adjutant General, A.C. Fuller, that numerous men wanted to join and requested permission to recruit them.[50]

Riots also occurred. Mob violence had been frequent in Cincinnati before the war, and it recurred in 1861 and 1862, when German and Irish workers in Cincinnati attacked African Americans in Bucktown because they believed free blacks were encouraging slaves to run away and to take low-paying jobs that would undercut their wages. The situation was especially bad in July 1862, when Irish American workers who had fallen on hard times engaged in two days of violent acts that stretched from the docks to blacks' homes near the levee. Petitions were sent to the General Assembly asking for the end of black migration to the state. A mob even attacked abolitionist Wendell Phillips at a U.S. Sanitary Commission rally in Cincinnati in March 1862.[51]

A race riot occurred in New Albany in July 1862. When African Americans allegedly shot and killed a white man and seriously wounded another, four were arrested, though they claimed they were innocent.[52] Thirty hours of

wanton acts of violence against blacks ensued. Several were shot, one mortally wounded. Sporadic outrages against blacks preceded the formation of a mob that descended on the largest black neighborhood in the city, beating and stoning blacks and vandalizing their property. Some of the group proceeded to the jail, where they were unable to force an entry and were dispersed. Patrols of soldiers arrived, bringing order to the city. But none of the rioters were arrested. The *New Albany Ledger* attributed the riot to blacks and abolitionists. "It is the strangers, who have no lawful homes here," intoned the newspaper editor, "who create nearly all the trouble."[53]

In the wake of this event, some New Albany blacks, paradoxically, crossed over the river to safety in Louisville. Others fled northward. Democratic editors, especially in Indianapolis, declared that the riot ought to alert blacks to the dangers of "impudence." But fugitives continued to come. Some came on their own, while others were contrabands who had encountered Union troops and been sent northward. The number of the latter steadily increased, especially in the spring of 1865. Often they "came in groups and were usually destitute and dependent upon the charity of local residents, white and colored."[54]

Men like Levi Coffin and Andrew Robinson sought to ease the lives of black newcomers. Coffin was the most influential member of the Western Freedmen's Aid Commission and was one of the prime movers in the formation of the Freedmen's Bureau in 1865. In addition to providing material aid, Coffin and his allies helped Cincinnati blacks understand and not fear the rules of civil society.[55] Robinson was in a powerful position between 1861 and 1865, as President Lincoln had named him Collector of Customs in Evansville. He "held almost unlimited authority in this section of the country."[56]

The Western Freedmen's Aid Commission was organized in January 1863. The WFRC had seceded from the Contrabands' Relief Commission of Cincinnati as a result of a disagreement over how to aid African Americans. It perceived its extensive aid—food, garments, and medicines—to be less important than educating and providing spiritual guidance to African Americans. It proposed doing those tasks on Southern soil, where blacks would be organized into self-supporting communities. Coffin, who raised funds for the agency in the North and in England, was the general agent. One of his stops was in Evansville on June 9, 1863, and local civic leaders contributed liberally.[57]

According to the 1863 report, since its inception the aid society had raised twenty-six thousand dollars and distributed nearly thirty tons of supplies, which included, among other items, 68,758 garments; hundreds of pairs of shoes,

socks, and stockings; and 4,611 cooking and kitchen utensils. The commission also provided farm and garden implements, garden seeds, sewing machines, and a cane mill and evaporator. It shipped eight portable hospitals and 19,860 feet of lumber. It also established schools in fifteen towns (including one at Cairo), hired sixty teachers, and furnished more than 41,000 new and 628 old schoolbooks, as well as pencils, pens, and paper. It was in the process of creating industrial schools. Given the recent appointment of John Eaton as superintendent of Freedmen in the Mississippi Valley, the commission sought to increase its efficiency by working with him. The commission closed its report with a special appeal for immediate help in collecting supplies to provide bedding, clothing, cooking equipment, and food and in generating money to help the burgeoning number of fugitives survive the cold and wet weather that was coming on.[58]

The problem was eminently practical. As the *Western Christian Advocate* of Cincinnati observed, before the war slavery was an abstraction: "everybody was ready to confirm the undesirableness of slavery as a social institution, and the abstract right of the negro to be free." It was now, however, "a subject of practical administration in the community's affairs."[59]

Prominent whites sensed that slavery was doomed. Members of the Cincinnati Methodist Episcopal Church Conference, for example, petitioned President Lincoln on September 8, 1862, to "fully and promptly carry out the Act of Congress for the Confiscation of the property and the emancipation of the slaves of all persons in rebellion against the Government of our Country" and to "use all constitutional means to secure universal emancipation." In his first lengthy commentary on the subject on February 24, 1863, F.M. Thayer, the Republican editor in Evansville, attacked the apprehension of blacks in that city as kidnapping. The day before, a former slave from Henderson had been captured while he was working near the waterfront. The black man had faithfully aided Colonel John W. Foster, an Evansville attorney who commanded Union forces in Henderson. This was "a naked attempt to steal a man and sell him for gain." Transactions like that were occurring almost daily, Thayer argued. Evansville had many churches, he added, but he questioned where their voices were in such matters. People were apparently too busy making money or too stingy to provide protection, compassion, justice, and the gospel for the poor, despised African. "Shame, shame!" he declared. In mid-October of the same year, the newspaper reported that a "gang of thirty negroes—slaves—were taken through this city last night to Kentucky" and inquired when this "infernal inhumanity" would cease.[60]

A few weeks later, however, a white man brought a black man named

Lafayette to the Vanderburgh County jail and declared that he belonged to a Tennessee slave-owner. He also stated that the jailer was required to safely keep the man until he was removed by proper authorities, and that he was entitled to one hundred dollars for apprehending the black. All other charges were to be paid by the owner. Although this claim was upheld, local officials were clearly uneasy. Shortly afterward a "black kidnapper" was arrested and sent to prison in Jeffersonville for attempting to take two boys from a steamboat and to sell them in Kentucky. When a Kentuckian attempted to bribe a white steward on a steamboat in order to lure a black man ashore, the steward turned the slave-catcher in. The following March the *Evansville Daily Journal* reported another slave-catching incident in upriver Crawford County. Negro stealing, like slavery itself, was "getting to be an uncertain business." The editor gleefully noted that blacks had strenuously resisted the would-be slave-catchers. Even with reinforcements and firearms, the slave-nabbers had been unable to carry out their mission.[61]

But some cases were not so clear. In August 1863 two black men were arrested in Spencer County and brought to Evansville for examination by a federal commissioner, a Democrat. The claimant was a Kentucky Unionist, entitled under existing law to his property. The attorney for the claimant was prominent Democrat Charles Denby, and the African Americans were counseled by Andrew Robinson. The two claimed that their owner was a Confederate, that they had escaped but had been captured and placed in a slave pen in Louisville, and that they had escaped at Rockport from a steamer taking them downriver to re-enslavement. The commissioner refused to uphold their claim. The Republican editor seemed torn on the merits of the case and observed that "we are told that he [Robinson] gave the boys excellent advice."[62]

Republicans also chided Democrats for what the editor in Evansville perceived to be a variety of outmoded and contradictory positions. For example, he pointed to their opposition to the War Department's use of contrabands to build entrenchments and fortifications while not finding fault with Confederates who used slaves to do the same thing. He criticized Democratic editors for saying nothing about mob rule during the draft riots in New York in July 1863. He also sneered at a distinguished politician in the region who had been a vocal opponent of the enlistment of black troops but had recently discharged a white servant and replaced him with a black. And he grew increasingly impatient with wanton acts of violence against blacks on the streets of the city. Thus it was not surprising to read about the facial expressions of two "conservative ladies sneering at and evidently dissenting from the sentiments of the prayer" offered by the Methodist minister, "in which he asked that 'if the

oppression of an inferior race was our nation's great sin, that the Lord would show it unto us.'"[63]

The increasingly apocalyptic war and the growing presence of former slaves increased many whites' charity and goodwill toward blacks. In Ohio they proceeded to establish schools, hospitals, and agencies to distribute food and clothing and to help freed people find employment.[64] Many churches in Indiana also supported field workers, missionaries, and other agents of aid to freedmen. They also initiated and contributed to educational programs.

Beginning in August 1863 the *Evansville Daily Journal* championed efforts to assist fugitives with money as well as prayer and sympathy. The number of fugitives in Evansville by the late summer of 1863 had risen dramatically, and their condition was desperate. Most were women and children. A public meeting was held at the Methodist Episcopal Church to discuss the need for relief of the wives and children of soldiers and men employed as laborers by the Union Army, and a few days later a committee comprising prominent citizens was formed to call upon townspeople for clothing, food, medicine, and money to help them. Perhaps typical was a case reported on February 19, 1864. Three men and four women, carrying three children, had arrived in town late the previous evening. In desperate condition, they were provided comfortable quarters for the night. The editor urged citizens to come to their aid.[65]

In July 1864 about 100 blacks, 91 of them women and children, families of Union soldiers, encamped at Blackford's Grove, on the outskirts of Evansville. Most were sick, and all needed clothing and food. The Republican editor, after visiting what he termed a "sad spectacle," urged his fellow citizens to come to their aid. The township trustee subsequently reported that the camp had been discontinued, as presumably most had moved on after being aided. The remaining refugees, about 40, were housed at the fair grounds. The trustee indicated he had spent $271. Of that, $183 came from contributions—$110 from local Jews. The balance was charged to the county. By the end of the year, as a result of a visit from a representative of the Indiana Freedmen's Aid Commission, a local effort was launched to provide more systematic and comprehensive aid.[66]

Fugitives in Cincinnati and Evansville were fortunate to have friends like Coffin, Robinson, and Thayer; the latter was an officer of a statewide organization that supported the Emancipation Proclamation.[67] Twenty-four former slaves who desired to form a Baptist congregation received Robinson's help in obtaining the use of a small building for their services. Robinson served as clerk at a meeting on May 13, 1865, called by deacons Green McFarland and Travis Ford to organize the congregation. He was one of the men elected

trustees at the meeting. Blacks appropriately named the church Liberty. That fall the congregation moved to a new structure at the corner of Seventh and Oak streets. The first pastor was a white man named Woods, but McFarland took charge in 1866 after he was ordained.[68]

Something even more substantial—a recognition of blacks' civil rights—was also emerging. In the early fall of 1863, for instance, an Irish American steamboat hand boasted brazenly that he had robbed a black man at a saloon on Water Street in Evansville. He asserted that the black man had no rights that a white man had to respect. In what was the first event of its kind in local records, the town marshal arrested and jailed him. The hand was convicted, fined, sentenced to prison for four years, and disenfranchised for ten years. At about the same time, the Republican editor took to task whites who had attacked an alleged house of ill repute run by a black woman and argued that the blacks who had attempted to defend it had the right to do so. "No men or boys," he declared, "have the right to take the laws into their own hands, even when a negro is in the case."[69]

In Illinois, Republicans gained control of state government in the fall elections of 1864. Whites' attitudes in the state on race matters had been tempered by then. The new legislature repealed the state's antebellum black laws barring black migration, restricting blacks' employment, and permitting the public auction of fugitives. It also endorsed passage of a federal civil rights bill.[70]

In Indiana, Baptists at their state convention in the fall of 1864 urged repeal of Article XIII and of the prohibition against public funding of blacks' education. They declared that "God [had] made of one blood, all nations that dwell upon the face of the earth." A few months later the Western Yearly Meeting of Friends "called for the removal of the prohibition against Negro suffrage and repeal of the law on testimony and other laws which embarrassed Negroes in the efforts at education." The General Assembly in early 1865 considered but did not pass such proposals, even though Republicans now controlled both houses. The Democratic *New Albany Ledger* attributed such efforts to "Boston Yankees" who sought to impose social equality on whites and praised Republicans who resisted change. Legislators also failed to alter the law prohibiting blacks' testifying in court. Indiana was the only Northern state to keep this offspring of the slave codes. In the meantime, Congress passed legislation permitting testimony of blacks in federal courts, and ironically the first case in which an African American's testimony was admitted was in Indiana in December 1864.[71]

To be sure, many whites' support of emancipation, African American sol-

diers, rudimentary civil rights, and philanthropy for refugees was motivated more by pragmatic than by moral considerations. Support for colonization and for the prohibition of interracial marriage also remained strong.[72] There is no question, however, that the war produced a fundamental shift in the attitudes of many north-bank whites.

The war also enhanced African Americans' self-confidence and produced both the expansion of existing black communities and the formation of new ones. As the story of the Black Brigade illustrates, blacks' desire to join in the war effort was amply evident. Notable men like John Carter of Evansville enlisted. So was their desire to aid newcomers. Evansville barbers actively helped slaves flee Kentucky and boarded them until they either enlisted or moved northward. Evansville blacks, like their counterparts in the larger towns up- and downriver, formed mutual aid organizations during the war: a Union Aid Society in early 1862, and a chapter of the United Brothers of Friendship in January 1864. These groups provided funds for the burial of fugitives and soldiers. The AME Church also provided financial and material aid. The war incubated a number of other black organizations. Places like Cairo boasted quite a few. Sundays and holidays brought out members of fraternal societies to parade in their multicolored uniforms, to the delight of whites as well as blacks.[73]

Support for African American schools also grew. In Shawneetown, for example, there had been some efforts to provide education before the mid-1860s, but these were short-lived. Sarah Curtis was brought from Evansville to establish a black school in the early 1860s, and she obtained—apparently with the aid of the Presbyterian congregation—a small room for that purpose. She was ostracized by white women, however, and returned to Evansville after only a few months. The census of 1870 revealed that by then there was a teacher for black students at the Presbyterian Church.[74]

In Evansville, where some schooling had been available through AMA aid in the 1850s, it was reported in September 1863 that philanthropic whites were planning to build a schoolhouse for colored children. For four years a school had been run by "a most worthy young lady, under the auspices of the American Missionary Society." She indicated that she was encouraged by her scholars' progress, but reported that the tenement in which she had been teaching was in dire shape. The Republican editor observed that blacks had been neglected and then blamed for being ignorant. Since the AMA had given Evansville a teacher, the editor urged, "let's give her a house."[75]

The campaign was apparently not successful, since another festival—this

time hosted by the AME pastor in April 1864—had a new schoolhouse as one of its goals. The school operated through the war years, and whites' beneficence played a prominent part in its existence. Several other festivals over the following year were held to raise funds. On the evenings of June 12 and 13, 1865, a large number of whites, many elegantly dressed, participated in one of these festivals. Africans "of all ages and colors" also attended. Two white women, a Mrs. Harvey and a Miss Johnson, organized the event. The latter was the white AMA teacher.[76]

As in the case of Liberty Baptist, whites' assistance was an important element in the development of black churches. The editor of the *Evansville Daily Journal* strongly encouraged whites to attend church festivals organized by blacks, as they did for the AME Church festival. In 1864 the pastor of the AME Church in Evansville, a Rev. H. Green, was the host for two events designed to raise money for a new church building.[77] Shawneetown blacks first worshipped in a congregation supported by white Presbyterians. By the end of the war, black Methodists and Baptists had created their own organizations there. A cooper, Cornelius Neal Elliott, was largely responsible for organizing the Methodists. Owing to costs and the small number of communicants in each congregation, however, they shared use of the Presbyterian Church.[78]

Blacks also began to participate in a free-labor economy for the first time. If Gallatin County, Illinois, was typical, most black newcomers were engaged in unskilled toil, whether on riverboats, on the waterfront, or in the hotels, restaurants, and other businesses. A number found employment on the farm, albeit as laborers, where they lived simply—bartering, hunting and fishing, and collecting herbs, roots, and other plants. Families commonly had two or more members in the workforce. Few blacks were skilled workers. The first postwar census identified, among blacks, just one blacksmith, two grocers, three draymen, two barbers, one teacher, one wagon maker, and one plasterer in the entire county.[79]

Similar patterns existed in upriver Vanderburgh County, where by 1870 only 42 of the 553 who listed an occupation were not employed in service or in unskilled labor. Slightly over half were common laborers, one-quarter were domestic servants, and about one-fifth worked in transportation, chiefly on riverboats. Ex-slave George Taylor Burns recollected that the war opened many opportunities for blacks as roustabouts and deckhands, because so many white men had joined the Union Army or Navy.[80]

The most important element in inchoate black communities was the family. One can infer from the federal enumeration schedules of Vanderburgh County in 1870—probably representative of all counties along the north shore of the

river—that many if not most blacks had arrived in family groups.[81] Nearly 59 percent of African Americans were natives of Kentucky, and another 15 percent, of other upper South states. Just 16 percent had been born in Indiana. The vast majority were newcomers to free-labor society. In Center Township in Vanderburgh County, for instance, farm laborer Louis Colwell and his wife, Jane, both 55, had four children, all born in Kentucky. Their ages ranged from 12 to 6. As the census was taken in late June of that year, one could reasonably conclude that they had arrived as early as 1863. But clearly they had come as a family. Anna Hutchinson, a widow, had four children. She and two children, ages 8 and 13, had been born in Kentucky. The youngest children, Lincoln, age 3, and Grant, age 2, were natives of Indiana. The ages of the 8-year-old and the 3-year-old suggest that the family may have arrived late in the war or shortly after it ended. Fifty-five families totaling 320 people in Vanderburgh County had similar characteristics—children born in Indiana and children who were natives of a slave state in the same family. Even more people were in families of which every member had been born elsewhere. Of the 1,408 blacks enumerated in 1870, moreover, all but about 250 lived in households headed by blacks. The others included 138 who worked as servants and 110 who were steamboat hands.[82]

Cincinnati teacher William Parham had anticipated the new challenges. After the war, "the next war will be against prejudice. . . . We shall need all the talent we have among us or can possibly command." Indiana's Democrats, for their part, showed how difficult that would be. Indiana's Democratic congressmen voted against the Thirteenth Amendment, as did Senator Thomas Hendricks. Democrats in the General Assembly railed against "'negro equality' and the much dreaded 'amalgamation' of the races. . . . They insisted that the Almighty had decreed that the Negro race should be inferior to the white." Declared the *Indianapolis Sentinel,* "Negro agitation has but commenced. . . . We wish we might see some little good resulting from a question so productive of evil."[83]

But a new era had begun. Blacks in Indiana, as in the Ohio Valley generally, "rejoiced in the extinction of slavery, and as the result of the part which they had played in the war, they looked forward optimistically to opportunities to assume new rights and responsibilities in the postwar period."[84]

PART THREE

THE POSTWAR YEARS

5

Population and Residential Patterns

The war brought unprecedented change to the former slave states, including loyal Kentucky, as slaves were freed and many ex-slaves moved to new environs. It also had extraordinary impact on the many communities located on the north side of the river. Tables 6–10 help to document the scope of that alteration (see appendix).

Most of the Bluegrass State's African Americans in 1860 were slaves, and about one-fifth of them lived in Ohio River counties (table 7). Of that number, one in four resided in Louisville and Jefferson County. Another one-fourth were found in three western Kentucky counties: Daviess, Henderson, and Union. Six counties—Mason, Boone, Oldham, Hardin, Meade, and Breckinridge—accounted for most of the remainder. Ten years later the state's African American population had declined by nearly 14,000, but along the Ohio there was an *increase* of almost 4,300 blacks. The increase occurred primarily in Jefferson, Kenton, and McCracken counties, all of which had cities and factories. Ohio River counties also claimed a larger share of the Kentucky's total black population (26%) than in 1860.

By 1880 river counties contained 27 percent of the African Americans living in Kentucky. Jefferson County was significant in that respect, as well as in the state's increased number of African Americans in the decade (16,500), since the county's total black population grew by 6,500. (Between 1870 and

1900, in fact, the number of blacks in Jefferson County increased by 161%.)[1] Moreover, four western Kentucky counties—Hardin, Breckinridge, Daviess, and Henderson—and one Purchase county, McCracken, grew by at least 1,000 each in the 1870s, for a total of approximately 6,300. These six counties accounted for four-fifths of the number of blacks added to Kentucky's population in the 1870s. In the remaining nineteen river counties, three experienced further declines, while in the rest there were modest increases. As in 1870, the counties with the highest rates of growth included major towns.

Across the river the decade of the 1860s also brought a transformation (table 6). First, about 20,000 more African Americans resided there in 1870 than in 1860. The rate of growth was well over 100 percent in sixteen river counties and between 50 and 99 percent in six others. Hamilton County, Ohio, experienced a sizable increase in African Americans, to 7,432, but its share of the region's population dropped to less than 25 percent. In 1860 it had been about 50 percent. Ohio's six counties opposite Kentucky now had 13,955 African Americans, or about 46 percent of all those living along the river's north bank. Downriver, though, the number and the rate of increases were striking. The number of blacks in Jefferson County, Indiana, nearly doubled. Clark and Floyd counties nearly tripled in black population, so that together they had more than 3,400 blacks. Vanderburgh County in Indiana and Alexander and Pulaski counties in Illinois, each of which had a mere handful of blacks before the war, now had well over 2,000 each. When nearby Massac County is added, Illinois's westernmost three river counties represented almost one-fifth of the total number of blacks residing in the twenty-five counties stretching from Ironton to Cairo. These three counties also had the highest proportion of African Americans on the north shore. Two, Alexander and Pulaski, exceeded 20 percent.

The shift that had begun in the war decade was even more evident by 1880 (table 6). The total number of African Americans rose to 41,341, one-third more than in 1870. Hamilton County experienced impressive numerical growth, to 10,533, an overall increase of 43 percent. But the county did not gain regionally, as its total remained at about one-fourth. Although neighboring counties—Brown, Clermont, and Scioto—experienced gain in the decade that ranged from 12 to 14 percent, six downriver counties in Indiana and Illinois grew from 57 to 99 percent, and another five rose between 21 and 39 percent. In Indiana, Vanderburgh County nearly doubled in black population, to slightly more than 3,800, well above second-place Clark County (2,536). The number in Spencer County (Rockport) grew by 57 percent, to almost 1,500. In Illinois, dramatic growth continued in the westernmost three coun-

ties, especially Alexander, whose black population nearly doubled to 4,568, a total exceeded only by Hamilton County. Alexander, Massac, and Pulaski counties together now had nearly 10,000 blacks, almost one-fourth of the region's total. Three of the top five counties in numbers of blacks were near the western end of the river—Alexander, Pulaski, and Vanderburgh, which among them claimed almost 30 percent of the total among the twenty-five river counties in the three states.[2]

Not all north-shore counties grew in number of African Americans in the 1870s. Four (Adams in Ohio and Dearborn, Jefferson, and Crawford in Indiana) declined, and two (Lawrence in Ohio and Harrison in Indiana) had slight increases in number but not in percentage. Minuscule rates of growth were recorded in Floyd and Ohio counties in Indiana and in Gallatin County, Illinois. African Americans were settling where the employment opportunities were greatest.

Continuities from the antebellum era were also evident. Although growth on the north bank of the Ohio was striking, there were considerably more blacks on the south bank. Of the nearly 114,000 living on both shores in 1880, nearly 64 percent were Kentuckians. One in five resided in Jefferson County, Kentucky. Those living in and around Henderson and Owensboro accounted for another 14 percent. By contrast, north-shore Hamilton County represented just 9 percent of the regional total, and collectively Alexander, Pulaski, and Vanderburgh counties slightly over 10 percent (table 6).

Some similarities tied these counties together. Service and river- and transportation-related job opportunities continued to attract and to retain large numbers of blacks. In 1880 blacks residing in Ohio River counties of these four states accounted for about the same share of the total of their respective states' African American populations as in 1870 (table 10). The same could be said about the percentage of blacks along the Ohio that the largest four counties claimed. In both 1870 and 1880, Jefferson County, Kentucky, possessed by far the largest share—about one of ten in Ohio River counties as well as in the commonwealth.

During and after the Civil War, moreover, African Americans tended to move from rural to urban areas because of job opportunities and the presence of Union troops and whites who provided a modicum of protection and encouragement. In 1870 (table 8) 21,024 African Americans lived in Kentucky towns of 2,500 or more, and they accounted for slightly below one-third of those dwelling in the state's river counties (table 7). Ten years later the number

had risen to just above 30,000, or 41 percent. Across the river, 12,918 resided in towns in 1870, or 43 percent of the African Americans residing in north-bank counties (table 9). Ten years later that number had risen to nearly 20,000, or just below half.

African Americans residing in cities represented a growing share of those who lived in urbanized counties. In 1870 African Americans in Cincinnati and Portsmouth, Ohio, represented over three-quarters of their respective counties' totals. Cairo accounted for 81 percent of Alexander County's blacks. Evansville and New Albany claimed slightly less than three-fourths of their respective counties' totals. Louisville had almost 80 percent of Jefferson County's blacks, and in Covington and Paducah the proportion exceeded 60 percent. By contrast, blacks in Owensboro, Henderson, and Maysville, like cross-river Madison, Jeffersonville, Mount Vernon, Metropolis, and Ironton, represented well below half of their predominantly rural and agricultural counties' total black population.

The same trends were even more evident ten years later. For instance, 77 percent of Hamilton County's blacks lived in Cincinnati. Nearly the same proportion of Vanderburgh County blacks were Evansville residents, and even higher percentages were found in Portsmouth and New Albany. By contrast, blacks in Madison, Mount Vernon, and Metropolis represented, as before, less than half of the total in their particular counties. Across the river, Louisville blacks accounted for slightly over fourth-fifths of Jefferson County's black population. In Covington and Newport, they represented slightly over seven-tenths of the county totals. By contrast, blacks in Maysville, Henderson, and Owensboro accounted for one-third or less. In Henderson, the Kentucky river county with the second-highest number of African Americans, only one-fourth of its population lived in the city of Henderson in 1870 and 1880. Blacks in nearby Owensboro accounted for a higher share—about one-third in 1880—largely due to the rise of employment opportunities at the waterfront, on the railroad, and in woodworking factories and distilleries.

Tables 6 and 7, compared to table 1, reveal another curious pattern, undoubtedly due to slavery and the large number of African Americans in most Kentucky river counties prior to the war. As late as 1880, with the exception of the Appalachian counties and a few on the north edge of the Bluegrass, the proportion of African Americans remained at least as high as in 1860. That was especially true of Jefferson, which rose from 12 percent in 1860 to 20 percent in 1870 and dropped slightly to 18 percent in 1880. Henderson rose from 40 percent in 1860 to 32 percent in 1870. The share declined to 31 percent by the end of the 1870s. As in Jefferson County, the ratio decrease was due to the

expansion of the white population, not to a decline in the number of blacks. By 1880 the average ratio of blacks residing in Ohio River counties was 17 percent, exceeded in seven counties.

Despite a huge increase in the number of African Americans on the north side of the river—about 200 percent in the 1860s and another 33 percent in the 1870s—the portion of the total population that was African American averaged just 4 percent in 1870 and in 1880. Fourteen counties, five in Illinois and six in Indiana, met or exceeded that percentage by 1880. The highest by far were the three westernmost Illinois counties.

A similar layout was evident in the cities and towns on either side of the river (table 8). Only one north-shore city, Cairo, where 37 percent in 1880 were African Americans, came close to the city of Henderson's proportion of blacks. Blacks accounted for at least one in six of the residents in five of Kentucky's river cities, as compared with just two, Cairo and Metropolis, across the river. Only two more, Jeffersonville and Mount Vernon, were in double digits. Cincinnati, with by far the most African Americans of north-bank cities, was 97 percent white.

Towns opposite each other on the river tended to resemble each other. In Appalachia, black populations in Ironton, Portsmouth, and Ashland in 1880 were below 10 percent. So were Cincinnati and cross-river Covington and Newport. Across the river from Louisville, 17 percent black, were Jeffersonville (13%) and New Albany (8%). An exception was downstream Evansville, which had 9 percent, as compared with 38 percent in cross-river Henderson, but the number of blacks living in the Indiana city had nearly doubled in the 1870s and would reach about 13 percent by 1900. Metropolis and Paducah had high proportions—20 and 32 percent, respectively.

In addition to demonstrating cross-river similarities, tables 6 and 7 also suggest that although the African American population on the north side of the river was growing steadily, and in some cases dramatically, the number of whites—especially immigrants—was increasing even faster in the most urbanized, industrialized counties. Almost 303,000 of Hamilton County's 313,374 residents in 1880 were white, and about 71,000 of the whites were natives of Germany and the British Isles. Downriver Floyd County, Indiana, had slightly more than 23,000 whites, approximately 2,200 of whom were German or British in origin. Of Vanderburgh's 38,345 whites, slightly more than 7,000 were from Germany or the United Kingdom. Only in the few industrializing counties in Kentucky were these trends approached. Kenton County, for instance, had 41,453 whites out of a total population of 43,983, and of them slightly more than 7,000 were British or German. Most notably, about 22,000

of Louisville and Jefferson County's 120,408 whites had the same origins. In most Kentucky counties, though, immigration was not an appreciable factor.[3]

The substantial increase in the number of African Americans residing on the north shore of the river in 1870 and 1880 was traceable largely to migration from Kentucky and Tennessee. One can reasonably infer that most of the Kentucky newcomers came during the middle to latter part of the Civil War and after it, and that they crossed over from adjoining or nearby counties—for instance, from Henderson and Union counties to Vanderburgh, and from Jefferson County to Clark and Floyd counties. (During the 1870s the population of most of Kentucky's river counties also increased [table 7]. This was the consequence of natural increase and of migration from counties to their south. Jefferson County's growth, by over one-third, was the most dramatic evidence that those counties with large towns received a large share of these newcomers.)

In Evansville, 59 percent of African Americans enumerated five years after the end of the war were Kentuckians. Indiana natives were a distant second: at 16 percent, barely above the percentage of blacks who had been born in other upper South states (15%). Upriver towns were similar. In Madison, a typical resident may have been Asa Gess, age 30. He and his wife had been born in Kentucky. Their three children, ages 3 through 7, were natives of Indiana, suggesting that the family had migrated during the middle of the Civil War. In Ohio Township, which bordered the river in Warrick County, 37 of 43 household heads were Kentuckians. Only 1 was a native of Indiana.[4]

In downstream Metropolis, Illinois, almost half of the heads of households in 1870 were natives of the Bluegrass State, and one-quarter were from Tennessee. A similar configuration existed in Gallatin County. In nearby Pope County, almost all of the heads of household enumerated in New Liberty, a tiny settlement on the Ohio near Golconda, were from Kentucky or Tennessee. Typical was John Standard, a farmhand who was thirty and a native Kentuckian. His wife was a native of Tennessee. Given the ages and birthplaces of their five children, it was evident they had migrated to Indiana within the past year.[5]

Ten years later, Kentucky remained the major source of Evansville's blacks, accounting for 52 percent of the total population. In neighboring Mount Vernon, slightly over seven in ten heads of household were Kentuckians. The same was true of upstream towns like Madison and New Albany as well as downstream communities like Metropolis, where 41 percent of household heads were Kentuckians. Another 30 percent were from Tennessee. Only 3 of 98 persons had been born in Illinois. In Pulaski County, the Bluegrass State was the birthplace of 169 of the 611 household heads, and 213 were born in Tennessee, reflecting the region's proximity to Tennessee.[6]

Another difference between north- and south-bank towns and cities was the way in which African Americans were dispersed (see table 9). On both shores, some neighborhoods had relatively large concentrations of blacks that accounted for a substantial share of the city's black population. There was a centripetal tendency toward concentration in one or several predominantly black regions. These usually acquired names. On the south bank, Smithland, for instance, had Brownsville, on a hilly part of the town, and Bucktown, which faced the Cumberland River. Many of Uniontown's blacks lived in Boxtown, located in the Ohio River bottoms. In West Point, just downriver from Louisville, many blacks resided in Salt Alley and East Alley.

Residential concentration was much more pronounced on the north bank. In 1870, for example, Cincinnati's Ward 13 had the largest number of blacks, 1,092, or 18.5 percent of the city's total. Evansville's First Ward had 415, or 29 percent. A single ward in Jeffersonville and Madison accounted for about half of the blacks in each of those cities, and in Portsmouth Ward 4 represented over 60 percent of the city's total. In Rockport, blacks lived in the river bottoms below the bluff that gave the town its name. In Metropolis, three-quarters of the black households bordered one another. In "suburban Metropolis"—a term used by the census-taker—all of the 53 blacks resided in fourteen adjoining households. Downstream, Alexander County gained 2,241 blacks during the previous decade. Slightly over half of them lived in the northern census precinct, where they represented 32.1 percent of the total population. Slightly more than one-fourth lived in the southern precinct, accounting for 18.4 percent of the total there. Blacks tended to live in clusters of numerous adjoining households where no whites lived.[7]

Cairo resembled towns in Kentucky more than those on the north shore, because there were so many African Americans and they were so widely dispersed. The census revealed that the percentage of blacks in the four city wards ranged from 20 to 32 percent (in Ward 3, which had 21% of the city's black population). Because the boundaries of the city were restrictive, limited by both terrain and decisions of absentee trustees, housing conditions were crowded. Population density was twice that of other cities the same size in the Midwest and the South. The rapid growth of the city during the war and the lack of both paternalistic and antislavery traditions created not only generally ramshackle housing and an environment conducive to vice and violence, but also confusion about the place of blacks in Cairo.[8]

Blacks in south-bank towns were more widely dispersed than their counterparts across the river. Although Ward 10 in Louisville had more than 2,200 black residents, the most in the city, it represented only 15 percent of the

aggregate number of African Americans. Ward 9 had 2,162 blacks. These two wards, near the city's center, accounted for only 29 percent of the total. Blacks lived in all of the other ten wards but were numerous in Wards 4, 5, 6, 7, 8, and 11, where they represented from 15 to 25 percent of the population. Only in wards 1, 2, 3, and 12 on the outskirts of Louisville were the numbers relatively small. Similar patterns existed in Covington, Henderson, Owensboro, and Paducah. In Henderson the black population of 1,489 resided in all four wards. Ward 3 had the highest number, 436, followed closely by Ward 4, with 432. The other two wards had 353 and 268. Covington had eight wards. The largest number of blacks (223, about one-sixth of the city's total) lived in Ward 4, but five other wards had between 125 and 165 each.[9]

Similar configurations were evident in 1880. In Evansville, for example, Ward 1 accounted for nearly one-third of the city's 2,686 blacks, and neighboring Ward 2, with 633, another one-quarter. Adjacent Ward 6, with 494, claimed one-fifth. By contrast, blacks in the other three wards, when combined, represented at most one-quarter of the city's African American population. Cincinnati's blacks were increasingly concentrated in a few wards. In contrast, blacks remained almost evenly distributed among the four wards in Henderson. In Covington Ward 4 had the largest number of blacks, 279, but they represented just 18 percent of the city's total. Two other wards had more than 200 each, and five more had between 100 and 199.[10]

On both sides of the river, however, few wards were predominantly black. In Louisville in 1870, for instance, Ward 9 was 28 percent black and Ward 10 was 20 percent black. Most of the other wards ranged from 15 to 25 percent. Similar proportions were found ten years later. In 1870 Evansville's Ward 1 was just 15 percent black, and only one more (Ward 3, with 11.6%) exceeded 10 percent. Ten years later, Evansville's Ward 1 had risen to 18 percent and Ward 2 to 14. The rest were well below that. In Cairo in 1880, though, 57 percent of households in Ward 3 were black. (The lowest percentage, in Ward 1, was 35.)[11]

Similar population distribution existed elsewhere. In Jeffersonville in 1870, Ward 1's 365 blacks—by far the largest number among the city's five wards—accounted for only 15 percent of that ward's population. In the same year the 1,092 blacks in Cincinnati's Ward 13 accounted for 14.5 percent, the highest proportion of any of the city's twenty-four wards. In Ironton, Ward 3 had 169 of the city's 306 blacks, but they were just 13 percent of that ward's residents.[12]

Cairo, as distinctive as ever, had much in common with Henderson, all of whose wards were heavily black. Percentages of African Americans there ranged from 33 to 44. This distinguished Henderson from all of its south-bank counterparts. Cairo's Ward 3 in 1880 was predominantly black, as before. Among

heads of household, 54 percent were Southern-born, and another 2 percent were Northern-born. This was the only ward with a majority black population, but in the other four wards the proportions were high, ranging from 30 to 40 percent. Blacks and whites, moreover, jumbled together residentially. There was no black ghetto, although about one-quarter of the city's blacks lived in Ward 3. Nearly 40 percent of that ward's whites lived next to blacks. (Ward 1 had the lowest percentage, 24.) Moreover, one-fourth of Ward 3's dwellings were multiple units that had black and white residents. For example, on either side of the home of William Mulkey, a young white attorney who had a wife and three children, were residences of blacks. Across the street were multiple residential units housing black and white families. There were whites dwelling "in the three tiny, heavily black but widely separated neighborhoods: the 'barracks' [where contraband laborers lived during the war] . . . the 'corral' . . . and the 'pinch,' a high crime area on the east side of Ward I in the business district." Blacks resided on most blocks in the city except for an upper-class, four-block neighborhood in Ward 2. In the remainder of southern Cairo, "more than a third of all white residences were adjacent to black homes and more than one out of six multiple-unit dwellings in the whole city provided shelter for both black and white households."[13]

Over time, though, north-bank neighborhoods that contained a large share of their cities' black populations became more racially distinctive. Some were predominantly white regions into which blacks moved, but others had been heavily black from the outset. Evansville was typical. The construction of modest cottages for blacks near the abandoned Wabash and Erie Canal attracted most of the postwar newcomers. A number of these dwellings were owned by Willard Carpenter and Thomas Garvin. This region, which extended generally to the northeast from Fifth and Canal streets and included parts of Wards 1 and 3, was close to the many service and transportation jobs found on or near Main and Water streets and at the Evansville and Crawfordsville Railroad terminal. By 1880 almost half of the city's African Americans lived within a four-block radius of Eighth and Canal streets, and of these, three-quarters lived on or near Canal and Fifth streets. Three smaller clusters were located elsewhere in the city. If one excludes blacks residing in white households and hotels or enumerated on steamboats, these sections accounted for 80 percent of Evansville blacks.[14]

These enclaves became the foundation for housing patterns that would predominate well after World War II. For one, the predominantly German American wards on Evansville's west side had few blacks. Another pattern was that in Ward 1 on the city's east side, where boundaries were unchanged be-

tween 1870 and 1880, nearly doubled its black population in the 1870s. The black population of adjoining Ward 2, also with boundaries unchanged, quintupled. Contiguous parts of Wards 1, 2, and 6 (the latter formerly part of Ward 9) claimed by 1880 three-quarters of the city's blacks, up from slightly over half in 1870. The number of blacks in that region, 1,979, had increased 300 percent.[15]

A third and perhaps most striking development in Evansville, as in many other towns, was that many streets or portions of them were by 1880 largely if not totally black: for example, Canal between Fifth and Eleventh, Oak between Sixth and Eighth, and Lincoln beyond Seventh (where Liberty Baptist Church was built). Gordon, Douglas, Bell, Reilly, Mitchell, Church, and Sumner streets, all near the old canal, were largely black, as were Oak and Chestnut alleys. Several streets in the three outlying clusters, such as West Virginia between Eleventh Street and St. Joseph Avenue, were also predominantly black. These patterns became more evident in the 1890s and the early twentieth century. By about 1890 the largest enclave accounted for four-fifths of all the city's blacks. Beginning in the early 1880s it was known as Baptisttown.[16]

Similar developments characterized upriver Cincinnati. The area derisively called Bucktown, situated in Wards 1 and 13 on the East End, held the largest concentration of blacks. This region was east of Broadway between Sixth and Seventh and ranged from Culvert through the bottoms. It comprised not only "the ordinary, hard-working poor but with a small admixture of the more affluent and a larger one of paupers, criminals and prostitutes." It was hardly a racial ghetto in 1870, though, as its population was only 15 percent black. Southwest of it, chiefly along Front Street between Ludlow and Walnut streets near the docks, was Little Africa. Located in portions of Wards 1 and 4, this region had about 400 blacks, approximately 7 percent of the city's total, who lived in sections named the Levee, Sausage Row, and Rat Row. Many of its residents were river men and dockworkers. Little Bucktown, located to the west in Wards 15 and 16 on Sixth Street, between Freeman and Baymiller streets, had about 900 black residents, about 15 percent of the total in the city.[17]

None of these three clusters were largely black at the outset. But "as the neighborhoods farther east of Little Bucktown became more devoted to wholesale business, mills, and factories with the decline in river trade, Little Bucktown became the major focus of black settlement in Cincinnati." And by the 1870s the other two "had become decayed, dirty, and congested, taking their place among the notorious slums of the era." Prone to flooding because they were situated in the river bottoms, they were poorly drained. One newspaperman in 1876 described an area "full of damp corruption and often under water, or

better expressed, liquid filth."[18] Little Bucktown, on the western edge of the central business district, more than doubled in size by 1910. The region around West Fifth and Central Avenue, several blocks from the Ohio, "emerged as the core of this West End community." It was situated in the basin portion of the city, where after 1870 a growing share of black Cincinnatians resided, since the adjoining hills were generally off-limits to them. By the early twentieth century, the proportion reached two in three, and over time the index of dissimilarity in that region grew steadily.[19]

Louisville, the river city with the most African Americans, had many north-bank characteristics. Well into the twentieth century, however, its black residential areas were more numerous and its black population more dispersed, even though Wards 9 and 10 near the center of the city contained the most blacks by number and percentage. These sections lacked adequate city services: police and fire protection, paved streets, city water and sewers, street lighting, parks, and schools. But Louisville did not have "'a distinct Negro world' completely isolated from the rest of society. The black ghettos around Chestnut Street and 'Smoketown' were not established by 1910." From the 1860s through the turn of the century, most African Americans who moved to Louisville were poor and thus "limited to certain areas. But during that time all blacks were not forced to live in one specific area." In the 1880s, whites attempted unsuccessfully to obtain an ordinance "restricting blacks to a designated 'colored district,' which suggests that blacks were living all over the city at that time."[20]

Blacks lived in most parts of the city as late as 1917. The notable exception was the affluent south side. Several neighborhoods with many blacks had existed since the Civil War era—especially California and Smoketown, west and east, respectively, of the city's center. In Smoketown, "blacks and whites often lived on the very same streets, and . . . some streets that had more blacks than whites in one given year did not necessarily become all-black streets." West Walnut and Chestnut streets, both lengthy east-west thoroughfares, could be described the same way. Within these streets, though, "the races were usually segregated."[21] Nevertheless, prominent professionals such as physician Henry Fitzbutler, attorney N.R. Harper, businessman William Spradling, and civic leader William H. Steward had black neighbors. Whites either lived across the street or were separated from them by vacant houses or lots.[22]

Many of Louisville's poor blacks lived near white businesses close to the center of the city—saloons and vice joints as well as hotels and restaurants, livery stables, and whiskey and tobacco factories. Whites who resided in these

districts were also poor and could not afford to move. A number of them were "undesirable" citizens—madams and prostitutes, for instance. Many blacks in these districts dwelled in alleys adjacent to white-occupied streets, even on the far east and west ends, which were predominantly black. All of the residents of Second Alley between Thirtieth and Thirty-Ninth streets in far west Louisville, for instance, were blacks, employed as domestics and day laborers. It was a legacy of slavery times that most blacks who lived in white areas were employees of the whites, not neighbors. According to George Wright, whites knew that blacks were "excluded or at least segregated from them in most aspects of city life. . . . [There was] little need for rigid segregation in housing." Whites who advocated residential segregation were those who "competed with blacks for employment and housing, not the upper-class whites who knew that the gulf between themselves and blacks could not be altered."[23]

California, located in the western part of the city and named by its first settlers, Germans, extended from Ninth Street west to Twenty-Sixth and south from Broadway to Oak. African Americans began settling here after 1865, thanks in part to the aid of a joint-stock company formed in 1866 to purchase land and construct cottages near Sixteenth Street. The California Colored School was built about a decade later. Whites began leaving this working-class region about 1900. Another neighborhood was Needmore, a swampy area named by poor black settlers and noted for its muddy streets and flimsy shacks. Known as Little Africa by the 1890s, the region was bounded by Virginia on the north, Wilson on the east, Algonquin on the south, and Southwest Parkway on the west.[24]

Smoketown, named for the many brick kilns located there, was the only neighborhood continuously occupied by African Americans from the Civil War onward. Cottages were built on Breckinridge Street in an area extending from Preston to Jackson to Caldwell and back to Preston. A compact area, it was eventually bounded on the east by what is now the CSX railroad, on the west by Floyd, on the north by Broadway, and on the south by Kentucky Street. It was distinguished by its narrow, shallow lots owned mostly by whites, who leased land to blacks. The latter erected small shotgun houses. With most of their capital tied up in their dwellings, the residents found that economic downturns led to loss of lease and home. The high degree of turnover made this a residentially and socially unstable neighborhood. Few blacks owned land in Smoketown, Washington Spradling Jr. being an exception. Whites in the region—who lived in brick and frame homes—were managers and skilled laborers, while blacks performed menial, labor-intensive work. Smoketown

soon contained a number of important black institutions, beginning with the Eastern Colored School (1874), one of the city's first schools for blacks.[25]

Other heavily black neighborhoods were Brownstown, Fort Hill, and Russell. Brownstown, centered around Second and Magnolia streets, was so named by the 1870s. Three black churches were established there between 1875 and the early 1880s. Fort Hill was a small, racially mixed settlement on the site of Civil War Fort Horton that came to be largely black. Most of the blacks lived on Meriwether and Bland streets and worked as common laborers in factories near the railroad line as well as in the brickyard, the lumberyard, and the sand and clay quarries. Russell, west of the center of the city, was situated north of California and named for noted black educator Harvey C. Russell. The eastern portion of the region had been inhabited by free blacks before 1861. Initially it was a suburb that attracted wealthy whites, and black residents built small frame, shotgun houses on minor streets and alleys. Whites began leaving in the 1890s, and middle-class blacks moved westward to this region.[26]

Upriver Covington, the second-largest town on the south bank of the Ohio, resembled Louisville in many ways. Although streets and neighborhoods contained both blacks and whites, racial separation existed within these regions. In Ward 4, which had the largest number and the highest percentage of blacks, clusters of black residences were much in evidence in 1870. For example, eight dwellings listed close together on two pages of the federal census contained fourteen families and fifty-one people, one-sixth of the ward's total. One household was Jourdan Finney's. Fifty-six and a day laborer, he had a wife, age 37, who was probably his second, since his son was 26. Living in the same building was the family of Cynthia Hawkins, 31 and a washerwoman, who had three small children. Another adult woman, perhaps a relative, lived with them. Also residing in Hawkins's household was Sarah Cobb, a 25-year-old domestic servant, who had a son age 10.[27]

Even greater clustering was evident ten years later, when the city had 1,788 blacks. About half lived in three of the eight wards—2, 3, and 4. If one adds the northern and southern portions of nearby Ward 5, these sections of the city held two-thirds of Covington's African Americans. Nearly 200 resided in alleys that were all or nearly all black. Covington's Ward 4 was a long, narrow rectangle stretching from the river south to Twelfth Street and east from Russell Street past the Kentucky Central Railroad line (which ran down Washington Street) to Madison Street, then north to Scott Street. Fifteen African Americans resided on Russell, 78 on Washington, 13 on Stewart, and 31 on Madison. Sixteen more lived in an alley between Russell and Washington.

Another 62 resided on Eighth, Tenth, or Twelfth streets. All of these homes were close to the railroad depot. Adjoining this ward to the east was Ward 3, another narrow section with the same north-south borders that ended at Scott on the east. Of its 203 blacks, slightly under one-third lived on Scott, mostly between Fifth and Sixth, on Sixth, or on Madison, near Second and Third streets. To the east of Ward 3, Ward 2, which also had the same northern and southern borders and extended east across Market to Greenup, had about 150 blacks. The new suspension bridge to Cincinnati entered this ward at Second Street.[28]

Western Kentucky's Owensboro, fourth-largest of the state's river towns, possessed comparable residential patterns. Although street names were not provided in the federal census of 1870, dwelling numbers disclose eighty-seven houses in Ward 1 located near each other that accounted for all but two blacks in that ward. Thirty-two mostly adjoining dwellings housed over half of the blacks in Ward 2. Living conditions in each ward were at best marginal. One residence in Ward 1 was that of Hannah Hankins, 60, whose occupation was listed as "keeping whorehouse." Two residents of the house were prostitutes, both age 20. Many of the men who headed black households, like Washington Jackson, age 55, were identified as tobacco stemmers or simply by the entry "works tobacco factory." Most women who had jobs were domestic servants.

Ten years later the city had 1,564 black residents, nearly all of whom resided in the 229 dwellings that had black heads of household. These inhabitants, though spread throughout Owensboro, lived near each other in relatively few neighborhoods. In one of the city's two census districts, number 165, 38 of the dwellings between numbers 401 and 453 had black residents. In the other district, 166, 15 residences of those numbered 88 to 107 had black occupants, as did 22 of the houses numbered 162 to 198.[29]

Paducah, the third-largest river city, had four federal census districts in 1880. Nearly 2,600 African Americans were enumerated, but slightly over 40 percent lived in Census District 125. The others had sizable black populations as well. Although the percentage of blacks in each was relatively small, all four had distinctive residential clusters where blacks lived near each other. In District 123, for instance, 88 of the 100 persons enumerated on Churchill Street were black. Large groups of blacks were also found on Clay, Campbell, Poplar, Harris, Harrison, Hickory, Madison, Gerard, and Trimble streets. Seventy-six percent of the district's African Americans resided on these streets. In District 124, two-thirds lived on two streets: in 31 residences on Court Street, and in 25 on Washington Street. In District 125, about one in four lived on Poplar Street. Nearly 40 percent of the blacks in the district had Adams, Hickory,

Jackson, Locust, and Washington street addresses. In District 126 households with black heads that adjoined one another were numerous on the west side of Broad, Locust, and Oak streets as well as on both sides of Chestnut.[30]

Across the river, in 1880 Metropolis had 534 blacks, the largest part living in 116 black-headed households. As in Kentucky towns, they accounted for a relatively high proportion of the town's total population. But as in other north-bank towns, a much higher level of residential concentration existed in one distinctive neighborhood. About 80 percent of the blacks resided in a region bounded by Sixth, Tenth, Court, Market, and Pearl streets and where most residences with blacks were close to each other.[31]

Madison, Indiana, was not much different. With nearly 8,800 residents, the city had only 454 blacks in 1880. Slightly over one-third of them were enumerated in Ward 5 and another one-quarter in adjoining Ward 4. Between them the two wards had 60 percent of those in the city. This section, informally known as Georgetown, was north of Fourth Street, between Walnut and Main. On the surface it would appear that residential concentration was a thing of the future, not the present, since even in Wards 4 and 5 blacks accounted for at most 12 percent of the total population. But appearances were deceptive. In Ward 5, for instance, 93 people were clustered together on Presbyterian Avenue and nearby Fifth and Cemetery streets. In Ward 4, 80 were enumerated around the junction of Broadway, West, and Fifth streets. Most blacks in Ward 2 lived on or near Walnut, Fourth, and Fifth streets, and in Ward 3 most were found around West, Mulberry, and Main streets. Seventeen more were found on the portion of Presbyterian Avenue that lay in Ward 6. Fifty of Madison's black residents, moreover, resided in alleys.[32]

As of the mid-1880s, however, the river valley's African Americans, like those of Louisville, "did not live in areas resembling the black ghettos of the second half of the twentieth century."[33] Many poor whites, native and immigrant, lived in the same areas as blacks. The formation of more rigid lines dividing neighborhoods by race came gradually—a product of whites' greater residential mobility and blacks' limited occupational and educational opportunities and of formal restrictions like restrictive covenants on the sale, rental, and leasing of property. The latter appeared in Evansville about 1909. Much more powerful, though, was word-of-mouth-communicated understandings about where blacks could live and occasional acts of retribution, including violence, against those who broke those rules.[34]

South-bank blacks were distinctive not only in being more widely dispersed in cities and towns, but also in living in households that whites headed, espe-

cially in rural areas. This was particularly evident in the immediate postwar census. The lower (southern) census district of Henderson County in 1870, for instance, contained 245 African Americans, but just nine households had black heads. Even in the town of Henderson, the proportion of black-headed households was relatively low. Whites headed slightly more than one-third of the households in which blacks lived, and one in six of the nearly 1,500 black residents resided in a white-headed household. Ten years later Henderson County continued to have a relatively large number of white households with black members. In town, whites headed about one in five households that contained African Americans. These accounted for just below one-tenth of the city's black population.[35] By contrast, of the slightly more than 2,700 blacks in Evansville in 1880, about 2,500 resided in the 574 residences headed by blacks. The 130 whites whose households contained blacks were keepers of hotels and restaurants, steamboat operators, and wealthy residents who employed domestics. In Enumeration Districts 77, 78, and 79, along the riverfront, 136 blacks lived in 90 white-headed households.[36]

It was not uncommon to find other vestiges of the slave past in rural south-bank counties. In Henderson County, entire black families were enumerated in white households, and frequently the African Americans had the same surname as that of the white head of household or of a prominent white living nearby. Wealthy farmer Payne Dixon's household included Henderson Alves, a black man whose given name reflected the locale and whose surname was that of one of the county's wealthiest men. Alves was a 47-year-old field hand, and his wife Patsay [sic], a cook, was 42. Both worked for Dixon. Also in the household was America Hatchett, 16; Jack Alves, a field hand who was 22 (perhaps the son of Henderson), and his wife, Amelia; another field hand who was 20 (possibly another son of Henderson); and a field hand and his wife in their late forties who had five children, ages 2 to 14. The household of wealthy tobacco dealer William Soaper, age 75, included his wife and children and nine African Americans, two of whom (one a tobacco stemmer) were also named Soaper. Also present was a black couple—a farm laborer and a domestic, and their children. In the town, Archibald Dixon, former planter and U.S. senator, had four black servants in his household of eleven members.

All told, 101 residents of the county had the surname Alves (or Alvis), and 65 of these were black. Sixty-eight were named Barret (or Barrett), of whom 44 were black. The surnames Dixon and Powell—names of the county's wealthiest planters and most prominent politicians—were ubiquitous: 253 of the former, of whom 166 were African Americans, and 218 of the latter, of whom 145 were black.[37]

In neighboring Union County, in 1870 whites headed 212 of the 459 households that contained black residents. Nearly one in four black inhabitants of the once slave-rich county lived in those households. That this vestige of slavery was not limited to rural portions of the county was evident in Uniontown, where whites headed 20 of the 50 homes that had black residents. These accounted for one-fifth of the town's black residents. As in Henderson County, the number of whites with blacks living in their households declined somewhat during the following decade.[38]

Posey County showed a different picture; across the river from Henderson and Union, it was one of southern Indiana's most productive agricultural counties, and one of its most rural. Outside of the town of Mount Vernon in 1880, there were 26 white homes in which blacks—mostly farm laborers—were enumerated. These represented only one in six of the households in the county in which blacks were enumerated. All told, these households contained just 53 of the county's 766 black residents. In Mount Vernon, 66 of the 71 households with black inhabitants had black heads.[39]

New Albany and Louisville were—like Evansville and Henderson—quite different from each other in this respect. Almost all of New Albany's 862 blacks in 1870 resided in dwellings headed by blacks. Across the river, although a sizable majority of African Americans resided in black-headed households, many did not. Quite a few were likely to be found in white-owned hotels and restaurants or steamboats as well as in white homes, where they were house servants.[40]

Contrast was also evident upriver, between Bluegrass Trimble County and cross-river Jefferson County, Indiana. In 1870 just 41 of the 119 households with black residents in Trimble had black heads. The remaining 78 white-headed homes accounted for nearly half of the county's 432 black residents. As in Henderson County, many had large numbers of blacks, often entire families. Such was the case of Jemima Townsend, a 40-year-old house servant, who resided with her six children, ages 1 to 22, in the home of a white farmer. Walker Baker, a farmhand who was 65, lived with his wife, Matilda, and a young house servant, possibly their daughter, and a 4-year-old girl, Ellen, possibly their granddaughter, in the household of a white farmer. Like downstream households, often the sole black member of a white household was a young black girl who was identified as "nurse." Such was the status of Emma J. Pitman, age 10, who lived in the home of a wealthy white merchant also named Pitman in the town of Bedford. That their surnames were the same was another vestige of slavery, one that was not uncommon in Trimble County in 1870. As in other rural river counties, the census ten years later disclosed that

a significant number of blacks continued to live in white-headed households but that the total had declined. In 1880, 426 of the 503 blacks in Trimble County resided in households that blacks headed.[41]

Across the river, Jefferson County, Indiana, had a relatively small black population in 1870, and most of the blacks (slightly over 90%) lived in black-headed households. Three in five of the 153 dwellings with black residents had black heads. Most of the white-headed families (27) were found in Madison, where the black members were household servants. Like families across the river, some included blacks who shared their surnames. Even though the number of black residents in the county dropped by nearly 50 percent by 1880, however, over nine in ten were enumerated in black-headed households.[42]

Upstream Covington and its rural environs in Kenton County resembled Louisville and Jefferson County. In the city, which had two-thirds of the blacks in the county, just slightly more than seven in ten resided in black households. In rural environs, the number dropped to about one in three. In Ward 4 of the city, with the largest number of blacks (223), 145 lived in black households. Similar proportions were found in Wards 7 and 8. By contrast, in Ward 1, which had 125 blacks, just 55 lived in black households. Here blacks were enumerated in such public places as hotels and in the homes of wealthy whites who had a number of black servants. Landen Stockton, a commission merchant in Ward 1, had 4 servants. A.B. Duke, a physician, had 6, and Otto Leopold, a bridge builder, had 5. In Ward 9, Henry Merton, a merchant with real property valued at nearly $54,000 and personal property at $47,000, had 4 domestic servants in his residence. Slavery's legacy was evident in Ward 4, where Levi Dougherty, a wealthy real estate agent, had 6 blacks, 5 of them servants, in his home. Ranging in age from 6 to 65, none possessed a surname.[43]

During the decade of the 1870s, more Kenton County blacks took up residence in black-headed households. The percentage of blacks living in black households in Covington rose to 87 by 1880. Outside the city, in rural Kenton County, the proportion reached 85 percent. Ward 4, which had the largest number of blacks, was slightly below the city average. As in 1870, Ward 1, with the lowest percentage residing in black households, had a number of wealthy residents who employed blacks. One of them, Amos Shricker, identified as a capitalist, had 8 servants, 3 of them black.[44]

Downstream counties in Kentucky and Illinois also demonstrated this divergence. In 1870, thirty-eight white households in Livingston County, Kentucky, across the river from Massac and Hardin counties in Illinois, had black residents. These included 102 persons, one-seventh of the county's African Americans. A number of these were farm laborers and domestic servants. A

significant number of the white households contained entire black families. One family of seven blacks, for instance, was enumerated in the household of a Dyer Precinct farmer: an elderly farm laborer, another laborer, a domestic servant who was probably his wife, and four children ages 6 months to 9 years old. A family of nine resided in the Salem Precinct home of a white widow, Ann Rutter, age 79. The family's head was a black man aged 36 whose surname was also Rutter. The family also included his wife, six children aged 2 to 13 (the eldest two of whom were farm laborers), and another person also identified as a farm laborer. Similar household patterns existed in ten other instances in the county.[45]

Ten years later, the number of those living in white households had dropped to 48 of Livingston County's approximately 1,000 blacks. As significant was the fact that just 34 white households—as compared with 167 black households—had black members, and only in a handful of instances (at most four) were black families living in them. Clearly blacks in that county, as elsewhere, were gaining greater independence from their former owners and other whites as time distanced them from slavery.[46]

A comparable pattern emerged in neighboring McCracken County. In 1880 the number of blacks in white residences had declined to 277, or just below 7 percent of the county's black populace. As elsewhere, the drop was greater in urban areas. Just 114 of Paducah's 2,498 blacks, or 4.5 percent, lived in white residences. All told, blacks were heads of 539 households in the city and another 274 in rural parts of the county.[47]

Across the river in Illinois, Gallatin County in 1870 had slightly over 600 blacks residing in 193 households, only one-fifth of which were headed by whites. In Shawneetown, just 14 of the 206 blacks in the village lived in 8 white households. All but 2 of the 62 blacks in nearby Hardin County were members of the 13 black families in the county. The same outline existed in Pope and Massac counties. In the latter, just 16 of the 169 households that contained African Americans, either as domestic servants or farmhands, were white.[48]

This pattern grew more pronounced during the 1870s. In the 1880 census of Gallatin County, for instance, only one-sixteenth of the 675 blacks in the county lived in white households. One-third of those were in Shawneetown. In one white home resided the family of Richard Suggs, a fifty-six-year-old laborer who was a widower. He had 4 children, the eldest of whom was a domestic. Another 7 blacks were enumerated in the household of hotel proprietor Charles Kampton—4 female servants and 3 children. Generally white homes contained only one or at most two blacks, usually servants or farm

laborers. Downstream Massac County had 1,645 blacks in 1880, and only 59 did not live in the 310 residences that blacks headed. Most of the 59 were servants living in Metropolis or neighboring Brooklyn (later Brookport). Of the slightly more than 3,000 blacks living in Pulaski County, just 54 were not enumerated in the 611 black residences. As elsewhere, most were household servants.[49]

A combination of factors—the level of urbanization and industrialization, the absence of a tradition of white control of black families, and the brand-new opportunity to advance on one's own—ensured that on the north side of the Ohio most blacks lived in their own households. In heavily rural north-shore counties, to be sure, there were some similarities to household life on the south bank. Nevertheless, on the Kentucky side of the river the incidence of blacks' residing in white households was significantly higher than on the north shore in 1870 and 1880, though it declined in the 1870s. This was clearly a reflection of some ex-slaves' unwillingness or inability to leave antebellum labor and family patterns.

A final point about postwar demographic and residential patterns is that blacks resided in inferior housing, usually in unhealthful areas, and as a consequence they experienced much higher mortality rates and had shorter lives than whites. In Louisville, for instance, few owned the dwellings in which they lived. Some were fortunate enough to live in poorly insulated, frame shotgun houses that had at most three rooms, but the vast majority resided in smaller apartments and tenements. Some neighborhoods lacked wells, so that residents had to haul in their water. Thousands of blacks lived in basements and poorly ventilated cellars. Housing was "congested and dilapidated, lacking modern bathroom facilities." The same could be said of poor whites' dwellings, "but the city did provide them with free public bathhouses, something not available to blacks. . . . Furthermore, most of the buildings were firetraps." In areas where blacks were concentrated, fire "caused a tremendous amount of damage in the entire period of 1870–1930." Yet fire stations in black neighborhoods in the west and east ends were not opened until the mid-1920s to mid-1930s, respectively. In addition, "unpaved streets, the absence of sewers, and the presence of litter characterized too many of the city's all-black neighborhoods." Health officials "consistently ignored sanitation in the black community, obviously never realizing that blacks could carry infectious diseases into the businesses and homes of their white employers." Poor sanitation and sewage drainage combined with overcrowded residences "led to higher rates of death and infant mortality for blacks and to a greater susceptibility to diseases like tuberculosis and pneu-

monia." The federal census reported that "far more deaths occurred from contagious and infectious diseases among blacks than whites."[50]

The *Louisville Courier-Journal* in 1873 lauded former slaves for having saved up $25,000 to purchase homes, but "progress for many was short-lived." The financial panic and its ensuing six-year depression devastated owners and renters of homes in black Louisville. Leading Louisville blacks formed a real estate and relief association in 1874 to help them with planning and purchasing homes, but the effort produced little progress. Residents of regions like Smoketown experienced periodic economic downturns after 1879, which created an endless cycle of exorbitant rents and high residential turnover. Blacks in Louisville also faced the prospect of increasingly segregated housing by the 1880s, as white leaders began openly to advocate confining blacks to specific parts of the city.[51]

Blacks' living conditions were little different in other places, whatever their size and regardless of which side of the river they were on, but there were a few exceptions. In rural Kentucky, some were able to purchase modest plots of land from socially minded whites and to erect small cottages. In towns like Louisville and Covington, middle- and upper-class blacks formed relatively affluent enclaves within largely black neighborhoods.[52] A similar outline was emerging in north-shore towns like Cincinnati and Evansville.

For the vast majority, though, residential conditions resembled those of ordinary blacks in Louisville. In Cincinnati, living conditions in Bucktown and the Levee were horrendous—five or six families crowded into seven rooms, often practically buried as a result of the city's efforts to fill the hollows with dirt to check erosion and disease. The Board of Improvements forced a cleanup of this region in the late 1870s, but the mortality rates for blacks and whites living there remained high, "and the damp and crowded tenements were prime breeding grounds for tuberculosis."[53]

Crime and vice were also prevalent, and these two sections of the Queen City were the "red light zones" of their day. Morphine use among prostitutes was widespread, and children of these women roamed the streets, dying of hunger and exposure or sometimes being taken in by kindly women. The police force interfered little with prostitution because of the political clout of brothel-keepers. What eventually led to a decline in violent crime was the sharp drop in the number of transients that coincided with the decline of the river trade. Prostitution and gambling, though, remained. Especially notorious were the varieties of brothels available on George Street, on the eastern edge of Little Bucktown. Poverty and squalor created a self-perpetuating cycle of life for those growing up here. That poor white migrants from the South and

from abroad—first the Irish and the Germans, and then those from southern and eastern Europe—also lived in these regions did not produce racial integration. Whites rarely lived with blacks in the same tenements, they distanced themselves from poor blacks, and they tried to escape these regions as quickly as possible. Unlike blacks, they usually succeeded.[54]

Evansville's Baptisttown was located in an undesirable part of town near the old canal and commanded higher rents than comparable shelter for whites. Other blacks lived in flood-prone areas on the north side of town. Blacks also occupied unkempt alleys near Main Street that, like other regions of the city, lacked paved streets and adequate drainage. Housing was densely populated. In Baptisttown, six persons on the average resided in each dwelling, a density 20 percent higher than the city average. By the 1880s, some prominent whites began, as in Louisville, to take public notice of the unhealthful, crowded living conditions, but only because they threatened whites' property values or because whites had to view them as they traveled to and from work. The location of such regions close to the city's vice districts reinforced whites' stereotypes of blacks as shiftless, unreliable, and loose-living, and those perceptions hindered improvement in the quality of housing. One modest sign of progress was the creation of an all-black fire unit at Olive and Governor streets in the late 1880s to serve all African Americans in Baptisttown.[55]

Early reports of the infant Indiana State Board of Health (1881), Vanderburgh County coroners' inquests, and other public records sharpen this picture. Statewide, the biggest killers of Indiana blacks in the year ending October 31, 1883, were what the health board termed "constitutional" ailments, primarily tuberculosis and pneumonia. Infectious and contagious diseases such as scarlet fever, smallpox, and typhoid fever were also major killers. Blacks accounted for 4.4 percent of those who died in that period, although they represented only 2 percent of the total population. State officials noted in their report that this death rate of blacks was lower than that of persons born in Prussia or the German Empire.[56]

Between 1880 and 1895 the annual rate of interments of blacks in Evansville's largest public cemetery, Oak Hill, ranged from 18 to 23 percent. In one six-year period, 153 of the coroners' 507 inquests involved blacks—nearly one-third of the total, although blacks made up less than 10 percent of the populace. Of these, 60 were children below the age of two. Thirteen of the remaining inquests indicated that tuberculosis was the cause of death. Mortality rates for blacks, especially among children and infants, consistently exceeded the rates for whites by at least 50 percent through the latter part of the nineteenth century.[57]

Such realities were, of course, not new to most African Americans. What was new was that the war had brought a change of status and residence for thousands in Ohio River counties. Many moved from rural to urban places in the Bluegrass State, as employment and security offered better chances for them. Others moved out of the state, mostly to towns and cities across the river. In either case, African Americans settled in distinctive racial clusters that laid the basis for twentieth-century ghettos. They would also encounter new challenges: relating to whites, and dealing with the vagaries of freedom.

6

Free and Equal,
with Opportunities and Pains

For Ohio River African Americans, mobility was the most immediate consequence of emancipation. Other stages followed: searching for long-lost
relatives, establishing legal existence by recording given and family names,
legalizing marriages and creating families, finding employment, and participating in public life. In Kentucky, the most pressing challenge was safeguard-
ing loved ones. Right on the heels of that priority came dealing with
homelessness, disease, and violence and finding a source of income. Blacks
"emerged from the Civil War into an atmosphere of confusion and uncertainty. Poverty-stricken, frequently the object of harassment and violence,
without basic state-supported human services, they suffered horribly during
the immediate postwar years."[1]

The next issue, for blacks on both shores, was coping with the promise of
freedom and equality—a struggle that blacks would ultimately have to engage
in on their own.[2] That is the focus of this chapter and chapters 7 and 8. The
other challenges are discussed in chapters 9–12.

Memories varied regarding when and how freedom came. George Arnold
recalled jumping ship near the end of the war and eventually making his way
to Evansville, where he got a job as a porter in a wholesale feed store. Grace
Monroe remembered being mistreated by her former master and driven from
the plantation at war's end. She found her mother, whom she had not seen for

many years, in Carrollton, Kentucky. She married and eventually had thirteen children in her new home across the river in Ohio County, Indiana. The master of John Rudd, born in 1854, forced him to remain on his farm and hired out his mother as a cook at a Louisville hotel. He was released through the efforts of an older brother, an army veteran. John took a steamer to Owensboro, where he worked briefly as a farmhand and a hotel porter before taking a job as a domestic servant in Evansville. Billy Taylor, who eventually settled in Jeffersonville, recounted his father's joining the army at Louisville and bringing the entire family across the river in 1865, when Billy was seven. Adah Suggs, born near Henderson in 1852, fled across the river to Evansville with the aid of Union soldiers. Her father was a soldier. Eventually his wife and family were freed. Employed by a prominent white family, Adah was married in 1872. Robert Cheatham was freed by his owner, a Henderson County physician, who brought the family Bible to Vanderburgh County court. Because it included records of slaves' births, marriages, and deaths, it was used to document the ex-slave's birth date and name. His given name was his father's, and his surname that of his former master.[3]

Samuel Watson remembered that emancipation made some slaves happy and others sad. "Many dreaded leaving their old homes and their masters' families." The former master of Watson's family "asked [Watson's] mother to take her little ones and go away." She took her family to a nearby plantation, where wages proved to be inadequate. She "worked from place to place until her children became half starved and without clothing." The older children left, returning to their old master, while the mother and young Samuel went to work for another planter, who indentured the young man for eighteen years. Samuel recalled that he had "a good home among good people." He was not paid for his work, however, until a sympathetic attorney brought suit against the master and gained a judgment of $115. Thomas McIntire, a slave in Ashland, Kentucky, recalled that his father and uncle enlisted in the Union Army and that their owner freed them before the end of the war. His father worked as a blacksmith, his mother sold chickens and eggs, and he worked on farms. The family saved enough to buy "a nice six-room house." One of his most vivid memories was that they were now able to purchase sugar instead of molasses as a sweetener.[4]

Determining whether freedom had been achieved by military service or by fleeing slavery was virtually impossible in Kentucky, especially after General Palmer's liberal issuance of passes in early 1865 and his speech to thousands of slaves on July 4, 1865. The imminent passage of the Thirteenth Amendment complicated matters, as it "annihilated many states' basic social institutions, in a

nation where federal power had never reached so far before." By giving freedom to blacks and confiscating whites' property, it produced a "gigantic shift in whites' view of the world."[5] Few freed slaves accepted offers of employment from former owners, because supervision by the old master was tantamount to a voluntary return to servitude. Blacks preferred freedom to slavery and accepted their new but fragile existence "with a 'becoming grace,' behaving 'like men of sense and character' as they went to work building a new life."[6]

Some former slaves moved to other states, mostly just across the river, while others decided to stay in Kentucky. They believed that "freedom was better than slavery and that, given a fair chance, they would eventually progress to the point of partaking of the good life they associated with freedom." They pursued freedom mostly on their own. The black family, "the rock of slave society, withstood the trials and tribulations of the immediate postwar years to become the foundation of postwar black society."[7]

A number of black and white philanthropic groups agreed that more was needed than freedom to ensure that blacks would not become a permanent subclass. With the urging of O.O. Howard, the head of the federal Bureau of Refugees, Freedmen, and Abandoned Lands, and the agency's director for Tennessee, Clinton B. Fisk—both former Union Army generals and abolitionists—Kentucky was made subject to the authority of that organization.[8]

The Freedmen's Bureau (as it was also termed) in the commonwealth sought to ensure legal justice and to promote education, industry, and order. The Kentucky branch was opened in late January 1866. During its brief, underfunded existence, the bureau mediated relations between black employees and white employers to ensure fair labor contracts. It also sought to force vagrants to seek employment. It made substantial contributions in promoting justice and providing educational opportunities. Fisk headed the bureau's Tennessee region until June 13, 1866, during which time three subdistricts were formed, two of which (Louisville and Paducah) were on the Ohio. Districts added later included Henderson and Owensboro. Pressured by Congress, the federal government began closing bureau operations in the late 1860s. Benjamin P. Runkle, who became head in January 1869, supervised this process. Educational programs ceased in the summer of 1870, but veterans' claims offices survived another two years.[9]

The bureau in Kentucky had limited success. It was tardily and poorly funded and had too few officials, especially field agents. At most it had fifty-seven employees. Superintendents sought to maintain goodwill by hiring local whites as agents, but meager pay discouraged the best people from seeking

employment. Agents faced harassment and death. Some were paternalistic, unconcerned about blacks' needs, and corrupt or abusive. There were too few federal troops, most of whom were used farther south. At most the army had twenty-one officers for the entire state. Troops were essential to bureau investigation of violence against blacks and settlement of labor contract disputes. From 1865 to 1870 the state experienced one of the most lawless times in its history because most whites—including state officials—believed the bureau was flouting the state's constitution and its social customs. Roving bands of Confederate veterans, combined with a population of former slaves in flux, created a volatile mixture that produced an unparalleled reign of terror.[10]

In the immediate postwar years, "the intensity of the actions directed against former slaves exceeded anything experienced by whites." Sometimes whites refused to sell land to blacks or to build black churches or schools. On other occasions there were threats of bodily harm. But "white hostility could explode directly into physical force. During a two week period in 1867 some sixteen whites . . . were arrested on separate charges of beating former slaves." In Boone, Carroll, and Trimble counties, blacks complained that slavery still existed. Mobs whipped blacks at random for alleged insults in Covington and Owensboro, where a black man asserted in December 1867 that the Freedmen's Bureau was blacks' only protection.[11]

Although relatively few whites engaged in terrorist acts, their actions were condoned by many others. Negrophobes sought to rid the state of all blacks, threatening blacks who sought to rent, lease, or purchase land as well as whites who offered land to blacks. Night riders, some of them members of the newly formed Ku Klux Klan, terrorized rural blacks. Families of black soldiers were favorite targets. In its annual reports between 1866 and 1868, the Freedmen's Bureau reported scores of murders as well as hundreds of cases of maltreatment—rapes, whippings and beatings, attempted murders, shootings, and the like. One-third of the 353 lynchings in the history of the commonwealth took place between 1865 and 1874. Ninety-two occurred between January 1866 and December 1870. Justice was neither swift nor fair. Between July 1, 1867, and June 30, 1868, for instance, "there were no arrests in ten of the twenty murders of blacks; in the other ten, four were acquitted, the court took no action in one case, and three remained before various courts."[12]

Nonetheless, the bureau provided some protection. In December 1867, for example, night riders warned whites renting to blacks in Daviess and Henderson counties that they would be burned out unless the black renters were gone by the following February. This occurred at the same time the bureau had been ordered to close operations there. The arrival of scores of

frightened blacks in Henderson and Owensboro prompted officials to remain and protect the freedmen. Bureau pursuit of justice in federal court under the provisions of the Civil Rights Act of 1866, moreover, led to some criminal convictions that would not ordinarily have been obtainable.[13]

In most lynchings black men were accused of assaulting white women. There were three such occurrences in Daviess County. Of one of those lynchings, in May 1866, a county historian wrote glibly that "while on his way to the jail, an unknown party placed one end of a rope over his [the black man's] head and threw the other end over a limb of a tree in the court-house yard." Whites often found blacks to be convenient scapegoats and engaged in random offenses, ranging from "the most trivial to the most odious of crimes, almost 'because they were there.'"[14]

During the summer of 1865, whites who aided freedmen in Henderson and Union counties were frequently beaten and threatened with lynching. Evansville's Andrew L. Robinson reported that whites had sought to re-enslave a number of wives and children of black soldiers and that night-riding former Confederate guerrillas were terrorizing the black families. Federal troops, often black men, provided some aid. In late November a number of black troops passed by the Evansville waterfront en route to Henderson, Uniontown, and Smithland, where they were to be garrisoned to restore law and order. The 5th Colored Cavalry Regiment, traveling downriver to do the same in Arkansas, drew a large crowd of local blacks, who admired "their sable brethren in Uncle Sam's uniform."[15]

In late July 1868, according to the report of a man visiting Henderson from Tennessee, some forty to fifty masked men, led by several men on horseback, reportedly marched through the streets of that city. The man recognized these men as a company of Klansmen. A month earlier, the Evansville Republican newspaper had reported the formation of a Klan company in that county. Klan activities in Henderson and other Kentucky counties to the south intensified and left a trail of violence against freedmen. A federal marshal arrived in Evansville on February 9, 1869, en route to Louisville. He had recently taken twenty-five soldiers and an officer into those counties to quell Klan activity. According to the marshal, the hooded order's machinations were worse than had been reported. Their "filthy bestiality" was of the sort that brought down "cities of the plain" in the Bible. He had arrested a number, including some "citizens of average respectability."[16]

For many blacks living in Kentucky's river counties, leaving the countryside was preferable to facing continual harassment. The notorious Shacklett family gang in Meade County, for instance, threatened to kill any African

American who did not leave for Indiana. About 500 regulators roamed Gallatin County, prompting 200 blacks to depart in a single day. Masked bands were also commonplace in western Kentucky and Purchase counties. Perhaps because of its long-standing tradition of Tidewater paternalism, though, "Henderson [town] was the only location in western Kentucky where civil officials provided assistance to black refugees fleeing violence." Alone among Ohio River towns, Henderson's town officials in 1868 passed an ordinance making the wearing of masks in public illegal.[17]

Blacks generally moved into towns, where they were not known, where their former owners could not easily reach them, where there was security in numbers, and where there were better job opportunities. The number of black residents in river cities and towns increased dramatically in the 1860s, but living conditions, as noted in chapter 5, were unenviable. Many blacks walked the streets, unable to find shelter. In Louisville in February 1866 alone, 135 died. Freedmen's Bureau officials reported similar conditions in Owensboro and Paducah.[18]

Whites were generally unaware of or unsympathetic to these needs. Kentucky legislators did pass a law in February 1866 that allowed revenues from a two-dollar poll tax on blacks to be divided between paupers and education, but little money was raised and most of it failed to reached the destitute. Blacks' protests led to an amendment of the law, permitting all the funds to go to the poor, but the results were about the same. City and county governments as well as private physicians "were only slightly more willing to assist sick and destitute freedmen." Louisville officials refused responsibility for the poor, because they said they did not control the pauper fund. Physicians often required a two-to-five-dollar fee in advance of treatment. Freedmen's Bureau officials concluded that the city would do nothing as long as the federal government aided blacks. The city did receive freedmen in its "pest house" when such communicable diseases as smallpox were involved. Covington provided coffins for poor freedmen and designated $800 for black paupers when state pauper funds became available in 1868. City officials used the remaining $2,700 from the state fund to build huts for blacks on the poor farm. They also rejected requests for reimbursement from whites who had assisted former family servants. Without their own charitable organizations, "postwar adjustment for Covington freedmen [was] especially difficult."[19]

Black paupers were somewhat better off in central and western Kentucky towns. Owensboro physicians cared for disease-ravaged freedmen, though city officials refused to provide aid. City government in Paducah collected the poll tax and appropriated modest funds for the poor, the sick, and the insane.

Henderson authorities in 1866, more than any other Kentucky town officials, "willingly adopted sanitary measures designed to prohibit the spread of disease in the black community" and "established a hospital for freedmen funded from the poll tax on blacks."[20]

Blacks in some towns formed their own organizations to aid the poor and the sick. In early 1866 several churches in Louisville commenced a drive to open a hospital. A few months later, the Freedmen's Sanitary Commission, led by John Fowles and supported by Washington Spradling and some white friends, opened one at Seventeenth and Broadway. The facility served at most thirty-five patients at a time and had a staff of four. Another group raised funds for a black orphanage. In Paducah, two freedmen's philanthropic societies were formed in 1865–66 to support orphans, the aged, and the infirm, but the high cost of burying the dead and the poverty of black Paducahans depleted their funds.[21]

Whites also helped. The Northwestern Freedmen's Aid Commission of Chicago came to the aid of blacks in Paducah. The Friends Association of Pennsylvania provided support for blacks in Louisville. Most of the humanitarian relief, though, came from the Freedmen's Bureau. Food, clothing, fuel, and medical care were the chief forms of aid. With limited success, agents implored former owners, local officials, white philanthropists, and blacks themselves to help the freedmen.[22]

Preventing starvation was the bureau's first concern. Beginning in 1866, it provided food rations. Most were distributed in urban areas, especially in Louisville and to those confined in the Refugee's and Freedmen's Hospital there. Covington, Newport, and smaller cities also received rations. Provisions were meager: one meal per day for hospital patients in Louisville in March 1868. Total expenditures for about 82,000 meals in Louisville in 1867 and 1868 were $17,714.07.

The bureau also provided clothing, fuel, and medical assistance in towns. All these efforts were insufficiently funded. At most five bureau dispensaries operated at any one time in the state between 1866 and 1869. The first was opened in Louisville at the corner of Center and Green streets in January 1866. Dr. John A. Octerlony received patients there three hours a day and made calls in the black community. By 1868 there were three dispensaries in the city, but they survived only a few months. A dispensary was opened in late 1866 in Covington and closed two years later. Owensboro's facility began providing services in May 1868 but ceased operations by midfall. In Paducah Dr. Fred Hassig was hired to run a dispensary in April 1867, but his services were terminated after eight months. Hassig and another doctor were left with the daunting challenge of serving the indigent free of charge.[23]

The Freedmen's Bureau's only hospital in the commonwealth, the Refugee's and Freedmen's Hospital at Fifteenth and Broadway in Louisville, began operations in July 1866. A monthly high of 308 patients was reached in February 1868. Inadequate meals, shortages of supplies, and administrative challenges plagued the facility. About 10 patients died each month. Bureau officials began reducing services in the fall of 1867, a time when occupancy was increasing dramatically. The building was sold in December 1868, and the 70 patients remaining at the time were transferred to Taylor Barracks. Three weeks later those still recuperating, along with twenty orphans, were sent by train to Washington, D.C.[24]

Bureau legacies also included programs for orphans, the handicapped, and the physically and mentally ill. Such federal aid was vital to blacks, who paid small fees for these services. A Home for the Destitute and an Orphan Asylum were combined in a building at Fourteenth and Broadway in Louisville. J.S. Atwell, later a prominent minister in Virginia, was the first director. State and local officials were unwilling to provide financial support. When the bureau terminated operations, the only program the state was willing to support was housing the insane—in a segregated asylum.[25]

These were not the only challenges. Fathers were often attacked, dragged from their homes, and tortured, and their homes destroyed or damaged. Family members could only watch helplessly. Some blacks were unable to reunite their families, even after passage of the Thirteenth Amendment. The case of William Boyd in Paducah was not unusual. In April 1866 he unsuccessfully sought bureau assistance to free his twelve-year-old sister, Ann, who had been kept in slavery by her former owners. Locating family members was daunting. After years of trying, Elisha Green eventually liberated and reunited three daughters owned by three white families in the Maysville area. He failed, though, in his efforts to locate and liberate a son. Mary Stowers, a former Owensboro slave, was more fortunate. She had been separated from her four-year-old son, Willis, in 1846, when he was sold to a cotton farmer in Alabama. After the war Willis moved to Evansville. In 1874 the Republican editor there reported that "an old woman" had recently arrived in the city and was inquiring about her son. The two were reunited. Black families were also threatened in other ways. A state law in 1866 gave county courts the power to take away children or relatives without their consent and to bind them in long-term apprenticeships. The removal of black children based on parents' poverty or alleged moral laxity was a subterfuge for reintroducing slavery, since former owners were given preference in such cases.[26]

Not all slave-era marriages survived, because of the adverse effects of sla-

very, poverty, and violence. Some black men and women wanted to start life over. The cost of purchasing marriage certificates led others to cohabit without benefit of marriage. Still others used their new status to leave a relationship they disliked. "An alarming number of fathers, lovers, or husbands deserted their children and young mothers." Such was the case of veteran Jackson Fields, who after the war did not return to his wife, Sarah, and two young children. Instead, he married another woman. Sarah asked the Freedmen's Bureau to help, and Jackson was ordered to pay her fifty dollars. Sarah was left to fend for her family on her own. Some women abandoned their children. Parents sometimes hired out their children and lived on their income. Women also turned to prostitution.[27]

For north-shore blacks, the immediate tasks were somewhat different. In most cases, blacks were newcomers in communities that previously had had few black residents. On the one hand, most whites had not encountered blacks before. How they would come to grips with thousands of outsiders who intended to take up permanent residence was initially unclear, though whites' stereotypes offered worrisome hints. On the other, blacks had to reorganize their lives, form families, get and keep jobs, and create social organizations. Location and population size made a difference. Cincinnati, with a huge number of African Americans before the war, had in place a critical mass for the creation of an even stronger community. It also had a relatively large number of Quakers and Yankees. The setting differed in almost every other place, and the small numbers and proportions of postwar blacks even by the mid-1880s made achieving community life challenging. By the 1880s, though, Evansville blacks represented nearly one-tenth of the city's population and had many social organizations and businesses of their own. Downriver Cairo had a distinctive experience. A rapidly growing town with few whites or blacks before the war, the lack of traditions of paternalism and antislavery convictions combined with the fluidity of socioeconomic change to effect what one historian has labeled confusion. For the first fifteen or so years after the war, whites and blacks shared neighborhoods, worked together, ran for public office together, and shared such public spaces as saloons, theaters, and parks. Over time, though, a color line came into being. Whites, lacking internalized standards of racial behavior and fearing the implications of a burgeoning black population, resorted to extralegal means of suppressing blacks, who turned increasingly inward to develop a separate community existence.[28]

The prospect of black settlement unnerved many whites. The *Cincinnati Enquirer* declared in May 1865 that the death of slavery, but not of African

Americans, created such an unfortunate situation that it would be better if they were dead.[29] Democrats were especially vocal in that regard. The *New Albany Daily Ledger* protested that there were not enough jobs for whites, let alone blacks. Angry whites in Evansville damaged the African Methodist Episcopal (AME) Church in August and attacked blacks attending a circus a month later. Fisticuffs between blacks and whites broke out when black soldiers entered Jeffersonville in December 1865.[30]

Anger sometimes took lethal forms. Although postwar violence against blacks was commonplace in Kentucky, lynchings also occurred, though less frequently, on the north bank: in Cairo, Charlestown, Evansville, Mound City, Mount Vernon, and Rockport. Evansville's only lynchings occurred in the summer of 1865, when a German American woman was allegedly "overpowered by two brutes" and "outraged." They reportedly attempted to murder her. Two young men, who claimed they were innocent, were apprehended. The next day they were dragged from the county jail, shot and clubbed, and hanged from a lamppost. Cigars were then stuck in their mouths. (A white child molester in the jail, though, was unharmed.) Lieutenant Governor Conrad Baker, an Evansville attorney, reported to Governor Oliver P. Morton that many blacks, including families of army veterans, had fled the city, fearing for their lives. Militiamen were sent to restore order, and blacks began to return to the city. The perpetrators were workers—Democrats of upper South and German origin—who resented the fact that local tobacco factories were employing former slaves.[31]

An incident three years later offers valuable insight into the justice system of that era. When a white steamboat fireman disappeared in the river at Evansville, purportedly after being chased by sixteen black deckhands, four of them were convicted of murder and imprisoned, although key witnesses were not called to testify. In 1871 the white "victim" was discovered living in Paducah. Affidavits were signed to that effect, including one by a black man who had seen the fireman swimming away from the boat. Andrew L. Robinson forwarded this information to Governor Baker, who pardoned the one man whose time in prison had not expired. No restitution was given the four men. The white fireman saw no reason to return to Evansville and went unpunished.[32]

Clark County, Indiana—bearing "the doubtful distinction in the postwar years of being the scene of more murder, violence, and general lawlessness than any other county in the state"—had a particularly gruesome lynching in 1871. A slow-witted black man was apprehended for allegedly hacking members of a white family to death. Acknowledging his assistance in the crime, he identified one man as the murderer and another as an accomplice. Although

the facts were so dubious that a grand jury failed to indict the three, a mob stormed the jail in Charlestown and hanged them in a nearby woods. A coroner's jury found that they "had met death by hanging at the hands of persons unknown."[33]

Antiblack rhetoric and harassment were commonplace. The provocation of blacks was a regular occurrence in contested public space—in Evansville near the waterfront, the railroad depot, and Liberty Baptist Church. In mid-July 1865, for instance, young white hooligans routinely robbed black newcomers residing in the vicinity of the Evansville and Crawfordsville Railroad depot on Eighth Street. The following summer roving bands of young white men, sometimes joined by girls, disrupted meetings at Liberty Church. In February 1868 a drunken young white man threatened black hotel employees on Water Street and called for a war to "get the g-d d—— niggers out of here." The Republican newspaper lamented the fact that "negroes go about the streets attending to their own businesses . . . [not] protected from the attacks of such characters."[34]

That editor, though, was not well-disposed to the presence of so many black newcomers. In the summer of 1866 a local businessman arranged for the transport of twenty-five or thirty blacks to Texas, where they would work in the cotton and tobacco fields. The editor noted that the city "could spare at least a thousand more and not miss them much." A half dozen families were "patching up some old houses on Locust Street between Water and First, as if intending to go into winter quarters there." Those houses, which were to have been razed, were a blight on the city.[35]

Efforts to drive out black newcomers and to prevent other blacks from arriving were commonplace. In upriver Boonville and its environs, prominent Democrats made an organized attempt during July 1865 to "wage war" on peace-loving blacks. Included was raising funds to hire an attorney to prosecute local whites for violating the still unrepealed Article XIII of the constitution. In December 1867 citizens in Center, German, and Knight townships in rural Vanderburgh County posted warnings to blacks that they would be driven out if they did not leave peaceably. Persons who rented homes to them were counseled to do otherwise or have their houses burned to the ground. The paucity of black residents in most rural parts of the county when the 1870 census was taken suggests that the warnings succeeded.[36]

Night-riding vigilantes also operated on the north bank. On several occasions in the early fall of 1868, a small group from Henderson "with funny outfits" was reported on the Evansville waterfront and on Main Street. The Klan was also present in southern Illinois, but Pope was the only river county

in which it was active. It was strongest in Illinois counties where per capita wealth as well as black and foreign-born populations were lowest. The Klan also thrived where Democrats and Baptists were numerous.[37]

The early postwar context established a pattern. Most whites—like those in Cairo, an "Ellis Island" for blacks, as one historian described it—were ever more insensitive if not hostile to black newcomers. Only in rare instances, as noted later, were blacks able to gain a modicum of political clout. Whites' negativity was especially evident in Indiana. Until the Indiana Supreme Court declared Article XIII unconstitutional in 1866, in theory blacks could not settle in the state, but come they did. Democrats like the editor of the New Albany daily railed that they were a drain on the state's resources. (Paradoxically, the state's commissioner of immigration declared in 1866 that there was plenty of good land, high wages, and good schools, as well as opportunities for employment and social intercourse.) Democrats made it clear that their chief objection was working and living side by side with blacks. A decidedly minority voice was that of a white pastor in Posey County, who wrote in October 1865 that a black had the right "to live where he may choose."[38]

Postwar Indiana was distinguished by having fewer black migrants than any other free territory bordering a former slave state. Declared one white, "the Hoosier state stands alone before the world unwilling that the native born citizens of the United States, with a colored skin, shall attempt to earn an honest living within her limits." In 1860 Ohio had 36,673 blacks, Indiana 11,428, and Illinois 7,628. Twenty years later there were about 80,000 in Ohio, about 46,500 in Illinois, and slightly fewer than 40,000 in Indiana. Opposition to blacks' migration was a convenient football for Indiana Democrats, but by 1880 its intensity had somewhat diminished. The state's Democrats that year adopted a platform that stated grudgingly that African Americans had the right to settle in the state, but derided Republicans for "importing paupers" for votes. Accusations to that effect would be a staple of Democratic politics for decades.[39]

Violence continued to surface. An egregious instance occurred in Mount Vernon in 1878, when four black men were hanged on the lawn of the county courthouse by a mob that had dragged them from the nearby jail. They had been accused of raping a white woman. A fifth man, Dan Harris, had allegedly shot and killed a sheriff's deputy attempting to arrest the four. The mob took him to the railroad yard and pitched him alive into the firebox of a locomotive.[40]

Lynch rule led Indiana governor James A. Mount to ask for legislation to deal with this shameful activity. The law that resulted was unworkable, even

though it provided for the removal from office of any sheriff who surrendered a prisoner to a mob and required the sheriff to call upon the governor to send militia if he believed a lynching would occur. The law also provided the death penalty or long prison terms for persons who joined in a lynching. The first violation of the law occurred in Rockport, the seat of Spencer County, in late 1900. Thousands watched and cheered a lynch mob that hanged three black men for allegedly murdering a white barber. Prominent citizens saw the mob's action as a warning to other "lawless Negroes." A U.S. marshal in Rockport said he was unsurprised by the incident, given the fact that "local Negroes had become 'overbearing and lawless.' He added that his fellow citizens had been forebearing [sic] in the face of an increase in crime by Negroes."[41]

Local and state histories published in the postwar years reveal much about the status of black newcomers and whites' perception of them.[42] Blacks' presence was at best grudgingly acknowledged. One does learn, though, that a number of vital institutions were created in African American communities along the river.

Something of an exception to the rule was Lewis Collins's *History of Kentucky,* published in 1874. The first volume contained "Annals," a chronological list of events in Kentucky's recent history that acknowledged guerrillas' attacking and killing black soldiers during the war and the issuing of free passes permitting slaves to leave the state. It cited Kentucky legislators' hostility to granting freedom, equality, and land to freedmen and documented at least twelve instances of lynchings and mob violence against blacks since 1866. Collins was openly opposed to Klan violence and reported with glee a case in which seven "radical negroes" had peppered a "Kukluxer" with birdshot. He indicated that in several counties, including Mason, the "colored people" held successful agricultural fairs in the fall of 1871. The "Annals" described the emergence of black political activism, beginning with the Republican state convention in Louisville in March, 1872, where a black man, J.B. Stansberry, was elected temporary secretary. It also provided accounts of blacks' participation in other conventions in Cincinnati and Covington.[43]

Collins also described sympathetically a state convention at Louisville in February 1873 where black men petitioned for equal educational privileges for black children. Claiming interest in no special legislation, delegates resolved to labor "honestly, earnestly, and amicably to secure equal educational privileges in common with citizens of Kentucky and with citizens of the United States, and to show ourselves worthy of the same." Collins included a flattering account of an assembly of blacks in Louisville in the spring of 1873

that had gathered to hear Frederick Douglass speak. Another gathering, he said, had demanded that a portion of public offices be given to black Republicans and that if that reasonable request was not granted, black men would cease to be indebted to the Republican Party. The same convention resolved that no citizen should be denied the right to serve on a jury because of color.[44]

Collins's second volume, which comprised county histories, offered virtually no references to African Americans. This was probably the product of his relying on local historians as writers of this portion of his history. Exceptions were the sections on Kenton and Mason counties, which noted that Covington and Maysville had two black churches each. His history also provided sobering detail when it compared and contrasted the wealth of black and white Kentuckians. Less than a decade after emancipation, whites' personal and real property was valued at $403,296,567, and they owned 22.8 million acres of land. Blacks' property was worth $3,569,040. Proportionally more of their wealth—about $1.5 million—was invested in town lots than the approximately $1 million in farmland, reflecting the movement off the land after the war.[45]

Kentucky's early county histories generally resembled each other in the way they portrayed blacks. The section on Jefferson County in *History of the Ohio Falls Cities and Their Counties, with Illustrations and Biographical Sketches* (1882) treated negatively the freeing of slaves and the use of black men in the army and excoriated General Palmer for violating state law. There were no references to black churches, fraternal organizations, or charitable organizations. There was one brief allusion to education—the opening of six schools in rented spaces, beginning in 1870, and the construction of an eleven-room brick school that was dedicated in October 1873. Buildings for black pupils were "in every respect equal" and were given "as good teachers of their own race and as ample facilities for acquiring an education as can be afforded." Whites were also portrayed as generous: taxes on blacks had risen only $1,440 the previous year, while trustees spent over $17,000 for black teachers alone.[46]

Upriver, blacks were virtually invisible in the first postwar history of Boone, Campbell, and Kenton counties. Atlases of Boone and Kenton counties showed no black schools, churches, or other organizations. In Newport, seat of Campbell County, there was just one evidence of a black presence—the First Colored Baptist Church, located on the corner of Jefferson and Columbia streets, about four blocks from the river.[47]

The first history of Daviess County, by contrast, was relatively expansive, as it identified schools, churches, and fraternal societies. A "colored school" was supported almost completely by state funds secured from taxes on blacks. A new brick building had been erected on Poplar between Third and Fourth.

Only 200 of the 500 black persons of school age regularly attended school, however, and there were just three teachers—Lewis Metcalf, principal, and Anna Vairian and Owen Barrett. Owensboro had three black churches—Fourth Street Baptist, Center Street (or "Snow Hill") Baptist, and Third Street Methodist Episcopal, identified as "Colored (African)." The Fourth Street church, located in a brick building between Elm and Poplar, had 500 members; its pastor was Moses Harding. Apparently Center Street Baptist was formed by some of Fourth Street's former members. The Methodist Church, which had had six pastors since its founding by a Reverend Dunahy, was located in a new building erected in 1873 near the corner of Third and St. Elizabeth streets. Its 119 members apparently were the most prosperous and influential black citizens of Owensboro. Two other matters regarding Owensboro's blacks caught the attention of its first historian. One was the fact that black men first voted in the city election of April 4, 1870. The other was the lynching of three men on May 17 and 20, 1866, and January 27, 1869. The author listed these atrocities without comment.[48]

Union County's first history was more typical. Slavery, for starters, seemed not to have existed there. No African Americans were mentioned in the lists of Union soldiers, churches, schools, and fraternal societies. The sole reference to blacks was derogatory. Noting that 20 percent of the adults in the county were illiterate, the writer declared, "Of course the uneducated negro population is to be blamed with a great portion of the illiteracy. Over 70 percent of the colored population cannot read or write."[49]

McCracken County's first historian was also nearly mute on blacks. A short paragraph mentioned two black churches, Methodist and Baptist, "all doing efficient work." The author observed that two of the six men hanged since 1832 were black. Like Collins, he compared the wealth of whites and blacks. Whites owned 152,057 acres of land worth $1 million, as compared with blacks' 1,391 acres valued at $10,840. Whites owned 2,747 town lots worth $2.2 million, as compared with blacks' 243 lots valued at $50,285. Whites owned 225 dry goods stores, groceries, saloons, and other businesses, valued at $446,000. The total value of black enterprises was $50![50]

But blacks in Henderson County received a great deal of attention in the paternalistic work by Edmund Starling, member of one of the county's most influential families. Unlike most early historians, though, he emphasized the antebellum period. Starling outlined the history of slavery from the founding of the county in 1798. He traced the increased incidence of slaves running away by that time to the interference in Kentucky's "property rights" by meddlesome Northerners and to lax enforcement of the law by north-shore judges.

Residents of Henderson responded by seeking to prevent blacks from securing weapons and to "suppress all Negro preaching and Negro meetings within the limits of the town." Because whites were "anxious and interested in their spiritual welfare," they organized a plan of worship for blacks and created the African Baptist Church in 1845.[51]

After treating the Civil War as a time of stress and lawlessness that was worsened by the enlistment of blacks in the Union Army, Starling expressed guarded optimism about the future. For one thing, emancipation had forced blacks to fend for themselves. Black Baptists—led by three trustees, Charles Livers, Thomas Goins Sr., and John Mackey—formed an independent congregation later named First Baptist, and on February 8, 1866, they were able to purchase the old white Methodist Church building for $3,000. Lewis Norris was called to pastor the church, and a campaign was launched to erect a new building. Members made weekly contributions of $60–$100, and white friends donated money. Norris, however, left in 1877 for a pastorate elsewhere as a consequence of internal discord that led to the formation of Fourth Street Baptist. His return ensured the completion of the building project in 1879 at a total cost of $7,000. Five years later the structure was destroyed by fire. Norris died in 1882. These two events led to the congregation's being scattered, according to Starling, to the four winds.[52]

Starling briefly described other black organizations. An AME congregation, whose pastor was R.W.T. Jones, was large and thrifty enough to build a commodious brick structure in the 1870s. The author also listed seven colored lodges, the oldest being St. John's Masonic Lodge, formed in September 1866. The United Brothers of Friendship (UBF) lodge was organized five years later, and four additional lodges were organized between 1879 and 1887.[53]

That was the extent of his treatment of Henderson's blacks in the new age. Schooling, for instance, did not interest him. He seemed relieved, in fact, that of the 6,058 increase in the county's population in the 1870s, "only" 1,578 were blacks. Regarding their behavior after obtaining freedom, he grudgingly acknowledged that they surprised him and "their most sanguine friends, who had viewed the situation with anxious solicitude. They came into this new life as though they had been drilled and tutored for months; they accepted the situation with a becoming grace; and while some few were disposed to behave unruly, the great majority behaved like men of sense and character . . . and going to work to build up themselves and growing families."[54]

For blacks living across the river, postwar histories were different in two basic respects: slavery had not existed there, and most African Americans were newcomers. Not surprisingly, these narratives were relatively vague. Some, like

the first history of Shawneetown, skimmed over the postwar era and harked back to the antebellum era to praise respectable white men who had risen up against the slave-catchers and regulators seeking to apprehend what the author called "wooly heads."[55] Local sentiment about blacks after the war was revealed in a brief section of the book. The Roman Catholic priest at St. Mary's parish in Shawneetown incurred the wrath of white parents when he admitted three children of colored members of his parish to the Catholic school. Irate whites appealed to the bishop at Alton, who upheld the priest, but their relentless pressure forced the priest to close the school and to leave town, along with nuns who taught in the school.[56]

The first postwar history of Pulaski County was somewhat more detailed. It documented three lynchings—in 1857, 1863, and 1883. The latest involved the alleged killing of a white man by a black. The author noted that both were outsiders who had been drinking on a train that arrived in Mound City. Masked men took the alleged killer from the jail on July 5 and hanged him. The incident sparked "much excitement . . . for some days afterward" among local black residents, "but it gradually subsided."[57]

That history also revealed there were four black churches and a black school in Mound City. Two of the churches were Baptist, one was Methodist, and the other was "Missionary Association." The First Free Will Baptist Church was the largest, with 111 members. The others ranged from 20 to 50 members. Although pastors' names were supplied, no other details—founding, charter members, and the like—were. The writer also identified a black Methodist church established in 1872 in Olmstead, a tiny upriver settlement. Mound City's black school received brief reference. It had two teachers, M.M. Avant and his wife, who between them earned $58 a month. (White teachers were paid $75.)[58]

The author of the first history of Cairo and Alexander County, H.C. Bradsbury, offered the most negative account among early north-bank histories. He included no references to black churches or mutual aid organizations and only alluded to the existence of blacks' education when he mentioned that there was one male teacher. He railed, however, about "negro raids upon the public schools. It seems they were not satisfied to be along in their own schoolrooms, and so they counseled together, and by concert of action, met at their churches and schoolrooms, and in bodies marched upon the white schools."[59]

Describing the effort of blacks to force whites to provide their youth a high school education in 1883 (see chapter 12), he declared, "The motly [sic] processions were headed by the most venerable old gray-headed bucks and

wenches, and tapered down to the most infantile, unwashed, bow-legged picaninnies." Then, he recalled, "all said, 'I recken we'uns wants to grandiate as well as white trash.'" This was "a great annoyance and interruption to the schools." The author asserted that tax revenues from blacks were "not enough to pay for the fuel used in the negro schools. But the young Solomons of Africa would have paid small heed to that, had it been presented to them."[60]

Postwar histories of Indiana's river counties were less vituperative but not necessarily sympathetic. The first history of Evansville (1873) did not mention African Americans. The first history of Warrick County (1868) also excluded blacks. The next (1881), was nearly as exclusive, though a passing reference to African Americans was buried in the report of the county school superintendent, who indicated that there were four colored schools in the county—one in Millersburgh, one in Boonville, and two in Newburgh. The history published in 1885 contained a little more detail. It reported that there were 292 black pupils among the 8,414 children of school age. C.S. Pritchard was identified as being at the colored school in Newburgh, and Minnie Clark was the teacher of 36 black students in Boonville. This history also briefly identified two black Baptist churches with seventy-seven members and property value of $150.[61]

The first histories of Perry and Spencer counties were also sketchy. The teachers of the colored school in Rockport were named. The only mention of blacks in Perry County was revealing. Residents of Cannelton, declared the writer, were disgusted when black troops were sent across the river in September 1864 to guard several Confederate guerrillas, prisoners in the town. This act was "so distasteful to a number of citizens that without his authority [that of the army officer in charge] they dismissed the colored men and placed white guards in their place." The band was led by the town marshal, who was subsequently arrested but released without trial.[62]

By contrast, the first postwar history of Clark and Floyd counties (1882) was relatively inclusive. For example, the anonymous writer identified all of the 104 local men who had served in colored regiments in the Civil War. He also listed all of the black churches organized before and after the Civil War. An AME congregation that formed in rural Clark County in 1842 moved into Jeffersonville and by 1880 began to erect its third house of worship. The First Colored Baptist Church was organized in 1861 on Illinois Avenue between Seventh and Eighth. Its first pastor, Philip Simcoe, led a group of dissidents out of this congregation in 1865 and formed Second Baptist, which met in a building at the corner of Indiana Avenue and Sixth Street. Black Baptists and Methodists near Memphis, in Union Township, held joint services in the black school there.

"The colored element has always been an important one in [New Albany]," declared this author. There was "quite a community" in West Union, on the north side of the city, and a Methodist church was organized there in 1840. Some members moved into the city in the early 1860s because of harassment by vigilantes, which also occurred in Clark County. The newcomers organized Crosley Chapel, named in honor of a bishop, at the corner of Lower Second and Elm, and Zion AME, or Jones Chapel, named after a pastor. The latter was organized by R.R. Biddle of Louisville. The city's largest congregation was the Second Colored Baptist, formed in March 1867 and located on Upper Fourth, between Main and Market. Its first pastor was a Rev. C. Edwards, a man "of considerable ability." He served nine years. The writer also named some of the original members, one of whom was a woman, Isabella Williams. Another was G.D. Williams, probably her husband. Like a number of other black congregations, when Second Baptist's members had saved enough money, they bought an old edifice that whites had abandoned—in this case the 1840 Presbyterian structure.[63]

Separate public schools for blacks were created in both counties in the late 1860s. In addition to the school near Memphis in rural Clark County, there was one in Jeffersonville on Court Avenue that apparently had once served white students. In Floyd County, 3 of the 13 schools by 1882 were colored. Blacks in New Albany also had three fraternal societies: two lodges of Odd Fellows and one of Masons. No lodges were listed for Jeffersonville.[64]

Generally blacks were also treated shabbily in the early postwar histories of Ohio's river counties. But the 1880 history of Clermont County, which lay on the eastern border of Hamilton, was very different, undoubtedly because many Quaker and Yankee opponents of slavery lived there. Both the tone and the breadth of the work set it apart. The author devoted a great deal of space to the Underground Railroad, which he described as the most worthy feature of the county's history. He spoke reverentially of heroic white men, regardless of party, who never refused bread to the "beseeching negro who turned away from chains and, with face turned toward the north star, fled." The alleged route of the Underground Railroad was identified, as were at least seven agents. (Only one black man—Mark Sims, a wagon master for two abolitionists—was mentioned.)[65]

The author also observed that "in all of the towns and most of the townships ample provision has been made for colored scholars, usually taught by intelligent teachers of that race." There were 588 black students in the county in 1878. Three black schools were identified—one each in Batavia, Franklin, and Ohio townships. The latter two adjoined the river. Franklin Township's

school, located in Felicity, was the earliest, created in 1852. Samuel Fox was the first teacher (1870) in Batavia Township, and H.F. Fox and O.S. Fox were the first in New Richmond, in Ohio Township. The latter subsequently taught in Batavia. The author also mentioned that Clermont Academy, in Clermontsville near the Ohio, was open to all, regardless of race, sex, age, or sect, but unfortunately he offered no detail of its history.[66]

At least four black churches had been established in Clermont County by 1880. Two were in Felicity, an AME Church (1859) and Zion's Baptist (1865). The first deacon of the latter, William Fry, served in that capacity well into the 1880s. The first pastor, James Fry, possibly William's brother or son, served for ten years. Two other churches were in New Richmond: a Baptist, established about 1850, and an AME, formed about 1851. The writer also named the deacons and trustees of these congregations, both of which built new houses of worship after the war. Both were considerably larger in membership than their counterparts in Felicity.[67]

Blacks in Brown County, which adjoins Clermont, also received some sympathetic attention, in an 1883 history. The largest settlement of blacks was in Ripley. The author noted that the county's whites had strongly opposed abolitionists, most of whom lived in that village. White opponents of slavery did not enter Kentucky to encourage escape, but they did assist runaways. The most celebrated case was that of Rev. John B. Mahan, who was apprehended and tried several times across the river in Mason County for aiding fugitives.[68]

Brown County's blacks were concentrated in its four river townships. Georgetown, in Pleasant Township, had 60 black students who attended a black school opened on Water Street a few years earlier. The Second Colored Baptist Church was organized in Georgetown in the summer of 1868 with the aid of antislavery white Baptists. The first deacons were Amos Young and John Shackelford. The congregation worshipped for a time in the black schoolhouse, but in the early 1880s built a frame house of worship to accommodate its 70 members. In the second township, colored Baptists in Ripley were organized about 1855 after years of worshipping with white Presbyterians. They numbered 175 by 1883. Black Methodists also organized in the 1850s and erected a structure that they still occupied. In the third township, school officials created a colored district near Higginsport in Lewis Township in 1870. Before that school-age blacks had had no access to schools. The first teacher was E.H. Jamison. About 30 pupils attended school by the end of the decade. The fourth river township, Huntington, had two schools—one in the country that was "furnished with the best school furniture"—and one in the village of

Aberdeen. The Colored Church of Aberdeen was organized about 1878 with the help of whites' subscriptions.[69]

Blacks' presence in the first history of upstream Adams County (1880) was hazy. An AME Church, organized in 1870, was located on the Cincinnati Pike, near Fairview in Liberty Township. That was the only black church listed for the entire county. Twenty-one pupils (out of a total of 375) in Wayne Township and 2 in Winchester Township were identified as black, but where they attended school was not revealed. The writer boasted, though, that 33 whites had organized one of the first antislavery societies "in the country."[70]

Early histories of Cincinnati were similarly foggy. One mentioned the existence of a colored orphan asylum supported by African Americans that was located in Avondale and accommodated 50 children. At the end of its list of public schools, it noted that blacks had four district and two intermediate schools and one high school. The district schools had 100 pupils and the intermediate and high schools had 70. These were the only references to African Americans in the book's 368 pages. Another history published six years later was completely silent on black Cincinnatians.[71]

Portsmouth and Scioto County's African Americans managed somewhat better. A relatively large amount of attention was given to education. In 1853–54, the town's school board "first recognized the man and brother with a black face." It took three years, though, for it to organize a school and to appoint a teacher, Mrs. E.E. Glidden, whose race was not identified. There was apparently a great deal of turnover in that position, possibly due to the fragility of the teachers' tenure. In March 1859, for instance, a Miss Jackson was named as teacher and paid $25 *monthly*—while at the same time white teachers were paid $550 by *yearly* contracts. In 1861, when there were 63 black pupils, O.M. Atwood was appointed as the first principal. Sometime in the previous year or two a second school building had been opened. Monthly contracts continued to be granted in the late 1860s, even for the principal, W.H. Holland, who was paid $50 a month. A new "colored school house" was erected at Eleventh and John streets during 1875–76. By the 1880–81 school year, there were 255 black and 3,013 white students in the Portsmouth public schools. That number of blacks showed a decline, as 347 had attended school during 1877–78.[72]

The only other reference to blacks in this account was the AME Church, about which the writer said it was "almost impossible to obtain any data." The first minister was a Reverend Charleston. A brick edifice was completed in 1846, several years after the organization of the church. Another building, located on the north side of Seventh, east of Chillicothe Street, was purchased in July 1868, and it served as a house of worship for a number of decades

thereafter. In typical Methodist fashion, pastors were rotated regularly. Phillip Tolliver, who served from 1875 to 1879, was the most prominent in the post-war era.[73]

The author, moreover, recalled "relics of barbarism": advertisements for runaways. He also reminded readers of "black Friday" (January 21, 1830), when all 80 blacks in town were forced to leave their homes and their belongings. About 200 white householders had signed a paper indicating they would not employ a black who had not complied with the law that required blacks to possess freedom certificates and post a $500 bond. Many of these whites, he added, celebrated the ensuing Fourth of July by listening to an enumeration of crimes committed by King George III and thanking God that they had not engaged in any activity as evil as that.[74]

These postwar histories at best hinted at the fact that constitutional and statutory changes at the federal level were shaping the lives of black and white citizens. Emancipation, citizenship, civil rights, and black male suffrage were guaranteed by three postwar constitutional amendments, and an 1875 law banned racial discrimination in selection of juries and in transportation and public accommodations. Congress and the Justice Department, however, were increasingly reluctant to enforce the Fourteenth and Fifteenth amendments, and the 1875 law was never actively enforced.[75]

Postwar governments in the four Ohio River states were uneven in their responses to these changes, despite enthusiastic support from blacks and some whites. Newly freed Kentuckians declared in their first postwar convention, "We love our country and her institutions. We are proud of her greatness, her glory and her might. We are intensely American." The role that they had played in crushing the rebellion against the Union was central. They portrayed themselves, moreover, as "neither 'docile' nor 'obedient.'"[76]

Not surprisingly, Kentucky's legislators strongly opposed the Thirteenth, Fourteenth, and Fifteenth amendments. The legislature that adjourned in early 1866 indicated clearly that it did not plan to make blacks legally equal, or even citizens. Whether because of spite or "to keep alive claims for compensation, conservative politicians, rather than eliminating all traces of slavery from state law, simply revised the old slave code, leaving much of it intact." Such regulations as those limiting the movement of free blacks were kept on the books, making second-class citizenship legitimate in the eyes of whites and ensuring that the memory of slavery would remain vivid in the minds of blacks.[77]

In essence, African Americans in Kentucky gained the status that *antebellum* free blacks had had. They could not serve on juries, testify against whites,

or vote. Whites alone could witness contracts. A black man who raped a white woman was punished far more severely than one who raped a black woman. Interracial marriages were forbidden. The exemption from state and local taxes for disabled Civil War veterans applied only to whites, and only whites' homesteads could not be sold because of debt. Marriage and tax records were kept according to race, and tax-supported institutions were racially segregated. Skin color determined how apprenticeships were arranged. When the federal Civil Rights Act of 1866 and the Fourteenth Amendment were passed, though, Kentucky officials had to adjust. Enforcement of federal law by state officials was at best unenthusiastic, reinforcing an atmosphere of intimidation and violence. Nonetheless, their efforts to perpetuate slavery in all but name would be difficult. Kentucky, for example, would be one of six former slave states not to require the poll tax for blacks, and voter registration procedures were comparatively uncomplicated.[78]

The performance of Cincinnati's Black Brigade and the nearly 5,100 black Ohioans who served in the Union Army encouraged Ohio blacks' hopes. Accordingly, they sought to gain the vote. Democrats were tough, however, and Republicans wanted to keep Unionist Democrats happy. Hence race had to be downplayed. Republican Jacob Cox, a war hero, was elected governor in 1865, but he had been nominated on the promise that he would take no stand on black suffrage. The race issue was so strong that he received fewer votes than the Republican candidate two years earlier had. Cox had a deep hostility to black equality. As governor he not only opposed giving the vote to blacks, but also advocated that African Americans be placed on a reservation in the Deep South.[79]

The inconsistency in Ohio Republicans' demanding citizenship and suffrage for blacks in the South but not in the North became increasingly transparent. When black suffrage was placed on the state ballot in the fall of 1867, Republicans lost control of both houses in the legislature and nearly forfeited the governorship. The enfranchisement of blacks failed by 38,353 votes—4,677 of them cast in Cincinnati. The 1868–69 legislature then attempted to turn back the clock, disenfranchising mulattoes and allowing challenges at the polls of anyone who appeared to be black. It also rescinded ratification of the Fourteenth Amendment and voted down the Fifteenth. The governor prevented those two actions from reaching Congress. The Fifteenth Amendment was narrowly passed in 1870 by a coalition of independent reformers and Republicans. Acknowledging the inevitable, Democrats soon thereafter began to court the black vote. But the context for that process had been clearly defined. The most recent historian of Ohio, Andrew Cayton, has ob-

served that the state's direction would be determined by its white, native-born, Protestant citizens.[80]

In neighboring Indiana, veterans of the 28th Regiment and other black units "were legally ineligible to return to Indiana at the war's end because they had first come into the state in violation of the exclusion article of the Constitution." The resolutions of black delegates to the first postwar state convention in October 1865 had some effect on a special session of the General Assembly the following month. Legislators enacted a partial removal of the ban on Negro testimony but refused to alter Article XIII. The futility of enforcing the constitutional exclusion of blacks' migration to the state and the actions of Congress on civil rights in 1866 made Article XIII increasingly questionable. The Indiana Supreme Court, observing that blacks were citizens of the United States under the terms of recent federal legislation, voided Article XIII later that year. The Republican-controlled legislature in 1867 refused to delete reference to Article XIII from the constitution, but it did repeal the 1852 law that enforced exclusion.[81]

Although white Hoosier Republicans endorsed the constitutional amendments abolishing slavery and granting citizenship and civil rights, they were reluctant to support granting the vote. As late as the 1868 election, most seemed to support black male suffrage only in the former Confederate states. It took a special session of the General Assembly in April 1869 and some clever political maneuvering by Oliver P. Morton, now U.S. senator for Indiana, to ratify the Fifteenth Amendment. "As a practical matter this ended efforts to block the enfranchisement of Negroes in Indiana, since the ratification of the Fifteenth Amendment had the effect of nullifying the parts of the Indiana Constitution which limited suffrage to white persons." Democrats, who in 1870 gained control of the legislature for the first time in years, commenced to seek ways of blocking implementation of African American suffrage, and for many years thereafter they acted as if black men did not have the right to vote. Not until a special election in 1881 were antebellum constitutional proscriptions of the rights of African Americans formally stricken from the Indiana constitution.[82]

In Illinois, in early 1865 the legislature repealed the state's "Black Laws" at the same time it ratified the Thirteenth Amendment, despite arguments that repeal would inundate the state with blacks. The predicted deluge of black migrants did not occur. The legislature, however, "moved very slowly in providing civil rights protection for its black inhabitants. Freedmen still could not sit on juries, vote, hold office, or send their children to common schools."[83]

As in Indiana, Democrats and some Republicans offered dire warnings about granting civil rights and the vote. Led by Governor Richard Oglesby,

both chambers of the legislature concurred in ratifying the Fourteenth Amendment in January 1867, but they failed to act on suffrage. To the surprise of critics, both houses ratified the Fifteenth Amendment in March 1869. A constitutional convention in May 1870, also dominated by Republicans and supported by black conventions in places like Pulaski County, adopted amendments that made no reference to race in such matters as the vote, the education of children, and the state militia. Despite strong opposition, especially in Ohio River counties, voters overwhelmingly approved these amendments in a referendum held in July. Even before that vote, Governor John M. Palmer—the general who had single-handedly doomed slavery in Kentucky—declared that "liberty was now on a permanent basis." He urged blacks to "love liberty, be grateful to the Republican party, work hard, educate their children, and become self-reliant." Concluded one Republican editor, "The negro is now a voter and a citizen . . . on an equal footing with the white man. . . . Let him hereafter take his chances in the battle of life."[84] Civil rights and politics could thereafter not be separated in Illinois or in any other Ohio River state.

7

Citizenship and Civil Rights
after the Fourteenth Amendment

Obtaining freedom was one thing. Securing citizenship was another. In all four states, conventions of black men in the immediate postwar period advocated a constitutional amendment guaranteeing citizenship rights. On paper, the Fourteenth Amendment, ratified in 1868, did so. The heart of that amendment was "due process" and "equal protection of the laws." Elimination of racial distinctions, however, "did not insure equality of treatment, and even the enactment of positive guarantees did not put an end to discrimination."[1]

Black leaders tended to focus on political rights and on education, subjects that are explored in more detail in chapters 8 and 12. The denial of the use of public accommodations and transportation was "approached with caution since Negro leaders were aware of the deep-seated prejudice which much of the white population felt toward anything which smacked of 'social equality.'" If they attacked such forms of discrimination, blacks "would weaken their position in the fight for schools and suffrage."[2]

Pervasive race consciousness enhanced their caution. In early histories, for instance, whites were always listed first and blacks second, if at all. City directories identified people of color with such markers as *c* or *col*. Local newspapers referred to alleged criminals as "colored brute," "colored man," or "colored boy," not by name. Kentucky authorities' perspectives on race were especially obvious. In the county tax lists prepared just after the end of the war, for instance, the printed forms, with columns for slaves and their value, were modi-

fied by hand. Those column headings were crossed out and replaced by entries for dogs over age two, sheep killed by dogs, and the value of those sheep.[3]

Progress toward freedom did occur, though rarely. In 1870, as a result of Louisville blacks' protests, one streetcar line permitted blacks, both men and women, to ride inside their cars; on another two lines black women only could ride inside. The Fourth and Main excursion route seated all blacks at the back. After several pastors organized a sit-in on the whites-only Market Street cars, the owners capitulated. Persistent, well-organized black resistance was the key. Over time, however, whites began to assert control of the front seats of streetcars. Segregation had returned by the 1880s.[4]

The Fourteenth Amendment had relatively little effect on north-bank African Americans, because it merely reaffirmed their citizenship, which they believed had already been recognized. Most whites perceived it, like the Civil Rights Act of 1875, as applying chiefly to blacks in the former slave states. Blacks rarely attempted to enter places that were by custom and cost off-limits to blacks. Typical was the advice of Alfred Carter, who had run a restaurant in Evansville since the 1850s. In a lengthy letter to African Americans in the March 12, 1875, edition of the *Evansville Daily Journal* that followed passage of the new Civil Rights Act, he emphasized the responsibilities that the new law had created. "Your prejudiced antagonists abhor it," he noted, "and employ every opportunity to express their disgust of the bill." Blacks should thus "perform no deed or act under the pale of this bill to give it the least semblance of the unjust measure that they represent, proving by your actions that you have not misconstrued the measure and the motives which prompted the framing of the bill."[5] Similar advice was offered about the same time by the young black constable Robert Nicholas, thus making problematic the argument that those who came of age in the slavery era were more deferential to whites than those who matured after emancipation.[6]

Even cautious optimism, though, proved to be groundless, because the U.S. Supreme Court soon gutted postwar civil rights legislation. In *United States v. Reece,* a case involving voting rights in Kentucky, and *United States v. Cruikshank,* which dealt with the 1875 Civil Rights Act, the high court effectively abandoned federal protection of blacks, leaving the matter to the states. It ruled in 1883 that the Civil Rights Act of 1875 did not forbid discrimination by private individuals.[7]

When black leaders in Evansville heard of the Supreme Court's ruling on the Civil Rights Act of 1875, they, like many elsewhere, met at a public hall to discuss a course of action. Present were men representing a variety of positions

on party politics whose interests in the race transcended partisanship. The young pastor J. Dennis Rouse called the meeting to order. Alfred Carter, veteran Republican loyalist and Evansville businessman, was elected chair, and Republican activist Frederick Douglass Morton was elected secretary. While the Resolutions Committee met separately to recommend what to do, Morton and Charles Sheldon, a political independent, addressed the crowd. The Resolutions Committee proposed that since the Civil Rights Act had been materially inoperative, the action of the Supreme Court would not hinder them. Citizens were encouraged to gain an education, to accumulate wealth, to purchase homes, and to cooperate with one another in seeking these ends. The resolution passed with few dissenting votes. By the time it was introduced, late in the evening, half of the audience had departed.[8]

One consequence of the Supreme Court's ruling was the passage of state laws in Illinois, Indiana, and Ohio in 1883–85. Indiana's, for example, stated that all persons were entitled to equal enjoyment of the state's public accommodations and conveyances and that no one should be disqualified as a juror on the basis of race. Passage by a Democrat-controlled legislature was politically expedient, since Democrats hoped to win blacks' votes. Most legislators, moreover, assumed that blacks would not venture into places frequented by whites because of their habits of diffidence and the cost and the unpleasantness of litigation. Proprietors could also find ways of refusing them. Occasionally tested, the law was "given the narrowest interpretation possible."[9]

In Indiana, "one symbol of racial prejudice which remained unchanged in the period after the Civil War was the legislation prohibiting mixed marriages." As in Ohio, persons with "pure white blood" could not intermarry or have "carnal intercourse with any Negro or person having a distinct and visible admixture of African blood." Persons of color (but not whites) who violated the law could be fined up to $100 and imprisoned for up to three months. A Madison man was jailed in 1884 for marrying a white woman. Judges "held that neither the adoption of the Civil Rights Act of 1866 nor the Fourteenth Amendment invalidated the Indiana law, and members of the legislature showed no disposition to modify the law."[10]

A county judge in Evansville upheld the marriage of a Dutch immigrant and a mulatto woman on the basis of the Civil Rights Act of 1866. In the same county one judge upheld the conviction of a black man who had married a white woman, but another judge quashed the decision, ruling that the Civil Rights Act and the Fourteenth Amendment contravened state law. The state Supreme Court reversed the second judge in 1871, arguing that the federal government did not have "the power to invade the police powers of the states,

and that neither [the Fourteenth Amendment] nor the Civil Rights Act had impaired or abrogated the Indiana law."[11]

Despite efforts by black conventions to modify the marriage law, it remained on the books through the 1880s. Enforcement was capricious, since "such unions usually went unnoticed unless brought to the attention of the authorities."[12] In October 1878, for instance, an Evansville black man, "black as black can be," sought to marry a woman "who would pass for white almost anywhere." The judge was eventually convinced that she "had colored blood in her veins," and the two were permitted to marry. Four years later a man who "looked white" and desired to marry an African American woman had to do the same thing: demonstrate that he was "a descendant of the Negro race and . . . has a right to be married to a coulared famel [*sic*] according to the laws of Indiana." Sometimes people went to other states to marry. The number of prosecutions under the law did not measure the true number of mixed marriages.[13]

Color was a pivotal issue in the legal system. After the war, Indiana blacks were permitted for the first time to testify in court, and restriction on the right to make contracts was lifted because of the elimination of Article XIII. In spite of the state civil rights law's provision for jury service, however, "the enactment of the law appears to have been a meaningless gesture, for the penalties were never invoked. In many cases Negroes were seldom called to jury duty and in some communities never."[14] On only two occasions were Evansville blacks called—in both instances, to serve on all-black juries convened to hear cases involving blacks (election fraud in 1870, and the theft of a mule in 1894). The *Evansville Courier* declared that the 1870 jury of "twelve black sovereigns were about the most uncouth specimens of *genus Africanus* it was ever our privilege to behold. We doubt if a single one could write his name or scarcely read the plainest printed copy." By contrast, the *Evansville Daily Journal* insisted, "We do not question the competency of the black man to sit as jurymen to decide the important questions of law and facts. Verily, the world moves! We repeat that this is an age of progress and advancement!" After 1894 no all-black jury was summoned in Evansville until 1946.[15]

The experiences of blacks and whites in the courts differed. Whites committing crimes against blacks were rarely punished, but woe to a black who was charged with a crime against a white. Wanton violence in the immediate postwar years was rampant, and guilty whites were rarely penalized. In the summer of 1867, for instance, the *Evansville Daily Journal* reported that a black man "stabbed on the wharf Monday morning died yesterday evening. There is no clue to the murderer and no effort to hunt him out. It was only a nigger."[16]

The next summer a white man shot and killed a black man in Spencer County who had thrown a rock at him for making insulting comments. The killer was found guilty of manslaughter and received a three-years prison term. Had the black man done the shooting, the penalty would have been much more severe.[17]

The Evansville newspapers regularly reported instances of crimes committed by blacks against blacks—fisticuffs, knifings, and even murders. Whites seemed unfazed: these activities confirmed racial stereotypes. Like urban white Southerners, they did not seek to understand the sources of such conduct or the travail that black newcomers faced when they confronted the legal system. Whites were concerned about control, not justice.[18]

Arrest and imprisonment records are revealing. During July and August 1870, for instance, 258 people were arrested in Evansville, and one-quarter of them were black—substantially more than the proportion of blacks in the total population. As in the urban South, moreover, they were often charged with petty crimes. Most arrests involved grievances between blacks. The proportion of blacks being arrested rose sharply, moreover, when Democrats gained control of the mayor's office and the city council, as they did in 1875. The arrest rate doubled in the following year. For the year ending March 31, 1876, police reported having arrested 1,311 persons, of whom 532 were "colored." To be sure, arrest rates reflected the fact that poor people were more likely to suffer at the hands of the law. Slightly more than 900 of those arrested in 1875–76 were common laborers. Race, though, was a powerful influence. Of the 84 placed in the Evansville city jail in December 1874, 28 were blacks, as were 56 of the 132 jailed in November 1875. In the 1880s the annual proportion ranged from 20 to 43 percent. If blacks were arrested, the odds were two in three that they would be convicted. For whites, the chances were about four in ten.[19]

The pursuit of justice and equality in Illinois was nearly as problematic. Illinois Republicans sought a middle way to protect the freedmen and to curb the vindictiveness of Southern extremists. Senator Lyman Trumbull, for instance, strongly supported the Freedmen's Bureau and the Civil Rights Act of 1866. Most legislators also endorsed the Fifteenth Amendment. But many Illinois Republicans cooperated with Democrats on a number of crucial issues and did not push for more sweeping change.[20]

The first test of newly acquired rights for blacks occurred in the schools. The new constitution of 1870, clearly influenced by the ratification of the Fourteenth and Fifteenth amendments, provided public education for all children. Laws in 1872 and 1874 required equal educational opportunity, but not school integration. As a consequence, virtually all black pupils in central and southern Illinois attended separate and poorly funded schools.[21]

In 1885 Illinois's Republican-dominated legislature passed a state civil rights law modeled after Ohio's. "That the bill became law with so little newspaper comment may, in fact, have been testimony to its necessity, political and otherwise." Shortly thereafter, though, Illinois Republicans turned their attention to other matters—temperance and railroad and warehouse regulation, among others—and became far less attentive to race. A consistent concern of many, including Republicans, was that the state might become a haven for blacks. The passage of the state civil rights law had recognized political reality—the fear of blacks' political independence—not Republicans' concerns about enhancing blacks' civil rights or promoting their political advancement.[22]

Blacks in postwar Ohio also had rocky beginnings after the war. Declared the Rev. S.D. Fox at an Emancipation Day celebration in 1865 in Clermont County, "We are now looked down upon . . . and excite only the pity of whites." In the same speech, he acknowledged the need for "a racial career of improvement." In areas not affected by political calculation or by federal enforcement, whites' support was knotty. Although by the 1870s exclusion from public places in much of the state was in retreat—for instance, streetcars, trains, hospitals, and state institutions—the same was not the case in Ohio River communities. In other public places—notably hotels, saloons, and restaurants—whites informally insisted on exclusion, and blacks acceded to them. Only two lawsuits were brought during the 1870s, because, for one thing, it was inconvenient to file federal suits: there were only two federal courts in Ohio (in Cincinnati and in Cleveland). And blacks did not use the state courts. Exclusion, moreover, was unevenly applied. Some upper-class whites tolerated light-skinned, relatively affluent African Americans but detested darker-skinned and usually poor ones.[23]

As noted in chapter 6, Ohio's Republican leaders took a cautious approach to civil rights issues. Democratic Party strength in the legislature made ratifying of the Fourteenth and Fifteenth amendments difficult. In 1869 the Ohio House of Representatives approved the Fifteenth Amendment by two votes, and the Ohio Senate passed it by just one. Although blacks' legal standing improved, whites' hostility persisted. Wilberforce College, for example, blacks' only higher education institution in Ohio, was burned to the ground by whites.[24]

Ohio's civil rights law created in the 1880s did not prevent blacks from being denied access to a number of public places, especially in Cincinnati. Blacks there could not use parks frequented by whites, attend events at theaters, or use the YMCA. They were blocked from entering most professions and skilled trades, could not attend the Medical College of the University of

Cincinnati, and were placed in Jim Crow cars of southbound trains. Although an early black historian of Cincinnati attributed these proscriptions to the licentious behavior of black newcomers, more fundamental was lower-class whites' resentment toward blacks, especially in times of economic distress. Furthermore, Cincinnati's white population included many people with Southern roots, and most of the city's trade was with the South. White leaders frequently complained that blacks were shiftless and lazy, that they were Republicans only because of spoils.[25]

South-shore blacks' status was even more tricky. On the one hand, black Kentuckians were on paper equal under the law, and black men could vote. On the other, the brief and impotent role that the federal government played in the commonwealth and the antagonism of most whites meant that racial progress was glacial. Many blacks departed for the North, where life was more promising and safer.[26] Those black men who stayed approached their newly gained powers with cautious optimism.

The state legislature did provide several significant guarantees for the freedmen. In January 1872 it permitted blacks to testify in court. Opponents had seen black testimony in federal courts as a major prop for the hated Freedmen's Bureau, but Governor Preston Leslie, a Democrat, backed the right to testify, as did Henry Watterson's *Louisville Courier-Journal*. Both were liberal or "New Departure" Democrats. This was a hollow victory, though, for it was not until 1882 that the legislature eliminated racial qualifications for jury duty in state courts. One should also note that in 1872 two black men, Nathaniel P. Harper of Louisville and George A. Griffith of Owensboro, were admitted to the bar.[27]

But Kentucky's black leaders could not prevent legalized separation of the races. Most recognized the limits of what whites would accept and focused instead on equal treatment in separate worlds. Segregation steadily increased, and "just about every community had its own rules and exceptions." In a number of places, for instance, vagrancy laws resembling slave-era controls were strictly enforced. Public schools were segregated from the outset. By 1884 separation by race was in place in such state institutions as the penitentiary, the school for the blind, and the hospital for the mentally ill. Residential segregation was on the rise, and blacks and whites generally worshipped separately. Yet black and white children often played together, and many black and white adults had strong bonds of affection. Some white leaders like W.C.P. Breckinridge openly championed a day when racial barriers would be removed and prejudice ended, but they realized that would take sacrificial and heroic acts.[28]

Kentucky's African Americans were by law and custom second-class citizens, and despite some evidences of progress, they remained victims of racism in the late 1880s. Financial exploitation, physical abuse, murder, and lynching were ever-present facts of life. Whites refused as a rule to accept the concept of civil equality, preferring a hierarchical relationship with blacks. Harassment and violence upheld the hierarchy when internalized values that both races inherited from slave times failed to control blacks.[29]

Although the vast majority of whites on both sides of the Ohio assumed blacks' inferiority, their responses to blacks continued to range widely, from paternalism to wanton violence. Reactions to the visits of Frederick Douglass, the most famous African American of his day, were illustrative. The *Evansville Daily Journal* responded warmly to his appearances in the city in 1869, 1870, 1876, and 1880. On each occasion the editor praised the intellectual power, articulateness, good sense, and oratorical skills of a cordial and dignified man. Douglass's 1870 lecture, for instance, was lauded as abounding "in healthy advice, broad and liberal ideas, sound political doctrines," dry and dignified humor, and "brilliant flashes of wit that served to convulse the house with laughter." The Democratic *New Albany Daily Ledger,* however, questioned Douglass's premises and expressed doubts about his intellectual and moral qualities.[30]

Editors portrayed black newcomers in substantially different ways, dividing largely along party lines. On the one hand, the *Evansville Daily Journal* initially praised the resourcefulness of the newly freed slaves but agreed with much of the Democrats' assessment of their behavior. Marital infidelity, sexual promiscuity, and sloth were all too common among blacks. But the editor at first attributed these faults to the legacy of slavery, which had prevented blacks from legally marrying. He also explained the presence of large numbers of mulattoes by recalling that white masters had often taken advantage of female slaves. The *Journal,* moreover, approved of the orderliness of black church gatherings and Emancipation Day celebrations. The Democratic *Evansville Courier* consistently ridiculed the behavior (and the aroma) of blacks at these events. This daily and its counterpart in New Albany traced blacks' behavior to inherent weaknesses: lack of enterprise, thrift, valor, honesty, moral rectitude, and mental acumen. Only those blacks who "knew their place" and took such positions as waiters and entertainers, for which they were naturally suited, could rise above the black masses. By contrast, the *Journal* editor on October 4, 1880, declared that the African American was "neither devil nor angel" but rather the product of the culture, economy, and political environment of the region.[31]

Throughout the 1870s and the 1880s, friendly as well as unfriendly whites commonly used the labels *nigger* and *darky* as adjectives as well as nouns. One dry goods merchant in Evansville placed an advertisement that listed goods for sale. After the list was a section for "Negro goods." He declared, "We advertise goods for the White race first and then for the Niggers." This, he added, set his firm apart from his Cincinnati competitors. Both Republicans and Democrats also identified African Americans by such sobriquets as "Ethiopians," "sooty fellows," "sooty beaux," "sable beaux," "dusty," and "dark-skinned and thick-lipped brethren." Editors of both political persuasions also printed jokes at the expense of black newcomers—for example, by making fun of the misuse and the mispronunciation of words by black preachers—and attempted to convey blacks' conversations in dialect.[32]

One reason most blacks on the north bank settled in towns and cities was that a number of rural counties created largely informal rules that prevented blacks from settling or even spending the night there. Population statistics beginning in 1880 demonstrate that trend. Utica in Clark County and Aurora in Dearborn County forbade blacks from settling. The black presence became a thing of the past in Dubois, Orange, Scott, and Washington counties, one county removed from the Ohio. In Washington County, for instance, the black population declined from 187 to 18 between 1860 and 1870 and to 3 in 1880. The *Salem Democrat* of July 1, 1883, boasted that no blacks resided in the county. By 1900 twenty-seven Indiana counties, many near the Ohio, had fewer than 50 black inhabitants each. The most notorious was Crawford County, which had had no black residents before or after the war. In the 1880s blacks employed in construction of a rail line connecting Louisville and St. Louis were attacked and driven out when they attempted to encamp in the northern part of Crawford County.[33]

On the north side of the river, few whites disputed the notion that blacks occupied a separate and inferior stratum of society. As noted earlier, neighborhoods increasingly separated north-shore whites and blacks. Cincinnati had its Bucktown, Little Africa, and Little Bucktown. Blacks in Evansville after the Civil War congregated near the defunct Wabash and Erie Canal in a region known by the early 1880s as Baptisttown. By 1880 about 44 percent of the city's blacks resided in the neighborhood, contiguous portions of Wards 1, 2, and 6, the center of which was Eighth and Canal streets. Ten years later, Baptisttown's share of the city's black populace had nearly doubled. At the same time, more and more streets and alleys—as in Cincinnati and other north-bank cities—were becoming predominantly black. Portions of twenty Evansville streets were at least 80 percent black, and another fifteen were between 50

and 79 percent. Most of these were in Baptisttown. Most streets in the city had no black residents. The index of dissimilarity—the segregation of any two groups in the population, on a scale of 0 to 100—rose from 28 in 1870 to 45 in 1900. Residential exclusion in Evansville was much higher than in such northern Midwest cities as Chicago, Detroit, and Cleveland.[34]

Alexander and Pulaski counties also had a large number and proportion of black newcomers. They resembled south-bank communities like Henderson, in that significant numbers of African Americans were found in most census districts. By the 1880s, for instance, slightly over 43 percent of the residents of Mound City were black, and they resided in most of the city's wards. Some blocks and regions of the Pulaski County seat, however, were predominantly black. The situation was similar in Louisville. In Cairo, the African American population skyrocketed in the 1860s and 1870s. The first city directory to indicate race (1868) disclosed that the races were nearly evenly distributed in city wards. It also revealed, like the federal census of 1880, which included street addresses for the first time, that Ward 4 had a larger number and proportion of blacks than any other.[35]

Residential segregation on the north shore resulted from many factors. Economic trends in American cities separated people by ethnicity and class. The rapid growth of cities, partly through annexation, combined with changing technologies in mass transit to produce increasing spatial separation of commerce, finance, industry, work, and residence. German newcomers to Cincinnati and Evansville, for example, clustered in distinctive neighborhoods. Over time, many moved elsewhere. For the increasing numbers of African Americans who were concentrated in one large and predominantly black region, however, moving elsewhere was unlikely for several reasons. Their homes were located relatively near places of employment. Relatively few were able to rise above poverty, which greatly limited the range of residential choices. Most important, continual white opposition to the threats to their space that they perceived blocked those blacks who could afford better housing.[36]

The predominantly black portions of Evansville, like their counterparts elsewhere, were located in the least desirable sections of low-income regions of the city and often commanded rents that were higher than comparable homes for whites. The stench and health problems associated with stagnant water in the old canal plagued Baptisttown. Streets and alleys were unpaved, and city services nonexistent. The number of households per dwelling in the two census districts with the largest number of blacks was 25 percent higher than in the city as a whole, and each dwelling housed an average of six people, one more than the city's average.[37]

Black neighborhoods were also situated near vice districts, a circumstance that was not unique to Ohio River communities. The proximity of black residents to gambling, houses of ill fame, and taverns reinforced the notion that that blacks were prone to loose morals and illicit behavior. The *Evansville Daily Journal,* ostensibly a friend of African Americans, regularly ran stories reinforcing the view that they were shiftless and unreliable. Usually such accounts dealt with petty crimes. Heavily black sections of the city were known for their "dives," and police raids on "low negro dens" became commonplace, especially on High Street in the lower part of Evansville as well as on Fourth Street between Walnut and Chestnut (the Midway). These regions were noted for their "unhallowed jubilees." Until the Panic of 1893, Cairo possessed a dual economy—one fueled by river and rail transportation, and the other by vice. Liquor and prostitution, which made the second economy prosperous, were also associated with places where blacks resided. Cairo, which became known as a "mean" town, had the highest crime rates in the state.[38]

Race relations in Evansville in the 1870s probably represented those throughout the north shore. In May 1872, for example, a young white woman was reportedly raped by a black man near the Ingleside Mine on the west side. A man was arrested a week later. Boys who had witnessed an assault on another white girl after the first incident described the attacker to the sheriff, who was convinced the black man was also guilty of the second crime. "His face is familiar to many citizens, and, for a negro's face, is very peculiar and easily remembered." Before the end of his second trial, which led to a second conviction, he had already been judged guilty in the Republican newspaper.[39]

In September 1876, while two Evansville policemen were watching the house of two white men suspected of robbery, they spied a black man whose behavior they deemed suspicious. When the African American fled on foot, the two gave chase. One of them fired his revolver at the man, who allegedly stabbed him. The second officer shot and killed the man, subsequently identified as Charles Barnett, a light-skinned man aged about forty who had done odd jobs since arriving in the city from Nashville in 1875. His wife was a laundress at the St. George Hotel. They resided at the corner of Eighth and Cherry streets. The story was printed under the headline "In Self Defense." The next day a coroner's inquest exonerated the policeman, whose fellow officer was the only witness.[40]

Like Republican newspapers elsewhere, the *Evansville Daily Journal* became, in ensuing years, increasingly ambivalent in its treatment of African Americans. By the early 1880s its coverage of blacks was little different from

that of its Democratic competitor. While lauding the virtues of the black elite, the *Journal* expressed contempt for the masses residing in Baptisttown, portrayed as a vice-ridden, immoral place. This epithet, possibly informally used for some time, was attached to a story about the abortion and subsequent death of a young black woman back of Beecher's Hall. The district was not named "because that is the prevailing belief, for an abhorance [*sic*] of water is most characteristic of true blood citizens of that locality. The houses are as irregular as the people."[41]

In Evansville, lines separating the races grew more distinct. The clearest and earliest form of separation was in public education, discussed in chapter 12. Neighborhood divisions were also congealing. In 1883 the city and county governments decided to erect separate orphanages for black and white children. The racial divide was also evident in public ceremonies. Black churches and societies were allowed to rent Peoples' Theatre and Evans Hall for fundraising lectures and concerts, but as the years passed, the number of whites attending such functions dwindled. Emancipation Day, celebrated, as a rule, in Evansville on September 22 well into the twentieth century, was the highlight of the year for African Americans.[42] Whites were rarely present after the immediate postwar period. Blacks and whites observed Independence Day separately. An exception occurred in 1876, when the most powerful black Republican, policeman Robert Nicholas, was asked to serve on the planning committee for the city's celebration of the nation's centennial. One float in the parade—sponsored by black Odd Fellows and members of the Benevolent Aid Society—was African American. When Labor Day ceremonies commenced in the 1880s, black workers—Hod Carriers—marched in the parades, but always at the end. Even that participation ceased, however, by the 1890s.[43]

By custom, black patrons did not frequent hotels, restaurants, and retail stores on or near Main Street or Water Street. Black boarding houses, brothels, and saloons emerged on the edge of the central business district. Beginning with the opening of the city's first hospital, St. Mary's, in 1872, medical care for blacks was spartan. The Daughters of Charity, like its members two decades later who established the Evangelical Synod of North America's hospital, Deaconess, offered service in a separate ward in the basement. A private clinic created a separate facility for blacks in a ramshackle house in Baptisttown. Given the size and the poverty of black Evansville, few black physicians settled there.[44]

Although Cairo's initial responses were somewhat confused, because of the newness of the city and the rapid growth of black and white populations, racial patterns by the late 1880s resembled Evansville's. At the city's leading

hotel, the Halliday House, whites no longer sought positions as barbers, porters, and waiters that required them to work with blacks. On the levees, whites no longer worked as roustabouts. The Episcopal Church of the Redeemer created a new edifice in 1888, open only to white members. Blacks remained in the older building, now known as St. Michael's. Black campaigners were no longer permitted to march in Republican parades. Most significantly, city officials refused to fund land improvements in the southern region, where most blacks lived. Sandy and low-lying soil produced continual seepage problems. Most of the new residences were built on the northern side of Cairo, which became predominantly white. Ward 3, which in 1880 contained one-fifth of the city's white residents, was one-tenth white thirty years later. Two-thirds of its residents, by then, were black. Less than one in ten whites in Cairo had black neighbors.[45]

Whites' responses to blacks in Ohio were little different. Several mitigating factors existed, though. First, Hamilton County was the sole Ohio River county opposite Kentucky that was generally Republican in politics. Second, Cincinnati had a rather large number of Quakers and Yankees, who had been strong opponents of slavery, and it possessed a relatively large free black community before 1865. Third, Wilberforce College, the only institution of higher education for blacks in the state, was established there. The college benefited from the largesse of white philanthropists, as well as a congressional appropriation in 1870. A center for training religious, educational, and civic leaders, the school added normal and industrial training in the 1880s. By then, state funding was its chief source of income. Students educated at Wilberforce had a strong and positive influence on the development of black society in Cincinnati and other river towns.[46]

But Ohio's whites did not advocate fundamental changes in white-black relations. Voters in 1874, for instance, rejected by an overwhelming majority a proposed new constitution that would have admitted blacks to the state militia. Rutherford B. Hayes was not an active supporter of the advancement of African Americans, either as Ohio governor or as president. Though hostile to blacks, Ohio whites rarely turned to lynching, but there was a lynching in Adams County in 1894, for instance.[47]

By the late nineteenth century, Ohio's major cities varied in the number and the percentage of blacks. Cincinnati ranked first in both. Cincinnati's customs were also the most restrictive, and even friends of blacks, such as the *Commercial Gazette,* perpetuated gross racial stereotypes. Blacks were also disproportionately arrested and convicted of crimes, a fact that reflected the city's ties to Kentucky and the upper South. The same was also characteristic of

southern Ohio generally, as separate lodges for fraternal societies and veterans as well as separate orphan asylums were commonplace.[48]

As noted in chapter 6, Kentucky law enforcement officials showed little interest in guaranteeing blacks' welfare after passage of the Civil Rights Act of 1866. The Civil Rights Act of 1875 also had little effect in the commonwealth. Kentucky's failure "to extend these and other basic constitutional guarantees to its black minority and the willingness of state officials to condone violence had the effect of fostering the abuse and harassment that characterized the 1870s and 1880s."[49]

The rule of law in Kentucky remained tenuous. A white plasterer in Uniontown shot a black farmer who had not responded properly to an order given him and got away, literally, with murder. Shortly afterward, a black man in Henderson was charged with having committed "a terrible crime"—an attempted rape of a little girl. He was apprehended on the packet *Grey Eagle,* bound for Evansville. The arresting officer disingenuously assured Evansville officials "there is no fear of a mob."[50] In another incident reported in the "Annals of Kentucky," the brother and the father of a white girl, age fifteen, shot and killed a black man who had allegedly attempted to rape her. The two surrendered and were tried and acquitted the same day. "The whole community," reported the historian, "justified the act."[51]

Regarding such acts, white leaders were either ambivalent, like Henry Watterson, editor of the *Louisville Courier-Journal* for fifty years, or supportive. Watterson portrayed lynching as an evil that was occasionally necessary. The author of the Union County history in 1886 had no qualms about the practice. White and especially black "troublemakers" were the target of white night riders, and in counties where there were few blacks, whites attempted to get rid of them, especially if they were successful. Whites were more likely to attack blacks in times of economic stress, and the panic years of 1873–78 were especially troubled in that respect.[52]

The General Assembly refused to pass a law outlawing mob violence. The 1890s, when 66 blacks died at the hands of mobs, were the most brutal statewide. A close second was the 1870s, when 58 died. The proportion of lynchings in Ohio River counties, though, was relatively low. In the years 1866–80, when 140 Kentucky men were lynched—107 of them black—only 12 of the cases occurred in river counties. Union County had the most, 5. Two took place in Gallatin County. During the years 1881–90, 54 lynchings took place, 9 involving black men in river counties. Henderson County had the most, 3, and Boone and Daviess counties had 2 each. Most Kentucky lynchings oc-

curred well to the south of the Ohio, especially in counties in western Kentucky or the Purchase, near the Tennessee border.[53]

In December 1874 the *Evansville Daily Journal* reported that three black men and a black woman in downstream Uniontown had been brutally attacked simply because of their race. The Democratic *Evansville Courier* sided with Uniontown officials, who declared these charges false and reminded Evansville that 50 percent of the town's purchases were made in Evansville. Uniontown's civic and business leaders lodged charges of slander in Louisville, St. Louis, and Indianapolis newspapers. They said they would boycott Evansville goods until the *Journal* retracted its story. They insisted that race was not involved and that no woman had been lynched. They granted, though, that three white men had been arrested for arson and that a mob had summarily dispatched them. The upshot was that the *Journal* acknowledged having received erroneous information but nonetheless condemned Uniontown for condoning lynching.[54]

The rare white who opposed lynching risked much. In July 1884 the white sheriff in Owensboro, a Confederate veteran, attempted to prevent a mob from removing from his jail a black man who had been accused of rape. The sheriff lost his life in the process. Blacks were, moreover, not necessarily passive about such activities. Ida B. Wells, famed "muckraking" student of lynching, described how blacks in Paducah armed themselves against white mobs, and retaliation by blacks who learned of lynchings elsewhere was not uncommon.[55]

Most racism, however, was expressed nonviolently. Kentucky whites' hostility drove blacks from most hotels in the state by the late 1870s. At restaurants, the declining quality of service and the refusal to permit blacks inside made it necessary for blacks to purchase carryout food at windows in the rear. Stores and shops were little better, "because clerks and managers were sometimes inattentive or rude."[56] Initially, theaters admitted blacks, but seated them in a separate section in the gallery—even when Fisk's Jubilee Singers performed at Louisville's Masonic Temple for the benefit of a black college. Harassment was also evident at ballparks and racetracks. The only black member of the Toledo baseball team, catcher Moses Fleetwood Walker, did not take the field in Louisville because of vehement protests from the white crowd. When the team returned to the city, Walker played but faced "a steady barrage of insults," and his play was adversely affected.[57]

Discrimination was also commonplace in rail transportation. During slavery days, blacks could sit where they wanted to, and while the Freedmen's Bureau existed they were able to thwart efforts to force them into second-class and inferior accommodations. Beginning in the early 1870s, though, separate

ticket windows and waiting rooms were created in railroad depots. Black men desiring first-class tickets had to ride in the men's smoking car or in second-class facilities, and those traveling long distances were denied sleeping berths. Although some railroad companies permitted black women to buy first-class tickets and sit in the ladies' car, more common was the experience of a Louisville woman who was denied access to the ladies' car by the conductor and ordered to sit in the smoking car. When she objected, the conductor stopped the train and ejected her. Segregation on Kentucky's rail lines was virtually complete by the end of the 1880s.[58]

Rural legislators initiated the call for a law mandating segregated coaches, because they objected to having integrated cars travel through their towns and villages. Implementation came slowly, as officials of the Louisville and Nashville complained of the cost of adding separate cars and insisted that few blacks rode the trains. Companies' policies were inconsistent, and officials were easily swayed by whites' objections. The climate of white opinion brought about the legislature's action on May 24, 1892, to mandate separate seating divided by a wooden partition.[59]

Louisville stood apart from most Southern cities in that whites were initially unable to enact an ordinance segregating streetcars. Certain whites' understanding of the essentially conservative character of blacks' protest may have been behind this failure: they sought to preserve the status quo, not to challenge the established order. Perhaps white leaders also were satisfied in not creating one more Jim Crow ordinance. As George Wright has argued, custom permitted them to segregate as they saw fit and to present themselves as progressive in comparison with the rest of the South.[60]

Nevertheless, Louisville's whites were united in their opposition to the Civil Rights Act of 1875. Henry Watterson called it "an insult to the white people of the southern states," a Republican tool dividing whites and blacks, who were as usual "blindly led to believe that a measure would lead to a 'Revolution' in their condition and elevate them to affluence, social status, and political power." The latter "could be obtained only through hard work."[61]

After passage of the bill, owners of Louisville restaurants and hotels indicated that they would ignore the law. Some declared that decent blacks would not mortify whites and themselves by seeking to implement the law. Louisville Republicans were embarrassed, since they perceived it as a threat to their efforts to broaden their base of support. They urged blacks to ignore the bill, work at self-improvement, and not foolishly attempt "to exercise their new privileges in an offensive way."[62]

Louisville's blacks generally resisted testing the Civil Rights Act, although

a handful unsuccessfully attempted to obtain tickets to theaters and to dine at a hotel. Leaders were "bitterly divided over what action to take." Ministers and teachers warned that demanding civil rights would produce racial friction. Some, led by physician Henry Fitzbutler and saloonkeeper William Spradling, who hosted at his saloon a meeting to discuss the matter, believed the law was "the culmination of their drive for all of their rights as citizens, and that though blacks should not throw themselves on whites they did have the right to public facilities."[63]

At a second meeting, held in a church, Fitzbutler and Spradling's group resolved that "judicious, prudent, and continuous use of the Civil Rights law by colored people in all necessary cases, is indispensable in securing good by the enactment of the law." William H. Steward and Nathaniel R. Harper, conservative black leaders, responded quickly and negatively. Steward, "a trusted employee of the president of the Louisville and Nashville Railroad, explained that . . . the black community should hold a quiet church service." Harper, "the first black admitted to the bar in Kentucky and a loyal Republican and office seeker," arranged that church service and "announced that his popular singing group would provide the entertainment." Fitzbutler's group canceled its plans, and the church service was the only public event held. Harper urged restraint: "We must educate ourselves to a higher morality than exists at present within the race." He also encouraged patronizing black businesses. "This will in time, make the Hotels, etc., of negroes as good as those of the whites, and do away with the necessity of troubling white people with their presence."[64]

There are no records that any Louisville blacks filed suit because they had been denied their rights under the new law. Most blacks "could not afford such luxuries as dining at the Galt House or attending the theater," anyway. Those who could faced "white resentment [that] might cost them their jobs or white patronage. They also knew that two blacks had already been assaulted after dining at a local hotel."[65]

In short, the Civil Rights Act of 1875 made little difference in Kentucky. When the Supreme Court declared it unconstitutional, some Louisville black leaders met to select an appropriate course of action. They agreed that the goodwill of whites was essential if they were to succeed as a race. They further urged whites to voluntarily admit respectable blacks to their establishments. And they "concluded with a familiar theme, that if blacks could somehow work hard and acquire wealth they would be accepted by whites." That blacks south of the Ohio had been generally unaffected by the Civil Rights Act of 1875 was the consequence, noted C. Vann Woodward, of blacks' being "bred to slavery [and] typically ignorant and poor and . . . not given to pressing [their]

rights to such luxuries as hotels, restaurants, and theaters even when [they] could afford them or [were] aware of them." There was "little need for Jim Crow laws to establish what the lingering stigma of slavery—in bearing, speech, and manner—made so apparent."[66]

By 1885 the racial divide was clearly evident. Blacks "were totally excluded from several white establishments and welfare institutions where previously they had been admitted." Although the four theaters in the 1870s had admitted blacks, reserving the dress and parquet circles for whites, by 1885 they denied admission to blacks altogether. The same occurred at the racetrack. Blacks were excluded from the grandstand when the Louisville professional baseball team played, and black newsmen covering the games were not given complimentary tickets. Annual fairs and expositions were closed to blacks, prompting blacks to create their own. One black newspaper noted the irony of "Colored Christians" being kept out of the Young Men's Christian Association.[67]

Blacks continued "to be totally excluded from or, at best, segregated in Louisville's welfare institutions." White juvenile delinquents, for instance, were sent to industrial schools, where they learned skills designed to help them find jobs, in lieu of going to jail. There was no such alternative for black boys until 1885, when pressure from black leaders led to city officials' opening a school. A similar school for black girls was not opened until 1896. Blacks were denied access to most of the free public bathhouses in the city. The number of beds and rooms for blacks at the public hospitals were not increased. City officials in the 1880s refused to hire a black physician, thus denying poor blacks the free medical services provided whites. Private clinics and the eight private hospitals did not admit blacks. Neither did the University of Louisville Medical School and the Hospital College of Medicine. Three physicians in Louisville and New Albany therefore in 1888 opened the Louisville National Medical College, which trained black doctors and offered medical care to black patients. (See more detailed discussion in chapter 11.) Perhaps most ludicrous of all was an 1884 law that segregated the races at the Louisville School for the Blind. Until the passage of a restrictive ordinance in the summer of 1924, though, blacks picnicked and even played baseball side by side with whites in public parks. They also used the public swimming pools and tennis courts.[68]

Abhorring mob violence, Louisville whites relied on the police force to keep blacks in their place. Blacks were far more likely than whites to be arrested—like north-shore blacks, chiefly for petty crimes. The percentage of blacks among those arrested rose from 22 percent in 1873 to 32 percent in 1881. In the meantime, the proportion of Irish arrested dropped from 17 percent to 7 percent. These changes were likely the result of the city's Demo-

cratic machine being taken over by John Whallen, who became police chief in 1884 and subsequently controlled virtually all appointments to city jobs. The city became "wide-open": the number of gambling houses and houses of prostitution grew, and city ordinances and Sunday closing laws were flagrantly ignored. Most of the houses of ill fame were situated near black neighborhoods. White offenders tended to receive lenient treatment at the hands of policemen. In spite of black leaders' complaints, policemen often used excessive force and sometimes killed alleged black criminals. "Especially vulnerable were blacks who were not well known by police officers or blacks who were engaged in activities that the police might label 'suspicious.'" Police "abused blacks at will, knowing that the courts would likely uphold their actions, even when the injustice to blacks was obvious."[69]

In some cities, such activities led blacks to respond with violence—for example, making it dangerous for one or two policemen to enter bars seeking to arrest black men. In Louisville, though, blacks' response was "resentment, suspicion, and disrespect for law officials." Black leaders did not advocate retaliation or self-defense. Whites "had no qualms about resorting to violence to suppress black aspirations for change." The difference between Louisville and Deep South cities was that suppression was "done legally"—through the police force, "the ever-present symbol of white authority."[70]

Whites' perception and treatment of blacks in Louisville was distinctive among Southern cities in other respects. No race riots or lynchings occurred between 1865 and 1930. Black men could vote. Some city leaders, like John Marshall Harlan and Louis B. Brandeis, were relatively free of race prejudice. Most white leaders practiced paternalism, a reflection of slavery times. In most of the South exclusion occurred first and segregation followed, but in Louisville exclusion was not uniform and segregation policies were often baffling. Schooling was segregated and unequal from the 1870s on, and yet beginning in 1871 blacks won (at least briefly) the right to sit where they wished on streetcars. Public parks were not racially segregated. Theaters, restaurants, and hotels eventually were. Large numbers of African Americans chose to migrate to and to remain in Louisville rather than traveling northward.[71]

Louisville's racial milieu was the result of three factors. First, the Civil War brought Northern troops and emancipation as well as a significant increase in the number of African Americans living in the city. Second, after the war there was an economic and political realignment. Wage labor altered life in rural areas and attracted black workers to the city. Many ex-Confederate officers and gentlemen settled in Louisville because of its reputation as a city of opportunity. And third, Northern political and economic influence was gradually

and systematically extended. One of its consequences was a transformation of the city's business elite and its workforce. Workers and leaders were "not united on racial policies nor consistent in their vision of the city's future development." What mattered most in the end was "the interplay of Southern racial traditions and . . . more general patterns of social inequality derived from immigration and [Louisville's] associated development as an industrial and manufacturing center."[72]

The "polite racism" of Louisville was not practiced in other river towns. Mob rule prevailed, especially in downstream communities like Owensboro, in July 1884, December 1889, and December 1896. In the first instance, Dick Mays—described by a contemporary historian as a "wretched negro"—was hanged for attempted rape. In the second, Doc Jones was lynched because he had been charged with murder. In the third, Alf Holt, portrayed by the same historian as a "typical darky," was dragged from the jail in the early hours of Christmas Day and hanged. Charged with but not convicted of having killed a white policeman during a disturbance in the "Negro quarter," he was, according to the historian, "like many of his race" in character. He was "ignorant, shiftless, and given to drink, but he had not been considered dangerous."[73]

On both sides of the river, as a consequence of deteriorating race relations, important blacks generally chose to preserve and if possible augment their ties to sympathetic whites. Louisville was probably representative of the region in this sense. The most prominent black leader during the 1870s, Horace Morris, was appointed as the first black steward at the Marine Hospital by President James Garfield. William J. Simmons, a Baptist minister, became president of State University in Louisville in 1880, an institution that received funding from whites. Simmons also founded the National Baptist Convention, served as its president from 1886 to 1890, established a Baptist newspaper, was elected president of the Colored Press Association, and in 1888 published a book of biographical sketches. He "was also adept at keeping white supporters while speaking out against overt injustices." As chair of the State Convention of Colored Men of Kentucky in 1886, he was the first black to address the state legislature. Like Booker T. Washington, he spoke of racial interdependency, declaring that all Kentuckians shared the "feelings and aspirations" unique to the state. "We come, plain of speech, to prove that we are men of judgment, meeting men who are desirous of knowing our wants."[74]

Although he was president of a liberal arts college, Simmons promoted vocational as well as moral training. Appearing at a black church with editor Henry Watterson, he spoke of the need for political independence and asserted

that educational progress had been made only under Democratic administrations. Simmons's protégé and successor, Rev. Charles Parrish, also railed about blacks' shortcomings, particularly those of the lower class, instead of focusing on racial discrimination. He, too, was placed on interracial boards and given prominent positions in the Republican Party.[75]

William H. Steward, born free in Brandenburg, Kentucky, in 1847, came to the city as a youth and attended the school operated at First African Baptist Church. From the outset he cultivated strong ties with prominent whites. A messenger and purchasing agent for the L&N, he accepted a position in 1877 as the city's first black letter carrier. He delivered mail to wealthy whites, strengthening his connections with them. A devout Baptist layman, he was the founder and chief black supporter of State University, the general secretary of the Kentucky Baptist Convention, and for fifty-six years the editor of *The American Baptist,* the official organ of the American National Baptist Convention and the General Association of Negro Baptists in Kentucky. He was also a longtime Mason, rising to leadership positions.[76]

Steward, whose black connections were important, was indebted to influential whites. Like Morris, he was a member of the Colored School Board of Visitors and responsible for the appointment of many blacks to teaching posts. His approval was required before white Republicans appointed blacks to political positions. Like Simmons, he deplored blacks' immorality and disunity. Superintendent of the Sunday School at Fifth Street Baptist for half a century, he "preached a gospel of abstinence, honesty, and hard work." Steward and Parrish "both courted the same influential whites, [and] it is not surprising that some bitterness existed in their relationship. Much of their disagreement centered on William J. Simmons."[77]

As elsewhere, black ministers were cautious in their approaches to racial discrimination. Whites' financial support was a major reason. William H. Craighead, pastor of Zion Baptist Church for half a century and trustee of State University, was undoubtedly typical, as he preached that paternalistic whites were largely responsible for blacks' progress.[78]

Black physicians, barred from white hospitals and in most cases from contact with white physicians and having only black patients to provide their income, had fewer reasons to counsel restraint. Henry Fitzbutler quickly became known for his advocacy of improvements in black education. He was sharply critical of segregated schools and unsuccessfully ran for the school board on several occasions. In 1879 he established a newspaper, the *Ohio Falls Express,* which for its twenty-two-year history was the leading critic of accommodators like Steward.[79]

But men like Fitzbutler were in a distinct minority, for black leaders pursued white leaders' approval and support as racial hostilities and Jim Crow intensified. Most of them comforted whites by preaching the gospel of self-help and targeting ordinary blacks' lack of refinement, which allowed them to appeal to whites while also seeking to preserve what little progress they had made.[80]

The accommodators' approach, with the corollary that the burden of proof lay with freed men and women, prevailed on the north side of the river as well. Evansville's first black constable, Robert Nicholas, focused his Emancipation Day address in 1875 on giving blacks a fair chance to earn the respect of whites through industry, thrift, and material progress. The same emphasis was evident in Alfred Carter's advice to his fellow citizens following passage of the Civil Rights Act of 1875. North-shore blacks in Indiana, like those on the south shore, "rarely attempted to invade the places designated by custom and economic circumstances for the use of white persons." Cincinnati blacks were advised to "go slow, uplift themselves, and forget about public accommodations."[81]

Carter, like most, did not challenge division by race, because he knew white businessmen and professionals would not risk alienating their white customers by attempting to please black clients. The accommodators also desired to please those few white civic leaders on whose financial and political support they depended. With the pool of political rewards shrinking, that strategy was increasingly essential. The "strive and succeed" approach later associated with Booker T. Washington was well entrenched in the cities and towns of both banks of the Ohio by the early 1880s. It echoed the experiences of middle- and upper-class black businessmen and professionals who had risen from desperate poverty to a modicum of respectability.[82]

Blacks in Evansville, like those in virtually all villages, towns, and cities on the Ohio, were, because of their relatively small numbers, more dependent on whites' resources than were blacks in Cincinnati and Louisville, which had black communities large enough to sustain institutions vital to blacks' well-being. Black dependency, born in slavery and strengthened by virulent racism, was strengthened.[83] But all black men could vote.

8

The Progress of Blacks
and the Ballot Box

As the memory of emancipation faded among whites living on the north shore of the river, the theme of national reconciliation fused with that of white supremacy. By 1890 few whites retained the ideal of civil equality. Most viewed the war as a time in which whites on both sides had served their respective causes loyally and sacrificially.[1] The restructuring of most whites' memories of the war made ever more daunting African Americans' quest for fair play in a time when formal and informal strictures based on race were being created. But black men never lost their right to vote, even on the south shore. The Fifteenth Amendment gave each black man, on paper, the same power as each white man.

Blacks' memory of liberation was formally celebrated on Emancipation Day. Although dates of the festival varied, the annual event recalled the race's achievements during and after the war and brought attention to obstacles to its development. In Evansville, Emancipation Day was observed on September 22, the date of the Preliminary Emancipation Proclamation in 1862. Elsewhere it occurred on January 1, the day of the Emancipation Proclamation in 1863. The Illinois river towns of Elizabethtown, Brookport, and Metropolis and the cross-river Kentucky towns of Paducah and Smithland celebrated Emancipation Day in early August, commemorating the time in the early 1830s when slavery was abolished in the British West Indies. The August day also coincided with

slack time before harvest. The celebration in Paducah assumed huge proportions by the 1880s: special trains and steamers brought blacks from Cairo, Chicago, Louisville, Memphis, and St. Louis. In 1887 a "grand excursion" to Paducah via the Henderson and Ohio Valley Railroad was organized by Evansville African Americans. Undoubtedly many had family ties, as ex-slaves, to that region.[2] In Kentucky, Jubilee or Emancipation Day was generally observed on January 1.

Wherever emancipation was celebrated, the apogee of the festivities was addresses by the "old soldiers": Union veterans who reminded black people of their former status, of the heroism of blacks in the war, and of the party that liberated them. Typically, issues relevant to blacks' future were also raised. In 1866 the well-attended celebration in Louisville included the adoption of a petition to the legislature for full civil rights. The 1869 event, the conclusion of which was held at Asbury Methodist Church, featured an oration by Rev. Henry J. Young. Like predecessors, he urged that blacks be given the vote.[3]

Independence Day provided blacks in Kentucky and elsewhere yet another opportunity to protest racial inequities and to demonstrate racial progress. The adoption of the Fifteenth Amendment gave them a momentous backdrop for the celebration in 1870. More than ten thousand gathered to observe a parade through Louisville to Courthouse Square, where slaves had once been auctioned. One highlight was an oration by Reverend Young. Another was the crowd's singing "The Fifteenth Amendment," composed by W.H. Gibson Sr. The song included these two lines: "For the Republican party will vote in a mass / For they have guarded well 'Thermopylae's Pass.'"[4]

Before as well as after the passage of the Fifteenth Amendment, black men on both sides of the river also participated in conventions that petitioned local, state, and federal officials on a variety of issues. For example, the Indiana Supreme Court's overturning of Article XIII of the constitution and the passage of the Civil Rights Act of 1866 enhanced the November 1866 convention in Indiana, which called for the removal of all restrictions based on race and for the granting of the vote. In November 1867 black citizens of Paducah sent a petition to the House of Representatives in Washington requesting the impeachment of President Andrew Johnson.[5]

In 1869 the legislatures of Illinois, Indiana, and Ohio endorsed the Fifteenth Amendment, despite Democrat-led protest rallies in places like Evansville and New Albany in March that railed against Republicans' perfidy and advocacy of "social equality." African Americans in all four states celebrated reaching this milestone, and they linked it to Republican leadership. Evansville's blacks celebrated the achievement "in a becoming manner" by organizing a

joint celebration with their brothers and sisters in Princeton, Vincennes, and Mt. Carmel (Illinois) at Princeton, north of Evansville, on May 26, 1870. This was the largest gathering to date of African Americans in southern Indiana. A lengthy parade preceded the service at the local AME Church. Seven men spoke, including George Jackson, James Townsend, and white attorney Andrew L. Robinson, all of Evansville. The president of the affair was Rev. W.S. Lankford of Evansville. About fifteen hundred African Americans rejoiced "that they were Americans at last."[6]

That fall, Indiana's Republican platform stressed three points: "the benefits Negroes had received from Republicans, the hatred of Democrats for Negroes, and the debt of gratitude that Negroes owed to Republicans." Republicans' support for the postwar constitutional amendments was not necessarily humanitarian, however, as the editor of the Evansville Republican newspaper disclosed. These acts were a means of guaranteeing that blacks would remain in the South where they belonged: "Show your disapproval . . . and you may have them leave the South in a body."[7]

Such words paled in comparison with the potent racism in Evansville and other Ohio River towns that tempered blacks' enthusiasm. Congressman W.E. Niblack, a Democrat, was one of thirty-two congressmen to vote against a resolution in July 1870 signifying that the Fourteenth and Fifteenth amendments were duly ratified and therefore part of the U.S. Constitution and binding on the states as well as the federal government. His district, the Indiana First, stretched along the Ohio from Posey through Jefferson counties. That fall he won reelection in large part by playing on racial fears: "We're not free because we cannot prevent whom we please from voting."[8]

Linkage between loyalty to the party of Lincoln and a racial strategy based on self-help was continually promoted after 1870. Evansville represented the region in this respect. Speaking at a ceremony commemorating the tenth anniversary of the end of the war, Robert Nicholas, the first black constable, declared that freedom had "imposed upon us a debt, which it will take generations to come to pay. It has been often repeated that we are incapable of comprehending the responsibilities upon us as citizens." He insisted that "we ask only a fair trial, and we are willing to abide the consequences, and we will in a few years demonstrate to the world that we are intelligent as well as free." Critical was educating "our children and ourselves in all the useful branches, and to strain every nerve, and leave nothing undone which shall tend to fit us for the duties and responsibilities of the undeveloped future."[9]

Few doubted at first that voting Republican would "open the way for the

elevation of the race." Evansville's experiences were typical. Evansville blacks elected a delegate to the state convention held February 22, 1872. The vast majority of black men supported the Republican Party in the first presidential election year after passage of the Fifteenth Amendment. A handful bolted the party of Lincoln because of Charles Sumner's and George W. Julian's appeal for blacks' support of Horace Greeley, the Democratic candidate for president. Both had been longtime abolitionists and friends of African Americans. Regular Republicans were frightened and attempted to discredit the two. Black political clubs organized to support Grant in Evansville and upstream Indiana towns, like those in Louisville, turned out the vote for the incumbent. Members of Evansville's Colored Grant Club included James Townsend, who denounced black supporters of Greeley for denying Alfred Carter, club president, the opportunity to speak at a Greeley meeting.[10]

Members of the black clergy were well recognized for their involvement in political life. Townsend (1841–1913), an AME pastor and the first black teacher in Evansville, was a veteran of the 54th Massachusetts who had attended Oberlin College for two years after the end of the war. He and another pastor, W.S. Lankford, were seated on the stage at the Opera House on March 17, 1870, during a speech by Frederick Douglass, and on August 15, 1870, when a large and racially mixed audience at the Opera House heard a lecture given by Hiram Revels of Mississippi, one of two African American members of the U.S. Senate. Clergymen were also prominent in the formation of the first political club, the Colored Grant and Wilson Club. The same club also selected Townsend as their representative on the Republican County Executive Committee—a practice that white Republicans permitted until the 1890s. Black Republicans held their first convention on February 20, 1872, at the AME Church. Two of the five members of the nominating committee were pastors.[11]

Members of the small black middle class played a vital part in politics. Vanderburgh County's Colored Central Committee for 1872 included George Jackson, a steward; and Frank Washington, Gus Carter, James Amos, and James Carter, who were barbers. Some other middle-class blacks in the county were Alfred Carter, who had a confectionery located on the corner of Sixth and Chestnut streets; James H. Gray, a janitor; James Mosley and Jacob Thompson, carpenters; W.F. Teister, a teacher; and Bushrod Taylor, a porter at the post office.[12]

The election of 1872 anticipated future politics in another respect. In Jeffersonville a fight between white backers of Greeley and black supporters of Grant "ended with the white guards riddling one of the Negro houses with

bullets and breaking up the furniture." In Evansville, Republicans charged that Greeley supporters had hired a naive black man to pay two dollars for each vote cast for the New York editor. Violence and allegations of fraud would persist during election times for years to come. Republicans accused Democrats of intimidating black voters, and Democrats charged Republicans with buying "imported" voters from Kentucky. Democrats—until they saw the value of courting black voters—also raised the red flag of miscegenation and social equality.[13]

Democrats and Republicans, as well as whites and blacks, recognized that the black vote provided a critical difference for Republicans, and in the early days Republicans actively courted blacks. The *Evansville Courier* observed in October 1870 that only black votes provided the means by which Republicans could outpoll the Democrats. Their initial response was to allege that Republicans imported illegal voters. That mantra recurred in city elections of 1871 and the state and federal elections of 1872. In river towns Democrats claimed that Kentucky blacks were being sent as far north as Indianapolis. They also offered rewards for those who could identify "floaters."[14]

The black vote gave the Republicans majority status in Cairo and Alexander County. Beginning in 1872, when the party won more than half of the vote for the first time, through the 1890s, Republicans claimed about 60 percent of the vote in local, state, and federal elections and consistently outpolled Republicans in the rest of the state. They elected John M. Lansden mayor in 1871, thanks in large part to the black vote that was organized by black politico "Dick" Taylor. A laborer, he was rewarded by being named a policeman. Blacks gained a number of other city jobs and were awarded contracts to repair sidewalks. Lansden also supported John Bird, a black expatriate from Canada, in his successful bid to become one of two elected police magistrates. (Bird's backing of a white candidate for school board the year before was a critical factor in his victory.) The experiences of Bird and Taylor demonstrated one result of Republicans' reliance on black voters: the creation of a black leadership base. For example, Bird became Rutherford B. Hayes's chief contact in patronage matters in southern Illinois. Another result was that the Democrats attempted to woo black voters, shifting from their initial harassment tactic. They also sought to portray Republicans as ungrateful to blacks and contemptuous of foreign-born workers, many of whom were Roman Catholic.[15]

There could also be penalties for political loyalty. After the spring elections of 1876, in the midst of the economic depression, a Democrat who was supervising a street project in Evansville dismissed thirteen black men who had not voted Democratic the previous day and filled their jobs with white

replacements. In the same election, George Buckner—at the time eighteen— was arrested for swearing in black Democratic voters because he allegedly owned no property. Later he produced a deed to some real estate.[16]

The fall election of 1876 was one of the nastiest in the city's history. Hundreds of black men were reported to have left places like the tobacco warehouses of Louisville for temporary sojourn across the river. Evansville Democrats enlisted the aid of the black former body servant of President James K. Polk, who at a rally on election eve insisted he would rather live in a slave state than in the North, "where the people treat the colored folks 'wusser than a dog.'" When he asked what civil rights had done for blacks, Robert Nicholas shouted from the audience, "It put you in the St. George Hotel [the city's finest] today." The same week Frederick Douglass addressed a large, racially mixed crowd, reminding blacks that it was the Republicans who had liberated and enfranchised them. He described the Democrats as "the sectional party and the party of the South. It is something like a snake which you catch by the head with a crooked stick. The tail slashes all around, but the head, the brains, are always in the same place."[17] James M. Townsend, who had been transferred to a church in Terre Haute a few years earlier, addressed the same theme at the Republican Colored County Convention. The opposition, though, was formidable. Forty-five "ruffians"—some black—were appointed special election officers by the Democrat-controlled city government. Black men were their special targets. Policemen liberally threw black men in jail and looked the other way when white Democrats harassed blacks.[18]

In the elections that followed, leaders of both parties uttered familiar themes. Republicans, especially loyalists like Nicholas, who depended on whites' favor for his job, used speeches and letters in the party newspaper to ritualistically plead with blacks to remember who had given them their freedom and the vote. Democrats predictably urged the party faithful to look out for black "repeaters." Wrote the Democratic editor in 1884, "Lest some of the rascals may escape, let the vote of every stranger be challenged, whether he be white or black."[19]

Blacks had consistently strong precinct, ward, and county organizations. Particularly important was Baptisttown, where most of their votes were located. Republicans sought—generally with success—to keep these crucial voters in line. In the 11 campaigns between 1870 and 1890 for city, county, and state offices, Republicans took 8 contests, losing 1 city race and 2 at the county level. The margins were generally close—five hundred votes or less.[20]

Republicans' operations in the 1884 campaign were typical. On the evening of October 22, 1884, a torchlight parade for James G. Blaine brought five

divisions of Republican loyalists to the city's streets. The one bringing up the rear, as usual, was black. Headed by Frederick Douglass Morton, a leader of the new generation of black men, it comprised a band and eight units representing local black political clubs. Each had a distinctive uniform: for example, Company E, 100 men dressed in blue capes and white caps; Company D, 60 men in red uniforms; a "broom brigade" of 15 men wearing silk hats and carrying brooms to signify a Republican sweep; and a glee club of 24 men and women wearing white suits and dresses trimmed with gold stars. The Republican paper reminded blacks of their indebtedness to the party of Lincoln and urged voters to avoid saloons, not to take offense at insults, and to go to the polls quietly and firmly. If challenged, they were to insist on their right to vote.[21]

Blacks' rewards, though, were always meager. From the early 1870s to the early 1890s, they were permitted one delegate to the Republican Central Committee. The first political appointee was apparently Alfred Carter, president of the Colored Grant Club, who was named city weigh master April 6, 1871. Republicans' fear of losing black votes prompted them to expand political rewards modestly. In April 1874 Andrew L. Robinson surprised black loyalists by declaring that the party was doing nothing for blacks and as a consequence he planned to switch parties. Some blacks followed him. Nicholas spoke in opposition to Robinson's position. In that election Democrats for the first time openly courted blacks. Nicholas was rewarded by being named city constable.[22]

After the early 1870s, Indiana Republicans included little in their platforms that had a special appeal for blacks. As in Illinois and Ohio, they were eager to strengthen their appeal to white voters and reluctant to appear to be a party that depended on blacks for their majority. That meant, among other things, a unwillingness to endorse blacks' efforts to campaign for public office. In turn, blacks' restiveness with the Republican Party grew increasingly visible, as evidenced by an active campaign on the part of dissidents to break from the Republican Party in Evansville during the municipal election campaign in the spring of 1877. Once more, Democrats openly courted the black vote. It is worth examining this event and those that followed in some detail.[23]

At issue in that election was the belief shared by a number of black men that they should be named candidates for three city offices at the upcoming convention. Alfred Carter and Robert Nicholas favored waiting to see what white Republicans desired. Said one dissident, however, "if we had waited for the apples to fall off we won't catch many good ones, but if we took a pole and pushed, a few of us would be more successful."[24] Some hinted that declaring

political independence would bring better rewards, as the two parties would compete for blacks' favor.

The controversy persisted. The next day, the Republican daily printed a statement by Frederick Douglass that urged blacks to stick with the Republican Party. It also published a letter from a black man who complained that blacks constituted half of the voters in the First Ward but were rewarded only with promises. Rejecting the notion of an independent party, the writer suggested that Republicans nominate a black for city council from the First Ward but not for city marshal or city recorder, since black candidates had little chance of winning those citywide races. Losses by black candidates would also hurt the party. The writer argued, moreover, that blacks needed to form their own executive committee, of which one member would be included on the Republican County Executive Committee. The Democratic *Courier* gave these matters unprecedented coverage, especially praising the speech March 12 of one dissident who decried Republicans' taking them for granted, and printing a letter from J.H. Carter that urged blacks to vote independently.[25]

On the evening of March 19 black men attended a raucous meeting where Charles Sheldon, who had urged independence March 12, was elected chair. Nicholas was elected secretary. That night, John Sanders was nominated as candidate for the First Ward city council position. Nicholas, who urged all to vote straight Republican, earned the scorn of several dissidents, who decried the Republicans' "trained monkeys." The chair of the meeting declared that given their seven hundred votes, perhaps blacks could "slip a coon in" if they nominated several candidates. Another participant stated that although it was too early to create a separate party, blacks should present their candidate before all political parties and ask for their support. After lengthy debate, Sanders's nomination was voted down, and participants failed to endorse any Republican candidates.[26]

White Republicans ignored the concerns of black voters. The First Ward Convention on March 22 nominated a white man to serve on the City Council. Two blacks—Sanders and the pastor of Liberty Baptist Church, Green McFarland—were among those selected as delegates from that ward to the city convention. Three black men were also chosen as delegates from the Sixth Ward. "A Word to Colored Men" appeared four days later in the Republican paper. The anonymous writer warned that Democrats had been attempting since the previous fall to trick blacks into supporting them with the promise of appointments. The author, possibly Nicholas, reminded blacks of Republicans' long-standing support and of what happened when Democrats ran the city two years before. Democrats had named Chesterfield Bailey to the police

force and promised three more black policemen, but had gotten rid of Bailey on trumped-up charges. The previous fall a few blacks had voted Democrat, and that party had responded by naming Alex Williams to the force. The changing of policemen's beats, though, placed Williams in the heavily black First Ward—"a bone to a dog."[27]

On the evening of March 26, 1877, Sheldon and Nicholas debated each other at the courthouse. At issue was which party could be trusted. Sheldon blamed Republicans for bringing on economic hard times and for providing no rewards. Nicholas claimed that in 1873 many blacks in two wards had voted Democratic in return for the promise of three policemen, but the victorious Democrats had dishonored the pledge. He also alleged that Democrats had offered him $500, or $1 per voter, and $300 more after the election.[28]

Blacks' impatience did produce some gains in the city election that followed. Republicans took most of the races, and the new city council named an unprecedented number of black men to city posts: three policemen (one for day duty and two for nights), a city hall janitor, a waterworks fireman (John Sanders), and a hose reel driver. Most black leaders seemed pleased with these gains.[29]

Every year thereafter a vocal minority in meetings of colored Republicans inquired what white Republicans were doing to repay them, and Democrats sought to obtain their votes. In 1880 Edwin Horn and Robert Nicholas were elected delegates to the city convention for the spring municipal election. Five blacks were named to the county convention to nominate candidates for county, state, and federal races. When Republicans won the election, the Republican mayor assigned three African Americans to the police force and one each to hose houses 5 and 9. Frederick Douglass Morton was named clerk of police court. At the county convention, black delegates nominated Willis Green, a physician, as a candidate for coroner. When delegates learned that Green was African American, however, he was defeated by a white candidate on the second ballot. Whites defended the outcome by saying that the party did not recognize race distinctions.[30]

In the fall elections, Republicans charged that Democrats were falsely accusing factory owners of importing blacks to displace white laborers, encourage pauperism and crime, and swell city and county government costs. They used Horn, "a colored man of education and information living in this city," to attack the *Courier*'s "intemperate zeal and unwarranted persecutions of a much abused race . . . [which were] steadily inflaming . . . the reckless hotheads of its party. . . . [who were] encouraged to set at defiance all law and order and begin a reign of violence." Republicans swept all of the county, state,

and federal races. William Heilman was reelected to Congress. His margin of victory in the county was approximately the same as the number of black voters.[31]

The rumblings that surfaced so publicly in 1877 were evident again in 1882. Once more the protagonists were Nicholas and Carter on the one side and Sheldon (along with William Beecher this time) on the other. A "Union Committee" was formed for the spring election. Carter was its chair and Nicholas its vice chair. More than thirty prominent black men, including Willis Green, Frederick Douglass Morton, and Green McFarland, were named to it. Carter and other blacks were selected as delegates to the city convention. In the First Ward primary, against the wishes of the regulars, James W. Henderson was nominated for First Ward City Council. Andrew L. Robinson was one of his most vocal supporters. Despite the Union Committee's plea for him to drop out in deference to the white Republican candidate, he stayed in the race— and the Democrats won the slot as well as the control of city hall. The party of Jackson also swept the fall state, county, and federal races. Among other strategies, Democrats locked up hundreds of alleged "floaters" before and during election day.[32]

Later in the decade Republicans, back in power, created Hose House No. 9 to serve the black neighborhoods east of the central business district. Thereafter black firemen were appointed only to that station. Black doctors pursued appointment to the newly created post of Pigeon Township physician, which brought modest income for serving black patients. Black men also continued to seek the posts of janitor in city hall and the county courthouse.[33]

In addition to a modest expansion in the number of political jobs, blacks' sometimes problematic loyalties produced a weekly "colored people" column in the *Evansville Daily Journal*. The earliest one appears to have been published in the summer of 1872. Edwin F. Horn was probably the editor of the column from the mid-1870s to the early 1880s. In the colored column a prominent black man would, in return for a few dollars and recognition by the white editor, provide white readers and those blacks who could read and afford to purchase the newspaper an opportunity to learn about the comings and goings of black people whose activities were deemed worthy of attention. This was also a means by which powerful whites could control who spoke for the black community. By the late 1880s the Democratic *Evansville Courier* instituted a similar column. (A coincidental consequence was that readers could learn that most blacks in Evansville were neither the brutes nor the perpetual children portrayed in the headlines and news stories of both newspapers—that they, like whites, revered families, churches, clubs, and dreams of upward mobility.)[34]

In the twenty years after passage of the Fifteenth Amendment, the ties between black and white Republicans on the north bank of the Ohio became increasingly frayed. Like his Republican predecessors, the first postwar Democratic president, Grover Cleveland, appointed blacks as ministers to Haiti and Liberia and as recorder of deeds in the General Land Office. He made more black appointments to minor offices, including postmasters, than Republicans had. By then the differences between the racial policies of Democrats and Republicans were so slight that the chief appeal white Republicans could offer was the warning of what would happen to Southern blacks if Democrats controlled the White House and the Congress.[35]

Serious efforts to woo blacks away from the Republican Party in Indiana occurred for the first time in 1888. Because of the revulsion that many had for the name *Democrat,* blacks were urged instead to be independent and thus to increase their power by dividing their votes and gaining greater political reward from both parties. The new black newspaper, the *Freeman* of Indianapolis, took this position. In July of 1888 a national convention of like-minded independents met in Indianapolis. Peter H. Clark of Cincinnati was elected president of the organization. Charles E. Sheldon of Evansville was selected as temporary chairman. Republicans attempted to discredit the group by playing on the fear—which proved to be groundless—that many blacks would support the group. The *Freeman,* in turn, claimed that Republicans had threatened Sheldon and others with bodily harm.[36]

Blacks predictably gained little as a consequence of this lively campaign, in which Benjamin Harrison of Indianapolis narrowly won the presidency. James M. Townsend, formerly of Evansville, was named recorder of deeds, a position that he resigned after a few months, and he was replaced by Rev. Dolphin P. Roberts of Evansville. Another Indiana black was named minister to Liberia. Meanwhile the condition of blacks in the South worsened. While the number of lynchings grew, most Northern Republicans joined with Southern Democrats in opposing a federal elections bill designed to protect voting rights of Southern blacks. As Emma Lou Thornbrough observed about blacks' circumstances by the end of the 1880s, "in spite of Negro grumblings white Republicans showed no disposition to give them any but the lowest offices." In Evansville, "where the Negro element was expected to be satisfied with the nomination of one of their members as constable," the Republican editor asserted that "not one colored man out of a hundred is fit to hold office. They are ignorant through no fault of their own." Republicans retained kindly feelings toward blacks, he asserted, but "they cannot hand the destinies of a community over to ignorant voters."[37]

Events in Indiana were typical of north-shore African Americans' experiences after 1888. As a consequence of blacks' disillusionment over the increasing contempt with which Republicans treated them—including the failure of the Republican chairman in Evansville in 1892 to appoint blacks to any party posts—Democrats' appeal for their support steadily gained ground. The first statewide colored Democratic convention in Indiana was held in July 1894. Although most blacks remained loyal Republicans in state and federal elections, at the municipal level the story was different, as evidenced by blacks' support of Democrats Thomas Taggart and William Akin, elected mayors of Indianapolis and Evansville, respectively, in 1895 and 1897. This was most likely a local and personal phenomenon and not a precursor of a major shift in blacks' loyalties, since both men had cultivated black voters and acknowledged their indebtedness to them. Both were also personally magnetic, drew on blacks' dissatisfaction with local Republicans, and spent a great deal of money on black votes. And they rewarded blacks with city jobs.[38] George Washington Buckner of Evansville, a teacher turned physician, was leader of the Colored Akin Club. His loyalties won him harassment from the school board and the local health department. He declared that "harsh treatment had been given him on account of his color."[39]

By the 1890s, though, north-bank blacks in Indiana had secured little political power. Elective and appointive offices were few. Republicans' margins of victories at the state level made the black vote less critical for their success. Blacks were ignored in selecting candidates for state office. Most Republicans' interest in the advancement of blacks was gone, replaced by a "lily white" strategy. One Indiana Republican editor put it succinctly: Blacks were prone to sell their votes and were not to be trusted. Hundreds of thousands of lives had been lost in the war so that they could vote. They should "scorn to make merchandise of the privilege purchased for them at such a tremendous cost."[40]

The increased segregation of the era produced a semiautonomous group of political leaders whose power rested on their ability to deliver the black vote—among Republicans, such older men as Frederick Douglass Morton and such younger men as the barber William Glover; and among Democrats, George Washington Buckner. In local elections the outcome was unpredictable. Increasingly the black clergy—inherently conservative and eager to court whites' favors—took a back seat in political affairs. Businessmen and professionals with black clienteles grew more prominent. Politics provided upward mobility to enterprising young men. Especially noteworthy in Evansville was a young Tennessee-born mulatto, Ernest Tidrington, who by the end of the

century was renowned as an energetic and resourceful ally of the independent-minded Republican saloon keeper Charles Ossenberg.[41]

Circumstances in other cities and towns up and down the Ohio were little different. Blacks' political behavior has to be understood within the context of virulent white racism, an inheritance of antebellum years. Their leaders emphasized self-reliance and avoided raising subjects, especially race-mixing and social equality, that would antagonize whites.

These themes were prominent, for instance, at the fiftieth anniversary of the AME Church in Cincinnati in 1874. The pastor, Benjamin W. Arnett, stressed the value of individuals' efforts as the key to racial progress. Political activist Peter Clark, principal of Gaines High School, declared that "Methodism is adapted to our wants, and we have therefore taken it to our hearts and made it our own." Methodism added "an opportunity to demonstrate more by deeds than works the ability of the colored man to plan, to lead, to execute." Civil rights legislation enhanced that strategy.[42]

Blacks predictably aligned themselves with white Republicans, but they also formed organizations that sought greater influence, representation, and patronage within the Republican Party.[43] Where their numbers were significant—Cincinnati, Louisville, and the river counties in southwestern Illinois—they secured more than token rewards.

In Illinois, African Americans secured political offices in the early 1870s both through appointment by the governor and via the ballot box. Beginning about 1870 and extending into the late 1890s, blacks in Metropolis obtained a "gentlemen's agreement" whereby one of the Republican city aldermen would be an African American. A black policeman was also appointed to serve in the town's west end. In 1873 Governor John L. Beveridge appointed John J. Bird, a black of Cairo, trustee of the Illinois Industrial University in Urbana. Blacks were numerous enough in a few Chicago wards and in only nine Illinois counties—among them Alexander, Gallatin, Massac, and Pulaski—to be of political significance in those places. Their votes supplied the margin of victory in a number of towns where they were numerous and well organized. In 1876 Bird and William T. Scott, editor of the *Cairo Gazette,* a black newspaper, campaigned statewide for the Republican slate.[44]

Democrats resigned themselves to reality and courted the black vote. A black minister warned that such appeals were deceptive and that in Massac County "Democrats had drunk 'the blood of one poor colored man in the past two weeks.'"[45] Although Republicans retained control at the state and national levels, they had distanced themselves from equal rights, making Illi-

nois blacks restive. Bird led Cairo's blacks in attacking the quality of public education. Cairo men also protested the lack of state and federal appointments—for instance, the failure of Governor Shelby Cullom to name a black man as commissioner at the Southern Illinois Penitentiary. In the fall of 1878, Cairo blacks "reaffirmed their discontent by calling on state and Federal officials to reward their faithfulness with 'suitable positions,' thereby giving 'practical effect to the genius and character of our free American institutions.'"[46]

Although a statewide meeting in July 1880 affirmed their Republican allegiance, it also produced nonpartisan committees, at the urging of Bird, that would monitor and advance blacks' interests. The convention decried the hiring of inferior teachers for black children and created permanent committees to implement the resolutions adopted at the meeting. Later that year the executive committee of the Colored State Convention endorsed a Democrat for secretary of state. Bird and Scott of Cairo were among those who took that unprecedented step. Most of Cairo's black Republicans denounced this action.[47]

As a consequence of threatened defections to the Democratic Party, Illinois Republicans named Dr. James H. MaGee of Metropolis, a black man who formerly lived in Cincinnati, to the State Central Committee in 1882. MaGee had been appointed to the Republican Executive Committee in 1878. Bird and Scott were increasingly independent, though, and with a sizable number of their brethren in southern Illinois induced a black man, Henry Nixon, to run for the General Assembly. Nixon's campaign was short-lived, however. MaGee, whom some hoped would run for Congress, declined the honor, saying a black man could not win. He added that he hoped Republicans would remove the color line from politics. Although most blacks were "natural born Republicans," they would be happier if they received more than token appointments.[48]

The following year, a state convention of colored men, meeting shortly after the U.S. Supreme Court had declared the Civil Rights Act unconstitutional, denounced the Republican Party and the highest court for breaking faith with them. They insisted they would vote only for men who recognized blacks' right to hold political office. Over the next year black men also debated whether another federal civil rights law was necessary. MaGee declared that he "made my own civil rights by my conduct." The Civil Rights Act had "done its work, which was to protect the freedman in his infant liberty. He is now of age, and can protect himself the same as other citizens."[49]

Most blacks, though, concluded that civil rights legislation was needed. They did not agree on how to obtain it. Many believed that pursuing federal

legislation would be fruitless. MaGee was the most vocal of those who advocated a *state* law. "The civil rights bill of Ohio, passed by democrats," he declared, "had caught not only many African fish, but also white whales." In the 1884 campaign African Americans were also "increasingly active as candidates for public office." In the election Richard Oglesby was elected to a third term as governor, and Republicans gained control of the General Assembly. Led by a white representative who had faced strong opposition from a black candidate the previous year, Illinois Republicans passed a civil rights law modeled after Ohio's, and Oglesby quickly signed it into law. The linkage of the vote and citizenship rights was clear. "Political participation at all levels was the only guarantee to full enjoyment of civil and economic rights."[50]

The number and the proportion of blacks in the electorate continued to be important. Cairo's blacks had helped to transform the city from a Democratic to a Republican bastion. Black leaders like Bird, Scott, and Rev. Thomas Strothers helped ensure Republicans' domination of Cairo. Bird, the police magistrate (1873–79), was especially influential. One newspaper reported that blacks in Cairo were the best off of any in the state, since they also had policemen, three state employees, a constable, several letter carriers, and a nominee for coroner. By 1895 four black men sat simultaneously on the fourteen-member board of aldermen. Pulaski County blacks nominated a candidate for office in the primaries rather than through the Republican Central Committee. In 1880 blacks there held the county posts of coroner and commissioner. In Mound City there were more black voters per square mile than in any other Illinois town. Whites' hatred of black newcomers nonetheless remained strong. Even "respectable" blacks joined whites in urging newcomers to settle elsewhere, as evidenced by a group formed by black leaders in 1879 to discourage destitute blacks from landing in Cairo by paying their steamboat fares to St. Louis. One Cairo black man reported in November 1882 that the hatred of blacks was even more intense in Mound City.[51]

White Republicans' resentment of blacks was a festering sore that in the 1890s—as in Evansville—split former allies. Whites began to refuse to endorse black candidates and, as in the case of Metropolis, ended informal agreements over political rewards. Some began to advocate disenfranchisement. Clearly this recommendation reflected Republicans' growing strength among white voters: they no longer needed the black vote in order to maintain power. That fact, though, needs to be placed within the context of overwhelming prejudice against people of color and the loss of memory of Civil War–era struggles for freedom and equality.

Upriver, Ohio's blacks were also emboldened, but the course they recom-

mended was limited: fair treatment and consideration as citizens of their common country. They recognized their obligations to use their freedom and their
newly gained rights for the cause of racial uplift. But ambivalence remained.
Some, such as William Parham of Cincinnati, had become pessimistic about
their chances, favoring and then turning against migration to Jamaica. But
emancipation and the vote changed things. Addressing the city's blacks before
the municipal election of 1870, the first in which blacks could vote, he declared, "Fellow citizens, see how it stands."[52] Speaking to Cincinnati blacks in
1874, he declared that even the humblest ruled: "Life and death, social standing, and the pursuit of happiness, are decided by the verdict of men chosen
from the masses."[53] Like Alfred Carter in Evansville, Parham mixed joy and
hope with awareness of whites' skepticism and hostility. For most blacks, though,
faith in American values remained strong. Echoing Robert Nicholas in Evansville, one Cincinnati black leader declared, "All we ask is give us our common
and natural rights as men, and every other condition of the human family will
find its own level."[54]

Ohio's river-city black leaders wanted to consolidate their leadership and
to expand employment opportunities. The exercise of political power and the
organization of an effective voting bloc was the best means to do that. They
were initially loyal and unapologetic supporters of the party of Lincoln, but by
the mid-1870s complaints that they were being taken for granted were, as in
Illinois and Indiana, unmistakable. Their political clout—considerably greater,
statewide, than in Illinois and Indiana—produced a state civil rights bill, helped
end the separate school and intermarriage laws, and expanded political opportunity.[55]

Blacks' votes were also a significant factor in Ohio's river counties. The
passage of the Fifteenth Amendment added 400 black votes in Brown County
and about 1,700 in Hamilton County, between 5 and 10 percent of the total
electorate. The black vote ensured Republican hegemony in two previously
uncertain congressional districts, the First and the Third. In Portsmouth, blacks
represented well over 10 percent of the voters. Their power in Cincinnati and
the state's largest towns was limited, though, because their population was
dispersed and they were vastly outnumbered by whites. Republicans' showing
in the April 1870 election was, nevertheless, impressive. Blacks enabled them
to defeat Democrats, supported by Roman Catholics, who among other things
campaigned against the use of the King James version of the Bible in the
public schools.[56]

In return, blacks sought political reward. Joseph Early, son of the first black
pastor in Walnut Hills in Cincinnati, was not only a renowned chef who pre-

pared dinners for three visiting presidents, but also founder of a black Republican club. He was probably the first black elected to political office in the state when he became constable in 1869. For years he reigned as "colored boss" and disbursed the limited political spoils that blacks were given. Another black, Robert Harlan, was named as one of two Cincinnati representatives on the state Republican Central Committee in 1871. Cincinnati's African Americans formed strong political bodies—the West End Grant Club and the East End Grant Club. Modest subsidies for these clubs from white Republicans helped to sustain them. Those who held offices in these organizations, though largely ceremonial, secured great prestige. Such positions, as well as political appointments, helped to enhance the small black middle class. The two political clubs also demonstrated the reality that only an organized black front would produce results, given the huge number of white voters.[57]

But the rewards were minuscule. The only federal appointment of note was Robert Harlan's being named "special postal agent." Republicans exploited the black vote rather than shared power. Black leaders' access to white Republican command was steadily weakened, and signs of political independence appeared. Nonetheless, a large majority of blacks continued to link their welfare to the party of Lincoln.[58]

In the years that followed, Republicans charged Democrats with being enemies of blacks and friends of Roman Catholics and portrayed them as bloodthirsty men who delighted in slaughtering blacks. Democrats accused Republicans of relying on ignorant voters whom they repaid poorly. Both sides, especially in 1876, used a variety of political tricks to gain the upper hand. Democrats claimed that Republicans were "importing" black voters from Covington and Newport as well as Chicago, and the Democrat-controlled police force rounded up and detained blacks. Republican marshals did the same with white rowdies. Purportedly about 1,800 extra votes were cast in that election. Eight years later, a Democratic police lieutenant, Mike Mullen, loaded up all the black voters he could find and locked them up in the basement of the Hammond Street police station until the polls closed. That sort of strategy helped maintain the power of Democratic Party bosses in the city between 1872 and 1885. Many observers deemed Cincinnati the worst-governed city in America.[59]

In Cincinnati, blacks' restiveness led white Republicans to provide some patronage concessions. In August 1873 Peter Clark organized a state convention that addressed blacks' political concerns and called for a more independent political strategy. The convention was denounced by Cincinnati black Republican loyalists Benjamin W. Arnett, William Parham, and John Harlan in

a meeting at Allen Temple. Democrats secured control of local government during the economic hard times, and a small group of black Democrats, led by a few well-financed black Democratic clubs, emerged. Black Republican loyalists liked to portray them as disreputable residents of Rat Row. But the reality was that Republicans no longer could take black voters for granted.[60]

By 1877 Clark had become a socialist and a champion of the poor of both races. That was also a watershed year for blacks in Cincinnati. White Republicans nominated and secured the election of George Washington Williams as the state's first black legislator. From that time until 1916, Cincinnati as well as Cleveland intermittently sent black men to the Ohio legislature. One was Arnett. Thanks to Ohio Republicans' awareness that black voters could not be taken for granted, especially in Cincinnati, it was now incumbent on blacks to use the political system to advance racial interests. The number of black appointees also rose from a negligible number in the late 1870s to 164 in 1891. The first black policeman was appointed in 1884. Black employees in city and county positions were mostly laborers and servants, but some blacks became clerks and sheriff's deputies.[61]

By 1882 Clark had left the Socialist Labor Party, but not his socialist loyalties, and had become a Democrat. He and his son Herbert formed the *Cincinnati Afro-American* as the organ of Cincinnati and Ohio black Democrats. Herbert took charge of the black Democratic campaign in 1883. The following year, Peter was elected as delegate-at-large to the Democratic National Convention. The *Cleveland Gazette* equated his acts with the greed of Judas and Benedict Arnold. "The good of the race is not," it insisted, "the burden of their heart's desire as they and their few friends would have the public believe."[62]

Integrationists in Cincinnati, like those in Cleveland, were by 1885 openly critical of Clark. Because he was helping Mike Mullen, the political boss, Clark—whom many had revered as much as Frederick Douglass—was "treading the downward path a great deal faster than his worst enemies dreamed of." Critics also railed against Clark's opposition to school integration and took on the teachers' lobby, which they believed he controlled. After Arnett and others introduced a bill in 1886 that proposed the end of segregation in public schools, the writing was on the wall for him. His Cincinnati critics—buttressed by the fact that Republicans had gained control of the school board—charged him with bribery and removed him from his administrative position at Gaines High School. Clark's departure weakened opposition to the desegregation bill, which went into effect in 1887. Clark wandered from job to job afterward; it was a sad end to the thirty-year career of a once revered and powerful man.

The *Cleveland Gazette* praised his stellar achievements in education and wondered why he had chosen to move into politics, where his actions proved to be ruinous to his career.[63]

Kentucky was forced to accept blacks' voting, just as it had emancipation and equal rights. Most of its postwar leaders, whether statewide or in Louisville, were former Confederate officers who had no use for black voters. But influential men like Henry Watterson took a pragmatic view: that it was better for the state's image and economic development to decry lawlessness in order to attract Northerners with capital to invest. And some strong Unionist leaders, like John Marshall Harlan, moved to the city after the war. The *Louisville Commercial,* beginning in 1868, was for thirty years a champion of racial moderation.[64]

Kentucky blacks, moreover, were not passive observers. At least four state conventions were held before 1870. Prominent in these were Rev. George W. Dupee of Paducah, Horace Morris of Louisville, and W.F. Butler of Jefferson County. Each of these black men addressed the challenges and the opportunities that freedom and citizenship offered. Conventions were held regularly from 1870 onward.[65]

In the spring of 1870, white Republicans selected blacks George A. Griffith of Owensboro and J.B. Stansberry of Louisville, among others, to canvass the state in order to explain the meaning of the newly adopted Fifteenth Amendment and to generate support for Republican candidates. White Republicans had earlier scorned blacks' efforts to participate in party affairs. A black Republican party was organized in February 1870 at a Louisville convention presided over by Rev. Henry J. Young, who declared that the vote would allow blacks to reverse the pattern of postwar elections dominated by Democrats.[66]

Kentucky black men voted for the first time in August 1870. Historian Edmund Starling recalled that the "election [in Henderson County] passed off as quietly as any that had . . . preceded it." That was not necessarily an apt description of events elsewhere. In some towns Democrats tried to get some blacks to run for office as a means of dividing the Republican vote. City fathers in Louisville altered the city charter to permit a municipal election to occur before the Fifteenth Amendment took effect. Some whites intimidated prospective black voters with loss of land and of jobs, and access to the polls was made difficult in many places. But black men voted in large numbers, and they voted Republican. Records indicate, though, that a higher percentage of white men were deemed eligible voters.[67]

As on the north bank, white Republicans' hold on black voters was not

guaranteed, largely because they failed to provide political rewards. In Louisville, no black was elected to office, and only a few received local or state political positions. Black delegates were seated at the state Republican convention for the first time in 1872. J.B. Stansberry was named temporary secretary. George Griffith of Owensboro, one of the black delegates, insisted that the party reward its black faithful. A compromise was achieved that satisfied few, and the matter of political spoils would remain a perennial issue thereafter.[68]

Some Kentucky blacks bolted the party in 1872 and voted for Horace Greeley. A number of black Republicans in Kenton County, for example, denounced the county convention's endorsement of Grant, and fourteen of the seventeen delegates (including all of the black ones) from the county walked out of the state convention when they were asked to support Grant. A national "Colored Liberal Convention" was held in Louisville in October 1872 to generate support for Greeley. A vast majority of black voters in Kentucky cities remained loyal to Grant, but black stump speakers competed with black regulars for their attention.[69]

During the 1870s, some blacks joined the Democratic Party, leaving the Republicans for good. Louisville's first black physician, Henry Fitzbutler, advocated political independence. For doing so, and for his outspoken opposition to segregated schools, he was ostracized by black Republican leaders. William H. Ward, who ran unsuccessfully for marshal of city court in 1877, was hired by the city's Democratic officials as janitor at the courthouse. Political favors also were provided several other prominent black men, notably Madison Minnis and William H. Gibson. But none of these men claimed to be Democrats, since that would have weakened their standing in the black community. Democrats did not depend on the black vote and offered these few political plums to blacks aspiring to hold office in order to buy them off.[70]

Although impatience with Republicans' failure to deliver rewards grew stronger, most blacks' suspicion of the Democrats persisted. Democratic legislators, for instance, failed to protect them from the threats of white regulators and did not permit blacks to testify in court. Impediments to voting were erected, including poll taxes, trick ballots, and especially election-day violence. But in 1873 black leaders praised the Democrat-controlled legislature for passing laws permitting blacks to testify and creating public schools for blacks. Both parties actively bade for the black vote thereafter. The *Louisville Courier-Journal* declared in the summer of 1877 that Republicans could not "calculate with any certainty on wielding the Negro vote as a unit."[71]

Marion Lucas has argued that blacks' best opportunity to share political

power with white Republicans, especially in cities, occurred in the 1870s. Where blacks had large numbers, they could influence party decisions, though they were rarely granted the right to hold office. More commonplace were racially balanced selection committees that gave blacks the chance to choose white Republican candidates. Louisville's blacks were neither aloof from political activity nor reluctant to effect change through the ballot box, and they remained frustrated by Republicans' manipulation and abuse. As on the north shore, white Republicans increasingly reached out to white voters and de-emphasized their connections with blacks, even though their power depended heavily on them. On the two occasions when they controlled city government in Louisville, Republicans hired blacks only as menial laborers. They repeatedly endorsed no black for public office. Increasingly Louisville's black Republicans pursued a policy of enlightened self-interest, voting only for those whites whose policies were deemed sympathetic. A few—notably Dr. Fitzbutler—defied party opposition and ran for political office.[72]

Black political clubs were essential to Republicans' chances at the polls. Since white Republicans were generally out of power, they offered modest financial support to these organizations as well as to the black newspapers that appeared in election years. Club members were patrons of whites, and hence their activities benefited themselves and not, as they claimed, the race. The clubs' duties were to get out the vote and to keep blacks in line. Some crumbs were offered their members. Clubs sought to ensure loyalty by offering political favors, and if that tactic did not work, they turned to face-to-face appeals for community solidarity. If these failed, they resorted to character assassination, getting out the vote to campaign against independents. When Dr. Fitzbutler campaigned for the school board in the 1880s, he had no chance of winning, but political clubs campaigned against him, making his margin of loss even greater. Fitzbutler's loss had a chilling effect on others. Black attorney Nathaniel R. Harper had thought about running for office, but in 1886 white Republicans co-opted him by offering him a job—a welcome source of income, given the poverty of his clients.[73]

The year 1886 was the first one in which the threat of political independence by Louisville's blacks paid off. Blacks were seated at the Republican state convention, and two black men were nominated for county office—Horace Morris for court clerk and W.H. Gibson Sr. for coroner. Both men lost in the general election. Blacks subsequently ran Gibson as an independent candidate for Congress, but on the eve of the election he withdrew under pressure from white Republicans. Blacks were embittered by the treatment they had received from both parties, but most returned to the Republican fold

the following spring, using the old strategy of pressuring the party for com-
promises. They also nominated a black man for superintendent of public instruction, but whites voted him down.[74]

Louisville's Democratic party, controlled by "Boss" John Whallen, ignored
and insulted blacks but did not practice the virulent behavior of its counterparts farther south. White Democrats' "polite racism" allowed them to pride
themselves on their "progressive" treatment of blacks—leaving them alone.
On those few occasions when Republicans had a chance of winning, though,
Watterson and other prominent whites used the race card to arouse whites'
fears. In 1887, when Democratic "reformers" ran a separate candidate against
Boss Whallen, Republicans assumed that the split would be to their advantage.
Reformers as well as regulars arbitrarily arrested blacks, bought votes, kept
many from registering, and used outright violence in order to ensure that the
black vote would not tip the balance. The "reform" slate won, but the tactics
used to gain its victory convinced civic leaders of the need for the secret ballot,
and Louisville became the first city in America to use it. Bribery was common,
especially of black men. A party worker would give a prospective voter a dollar
or two, and then the party worker would mark the ballot for the voter if he did
not do it himself.[75]

By the mid–1880s south-bank blacks were of two minds—going slow or
demanding a share of political offices. Younger leaders were less conservative.
Delegates to one convention addressed twenty questions, including one asking
whether blacks owed the party of Lincoln any loyalty. Each debate led to the
same two answers: the Republicans were superior to the Democrats, but they
refused to treat blacks as equal partners. Six hundred gathered in 1887 and
formed the Independent Party of the Colored Race, claiming to be neither
Republican nor Democrat and to be for the party that befriended African
Americans. Some talked a few months later about running an independent for
governor. Nothing came of these efforts.[76]

Political rewards for Kentucky's blacks were extremely limited. More of
them were given in districts where blacks were in a clear majority of the
Republican Party and could potentially run a candidate of their own, or where
their numbers forced whites to make concessions on candidates and spoils.
Other achievements were invisible—when, for instance, black individuals were
able to make deals with white leaders that, typically, padded the pockets of
those making the deals.[77]

Increasing impatience in Louisville gave blacks more patronage positions
than in any other town along the lower Ohio. But the positions were menial
ones—primarily jobs as porters, janitors, and sanitation workers. Few were

employed in skilled, professional, and clerical positions. City and county workers received coal and food assistance during hard times and unemployment.[78]

The signs of the times were obvious when white discontent with Democratic rule helped to lead to the first Republican victory: the election of a congressman in 1894. White Republicans refused to endorse the aims of a club formed by Dr. Fitzbutler that sought, among other things, to elect blacks to office. When Tenth Ward members helped elect Nathaniel R. Harper as their candidate for the state legislature the following year, white leaders changed the rules for nominating candidates and offered Harper, a struggling attorney, a job speaking to black voters in the fall if he dropped his candidacy. Fitzbutler's club was so angered that it did not endorse Republicans in the 1895 city election, but the Republicans won anyway. Despite an appeal from loyal black leaders, blacks were not added to high level patronage jobs. In fact, none would be hired on the police force until 1923, the same year that the first all-black fire company was created.[79]

It was clear by the mid-1880s that the national mood about the status of African Americans was changing, and not for the better. What else could be done than to encourage blacks to "strive and succeed"? Formal and informal segregation along racial lines was being intensified. Decades-long agreements between white and black Republicans were eroding, and Republican and Democratic newspapers on both sides of the river spoke of the growing menace to public safety and morals that the "shiftless" element represented.[80]

North-bank civil rights laws made those states appear more tolerant than Kentucky. In practice, the treatment of blacks differed only by degree. Obsession with the "Negro problem" was omnipresent. By the 1890s it was apparent that in a number of Ohio River cities and towns there were organized efforts to rid communities of the "shiftless" element. Consequently, for instance, the percentage of African Americans in the twenty-four counties on both banks of the river below the Falls declined between 1880 and 1900. Whether the decrease was traceable solely to economic conditions is worth examining.[81]

9

Making a Living

The ending of the Civil War transformed labor on both banks of the Ohio. Emancipation offered thousands a chance for a new start. Many blacks moved to cities and towns, although in Kentucky most remained on the land. The larger places—Cincinnati, Evansville, and Louisville—became sprawling, manufacturing-based towns that created new forms of blue- and white-collar employment. That meant little to African Americans, though, because most of them would be mired in the same menial labor and service positions that they had held for decades.[1] Nonetheless, a small number of black men and women created businesses and professions, acquired property, and rose well above their humble roots.

Employment patterns in north-shore states were similar. In Indiana virtually all of the blacks who worked the land were farm laborers or renters of farms. Those settling in cities and towns found most types of employment closed to them, not primarily because they lacked skills, but because of racial discrimination.[2] A few opened their own businesses, and some entered government service. Most, though, were laborers or servants—for example, in Evansville in 1880, 91 percent of black workers were in those categories; twenty years later, the figure was 93 percent. The vast majority of New Albany's black male workers were employed at the city wharf or in street maintenance. Married females also made up a large part of the black workforce. Most white women shunned employment as "unbecoming," but black women worked because of economic necessity. One consequence was that a consid-

erably higher proportion of blacks than whites participated in the labor force. Hard work did not guarantee progress, though, since labor and service jobs paid less than factory and clerical work.[3]

Even the jobs that blacks could get were not secure. A combination of hard times, unemployment, and hardening racial views led whites to covet certain jobs in the service sector and to replace blacks in them. Technology also worked to the disadvantage of blacks. The declining use of steamboats for passenger traffic cut drastically into the black workforce. In Cincinnati, for instance, the percentage of black men working around and on steamboats between 1860 and 1890 dropped from 13 percent to less than 2 percent. (Subsequently, motorized delivery vehicles would displace black teamsters, cabbies, and draymen.)[4]

By 1890 only 2,287 Indiana black men out of a black population over 45,000 were "engaged in trades which could in any sense be classified as skilled." Lack of training was a factor, but even more significant was the negative attitudes of whites. Most employers refused to hire blacks, and almost all unions barred blacks from membership. The short-lived Knights of Labor created colored chapters in several Indiana cities, including Evansville. There "were a few black members of the United Mine Workers, but probably none in any of the other A. F. of L. affiliates." Some belonged to unions of black teamsters, hod carriers, pottery makers, shovelers, and blacksmiths.[5]

Occupational prospects declined while, coincidentally, educational opportunities increased. This state of affairs demoralized black youth and led to cutthroat competition for the few relatively good jobs. Many black men were willing to engage in strikebreaking, which was most widespread in the coal mines as early as 1880. At that time black men were brought from Kentucky to break strikes in the coal-rich region of Indiana that extended northward from Vanderburgh and Warrick counties.[6]

A small business and professional class emerged in cities that had black populations large enough to sustain it. As of 1880 black Evansville had a grocery, three saloons, and an "eating house." In the decade that followed, it also gained an insurance agency, a pharmacy, and a few small black-owned hotels on Water and Walnut streets. There were more black barbers, whose customers were mostly white. Black-owned barbershops in Evansville, Jeffersonville, Madison, and New Albany were smaller in scale and number, though, than in Indianapolis. In Evansville, four men whose careers can be traced from the 1870 census to the 1891 city directory—James Amos, Augustus Carter, John Grandison, and William Jones—established barbershops.[7]

Ministers and teachers dominated the black professions. They served an

exclusively black clientele and had enormous influence in community affairs. Black doctors and lawyers also served only black clients, but there were few of them outside of Indianapolis. Evansville and New Albany had the only black physicians among the state's Ohio River cities. In 1880 Evansville's Willis Green was the first African American certified by the county clerk to practice medicine. Tradition says that he learned medicine sitting in the back of a lecture hall at the Evansville Medical College while the white man who employed him as chauffeur took classes. Two others, Jeremiah Jackson and George Washington Buckner, opened practices around 1890. Denied admission to the city's white hospitals and serving poor clients, black doctors faced formidable odds trying to make a living. Racism also limited blacks' access to medical care: Evansville had one black physician for every 1,234 blacks, as compared with one white physician for every 400 whites. Evansville did not have black lawyers until the early 1890s, when there were two in practice, and both departed within a year or two because of the lack of business.[8]

Patterns in Ohio and Illinois were similar. Black businesses and professions were most numerous and diversified in Cincinnati. A few black men in southwestern Illinois achieved prominence in law and the newspaper business. In counties across from Appalachian Kentucky, some found jobs in coal mines. Increasingly, black barbers lost out to white competitors, who played the race card to lure white customers away from them. Few blacks worked in factories, and blacks were barred by unions from the skilled trades. In accordance with these factors, by 1890 19 percent of Cincinnati's male laborers and 22 percent of male servants were African American. Among women, 46 percent of the servants and 38 percent of the laundresses were nonwhites.[9]

In south-bank towns also, competition from whites and frequent economic downturns meant that even menial employment was uncertain, and unemployment rates were high. Often the only choice for a black man was between remaining idle and becoming a strikebreaker. The reality of the workplace was stark. Whites were hostile to blacks who sought occupations that were not perceived as "nigger work." Unions excluded blacks, although some all-black locals, notably the Hod Carriers Union in Louisville, were organized. In rural areas, the options for the vast majority of workers were domestic service, farm labor, or apprenticeships—the latter a thinly veiled form of slavery. Efforts of sympathetic whites to advance the race were rebuffed. John G. Fee, for example, was unable to organize companies that would purchase land and then sell lots at reasonable prices to blacks. Nonetheless, some African Americans were able to buy farms, and in cities and towns a small but impressive number

purchased lots and dwellings. In Louisville and some smaller cities, moreover, black businesses were created.[10]

The situation was especially harsh in the winter of 1865–66, the first one after passage of the Thirteenth Amendment. The end of slavery created an agricultural labor crisis and sparked efforts by whites to establish new forms of control over blacks. The legislature fashioned a contract labor system that favored the master: for example, it permitted him to negate a year's pay, near the end of the annual contract, for behavior deemed inappropriate. The Freedmen's Bureau sought—often unsuccessfully—fair enforcement of labor contracts and refused to permit an overseer system.[11]

The bureau's courts took action in about one thousand cases, mostly grievances against employers' efforts to drive blacks from farms, not efforts to settle contracts. The bureau ensured that many labor arrangements were for wages, more secure than annual contracts. Regulators, however, continued to operate freely, notably in Daviess, Boone, and Kenton counties, thereby encouraging migration to towns in the summer of 1867. An economic downturn in late summer accelerated the process, which exacerbated overcrowding in towns like Covington and Owensboro. Improved economic circumstances and lessened vigilantism led some to return to the land the following spring, but regulators' outrages persisted, especially in January, the hiring time for the year. Violence was particularly malevolent in 1871.[12]

To woo black laborers, white farmers—who needed a reliable supply of farm workers—persuaded the legislature in 1871 to abolish the contract labor law, thus (on paper) giving black and white tenants equal status. The 1871 and 1873 legislatures also attempted, with some success, to minimize white vigilantism. Consequently the number of blacks who owned their own land increased modestly. Blacks' economic and social gains were chiefly due to whites' pragmatism, not legislative benevolence.[13]

When cross-river settlements are compared and contrasted, the similarities and differences are striking. In general, predominantly agricultural and rural north-shore counties—for example, Hardin and Pope counties in Illinois; Posey and Warrick counties in Indiana; and Adams and Brown counties in Ohio—had much in common with their south-shore counterparts. Most men worked on farms they did not own, and women were engaged in domestic service. Kentucky laborers, though, faced several idiosyncratic circumstances: the state's apprenticeship law; involvement in a distinctly Southern kind of farming, share-cropping; and pervasive vigilantism. Terrain and local agricultural and natural resources also shaped employment patterns on both sides of the Ohio.

In Appalachian Boyd County, Kentucky, for instance, one-quarter of the 206 black residents in 1870 lived in Ashland and about one-third in upriver Catlettsburg. Virtually all African Americans were enumerated in black-headed residences. Of the 35 black heads of household, 18 were laborers. Just 4 were farmers—a reflection of the fact that agriculture in that part of the state was not particularly lucrative. The most affluent was Alex Jamison Sr., age fifty and a blacksmith. One of his seven children, Alex junior, was a carpenter who lived next door. The oldest son living in the elder Jamison's home was a plasterer.[14]

Ten years later the growth of coal mining and railroads in that part of Kentucky and neighboring West Virginia was manifest in the African American population, which had nearly tripled. Those residing in or near Ashland accounted for about half of the county's blacks. A number of the men were railroad hands, coal diggers, and workers in coal tips. Most, however, were common laborers. Six household heads were employed as domestics or as servants in newly established hotels and restaurants.[15]

Campbell County, with a relatively small black population, was somewhat similar to Boyd. About half of the blacks lived in Newport, where almost all adults were domestics or laborers. Significantly, one-quarter of the black population lived in white households, employed as servants or farmhands. Campbell County experienced some change in the 1870s. Newport's black population more than doubled, to 242—four of five black residents in the county, reflecting distress in the rural economy and job opportunities in the city. But remnants of the past persisted. In Newport, as elsewhere on the south bank, a high proportion of blacks continued to live in white households—in this case, one in six. The social significance of this pattern is developed in chapter 10.[16]

Downstream Kenton County was larger and more economically advanced than Campbell County before the war, owing to its proximity to Cincinnati's waterfront. The completion of the Roebling suspension bridge in 1867 further increased the difference. African Americans numbered nearly 1,700 by 1870, nearly three times the 1860 population. Almost 1,100 lived in Covington, where most were employed as laborers or servants. The largest number resided in Ward 4. In Wards 1 and 2, where a number of wealthy whites lived, two-fifths of the blacks resided in white households and worked as servants. In the other wards, relatively few lived with whites.[17]

Kenton County grew during the 1870s, as did its African American population. Three in four blacks lived in Covington, a ratio similar to neighboring Campbell County's town-country ratio. Otherwise, little had changed. Most workers outside the city were farmhands, and inside the city common or day laborers, washerwomen, and servants. In Wards 3 and 4, many household heads

worked in coal yards and in factories, principally glass factories. A large proportion (40%) residing in the wealthiest ward, Ward 1, were servants living in white-headed households. There were also five clergymen, and the city had a black teacher: John S. McLeod, a native of Ohio, who had arrived with his wife and children sometime between 1874 and 1878.[18]

Across the river, Cincinnati had a large enough black community to sustain a number of businesses and professions, though the number was small compared with Cleveland and Louisville numbers. The first businesses were barbershops, the earliest of which had opened in 1845. In the early 1880s prominent black "tonsorial parlors" were George W. Stevens's at 172 Central Avenue and Hogan's on Sixth Street, near Race. The African American Republican newspaper the *Cleveland Gazette,* which was launched in August 1883 and had a Cincinnati column, was sold at these two businesses. Undertaking had also been an early and lucrative line of work for blacks. A number of other black businessmen earned fortunes: Robert Harlan, who bought and sold racehorses; Robert Gordon, who ran a coal firm; Thomas Schooley, who owned a pickling company; Alfred Thompson, who had a tailoring business; Pressley Ball and Alexander Thomas, photographers; and Samuel Wilcox, a grocer. The black aristocracy also included African American butlers, light-skinned mulattoes like Ben Hunter, considered the "prince" of the city. Such men, like barbers, served white clienteles.[19]

The editor of the *Gazette* labeled Cincinnati's black community the "Paris of America" because of the large number of wealthy and intelligent black citizens and its good schools. Nothing, he asserted, would demonstrate racial progress more than the establishment of a black newspaper, but limited capital and advertising income prevented that from occurring in Cincinnati. Articles in the *Cleveland Gazette* or in the white local dailies had to suffice. A "colored column" was created about 1884 in the Republican *Cincinnati Commercial Gazette* and in December 1887 in the Democratic *Cincinnati Enquirer.*[20]

Lack of capital and black patronage also thwarted the establishment of black hotels until the early twentieth century. The absence of such accommodations proved embarrassing when black visitors from the north came to town. J.P. Green, a black legislator from Cleveland, arrived in Cincinnati for Labor Day celebrations but was denied a room at all the city's hotels, despite entreaties by the welcoming committee. He was forced to spend the night in a cheap restaurant.[21]

African Americans in Cincinnati faced strong opposition from white trade unions. One factor was that although their numbers were large, their proportion of the total population was small, and it declined as the number of white

newcomers grew. Cincinnati's Trades and Labor Assembly, reorganized in 1864, refused to admit women and black laborers. Iron workers in the foundries of Cincinnati prohibited black membership, and the bricklayers union of the city refused to honor the travel cards of visiting union-affiliated black bricklayers. The Knights of Labor attempted to transcend race and gender barriers, but there is no evidence of black participation in local assemblies. Blacks did form a union of hod carriers.[22]

A notable exception was the short-lived Union Labor Party (ULP). Linked to the Democratic Party, it was class- rather than race-oriented, but its clubs were racially segregated. In 1888, to reach out to black Republicans, the ULP nominated Alfred R. Paige, a waiter and the president of the Ward 5 Colored Union Labor Club, as a candidate for the state legislature. The ULP faded from the scene after the election, in which Paige and party candidates were defeated.[23]

Downriver Trimble County, Kentucky, offered evidence of continuity with antebellum labor patterns. Not only did it remain rural and agriculture-dependent, but also about half the blacks in the county lived in white households as farmhands, domestics, cooks, and nurses (the nurses were girls of ages ten to fifteen). Entire black families lived in these households, often sharing the surname of the white head of household. Some change was evident by 1880. Slightly more blacks inhabited households that blacks headed. For example, in Milton Precinct, opposite Madison, Indiana, about two of three households with black residents had black men or women at the head.[24]

Across the river, the African American population of Jefferson County, Indiana, in 1870 was somewhat different from its prewar configuration. It was about 50 percent larger, and nearly three in four of the blacks resided in Ohio River townships or in the city of Madison. The majority of black workers outside of Madison were farmers and farm laborers, but only a few owned their farms. A huge majority, 90 percent, dwelled in residences headed by blacks. In Madison, although most household heads were employed in common labor or service, some had skilled employment: there were a plasterer, a carpenter, an engineer, three barbers, and three engineers. Over the following decade, black employment in rural Jefferson County declined somewhat, but it doubled in Madison. About one-third of the blacks resided in Wards 4 and 5. Labor patterns resembled those of 1870.[25]

Louisville resembled Cincinnati more than its south-shore counterparts. Jobs and public schools, along with the freedom associated with big-city life, attracted a steady stream of newcomers. This was part of a larger sectional trend, the migration of blacks to urban areas. In 1870 Louisville ranked elev-

enth among cities with sizable black populations. In the decades that followed, decennial increases ranged from 37 to 40 percent, the highest or second-highest among those cities. By 1900 it was the seventh-ranked city in number of blacks.[26]

Jobs were plentiful, but vestiges of slave labor remained. Barbering and cartage were lucrative occupations. In 1870 an estimated 150 black draymen owned their own horses or mules and wagons. Carpenters, blacksmiths, painters, builders, and bricklayers also made a relatively easy transition to freedom. A few blacks found profitable employment as messengers for banks, railroad companies, and other businesses. Others established groceries, restaurants, realty agencies, and furniture dealerships. A short-lived black newspaper, the *Weekly Planet,* was established in 1874. Blacks also organized the Louisville Cemetery Association in 1886.[27]

A branch of the Freedmen's Savings and Trust Bank—the largest branch of that bank—was opened in Louisville in September 1865 and was strongly supported by blacks. Aware of the value of deferring pleasure and saving for homes, schools, and other necessities, black depositors numbered three thousand by 1874, and deposits totaled $3 million. Horace Morris, the cashier, was an excellent administrator. The branch had an advisory board that was considered one of the best in the Freedmen's Bank: Morris, Washington Spradling, and Henry Adams, as well as several eminent whites. Unfortunately, fraud, inept bookkeeping, and economic depression—none the fault of this branch—led to the bank's demise in 1874. Thousands lost their savings.[28]

The inability to organize another bank symbolized the plight of African Americans in the years that followed. Few gains were realized by the early twentieth century. Most blacks performed menial day labor that was "dirty, unpleasant, and often dangerous." Some black men, though, gained respect from whites because of their skill and diplomacy in certain positions. The highest-prestige jobs in Louisville, as elsewhere, involved close contact with whites that required blacks to be discreet as well as deferential: barber, messenger, janitor, and waiter, among others. Louisville's whites liked to think that blacks there were better off than in other Southern cities, because their wages were higher and servants were treated like family members. Unlike other Southern cities, however, Louisville barred blacks from serving as firemen, policemen, clerical workers, and so forth, for the local government. A city ordinance of 1877 required that the city hire only white employees.[29]

Blacks' successes in business came chiefly in barbering and in undertaking. Most establishments were marginal; they were vulnerable to technological change, fluctuations in the size of the black community, and the vicissitudes of

the economy. The decline in passenger steamboat traffic eroded the number of river-related jobs, and the internal combustion engine would soon destroy the transfer businesses. But there were enough black residents of the city to support black attorneys, dentists, and physicians.[30]

Louisville's economy, like Cincinnati's, was transformed in the decades after the war. Rail connections enhanced the city's strength as a wholesale and retail trade and manufacturing center. As in Cincinnati, though, occupational patterns among blacks were not altered in the process. In 1890, 65 percent of the female servants and 60 percent of the male servants in the city were African Americans. Such work was "demeaning and unappealing and the wages were too low. Indeed, in 1885 and again in 1886 . . . black female servants worked sixty hours a week for $3.00."[31] Half of Louisville's black domestics were married.

Black men continued to be overrepresented among waiters and barbers. In the first census to identify the position of waiter, four of five were African Americans. The city's leading hotels and private clubs used only black waiters. Most of them worked long hours and received low pay. Since remuneration was based on tips, it was uncertain. Only headwaiters, esteemed by white patrons, were paid adequately. Barbering paid the best wages. Barbers often rented space in white hotels and served the local elite and visitors to the city. They held their own, unlike barbers in Cincinnati. At the end of the 1880s, about 30 percent of the city's barbers were black. Louisville whites "felt secure with blacks performing services for them, since they deemed this as part of the southern tradition. They were unaffected by the argument that black barbers and waiters were taking jobs from whites."[32]

Most blacks, however, were common laborers—digging ditches, hauling boxes, cleaning streets, working in the sewers, and sweeping floors. All of these were poorly paid at work that was often seasonal. Half of the common laborers enumerated in the 1890 census were African American men. Black women were also laborers, primarily in laundries and food processing or tobacco factories. In 1890 84 percent of the city's laundresses were African Americans. In tobacco factories most of the black workers rehandled tobacco, turning it into snuff, cigars, and cigarettes. It was a dusty and unhealthful task that paid less than a dollar a day. Unlike white women, who were paid by the week, black women were paid a piece rate and sat at their desks all day, even eating their lunches there. Because opportunities for employment in clerical and telephone positions siphoned off many white women, the proportion of black female tobacco workers grew steadily. African American women were denied employment in the city's woolen mills.

Black men engaged in arduous and disagreeable work that whites avoided. Most of the sewer workers, for instance, were blacks who worked long days in unsanitary conditions, earning $1.50 a day. In July 1877—a time of national worker restiveness—they went on strike for better wages and working conditions as well as for union recognition. The mayor organized a militia that quickly crushed the strike, and he fired strike leaders. Blacks were also predominant among livery stable keepers, cleaning the stables and feeding and washing the thousands of horses and mules that were essential to transportation. City government used black men on road and bridge crews and to demolish old buildings.

Blacks were also ubiquitous among L&N Railroad workers, although the small number of conductors, engineers, firemen, switchmen, and brakemen declined over time. Newly organized railroad unions generally barred blacks, and white workers often struck to ensure that black workers were replaced with whites. Most blacks had the most unskilled and grueling jobs—laying and repairing track, serving as water boys and cooks in the camp cars, cleaning coaches, and loading and unloading freight cars. The most desired positions were those of waiter, cook, and porter, which despite long hours and low pay carried the potential for whites' esteem and reward.

Initially many skilled black workers were blacksmiths, carpenters, brick makers, cabinetmakers, and painters—a reflection of skills gained during slavery. Black leaders like William J. Simmons promoted such employment through "industrial education." But over time the proportion of blacks in such positions dwindled. Denial of access to the building trades was an important factor; by the 1890s most apprenticeships were closed. Another was pressure from white competitors, such as those who unsuccessfully attempted to force the city's only black brick maker out of business in 1890. A third factor was that skills like blacksmithing and shoemaking that were taught boys at Central High School were becoming obsolete.

Louisville was also an anti-union city. Large employers like the L&N Railroad regularly and arbitrarily cut wages. Most blacks were employed in occupations that had little bargaining power and were unable to form unions. Hod carriers, musicians, and brick makers, who competed successfully with whites, were admitted to unions, but this achievement amounted to "a move by whites to control blacks as much as anything else." White musicians, for instance, were "tired of seeing blacks get the better jobs, [and] encouraged the formation of a black musicians' union in an attempt to regulate the number of black musicians in Louisville." Denied membership in the white local, blacks were permitted to serve on the consolidated union board.[33]

Most of the city's organized black workers in the 1880s belonged to the Knights of Labor. The high-water mark for interracial cooperation was May 1, 1886, when six thousand black and white workers joined together in a daylong demonstration for the eight-hour day. By contrast, when American Federation of Labor (AFL) president Samuel Gompers came to Louisville for the May Day parade in 1890, blacks marched at the end of the grand parade. Afterward, blacks and whites held their picnics and festivities in separate parks.

Some unions were African American: waiters and cooks, hod carriers, coopers, teamsters, and hacks organized locals. The most active of them was Waiters' and Cooks' Alliance no. 261, whose business manager found employment for blacks in hotels, clubs, and restaurants and at banquets, balls, and receptions. The union's rented room on Fifth Street was used for social and recreational purposes as well as for union meetings. There was at least one racially integrated local, Rainbow Union no. 14, an organization of tobacco workers. Blacks constituted one-quarter of the city's tobacco workers. Thomas N. Williams, the first African American member of the union, recruited a number of his fellow workers. He rose in the ranks, representing the local at the international meeting of tobacco workers and becoming a vice president of the union.

Rarely was a black hired in a position of authority in local government or private business. For educated blacks, the most attractive employment was in the post office. Gained through taking the civil service examination, such positions as clerk and letter carrier provided security and status and allowed some blacks to pursue additional business ventures or to attend school. William H. Steward, for example, worked at the post office and also published a religious newspaper, the *American Baptist*.

Blacks could avoid insults and discrimination by forming their own businesses. "Of all the ideas in the late-nineteenth-century Afro-American community, blacks put most faith in business ownership as a way to economic independence." A black newspaper in 1885 highlighted Louisville's achievements. In addition to three furniture dealers who had been in business since the late 1860s, there were "fine" black-owned barbershops that served white men, eight groceries, and several other establishments. Two men ran the most lucrative business, undertaking. Ten years later another newspaper listed these black businesses: "two tailor shops, twenty restaurants, ten saloons, three newspapers, twenty barbershops, three carpenter shops, three blacksmith shops, and several funeral homes."[34]

The most successful black-owned businesses were those catering solely either to white or to black customers. Two of Louisville's most successful black

businessmen were E.I. Masterson and David L. Knight. The former, a graduate of the tailoring department at Tuskegee Institute, made fashionable and expensive gowns, suits, and other clothing for white patrons in his shop at West and Walnut streets. Knight formed the Lightning Transfer Company, a firm that secured many contracts with white customers and lasted thirteen years. The steady growth of white racism in the late nineteenth century eroded white customers' patronage of such firms. The businesses that survived were of the mom and pop variety with little capital and marginal profits. So few blacks accumulated business experience that highly profitable enterprises like furniture-making ceased to exist when their owners died.[35]

Some successful black ventures depended only on black customers. Before the middle of the 1880s, black undertaking establishments failed, as a rule, because of competition from white funeral homes. But white customers increasingly disliked having white undertakers serve blacks; the blacks were either denied service or charged twice the regular price. The door was opened thereby for enterprising black undertakers like William Watson, who formed a company in 1887 and earned a great deal of money. He was probably the city's wealthiest black man when he died in 1905. By 1908 there were ten black undertakers in Louisville.

Louisville's large black professional class distinguished it among cities of its size. At the end of the 1880s there were 59 clergymen, 8 lawyers, 13 physicians, and more than 100 teachers. Louisville had more black attorneys than the whole state of Georgia and more black doctors than any city in Ohio. The challenges facing black attorneys and doctors, however, were enormous. Totally reliant on poor blacks for their livelihood, many either left the city or found other forms of employment. The medical practice of Henry Fitzbutler, established in 1871, suffered for years because of his patients' poverty. Black physicians were also denied access to the city's hospitals.

The careers of George A. Griffith of Owensboro and N.R. Harper of Louisville, the first attorneys to receive their licenses to practice (in 1871), faced similar tests. By 1893 there were seven black attorneys in the commonwealth—three in Louisville, but none in any other Ohio River community. Harper, the most influential, was a native of Indianapolis who was educated in Detroit before coming to Louisville in 1869. Enduring years of racial prejudice, he became the first black to preside as a city court judge and won for blacks the right to sit on Kentucky juries. His clients eventually included not only prominent and ordinary individuals but also the city's black Methodist churches and its real estate and relief association. Harper survived financially, however, by securing Republican Party appointments to several minor posts.[36]

Quite a few professionals were full-time teachers. Black leaders, who often disagreed bitterly over how the schools were run, "at least had a say in who taught at the schools. Like the U.S. Post Office, the school system offered more security . . . and a higher wage than most jobs." There was intense competition for a limited number of positions, and black leaders "used their influence to win jobs in the school system for themselves, their friends, and, most especially, their children. In fact, a group of black teachers and principals developed a vested interest in running the black schools."[37]

In general, blacks in Louisville "made few gains in employment between 1870 and 1915." Whites had a large pool of cheap and exploitable labor at their disposal and a means of coercing blacks into supporting the white power structure. African Americans were underrepresented in most occupations and overrepresented in others. The relatively large number of black professionals was a consequence of the large size of the black community, but even the white-collar blacks eked out marginal incomes. Most black businesses could not compete with white businessmen who wished to tap the black market.[38]

Across the river in New Albany, the small size of the black community made for a bleaker situation. In the first postwar census, the number of blacks was substantially higher than ten years earlier, but the total population was infinitesimal compared with Louisville's. The proportion of African Americans was also much smaller, about 8 percent. In 1870 all but 258 of Floyd County's 1,462 blacks lived in the city.[39]

Outside New Albany, most household heads were farm laborers. A handful, like Josiah Finley, a native of Kentucky, farmed their own land. In New Albany virtually all men were common laborers. In 1870 in Ward 5, which had the largest number of blacks in the city, a representative household was that of Washington Broomwell, a laborer age 27, who resided with his wife, Priss, 20, and their daughter, Josephine, who was 2. Since all were Kentucky-born, it is likely that they migrated to New Albany between 1868 and 1870. Ward 5 also had a large number of steamboat hands, cooks, and chambermaids. There were also four barbers and several blacksmiths and carpenters. Three of the most prosperous blacks lived in Ward 6. James S. Berkshire, 53, was a house carpenter, as was his son John, age 20. Morgan Blackburn, 42, was a porter on a steamboat. Some clergymen and teachers also lived in New Albany, but no businessmen.[40]

Downstream, blacks on the Kentucky side of the river as a rule did not have communities large enough to sustain a business and professional class. The legacy of slavery was also powerful. Those on the north side of the river gen-

erally fared better, although the economies of most Illinois and Indiana counties resembled those to the south, as they were quite rural and heavily dependent on agriculture.[41]

In Hancock County, Kentucky, for instance, the 1870 census revealed that
with the exception of 127 blacks living in the town of Hawesville and 41 in
the village of Lewisport, the vast majority of the county's 703 African Americans worked on farms. Four household heads in Hawesville were coal miners,
three worked in the local tobacco factory, and one was a steamboat hand.
Similar patterns were evident ten years later. Blacks did not perceive cross-
river Perry County, Indiana, as a better place to live. In the first postwar census
only 44 lived there, half in the town of Cannelton. Heads of household were
common laborers or servants. Just 10 black persons were enumerated in the
Swiss-German town of Tell City, a rapidly growing furniture-making center.
Blacks living outside of these towns were employed as farm laborers. Little
changed by 1880.[42]

Just downriver, Daviess County, Kentucky, reflected antebellum labor patterns. In the 1870 census most household heads were farmhands. In Owensboro,
about one-quarter of the city's 654 African Americans dwelled in white homes,
usually employed as servants. Those who headed their own households were
characteristically unskilled workers who stemmed tobacco. Most of the twenty-
three women who headed black households were washerwomen. Although
the number of blacks in Owensboro more than doubled over the following
decade, employment patterns in the county remained unchanged.[43]

Here, as elsewhere, change and continuity intermingled. On the one hand,
African Americans in Owensboro made several abortive efforts to organize
unions, both during the Panic of 1873 and subsequently. The United Brothers
Foundation, formed in May 1875, whose members demanded a raise of $.25 a
day, to $1.50, and the Ancient Order of United Workmen, created in March
1877, were unsuccessful. On the other, legalized slavery persisted here, as in
other Kentucky counties, as a result of the state's apprentice law. Teens designated orphans and delinquents could be bound as apprentices until age twenty-
one. This law was not abrogated until the early twentieth century. Daviess
County court records of 1885–95 disclosed 105 such cases.[44]

Across the river, postwar Spencer County attracted a relatively large number of African American newcomers. The county's black population expanded
dramatically, from 949 in 1870 to 1,492 by 1880. By 1900 blacks accounted
for 19 percent of Spencer County's population.[45] Most of them resided in
Rockport. Racial discrimination and the lack of financial resources to purchase farms barred blacks from the largely German Catholic and agricultural

(Above) The office of the quartermaster and the commissary at Camp Nelson, Kentucky's largest refugee camp, located south of Louisville. Most of the camp inhabitants were wives and children of African American men who had joined the Union Army and were, as of March 1865, free people. Courtesy of the Audio-Visual Archives, Special Collections and Archives, Univ. of Kentucky Libraries. (Below) About fifty-five African American young women and two bearded white men in 1864 with a white female teacher, possibly from the American Missionary Association, at Camp Nelson. Courtesy of the Audio-Visual Archives, Special Collections and Archives, Univ. of Kentucky Libraries.

THE OHIO LEVEE AT CAIRO.—[SKETCHED BY ALEXANDER SIMPLOT.]

(Above) This 1865 view of the Cairo levee illustrates one aspect of life along the Ohio in this era—the ubiquity of African American workers on the wharves and the riverboats. Courtesy of the Abraham Lincoln Presidential Library, Springfield, IL. *(Below)* This simple log structure, perhaps typical of those housing rural blacks on both sides of the Ohio, was the residence of a farm family in rural southwestern Indiana. Courtesy of Univ. of Southern Indiana Special Collections and University Archives.

Liberty Baptist Church, formed in March 1865, was located at Seventh and Oak streets in Evansville, Indiana. A cyclone in the spring of 1886 destroyed the predecessor of this edifice, which was completed seven months later. Courtesy of Univ. of Southern Indiana Special Collections and University Archives.

Alexander Chapel AME, on Church Street in Evansville, is shown here just before it was razed for urban renewal in the 1960s. It traced its roots to early 1843, when a building was erected in the "lower" part of the city. The congregation moved to this site, near Fifth and Walnut streets, and erected this structure in 1889. Courtesy of Univ. of Southern Indiana Special Collections and University Archives.

The Second Baptist Church, New Albany, Indiana. African American congregations often purchased houses of worship that white Protestants had abandoned for newer structures. The Second Baptist Church was organized after the Civil War. In 1889 it was prosperous enough to secure this Greek Revival structure from local Presbyterians. Built 1849–52 at Main and Third streets, the church was a station on the Underground Railroad. It is known locally as the "Clock Church." Author's collection.

(Above) The Fourth Street Market in Evansville in the 1880s was on the dividing line between black and white Evansville. Control of the territory was increasingly contested. Courtesy of Univ. of Southern Indiana Special Collections and University Archives. *(Below)* A row of dilapidated homes in the 300 block of Clark Street, photographed in the 1950s prior to urban renewal. This part of "lower Evansville" was the core of the early black community. The first black church and school were located near here. Courtesy of Willard Library Archives, Evansville.

White diners on the steamer *Crescent City* in the 1890s. Six black men waited on them. By this time work for blacks on such vessels was becoming rare, because of declining passenger traffic on the Ohio and its tributaries. The riverboat plied the waters between Evansville, Indiana, and Bowling Green, Kentucky, via the Green River, which entered the Ohio in Henderson County. Courtesy of Willard Library Archives, Evansville.

The steamer *Park City* at an unidentified lower Ohio River landing in the late nineteenth century. Black roustabouts, once omnipresent on Ohio River waterfronts, were by then, like blacks who worked as waiters, a small proportion of river towns' workforces. Rail traffic had cut drastically into river freight and passenger service. Courtesy of Willard Library Archives, Evansville.

For boys and young men in Kentucky, one promising career in the postslavery era was that of jockey. The most storied career was that of Isaac Burns Murphy, shown here. He was born in 1861 or 1863 in Lexington, the son of a free man, James Burns, and began riding as Isaac Burns at the first meeting of the Louisville Jockey Club (now Churchill Downs) in 1875. He placed fourth in the Kentucky Derby two years later. By that time he was using his mother's maiden name, Murphy. He rode in nine Derbies, winning three (1884, 1890, and 1891), a record not surpassed until 1948. By his account he won 44 percent of all his races. According to the *Encyclopedia of Louisville* (Lexington: Univ. Press of Kentucky, 2001), 636, his brilliance dispelled the notion that the jockey's skill was insignificant, as compared to that of the horse. He died in 1896. Courtesy of Special Collections, Photographic Archives, Univ. of Louisville.

Benjamin W. Arnett (1836–1906) served as a Republican representative in the Ohio House of Representatives during the 67th session (1886–87) of the General Assembly. Arnett was a Bishop in the AME Church, president of Wilberforce University, and the author of legislation for repeal of Ohio's "Black Laws." For many years he was pastor of Allen Temple in Cincinnati, the oldest AME congregation on either side of the Ohio. Courtesy of the Ohio Historical Society.

Peter H. Clark, described by William J. Simmons in his book *Men of Mark* as an "editor and agitator," was born in 1829 and educated in Cincinnati, where for many years he was the most eminent educator in the colored public schools. Outspoken on a variety of issues, his political independence and his opposition to desegregation cost him his position as head of the black high school in Cincinnati in 1886. His career after that was checkered. Courtesy of the Ohio Historical Society.

J. Dennis Rouse, born a slave in the 1850s, came as a boy with his family to Evansville at the end of the war. His father, Adam, helped to found Liberty Baptist Church in March 1865. Seventeen years later, J. Dennis Rouse was elected pastor, a position he held until his death in 1929. Rouse was a prominent civic as well as religious leader. Courtesy of Willard Library Archives, Evansville.

(Right) Henry Adams (1802–1873) was ordained in 1825 and came to Louisville as pastor of the First Baptist Church in 1829. The congregation, which later was known as Fifth Street, separated from its white sponsors in 1842. In 1865 Adams was the first moderator of the General Association of Kentucky Baptists. Light in complexion, he advocated a cautious approach to racial progress. Courtesy of University Archives, Univ. of Louisville.

William J. Simmons (1849–1890) became president of the fledgling school organized by Kentucky Baptists in 1879 that was renamed State University. Through his leadership State University—the only institution of its type on either side of the Ohio—became a respected center for training ministers, teachers, and physicians. After his untimely death, the institution was named in his honor. Courtesy of University Archives, Univ. of Louisville.

RULES AND REGULATIONS.

1. Students must attend Church and Sabbath-school at least once each Sabbath, unless excused by the President.

2. Punctuality, regularity and obedience to all rules and regulations and faithful study particularly required. Habitual indolence and inattention to study will be regarded as an offense against the spirit of the laws of the Institute, constituting a sufficient reason for reprimand or dismission.

3. Profanity, gambling, fire-arms and other dangerous weapons, games of chance, the use of tobacco in any form, the use of intoxicating drinks, attendance at any place of amusement of corrupt influences, are strictly forbidden.

4. No male student may room or board in any place disapproved by the President.

5. The association of the opposite sexes is disallowed. No correspondence allowed except with those designated by the guardian, or parent.

6. Students must keep their own rooms clean, and open the door for inspection by officers of the Institute.

7. All bills must be settled before the first of each month, and on the fifth of each month the receipts must be shown the instructors before further recitation.

8. All students are required to do their part and take their turn in taking care of the grounds and public buildings.

9. Verbal order or announcements, made from time to time by the proper authority, are as binding as the printed "Rules and Regulations."

10. All pupils are required to be in the chapel at 9 A. M.; no one allowed to be tardy. The first tardy in any one month, for good reasons, will be excused. The second will not be excused, the pupil must not enter classes, but return home. The parent or guardian shall be notified of the fact. When this process shall have been gone through and the pupil sent home the second time in any month, he or she shall not return until the parent or guardian has given satisfaction personally. All absences must be strictly accounted for.

Parents and guardians having friends in the Institute, are required to send all money to the President. This rule must be promptly observed. Too much spending-money teaches the student extravagance.

A page from the 1881–82 bulletin of the Kentucky Normal and Theological Institute, later known as State University, discloses the intense interest of school officials in propriety, a central theme in blacks' quest for respectability and recognition from whites. Courtesy of University Archives, Univ. of Louisville.

(Above) Few late-nineteenth-century school buildings for African Americans survive. The Division Street School, erected in the east-side Providence neighborhood of New Albany in 1885, is being restored by preservationists. It is located just south of the intersection of Spring and Eighteenth streets, at 1803 Conservative Street. Author's collection. *(Below)* The Corydon Colored School building was completed in 1891 and recently restored. Located on Summit Street, near High, it graduated its first pupils in 1897. The Harrison County school officials, like those in all other southern Indiana school districts, opened racially segregated schools shortly after the General Assembly provided for publicly funded education for blacks in 1869. Author's collection.

Evansville's city officials created an all-black fire company in the 1880s. This one, shown at the turn of the century, served Baptisttown. Service in the company was a prized political plum, especially since no other fire companies had black members. Courtesy of Univ. of Southern Indiana Special Collections and University Archives.

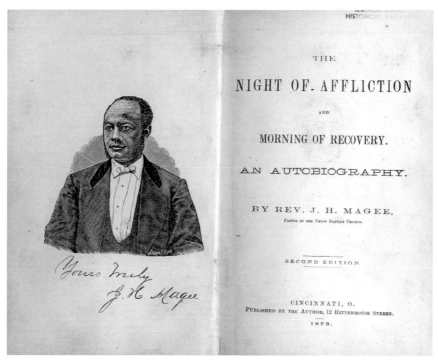

THE

NIGHT OF AFFLICTION

AND

MORNING OF RECOVERY.

AN AUTOBIOGRAPHY.

BY REV. J. H. MAGEE,

Pastor of the Union Baptist Church.

SECOND EDITION.

CINCINNATI, O.
PUBLISHED BY THE AUTHOR, 12 RITTENHOUSE STREET.
1873.

J.H. MaGee, who died in Springfield, Illinois, in 1912, had a long and illustrious career as educator, church leader, and government official. He was well educated, obtaining part of his schooling in England. He pastored Union Baptist Church in Cincinnati, taught school in Metropolis, Illinois, and was one of the region's most eminent black Republicans. Like a number of other black politicos frustrated with white Republicans' abandonment, he departed the Ohio Valley for greener pastures to the north—first in Chicago and then, during the last twelve years of his life, as messenger in the office of the state printer. His obituary is found in the *Illinois State Register* of May 30, 1912. Courtesy of the Abraham Lincoln Presidential Library, Springfield, IL.

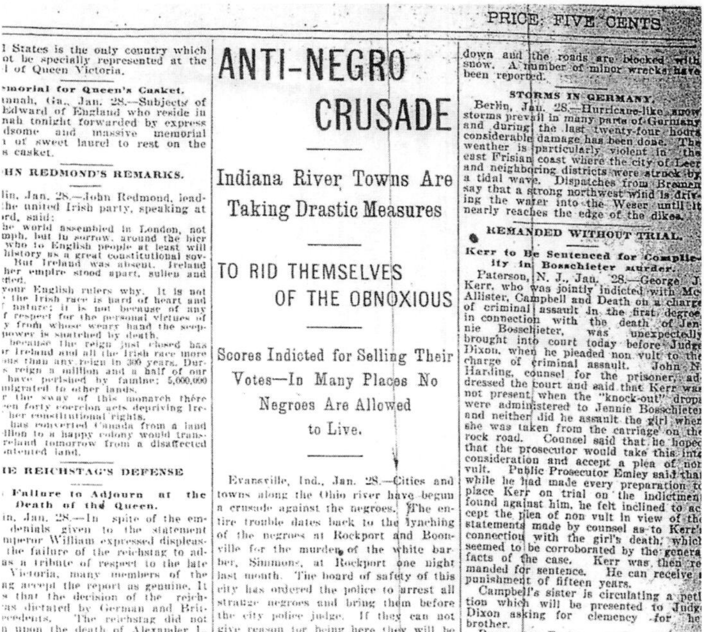

ANTI-NEGRO CRUSADE

Indiana River Towns Are Taking Drastic Measures

TO RID THEMSELVES OF THE OBNOXIOUS

Scores Indicted for Selling Their Votes—In Many Places No Negroes Are Allowed to Live.

Evansville, Ind., Jan. 28.—Cities and towns along the Ohio river have begun a crusade against the negroes. The entire trouble dates back to the lynching of the negroes at Rockport and Boonville for the murder of the white barber, Simmons, at Rockport one night last month. The board of safety of this city has ordered the police to arrest all strange negroes and bring them before the city police judge. If they can not give reason for being here they will be sentenced to the rock pile. The object of this order is to rid the town of an obnoxious class of negroes. It is estimated that there are two thousand colored men in this city who absolutely refuse to work. They spend their time in the colored saloons and low dives of the city and live the best way they can. On election day they are in the market and the man who bids the highest is the man who lands them.

The board of safety was led to take this step by the action of the Spencer county grand jury in indicting 159 negroes of Rockport for selling their votes on election day. The citizens' committee have been actively at work for the past month arranging the preliminary evidence to be presented to the grand jury. It is said an attempt will be made to have the blacks who are indicted arraigned in court in one day and it is desired that they be sent to state prison at the same time. Such a proceeding would be a novel thing in the history of Indiana jurisprudence.

Other towns in Indiana along the river are taking steps to drive the worst element of negroes away. In some towns no negro is permitted to live. Vigilance committees have been appointed at Grand View, Enterprise, Tell City and Leavenworth. Since the recent trouble at Newburg many of the colored people have left that town.

DEWET'S OPERATIONS

With Force of Five Hundred in Vicinity of Ventersburg Road.

Ventersburg, Orange River Colony,

STORMS IN GERMANY

Berlin, Jan. 28.—Hurricane-like snow storms prevail in many parts of Germany and during the last twenty-four hours considerable damage has been done. The weather is particularly violent in the east Frisian coast where the city of Leer and neighboring districts were swept by a tidal wave. Dispatches from Bremen say that a strong northwest wind is driving the water into the Weser until it nearly reaches the edge of the dikes.

REMANDED WITHOUT TRIAL

Kerr to Be Sentenced for Complicity in Bosschieter murder.

Paterson, N. J., Jan. 28.—George J. Kerr, who was jointly indicted with McAllister, Campbell and Death on a charge of criminal assault in the first degree in connection with the death of Jennie Bosschieter, was unexpectedly brought into court today before Judge Dixon, when he pleaded non vult to the charge of criminal assault. John N. Harding, counsel for the prisoner, addressed the court and said that Kerr was not present when the "knock-out" drops were administered to Jennie Bosschieter and neither did he assault the girl when she was taken from the carriage on the rock road. Counsel said that he hoped that the prosecutor would take this into consideration and accept a plea of non vult. Public Prosecutor Emley said that while he had made every preparation to place Kerr on trial on the indictment found against him, he felt inclined to accept the plea of non vult in view of the statements made by counsel as to Kerr's connection with the girl's death, which seemed to be corroborated by the general facts of the case. Kerr was then remanded for sentence. He can receive punishment of fifteen years.

Campbell's sister is circulating a petition which will be presented to Judge Dixon asking for clemency for her brother.

Prosecutor Emley announced today that he would have McAllister, Kerr, Campbell and Death arraigned for trial tomorrow and move that sentence be pronounced at once.

It is the general opinion here that all the prisoners except Kerr will receive the extreme penalty for murder in the second degree of which they were convicted. The full penalty is thirty years' imprisonment at hard labor. It is also believed that Kerr will be sentenced to the full penalty of the law on the plea to which he has pleaded non vult, which is fifteen years' imprisonment at hard labor.

NEELY'S STATEMENT

Pleads Innocence of Fraud in Cuba But Says He Cannot Prove His Innocence.

New York, Jan. 28.—A long dictated statement from Charles F. W. Neely, who has just been taken to Cuba for trial, was printed here. In the course of this Neely describes in detail how an after-issue of stamps had been made for the Cuban service were destroyed. For the purpose of conducting the destruction Director-General Rathbone appointed a commission, says, composed of himself (Neely), Auditor Reeves, of the registry division, an Marfield, an Ohioan. It has been alleged that Neely stole many thousands dollars' worth of stamps by burning their place packages of waste paper, reference to this charge Neely about these stamps:

"The man who says they were destroyed, or who says that I said it destroyed, or who says that the packages contained only brown paper...

[Left column — partially visible]

States is the only country which not be specially represented at the f of Queen Victoria.

morial for Queen's Casket.

annah, Ga., Jan. 28.—Subjects of Edward of England who reside in nah tonight forwarded by express some and massive memorial of sweet laurel to rest on the casket.

HN REDMOND'S REMARKS.

lin, Jan. 28.—John Redmond, leading the united Irish party, speaking at rd, said:

IE REICHSTAG'S DEFENSE

Failure to Adjourn at the Death of the Queen.

in, Jan. 28.—

RVICES AT WASHINGTON.

mory of the Queen Will Be Held Feb. 2.

hington, Jan. 28.—

NEW CREDENTIALS

Be Given Ambassador Choate and Lord Pauncefote.

hington, Jan. 28.—

This article, which appeared in the *Chattanooga Daily Times* of January 29, 1901, provides some insight into efforts by white leaders in Ohio River towns at the turn of the century to eliminate "obnoxious" blacks. Such "crusades" were one reason for the decline in black populations after 1900 in Indiana river towns. The trigger in this instance was the lynching of several blacks in Boonville and Rockport the previous December for the alleged murder of a white barber. Evansville authorities estimated that about two thousand "worthless" blacks resided in that city, and responded by sentencing them to the "rock pile" if they could not provide a good reason for being in the city. Otherwise, they would spend their time in saloons and "dives" and sell their votes to the highest bidders in elections. More severe punishment was planned for Rockport. Many blacks had already left Newburgh. Author's collection.

northern section of the county. Job opportunities in Rockport, though, were abundant. Spencer County was the state's leading tobacco producer, shipping an average of 5 million pounds each year between 1875 and 1885. Many black men worked in the firms that supplied downstream Owensboro's stemmeries. Others were employed on riverboats, on the riverfront, or in sawmills. Women worked as domestics and washerwomen.[46]

Change and continuity were also evident in Henderson County. Emancipation brought not only a dramatic change in labor relations, but also a shift in residence. Slightly below one-quarter of blacks in the county lived in the town of Henderson by the summer of 1870. All but 270 of the 1,489 blacks in the town, moreover, lived in the 235 households headed by black men or women, a sign of greater self-sufficiency than was apparent in the surrounding countryside. Henderson's role as a major exporter of plug tobacco was evident in employment patterns, because the occupation most frequently listed by black household heads was "works in tobacco stemmery." Day laborer, farm laborer, and drayman or teamster were also frequently cited occupations. Female heads of household were employed as domestics, servants, cooks, washerwomen, and nurses. Some women worked in the tobacco stemmeries. As in Jefferson County, Kentucky, skills acquired in slavery were evident in the number of barbers (3), carpenters (3), plasterers (5), blacksmiths (4), and coopers (4). One black household head was a horse trainer. There were also some businesses—three saloons and the grocery of Henry McFarland—as well as three teachers and two ministers.[47]

Nearly 4,500 Henderson County blacks lived in the country, where vestiges of slavery remained strong. Most males above age 12 were farmhands. Female heads of household who did not keep house were domestics or washerwomen. As elsewhere on the south shore, a large proportion lived in white households, where adults worked as farmhands or servants, and girls between 10 and 15 were frequently identified as nurses. Lower Henderson Precinct, for example, had 245 blacks, but only 9 of the 57 households had black heads. The household of Archibald Dixon, a prominent attorney and a former U.S. senator, included 14 black servants.[48]

Ten years later the situation was slightly changed. The ratio of blacks living in the town had risen to 27 percent, and the total black population of the county was somewhat larger. At the same time, the proportion of blacks in the county dropped to 31 percent, because of the substantial growth in the number of whites. Generally the occupational patterns were unchanged. The chief difference was that fewer men and women in both the town and the country lived in white-headed households, suggesting that blacks' economic and social autonomy was increasing.[49]

Cross-river Vanderburgh and Warrick counties offered striking differences and similarities. Warrick's overwhelmingly rural and agrarian economy, combined with the venomous treatment of blacks by whites of mostly upper Southern extraction, made it a destination that most migrant blacks avoided. The number of blacks in the county increased slightly in the twenty years after the war. Most resided in and around Newburgh in Ohio Township. The village had a tobacco warehouse and a stemmery, where some blacks worked as common or day laborers. Most of the thirty-nine heads of household, though, were farmers or farmhands, and a few owned their farms. Employment patterns changed little during the 1870s and 1880s; however, the development of coal mining brought some employment in that sector to blacks.[50]

Vanderburgh County gained substantial numbers of blacks during and after the Civil War. Most settled in Evansville. After 1870 the black population of Evansville nearly doubled in each decade, by 1900 reaching 7,405, almost 13 percent of the total population. Although the rural black population of the county also grew, by the end of the 1880s 92 percent lived in Evansville. In this respect Vanderburgh County resembled Hamilton County, Ohio, and Jefferson County, Kentucky.[51]

The growth of Evansville, the only metropolis and the largest wholesale and industrial center between Louisville and St. Louis, brought (on paper) the chance for a better life for thousands of former slaves. By the end of the century, spurred by commercial expansion via river and especially rail transportation, Evansville was a major hardwood manufacturer, with a number of large furniture factories. Drawing on ample coal and iron ore nearby and a large number of German-born artisans, the city boasted thirteen foundries, several machine shops, and a rolling mill. It had one of the nation's largest tobacco markets and one of its largest cotton textile mills. Its hinterland stretched 75 to 100 miles. This industrializing city offered a wealth of new types of jobs.[52]

River traffic initially accounted for the occupations of many former slaves. One-fifth of the 553 black workers in 1870 were boatmen, cabin boys, chambermaids, cooks, porters, or stewards. Theodore Dreiser, who resided in the city as a youth, recalled "scores of small mule-drawn drays driven by Negroes in sleeveless cotton undershirts and batted trousers gripped tightly about the hips." Half of the city's black workers were common or day laborers employed at the waterfront and in other parts of the city. Second in number were servants, who worked in homes, hotels, and restaurants.[53]

Several aspects of Evansville's black workforce are striking. From the outset married females made up a significant portion, and by the end of the

century that portion had risen to one in three workers. Over time, moreover, there was only a slight variation in the sector of the economy in which blacks worked. In 1870 nearly half worked in service occupations or in transportation. Slightly more than half were employed in industry, but mostly as common laborers. By the turn of the century, the proportion of those in service and transportation had grown to two in three. Blacks employed in industry increased in number but decreased in proportion. There was also a slight increase in agriculture and mining: about 3 percent were employed in coal mining.[54]

The status of employment was little changed. Here, too, Evansville resembled Louisville and Cincinnati. Most black men were blocked from factory jobs, and black women were denied the opportunity to become white-collar workers. Reflecting a regional trend, the percentage of skilled workers dropped from 5.2 in 1870 to 3.3 by 1890. The number of black professionals increased steadily, to twenty-seven in 1880 and more than twice that number twenty years later. Most of the professionals were clergymen and teachers. The reason for their increased numbers was similar to that for Louisville's—the growing segregation of blacks.[55]

As elsewhere, political jobs were prized. Appointment to the police or fire department was especially desirable, and black men eagerly sought to be custodians at the city hall and the courthouse. High status was accorded positions that gained blacks access to whites' confidence. When George Jackson, longtime black steward on the packet boat *Idlewild,* died at age seventy-five, the daily newspapers devoted an unusually large amount of space to his passing, praising him as a faithful, loyal servant.[56]

By the 1890s at most twenty black men were employed as skilled workers in factories. Nearly all of the blacks working in factories were menial laborers, mostly in brick and tile works or in lumber and saw mills. Unions, mostly without formal prohibition of Negro membership, found ways to keep blacks out. An exception was Local no. 15 of the National Brotherhood of Operative Potters. Apparently the United Mine Workers' local admitted some black members. The hod carriers had an all-black local, no. 11, later renamed the Building Laborers' International Protective Union of America.[57]

The racist practices of most unions and employers were not conducive to workplace collaboration, but there were rare exceptions. During the turbulent summer of 1877, Bushrod Taylor, a black Democrat, organized black steamboat workers, who were paid just sixty-six cents a day, and led them out on strike. Taylor's men were welcomed into the newly formed Workingmen's Protective Union. The WPU's life span, unfortunately, was brief. Blacks were

frequently used as strikebreakers. Hence black roustabouts' periodic strikes for better wages evoked little if any sympathy from whites, and often their jobs were filled by whites if white unemployment was high. White workers strenuously resisted when black workers entered places they deemed their own—for instance, when teams with black drivers were sent into the city's predominantly German American west side to repair streets.[58]

The city's occupational index—aggregate employment ranked on a scale of 100 to 700, with the latter the lowest in prestige—is revealing. In 1880 black males ranked 656 and black females 626. Twenty years later those numbers were, respectively, 626 and 608. There had been some progress, but by then white men with native-born parents had an index of 490 and foreign-born white men 463. Among white women, the numbers were 496 and 504.[59]

Such numbers belie other patterns of racial discrimination similar to those found in Louisville. Black men accounted for three-quarters of the boatmen, two-thirds of the hostlers, four-fifths of the servants and waiters, and slightly over half of the brick and tile workers. Black women were two-fifths of the servants and waitresses and two-thirds of the laundresses and washerwomen. By contrast, there were no black salesmen or saleswomen, stenographers, clerks, or bookkeepers. Socioeconomic advancement was limited. Of the 23 heads of household who can be traced from 1870 to 1891, 10 experienced modest advancement. Four became owners of barbershops, 2 sextons or custodians, 2 engineers, 1 a foreman, and 1 (Willis Green) a physician. The other 13 remained in the same sort of employment or declined somewhat in rank.[60]

Patterns were similar downstream. Union County, Kentucky, resembled neighboring Henderson, as nearly one-fifth of its 2,574 blacks in 1870 resided in rural white households, and many shared the surnames of the whites they lived with. Some resided in the county's small river towns, Caseyville and Uniontown, where most worked as servants, washerwomen, laborers, and teamsters. The majority of the blacks lived in the country, where they were employed as farmhands. Few owned their land. During the 1870s the number of blacks grew and the percentage of blacks residing in white households declined, although the number remained high—280 in 1880. The number of blacks living in the county's towns and villages increased slightly, especially in Uniontown, where many worked in the tobacco factories.[61]

During the 1860s and 1870s some blacks migrated from Henderson and Union counties to Posey and Gallatin counties across the river. About half of this group lived in Mount Vernon and Shawneetown, where they found employment as laborers and servants. Those living in the country were generally

employed as farmhands. From these counties to the mouth of the Ohio, similarities in patterns of employment in the rural counties of Illinois and Kentucky—Hardin and Pope on the north bank, and Crittenden, Livingston, and Ballard on the south—were very much in evidence. There were few skilled workers, and black populations remained small. The chief difference, as in upriver counties, was that a significant proportion of south-bank blacks resided in white households.[62]

A notable exception was McCracken County, Kentucky. Not planter-dominated before the war, it was tied by rail to the Mobile and Ohio Railroad, blessed with a relatively large number of factories, and able to attract immigrant workers. Paducah resembled Evansville and Louisville more than Henderson or Owensboro. During the Civil War decade, Paducah's black population nearly doubled, and it increased by one-third in the 1870s. Three of four blacks in the county in 1880 lived in Paducah. Few, moreover, resided in white households, whether in town or in the countryside. Enumeration District 125 had the largest number of African Americans, about 1,050, who resided in 240 black-headed households. Many were common laborers, working in either sawmills or tobacco stemmeries, or domestic servants.[63]

Employment opportunities were also broader than in most Purchase and southern Illinois counties. By the early 1880s black Paducah had two businesses. Phil Williams, a boot and shoemaker, had a shop on the southeast corner of Locust and Washington streets. Lawrence Glore had a saloon on the southwest corner of Court and Main streets. About a decade later there were thirteen black barbershops (out of a total of sixteen in the city), four boot and shoe makers, a saloon keeper, a horse-shoer, and a physician, C.I. Isbell.[64]

Massac County, Illinois, directly across the river, grew from a mere handful of blacks to 956 by 1870. During the 1870s, it expanded by slightly over 78 percent. The county's seat, Metropolis, remained a relatively sleepy market town with a few firms that processed grain and timber. Adjoining Brooklyn, later renamed Brookport, also grew slowly. These two settlements resembled New Albany and Jeffersonville, as the more dynamic economy, Paducah, lay on the south bank of the river. Massac County's black population was mostly rural. Few blacks resided in Brooklyn. In 1870 many lived near tiny Pellonia, on the river. Most male household heads worked as farmhands. In Metropolis, where one-tenth of the population was black, 17 of the 46 heads of household were sawmill hands. Nine were common laborers or workers in the town's small factories. Probably typical was Marshall Adams, a forty-five-year-old tobacco factory hand. Married, the native of Virginia had eight children, and two sons were also tobacco factory workers. The family migrated to Metropolis

between 1868 and the winter of 1869–70. Metropolis also had four teamsters, a barber, a house carpenter, a blacksmith, and a shoemaker among its household heads.[65]

By contrast, the black and white population of downriver Alexander and Pulaski counties exploded in the 1860s and 1870s. The increase reflected war-induced growth in that part of Illinois, since both counties had Union Army and Navy bases and were supply centers for the Union armed forces. In 1870 the two had the highest percentage of blacks of all twenty-five counties across the river from Kentucky. Blacks accounted for one in five of Alexander County's residents in 1870 and 1880. In neighboring Pulaski County, the proportion of black residents in 1880 was one in three. A large number of black newcomers were from Tennessee and states to the south and west, primarily Arkansas and Missouri. Like other north-bank settlers, they established their own households, however poor they were. In Alexander County in 1870, for instance, just 116 blacks lived in white households.[66]

Alexander's population was much more urbanized than Pulaski's. Well over 80 percent of Alexander County's blacks in 1870 lived in Cairo, but only about 30 percent of Pulaski County's resided in Mound City. These proportions remained about the same over the following decade. The number of blacks in Pulaski County was also comparatively small. Hence they were unable to establish the range of business and professional activities found in Cairo. There were only about 800 blacks in Mound City in 1880. Over twice as many were scattered among rural precincts adjoining the river, where most heads of household were farm laborers. A few owned their land. Typical was Cezar McKee, fifty-five, a Tennessee-born farm laborer, who was married and had two children. One can infer that the family migrated to Illinois in 1867 or 1868. Over three-quarters of the 138 black heads of household in Mound City were common laborers.[67]

One factor in the growth of the African American population in Pulaski County was recruitment by the Illinois Central Railroad, which owned a great deal of land that had been granted by Congress in 1850. At the annual conference of the Mt. Olive Baptist Association in Cairo in 1881, a Cairo man named Gladden, general superintendent of the Freedmen's Relief Association and land agent for the Illinois Central Railroad, urged men to take advantage of cheap and plentiful farmland ($5 to $8 an acre) and to settle in the country, where they could build a solid foundation on which to compete.[68]

In Cairo, many blacks who had settled in the town's wartime contraband camp decided to remain. With few exceptions, they had arrived with nothing more than the clothes on their backs. Local whites were generally hostile to

them. Only a handful of black newcomers found work in Cairo's factories. Instead, almost all worked long, irregular hours as common laborers or in service and received low pay. Others worked as deckhands on riverboats. Some, like Abram Jackson, a house carpenter, were artisans.[69]

The size of Cairo's black community permitted the creation of a small business and professional class, as noted earlier. The town boasted, for example, three black newspapers between 1862 and 1890: the *Weekly Gazette* (1862–81), edited by William T. Scott; the *Cairo Gazette* (1881–90), a monthly paper also edited by Scott; and *Three States* (1881–83), a weekly edited by Gladden. In the 1870s and 1880s, Cairo had black doctors, physicians, judges, policemen, and constables as well.[70]

Cairo's laborers, moreover, were not passive—perhaps a reflection of the fluid state of race relations in a rapidly growing town. Several hundred water-front workers, enraged at wage cuts in the summer of 1877, gathered at the Cairo levee to protest: the Mississippi Valley Transportation Company (MVTC) had hired replacements at 2.5 rather than 3 cents per container, as strikers had demanded. The strikers drove away the scabs and met the next day to continue the strike. Local authorities urged the governor to send help, but he asked them to take care of their own problem. The strikers prevailed, and their action set the basis for greater militancy among roustabouts. The MVTC understood that time was of the essence in their business, and that delays were costly. Black workers' actions against the strikebreakers had also been important. After 1877, until the Panic of 1893, the unity and power of waterfront workers blunted company efforts to cut wages.[71]

The successful strikers stood outside the norm. Nearly all Cairo workers were unorganized servants and common or day laborers. Perhaps typical was Archer Foster, a laborer, who in 1870 was twenty-six and a native of North Carolina. He and his wife Hannah, a Kentuckian, had moved to Cairo only about two years earlier. Women worked mostly in whites' homes and hotels as cooks, laundresses, nurses, and maids. Like their counterparts upriver, they cared for two families—the white family as well as their own. Their days were long and exhausting. Furthermore, the white household was as much con-tested terrain as the waterfront was. Although many black servants were treated like family members, white mistresses could be cruel as well as kind. Those servants who felt mistreated could leave without giving notice, fail to show up for work, or choose not to apply for work in white households with a bad reputation. Cairo's black domestics, in fact, formed their own chapter of the local Knights of Labor in 1886.[72]

One historian of Cairo has described the city as having two economies—

one dependent on river and rail transportation, and the other based on liquor, gambling, and prostitution. The city's rapid growth prior to the Panic of 1893 sustained both and mitigated clashes between African American workers and their white counterparts, especially the German- and Irish-born. Prosperity also deflected efforts on the part of the white elite to create political reform. The depression that followed the economic crash of 1893 gravely injured the city's economy: fewer steamboats stopped in Cairo and rail traffic increasingly bypassed it, in part because of the completion of a railroad bridge in the late 1880s. The decline of the first economy facilitated the rise of the second and also exacerbated clashes between black and white laborers.[73]

Property ownership was one measure of the progress of former slaves. The records are unfortunately thin. Federal enumeration schedules, for instance, included the value of real and personal property only through 1870. Local tax records are also spotty. What we do have suggests that within the brief period of two decades some African Americans acquired an impressive amount of wealth, by the standards of the time. Before the war, the few free blacks on either side of the river held property of negligible worth, and slaves represented a significant portion of Kentucky whites' wealth. In Mason County, for instance, the 2,614 slaves in 1860 represented $1.06 million in property value for their 551 owners. In the year after the end of the war, the value of blacks' taxable property in the entire state of Kentucky was $976,956. Seven years later, Kentucky whites' real property value was $403 million, but blacks' had risen to $3.6 million. By 1885 it was about $4 million.[74]

Progress was especially striking in Jefferson County, Kentucky. The tax lists for 1875 disclose that 662 blacks owned property valued at $406,755, or $614 per person. These blacks represented only about 7 percent of those on the tax lists, although blacks constituted about 20 percent of the population. A more positive way of looking at the matter is that hundreds of former slaves had become property owners. The largest number, 429, resided in Louisville. The 233 blacks who paid taxes in the rural districts of the county had property valued at about $42,000. So slightly over $362,000 of assessed wealth of blacks lay in town lots and improvements in Louisville.[75]

The Third District was by far black Louisville's wealthiest: its 140 black taxpayers accounted for about half of the county's assessed valuation. The town lots owned by these blacks were valued at $99,900, and improvements at $78,850. Per capita valuation was $1,311. The leading taxpayer was Louisa Spradling, who owned five lots worth $11,600 on Walnut and Madison streets, between Eleventh and Twelfth streets. Members of the Spradling family were easily the

city's leading property owners. Among them, the four Spradlings had nineteen town lots worth $42,900, more than one-tenth of the assessed value of black-owned property.[76]

Downriver, blacks' financial progress was at best modest. In Breckinridge County, for instance, 309 African Americans were registered on the tax lists of 1875, but less than half paid any taxes. Of those, only 34 owned real property—a total of 2,543 acres assessed at $34,460. Just 5 had property worth more than $1,000. The typical black taxpayer owned no land but paid a tax on a horse or a mule. In Hancock County in 1875, whites' property was worth $1.6 million and blacks' only $10,080. Only 6 of the 59 African Americans with assessed property owned land: 541 acres valued at $4,370, and two town lots assessed at $300. They also owned 88 horses and 7 mules.[77]

Property records in Henderson County provided a somewhat more encouraging picture. The tax list dated January 1, 1873, disclosed that whites owned property worth $9.6 million. A separate section included the names of 1,437 African Americans, few of whom had any property. Their total assessed value was $108,520: $25,635 in horses and mares, $14,440 in mules, and a minuscule amount in such property as watches, silver, and clocks. One-quarter was farmland: 2,886 acres valued at just under $26,685, or about $9 an acre. More than one-third of the blacks' assessed property lay in the city, where economic advancement was more promising: 112 town lots worth $38,400.[78]

McCracken County resembled Henderson County in black-owned property. In 1873 the total valuation of blacks' property was $56,590. Most of it was in town lots. In 1885, their property was assessed at slightly under $69,000. Black-owned farmland represented a small part of the total: 1,391 acres, worth $10,840. By contrast, whites owned 152,057 acres, valued at slightly over $1 million. Blacks' 243 town lots were appraised at $50,288. The financial gap between them and whites remained enormous, as whites owned 2,747 town lots assessed at $2.2 million.[79]

Property values listed in federal enumeration schedules in 1870 enhance the conclusions gained by examining tax records: that blacks in Kentucky towns were better off than their rural brothers and sisters, and that on the whole those living on the north bank were more prosperous than those on the south. Some examples by region will suffice.

Most of Appalachian Boyd County's small black population resided in Ashland and Catlettsburg. The wealthiest were a father and son, Alex Jamison senior and junior of Ashland. The elder Jamison had real property worth $1,125. The realty of Alex junior, who lived next door, was valued at $400. Just four blacks in the county owned real estate, worth a total of $2,345. Six had per-

sonal property valued at $929 in all. Blacks in Bluegrass Campbell and Kenton counties who had property of value also resided in towns, Newport and Covington. The amount of aggregate wealth, though, was minuscule. John Crocker, a thirty-three-year-old servant residing in Covington, had real property valued at $100 and personal property worth $200. His wife also had personal property valued at $100. In rural Trimble County, just one black man, George Green, had real property, valued at $1,500. Blacks' personal property in the county was worth $500.[80]

Blacks in western Kentucky and Purchase counties—with the exception of those residing in the towns of Henderson and Paducah—also had little real and personal property. Only 9 of Union County's nearly 2,000 blacks owned real estate, which had an aggregate value of $3,975. Two people accounted for half of that total. Thirty-one had personal property valued at $10,350. In Livingston County, where nearly 800 blacks lived, only 44 heads of household owned real or personal property; the total worth was $15,495.[81]

Across the river, the majority of blacks with property were as a rule found in cities and towns. In Jefferson County, Indiana, the most well-to-do African American was a mulatto resident of Madison, John Carter. At 56, he had acquired real estate worth $3,500. In the rural part of the county, probably the wealthiest black was a farmer, 41-year-old Thomas Young, who lived in Madison Township. He possessed realty worth $300 and personal property valued at $175.[82] Downstream Floyd County was similar. In rural parts, the most prosperous black was Josiah Finley, a mulatto farmer and a native of Kentucky, who had real estate worth $5,000 and personal property valued at $400. In New Albany, Morgan Blackburn, 42 and a steamboat porter, had real property valued at $9,000 and personal property valued at $300. Nelson Fields, a pastry cook, was also comparatively affluent, with real estate listed at $2,000 and personal property at $1,900. They and six other men owned realty valued at $16,900 and personal property worth $4,300, most of the county's total for blacks in each category.[83]

Vanderburgh County offers a somewhat similar portrait. Of the approximately 2,150 African Americans in the county in 1870, just 29 owned real estate, and 93 had personal property worth $50 or more. The combined value of blacks' realty and personal property was, respectively, $46,600 and $10,000. Twenty-five in Evansville owned realty and personal property that accounted for about three-fourths of the county's total for blacks. A notable exception was Daniel Liles (or Lyles), a farmer residing west of the city, whose realty, worth $15,000, was the highest in the county among blacks. He and three other men, in Center Township, were the only black farmers who owned land.

His wealth in personal property was also comparatively high, at $700. Liles, a native of Virginia, was 75, and his wife, Nancy, also a Virginian, was 60. The household included a son, Wester (Western?), 30, and six very young children, probably Daniel's grandchildren, all of whom were born in Indiana. The family had returned to the county in about 1862 or 1863, having been driven out in 1857 (see chapter 2). The second-wealthiest was Evansville's Mary Morton, also a native of Virginia, who was 38 and a widow. Her realty was worth $3,000 and her personal property $200. All told, fifteen blacks in Vanderburgh County in 1870 possessed realty valued at $1,000 or more. The progress of these and other property owners in the brief time that most had resided in the city compared favorably with that of blacks living in the town of Henderson.[84]

In the long run, though, black property ownership remained an exception to the rule. By 1890, for instance, Evansville was one of fifty-eight American cities with 50,000 or more blacks. One-fourth of its heads of household owned their homes, but only 9 percent of black heads of household did, as compared to 32 percent of German Americans. Ten years later, the overall rate of home ownership had risen to 32 percent, but for blacks it remained at 9. Black Evansvillians, moreover, were concentrated in Baptisttown, where just 6 percent were home owners, and virtually all of the residences were substandard in quality.[85]

Property ownership in Illinois's river counties resembled that in Indiana's. In the five rural precincts of Alexander County, for instance, only two blacks owned real estate—farms worth a total of $1,300. Seventy-six heads of household had personal property worth $4,330, or $57 per capita. In Cairo, where most of the county's blacks lived, some were able to secure wealth on the level of blacks in Evansville and New Albany. Two-thirds of the black population resided in the North Precinct, but only 179 of the 263 black heads of household had any property of value. Most of that was personal property, valued at $10,125, or $57 per person. Just 3 owned realty, worth a combined $300. In South Precinct, 4 people owned real estate valued at a total of $4,200. One was saloon-keeper W. T. Scott, whose realty was worth $1,500. The other 2 of note were Stephen Bradley, a drayman, whose realty was valued at $1,200, and Susan Brown, a widow, with realty worth $1,000. Blacks' personal property was worth a combined $8,985, or $76 per capita.[86]

In the other river counties, few owned real estate. In one rural precinct near Grand Chain in Pulaski County, for instance, there were 145 black-headed households. None of the heads owned any realty. Exceptions in another precinct along the river were Christopher and Alexander Cross. Father and son, they owned realty worth a combined $1,400 and personal property worth

$600. The elder Cross was a blacksmith, and the younger a brick mason. In the adjoining precinct, Jackson Johnson, a farmer who was fifty, owned land worth $2,000 and personal property worth $500. He was by far the wealthiest black man in rural Pulaski County. Just one other farmer owned his land. By contrast, African Americans in Gallatin County in 1870 owned real property valued at $84,005—mostly their 5,791 acres of farmland. Personal property was valued at $31,145. Most realty and personal property wealth was found in rural areas and reflected the relatively old age of quite a few of the property owners, who also had resided there for a number of years prior to the Civil War.[87]

Several conclusions seem apt. First, on the south side of the river, especially in counties with large black populations, some blacks possessed skills acquired in slavery that allowed them to find work in their crafts after war's end. Over time, though, skilled employment declined as a result of technological obsolescence and white unionists' resistance to black membership. The same fate faced skilled workers on the north shore.

In rural Kentucky, where most of the Kentucky blacks along the Ohio lived, the legacy of slavery remained powerful, but by the 1880s fewer African Americans lived and worked in white households; blacks had more autonomy than they had had in 1865. Most of them remained farmhands and domestic servants, but some acquired taxable property. A growing proportion resided in cities and towns, especially Louisville, where the large antebellum free black and relatively independent slave population became the nucleus of a large, but economically fragile, community.

In most north-shore counties, blacks generally settled in towns and took menial employment in labor, service, and transportation. Significant differences existed within states and even within regions. Most were locked in unskilled labor and were propertyless, but some gained property and moved upward into middle- and upper-class status. Even in the largest black communities, though, black attorneys, doctors, and businessmen had a problematic existence because of their clients' poverty.

However slight the difference may appear to us, the futures of north-bank African Americans were more promising than those of blacks across the river, except for blacks living in Jefferson County, Kentucky.[88] However much racist values of the upper South permeated the lower Midwest, there were mitigating factors there that did not exist on the south shore—a relatively large number of whites in larger towns who were natives of the Middle States and New England and tended to be more tolerant of blacks, greater receptivity to the

Republican Party and its modernizing ethos, a higher degree of urbanization and industrialization, and weaker legislative and court support for de jure segregation. Black men and women on the north shore had greater opportunity to climb the economic ladder, however slippery its rungs were. They were unbound by slave-era proscriptions. To be sure, many whites sought to keep them apart, visually and physically, but they did not erect the array of legal barriers that emerged in Kentucky.

Freedom brought chances to make a new start. And it brought hope. As one of the nation's first African American historians, George Washington Williams, declared to an assembly near Cincinnati on July 4, 1876:

> By faith and hope we look into the future; a propitious future, inviting us to share its duties and enjoy its honors. Forgetting the flesh-pots of Egypt, and leaving the superstitions incident to our bondage beyond the Red Sea of our miraculous deliverance, let us press forward to the promised land. Let us move on with alacrity, while over us is spread a bright sky, and a redolent atmosphere about us, invigorating our lungs and making glad our hearts. We march into the future with joyful anticipation of the immortal work that awaits us.[89]

10

Families and Community Life

During the unsettled times after the Civil War, African Americans sought to create new ways of organizing their lives as well as their relations with whites. Soon the relations between blacks and whites on both shores of the river assumed a form that would prevail well into the twentieth century. African Americans' major achievement was the creation of a distinctive society and culture. Former slaves could "point with pride to their achievements as a people freed from slavery, if not from racism."[1] The new order was founded upon family, church, fraternal and benevolent associations, recreation, and schools.

The most essential element was the family—an aspect of black life that historians of this region have largely overlooked.[2] The ending of the war brought enormous change, since marriage had been illegal for slaves. Ex-slave women often severed ties with white men and pressed claims with the Freedmen's Bureau against white fathers of their children. They also filed claims of sexual abuse against white men, but ex-slave husbands and fathers could not prevent their wives and daughters from sexual insults and abuse. Records also disclose a strong desire to legalize slave marriages as well as to register unions that occurred after the war. A largely illiterate population quickly learned the rules of civil society, creating vital family and kinship values and ties. Blacks' choices immediately after the war and before the granting of substantial new rights reflected values learned in adapting to slavery, and the Thirteenth Amendment facilitated their decision-making.[3]

Camp Nelson, near Louisville, where wives and children of many black

Union soldiers flocked in 1864–65, had a seven-room schoolhouse, four large wards, a dining room, sixty government tents, fifty cabins, and ninety-seven two-room "cottages." But disputes between slave-owners and camp officials persisted into late 1865, and soldiers continued to report mistreatment of their wives and children by owners. Most controversial of all were the liberal policies of General John M. Palmer, who continued martial law until October 1865 (see chapter 3). Thomas James recalled the claims of a slave-trader who demanded that he give up a woman living in his refugee camp. The woman asserted that her husband was in the army and that she had a rail pass to Cincinnati. Palmer ordered a hearing, following which he had her taken across the river to board a train safely for Cincinnati.[4]

White opposition remained adamant. Advertisements promising prosecution for people harboring runaways continued to appear in Louisville papers. Although President Andrew Johnson ended martial law in the commonwealth October 12, 1865, and refused to remove Palmer, obstructionism persisted. A Covington railroad official denied an ex-slave transportation across the river to Cincinnati because he had lost the pass given him by his former owner. The black man was on his way to gather his family, sent there for safety during the war. Only the protection afforded by Union troops enabled blacks to use the ferry between Louisville and Jeffersonville. Kentucky courts lodged a series of charges against Palmer until the ratification of the Thirteenth Amendment made them moot. Nevertheless, "the Kentucky legislature denounced him at the very moment that Louisville blacks 'extensively' signed petitions urging that body to define the 'rights, duties, and interests of the colored people within the general laws of marriage, divorce, and legitimacy.'" A year later, a court convicted him of a felony—aiding a woman's escape to Indiana.[5]

The social upheaval in Kentucky was mirrored elsewhere in ex-slave states and "tested the strength of slave family ties among soldiers and other slaves." An agent of the Freedmen's Bureau reported many instances of brutal treatment of soldiers who sought to claim their wives and children at their former homes. The lives and personal property of family members were also threatened. This was hardly Palmer's responsibility, for abuse of the families of black soldiers antedated his arrival and also occurred in other former slave states. A number of Union officers outside Louisville, refusing to follow Palmer's orders, denied wives the opportunity to visit their soldier husbands in camp. One soldier wrote Stanton, "Our wives and children are laying out doers and we have no chance to get a home for them we havent had six days furlough to see our wives and we have been in the army fourteen months."[6]

Emancipation, in short, did not alter "the sexual beliefs of southern ex-

slaves, southern whites, and northern whites. But the social upheaval associated with the war and emancipation allowed ex-slaves to act upon their beliefs in a changed setting and even—for some—to try to reverse sexual and social practices that violated prevalent slave moral and social norms. The task proved difficult."[7]

Even after the passage of the Thirteenth Amendment, stresses on the black family were gargantuan. Reuniting families torn apart by sale or flight was a major challenge, and generations-old patterns of black-white relations were difficult to change. Agents of the Freedmen's Bureau in Boone County, for instance, were urged not to interfere with white families that continued to hold slaves after 1865. The efforts of Elisha Green of Mason County and Mary Stowers of Daviess County, described earlier, help to document the challenges facing blacks who sought to reconstitute their families. The 1870 census revealed that in largely rural counties and even in small towns, a large proportion of blacks continued to reside in white households, often as complete families that shared the surnames of white heads of household. Although the percentage of blacks in this residential pattern declined in the 1870s and the 1880s, it remained a distinctive feature of south-shore social and economic life. Another exceptional characteristic was the state's apprenticeship law, which gave preference to former masters.[8]

On February 14, 1866, the Kentucky legislature declared cohabiting couples legally married and their children legitimate if they paid a fifty-cent fee and registered with the county clerk their intention to be together. For an additional quarter they could obtain a marriage certificate. When some clerks refused to cooperate, agents of the Freedmen's Bureau assisted blacks. The law also proclaimed future marriages of blacks and mulattoes legal if performed by a "minister in good standing" with a "recognized church of colored persons." That destitute blacks actively took advantage of this law, even paying for a certificate, testified to the importance of the family.[9]

Slavery, poverty, poor housing, and violence all shaped marriage and family. After the war's end some blacks who had been forced into an unwanted marriage by their owners abandoned their mates. Some of them, like others, decided to start over with new families. Some men abandoned wives and children, and some women, lacking income and public assistance, deserted their children or hired them out. A number of destitute women turned to prostitution. For most blacks, though, legalization of marriage and protection of family life were paramount. In Louisville, for instance, most black families in 1870 and 1880 were headed by a male and contained two parents. In 1870, 71

percent of black children resided in two-parent households, and ten years later 76 percent did.[10]

Examination of local records reveals somewhat uneven patterns of black marriages after the passage of the 1866 law. Meade County had just one black marriage recorded between 1865 and 1884, between Squire Pate and Jane McKeel on April 22, 1866. The minister who performed the service was E.T. Hickerson, a white Baptist clergyman. (The license had been issued the day before by an agent of the Freedmen's Bureau.) Henderson County's records contain no entries for black marriages between 1865 and 1900. By contrast, in sparsely populated Crittenden County, 22 marriages were registered between 1866 and 1872 in the "Declaration of Marriage of Negroes and Mulattoes— Commonwealth of Kentucky." The first 2, on July 4, 1866, were those of Reuben and Matilda Wheeler, who indicated that they had lived together 20 years, and Glasgow and Harriett Leigh, who had cohabited for 5. An additional 3 marriages were recorded that year, and 10 in 1867. The next-highest number in one year was 6, in 1872. Handy and Tobitha Cruce, who registered on November 13, 1867, had lived together since 1827.[11]

The first marriage of free people of color in Crittenden County under the new law, the marriage of Edmond Mills and Esther Butler, was recorded on February 12, 1867. The two had not lived together as man and wife during slavery. Over the following twenty years, about 5 percent of all marriages involved African Americans; that ratio amounted to about half the total percentage of blacks living in the county. The low percentage probably was related to the declining proportion of younger people, who were moving away and marrying elsewhere. Relatively few marriages were recorded in 1867–69. The largest number, 11, were entered in 1877. Eight or 9 marriages were recorded annually in 1870, 1872, 1879, 1882, 1885, and 1886. The ministers most frequently identified were Willis Clark and Lank Grissom, and Mt. Zion Baptist Church was the site of most church marriages.[12]

In neighboring Livingston County, also thinly populated, 13 ex-slave couples took advantage of the new law between 1866 and 1871. The first was Thomas Gray and Sarah Jane Gray, who certified by their mark (all other black couples also signed by a mark) on June 16, 1866, that they had lived together for 15 years. All told, the slave marriages ranged in length from 6 to 35 years; 8 had lasted at least 12. In a separate book, "Marriage Bond Book and Register for Freedmen: Negroes and Mulattoes," 79 marriages were recorded between May 1866 and December 1871. The largest number, 21, occurred in 1869, and the smallest, 12, in 1866.[13]

Many ex-slave couples crossed the river to make a new start in Illinois,

Indiana, or Ohio. One can infer from the 1880 federal population schedules of Vanderburgh County, Indiana, for instance, that 40 percent of the 210 rural families and 30 percent of the urban families had been created in a slave state (primarily Kentucky) and had migrated to Indiana after 1865. A majority of the families, though, were commenced in Vanderburgh County by free black men and women. In Hamilton and Floyd counties also, more than half of the black families had begun on the north bank.[14]

Similar patterns were evident downstream in Illinois. In rural Massac County in 1870, for instance, the family of Charles Moore, a farmer, had been started in Tennessee; one of his two children was born there about 1859, but the other child, age 5, was born in Illinois about 1865. The same was true of the family of Sandy McBride, whose oldest child was a Tennessean and whose other two children, 5 and 3, were born in Illinois. By contrast, both of farm-hand Robert Loury's children, ages 2 and 12, were Tennesseans, suggesting that his family had arrived in 1868 or later. In five rural districts as well as in the town of Metropolis, the number of families with children born elsewhere as well as in Illinois was the same as those with children born in slave states only.[15]

In the same year, South Cairo Precinct of Alexander County had 136 black-headed households, and well over half of them had children. Twenty-six included Illinois-born children. These families were evenly divided between those begun elsewhere and those commenced in Cairo. Illustrative of the former was washerwoman Winnie Wiburn, apparently a widow, who had five children. Three (ages 15, 13, and 4) were natives of Kentucky, and two (ages 3 and 1) were Illinoisans. Apparently she and her husband had migrated to Cairo sometime after 1866. All of the children of John Bennett, a barber, had been born in Arkansas. One can infer that he and his wife, also from Arkansas, had moved to Cairo near or after the end of the war. In contrast, laborer James Orange and his wife had two children, 3 and 1, who were natives of Illinois.[16]

Marriage records in north-bank counties suggest that during the latter part of the Civil War and in the immediate postwar years there was a steady but not dramatic increase in the number of black marriages. Clermont County, Ohio, across the river from Bracken and Campbell counties, was probably typical. Between 1850 and 1874 its county clerks recorded 160 black marriages. (In 14 cases, only one of the partners was identified as black.) Slightly over 60 percent were registered before the end of the Civil War, and these were evenly divided between 1850–59 and 1860–64. The remainder occurred in 1865 or later. The first postwar marriage was that of Moses Gales, 28, and Disey Powell, 18, in July 1865. Just 3 weddings were recorded in 1865 and 6

the following year. There were 8 in 1867, 10 in 1868, and 13 in 1869. Between 1870 and 1874, 27 were registered.[17]

Ohio County, Indiana, across the river from Boone County, Kentucky, had 15 marriages of black couples between 1844 and 1881, but only 1 of them occurred before the end of the Civil War. The first postwar marriage was that of William Brown and Elizabeth Coleman on July 6, 1867. Just 4 took place between 1867 and 1869, and the remainder in the 1870s and early 1880s. By contrast, the clerk of rural Spencer County, Indiana, registered 22 black marriages between 1865 and 1869, a significant increase over prior records. Between 1870 and 1879, 13 more marriages occurred, and the number jumped to 36 in the 1880s. The earliest was that of Sarah Butler and Medford Shaw, married on May 28, 1865. It was followed by the union on July 2 of Harriet Ross and Don Quixot [sic]. Only 3 marriages were registered that year. Six or 7 were recorded annually between 1867 and 1869.[18]

In neighboring Warrick County, the first black marriage, that of John Birch and Victoria Hardin, was entered on March 19, 1867. The couple was married by a justice of the peace. The next entry appeared five years later, on April 6, 1872. That time a clergyman performed the ceremony. Three more marriages took place that year. Twenty-one were recorded between 1873 and 1879, and twenty-five between 1880 and 1889.[19]

In Vanderburgh County, race was not indicated in marriage records until about 1900. It is possible to make some inferences, though, based on surnames of African Americans mentioned in newspapers and other records. One of the earliest black marriages in the 1860s was that of Augustus Carter and Sarah Bugg, which occurred December 29, 1863. Green McFarland, pastor of Liberty Baptist, wed a Miss C. Chambers on November 29, 1865. Amos Thompkins wed Polly Lyles on December 23, 1867. Alfred Carter, brother of Gus and son of restaurateur James, married Eliza Morton, daughter of the wealthiest black woman in Evansville, in October 1868. All told, at least eleven marriages involving blacks occurred between 1863 and 1869. Notable marriages after 1869 included that of George Jackson and Lydia Carter in March 1873; Robert Nicholas and Mattie Duncan in December 1874; Dennis Rouse (second pastor at Liberty) and Susie Jackson in September 1876; and Willis Green (the physician) and Sarah Morton in June 1883.[20]

Rural Posey County marriage records do not include racial identification until 1880. Over the following two decades there were 132 weddings involving African Americans. These were as a rule between men and women who indicated their birthplace as Kentucky. Typically, the male was a laborer or engaged in farming. One such marriage was that of Samuel Baker, a laborer,

and Bell Webster, both of whom lived in Mount Vernon. Both had apparently lost previous spouses by death. He was 37 and she was 39. They were married on December 30, 1885. Officials here, as in several other river counties, used a variety of terms to describe African Americans: *light brown, light-complected, yellow, ginger, dark brown,* and *black,* as well as *colored* (sometimes *culard*) and *Negro.*[21]

Downriver Illinois counties disclose somewhat similar patterns, and records there are also uneven. Gallatin County had at least 76 black marriages before February 1874. There is no evidence of a flood of applicants for the legalization of marriage immediately after the war, as the earliest ones transpired in 1867: Major Johnson and Leanne Ray in August and David Jackson and Judy Simpson in December. Eighteen more occurred between 1868 and the end of 1870. Another 66 weddings were registered between March 1874 and the end of 1882.[22]

Tiny Pope County, across from Livingston County, Kentucky, recorded the marriages of 12 black couples before 1860 and 3 during the Civil War. The first postwar marriage was that of Richard Johnson and Celia Sides on June 25, 1865. Two more occurred between 1866 and 1869 and 1 in early 1873. As in upriver Gallatin County, there was no evidence of a rush of Kentucky blacks to cross the river and legalize slave unions—perhaps because Pope was a thinly populated, rural county with no large town.[23]

Family authority, organization, and size on either bank of the Ohio exhibited a great deal of continuity. In rural counties, families were as a rule headed by males, included a wife, and were nuclear— typically parents and children. Sometimes they were extended—that is, they included other family members, such as parents or siblings of the husband or wife—but they were rarely augmented with boarders and lodgers. Rural households were on the average larger than urban ones. The chief difference between settlements on the river's banks was that in Kentucky, especially in the immediate postwar years, a relatively large portion of rural blacks resided in white households, often as complete families. A legacy of slave times, this was especially evident where slave populations had been high.

In the cities and larger towns on the north side of the river, as well as in Louisville, Covington, Newport, Owensboro, and Paducah, the proportion of male-headed, two-parent families was lower and the percentage of extended and augmented families was much higher than in the countryside. Families in cities and towns were more likely to have a single parent, usually a woman, as head. The incidence of female-headed families was a symptom of the greater

number of employment opportunities in urban areas. It also reflected the fact that the urban environment was more conducive to family disintegration due to death, desertion, or divorce. Married women in the city, unlike their rural counterparts, were often employed, mostly in service-related work such as taking in washing. Families in cities and towns were more likely to be augmented or extended, although they were also somewhat smaller in size than those in the country. In Evansville in 1880, for instance, only slightly more than half of the families were nuclear—a smaller percentage than in Portsmouth (about 67%), Cincinnati (65%), and Louisville (65%).[24] Whether urban or rural, relatively few black heads of household owned their homes.

Family extension and augmentation provided income for families and shelter for newcomers in cities and towns, since rents were high and living space was limited. In addition, the proportion of youth living apart from their families was higher in urban areas. Contributing factors were the scarcity of schooling and employment opportunities in the countryside and the fact that urban poverty forced family members—female as well as male—to find employment away from home. This was at variance with the middle-class view of the family as a shelter for children in a heartless world. Rural young women were more likely than rural young men to remain at home, and when they left, their purpose was marriage. The size of the town was not a factor. In 1880, for instance, only 65 percent of persons in Evansville who were age 15 or less lived with both parents, as compared with 87 percent in rural Vanderburgh County. In Cincinnati and Louisville, and also in Portsmouth, Ohio, three-quarters of those 15 or less lived with both parents. In addition, about 15 percent of the heads of household in Portsmouth between ages 21 and 30 were incipient, or childless. The proportion of such families there was significantly lower than in Cincinnati (28%), Evansville (30%), and Louisville (24%). These rather high rates of incipience resulted from the migration of younger families to cities, especially on the north shore. Cities attracted not only younger families but also young single males. Hence there were about 10 more black males for every 100 black females in Cincinnati and Evansville in 1880. Louisville had almost 27 more. Undoubtedly these figures had to do with the less desirable conditions for young males in rural Kentucky.[25]

It is helpful to examine these generalizations by region, by cross-river comparison, and within counties. In Boyd County, Kentucky, an Appalachian county where slavery had had a minimal presence, 7 of the 9 black household heads in Ashland in 1870 were males, as were 8 of 10 in nearby Catlettsburg. In rural parts of the county, 10 of the 13 black households had a male head. There was little difference between town and country in patterns of family authority;

the two-parent family was the rule. There were some differences, however. In Ashland and Catlettsburg, 10 of the 19 black-headed households had a boarder or a lodger. None of the rural households did. Rural households were slightly larger than those in Ashland. A relatively small proportion—about one-fifth—of the county's black population resided in white households, and almost all of these lived in rural parts of the county. The most significant change that occurred by 1880 was that proportionately fewer blacks resided in white households.[26]

Just downriver, the seat of Ohio's Scioto County, Portsmouth, was more typical of larger towns and cities in the region, in that a smaller percentage of black households in the city, as compared to rural areas, resided in male-headed, two-parent households. In addition, one-third of city households were either extended or augmented. The urban experience—the availability of work, the presence of social stress, the prevalence of disease, the death of spouses, the opportunity for desertion, and other aspects of city life—is generally considered by historians of the black family to have been more disruptive than slavery in accounting for female-headed black families.[27]

In Kenton County, opposite Cincinnati, blacks in 1870 who lived in Covington were much more likely than their rural counterparts to live in a household headed by a black (3 of 4, as compared with 1 in 3). Most female-headed households were found in Covington. Typical of the latter was the family of Harriet Crawford, age 48, a washerwoman who lived in Ward 7. She had sons George, age 19, and John, 18, both of whom worked in a tobacco factory. Her home also included a 12-year-old girl, Angeline Morris. Families were also somewhat smaller in size in the city, averaging 4 persons, as compared with 4.5 in the countryside. Covington families were more likely to include nonrelatives. The household of George Washington, 50 and a hod carrier, also included his wife, Meda, also 50, who was a washerwoman; Betty Small, 23 and a domestic; and Millie White, 18, also a domestic. In Covington, as in other cities, rental costs and the scarcity of housing produced multifamily residences. In Ward 4, which had the largest number of African Americans in the city, for example, three dwellings adjoining one another contained 7 households and a total of 15 people. Nearby, five adjoining abodes had 11 families and a total of 40 people. Ten years later these configurations were little changed, except that proportionately fewer families, rural as well as urban, lived in white households: 202 of 1,565 in the city and 66 of 554 in the countryside.[28]

In contrast, in Trimble County, heavily rural and agrarian, about half of the county's blacks resided in white-headed households in 1870. There were just 41 black-headed families in the entire county, and they averaged 5.3 persons each. All but a handful were nuclear, and none lacked children. Typical

was the family of William Thomas, 26 and a farmhand, who had a wife, Martha, and three children, ages 1 to 6. Little changed in the decade that followed, except that the number of black-headed households rose to 71, and these constituted slightly over four-fifths of the county's black population. All but 3 were male-headed, two-parent families. Virtually all were nuclear.[29]

Cross-river Jefferson County, Indiana, offered some striking contrasts. In 1870, slightly over three-fourths of the black population resided in households that blacks headed. Nearly half of those living with whites were enumerated in Madison, and most of them were domestics. Rural households averaged 6.7 persons, as compared with 3.8 in the city. As in other north-shore communities, most female-headed families lived in the city, as did all eleven families with boarders and lodgers. Female-headed families typically included several wage-earners. Maria Wilson, 45, took in washing. Her son William, 22, was a hostler. Both were Kentuckians. The other children—Samuel, 18, a laborer, and four other children, ages 16 to 9, all of whom attended school—were natives of Indiana. Ten years later, an even higher proportion of blacks lived in black-headed households, half of which were in the city of Madison. As before, most female-headed families (20 of 26) resided in Madison, as did all of the augmented households. Family structure in downriver Floyd County, Indiana, was similar to that of Jefferson in both 1870 and 1880.[30]

These rural-urban patterns were replicated downriver from the Falls of the Ohio. In 1870 Hancock County, Kentucky, heavily agricultural and rural, had just under 100 black-headed households that accounted for 579 of the county's 729 blacks. But nearly 18 percent resided in white households—as elsewhere, mainly in rural precincts, but also in the village of Lewisport. In the county seat of Hawesville, by contrast, 100 dwelled in 22 black-headed families. The average household was 4.5 persons, less than the county average of 6. Five of the 8 female-headed families in the county were in Hawesville, and one-third of the town's families were either extended or augmented. The same change that occurred in upriver south-bank counties over the following ten years was evident in Hancock County. The percentage of blacks living in black-headed households rose to just over 83 percent. Countywide, most families had two parents and were nuclear. The family of Hawesville's Randall Lander, 40 and the Kentucky-born driver of a team, was representative. His wife, 39, took in washing, and a 17-year-old daughter was a servant. The household also included five more children, ages 11 to eleven months. Cross-river Perry County, with relatively few blacks, differed from Hancock in the same way that Jefferson County, Indiana, contrasted with Trimble County, Kentucky.[31]

Rural blacks residing in downstream Daviess County far outnumbered those living in Owensboro. Many of the rural blacks lived in white households and shared the surnames of nearby whites or those with whom they lived. Even in Owensboro, prewar patterns persisted, with well over one-quarter of the town's African Americans living in households that whites headed. For example, George Buckner, 14—later a physician in Evansville—lived in Ward 2 with his sister and brother in the home of William and Nancy Buckner, whites, ages 60 and 45. The county had 93 black-headed households, 23 of which had female heads. Most of the latter, like the 35 augmented or extended families, were in Owensboro. The average household size in Owensboro, 4.8, was slightly smaller than that of rural Daviess County, 5.2.[32]

Conditions changed somewhat in the 1870s. The number of blacks residing in Owensboro doubled, but almost three in four in the county were enumerated in rural precincts, many in white-headed households. Typical of these was Henry Glover, 44, who lived with his wife, 34, and three children, ages 11 to six months. They provided labor for white farmer S.R. Ewing, who lived in Lowertown Precinct. The proportion of Owensboro's blacks residing in white households, though, had dropped to about 14 percent. Of those in black-headed households in the town, almost one-third (72) had a female head. Nearly half (98) included relatives, boarders, or lodgers, or some combination of these. Outside city limits, few families had female heads, and almost all were nuclear. As in 1870, rural families were slightly larger than families in Owensboro.[33]

Nearby Warrick County was also rural and agricultural, but it, too, differed from its south-shore neighbors in some fundamental ways. In 1870 over half of the county's blacks resided in Ohio Township, which included the village of Newburgh. Nine of ten of the county's African Americans lived in black-headed households. All but 2 of the 70 households had male heads. Slightly over one-third (25) were extended or augmented, and these resided in the county seat or Newburgh. Probably typical was the family of John Staples, a 40-year-old Kentucky-born farmer. He had a wife and nine children, ranging in age from 17 to three months. That the youngest, twins, were born in Indiana and the next youngest, age 2, was born in Kentucky suggests that the Staples family migrated to Ohio Township sometime during or after 1868.[34]

Cross-river Henderson County remained distinctive. For one thing, the vast majority of African Americans resided in rural parts of the county. For another, many there lived in white-headed households. In the town of Henderson, by contrast, just one in five did. The average size of the town's 235 black-headed households was five. One in ten of them had female heads. Un-

like rural black families, almost all of which were nuclear, about half of the households in the city of Henderson included boarders or relatives or both.[35]

In rural Henderson County, patterns of living evoked antebellum times. For example, the household of Payne Dixon, a white farmer, comprised Henderson Alves, 47, a field hand; Patsay, 42, a cook and probably Henderson's spouse; America Hatchett, 16; Jack Alves, 22, a field hand, and Amelia Alves, 20, possibly Jack's wife; Zeptha Alves, 20, a field hand; and Bejar Watson, 48, a field hand, and his wife Elmia, 49, as well as their five children, 2 to 14 years in age. Tobacco dealer William Soaper, 75, and his wife and children, resided in Upper Town Precinct. His home included ten African Americans: Miles Lambert, farm laborer, his wife, Louisa, a cook, and their 4-year-old son; Dick Soaper, 16, a tobacco stemmer; Frank Soaper, 10; and Thomas Black, 45, a farm laborer, his wife, Arianna, a servant, and their three children, ages 8 to 14.[36]

Blacks' surnames evoked memories of slave times in Henderson County. By far the most common one was Dixon, the name of the noted planter and politician. Of the 253 Dixons listed in the 1870 census of the county, 166 were black. The county's African Americans also included 145 Powells, 65 Alveses, and 44 Barrets. The home of Harvey Dixon, white, who had a wife and five children, included three colored Dixons: Nancy, 16; William, 14; and Ann, 10. White physician James Powell, 32, had a wife, four children, and a sister. His household also contained two black Powells: Martha, 48, a domestic; and Addie, 6.[37]

Over the following ten years, the proportion of blacks living in the town rose slightly, and the percentage living in white-headed households in town dropped to 8 percent. Both changes suggested that blacks' autonomy increased significantly during the 1870s. But urban conditions brought a higher level of one-parent, female-headed households—just below one in four in 1880. Family extension and augmentation remained high, nearly 40 percent of black households. In the countryside, however, the male-headed, two-parent, nuclear family predominated. Average household size there continued to be higher than in the town. Antebellum social patterns, though, persisted in rural Henderson County, not only in blacks' surnames, but also in the number of blacks who still lived in white families. William Soaper, now 85, still had Frank, a servant in 1870, in his household. Frank had married during the decade, and his wife, Susan, was also a servant. William's household also included Laura Soaper, 35 and a cook. The latter had two children, Eli and Mattie Soaper, ages 10 and 6.[38]

The structure of black families across the river in Evansville and Vanderburgh County was substantially different. For one thing, most of the hundreds of black newcomers resided from the moment of their arrival in households that

they headed. In 1870, just 48 of the slightly more than 700 African Americans in rural Vanderburgh County lived in white households. The same proportion was evident in the city of Evansville. Ten years later, the number of blacks living in rural white households had risen to 113, but that amounted to only about 8 percent of blacks living in the country. Most, as in 1870, were domestics or farmhands.[39]

The impact of the urban experience on family life was manifest in Evansville, and it can be assumed that in Cincinnati and Louisville African American family life was similar. In 1880 almost 98 percent of all households in rural parts of Vanderburgh County were male-headed, with two-parent families, as compared with 78 percent in the city. Twenty years later the numbers were, respectively, 84 and 72. That 83 percent of female heads of household had no occupation, and that 75 percent were widows underscored the social and economic fragility of such families. This may help to explain family augmentation, present in slightly over 33 percent of all Evansville households in 1880, as compared with only 14 percent in rural Vanderburgh County. About 75 percent of rural households were nuclear, as compared with 50 percent in Evansville. (The proportion of families that were extended was nearly the same in both sections, about 11%.) The same pattern prevailed twenty years later.[40]

Urban dwellings in 1880 were more likely than rural ones, moreover, to include more than one household: there were 1.2 families per dwelling in the city, as compared to the nearly even ratio in the countryside. In contrast, urban households were smaller: 4.3 persons, as compared with 4.7 in rural areas. This difference reflected several factors: the scarcity and the cost of urban housing, the higher incidence of one-parent households and the greater number of incipient (childless) families in the city, and the desirability of large families in agricultural regions. As noted in chapter 9, many black women in Evansville worked (about one in three) and were married (about two in five) by 1900.[41]

Several examples are useful. In 1870 rural Center Township's blacks were mostly newcomers from Kentucky, like the family of David Morton. Age 38, he was a farm laborer. His wife, Ann, was 30. They had six children, ranging in age from 15 to 3, all of whom had been born in Kentucky. The family had migrated to Vanderburgh County sometime after 1867. Like most of their neighbors, the family had no real or personal property of value. George Walz, 24 and an Arkansas-born laborer, dwelled in Ward 1 of the city. He and his wife, Peckey, 23 and a native of Kentucky, had two children: Maggie, 3, and George, ten months. Both children were natives of Indiana. The couple had either migrated to Evansville or been married there sometime before 1867. Their household also included another family, which was headed by a widow,

Margaret Monroe, 40. She had no occupation, but her son, Samuel, 21, was a laborer. Her household also included Julia Taylor, 50, and Maria Jean, 13. Their relationship to Margaret or to either Walz was uncertain.[42]

In the 1880 census, David Morton and his family no longer resided in Center Township. Where they moved is unclear. Probably typical of those who remained in the country was the household of Napoleon Matthews, 55 and a farmer. He and his wife, Willie, 48, had five children, the eldest of whom, Couch, was 27 and a farm laborer. The youngest, Charles, was 5. The youngest four had been born in Indiana, and the parents as well as Couch in Kentucky. Since the next oldest, Eliza, was 12, it is likely that the family moved to Indiana sometime before 1868. (Possibly Willie was his second wife, given the gap in their ages.) In Evansville, Preston Glass, 23 and a native of Kentucky, was a roustabout. He and his wife, Sarah, 23, had two children: Edward, 5, and Albert, 1. They resided at 620 Campbell Street, near Washington Avenue and Second Street in Ward 1. As Sarah and the children were natives of Indiana, one might infer that Preston and Sarah met and were married in Evansville sometime before 1875.[43]

Typical of augmented families was that of Henry Johnson, 53 and a laborer, who lived with his wife, Winfred, 38 and a cook, at 906 Gum Street. Possibly she was his second wife. Both were natives of Kentucky. Their household of seven people included Rebecca Jones, 20, who kept house. Henry's stepdaughter, she was married, but her husband was not present when the census-taker came by. She and Laura Jones, 16, and Samuel Jones, 12, also listed as stepchildren, were natives of Arkansas. Ora Jones, 2, was identified as Henry's granddaughter and a native of Indiana. It is unclear when Henry and his wife arrived in the city. Henry's home also included a boarder, Charles Dawson, 33, who was an engineer and a native of Missouri.[44]

Downstream, both sides of the river were mostly rural and agricultural. The contrasts resembled those upriver. Many south-bank blacks resided in white households, though the number and the proportion declined somewhat in the 1870s. Across the river, most blacks lived in households that they headed. Rural families were mostly nuclear and male-headed and were larger in size than their counterparts in villages and towns.

Union County, Kentucky, for example, was in many respects a mirror image of Henderson, and in many respects cross-river Posey and Gallatin counties, which were similar to each other, offered significant contrasts to Union. In 1870 Union had about 2,500 black residents, most of whom lived outside of the river towns of Uniontown, Caseyville, and Raleigh and the interior county seat, Morganfield. About 25 percent of them resided in white house-

holds, and in a number of instances blacks shared the whites' surname. Just about as many white households had black residents (212) as ones headed by blacks (247). Only 18 of the latter had female heads, and most of those were in Uniontown and Morganfield. About two-thirds of the 247 black families were nuclear. Of the rest, most (about 60) were extended. Approximately 30 families had a boarder, typically a single male who was a farmhand. Most male household heads were laborers, usually on farms. The average black household had six persons. Circumstances were little different ten years later. The major change was that the number of blacks living in white households had dropped to about 10 percent of the total black population. The number of white households with blacks also declined, but the number remained relatively high (140). All but 59 of the 445 black-headed households were nuclear. The average rural family size was about the same (5.7 persons) as in 1870.[45]

Cross-river Posey County, Indiana, also had a productive agricultural economy. It differed in several ways, however, from Union County. In 1870 and 1880, more than nine in ten blacks lived in black-headed households. Almost all of those enumerated in white-headed households were farmhands. Slightly over half of the black households (66), accounting for half the county's black population, were located in Mount Vernon, not in the country, because job opportunities existed there. A third difference was that the number of augmented and extended families was much higher (about one in three households) than across the river, and the majority resided in the county seat. In addition, although nearly all black households in the county had male heads (111 of 126), 15 had female heads, and 12 of them resided in Mount Vernon. Countywide, black households had about 5.5 persons on the average, but in Mount Vernon the number was slightly smaller. Comparable observations can be made about patterns ten years later as well as in neighboring Gallatin County, Illinois, in 1870 and 1880.[46]

Family patterns in downstream Ballard, Crittenden, and Livingston counties on the south shore and Hardin, Pope, and Massac counties on the north shore were generally similar to each other, probably because slavery had a much smaller imprint in that region as compared with Union County and its neighbors upriver. In all six counties virtually all black families lived in the countryside. In Livingston County in 1880, for instance, less than one in four African Americans lived in the largest settlement, Smithland. Black families in that village were fairly small: slightly over 4 persons each, as compared with 5.4 for the county as a whole. Half of the thirty-six female-headed households in the county were located there, and they represented one-third of all the black households in that community. About one in four families in Smithland in-

cluded relatives or boarders or both. Just 11 of the 228 black residents of the village resided in white households. Outside Smithland, 37 blacks (out of a total rural population of 685) lived in twenty-eight white households. Family configurations in the other two Kentucky counties and their cross-river neighbors resembled those of Livingston.[47]

McCracken County, which lay immediately to the west in the Purchase, was an exception. It differed in household arrangements from its south-bank counterparts and resembled upriver Jefferson and Kenton counties in Kentucky as well as downriver Alexander County in Illinois, largely because of the presence of Paducah. Most of the county's blacks (92%) resided in black-headed households in 1880. The percentage was even higher (95) in Paducah. In addition, a majority of the black population (just under 60%) lived in the city. Countywide, black families averaged slightly over 5 persons in size; in Paducah the average was 4.6. Of the 813 black-headed families in the county, 189, or 23 percent, had female heads. Most of these resided in Paducah, and they represented almost one-third of the 539 households in the city. Twenty-five percent of Paducah's black households included relatives or boarders and lodgers, compared to just under 14 percent in rural McCracken County. Put another way, about seven in ten Paducah black families had a male head and two parents, and about three in four were nuclear. Outside of the city, nine in ten had a male head and two parents, and between eight and nine in ten were nuclear. The household of Paducah's Jasper Robertson, 37, a mulatto, was representative, as he worked in a tobacco factory. He and his wife, Kate, 29, had a son, 11. His household also had five boarders, ages 25 to 40, all of whom worked as laborers or servants.[48]

Cross-river Pulaski County differed in two respects: it had a much higher proportion of African Americans, and they were concentrated in the village of Mound City and bottomland precincts adjoining the Ohio. Virtually all were employed as farmhands. Few blacks lived in white households, and all but a handful of black households had male heads and were nuclear in form. Little changed in the 1870s. By 1880 Mound City Precinct accounted for about one-quarter of the county's black population. Half lived in four other river precincts: Grand Chain, Junction, Ohio, and Villa Ridge. The size of the average household was 5 persons.[49]

Probably typical was the family of Jasper Perkins, 40, a farmer and a native of Tennessee, who was enumerated in Villa Ridge Precinct. His wife, 30 (possibly his second wife), was also from Tennessee. So was the eldest son, 17. But seven other children, ranging from 15 to 1, had been born in Illinois. This would suggest that the elder Perkins moved to Pulaski County near the end of

the Civil War. Close by were five other households headed by persons named Perkins whose ages ranged from 25 to 48. All were from Tennessee. The ages and birthplaces of their children suggested that they were siblings and probably migrated at about the same time.[50]

Next-door Alexander County, where most blacks lived in Cairo, more closely resembled Vanderburgh and McCracken counties. In its rural precincts in 1870, only 7 of the 84 households had female heads. About one-third included relatives and in a few instances boarders. In Cairo, by contrast, females headed a much larger number and percentage of families, and household augmentation was common. In South Cairo, for example, females headed 39 of the 136 black families, or 29 percent of the total. Boarders and lodgers, and to a much lesser extent relatives, were enumerated in approximately 54 percent of the households. Females who headed families often secured income by taking in boarders and lodgers. Such was the case of Emily Newman, 38 and a native of Maryland, who listed no occupation. She had a son, Alfred, who was 10. Her home also included four adults ranging in age from 21 to 40. Some may have been her relatives or related to each other.

The same configurations existed in North Cairo Precinct. Typical of nuclear families was that of Stephen Hunter, 30 and a laborer. He and his wife, 25, had a son, Peter, who was 1. The child had been born in Illinois. Like virtually all of the black population of Cairo, the couple had arrived sometime near or after the end of the Civil War. Many families were augmented. Such was the case of laborer Thomas Johnson, 35, and his wife, Frances, 30. Both were Virginians. Two children, 8 and 10, had been born in Kentucky, and the youngest, 5, in Illinois. The household also included a man and a woman in their twenties whose name was Robins—possibly husband and wife and related to Frances.[51]

Marriage and the family mattered much to African Americans on both sides of the Ohio in postwar years. Most blacks lived in two-parent families. Employment opportunities, death, desertion, and divorce explained the higher proportion of one-parent, female-headed households in cities and towns. It was no coincidence that families in towns and villages often included boarders, lodgers, and relatives. They could enhance family income this way in an environment of poor-quality, high-rent housing. Families in towns also provided nurture and shelter for newcomers, whether relatives or not. Because of the higher incidence of female heads and of younger couples who had either no children or a few young ones, urban families tended also to be smaller than their rural counterparts. Those counties with cities attracted the largest num-

ber of black families, and over time they accounted for an increasing proportion of the region's black population.

Although there was a great deal of continuity in form and function of
families on either side of the Ohio, a significant difference was that in Kentucky—with the notable exception of Louisville, and to a lesser extent
Covington and Paducah—a relatively large proportion of blacks, including
black families, resided in white-headed households. The proportion declined
somewhat during the 1870s but remained a distinguishing feature of black
society—as did the use of surnames of former owners—into the 1880s.

The black family was the pillar of black society. Too often historians have
overlooked its importance. But it is now to the other elements of black society
and culture that we shall turn our attention.

11

Black Society

After the family, blacks valued the church as the most vital element in their lives. The church provided social as well as spiritual nourishment in a time when racial bigotry prevented blacks from engaging in what we in the twenty-first century consider normal relations among human beings. Closely associated with blacks' religious institutions were benevolent and fraternal organizations that helped African Americans form a distinctive culture.[1] The establishment of public schools, discussed in chapter 12, was also a noteworthy achievement of postwar black society, and it went along with the development of churches and other social organizations.

The transition to all-black churches occurred rapidly after the war. Prior to the war African Methodist Episcopal (AME) churches prevailed among north-shore blacks, while on the south shore Baptists were predominant. In rural areas and small towns, many south-bank blacks worshipped in white churches (as noted in chapter 6). Such mingling was less common across the river. The Hanover Presbyterian Church in Jefferson County, Indiana, like its counterpart in Evansville, had only one African American member before 1865. A dozen or so blacks belonged to the Methodist churches in Lawrenceburg and Madison. New Albany's Presbyterians included some black members.[2]

But most blacks ended up leaving white churches. They did so to avoid insults, to express resentment over exclusion from church activities, and to select their own ministers and forms of organization. Some blacks resisted the trend toward segregation because whites ridiculed blacks' modes of worship;

in addition there were blacks who believed an integrated setting promoted a better quality of leadership. Black churches were institutions that they could control, however, and for most blacks this was the deciding factor. By 1870, for instance, there were eleven black meetinghouses in Ohio River towns of Indiana. Thirteen more followed in the 1870s.[3]

There was no dearth of men to serve as pastors. The constraints of slave society were gone, and the number of black preachers grew dramatically. Their styles had enormous influence not only on African American Christianity, but also on black society and culture. Following "the model of the paternalistic master in their relationships with their congregations," preachers "coached their congregants in everything from relating to God to coping with the mundane minutia of daily life."[4]

From the outset black churches elicited a wide range of responses from whites. Evansville may have been typical. There Democrats, especially German Americans, sought for at least ten years after the end of the war to get the City Council to close Liberty Baptist Church, because they said the members' forms of music and worship offended them. Even the Republican editor in 1875 described revival meetings at Liberty Baptist and the AME churches as a "painful state of excitement" characterized by the singing of "unchurchlike songs, the groans of mourners at the anxious seat . . . the entreaties and menaces of friends and relatives . . . [and] the shouting and screaming of men and women in a ferment of real or assumed enthusiasm." He also derided the "absurd and laughable" visions of Sunday night worshippers.[5] Although the black elite shared his contempt for this form of worship, ordinary blacks enjoyed the enthusiasm of church rituals, especially the emotional climax that the sermon provided.

Some whites—at least in the immediate postwar years—supported blacks' efforts to worship on their own terms. Andrew L. Robinson of Evansville was one of their strongest advocates. This Baptist layman and antislavery attorney was approached by Green McFarland and twenty-three other newcomers to arrange for the organization of a black congregation. The meeting to create Liberty Baptist Church took place in the Baptist Lecture Room at Fifth and Chestnut streets on May 13, 1865. Robinson served as the first clerk. A white man named Woods served as pastor until McFarland was ordained in 1866. Robinson and businessman Asa Igleheart, agents of a philanthropic group, also worked with Evansville blacks to aid newly freed slaves across the river. For many whites, having black Christians in their midst for the first time created spectacles to be enjoyed—like blacks' baptismal services in the Ohio and their musical concerts in public halls.[6]

The Baptists became the largest Protestant denomination among blacks.

The number of black Baptist churches in Cincinnati rose from 6 shortly after the end of the war to 13 by the turn of the century. Membership doubled. In Indiana, by 1887 there were 5,565 black Baptists. Liberty Baptist, the largest black Baptist church outside of the capital, boasted 800 members. By the early 1890s four new Baptist congregations had sprung up in Evansville. McFarland, the second-largest, was formed in 1882 by dissidents at Liberty who objected to the hiring of J. Dennis Rouse as pastor. Their church was named for Green McFarland.[7] Louisville's black Baptists were even more numerous. Fifth Street Baptist Church was the oldest and the state's largest in membership. Led by three pastors whose tenures ranged from 14 to 53 years, Fifth Street ministered to a variety of social and spiritual needs. Its leaders helped to form the General Association of Negro Baptists in Kentucky and the Kentucky Normal and Theological Institute.[8]

Black Methodism grew also, although at a slower pace, because black Methodists had a centralized hierarchy that encouraged concentration of resources. Churches were found in most towns and cities, but usually not in rural areas. Pastors, rotated as a rule every two years, were unable to develop the level of influence over their flocks that Baptist ministers had.

The founder of most of the AME churches in the region was William Paul Quinn. The fourth and senior bishop of the denomination, he died in Richmond, Indiana, on February 21, 1873. Accompanying his casket to the cemetery were the AME pastors from a number of cities of Indiana and Ohio, including Benjamin W. Arnett of Cincinnati and W.S. Lankford of Evansville. Arnett's church, Allen Temple, was the oldest (established in 1824) and the most influential congregation of that denomination along the Ohio. By 1890 there were fifty-one AME churches in thirty Indiana counties, with a total membership of 4,435. Second to Indianapolis in membership was Evansville, where the congregation hosted the week-long state conferences in the summers of 1872 and 1880. The number of delegates and onlookers at the latter event was impressive, as 1,200—too large a crowd for the church—assembled in Evans Hall, the city's largest public meeting place.[9]

Religious affiliation was one means of demonstrating class and status differences. Because of their organization and their emphasis on an educated ministry, black Methodists offered a more restrained, intellectual approach to religion. The black elite tended to be attracted to the AME Church, whose better-educated clergymen were critical of the emotionalism that had strong appeal to the masses.[10]

As Quinn's funeral services revealed, though, racial unity transcended denominational lines when events vital to a black community occurred. The

anniversary services of black ministers and of churches were interdenominational affairs. The proceedings of the fiftieth anniversary celebration at Allen
Temple included histories of the other churches in the city as well as its own.
The laying of the cornerstone for the new AME meetinghouse in Evansville
in June 1874 was an interdenominational event capped by a grand picnic that
the United Brothers of Friendship sponsored. Dedication services in July 1879
attracted all of the city's black ministers and clergymen from outlying towns.
Annual revival services at the largest AME and Baptist churches in Evansville
were collaborative. Black clergy also cooperated in planning annual Emancipation Day proceedings and were prominent figures at school graduation activities. When civil rights were at stake, as noted in chapter 6, denominational
lines were relatively unimportant. During Thanksgiving week in 1872, for
instance, Liberty Baptist and the AME Church in Evansville sponsored a rally
that attacked racial segregation in the schools.[11]

The struggles encountered by impoverished blacks in smaller towns and
villages to sustain religious life—arranging for meeting places, paying for clergymen, and providing philanthropic assistance to members—must have been
monumental. These tasks were difficult enough for brothers and sisters in larger
places. Although many of the histories of towns and counties published in the
two or three decades after 1865 either ignored or denigrated blacks, some
document the formation of churches in predominantly rural counties (see
chapter 6).[12] Where blacks were scattered and few in number—as in Perry
County, Indiana, or Pope County, Illinois—one can only speculate, given the
lack of records, about where worship occurred and who provided religious
nurture. Services may have been held in the homes of residents, in barns, or in
whites' churches, with the aid of black laypeople or white clergy.[13]

By contrast, contemporary accounts by Cincinnati blacks portray a rich
religious life that must have been found in other large towns on the Ohio as
well. When Allen Temple AME held its semicentennial celebration, its proceedings noted that there were three black Methodist, six black Baptist, and
one black Christian (Disciples) churches in the city. Five of these ten churches
had been established since the end of the Civil War. In value of property, Allen
Temple, located on the corner of Broadway and Sixth streets, in the heart of
Bucktown, was the wealthiest, at $75,000. The former Sephardic Jewish Temple,
which Allen purchased in 1870, seated hundreds and boasted rows of chande-
liers valued at $1,000 each. Most congregations elsewhere could not afford
such expensive fixtures, but a number of black churches had stained-glass windows, varnished interiors, carpeting, parsonages, small libraries, kitchens, and
pastors' studies. Eventually most paid their pastors.[14]

Second in value of its property was Zion Baptist, on Ninth near Central Avenue. Third was Union Chapel, on Seventh near Plum. According to the Allen Temple's proceedings, three black church properties were valued at $10,000 or less. In number of members, the largest was Union Baptist, located at the corner of Mound and Richmond, which had 512. Next was Allen Temple, with 390, and in third place was Zion Baptist, with 200. Mount Zion Baptist, on Ninth, near John, had 150 members. Brown's Chapel in Walnut Hills and Union Chapel each had 100 members. The other four had between 50 and 80.[15]

As noted earlier, Evansville's first comprehensive history, like its antiquarian counterparts in Clark, Floyd, Perry, Spencer, and Warrick counties, listed all black organizations. There were ten congregations in the city by the late 1880s. Five were Baptist: Liberty and McFarland, located near Baptisttown; Independence, on the west side; and Mt. Zion and Free Will, on the north side, where black coal miners resided. Four were Methodist: Alexander, Hood's Chapel AME Zion, Fifth Street ME, and St. John's ME, the latter two affiliated with the Central Conference of the white Methodist Episcopal Church, North. A Colored Christian Church was also established.[16]

Three congregations were the most influential: the AME, the oldest, which was named Alexander in the 1870s in honor of a beloved pastor; Liberty Baptist, the largest in membership; and McFarland Baptist. These three served all classes, though their lay leaders tended to come from the black elite. Most black churches were tiny and served day laborers, servants, and miners. When Hood's Chapel filed its articles of incorporation in the county recorder's office in 1886, for example, 23 of the 36 people entered an X after their names.[17]

Cincinnati's and Louisville's Roman Catholics witnessed the creation of black parishes shortly after the Civil War, but Evansville's, most of whom were German Americans, strongly opposed not only the idea of separate black parishes but also having blacks sitting with whites in church services and allowing them to attend parochial schools. In the late summer of 1868 the *Evansville Daily Journal* chided local Catholics for being so hostile to the Negro. The most violent opponents of blacks in the region, asserted this evangelical Protestant, were Roman Catholics. The scant surviving evidence suggests that a handful of black Catholics worshipped separately in the basement of Holy Trinity Church, probably thanks to the support of John A. Reitz, a prominent citizen who had helped to create the parish.[18]

Similar patterns appear in early histories of Illinois's river counties. Pulaski County's first history, as noted in chapter 6, documented the existence of three churches by the early 1880s. As of 1883 Cairo had several black Baptist churches. Its black Episcopalians worshipped with whites until 1888, when a new edi-

fice was completed that was open only to whites. Blacks used the older church, renamed St. Michael's.[19] Massac County had two black churches by 1874. First Colored Baptist was established in Metropolis in 1866. Ferdinand Robinson was an early pastor and held his post longest—twenty-seven years. Bethel AME was organized in 1874 in adjacent Brooklyn, later named Brookport. It was much smaller in membership than First Baptist.[20]

All-black churches were also an essential part of the lives of Kentucky's African Americans. Many had their roots in white congregations. For sentimental or emotional reasons—for instance, the desire to be buried with loved ones in the black portion of graveyards—some members chose to remain in the white churches. But by the 1870s, it was rare to find blacks in a white church. Whites reinforced the trend by insisting that white clergymen should minister only to whites. As on the north bank, Baptists were the most numerous. Led by Rev. Henry Adams of Louisville's Fifth Street Church, they created the State Convention of Colored Baptists at a conference in the city in August 1865. The delegates elected Adams moderator, adopted a constitution, and formed committees on education, missions, and membership. The actions of the convention accelerated blacks' departure from white congregations.[21]

The State Convention met three more times before reorganizing as the General Association of Colored Baptists in 1869. Total membership in the state was 12,520. After Adams's death in 1871, Rev. George W. Dupee of Paducah led the organization. During his tenure the number of churches grew to 239 and membership to nearly 42,000. The General Association boasted 57,285 members by 1891. In 1875 the organization also took over publication of Dupee's *Baptist Herald,* renamed the *American Baptist* in 1879.[22]

A prominent issue at these meetings was the education of ministers. The cost of building a seminary was staggering for former slaves. Some churches and lay people made generous donations, while the General Association assessed each member five cents monthly. Whites were also approached for their support. During Dupee's tenure the General Association opened a seminary in Louisville in 1874. Poorly funded and poorly attended, it lasted only five months. Led by H.C. Marrs and his brother, Elijah, the association purchased land and a building for a theological school on a block bounded by Seventh, Eighth, Kentucky, and Zane streets in Louisville. Classes began in November 1879. The following year the trustees hired William J. Simmons to run the school, named Baptist Normal and Theological Institute.[23]

Simmons, born a slave and a veteran of the Union Army, graduated from Howard University in 1873 and became a minister in 1878. His fledgling

school grew despite a number of challenges. Most teachers, for example, lacked college degrees, but by 1891 over half of the faculty were college graduates. Academic standards rose somewhat, but students were selected for their religious proclivities, not their academic achievements. Tuition was nominal, and the school's financial state was always precarious. A superior publicist, Simmons established an awards program for outstanding students and promoted their achievements among influential whites. Religious services at the school—renamed State University in 1883—displayed the accomplishments of black clergymen, singers, and musicians before white audiences. Simmons's unflagging efforts to raise money from black and white churches, black and white leaders, and northern philanthropic and missionary societies ensured the institution's survival. Support from Fifth Street Baptist was also important, as it provided space for university services and often funded the school during its all-too-common fiscal crises. Most important was the annual subsidy from the American Baptist Home Missionary Society. The women's group of the Northern Baptists also helped to support teachers' salaries. Baptist millionaire John D. Rockefeller gave $500 in 1884, and the Slater Fund donated $1,000 a year later.[24]

Simmons broadened and improved the curriculum. He created a College Department that offered training in the liberal arts. In the mid-1880s Louisville National Medical College and Central Law School began an affiliation with the school. State University also created a Theological Department that offered a two-year program leading to a B.D. degree for those with college degrees and a series of courses for pastors without college degrees. Also offered were extension courses for pastors. These outreach programs led Simmons to advocate formation of a national organization to strengthen the work of black clergymen. In 1886 he was selected president of the newly formed American National Baptist Convention. Simmons was the heart and soul of State University until his resignation in 1890 to head a new black institution that stressed industrial education.[25]

Emancipation greatly increased the mobility of pastors: for the first time they could move to new charges as they saw fit. The most talented pastors could climb far up the ladder of success. A notable success story was Allen Allensworth's. After serving in the Union Navy, Allensworth returned to Louisville, where he was converted at Fifth Street Church. He worked as a sexton while enrolled in a school run by the American Missionary Association. He then taught school for the Freedmen's Bureau. After taking some courses in Nashville to prepare for the ministry, he served as financial agent of the General Association. He gained a reputation as a strong lecturer and "teaching"

minister at several churches. Following a stint as field representative for the American Baptist Home Missionary Society, Allensworth became pastor of Union Baptist Church in Cincinnati, where he served until 1886. Later he was the chaplain for the 24th U.S. Colored Infantry Regiment and rose to the rank of lieutenant colonel.[26]

Louisville had the most black houses of worship on the Kentucky side of the river—twenty-four by 1880. First Baptist, which was renamed Fifth Street in 1870, was the oldest and the largest, with about 1,200 members. Second-oldest was Green Street Baptist. Henry Adams was the longtime pastor of the former, as was Richard Sneethen of the latter. The national convention of the Colored Baptists was held at Green Street in 1879. The oldest Methodist church, Quinn's Chapel AME, antedated the Civil War. Membership grew substantially, in part because of the church's prominent role in civil rights activities. Young's Chapel AME, formed in 1869 by Rev. Octave Double, was located on Fifteenth Street. Originally known as the California Mission Church, it was renamed in honor of Rev. Henry Young of Quinn's Chapel. The first state conference of the African Methodist Episcopal Church, Zion, took place in the city in June 1866 at Center Street Church, which sought to secede from the white Methodist Episcopal Church, South. A court fight with whites over ownership of the property ended with an 1868 decision that left the title with the whites. Most of the parishioners then left Center Street to organize Fifteenth Street AME Zion. Some of its members, in turn, withdrew to establish Curry Chapel, named for Rev. E.H. Curry. Curry Chapel soon became one of the largest and most influential Zion churches in the city. Broadway Tabernacle AME Zion "rivaled Fifth Street Baptist in the makeup of its members and its varied program."[27]

One of the greatest preachers in the state, Alexander Walters, was associated with Fifteenth Street Church. A native of Bardstown, he was educated in Louisville and was a brilliant student. In 1877 he was licensed to preach in Indiana, but he returned to the Kentucky Conference a year later. In 1881 his bishop assigned him to the Cloverport Circuit, where he created five Zion churches. There, as before, he supplemented his income by teaching school. When Fifteenth Street Church decided to move to a new edifice on Twelfth Street, Walters became pastor of a group of twenty-five that refused to depart. His rise in the denomination was spectacular. He was elected bishop in 1892.[28]

Some of Kentucky's African American Methodists remained affiliated with the Colored Missionary District of the Colored Methodist Episcopal Church, South (CME), that was part of the white Methodist Episcopal Church, South. Formed in 1866 to organize recently freed black preachers, the CME was

governed by whites. The state had two administrative districts, one of which was centered at Jackson Street Church in Louisville, founded in 1870. The largest congregation was on Center Street, between Green and Walnut. This congregation had a series of well-educated pastors with a strong commitment to civic progress and racial justice. It was later renamed in honor of its first and longtime pastor, C.H. Brown.[29]

Some Kentucky African Americans belonged to other groups, most of which were controlled by white denominations. White Presbyterians provided pastoral training for black ministers, but congregations for black Presbyterians were not formed until the late 1870s. Black Cumberland Presbyterians held an organizational meeting in Henderson in 1868. For a time they met in white houses of worship, but in 1874 they were permitted to form a separate General Assembly. With whites' assistance, they opened an institution to train clergymen in the early 1880s. The Protestant Episcopal Church had some black adherents. Most notable was St. Mark's Episcopal Church, Colored, formed in 1867 as a mission in Louisville. The congregation purchased the former German Lutheran Church structure on Green Street, between Ninth and Tenth streets. After its first pastor, the energetic Joseph S. Atwell, departed the following year, the congregation disbanded. A few years later whites helped blacks to form the Church of Our Merciful Savior on Madison, between Ninth and Tenth streets.[30]

After the Civil War the white pastor of the Disciples of Christ Church in Louisville, W.H. Hopson, organized a black congregation, which had a white pastor, J.D. Smith. The need for a school to train black ministers led to the opening of the Louisville Bible School on Seventh Street in 1873. Hopson and Smith worked tirelessly to educate and place students in Disciples pulpits in Kentucky and states to the north. Preston Taylor, supported by other black leaders, moved the school to New Castle in 1884. Before becoming a pastor, Taylor had been a stonecutter, a railway porter, and a contractor; he was trained for the ministry at Louisville Bible School, which suffered financial problems and was closed in 1892. In the same year, white Disciples reopened the school in Louisville.[31]

A Roman Catholic parish for blacks, St. Augustine, was created in February 1870 through the leadership of Fr. John Lancaster Spalding. The small congregation had been meeting in the basement of the Cathedral of the Assumption since 1868. The newly built church, which initially served seventy-five members, was located on Fourteenth Street, near Broadway, on the grounds of the Civil War barracks and hospital. The school was on the ground floor and the sanctuary on the second. Members of the Sisters of Charity of Nazareth

served as teachers. Spalding was pastor until 1873. In its early days several eminent Baptists served as choir directors. The parish had a modest program to aid poor and elderly members.[32]

Kentucky also had "a small but dedicated movement of independent black churches following the Civil War. These churches, congregational in polity, grew out of the activities of the American Missionary Association . . . and from the specific efforts of John G. Fee." The AMA's shift of emphasis to education hurt these churches, as support for pastors' salaries dried up. Most did not survive the 1880s. The Plymouth Congregational Church of Louisville became one of the most prominent in the city. Its pastor, E.G. Harris, like Rev. Leroy Ferguson of the Church of Our Merciful Savior, had close ties to white leaders and exerted great influence among blacks. Harris combined an emphasis on self-help and the closing of "dens of sin" with the social gospel. He purchased and leased space in tenement houses and opened a settlement house. A major reason for his appeal was his authority among whites—his ability, for example, to find jobs for blacks.[33]

Blacks formed churches in other Kentucky river towns, and a number of their meeting houses were by standards of the day impressive. Two stood out. Owensboro's Third Street AME erected a large edifice in 1873 that cost sixteen thousand dollars. The largest black Baptist church in the western part of the state was Washington Street in Paducah. Its pastor, George W. Dupee, was widely respected as a revivalist and church organizer. The city had four other churches in 1881—two of them Baptist, one Christian, and one AME.[34]

Even though most black pastors were poorly educated, they were the most prestigious members of their communities. Some better-educated black clergy ridiculed them, and whites—for example, those who attended black camp meetings—found their antics amusing. W.E.B. Du Bois described the Baptist pastor as "the elected dictator of a pure democracy, who, if he can command a large enough following, becomes a virtual dictator; he thus has the chance to be a wise leader or a demagogue, or, as in many cases, a little of both." Black clergymen offered a message that was usually conservative in theology and social theory. So did their lay supporters. The Sunday School superintendent at Liberty Baptist, J.D. Cox, admonished parents to "help solve the race problem . . . by having good principles instilled in your boys and girls."[35]

The black ministers' duties were multifaceted: to stimulate membership growth; to build, enlarge, and refurbish church edifices; to represent their people in the white community; and to symbolize the progress of a once-downtrodden people. Pastors provided family and personal consultation; found work for the

unemployed; baptized, married, and buried members; and visited the sick and bereaved. A major responsibility was leading a congregation out of debt. Financial skills, including raising money among white benefactors, made a substantial difference in a black minister's career. Congregational histories are filled with references to the financial ability of pastors the members considered able leaders. On one end of the scale was Allen Temple, which paid its pastor $1,300 in the late 1880s and provided a comfortable parsonage and other perquisites. On the other lay the vast majority of congregations—small, impoverished churches in small towns and rural areas where the pastor's salary was perhaps $300. Secular employment to supplement such an income was obligatory.[36]

Leading clergymen often held their posts for many years and died in office. They were usually replaced by assistant ministers whom they had apprenticed or by other men closely tied to the church. Henry Adams of Fifth Street Baptist in Louisville, who had begun serving as pastor in 1839, died in 1872 at the age of sixty-nine and was succeeded by Andrew Heath, his assistant, who continued in the pastorate until 1887. Heath's assistant, John H. Frank, followed him and held the post for more than 40 years. After the death of the longtime pastor of Green Street Baptist Church, Richard Sneethen, Daniel A. Gaddie succeeded him, serving for 40 years. W.W. Taylor was pastor of the influential York Street Baptist Church from its founding in 1845 to his death in 1882. Renamed Calvary Baptist in 1883, the congregation hired Charles H. Parrish in 1885, and he served 46 years.[37]

In Paducah, the "great revivalist and founder of churches" Rev. G.W. Dupee was pastor of Washington Street Baptist Church from the end of the Civil War until his death in 1897. "Dupee reportedly baptized ten thousand converts." Across the river, the first black pastor of Liberty Baptist in Evansville was Green McFarland, who toiled from 1866 to 1882. J. Dennis Rouse, also a former slave, succeeded him and served until his death in 1929. Rev. W.H. Anderson, a Union Army veteran, pastored the rival McFarland Church from 1882 until he died in 1919.[38]

Black pastors were often educators as well. The case of Rev. Alexander Walters in Kentucky is illustrative, as is that of Rev. James M. Townsend, who like Walters was a Methodist clergyman. In 1869 Townsend became the first black teacher (one of two) of the newly opened public schools in Evansville. He left Evansville to assume a pastorate in Terre Haute, Indiana, in 1873. Later he was the first black elected to the Indiana General Assembly.[39]

The level of pastors' political involvement varied, given the tradition of separation of church and state and the belief among many that the church had

primarily a spiritual mission. Financial implications—that is, white supporters' views of activism—also were important. Arnett of Cincinnati and Townsend of Evansville typified the politically active. Others believed that such activities diminished the value of the minister and of his church. Public utterances were to be limited to vice, the Sabbath, and the use of the Bible. There were also denominational differences. Baptists tended not to make statements on national issues at their annual meetings, whereas Methodists—who had a much better educated, more literate clergy—annually produced "pious, polite, and reasoned reports on secular issues, with occasional comments on controversial ones." These documents were not, however, designed to stimulate debate and forge "a connectional stand." Though not avoiding "a broad defense of racial interests, they were more for the purpose of reference for posterity and served a largely symbolic fulfillment of moral obligation to see Christian values realized in the world." There was "a ritualistic quality in the way the reports were read into the record, and succeeded by the next order of business."[40]

Conservatives' critics insisted that the church do more to reach out "beyond the sphere of their normal activities." Especially important was the development of programs like the YMCA and the education of young men for the ministry and teaching. This was a theme in Arnett's anniversary sermon at Allen Temple in 1874. Other concerns addressed the recreational needs of children and youth and the failure of the church to win the hearts and minds of young people, especially when it came to saloons and houses of ill repute.[41]

Whether their churches were large or small, urban or rural, Baptist clerics' message was traditional. They insisted that members legalize their marriages and excluded from church services persons who attended the theater, dances, circuses, or minstrel shows; who participated in games of chance; who visited brothels; or who were pregnant out of wedlock. Ministers were paternalistic, promoting good citizenship and hard work and denouncing activities that made blacks look bad. Members were required to attend all services, including prayer meetings and special events during the week, and to live exemplary lives. Rev. Henry Adams of Louisville, like most of the black elite in the postwar era, made few demands of whites. He disappointed some newly freed blacks by encouraging them to strengthen their relationships with their former masters. He urged that blacks lift themselves up, for whites' goodwill was essential to their progress. As time passed, older leaders lamented what they felt was a loss of standards among younger clergymen and their congregations, who were less patient with whites' paternalism.[42]

AME pastors across the river delivered a similar message. At the end of the thirty-third annual conference held in Evansville in August 1872, delegates

passed resolutions condemning the use of alcohol and tobacco and praised the efforts of church members to secure a good education for their children. Speakers at the fiftieth anniversary of Allen Temple linked the progress of the race, both material and spiritual, to the church's leadership. Pastor Arnett noted that the development of that congregation had been inseparable from the efforts of free people to help themselves. "Certainly there is not a heart here which does not beat with pride at the material progress we have made in fifty years," he declared. "The Lord has done great things for us, whereof we are glad. There is not a finer site in the city than ours, and the accommodations are superior to any in the State, in my opinion."[43]

Arnett insisted that good character was fundamental to success, offering as proof the career of Dr. Commodore F. Buckner, steward and trustee of the church, who had been born a slave in Newport, Kentucky, in 1824. He moved to Cincinnati with his mother and siblings after his father died. As a youth he worked on the steamer *Monmouth,* which plied the rivers between Cincinnati and New Orleans, and then went to work as a hotel cook. Next he worked on canal boats on the Whitewater Canal, using his spare time to read, especially books on medicine. He received training from some physicians in Cincinnati and opened a private practice in 1849. "The black physician" was praised by his white counterparts as a man "of respectable associations and habits" whose practices among blacks gained "fair success" and were based on "honorable principles, without deception or charlatanism." Having a large practice, he was nonetheless denied a medical diploma, because that "would be putting a negro on an equality with white men." Arnett asserted that "Dr. Buckner . . . has done more without a sheepskin than some have done with one. Sheepskins or diplomas are a good thing, but common-sense, intelligence, and success are better."[44]

Arnett concluded by stating:

We must not look to others to do our work, but we must be up and doing and prove our capabilities for the enjoyment of religious and political liberty. We must as a race secure the good will of the community in which we reside, and the way to accomplish that effectually is to secure the four elementary powers of our civilization— religion, education, wealth, and integrity, and with a ballot cast by intelligent men, and our children raised by educated mothers, we will conquer a peace before the Centenary Celebration of African Methodism in this city. Fathers and mothers, you must do all you can to educate your children. It is not enough for you to train your children morally, but you must spend much time and money to see that the

intellect is properly cultivated for usefulness. . . . This life has something for us if we will only be industrious.[45]

Members contributed generously to their churches and engaged in many forms of community service. After Allen Temple, the most impressive in this regard were Fifth Street and Green Street congregations in Louisville, whose members contributed on the average $2,500 annually after the war. Pastors were paid $900 to $1,200 each year, and their assistants one-third to one-half as much. Larger churches also paid sextons, organists and their assistants, clerks, night watchmen, and other personnel and had a fund to assist the poor.[46]

Black Christians served their communities in a variety of ways. Church choirs often sang at dedication ceremonies of schools, and sanctuaries were auditoriums for public events. Churches supported fund-raising events for schools and fraternal and benevolent organizations, as well as for their own activities. In Evansville, as elsewhere, several times a year black Baptists and Methodists held festivals and other public events that were open to both whites and blacks and sought to raise money for pastors' salaries, building construction, school programs, and benevolent causes. On the evenings of June 7 and 8, 1869, for instance, Mozart Hall was crowded with people—about one-third of them white—to witness a "grand tableaux and concert of the colored ladies of the African M.E. Church." The Republican editor marveled at the number of whites present, especially the highly conservative "first families" of the city, who were evidently "highly delighted with the entertainment." In October, Mrs. F.E.W. Harper, a "lady of color," gave a lecture, "Our New Citizens—The Work before Us," to benefit the AME Church. The Republican editor encouraged whites to attend, observing that the objective was worthy and this "entertainment somewhat novel" and that the cost was only twenty-five cents. Over time, though, white editors published less news of black events and relegated such coverage to the "Colored Column" appearing weekly.[47]

Fifth Street Baptist in Louisville began a fund drive to open a hospital for blacks in 1866, and in the 1870s revolutionized the concept of social welfare by assigning deacons to supervise visitation in each ward of the city and to provide food and clothing for the poor, even nonmembers. During the depression that began in 1873, the church provided up to three dollars per week for unemployed workers, the equivalent of a laborer's weekly wage. Fifth Street also established branch mission churches and sponsored missionary work in Africa. Green Street Baptist created a day school for newly freed slaves. Tiny St. Augustine Catholic Church, which never had more than 120 members, had a number of programs to help the poor. Louisville Catholics established the

House of the Good Shepherd, which cared for about 105 girls a year in cooking, sewing, and citizenship classes that were designed to keep them out of the city jail. St. Augustine supported a small house where the elderly poor were cared for, and it had a school.[48]

In Cincinnati, Union Baptist established a cemetery two miles west of the city in Price Hill. The first burial recorded there was September 2, 1865. Originally housed in a sixteen-acre plot, the Union Baptist African American Cemetery began keeping official records in 1884. Records for the years 1884–89 disclose that the majority of those buried, 365 of the 635 entered, were natives of Cincinnati. Another 141 had been born in Kentucky. The chief reason for the high proportion of Cincinnatians was infant and early childhood mortality: 223 entries were for children age 2 or under and 78 were for those between 2 and 5. The main causes of death for adults were giving birth, being shot, being hit by streetcars or trains, having an accident on the job, and contracting diseases like consumption and cholera. Just 47 of the people buried were over age sixty. Union Cemetery's burials reflected the occupational composition of black Cincinnati. Of the 100 or so whose jobs were listed, almost all were domestics, steamboat hands, cooks, laundresses, porters, and coachmen.[49]

Black churches also promoted educational and social uplift. The superintendent of education for the Freedmen's Bureau in Kentucky observed that black churches were usually the only available schoolhouses for blacks in the state. The same was true on the north shore of the river. Black churches also took the lead in promoting educational advancement, as evidenced by the statewide conference for teachers held at Quinn Chapel in Louisville in 1870. Many pastors, moreover, saw the church as a fulcrum in the struggle for racial advancement. In the same year Quinn Chapel provided leadership in organizing protest against the segregation of streetcars. Rev. J.C. Waters, pastor of Asbury Church, organized several protest rallies at his church. Rev. Thomas Strother of Cairo wrote Senator Richard Yates in July 1868 that he represented "a large portion of the despised race in this community," whose freedom was meaningless without the vote. He was also a prominent advocate of school desegregation, as was Rev. Nelson Ricks, also of Cairo. Rev. James H. MaGee of Metropolis, Illinois, a minister and a teacher, was a prominent advocate of civil rights legislation in the 1880s. Ricks led the effort to admit blacks to Cairo's white high school in 1883. Green Street Baptist Church in Louisville hosted a conference in 1886 that was designed to press the state legislature to enact civil rights legislation.[50]

Black churches were closely tied to a plethora of benevolent and fraternal societies. Such groups met many social and recreational needs, and their an-

nual meetings, with parades, excursions, and merrymaking, were highlights of black community life. Initiations, rituals, and uniforms provided a sense of identity and camaraderie. These societies also aided widows and orphans of members, provided death benefits and health care for ill members, and raised a great deal of money for worthy social causes.[51]

Slightly less than ten years after the end of the Civil War, Cincinnati boasted thirty-eight black benevolent and fraternal societies, the most prestigious of which were the Masonic lodges. The oldest had been formed in 1848. About four in five of the organizations had been organized since 1864, reflecting migration patterns in that decade. Many were women's societies, and virtually all had benevolent purposes. Typical was the Dorcas Relief Society, established February 22, 1866, by Minnie Mitchell and others to help the poor, relieve the sick, and bury the dead. Some societies had both male and female members. The Christian Aid Association was created October 8, 1872, to assist Allen's Temple in paying off its debts. The vice president was a woman, as was the treasurer, while the president, the secretary, and the assistant secretary were men. More commonly seen were men's lodges and women's auxiliaries of them, such as the male Grand Chapter for the West and the female Salem Court, no. 2. Other groups had entrepreneurial aims. The Sons of Enterprise sought to purchase real estate and erect public halls as well as to support members' industry, temperance, and virtue. A regiment of militia, headed by Colonel Robert Harlan, organized in 1870, represented another kind of organization.[52]

The oldest extant black society in the Queen City was the United Colored American Association, formed in 1844 to purchase and maintain land for a burial ground. The Colored Orphans Asylum was created later that year as a result of the visit to Cincinnati by Quaker Lydia P. Mott, who wished to help blacks establish such a facility. Whites—among them Salmon P. Chase, who wrote the charter that was granted by the Ohio legislature—assisted blacks in this venture. Three of the nine trustees were whites. Trustees rented, repaired, and eventually purchased a dilapidated building on Ninth Street owned by Nicholas Longworth. In 1867 the property was sold, and an old building in Avondale, along with six acres, was purchased and remodeled. The name of the society was changed to the New Asylum for Orphan and Friendless Colored Children. Charles Armstead served as longtime superintendent, beginning in 1862, and his wife, Eliza, was matron. Peter Clark served for many years as president of the board, as his father also had done. The black churches of the city made quarterly contributions to the institution.[53]

Like the records of Union Cemetery, black organizations' records reveal much about the nature of black society. Prominent men and women served as

officers or trustees of many fraternal and benevolent societies, but quite a few of these groups operated on modest revenues. The Relief Union of Plum Street Baptist Church in Cincinnati, for instance, began in 1868 with initiation fees of $0.15 and monthly dues of $0.12. By 1874 these were, respectively, $3.00 and $0.25. Membership as of February 1874 was "about thirty," meaning annual income would have been about $30, in addition to, at most, about $99 from initiation fees. The fund-raising efforts of these societies, nonetheless, were impressive. The Sewing Circle of Allen Temple, organized in 1864, raised more than $2,500 by 1874. The church's trustees collected $12,000 for the orphan society's land and buildings and contributed annually to defray its operating costs.[54]

In Louisville, such groups were distinguished by not only their number but also their variety and scope. The Louisville black community was much larger than that in Cincinnati, and there was a huge gap in social services that had to be filled following the closing of the Freedmen's Bureau. Meager public funding and whites' insistence on racial separation meant that blacks had to help themselves. State institutions were generally not created until the mid-1880s. Mentally ill blacks received state-assisted care beginning at a temporary, segregated structure in 1868, but in 1876 the state began housing them in racially separate sections at all of the state's asylums. In contrast, care for the poor and those orphans who were not apprenticed "fell almost entirely upon the black community. Churches and concerned citizens united, creating numerous organizations which cared for the indigent until local and state governments could be persuaded to accept at least partial responsibility."[55]

To care for fatherless and orphaned children, some members of Louisville's churches and lodges created the Union Benevolent Association in the early 1870s. After one initiative failed, Peter Lewis and Shelby Gillespie successfully led efforts to create the Orphans Home Society, which admitted its first child in 1878. Its leadership included whites as well as blacks. It secured a meager endowment of $6,500 through the help of such groups as the Ladies' Sewing Circle. By the 1890s the Orphans Home Society housed eighteen black orphans.[56]

Pressure from black leaders, supported by prominent whites, led to the opening of an industrial school for delinquent black youngsters in 1877, six years after one for whites had been opened. By the late 1880s the home had an average annual enrollment of 111 children and a turnover rate of 25 percent. Because 25 percent of them were illiterate, pupils received a basic education in addition to industrial training. Inadequate funding forced churches and benevolent organizations to contribute to the school frequently. A similar school for girls was established in 1893.[57]

Louisville's black churches and benevolent societies created other institutions. The Louisville Cemetery Association, one of several in the state, was chartered in 1866. About five hundred people contributed to the purchase of thirty-three acres on Goss Avenue. The St. James Old Folks' Home was established in the late 1880s, about the same time that the United Brothers of Friendship established a Widows' and Orphans' Home for its members. Because black men were denied access to the YMCA that opened in the 1880s, a separate facility was established.[58]

Arguably the most distinctive organization in Louisville, aside from State University, was the Louisville National Medical College (LNMC), opened in 1888, which also provided a free dispensary. There was nothing like it on either side of the river. The brainchild of Dr. Henry Fitzbutler, it reflected two realities: white hospitals refused to serve blacks, and the state's medical colleges would not admit blacks. Several other physicians assisted Fitzbutler in forming LNMC, including W.A. Burney of New Albany, who extended his practice across the river, and Rufus Conrad, a native of Louisville. Within several years the school had thirty students in a three-year program, and a number of graduates remained in the city to practice. LNMC became affiliated with State University and established its own hospital and nursing program in 1892.[59]

This was a major exception to the rule regarding medical care. Typical of larger river towns was Evansville, which by the early 1890s had three hospitals, all private. The oldest, operated by the Daughters of Charity since 1872, operated one ward for blacks, regardless of their medical condition, in the basement. So did Deaconess Hospital, which opened about two decades later. The third, not affiliated with a church, provided modest services in a separate, ramshackle building. Blacks in Metropolis could cross the river to Paducah to receive care at a hospital run by the Illinois Central Railroad. In smaller places like Shawneetown and Portsmouth, medical care was at best capricious.[60]

The development of a medical school in Louisville reflected the size and influence of its professional groups—medical, legal, and journalistic—that were at the forefront of the cultural and intellectual efflorescence that followed emancipation. Mobility gave such black men as the editors of the four religious newspapers published in the 1870s and 1880s opportunities to inform, to stimulate, and to uplift thousands of freed people. A popular form of entertainment was the public lecture, provided by politicians, former Union Army officers, and ministers. River and rail transport permitted Louisville to become a regular stop on these circuits. Literary, musical, and benevolent societies such as the Frederick Douglass Lyceum and the Nat Turner Club were formed to

cater to the elite. The Elite, Fantasma, and Quid Nunc clubs of Louisville were open only to the wealthy. These groups, which emulated white society, "had enormous prestige in the black community, and their large weddings, impressive receptions, and gala parties were thoroughly covered in the black press."[61]

The largest and most popular of such groups for blacks were lodges and fraternal orders. The top three in the level of organization and activity in Louisville were the Masons, the Odd Fellows, and the United Brothers of Friendship (UBF). The Masons, organized before the war, had fifteen lodges by the mid-1880s. The Odd Fellows boasted the city's largest lodge, which had 1,500 members and its own hall, built in 1880 and valued at $2,500. Ten years later it moved into one worth four times that amount. The UBF was distinctive: it was a home-grown relief association for ex-slaves. Established by three men in 1861 and open to slaves as well as free persons, the UBF spread across the country and the globe, becoming a major international body with headquarters in Louisville. The Sisters of the Mysterious Ten, its women's auxiliary, also was based in the Falls City.[62]

In addition, Louisville blacks had a number of church choirs, glee clubs, and bands, as well as such musical societies as the Treble Clef Club. W.H. Gibson Sr. and Nathaniel R. Harper organized Louisville's Colored Musical Association, which sponsored the city's first music festival in May 1880. The CMA hosted four such events by 1888. These attracted a number of noted soloists, orchestras, and choral groups from such other cities as Cincinnati, which had a Choral Association that participated in the 1881 festival.[63]

Because of the size of black Louisville, its societies greatly exceeded the number and the variety of those in other cities and towns.[64] The basic pattern, though, was similar elsewhere. Owensboro's first history included reference to four black associations: two United Brothers of Friendship lodges and their female counterparts, the United Sisters of Friendship. Four men established the first UBF lodge of the city, number 7, in the winter of 1866–67. Initially the purpose of the lodge was benevolence, but it expanded to provide burial insurance for its eighty members. Its property, valued at $4,000, included a hall, where members met twice monthly. The second lodge, formed in 1872, had 60 members. Lodge number 8 of the sisters, organized in 1868, had 300 members in the early 1880s. Its "Princess" was Mrs. Lizzie Daws. The other sisters' lodge, which numbered about 50 members, was established in August 1881. Similar patterns emerged in Henderson and Paducah.[65]

Indiana's blacks also organized a plethora of groups, most of which were in the largest towns. Masons had twenty-two chapters in Indiana by 1888,

including several each in Evansville and New Albany and one in Mount Vernon. The largest organization was the United Brothers of Friendship, which had about 3,000 members in fifty-one lodges, a number of which were located in Ohio River towns. The Knights and Daughters of Tabor was also popular, as were the Independent Sons of Honor and its women's branch, the Daughters of Honor. There were also black branches of the Odd Fellows and the Knights of Pythias.[66]

Historical accounts from the postwar era provide scant detail about black organizations. An exception was New Albany's history, which listed three black lodges—two Odd Fellows and one Masonic. Edmonds Lodge number 1544 of the IOOF met twice monthly at their hall on the west side of State Street, between Elm and Oak. St. Paul's number 1540 also met twice a month in its hall on Lower Fourth. St. John's Lodge number 8 of the Masons met in the same building as Edmonds Lodge.[67]

The activities of benevolent and fraternal societies were inseparable from community rituals, as was vividly illustrated on Emancipation Day in Evansville. That day featured a grand parade, followed by a picnic, where prominent men, veterans of the Civil War, delivered orations and children performed "broom drills" to remind observers of slavery. On September 22, 1869, the Mutual Aid Society, led by a brass band and followed by a large crowd, paraded to Blackford's Grove for a picnic and speeches. The same organization had sponsored a concert at Mozart Hall to raise funds for needy residents earlier that year, and a few months later it hosted a fund-raising fair at the Masonic Hall. By the end of the century the city had at least twenty-two African American social organizations.[68]

The most important groups in Evansville, as in Cincinnati and Louisville and smaller cities and towns, were the United Brothers of Friendship, the Masons, and the Odd Fellows. Often men and women belonged to several of these. The Masons had four men's lodges and a chapter of the Order of the Eastern Star for women. The Odd Fellows had two lodges for men and two chapters of the Household of Ruth for women. Blacks organized a number of other groups—for instance, Richard Amos's Evening Star Brass Band, formed in June 1868, which lasted until about 1892, and Augustus Carter's Quadrille Band, formed in 1878 and active until about 1895. Veterans also created the Colonel John F. Grill Post No. 541 of the Grand Army of the Republic in 1888.[69]

The largest society, in number of lodges and members, was the UBF, created to "visit the sick, relieve the distressed, watch over and bury the dead, comfort the widow, and guard the orphans." Evansville's earliest lodge, named for Charles Asbury, was created shortly after the end of the Civil War. The first

newspaper record of its existence appeared in May 1867, when it sponsored an Ethiopian Festival at the Masonic Hall: "The Ethiopian damsels were arrayed in the most gorgeous attire, and we presume to their sooty beaux looked extremely fascinating. Out of curiosity we looked in for a moment, and must confess that the order prevailing would have done credit to any assembly."[70]

The UBF was reorganized in the summer of 1872, and to celebrate, its members, led by Rev. Green McFarland, saloonkeeper J.H. Gray, confectioner Alfred Carter, and teacher James M. Townsend, organized a parade and a gala picnic. A year later, members sponsored an excursion to Henderson to socialize with members of the lodge there. Like other fraternal organizations, it was a sponsor of annual Emancipation Day festivities. The most important event on its calendar, as with other groups, was the "annual sermon," usually held in the spring. This included a parade to a church, where members participated in organizational rituals and heard a sermon given by one of the city's leading clergymen. By the late 1880s, the UBF had eleven lodges, male and female, in Evansville. The wife of James Townsend was the first "worthy princess" of Mt. Carmel Lodge, created about 1868. Of the approximately 300 members by 1889, the majority were from the black middle and upper classes. Members of the Evansville UBF were prominent in state and national affairs. Charles Asbury became a state grand master, and Frederick Douglass Morton national grand master.[71]

The Masons were also noteworthy. McFarland Lodge, the first (1870), was named for the pastor of Liberty Baptist Church, who was also active in the UBF. Other members included Adam Rouse, a janitor, and John Banks, foreman at a tobacco factory and a trustee of the AME Church. Worshipful masters of this lodge included J.D. Rouse and Lewis Anderson, longtime trustee of Independence Baptist Church. The leadership of another lodge, Pythagoras, formed in the 1880s, included two trustees of the AME Church. By the late 1880s there were about ninety Masons in Evansville.[72]

The original lodge of the Odd Fellows was formed in January 1876. On July 4 of that year they, along with the Colored Benevolent Aid Society—150 men in all—marched in the parade celebrating the nation's centennial. Their growth was so substantial that they hosted the state convention. In 1893, both lodges were joined by members of the Henderson society to celebrate the "annual sermon." Membership in the late 1880s was seventy-five.[73]

Many activities like Emancipation Day brought black citizens together. Black baseball in Evansville dates to at least the summer of 1869, when the club was bold enough to challenge (unsuccessfully) the white Evansville squad to a game. African Americans had at least one baseball team every summer thereaf-

ter, and its exploits transcended boundaries of class and status. In Louisville, members of different churches, clubs, and cliques "had only one high school. Central was unquestionably the pride of the black community and would remain so for decades."[74]

Many black organizations, though, were part of "a broad nexus of socio-economic relationships and cultural values" that separated the black elite from the majority of the black citizens.[75] They tended to represent bourgeois values and lifestyles and the chance to distance members from the presumably dissolute residents of the "lower" parts of their towns, whether Little Buck in Cincinnati or Baptisttown in Evansville. Dress, manners, and lifestyles differentiated members from the lower classes. Clubs provided opportunities for contact with men of power and for social advancement. Despite the fact that many of the clubs were financially strapped, hardly able to rent, let alone purchase meeting halls, they provided entertainment, accouterments, and benefits for members.[76]

In Evansville, as elsewhere, there was a small upper class—perhaps at most 2 percent of the black population—comprising barbers, shopkeepers, artisans, physicians, lawyers, and some teachers and clergymen. Some had been prominent before the war (Lena McDaniel, Mary Morton, and James Carter) but most either arrived in the city or came of age after it. James's sons Alfred, a confectioner, and Augustus (Gus), a barber, were important citizens after 1865. James and Richard Amos, sons of a relatively wealthy farmer who lived just outside Evansville, were also distinguished—one as a barber and the other as a musician. Adam Rouse, who came to the city just after the end of the war, became courthouse janitor in 1880, a position that blacks prized because it signaled access to and acceptance by white leaders. Willis Green, the physician, was another member of the city's black elite.[77]

Unlike the African American elite in more northerly cities, Evansville's influential men and women, and those in other river towns, resided in or near the incipient ghetto. With the exception of barbers, their clientele was exclusively black. Initially most had little or no formal education, but toward the end of the century an educated upper class appeared. They represented an interlocking directorate, because they served as leaders in churches, schools, and social organizations. As elsewhere, virtually all were defined by census-takers as mulattoes; lighter skin both symbolized and made possible higher status. Emulating and being accepted by affluent whites was paramount, and toward that end separating themselves from ordinary blacks whose behavior was deemed reprehensible was essential. But such values, like appearing white, did not guarantee whites' acceptance.[78]

A similar pattern existed in Louisville, where the black elite—self-named the Four Hundred—set themselves apart because of their level of education, their contacts with whites, their occupations, and their lifestyles. According to Gunnar Myrdal, such an elite provided standards and values and epitomized the hopes of the black masses. Because they were articulate and successful, their views and interests were usually considered synonymous with those of the larger black community. Beginning with the antebellum period, "when Washington Spradling and several other mulatto children were freed by their white fathers, Louisville's elite Negro group was dominated by light-skinned persons." Only one of the city's leading black men before World War I was dark-skinned, and just about all of the women in exclusive clubs were light-skinned. Admission to the Four Hundred also reflected access to prominent whites, since members were porters, head waiters, or domestic servants in the homes of the wealthy. The elite threw lavish parties and "spent considerable time and money on furnishing their homes and showing them off to friends and neighbors."[79]

A small middle class was slightly below this group in level of income and status. If occupation is the chief yardstick, this cohort comprised most of the artisans, teachers, clergymen, small businessmen, and clerical workers. At most they represented 8 percent of Evansville's blacks, less than half the proportion in Boston and Cleveland. Some service workers, especially janitors, were included in this group. Most had little or no daily contact with whites. They, too, developed lifestyles that distinguished them from the black masses, mostly through church and club activities. They advocated the "strive and succeed" ethic of Booker T. Washington. Many formed and belonged to literary, social, and recreational organizations.[80]

At the bottom were the 90 or so percent of blacks in Evansville and other river towns. These were primarily unskilled, illiterate laborers, more than half of whom were unemployed on the average of four months a year. The vast majority, however, did not engage in the sort of promiscuous lifestyle that prominent whites and the black elite accused them of. They resided in ramshackle homes in two-parent households that often included boarders, lodgers, and relatives. There was, to be sure, a "deviant subculture" involving drinking, gambling, and sexual promiscuity that, in Evansville, existed in Baptisttown, along the Midway (Fourth Street), and in the Tenderloin, the red-light district near the river on High Street. Newspapers, especially the Democratic daily, were fond of portraying black men as dandies who dressed garishly, wore bowler hats, and smoked Havana cigars. Most black men, in fact, were concerned for the welfare of their families and struggled to make a living.[81]

As Marion Lucas concluded in his history of blacks in Kentucky, the greatest attainment of postwar blacks was "a distinct society and culture, with black professionals in medicine, law, journalism, and religion providing the leadership." Neighborhoods in Ohio River cities and towns "could point with pride to their achievements as a people freed from slavery, if not racism."[82] Their churches and their benevolent and fraternal organizations—built on strong family ties—were central to those securing those achievements. No achievement was as satisfying as the establishment of schools, which made it possible for blacks to break free from ignorance and dependency.

12

Schools for Blacks

Public education was crucial for racial uplift. Post–Civil War conventions of black men stressed that fact even as they called for protection of their civil rights and for the right to vote. White leaders in the four states along the Ohio responded in ways that were often similar. By the mid-1880s even high school education was available for black youth. But schools were segregated and assuredly inferior in quality. Illiteracy remained a major obstacle to racial progress, especially on the south bank. In 1880 the percentages of persons over age ten in Illinois, Indiana, and Kentucky who could not read were, in order, 4.3, 4.8, and 22.2. Among blacks the percentages were 37.2, 38.6, and 70.4. The percentages of the same age cohort who could not write were, in the same order, 6.4, 7.5, and 29.9. For blacks they were 26.7, 15.6, and 62.7.[1]

At the second postwar black state convention in Illinois, held in October 1866, Bryant Smith, a delegate from Shawneetown, joined others in endorsing public funding of black schools. Republican hesitancy and Democratic opposition delayed action for a number of years.[2] The revised constitution of 1870 provided for free public schools, and the legislature in 1872 mandated education in public or private schools for those between ages seven and sixteen. Funds for black schools, though, were to come only from black taxpayers. Another law passed two years later imposed fines on those who excluded black children from public schools and required school officers to provide for the education of all children. It did not mandate school integration or equal funding. Nearly all schools in the southern part of the state were racially segregated.

Several suits brought before the state supreme court challenged school segregation, but only one of these involved a southern Illinois town—Alton, near St. Louis.[3]

Indiana was little different. Prior to 1869 the only formal education for blacks was privately funded. Democratic voices such as the *New Albany Daily Register* of February 5, 1867, complained that blacks contributed nothing to the state's revenues and could therefore claim a share of public education only "on the plea of charity." Many Republicans responded that blacks paid taxes, that their progress through education would bring in more revenue, and that poorly educated citizens increased the crime rate. In 1870 eight of the ten Indiana counties with the highest proportion of illiterates also had the highest percentage of blacks. Five were on the Ohio River.[4]

Through the leadership of Conrad Baker, a native of Pennsylvania who had practiced law in Evansville and become governor in 1867, a special session of the Indiana legislature in 1869 not only ratified the Fifteenth Amendment but also required trustees to create separate schools for black children where there were enough of them to warrant such a school. If there were not, districts might be consolidated. If not enough blacks resided within "a reasonable distance," trustees were permitted to "provide such other means of education for said children as shall use their proportion, according to numbers, of school revenue to best advantage."[5] The law also "put the property of white and colored owners on the same basis for assessment and collection of school taxes."[6]

Many school districts were dilatory in implementing the law, and those that did provided inferior facilities and paid teachers poorly. Evansville opened two schools for about 250 black pupils in September 1869. A year later, New Albany reported that its colored school had 200 students. By 1875 enrollments in the river counties of Vanderburgh, Clark, Floyd, Spencer, and Jefferson were, respectively, 537, 427, 309, 347, and 278. About two-thirds of the black students in the state were enrolled in just nine counties, mostly along the Ohio.[7]

Two problems existed. The first—tested initially in New Albany—was the definition of "colored." The state superintendent of public instruction resolved this one, overruling a local decision barring students with one-sixty-fourth black ancestry and declaring that the criterion ought to be the same as that of the state's antimiscegenation law: one-eighth or more. The second was more perplexing: what to do with black children when there were too few to warrant a separate school. Some officials, especially in northern Indiana, admitted them to white schools. In 1874 the Indiana Supreme Court overturned a lower court ruling that permitted black children to enroll in a white school

because a colored school did not exist. That action prompted the legislature in 1877 to revise the law to require school districts to admit black students when they did not supply separate schools. Furthermore, black students showing sufficient academic achievement to enroll in higher grades than those provided in black schools were to be admitted to white schools, and no distinction was to be made on account of race or color. Local officials were left with the power to decide whether schools would be integrated. Not surprisingly, glaring inequities persisted.[8]

These were most evident in southern Indiana, where the proportion of school-age children attending school was the smallest in the state. In Evansville in 1887 there were three black schools and eighteen teachers for about one thousand students, less than half of the school-age population. In 1888 Mount Vernon's black students represented slightly over one-third of the school-age population. In Jeffersonville and New Albany they accounted for 45 percent, and in Madison 50 percent.[9]

Black students, moreover, rarely attended beyond the sixth grade, for a number of reasons. The poverty of most black parents, who needed income that their children could secure, was one. The lack of a tradition that schooling mattered was reinforced by the limited range of jobs available. The low quality of educational facilities and of instruction also tended to discourage a commitment to more than the most basic education. But over time the number of black children in school rose, partly because of the passage of a compulsory school law in 1897. One consequence was a decline in blacks' share of the state's illiterates, from 35 percent in 1880 to 22 percent twenty years later.[10]

High school education for blacks outside of Indianapolis, where Indianapolis High School admitted black students in 1879, was rare. By the 1880s there were high schools that blacks could attend in three Ohio River cities—Evansville, Madison, and New Albany—and all were segregated. Evansville's "high school" for blacks, for example, opened in the fall of 1878. Ten years later it had 80 students and 4 teachers. New Albany had 32 pupils and 2 teachers. Many students supported themselves financially.[11]

Educational opportunities were somewhat better in Ohio. A state law in 1864 permitted school officials to bar students from white schools if their "blood" was deemed black, but it also required them to establish a public school for blacks when a district had at least twenty black pupils. School attendance was highest in cities and towns. Even so, only two in five school-age black youth in Cincinnati attended school. In 1866 Cincinnati established the state's first black high school, named for John Isom Gaines, who had championed black schools as the chief means of securing moral and social uplift.[12]

The provision of schooling for African Americans came slowly. Five years after the end of the Civil War, only about half of Ohio's school districts had black schools, and relatively few blacks attended school, for the same reasons as those in Indiana. The diffusion of the black population prompted township officials to combine districts and to support only one school in the township. Consequently, many youngsters faced long trips each day. City officials did the same thing. Whites generally resisted the admission of blacks to white schools, even if separate schools had not been created. Just 52 percent of Ohio's school-age black children, as compared with 77 percent of whites, were in school in 1870.[13]

Cincinnati's black schools boasted skilled administrators and teachers, decent school buildings, and a curriculum not that different from whites', but they were overcrowded and understaffed. In 1874 there were three elementary schools and one high school—and twenty teachers—for one thousand students.[14] Black leaders protested these conditions, but most did not advocate school integration, partly because the state's supreme court, like Indiana's, had ruled against those who sought to enroll their children in white schools that were closer to their homes than black schools. An exception occurred in Portsmouth, where beginning in the mid-1870s blacks objected to the absence of high school education. For about ten years, a modicum of high school training was offered in separate facilities, but in the fall of 1885 black students were admitted to Portsmouth High School, formerly an all-white school.[15]

When the Ohio legislature began to debate changes in the school laws in 1871, Cincinnati blacks were openly divided on the issue. Superintendent William Hartwell Parham wrote to the *Cincinnati Commercial* that integration would be agreeable if all barriers of prejudice were removed and all caste discriminations ended. He cautioned, "We have not forgotten what was the condition of our schools before the control was placed in our hands." Several meetings were held in which most voted to retain racially separate schools and a separate school board. Peter H. Clark led this effort. "In a school of mixed races," he wrote to the *Commercial,* "the colored children would be neglected by the teachers, who could not but be prejudiced against them in the interest of their own race." But in 1873 the legislature returned oversight of black schools to white-controlled common school boards.[16]

Five years later, moreover, Republican legislators passed a law enabling school districts to decide whether they desired segregated schools. Although many blacks favored school integration, Clark remained strenuously opposed. To him, separate schools produced self-esteem, were the objects of community pride, and employed teachers who were role models and who stood to

lose their jobs if segregation ended. Clark declared that the real need was equal funding. Whites opposed race-mixing, and integrating schools, he insisted, would aggravate that problem. A number of black teachers and parents agreed, decrying whites' growing interference in black institutions.[17]

Gaines High School offered a high-quality education in the face of great obstacles. A faculty of four was forced to teach both the intermediate and high school grades. Many students dropped out before graduation to take up teaching positions in rural areas, where certification standards were less stringent. The city's poor racial climate also made the retention of Gaines's graduates difficult. Just 20 percent of its graduates were teaching in Cincinnati in 1876. Three of the four graduates in 1877 left town to take positions elsewhere.[18]

Despite disparities in funding, average daily attendance at the black schools remained relatively high—95 percent in district schools and 98 percent in the high school, a significant improvement over the period before 1873. Rates of attendance increased steadily, on par with those of whites. Possibly one factor was the more efficient operation and better financing provided by a common school board. Another was Ohio's first compulsory attendance law, passed in 1879. The average number of pupils per teacher varied from school to school, though on the whole it was higher in black schools than in white ones. By 1885 there were 1,285 black students in Cincinnati's district schools, 205 in intermediate grades, and 75 at Gaines. The number of teachers had risen to 31. All but 5 were black.[19]

The debate over separate schools heated up in 1884, when the governor of Ohio called for their elimination because they were usually inferior in quality and distant from students' homes. A legislative amendment permitting racially separate schools if a majority of black voters wanted them did not pass, despite strong support from a group of Cincinnati blacks that Clark headed. The men expressed doubts similar to those voiced by Parham in 1872 and articulated the fear that they would lose their teaching positions and the thousands of dollars that separate black schools generated.[20]

The legislature repealed the separate school law in 1887. The coauthors of the measure were two of the three blacks in the Ohio legislature. One was Benjamin W. Arnett, former pastor at Allen Temple, who had become a bishop in his denomination and an organizer of Wilberforce University. The sponsors stressed that separate schooling for blacks was class legislation and that these schools were inferior in quality, made students attending them think they were inferior, denied black children the same rights as those enjoyed by white children, undermined the organic and moral unity of the state, paid black teachers less, and represented an anomaly among northern and western states. Political

expediency and financial concerns, not those that the sponsors raised, probably ensured passage of the bill. As noted earlier, Clark's opposition cost him his job at Gaines High School and eliminated his leadership of the antidesegregation lobby.[21]

Thereafter, legal separation of the races ended. Technically no new racially separate schools were to be constructed. De facto segregation developed, however, at the legally defunct colored public schools, and in Cincinnati black parents and civic leaders supported the situation. The Cincinnati school board announced its intention to integrate schools for 1887–88 but yielded to black parents' preference to have their children educated by black teachers.[22] Opposition to desegregation was especially strong at Walnut Hills. Integrationists chided them for taking what they deemed a backward position. They declared that blacks should seek to have their quota of teachers in "mixed" schools.[23]

Subsequently, black schools were described as "voluntary branch schools open to both races." In fact, they remained totally black, and 90 percent of the black pupils attended them. The superintendent observed that most black families lived near the black schools, that they preferred to be taught by teachers of their own race, and that many children were strongly attached to their teachers. So long as these schools were open to whites as well as blacks and sustained at a reasonable expense, he recommended the board retain them. He did note that the cost of educating black youth would be lower in integrated schools and that the quality of teaching would improve, since black teachers taught two grades of pupils together.[24]

By 1890 the number of blacks enrolled in white primary schools had risen to 800. Soon most of the previously all-black schools were closed, but owing to residential patterns certain schools became predominantly black. Most black high school students attended Gaines, where Parham was named principal in 1887. Eleven graduated in the spring of 1888, out of a total of ninety-eight enrolled. The normal division was eliminated that year, and the school was closed in 1890.[25]

Some have argued that the black schools of Kentucky were more successful in terms of funding and quality. Three critical turning points are usually cited: the creation of a poll tax to fund black schools in 1867; the legislature's enhancement of the black school fund in 1874; and the school equalization law of 1882. The reality was that grossly unequal conditions persisted, and many youth attended school irregularly, if at all. One of the results was high illiteracy rates.[26]

From the outset free blacks' thirst for education was immense, but so were the obstacles to their quenching it. Whites were hostile, fearing the loss of

social control. By far the most significant factor was poverty. Suddenly freed, with no means of supporting themselves, African Americans had to find means to survive.[27]

Initially the only schools were provided by religious groups and the Freedmen's Bureau. Local officials and legislators, many of them Confederate veterans, were openly antagonistic to the presence of Northern teachers sent by such groups as the American Missionary Association. Laws were passed in 1866 and 1867 that reflected legislators' insistence that blacks help themselves. Taxes on blacks were instituted, the revenues from which were to support paupers and schools—the latter if local officials wished to do so. County governments were made responsible for black schools and authorized to spend $2.50 for each pupil who attended school for three months. Funding was not provided for buildings. An 1868 law required that paupers be paid first. In theory, about six cents per pupil was raised, but little of that reached black schools. There was no mandate that public schools be created or that counties disburse funds for schools, even when the legislature in early 1871 repealed the 1867 law, splitting pauper and education funds.[28]

Statewide, the short-lived Freedmen's Bureau opened 97 schools and provided 117 teachers, mostly black, by the fall of 1867. Schools were supported by patrons' subscriptions and pupils' tuition as well as bureau funds and contributions from Northern philanthropists. A year later, there were 267 schools—87 entirely supported by freed people—employing 284 teachers and enrolling almost 13,000 pupils. Since the bureau did not maintain attendance reports at the many schools opened in black churches, more blacks attended schools than bureau records indicated. Much of the schooling, moreover, occurred on the weekend and in the evening for adults who wanted to learn how to read and write.[29]

The Freedmen's Bureau played a central role in the education of black youth in river towns and cities. In Smithland and Paducah, monthly reports stated that fifty or more students were enrolled in each classroom. Actual attendance was perhaps 70 percent, since a number of pupils attended irregularly or for only a few days or weeks. These schools were typically held in black churches, usually in single rooms lacking stoves and windows. Terms were brief in rural schools—from November through March, reflecting seasonal farming needs—and somewhat longer in towns. Education was basic, and few students went on to graded schools. No one received more than a third-grade education. Desks, textbooks, and classroom supplies were meager. But despite those impediments, the schools created the foundation for postwar public education in the commonwealth.[30]

The drive for education was strongest in the cities, especially Louisville. General Palmer's coming to Louisville in 1865 encouraged black churches, led by Henry Adams at Fifth Street Baptist, to open schools. Fifth Street's school had been closed by authorities four years earlier. By July it had 250 pupils attending classes five and a half hours each weekday. Adams was a teacher, as were his daughter and another woman. Within a year, seven more schools in the city enrolled nearly 1,000. Bureau and missionary aid were vital, but blacks' support—in providing classrooms in churches and finding housing for white teachers—was also critical. A shortage of teachers and classrooms forced educators to limit enrollments, but parents continued to seek space for their children. Officials were surprised that so many were willing to pay tuition or to sacrifice income their children might have secured by working instead of going to school. By 1870 there were at least fifteen schools in Louisville, serving 1,500 students.[31]

Blacks' initiative also created the Ely Normal School, dedicated in April 1868 in a festive atmosphere that attracted many black and white citizens. Named for the Freedmen's Bureau superintendent for Kentucky, Ely was a joint venture of two Northern benevolent societies and the Freedmen's Bureau. It met a basic need, the training of black teachers. Located at Broadway and Fourteenth streets, the school was, unfortunately, "little different from most schools in Louisville. Its 'normal department' consisted of 'special instructions' for 40 of the 396 pupils." Six of its seven teachers were white. Ely closed after just a few years, and in 1871 the American Missionary Association leased the building for the first black public school.[32]

Interest in education was substantial elsewhere on the Ohio. In Gallatin County, freedmen organized a board of trustees and raised money for a school. Similar efforts in Covington led to the opening of two schools in the fall of 1865. In both cases benevolent societies and the Freedmen's Bureau helped. In Breckinridge County, a freeman, Marshall W. Taylor, taught at the Noble School on the basis of a modest education he had gained in slave times. The bureau contributed $250 to building the school and $15 per month for operations. Daviess County blacks, with the aid of the bureau, opened a school for 150 in the fall of 1866. Blacks had already secured $300 via a loan from a white benefactor to acquire land for the school. A large brick school, named after Ely, was constructed thanks to $400 from the bureau. In the fall of 1867, parents of 140 pupils collectively paid $33.50 tuition each month, and the bureau gave another $40. In Paducah, white missionaries opened one school in 1865, and two more were organized a year later. In 1868 the bureau funded the erection of a large brick schoolhouse capable of housing 250 students. Baptists in the town also had a tuition school with 125 students.[33]

Black leaders were aware that support from Northern benefactors and the bureau was temporary. Accordingly, in December 1867 they organized the first of a series of (unfortunately, unproductive) statewide conventions. The Colored Education Convention at Louisville in July 1869 created a "gala atmosphere of the marching bands and colorful uniforms of local benevolent societies [that] could not conceal the bleak future of black education in Kentucky." Benjamin Runkle of the Freedmen's Bureau announced there that his agency was ending its educational programs the following summer. "The message was clear: blacks must assume responsibility for whatever educational progress they hoped to make."[34]

The 250 delegates to the 1869 gathering called on the legislature to create black public schools and formed a "Kentucky State Board of Education." They also wrote a constitution and bylaws, created a plan for annual meetings, organized committees, and encouraged cities and towns to establish their own school boards. Over the next four years, however, many of the private schools were closed because of funding problems, and the state government did nothing. These years represented "the nadir of black education in Kentucky."[35]

The 1870 census of Louisville supports that evaluation. Although blacks accounted for about 15 percent of the total population, just 7.3 percent of the city's school enrollment was black. Almost 60 percent of blacks in Louisville could not write, as compared with just under 6 percent of whites. Although those who could not read (11,855) were not identified by race, it is reasonable to conclude that most were African Americans.[36] In this context, adults' desire to get an education was especially impressive. Many worked all day and then attended night school, for which they paid ten cents a week. Said one hotel worker, G.H. Richardson, "I go to help build up my race. I am educating my children and want to keep up with them and give them encouragement."[37]

Publicly supported schools for blacks received their first boost in Louisville, where white leaders adopted a new charter in March 1870 that created separate black and white school funds. A month later, a committee of whites recommended that the nearly $3,700 in taxes that blacks had paid over the previous year and the $730 due from the state be placed in a "colored school fund," to which the city should add another $3,500 in appropriations. The committee suggested the creation of schools at Fifth Street Baptist and Center Street Methodist churches. The school board endorsed these recommendations. Within several months, a third school, at Jackson Street Methodist Church, was added. During 1870–71 the total budget for all three was exceedingly small, however—less than $1,000.[38]

In July 1871 the school board created a Board of Visitors comprising nine

prominent black men. Horace Morris was named secretary of the board.[39] The board encouraged city officials to place all taxes paid by African Americans for five years into the school fund. Morris arranged the lease of the former Ely Normal School. Although it was near railroad tracks and not centrally located, the consolidated school opened in September 1872. The principal was Joseph M. Ferguson from Cincinnati, a Gaines alumnus. Most of the teachers from the church schools also relocated there. The dilapidated building was used for only one year. The following year black students enrolled at four different buildings: Eastern, Western, Portland, and Central. All but Central were housed in rented quarters—small, dark, overcrowded rooms.[40]

The opening of the new Central Colored School offered hope for fairer school funding. (The choir of Fifth Street Baptist Church sang Psalm 40 at the dedication—titled, appropriately, "I Waited Patiently.") The "crowning achievement of early black education in Louisville," Central was dedicated October 7, 1873, in "one of the grandest events ever held in the black community." The three-story building was located at the southeast corner of Sixth and Kentucky streets. Morris, who delivered the dedicatory address, emphasized the progress blacks had made with white school board assistance. Central enrolled 457 in its first year and doubled in size the next year. Citywide, by 1873–74 school enrollments had risen to 1,847 and the number of teachers to nineteen. The pupil-teacher ratio, though, remained high.[41]

Outside of Louisville the level of support for public schools was even more uneven. In 1871 the legislature permitted Owensboro to create public schools, but that law excluded blacks. The city of Henderson opened a tax-supported school for blacks in 1871, and Covington did the same in 1873. The school system for Hancock County's blacks was a plan that existed only on paper. During 1870–74, however, some churches and towns maintained modest schools for blacks in communities along the Ohio. Catholics, for instance, "played a small but important part in educating freedmen." The first Catholic school in an Ohio River community was St. Augustine's School, opened in Louisville in 1871. The Methodist Episcopal Church's Freedmen's Aid Society provided support for a small school in Cloverport, as well as for schools in two interior towns. Baptists supported schools in Owensboro and Paducah.[42]

During the nadir years, the desire for public schools intensified. Black leaders met with the superintendent of public instruction in January 1873 to attempt to gain his support. Regional meetings called on the legislature to act, and leaders indicated that otherwise they would pursue their goal in federal court. Some whites expressed support because of the moral obligation that they perceived. Others took the pragmatic approach, linking civil order to

education. For many whites, the imminent passage of Charles Sumner's civil rights bill raised the specter of race-mixing, and the creation of black schools would ensure racial separation. H.A.M. Henderson, a former Confederate general who was superintendent of public instruction, argued that failure to act would prevent the state from receiving its share of federal funds for black education in the South that depended on creation of black schools. An outspoken critic of racial mixing, he "could not resist the bait."[43]

In February 1874 the Kentucky legislature authorized the creation of segregated public schools. White county school commissioners were to appoint three black school trustees, who were to establish schools in their districts that would not be near white schools, hire teachers to teach six hours daily, and keep adequate records. Black trustees were, in turn, accountable to white school board members. School terms were to be at least three months, but in districts with fewer than sixty pupils, eight weeks. There was to be at least one black school in each county. Funds came from taxes paid by blacks: the $1.00 poll tax on all men twenty-one and older, and all fines, fees, and forfeitures. Legislators, their niggardliness betraying their racism, estimated that the cost per pupil would be $0.50. They assumed that federal appropriations, blacks' contributions, and local revenues would provide additional funding. Over the next eight years, black residents and some cities and towns supplemented the black school fund, but federal funds did not materialize. The number of pupils doubled, as did appropriations, but the latter ranged, per pupil, only from $0.30 to $0.58. To one historian, this amounted to "making educational bricks without straw." In 1880 the per capita annual expenditure for white students was nearly four times that for blacks. The amount in the colored school fund peaked at $40,733 in 1881. In that year 844 schools enrolled 30,000, less than half of the school-age population.[44]

Equal educational opportunity was illusory. John Marshall Harlan, later a U.S. Supreme Court justice, was one of a few whites who advocated equality in funding. Taking that position contributed to being badly defeated in his campaign for governor in 1875. Overcrowding of classrooms—sometimes 100 to 120 pupils per room—was commonplace. No black school had a library before the early 1900s, and black churches housed one-fifth of the public schools in the late 1880s. The superintendent of public instruction stated that slightly more than 40 percent of school buildings were in poor condition and that another 33 percent should be condemned.[45]

The quality of blacks' schooling remained challenging. Most teachers in the black schools were African Americans. By the late 1880s, few had normal school degrees, and about 13 percent had had no teaching experience at hir-

ing. Fifty percent held third–class teaching certificates, but only 18 percent possessed first-class certificates. About 30 percent taught without any certification. In the 1880s elementary teachers earned between $37 and $47 a month, and high school teachers were paid between $83 and $95. Males earned more than females, and teachers in cities and towns were paid more than those in rural schools. Salaries were not dramatically lower than those given to white teachers, but black schools had shorter terms—in the early 1880s, an average of sixty-six days. By the end of the decade, the average term had increased to six months, although in more than 100 districts, all rural, it was three months. The pupil-teacher ratio remained high, an average of fifty to one. Deficiencies in instructional materials and school supplies persisted.[46]

The 1882 history of the Falls cities offers insight into whites' thinking about these schools. Louisville's black school enrollment was slightly more than 2,000. Principals' salaries had risen to about $1,100, and teachers' salaries ranged from $310 to $500. To the white author, pupils' education was "in every respect equal," and black children were provided "as good teachers of their race and as ample facilities for acquiring an education as can be afforded." This was due primarily to whites' generosity, he noted, because revenues from taxes on blacks raised only $1,441 the previous year, and trustees spent $17,183 for teachers alone.[47]

A unique test faced black teachers in Louisville and elsewhere. Louisville's Board of Education inserted morality clauses in the contracts of black teachers but not those of whites. Accordingly, "much apprehension and speculation surrounded the annual July school board meeting when blacks from the two committees [the Board of Visitors and the Committee on Colored Schools] would advise the school board on teacher appointments for the coming year." These meetings attracted large crowds, which "heard a series of charges and countercharges with each teacher's nomination."[48]

Four black ministers, led by William H. Seward, dominated the hiring and firing of black school employees. Some clergymen "became notorious for soliciting church contributions from teachers and principals, explaining that their blessing would help the teachers keep their jobs. . . . obtaining a teaching job took 'influence' rather than 'ability.'" These clauses "proved to be an effective method of control. Black teachers, realizing that any questionable action on their part could lead to dismissal, remained aloof from controversial issues." In some cases "charges of 'immorality' might have actually meant 'militancy,' that black teachers were disciplined after speaking out against white racism or criticizing established black leaders."[49]

Inadequate funding was a festering sore. One strategy that leaders adopted

was the creation of the Colored Teachers' State Association in 1877. Led by such prominent men as Horace Morris and John H. Jackson of Louisville, the group eventually turned to the federal courts after the state legislature failed to respond. Paducah parents sued the state for levying a poll tax on blacks but not on whites. In early 1882 a federal court upheld their claim. The legislature responded about three weeks later by passing a law authorizing equal funding, repealing the poll tax, and increasing the school property tax. The alternatives were either integration or shutting down the schools. A referendum on this issue was required so that the action appeared to be the will of the people. The equalization law illustrated the growing power of such "New Departure" Democrats as Henry Watterson of Louisville.[50]

Black voters faced a dilemma. A vote for the measure seemed to endorse segregation. A negative vote could be interpreted as a vote against segregation or for inequality of funding. Mass meetings generated heated debate. Many speakers attempted to take a middle road by denouncing segregation and endorsing the benefits brought by equalization. In the end, a majority of 17,000 supported the legislation.[51]

Equalization did not occur immediately, since the law applied only to state funding, and local boards retained substantial power over school finances. Only in Louisville and Paducah did school boards equalize funding for the 1882–83 school year. Blacks elsewhere turned to the federal courts. In late August 1882, for example, Owensboro blacks unsuccessfully attempted to enroll pupils in the Lower Ward white school because equalization had not occurred. The following April a federal court ruled that legislation permitting school boards to discriminate in the collection and the distribution of school funds violated the Fourteenth Amendment. The school board reluctantly accepted the ruling. A new state law in 1883 increased per capita school funding for blacks as well as whites, but prohibited the use of whites' tax revenues to repair black schools. Segregation became even more deeply entrenched in 1891, when the state's constitution was amended to require racially separate public schools.[52]

However limited its scope, "equalization" doubled the size of the black school fund between 1882 and the end of the decade. During those eight years per capita spending rose from $1.30 to $2.25. Equalization also brought an extension of the school age to twenty and increased the number of eligible students in the state to 113,000.[53]

A number of new elementary schools were created in Louisville, beginning with Fulton and Portland schools in the late 1870s. California Elementary on Kentucky Street (1882), Main Street Elementary (1884), and Maiden

Lane (1890) followed. Total enrollment rose to 5,000 and the number of teachers to eighty-four. Overcrowding persisted, though, and the average teacher had 45 students. In some schools 100 students were crammed into one room, and they were forced to take turns sitting at the desks.[54]

A high school was opened in 1882, when Central Elementary added a three-year curriculum. It was essentially a junior high school until 1893, when a four-year course of study began to be offered. To blacks, however, Central was synonymous with strong teaching and rigorous discipline. Although inferior in facilities to white high schools, its teachers offered dedicated service and top-notch instruction. Athletic events as well as concerts and other special events at Central attracted large numbers of parents and other adults.[55]

Blacks in Louisville also took great pride in their night schools. At their peak in the late 1870s, Eastern and Western elementary schools had five hundred students each. The sight of a child and a 40-year-old man sitting side-by-side in grammar school was not uncommon. The school board became skeptical of the value of these schools, though, and enrollments dropped in the 1880s. In early 1886 all pupils over age 20 were expelled, but a compromise allowed those who had already enrolled before they were 20 to remain until age 25.[56]

Outside of Louisville, the quality of education after 1874 varied. Rural Jefferson County's twenty schools were one-room structures that offered just a few months of education annually. In Owensboro, a new brick building on Poplar Street between Third and Fourth streets was opened in 1879, and about 200 students attended daily, instructed by principal Lewis Metcalf and teachers Anna Varian and Owen Barrett. But only 40 percent of the town's school-age black population was enrolled. Equalization permitted officials to open a second building and hire teachers from Cincinnati and Louisville. A third schoolhouse was built in the upper ward, but its destruction by fire forced officials to rent space in the African Methodist Episcopal (AME) Church on Third Street. Total enrollment by 1891 was 574, and the proportion of school-age children attending school was about twice that of 1874. In 1887, unaccountably, city officials—probably fearful of the leadership that black teachers provided in the community—replaced all the black teachers with whites. This ten-year-long policy turned out to be quite divisive among Owensboro blacks.[57]

Downstream conditions varied enormously. In Henderson, John Mason and his wife Martha were hired as teachers in the first black public school in 1874. Another room was added in 1878, and a graduate of the school, Virgie Harris, was hired as an additional teacher. In 1882 the school had four teachers and 386 pupils. A second building was opened by 1891. Crittenden County, like most rural counties along the river, had separate black school districts

beginning in 1874. Teachers were paid twenty-four dollars a month, and school terms were brief. The total black school enrollment by the late 1880s was 367, and about one-fifth of the students were in Hurricane Landing (later named Tolu) on the Ohio. When a high school was opened, blacks were denied admission to it, and county officials paid their tuition and transportation costs to attend black high schools in neighboring counties. As a result of "equalization" in 1882, the state revenue provided per student per year was raised two cents, to twenty-two cents![58]

Statewide, black school enrollments in the late 1880s continued to lag behind those of whites. Just 36 percent of school-age black youth attended school, as compared with 50 percent among whites. Only three former slave states had lower rates of black school enrollment. This was not limited to public education. Kentucky, one of the three former slave states with the largest number of black Catholics, had just a handful of blacks in its Catholic schools. The policies and practices adopted after 1865, one historian aptly observed, created "a legacy of poverty and suffering that haunts Kentucky to this day," because blacks were placed "in the position of an underclass." The state of education for blacks reinforced "the idea that they rightfully belonged at the bottom of society."[59]

On the north shore, in the rural counties upriver from Cincinnati, the best that black students and parents could hope for was a single all-black school that served a town or an entire township. Whites perceived this as progress. The first history of Clermont County, for example, boasted that "in all of the towns and most of the townships ample provision has been made for colored scholars, usually taught by intelligent teachers of that race."[60]

Matters were comparatively better in Hamilton County. A high illiteracy rate was symptomatic of the slave origins of virtually all newcomers. But the rate was considerably lower than Louisville's, reflecting the fact that public schools had existed since the antebellum era. In 1869–70, nearly 800 black youth attended school. The largest number, 152, resided in Cincinnati's Ward 13. Of all the cities and towns on the north bank, Cincinnati had the most black schools and educators, but classrooms were inadequate and crowded. The presence of hundreds of black newcomers placed great strains on the system, especially in the Western District. In addition, the "colored school fund," determined by a levy based on the census of school-age persons, was underfunded. Based on the city census of 1865, the fund should have amounted to $20,120, wrote Peter H. Clark in the *Colored Citizen,* but school officials had deposited considerably less.[61]

The ending of the war brought a great sense of urgency to the Colored School Board. The school year beginning in the fall of 1866 was one of unprecedented breakthroughs, including legislation providing the capital needed to build and to expand elementary schools as well as to open a high school. The position of superintendent of the colored schools, moreover, was reinstituted. William Hartwell Parham, a teacher in the Cincinnati schools since 1860, was named to that position.[62]

Parham's first responsibilities included alleviating crowding in the Western District. He adjusted the boundary between the Western and Eastern districts and opened two schools, one in the Northern Colony and the other in the Southern Colony. The number of teachers was increased to 11, 4 each at the district schools and 3 at the others. Parham also served as principal and teacher at Southern. Although Clark strongly championed Parham's decision to open the high school, Western District trustees vehemently opposed it. They favored additional funding to alleviate the crowded elementary schools. The board approved its creation by just one vote.[63]

Gaines High School was first located on the upper floor of the Court Street schoolhouse in the Western District. Its initial faculty numbered seven, and three of them—teachers of drawing, German, and music—were whites. Several of the teachers added in following years were, like the white teachers, specialists who traveled to all of the schools of the district. Monthly teacher-training sessions were held at Gaines for two years, and in 1868 a normal school division was opened that held classes from 5:00 until 7:00 p.m., three days a week. Teachers in the colored schools were required to attend. Seniors in the high school desiring to teach were also permitted to enroll in these classes.[64]

The annexation of Walnut Hills by the city added about 200 more black students in a third school district. The region had been the first of the suburbs in the hilltops to receive black migrants from the basin along the Ohio. Its pastor's home had served as the school for blacks since 1859. A new three-story school building with eight rooms was opened in 1872 and considered by blacks to be "the jewel of the black school system. . . . It was located on Elm Street (now Alms Place) near Chapel Street. . . . The school building and its spacious playground cost $23,997.88."[65]

Allen Temple's fiftieth anniversary celebration demonstrated the close ties among teachers, clergymen, and members of benevolent and fraternal associations. The proceedings traced the history of the local schools and listed their principals, teachers, trustees, and graduates. Details of school enrollments and expenditures were also included. The number of students had risen to 1,162 in

1873, and total expenses were $24,699—less than half of which went to salaries. Many of the teachers belonged to Allen Temple or other churches.[66]

The proceedings of Allen Temple's celebration included Parham's address, "The Common Schools, the Citidal [sic] of Liberty and the Bulwarks of Christianity." He described the public school as the foundation of American freedoms. "If liberty is to find a secure and a permanent abiding place, a fortress of defense against threatenings [sic] and assaults within our land," he insisted, "that place must be within the walls of our Public Schools, where the hearts of the nation are moulded, and where the seed of future fruit is sown." These institutions were also critical to black churches, because ministers "must be men ready to teach. . . . [and] able to read the word, with sufficient culture to comprehend it, and ability to expound and defend it." Nine in ten ministers "will be men whose only educational facilities they will find within the walls of the Peoples' College."[67]

Schools' connections to civic leaders were evident in other ways. Clergymen typically had to supplement their meager incomes. Some earned money as school trustees. One Cincinnati pastor, a school trustee for fourteen years, was also in the carpentry and repair business and found lucrative employment in the schools. Rev. William Buckner, trustee between 1871 and 1874, was a school watchman. Other trustees were prominent in business as well as church affairs. Parham's father, a trustee between 1856 and 1873, was a successful tobacco merchant, and his business affiliate, Frank Rieder, was also a school trustee (1870–71). Isaac M. Troy, a shoemaker and a longtime trustee of Zion Baptist Church, served as school trustee for eight years. Robert Gordon, trustee from 1871 to 1874, was in the coal supply and real estate businesses. His daughter married George H. Jackson, a teacher in the Cincinnati schools. Joseph Early, trustee for the Walnut Hills district during 1870–74, was the son of the first black clergyman in that part of the city. A chef, he became a prominent Republican and was the first black elected to office in Ohio. A "colored boss," he distributed political spoils to black Cincinnatians.[68]

Arguably the two most eminent black civic leaders in postwar Cincinnati were educators. Peter H. Clark, described as the "greatest black school teacher of the century," was born in Cincinnati in 1829. Educated in Cincinnati and at Oberlin College, he began teaching in 1849. Soon he branched out into other activities. He served as a trustee of the Colored Orphan Asylum, was associated with Levi Coffin and Frederick Douglass in antislavery causes, and became president of the black lyceum. He was elected president of the Ohio Civil Rights League in 1865 and presided at the first national convention of black newspapermen in Cincinnati in 1875. He was also an active Mason. A front-

page story in the *Cincinnati Commercial* of March 31, 1867, described him as the "life and soul of the colored schools. . . . and justly regarded as a man of unimpeachable integrity and the utmost purity of life."[69]

Parham (1829–1904), superintendent of the colored schools, was born in Virginia, educated in Philadelphia, and came with his family to Cincinnati in the 1850s. While he worked on the steamboats, he gained additional training under Clark. He became a teacher in the Cincinnati schools and pursued legal studies, becoming the first black graduate of the Cincinnati Law School (1874). Longtime superintendent of the Zion Baptist Sunday School, he was 12th Grand Master of the Freemasonic Colored Lodge of Ohio. After Gaines was closed, he practiced law and resumed political activities.[70]

Details about downstream Indiana blacks' education are scant. Jefferson County's first history, for instance, contained a brief reference to a school for blacks located on North Broadway in Madison that was one of six public schools in the city. The first historical account of the Falls cities of the Hoosier state was relatively expansive. After passage of the state school law in 1869, black schools were established at Memphis in Union Township, in rural Clark County, and on Court Avenue (the New Market School) in Jeffersonville. This work revealed, unwittingly, a sobering statistic—that just 33 percent of the 689 black youth of school age in Floyd County in 1878 attended school. This figure was considerably lower than the 45 percent overall average for the county, which was low to begin with.[71]

As of the mid-1880s there were several elementary schools and one high school for blacks in New Albany. These were situated where most blacks in the city resided. West Union and Upper Fourth Street schools were the first, created in 1870 and 1874, respectively. Both were closed by 1879. A new building was erected in 1875 on Lower Second, at the corner of Elm, that operated until 1907. Another school was in a leased building on Upper Eleventh at the corner of Market (1877 to 1883). A new building was erected on Division Street in the eastside Providence neighborhood in 1885. Scribner High School was opened in an 1822 structure in 1880.[72]

Separate and unequal education was also the rule in downstream Rockport. The first history of the county identified three black men who taught at the colored school between the opening of the school in 1874 and 1885: A. Hall was the first (1874–75), and he was followed by Charles Martin and D.R. Cunningham. The record is unclear whether continuous service was provided black students, but clearly there was only one teacher at a time. In neighboring Warrick County, in 1883 there were 8,414 children of school age, about 5,300

of whom attended school. Of those, 292 were black; they constituted a proportion of the black school-age population that was much smaller than the proportion of whites who attended school. There were two black teachers: Minnie Clark, one of the nine public school teachers in Boonville, who had thirty-six black pupils; and C.S. Pritchard in Newburgh.[73]

In Evansville, in the summer of 1865 industrialist Samuel Orr asked the Evansville City Council to fund a school for blacks. He argued that it was "a matter of humanity and policy" and also cheaper in the long run "to provide a school room for them now, than it would be to provide prison room for them if permitted to grow up among us without proper instruction."Vermont-born attorney Horatio Q. Wheeler, a school board member, donated the land, and the city council, despite strong Democratic opposition, appropriated $1,000 for a building.[74]

In early December 1865, scholars and their teacher at the new school, located at the corner of the defunct Wabash and Erie Canal (Fifth Street) and Chestnut Street, organized a festival to raise money so that the teacher, a white woman identified as "Miss Johnson," could employ an assistant. The school was "too large for any one teacher to do it justice."[75] The following June the "Misses Johnson" presided over the public examinations of pupils—a common practice of teachers in those days. The audience, racially mixed, was delighted. The number of pupils was huge: of the 273 registered by the school, 114 demonstrated their progress in reading, geography, spelling, and arithmetic. Some spoke with great enthusiasm, "especially of the excellent teachers, who have braved public opinion and labored quietly, earnestly, faithfully, and assiduously to elevate the offspring of an unfortunate race." The Republican paper added faint praise: "a great deal could not be expected of those scholars, who have never had the advantages of parental training."[76]

The teachers the following year were John Tennis and his wife, apparently whites, and the school term was six months long. The annual examination attracted the attention of many whites. The report also revealed that most of the funding—sixty dollars per month, for four of the six months—had come from the American Missionary Association. During the last two months, parents' subscriptions had provided the only revenue. Enrollment was high (178 students) but average attendance was slightly below 30 percent. The recitations were described as "highly creditable, and considering the circumstances, some classes exhibited extraordinary progress." One pupil had not known how to read six months earlier and had advanced to his fourth reader. Another was a woman in her early twenties, who had learned to read and write. She did washing most days and attended school when she could, a few times a week.

"Those who profess to doubt the capacity of negroes to receive education," the reporter concluded, "should visit this school."[77]

Funding remained modest and came mostly from the AMA. In early 1867, Governor Conrad Baker and Judge Asa Igleheart, prominent Evansvillians, urged members of the Evansville Presbyterian Church (New School) to raise money for the school at Fifth and Chestnut. The congregation agreed to take up a collection if other churches joined them, but their challenge was not met. Individual members contributed, however. The following year enrollment increased to 231, but there was just one teacher, Mrs. Tennis, who received less than half her salary from parents' subscriptions. The remainder came from the munificence of whites.[78]

Attendance records revealed the challenges that poverty and racism posed— a pattern that persisted after the creation of public schools. Enrollments were highest in February; afterward many students left to work on area farms or stay home so that their parents could go to work. The absence of compulsory school legislation abetted this situation. But interest was high. The age range of pupils remained broad—from six to middle age.[79]

The black school, like Liberty Baptist Church, continued to offend Democrats. Some petitioned the City Council to close it, and they were supported by the cigar maker, Herman Fendrich, a member of that body, during the city elections of 1866. Whites complained about the proximity of the school to their residences and alleged that black school children engaged in lewd conduct. The school survived, though.[80]

When school officials began to explore schooling for blacks after the legislature authorized tax-supported education, they did not seriously consider school integration. Neither did black parents, who petitioned that "colored teachers might be appointed to teach the colored children."[81] The closing ceremonies of "Mrs. Tennis's Colored School" in June 1869 were especially joyous. Afterward, hundreds attended a picnic at Blackford's Grove to celebrate the passage of the public school law. In August the school board hired two teachers: one for a school on Clark Street, in the "lower" part of the city, and the other for Fifth Street. George Jackson Jr. was to be the teacher at the former, known as Clark Street, and James Townsend was hired for Fifth Street. Jackson was a son of the highly respected steward on the steamboat *Idlewild*. Townsend, as noted earlier, was an AME clergyman.[82]

Registration was brisk. In October the school board requested a twenty-cent tax levy to support the unexpectedly high enrollments. The first annual report of activities in these schools was published in May 1870. High enrollment clearly indicated black parents' desires for their children's development.

That scores of adults enrolled in Townsend's night school attested to their thirst for learning. Two teachers were added in the fall of 1871. Large numbers enrolled in night-school classes well into the 1870s. Edwin F. Horn's night school for 1875–76, for example, ran between early October and late February. On the average, 67 attended—40 women and 27 men. At the closing ceremony the white school superintendent congratulated the students on becoming a reading people. Horn's pupils presented him a gold-headed cane.[83]

Horn, a bright young man who was part Indian, also covered black community news for the Republican paper in the 1870s. Like most, he did not challenge the existence of separate schools. His speech to the school board upon completion of the new consolidated school on Governor Street in 1875—opened to serve all Baptisttown children—emphasized the pride that blacks had in the new structure. The keys to advancement were education and wealth: "Give *our* people as much education as they have, and as much wealth, and I care nothing about what the *law* may read." It was parents' "*imperative and duty* to send your children to school. . . . If [children] be educated and virtuous, the greatness of our people is assured."[84]

The black schools—as evidenced by the Strawberry Festival at the home of Mrs. James Carter in the spring of 1870 that honored the work of James Townsend—became the center of black culture and society. Closing examinations and commencement ceremonies demonstrated the progress of a race as well as that of young scholars. The closing ceremonies for the first year, 1869–70, were the most distinctive. This was an event marked by music led by John H. Carter and the attendance of prominent whites. Almost as significant was the first graduation at the Colored High School on June 14, 1882. The ceremony was held in Evans Hall, the city's largest public hall. In succeeding years, the black community united behind its young scholars, proudly displaying their achievements for white as well as black observers.[85]

As of the late 1880s, blacks in Evansville attended three elementary schools: Governor Street, Independence (on the northwest side), and Clark Street, where a new building was opened in 1889. The black high school was moved there from Governor Street. Initially those in rural Vanderburgh County attended three schools, one of them on Daniel Lyles's land southwest of the city. Rather than building separate schools for blacks, however, trustees in all but one of the townships began paying the tuition for black pupils to attend schools in Evansville. This included pupils at the higher grades. In 1877 black parents in Knight Township unsuccessfully petitioned trustees to admit their children to the eighth grade in the nearby white school, "to receive the benefits of public

schools in common with others of like grade, there being no adequate provision made for colored children for that grade."[86]

As elsewhere, the quality of segregated education remained inferior. By the 1889–90 school year, the number of black pupils in the city was 700, all but a handful of whom were enrolled in elementary grades. The pupil-teacher ratio was high. Salary differentials provided additional evidence of discrimination. For example, in the early 1870s, Townsend, with an annual salary of $700, was the highest-paid of the four black teachers, but that was the amount paid to the heads of the smallest white schools. The other black teachers received an average of $400. In 1889 the value of black school buildings was 9 percent of the city's total, although blacks constituted 14 percent of school enrollments. Per capita expenditure for all students was $24 per year; for blacks it was $13.[87]

Additional signs of racial discrimination were transparent. The first state-licensed black teacher was not hired until 1884, when there were already twelve licensed white teachers. There were no kindergartens in the black schools, although five of the nine white schools had them. Inequality was evident in other ways. Newspaper accounts diminished the importance of the black high school by continually referring to (white) Evansville High School as "the crowning glory of the public schools" or "the public high school." Newspaper coverage of black school graduations emphasized the crowd's orderliness and its love of music. Black teachers were invited to attend the monthly meetings of the public school teachers, but newspaper accounts suggest that they were invited more as entertainers, singers of spirituals and dancers, than as educators.[88]

Passage of the revised 1877 school law occasioned Evansville whites' reinforcement of second-class education. As in New Albany, black parents faced cynical white responses to their demands for educational equality. On September 3, 1877, Charlotte McFarland, wife of the pastor of Liberty Baptist, called on superintendent of schools J.M. Bloss to make a request that was later in the day "sprung"—as the Republican editor put it—on the school board. Her daughter and another student had successfully passed the examination for promotion to the grade above the highest grade taught by Z.M. Anderson, who taught forty-five students in grades five to eight at Governor Street School. She requested that the school board either provide schooling at the grade to which they were entitled or admit them to the white high school. A week of heated public discussion ensued.[89]

In the first school board discussion of the request, its president, a Democrat whose party controlled the board, insisted that the issue was race-mixing, that Republicans on the board had political motives, and that Mrs. McFarland

wanted to "cause trouble, that she did not care if she broke up every school in town in the effort to force her child into the white schools. . . . The moment it became known that Evansville schools were mixed it would deter people from coming here." He claimed that many whites came "to the city with their families chiefly for the benefit of the public schools. . . . ninety-nine out of a hundred would prefer to see the children separated in the schools, and he did not believe it was the right time to compel their intermingling."[90]

The leader of the Republican minority responded that his only interest was "the principle of equal human rights under the law." He declared that he wanted the matter to be handled deliberately and asked that the superintendent be instructed to report whether "other provision could be made for them. . . . If it became necessary to admit the children to the High School, they were simply doing their duty and enforcing the law of the State."[91]

A number of citizens, some African American, voiced their opinions in the newspapers the next day. Virtually alone, white merchant C.H. Butterfield said blacks had the legal right to enter the high school if other provisions were not made, and that the city would outgrow its fears should that occur. Judge Asa Igleheart's position, like that of most Republicans, was that the school board should provide equal quality education for blacks and whites, not mix the races. Some asserted that admitting blacks to the high school would encourage white parents to enroll their children in Catholic schools. An unidentified black man wrote that the law required the board to act, and that it was unfortunate if some whites were upset by that. Black people, he said, preferred separate schools and no special privileges.[92]

The following day a black man who identified himself only as "Free Black" expressed a different view. He wrote that Bloss's disapproval of Mrs. McFarland's request did not provide a "fair chance for future promotion." Distributing black students among the higher grades in white schools would cost less than creating a separate school. If Bloss's definition of rights were followed, blacks should not reside in Indiana, vote, or testify in courts. A day later, an unnamed but purportedly prominent black man offered a more nuanced argument when he declared that black parents and students desired a good high school education in a separate school, but that the board would be unlikely to provide such costly programs as chemistry, Latin, and German, even though blacks paid their fair share of taxes. Whites were not more prejudiced in Evansville than elsewhere, he added, but they violated the law by not providing equally for black and white students. Another black man was more direct, as he commented in the same day's newspaper, chiding the superintendent for acknowledging that Anderson was currently handling four grades and more than forty

students, while no white teacher had to teach more than two grades. One result was that some good students became disheartened and left the schools. Poor parents, who labored hard to feed and clothe their children, saw little improvement in their learning. He inquired what white parents would do if their children were crammed together for years and at the end of their schooling be placed in a little closet with "an incompetent teacher to continue the work of destruction."[93]

During that week the Republican daily reported on what was happening around the state as well as in the city. Labeling as cowards whites who during the week proposed closing the high school, the editor pointed out that several Indiana school boards had decided to admit blacks. The Democratic daily's comments were visceral: "The colored race [should have] the same opportunity for educating their children that white people enjoy," but this should "not be done by giving it to them at the expense of others." Its editor said the two black youngsters could receive an excellent high school education by spending a thousand dollars or so to "secure the services of a college-bred tutor . . . [for themselves and for] such other colored children as may pass the proper examination." To admit them to the high school would create "constant discomfort and humiliation." For whom, the editor did not indicate.[94]

The Democratic daily reflected the position of the Democratic majority on the school board by insisting it was not opposed in principle to admitting blacks. Arguing that the timing was poor, it also printed letters from "sensible" blacks who opposed integration for the same reason. One man observed, for instance, that they would have themselves to blame "if by an unwise and indelicate attempt to force their children into the white schools," they aroused white opposition to public schools that would deprive all children "of the inestimable blessings of a free common school education."[95]

The Democratic paper also published what would today be considered the results of a focus-group discussion among black leaders, although Z.M. Anderson, whose job was tenuous, refused to comment. Robert Nicholas, the former policeman and now proprietor of a restaurant on Fourth Street, said he and other prominent black men, like Reverend McFarland, wanted equal rights but were willing to accept separate accommodations if they were equal in quality. A few, though, agreed with the policeman Jacob D. Thompson, who said he "had talked with a great many of his race and they were opposed to a separate High School, as they believed that if that were provided, no matter how careful they might be in providing for a teacher, the course would be inferior to the regular High School." One teacher could not possibly teach all of the courses necessary to provide a solid high school education.[96]

On September 9 the *Courier* indicated that some prominent blacks agreed with Thompson and others that the high school should either be integrated or done away with altogether. It pointed out that abolishing the high school might be a good step, because it was expensive and stuffed youngsters' minds with "disgusting conceit." The editor aimed most of his ire, however, at "insolent" blacks who pushed for admission to white institutions. "It would be graceful for them to remember that within the short span of thirteen years they have been freed from slavery . . . been given the right of suffrage . . . [and] made equal before the law with their former masters and with all other citizens." Two days later he denied "that the white people of this country have indulged their prejudices in dealing with the colored people. On the other hand they have been treated with exceptional favor."[97]

On the evening of September 10, Bloss offered two solutions that the board accepted. Anderson's teaching would be limited to grades seven and eight, and another teacher would be hired for grades five and six. For the black youth eligible for high school, he proposed opening several rooms in the library building on the Evansville High School lot on Seventh Street. A graduate from the Pennsylvania Agricultural College (whose race was not identified) would be hired to teach there. That "solution"—separate and unequal—seemed to satisfy most whites. Blacks' subsequent silence on the matter could have been interpreted differently. A room was subsequently rented at St. John's Evangelical Church, near Clark Street School, for seventh- and eighth-grade students. In the same term, 1878–79, the "high school" for blacks was opened. Democrats complained that this meant "a mixed recreation ground for both colors and no separate recesses."[98] The following year the school was moved to Governor Street School.[99]

Many prominent blacks in Evansville, unlike those in Cincinnati, had opposed the creation of a separate black high school because they believed it would be inherently inferior. Most acceded to its formation, though, because they were happy to get anything. As in Louisville, however weak its offerings, the black high school became an object of great community pride. Its principals, beginning with Lucy Wilson McFarland, were highly literate individuals who assumed positions of leadership in all aspects of black community life. Black teachers, many with degrees from schools like Fisk and Wilberforce, became the moral and social as well as educational backbone of middle- and upper-class black Evansville. Their dedication extended well beyond the classroom. A number of them taught for many years. Pinkney Miller, hired at Governor Street in 1884, was typical. He became principal in 1890 and served there until the school closed in 1928.[100]

Elsewhere the educational offerings were considerably bleaker. Neighboring Posey County, in area one of the largest on the Ohio, had one black school, located in Mount Vernon. Blacks living in the country (about half of the black population) had to find a means of traveling up to ten miles each way daily. This first school for blacks was opened shortly after the passage of the 1869 school law in the former county seminary building, constructed in 1843. As of the mid-1880s there were two teachers: Ollie Cooper, the principal, and Gertrude Bland, his assistant.[101] Samuel Anderson and Solomon Wilson, residents of Shawneetown, were leaders of an organized protest against the exclusion of blacks from the public school tax fund. In 1872 the legislature responded by permitting a percentage of tax revenues paid by blacks to be used for the education of black youth. Enrollment at Gallatin County's black school, not surprisingly, was relatively low. About one-third of black youth of school age attended it; at the same time approximately two-thirds of white youth were in school.[102]

Illinois census records for 1870 disclose that the same school attendance proportions held, on average, throughout the state. Statewide, 6 percent of white males and 8 percent of white females ages ten and above were illiterate; for blacks the percentages were, respectively, 44 and 49. Rates for both races were higher in Gallatin County. Among whites, 30 percent of persons age ten and above were illiterate; for blacks it was 74 percent. Forty percent of Gallatin County's illiterates were black.[103]

Similar patterns existed downriver. There was one school for all of the blacks in Pulaski County, opened in Mound City in the early 1870s. The first teacher was Wren Harris, an Illinois native who had moved to the county in the late 1860s or early 1870s. The teacher during 1882–83 was M.M. Avant, who was paid $40 a month for a relatively short academic year. (Whites received $75.) His wife, his assistant, received $18. The first school for blacks in Cairo opened in a small frame building that had housed the town's first public school. After the war the Freedmen's Bureau and northern missionaries provided some schooling, but black parents demanded more. Because of their persistence (and large numbers), the town's Republican school superintendent responded by creating the African Union School on August 30, 1867. Blacks raised money for this free school, which whites saw as a private institution that they would support through charity. T.J. Shores, one of the town's leading black men, was selected as teacher.[104]

Shores, a rival of Rev. Thomas Strother, was influential among migrants from the rural South, while Strother appealed to natives of the North. Strother and his supporters occupied the white school on Thirteenth Street on Octo-

ber 11, 1867, and called on whites to admit black students or to support the black school with tax revenues. Whites' resistance was vehement. The Democratic newspaper declared that no resident would tolerate race-mixing. Other prominent whites said blacks paid virtually no taxes and were not entitled to public funding. A week later, Strother organized the Cairo Educational Association to assuage whites. Clearly his goal was obtaining equal funding, and he called for and received whites' charitable support of the black school. Shores's teaching certificate was revoked by the school superintendent, and he left the city. As a consequence of the 1874 school law, most black pupils enrolled in the tax-supported Greeley Grammar School, a two-story, wood-frame building with four rooms that was located on the corner of Nineteenth and Walnut streets. As of 1877 five teachers taught 220 pupils in five grades. There were also several private schools for blacks. All were inferior in quality. Reuben Smith, a janitor, was one of a handful who protested this state of affairs publicly, writing a letter to the newspaper in May 1878 that objected to the poor quality of the buildings and the teachers.[105]

Between 1880 and 1883, Cairo blacks organized several means of seeking change. John Bird, a former police court judge and postal carrier, led a group of blacks that met with Governor Cullom to request, among other things, educational reform. Bird, along with James Scott and Alex Leonard, organized a colored state convention in July 1880 that petitioned for better schools. On the afternoon of March 3, 1883, Nelson Ricks, pastor of Free Will Baptist Church, led 125 children and their parents to Thirteenth Street School, which housed the high school, and refused to leave until improvements in the black school were assured or blacks were admitted to white schools. They also called for qualified teachers and schooling above the fifth grade level. Without adequate education, Ricks declared, they had no chance to improve themselves. The protests lasted a week. White leaders first threatened to close the black school, but relented and promised to repair Greeley School and to create a high school for blacks. Not all demands were met—for example, a school library and adequate funding for textbooks. Sumner High School, for blacks, graduated its first class in 1893.[106]

On both sides of the river, separate and unequal were the rule, and this condition remained so by the late 1880s. Black teachers had more students per capita than white teachers did, regardless of the state or the side of the river on which they lived. The same applied to teachers in country as opposed to city or town schools. The ratio in all Kentucky classrooms was much higher than in those across the river, and it was especially high in black schools. One should also note that according to the census of 1890, fifteen of the fifty counties

along the Ohio had no black teachers. Ten were in Indiana, three in Ohio, and two in Illinois. Three more counties, two in Illinois and one in Kentucky, had just one black educator each. These were rural counties with relatively few blacks.[107]

Location seems not to have made a difference in the percentage of blacks in the total black population attending school. Among the largest three urban counties, Hamilton had the lowest (11%) and Jefferson County, Kentucky, the highest (17%). Vanderburgh's percentage was 15. Among smaller counties— Alexander, Floyd, Henderson, McCracken, and Scioto, for instance—the percentages were similar, about 20.[108] Not all differences were north-south in origin.

Education, in essence, provided a fragile but vital means of individual and collective advancement. By contemporary standards black schools were decidedly inferior in quality. Black parents and civic leaders did not, as a rule, advocate racial mixing, except when whites, like those in Cairo and Evansville, prevented them from securing the same level of education as white pupils. Some blacks, notably in Cincinnati, preferred separate schools because they guaranteed a known quantity and quality of education. African Americans were not passive recipients of meager handouts, in general. Black schools, moreover, attracted dedicated teachers who served as role models for their students and as leaders in religious and civic affairs. The black school was an object of pride and a beacon of hope.

Epilogue

From the 1890s to the Great Depression

Before 1861 relatively few African Americans resided on the north bank of the Ohio, and the large black population on the south bank was mostly enslaved. The Civil War set unanticipated forces in motion. Thousands of men, women, and children moved—from farm to town in Kentucky, and from Kentucky northward. On the north bank, most black newcomers migrated to towns. They encountered large numbers of white people for the first time. For both white and black, the immediate postwar years brought great promise and uncertainty.

Newly freed blacks did what whites had been doing all along: they created families, built homes and neighborhoods, established churches and benevolent organizations, formed schools, and developed community rituals. At first, some sympathetic whites reached out to support them. By the mid-1870s, many whites had either lost interest or grown impatient. Racial separation, in the meantime, became increasingly prevalent. All settlements had sections that were considered "colored." In Kentucky blacks "lived close to but not in white neighborhoods . . . [and] some marker . . . usually separated black residential areas from white neighborhoods."[1] Most African Americans accepted such divides and understood that success depended on their helping themselves.

By the mid-1880s patterns of employment, housing, education, religious and cultural life, and race relations—soon known as Jim Crow—were well in place. They would dominate African American communities well into the

twentieth century. Variations existed. One factor was the number of blacks residing in black communities. Evansville's, Cairo's, and Cincinnati's blacks, for instance, were able to create and to sustain economic and social organizations that were not feasible for blacks in smaller places like New Albany. The founding of a community was also significant. Cairo's black community grew at a fast pace, but its roots were quite shallow, unlike Cincinnati's.

A third factor was the percentage of blacks in the general population. Because they represented a high proportion of the population, Cairo and Mound City blacks, at least until the 1890s, gained a modicum of political power that those in Evansville and Cincinnati did not. In most places, the proportion of blacks was small, and thus they were not perceived to be a threat to whites' interests. When that balance was upset, whites responded negatively and sometimes extralegally. A fourth factor was the degree to which the legacy of paternalism associated with plantation culture persisted. In rural regions and towns like Henderson that had a high percentage of ex-slaves, blacks continued to be treated as perpetual children. Cairo and some other north-bank settlements lacked that tradition. And there were significant regional variations. In Louisville, blacks had a long history of autonomy. The farther downriver one traveled, the closer one approached Deep South values and institutions. Such regional variations were reflected on the north side of the river. Southern Illinois was quite different, culturally, from southern Ohio. Finally, the ebb and flow of population shaped black community life. In most cases black population on the south shore began to decline in the 1870s. On the north shore, with the exception of Cincinnati, declension accelerated after 1900. The reduction in size of black populations had enormous implications for what blacks could do for themselves.

Whites' responses to blacks in Illinois, Indiana, and Ohio had much in common with those of whites in Kentucky. Legalized separation of the races, however, occurred earlier and was more extensive on the south shore of the river. In addition, the presence of significant numbers of New Englanders and migrants from the Middle States in Cincinnati and Evansville mitigated the virulent racism prevalent in the southern Midwest. Although most whites on the north bank preferred not to reside close to blacks, they were less inclined to discourage blacks' rising in class and status. African Americans in Louisville, however, enjoyed a more vibrant community life than many across the river.

Similarities and differences also could be seen within states. African Americans in towns located in counties with a strong plantation heritage had less control over their lives than those living in counties where slavery had been a relatively insignificant factor. Hence Henderson, Owensboro, and Uniontown

were quite different from Covington and Newport. Because of numbers of black residents, there were differences within states: for example, between Cairo and Shawneetown; Evansville and New Albany; and Cincinnati and Portsmouth.

Despite enormous odds, African Americans were for the most part able to create a viable way of life after emancipation—whenever emancipation occurred for them. Careful to keep to the places that convention assigned them, they nurtured individuals and organizations on their own and were invisible to white people, who could not prevent those considered inferior from persisting and hoping.

Most communities had moved toward formalized racial separation by the mid-1880s, but the forms of separation along the Ohio were more nuanced than farther south.[2] The intersection of race, place, and space in the postwar period required whites and blacks to negotiate—though not equally—the meaning of freedom. Segregation in that era was commonplace, as whites generally thought of culture and society through the lens of race, whether Native American, Hispanic, Asian American, or African American. Keeping blacks in their place required "a permanently separate and dependent underclass."[3] As David W. Blight has observed, "the 'peace among the whites' that [Frederick] Douglass had so feared in 1875 had left the country with a kind of Southern victory in the long struggle over Civil War memory."[4]

Roger A. Fischer has described "an evolutionary concept of segregation."[5] Segregation antedated the 1890s. What changed was "the precise manner and intensity with which such separation [was] maintained."[6] The growing dissatisfaction with blacks' assertiveness and numbers, as demonstrated by the editor of the formerly sympathetic *Evansville Daily Journal* by 1890, was undoubtedly common among whites. Urban blacks initially resided in small, segregated neighborhoods that were largely created by their choice. Churches, schools, fraternal and benevolent organizations, small businesses, and professional services attracted them. Their neighborhoods became their basis for a biracial society. Whites viewed the matter differently. Fears of blacks produced various forms of residential restriction—restrictive covenants in Evansville in 1909 and a zoning law in Louisville in 1914, for instance. In *Buchanan v. Warley,* though, the U.S. Supreme Court ruled on November 5, 1917, that the Louisville ordinance, which prohibited a person from moving into a block where a majority of the residents were of another race, was unconstitutional.[7]

Distance between the races was defined in social as well as spatial terms. Blacks were expected to be deferential—to address whites by some title of respect, for example, whereas whites typically called blacks by their given names.

Along the Ohio, this social rule was undoubtedly most pronounced in the rural villages and small towns.[8] Leon Litwack has observed that "what made the laws increasingly urgent was the refusal of blacks to keep to their place." He quotes an Episcopal minister from Louisville, who points out that Jim Crow laws required a black to make sure "the manner of his doing and his going [was] that of an inferior."[9]

Kentucky was distinctive from the north bank and the Deep South in one respect. Removed from populism and disenfranchisement, it had "a remarkably high rate of lynching." Rural parts of western Kentucky and the Jackson Purchase had "few towns, weak law enforcement, poor communications with the outside, and high levels of transience among both races." Lynching "flourished where whites were surrounded by what they called 'strange niggers.'"[10] Nearly half of the 353 lynchings that took place in Kentucky between 1865 and 1934 occurred in those two regions. The last ones on the lower Ohio were in Henderson and Paducah in 1915–16.[11]

Racial violence was not limited to the south shore, however. Between July 4 and 10, 1903, a shooting incident in Evansville led to a riot that caused the death and wounding of scores of blacks and whites and inflicted substantial damage to blacks' homes and businesses. Hundreds of African Americans fled the city for safety, many of them permanently. Governor Winfield Durbin sent the state militia to restore law and order—the first time an Indiana governor had taken such a step. Two lynchings took place in Rockport in the fall of 1900. One occurred in Cairo on November 11, 1909, that was emblematic of growing segregationism buttressed by vigilante justice.[12]

Some of the population patterns created in the twenty years following the end of the Civil War persisted, while others did not. The aggregate black population of Kentucky's river counties continued to far surpass that of north-bank counties. Within south-bank counties, blacks continued to move to towns and cities, notably Louisville, whose African American population rose to 47,354 by 1930. Nevertheless, in a pattern different from that in cities to the north, the proportion of black inhabitants of Louisville declined steadily—from a high of 19.1 percent in 1900 to 15.4 percent in 1930—because the influx of white newcomers was significantly higher. By 1930 Cincinnati's African American population reached 47,818, surpassing that of Louisville. The proportion of black residents increased steadily, from 3.9 to 10.6 percent. Cincinnati's overall rate of growth, though, was lower than the rates of all major northern cities except Pittsburgh.[13]

A notable exception among river cities was Evansville, whose African American population reached 7,405 in 1900, nearly 13 percent of the total

population. Thereafter it declined—to 6,266 in 1910—and over the following thirty years hovered between 6,400 and 6,800. Evansville blacks accounted for 6 to 7 percent of the city's population between 1910 and 1940. The race riot was a factor, but it was symptomatic of larger forces at work in the lower Ohio valley: among others, systematic efforts by fearful whites to intimidate the rapidly growing black population into leaving and to erect more rigid lines separating the races. Declines in black population occurred in other Indiana and Illinois river cities in this period. Probably more important, though, was the "push" of inferior employment and the "pull" of job availability in the north that was enhanced by improvements in north-south rail transportation.[14]

Regional changes were significant. In Kentucky, the proportion of blacks living in cities steadily increased—to 55 percent by 1940. Cincinnati also gained an increased share of the black population in southern Ohio. The rural counties on the north bank experienced declension in the proportion of their black residents; in some cases it occurred as early as the 1880s. In the eleven Kentucky counties below the Falls, decline began after 1860. The exception was McCracken County, which rose from 17 to 27 percent blacks by 1880; thereafter the percentage dropped steadily. In 1860 all but one of the eleven counties had been at least 13 percent African American. By 1920 only two were, Henderson and McCracken.[15]

Declension occurred in numbers as well. Between 1880 and 1890, 29 of the 50 counties along the Ohio lost black residents. Eighteen were in Kentucky, 3 in Illinois, 5 in Indiana, and 3 in Ohio. These were rural counties with relatively few blacks to begin with. The number of blacks continued to drop over the next thirty years. Counties with the largest towns experienced substantial numerical growth through 1910. But between 1900 and 1910, the number of counties with an increase of blacks dwindled to eleven, and for the first time all of Indiana's Ohio River counties lost black population. Chief among these was Vanderburgh. Daviess and Henderson counties in Kentucky also experienced declension for the first time. Between 1910 and 1920, the same thing occurred in Alexander, Jefferson (Kentucky), McCracken, and Pulaski counties. Just five counties gained black population between 1910 and 1920, the most prominent being Hamilton.[16]

In short, until 1900–1910, river counties with large towns provided job opportunities and relative safety from the whims of white racists. While prospects for employment—for example, on riverboats or in horse-drawn freight delivery—dwindled, jobs in industry and in service in cities to the north expanded, especially when World War I shut off immigration.[17]

A generally low quality of education, of which illiteracy was a major symptom, may also have impelled people to leave the region. In 1900, for persons ten and above, regional differences were a matter of degree rather than kind. Among the most urbanized counties, the percentage of illiterate blacks was lowest in Hamilton (17.8) and highest in Jefferson (Kentucky) (27.2). Vanderburgh's was 22.2. The percentages in McCracken County, Kentucky, and Alexander County, Illinois, were, respectively, 32.2 and 26.2. Among rural counties, cross-river differences were relatively slight: 25 percent of blacks over age ten in Posey County were illiterate, as compared with 33 percent in Union County, 20 percent in Lawrence County, Ohio, and 25 percent in Boyd County, Kentucky.[18]

The experiences of African Americans in the largest three cities after 1890 are revealing. In Cincinnati, most black leaders remained committed to racial separation as a means of ensuring greater community autonomy. The twentieth-century pattern of de facto segregation originated in the decade following passage of the 1887 school law. Walnut Hills District School, eventually housed in a new building named Frederick Douglass, enrolled increasing numbers of black students. Walnut Hills evolved into a racially polarized part of the city. Two other schools, which became all-black, were constructed between 1888 and 1914.[19]

The number of white allies in these three cities was small, and interracial cooperation was weak. African Americans had to rely increasingly on their own resources. The expanding black working class was the economic foundation of community life and enabled some blacks to move into the middle class. In Cincinnati, those who were better off purchased or rented nicer homes on the edge of the east and west ends, and those in the black upper class moved farther out to sections of hilltop neighborhoods, especially Cumminsville and Avondale. In Louisville, affluent blacks clustered in the area of Chestnut Street. In Evansville, families of the most prominent educators and businessmen built homes across the street from the new Lincoln School.[20]

Churches also reflected class disparities. Allen Temple in Cincinnati, Quinn Chapel in Louisville, and Alexander Chapel in Evansville—all African Methodist Episcopal—appealed to the black elite. Baptist churches tended to attract a broader range of classes. Some congregations—notably Fifth Street in Louisville, Union (formerly First) in Cincinnati, and Liberty in Evansville—were affluent enough to erect new houses of worship and to employ relatively well-educated and well-paid clergymen.[21]

Educated blacks sought to ensure that black workers' behavior was appropriate. Denouncing dancing, drinking, gambling, prostitution, and other forms

of vice, they argued that such behavior weakened the mind and the spirit of ordinary blacks and made them less law-abiding and productive. Cincinnati black leaders, for instance, organized the National Negro Reform League and Criminal Elimination Society in 1914.[22]

Such strategies reflected the capricious racial climate. In Evansville, for instance, a white railway foreman shot and killed a black man who he alleged had threatened him. The county coroner promptly ruled the shooting self-defense, and the white man was freed. Six years later, in February 1913, the son of a prominent white furniture maker shot and killed three black workers in cold blood at his father's factory. His sentence was two years in prison for manslaughter. Two weeks after these shootings, a black man shot a white man in what he argued was self-defense. The next day an all-white jury convicted him of murder, and he was sentenced to life imprisonment.[23]

Most ordinary blacks worked hard and productively and supported the interests of their employers. They developed strategies to protect their fragile place in the urban economy that included strike-breaking and forming unions. Sometimes they refused to support black businesses and professional people who acted in ways that they deemed detrimental to the race. Like their more affluent brothers and sisters, they were class- and race-conscious.[24]

Gender also shaped black society. The reform organization in Cincinnati noted earlier, for instance, reflected a widespread concern for the welfare of young single women. Black women faced three forms of discrimination: race, class, and gender. Most could not escape menial employment as servants or service workers. Even black women with higher levels of education were blocked from such occupations as attorney and physician and only gradually became nurses and clerical workers. Most turned to teaching, and their contributions were enormous. An exemplar was Sallie Stewart, longtime teacher and dean of girls at Douglass (later Lincoln) High School in Evansville. Revered for her loyal support of women's interests, she created a day nursery and started a drive to eradicate tuberculosis, among other projects. She was a founder of the Evansville branch of the National Association for the Advancement of Colored People in 1915 and of the Inter-Racial Commission in 1927. Women's groups demonstrated the importance of building bridges, since class and gender interests were defined in racial terms.[25]

The need for laborers during World War I and the boll weevil infestation of cotton-growing regions of the South produced a massive migration of African Americans northward.[26] Most bypassed the Ohio Valley, except for Cincinnati. Jobs and good wages were the primary appeal, and labor agents for railroads and factories went south to recruit workers. The blacks came primarily by rail.

Most employment remained menial. In 1930, just 4.4 percent of Evansville's black workforce was employed by factories, mostly as custodians, janitors, or drivers. Of the 3,294 black men and women who had jobs, 2,937 were either common laborers or servants. Just 6.4 percent of the city's population, blacks represented 92 percent of the porters, 61 percent of the laundresses, 50 percent of the janitors and sextons, 42 percent of the common laborers, and 39 percent of the domestic servants. The occupational index for all black workers was substantially higher (599) than it was for whites (487). The same patterns existed in Cincinnati and Louisville. Compounding the problem was the fact that blacks as a rule were unemployed twice as long annually as whites, and during the first year of the Great Depression the situation worsened. Among black women, domestic service remained the most prominent line of work. Few black women gained access in any of these cities to the growing white-collar sector.[27]

Although the lower Ohio did not have the level of racial violence that struck East St. Louis and Chicago in 1917 and 1919, its cities increasingly restricted "access to housing, social services, public accommodations, and places of leisure and entertainment."[28] In Louisville, informal segregation in public transportation increased. In 1924 the city barred blacks from its public parks. Similar exclusion occurred in hospitals, clinics, and professional schools, where training was permitted only on a segregated basis. In Cincinnati and Evansville, de facto segregation, especially in housing, prevailed. In Cincinnati, hotels, restaurants, and soda fountains refused to serve blacks. There, as in Evansville, blacks could gain access to some theaters only by entering through a side door and by sitting in a separate section in the balcony. By 1910 custom blocked Evansville blacks from entering any park in which refreshments were served. In 1918 the Evansville school board segregated black parents at any concerts in which their children performed. By then the board had cut high school graduation requirements for black pupils from four to three years, had made Latin optional, had reduced the number of higher mathematics courses, and had added a number of commercial and vocational courses deemed "very essential . . . [for] . . . their life work."[29]

The 1920s were also a time of Ku Klux Klan revitalization. Proportionally, Evansville had the most members—an alleged roster of about 4,000 in a city of about 90,000. Numerically, Louisville had the least, approximately 3,000, and Cincinnati the most, 12,200. The face of the Klan varied from place to place. Purportedly it was officially denounced by Louisville authorities and banned from distributing literature on city streets. In Cincinnati and Evansville, members held a number of public concerts and rallies. In the Indiana city

the Klan's special targets were bootleggers and their alleged compatriots, German Catholics. It controlled county and city government from 1922 to 1928.[30]

In each city, the Klan's support for "100 percent Americanism" strengthened legalized and informal segregation. An ordinance passed by Cincinnati officials in 1924 limited new residential construction by blacks within the basin while encouraging it outside the region. Within six years just 2.5 percent of the city's homeowners were black, and the median value of their homes was about half that of whites' homes. High rent, building codes, zoning laws, the city plan of 1925, and subdivision regulations fortified the wall dividing blacks and whites. The Cincinnati Real Estate Board instructed its employees not to rent or sell property to blacks in white areas. The West End as a consequence absorbed most of the black newcomers. Between 1910 and 1930, the white population in the basin area, near the river, dropped by more than half, to 59,000, while the black population in the region rose from less than 13,000 to 32,728. The index of dissimilarity in the city escalated to nearly 66 percent.[31]

Centripetal tendencies in Evansville also intensified. Especially important was the decision of the school board in 1925 to erect a new school for blacks that consolidated all but one of the black schools. Toward that end, it launched a study that identified the "principal Negro district," an area to the east and northeast of the Chicago and Eastern Illinois Railroad terminal. Almost three-quarters of the city's blacks lived there. Five years later, the proportion of blacks in Evansville living in that region had risen, in part because of the opening of Lincoln School in 1928. The index of dissimilarity, which had been considerably higher than Cincinnati's in 1900 (45), was well over 75 in 1930. No blacks lived on nine out of ten Evansville streets in 1930.[32]

Louisville's blacks faced an even more restrictive environment. City officials accelerated the trend toward physical separation after 1915. They changed street names where whites and blacks lived on the same streets, for instance, and the new names ensured that blacks knew where the dividing lines were. Thirtieth Street, for example, was the dividing line for the West End, where most blacks were encouraged to live. Some moved to the East End, where they lived in Smoketown.[33]

In all three cities, housing in areas where lower-income blacks lived was overcrowded, unsanitary, dilapidated, and overpriced. Most of Evansville's housing stock was substandard, and few dwellings had running water or were connected to sewer lines. In the early 1920s a study of Cincinnati homes disclosed widespread overcrowding: for example, 94 blacks lived in a twelve-room tenement, and 20 lived in a three-room flat.[34]

In all three cities, nonetheless, community-building enterprises contin-

ued, from churches and schools to professional, business, civil rights, and political organizations. One black newspaper reported in 1924 that Louisville had a number of black-owned businesses, in addition to restaurants and barbershops: eight undertaking establishments, three drug stores, two building and loan associations, two photographers, six real estate companies, three architectural firms, four newspapers, three movie houses, fifteen groceries, two banks, and four insurance companies. The most impressive of the latter was the Mammoth Mutual Company, which built a six-story edifice to service thousands of customers in the city and elsewhere.[35]

Louisville's relatively large black business and professional community also supported the establishment of a chapter of the National Urban League before World War I. Its special interest was expanding employment opportunities. Some black civic leaders joined the Commission on Interracial Cooperation (CIC), created by whites to foster better race relations; it was not unlike the Inter-Racial Commission in Evansville, which began in 1927.[36]

Changes were far more modest in Evansville. The number of black businesses rose from 47 to 51 in 1920. Most were financially marginal, and some—like Black's Hotel on Walnut Street, near Fourth, and Logan Stewart's life insurance and real estate business—did not survive the 1920s. The most significant addition was the undertaking business of W.A. Gaines, who had established similar firms in Covington and Paducah before coming to Evansville in 1907.[37]

Blacks' religious, fraternal, civil rights, and political activities also expanded. The number of religious institutions grew steadily, and black ministers remained central fixtures in the affairs of black men and women. Clubs, fraternal societies, and social welfare organizations continued to mirror as well as to bridge the gaps among black residents. Ernest Tidrington of Evansville, for instance, served as state "grand chancellor" of the Knights of Pythias from 1909 until his death in 1930. There were also such groups as Cincinnati's Negro Civic Welfare Association (NCWA), created during World War I through the leadership of sociologist James Hathway Robinson, who moved to Cincinnati in 1915 to take a teaching position at Douglass School. The NCWA helped to create a wide range of social services available to black workers.[38]

African Americans in all three cities also formed branches of the NAACP. Louisville's branch was created in 1914 to fight the residential segregation ordinance, while those in Cincinnati and Evansville arose in (unsuccessful) opposition to the showing of *Birth of a Nation* in 1915. Two years later the Louisville branch led the successful effort to secure an antilynching law. In the 1920s the branch also "initiated the movement that led to municipal restric-

tions on Klan activities."[39] Its primary interest during the decade remained residential segregation, and its achievements were, unfortunately, few. The Cincinnati branch was also active in the 1920s. It helped to kill a bill in the legislature that would have outlawed racial intermarriage. In Evansville, by contrast, the NAACP chapter became moribund after 1915, a reflection of the small size and limited resources of the black community.[40]

Until the 1930s, most blacks voted Republican in state and national races, but at the local level they became more independent. A new generation of black leaders, all prominent businessmen, challenged the Republican establishment in Louisville in the early 1920s by forming an Independent Party. Although unsuccessful at the polls, their efforts prompted Republicans to expand the number of blacks hired at city hall and, for the first time, to appoint blacks to the police and fire departments.[41]

In Cincinnati, blacks pressed whites for greater reward for their loyal support. Their challenge after 1924 was unique, because Cincinnati adopted a new form of government that abolished ward lines, created a nine-person city council, all elected at large, and instituted a city manager. Established to eliminate Republican corruption, the system theoretically allowed any group with at least 10 percent of the total votes plus one vote to elect a person to the council. Not until the early 1930s, though, were blacks able to elect one of their own.[42]

In city races Evansville's blacks began to demonstrate independence and helped to elect a series of Democratic mayors beginning in the late 1890s. After 1905 a white saloon-keeper, Charles Ossenberg, and his black ally, Ernest Tidrington, were the key figures in delivering the black vote. The two aided Democrat Benjamin Bosse in 1913, for example, and as a reward Tidrington became the city's first black detective. In 1925, though, the two strongly supported the candidacy of Klansman Herbert Males, a Republican. After his election, Males named more than 100 blacks to city jobs, 80 more than his predecessor. Black leaders also admired his building of Lincoln School. In the city election of 1929, "good government" forces defeated Males in the primary, and Tidrington threw his support to the Democrat, who won in the November election. In early 1930 Tidrington was shot and killed, reportedly as retribution for his disloyalty.[43]

In Cairo, white Republicans were increasingly resentful of blacks' assertiveness, especially after their protest against the local school system in 1883. The number of black voters, combined with whites' moving north of the city center, gave black Republicans even more power. State Republicans saw Cairo as a bastion when their influence was waning in the state, and Cairo

blacks perceived them as their chief protectors. John C. Walton, a black man, was elected to the city council in the late 1880s. William T. Scott of the black *Cairo Gazette* secured the contract to print city documents. In 1895, Dick Taylor was one of four African Americans elected city alderman. Two years later, ten black men held elective office in the city and county.[44]

In the meantime, local white Republicans sought means of diminishing blacks' influence. The souring of the economy after 1893, as noted in chapter 9, enhanced racial tensions and encouraged vigilante justice. The first historian of Cairo—John M. Lansden, who, ironically, was elected mayor in 1871 primarily because of black votes—commented that whites had never wanted blacks as voters, officeholders, or citizens. In fact, he declared, they did not want them at all. Lansden successfully led Progressive-era efforts to curb blacks' clout by creating a new voter registration act and a city-commission form of government in 1913 that had at-large seats. As the Democratic Party's strength in Alexander County waned, because of the Panic of 1893 and the unsuccessful presidency of Grover Cleveland, partisan competition declined, and party politics became a contest among Republican factions. White votes in the northern part of the city helped Lansden and others diminish blacks' political strength. John J. Bird, a black, had once served Rutherford B. Hayes and others as a consultant on politics in the region. Now Lansden, elected mayor with black votes, called "the elective franchise in their [blacks'] hands" a "political travesty."[45]

In the interim, Bird and Scott had moved to Springfield in the early 1890s and had become key members of a group of influential black leaders who had close ties to national leadership and also played an important part in the struggle against racial injustice in Illinois. Joining them was Jacob Amos, an engineer at Cairo's electric light and power plant and a former city alderman. All criticized white Republicans' perfidy.[46]

Black women were also involved in the political struggles of blacks in these cities, especially after 1920. These political activities were "deeply embedded in their support of churches, fraternal orders, and social clubs." Noteworthy was Cincinnati's City Federation of Colored Women's Clubs, which purchased an impressive brick building on Chapel Street, near Gilbert Avenue, in 1925. In addition to her many other interests, noted earlier, Sallie Stewart of Evansville was active in the National Association of Colored Women and served as its national president in the 1930s.[47]

Class and culture sometimes divided African Americans. The formation of the Universal Negro Improvement Association of Marcus Garvey in 1914 was probably the strongest evidence of division. The UNIA strongly appealed to

ordinary black men and women with a message of racial pride and unity. It attracted many adherents in Cincinnati and Louisville, but not in Evansville. William Ware of Cincinnati, a founder of the Welfare Association for Colored People in 1917, succeeded in getting Garvey to visit Cincinnati in February 1921 and formed a chapter of Garvey's organization that reportedly gained eight thousand members. In Louisville, editor I. Willis Cole and pastor Andrew W. Thompson backed the Garvey movement.[48]

Reuben Gold Thwaites's account of his trip down the Ohio in 1894 provides a glimpse into the dynamics of race in the smaller places of the region. Cloverport, in Breckinridge County, Kentucky, had a bustling riverfront where black roustabouts loaded freight onto steamboats while "singing in a low pitch an old-time plantation melody." Paducah was "a stirring little city with the usual large proportion of negroes, and the out-door business life met everywhere in the South."[49] Contemporary accounts of African Americans' life in such places are scarce. As a rule, early (and even recent) histories of most towns and counties are silent about the experiences of African Americans. Some primary records—notably federal census schedules and tax records—help fill that gap. Most of these places had few black residents, who lacked the critical mass to support many black-controlled institutions beyond churches and clubs. Their numbers were large enough in Cairo, Metropolis, and Mound City, though, to ensure for a time a degree of influence in local and state decision-making that most blacks did not possess elsewhere.

Occupational patterns in the villages and rural environs of the south shore of the river remained virtually unchanged. Some small businesses lasted until the Great Depression. Owensboro, for instance, had black-owned barbershops, groceries, saloons, restaurants, and one photographic studio—perhaps the only one owned by a black in the state in the 1890s. Paducah had three black doctors who formed a partnership and operated a pharmacy. Among smaller cities, Henderson had the most black business and professional establishments. Until the 1940s a number of black entrepreneurs operated in the heart of the city's business district. Their success resulted from their location and from patronage by whites as well as blacks.[50]

Blacks were reminded daily that they were deemed inferior. Hotels and restaurants were off-limits, for instance. Nonetheless, much of the proscription occurred as new opportunities and thus new challenges arose. Paducah created separate public facilities for blacks—lavatories, restaurants, and waiting rooms—in train stations. Black women were permitted to shop in downtown stores but not allowed to try on articles of clothing. Henderson's Barret Park was

segregated in 1903 at the insistence of white civic leaders. Black clergymen acceded. Blacks were thereafter permitted to use only the section of the riverfront park abutting the city wharf. Kentucky's newly created public libraries admitted only whites. Henderson's library board, which opened a facility in 1904, declared that blacks' presence "would totally destroy the usefulness of the Library to this community." Responding to blacks' complaints about exclusion "from yet another public institution, library officials moved a few books, which were 'suited to the needs of the colored population,' to the Eighth Street Colored School."[51]

Schooling, always segregated, remained grossly inferior. The commonwealth's black elementary schools had no libraries, and even worse, the same was true of the few black high schools. (Few blacks attended high school.) Only donations from concerned teachers and parents provided books for secondary schools. Normal school training, available for whites in most cities, was offered to blacks only in Louisville. Equal school funding was illusory. Equalization was consistently overlooked in the interest of providing better facilities, supplies, and teachers for whites. Some counties provided no schools for blacks at all. Increased funding for and attention to blacks' education did, however, diminish the overall illiteracy rate: it was only 15 percent in 1930.[52]

Well into the 1920s, the school year for black youngsters in rural Kentucky was shorter than for whites—typically three to six months. One reason had to do with the circumstances of rural families, which needed their children to work. Sometimes, though, the shorter school year was the result of caprice. The Henderson County superintendent in 1923 arbitrarily closed a colored school after three months, even though the teacher had a contract for seven months and parents had paid taxes on nine hundred acres of land to support the school and purchased books and clothes for nineteen pupils.[53]

White school officials found plenty of reasons to drag their feet on adequate funding, and usually they blamed the victim. For instance, they accused black preachers of meddling in school affairs, but without the clergy little educational opportunity would have existed. In many counties the only schools for blacks were provided in black churches. "Foot dragging" was clearly evident in the creation of high schools. After the establishment of one in Louisville in 1874, there was no other black high school in the state for about twenty years. Five were established in the 1890s—two in Ohio River towns, Covington and Owensboro. A state law in 1908 requiring each county to create a public high school did not mention blacks. As of 1916 there were only nine black high schools in Kentucky, including one in Henderson. The curriculum there stressed vocational training.[54]

Henderson's Frederick Douglass High School demonstrated the challenges facing blacks. Adults were doubly taxed: first, to support *all* the schools, and then to finance school equipment and supplies as well as land and building materials for the black schools. Henderson school officials grudgingly funded a few high school teachers for blacks in 1905, but a building was not opened until ten years later, after parents purchased a lot and began construction.[55]

The only black college on the Ohio outside of Louisville was Dennis Henry Anderson's Western Kentucky Industrial College, established in Paducah in 1910. His tuition-free school, which provided teacher and vocational training, was small and unaccredited. State appropriations were ended in the 1930s, effectively closing the institution. The legislature created the West Kentucky Vocational Training School for Negroes on the site, and it operated until desegregation in the late 1950s.[56]

In smaller towns, as in Louisville, the relatively high incidence of petty theft and such vices as gambling, prostitution, and drunkenness among blacks continued to be a drag on educational progress. Occupational and residential proscriptions were largely to blame. Whites' unwillingness to end illegal activities in and around black neighborhoods was also a factor, because it displayed their assumptions that criminality was to be expected of blacks. At the same time, whites went unmolested. Instances of police brutality toward blacks also became more numerous.[57]

Across the river, the passing of time brought a higher level of segregation. Separate schools for blacks persisted in all cities and towns along the north shore of the river. In predominantly rural counties and small towns where high schools were not provided, blacks seeking further education had to travel to the nearest community that had one. Black pupils in Brookport, Illinois, for example, had to go to nearby Metropolis for high school. Massac County was representative in other respects. The Oak Grove neighborhood in Metropolis accounted for a higher percentage of the town's black residents and had higher indexes of dissimilarity as the years passed. Custom dictated that blacks must stay out of the eastern part of Metropolis. Massac County had no black doctors or dentists. Black residents needing medical care had to go to Cairo or cross over to the Illinois Central Railroad Hospital in Paducah.[58]

The patterns that governed blacks' lives on either side of the Ohio were well in place by the late 1870s, and over the succeeding sixty years they became more deeply entrenched. In such an environment, blacks, mostly on their own, created a variety of means of coping with second-class status and built an impressive number and array of organizations. The character of their responses

varied according to their numbers or their share of the total population as well as their location.

On both sides of the river, these patterns began eroding in the 1930s. The days of Jim Crow were clearly limited, and blacks' self-confidence was a major reason. The rechartering of the Evansville chapter of the NAACP in 1938 occurred because of two cases its members took on: they sought justice for a young illiterate man charged with murder, and they tried to achieve desegregation of the new vocational high school. Although unsuccessful in both initiatives, the chapter gained 175 members in that year. At about the same time, Alfred Porter, director of the Lincoln High School band, did the unthinkable. When asked to have his band "just fall in" at the end of the line for a holiday parade downtown, as tradition dictated, Porter refused to comply. Flabbergasted parade organizers resorted to drawing lots for the order of march—a pattern that persisted thereafter. In 1940 the Kentucky Negro Education Association publicly stated its willingness to consider litigation if blacks were denied admission to the state's white colleges. This act went far beyond previous calls for equal but separate education.[59]

The sad fact is that such winds of change were so belated. Whether first-class citizenship could have been achieved in the two decades after the Civil War remains debatable. Egregious, venomous racism on both sides of the Ohio probably ensured that it could not have been. Perhaps it was naive for blacks to think that success "only required that they build respect for their race by becoming responsible, hard-working citizens."[60] What is remarkable, though, is what was achieved by African Americans in these circumstances.

Appendix

Population Tables

315

Table 1. Population of Ohio River counties of Kentucky, 1860 (east to west)

	Total	Whites	Blacks	Free blacks	Slaves	Slaves as % of blacks	Slaves as % of total pop.
1. Appalachian							
Boyd	6,044	5,871	173	17	156	90.2	2.6
Greenup	8,760	8,350	410	47	363	88.5	4.1
Lewis	8,361	8,114	247	17	230	93.1	2.8
2. Bluegrass							
Mason	18,222	14,065	4,157	385	3,772	90.7	20.7*
Bracken	11,021	10,188	833	83	750	90.0	6.8
Pendleton	10,443	9,975	468	42	424	90.6	4.3
Campbell	20,909	20,705	204	88	116	56.7	0.6
Kenton	25,467	24,815	652	85	567	87.0	2.2
Boone	11,196	9,403	1,793	48	1,745	97.3	15.6*
Gallatin	5,056	4,334	722	14	708	98.1	14.0*
Carroll	6,578	5,491	1,087	42	1,045	96.1	15.9*
Trimble	5,880	5,044	836	5	831	99.4	14.1*
Oldham	7,283	4,815	2,468	37	2,243	90.1	30.8*
Jefferson	89,404	77,093	12,311	2,007	10,304	83.7	11.5
3. Western							
Hardin	15,189	12,626	2,563	33	2,530	98.7	16.7*
Meade	8,898	6,944	1,954	22	1,932	98.9	21.7*

	Total	Whites	Blacks	Free blacks	Slaves	Slaves as % of blacks	Slaves as % of total pop.
Breckinridge	13,236	10,879	2,357	17	2,340	99.3	17.1*
Hancock	6,213	5,382	831	13	818	98.4	13.2
Daviess	15,549	11,958	3,591	76	3,515	97.9	22.7*
Henderson	14,262	8,418	5,844	77	5,767	98.7	40.4*
Union	12,791	9,666	3,125	20	3,105	99.4	24.3*
Crittenden	8,796	7,838	958	19	939	98.0	10.7
Livingston	7,213	5,955	1,258	36	1,222	97.1	16.9*
4. Jackson Purchase							
McCracken	10,360	8,554	1,806	68	1,738	96.2	16.8*
Ballard	8,692	6,943	1,742	24	1,718	98.6	19.7*
Total	355,823	303,426	52,397	3,322	49,075	93.7	13.8
State total	1,155,689	919,522	236,167	10,684	225,483	95.5	19.5
Regional % of State total	30.8	33.0	22.2	31.1	21.8		

Sources: Marion B. Lucas, *A History of Blacks in Kentucky*, vol. 1, *From Slavery to Segregation, 1760–1891* (Frankfort: Kentucky Historical Society, 1992), xx; Joseph G. Kennedy, *Population of the United States in 1860* (Washington, DC: Government Printing Office, 1864), 180–83; Francis A. Walker, *A Compendium of the Ninth Census (June 1, 1870)* (Washington, DC: Government Printing Office, 1872), 48–52; U.S. Bureau of the Census, Tenth Census, 1880, *Statistics of the Population of the United States* (Washington, DC: Government Printing Office, 1883), 392–93.

* Above the average percentage for Ohio River counties

Note: My definition of regions reflects that of Lucas, *History of Blacks in Kentucky*, xx. A more complicated description of the state's physiographic regions is found in Lowell H. Harrison and James C. Klotter, *A New History of Kentucky* (Lexington: Univ. Press of Kentucky, 1997), 22–23. Technically, Hardin, Meade, Breckinr idge, and Crittenden counties and parts of Lewis and Livingston lie in the Pennyroyal region, which encloses the "western coal field." Instead of "Appalachian," they use "Eastern Coal Field." Lucas's simpler terminology allows, among other things, for less visually cluttered tables.

Table 2. Slaves and slave owners in Kentucky's Ohio River counties, 1860

	Slaves	Owners	Average owned	No. owning over 10	No. owning over 20
Appalachian					
Boyd	156	48	3.6	3	0
Bluegrass					
Bracken	750	170	4.4	15	1
Campbell	110	49	2.2	0	0
Jefferson	10,315	2,226	4.6	205	27
Kenton	568	224	2.5	6	1
Mason	3,692	768	4.8	97	11
Trimble	797	175	4.5	14	1
Western					
Daviess	1,768	340	5.2	43	10
Hancock	823	194	4.2	18	5
Henderson	5,856	943	6.2	169	67
Meade	1,932	370	5.2	55	11
Union	2,560	526	5.8	96	24
Purchase					
McCracken	1,738	364	4.8	33	9

Source: Eighth Census, Kentucky Slave Schedules, 1860, National Archives Microfilm Publications, M653, rolls 401–6.

Note: I have listed a representative mix of counties, not all twenty-five.

Table 3. White and black population of towns with 2,500 or more residents, 1860

	Total population	Percent black
Cincinnati, Ohio	161,044	2.3
Louisville, Ky.	68,033	10.0 (7.2% slave)
Covington, Ky.	16,471	1.7 (1.2% slave)
New Albany, Ind.	12,647	7.5
Evansville, Ind.	11,484	0.8
Newport, Ky.	10,046	0.9 (0.4% slave)
Madison, Ind.*	8,130	3.0
Portsmouth, Ohio	6,268	3.4
Paducah, Ky.	4,590	14.6
Maysville, Ky.	4,160	9.4 (6.1% slave)
Jeffersonville, Ind.	4,020	15.6
Ironton, Ohio	3,691	3.2
Lawrenceburg, Ind.	3,599	0.1
Charlestown, Ind.	3,161	6.2
Aurora, Ind.	2,990	2.4

Sources: Darrel E. Bigham, *Towns and Villages of the Lower Ohio* (Lexington: Univ. Press of Kentucky, 1998), 255–57; Kennedy, *Population of the United States in 1860*, 112–28, 182–83, 373–96; Walker, *Compendium of the Ninth Census*, 166–77.

* The Madison total does not include North Madison, annexed after the war. Its total was 938, and 19 blacks lived there.

Table 4. Percentage of blacks living in urban areas, Ohio River Valley, 1860 (east to west)

County	Percent in county residing in places of 2,500 or more population*
Lawrence, Ohio	17.2 (Ironton)
Scioto, Ohio	65.9 (Portsmouth)
Mason, Ky.	9.3 (Maysville)
Hamilton, Ohio	80.4 (Cincinnati)
Campbell, Ky.	44.1 (Newport)
Kenton, Ky.	42.9 (Covington)
Dearborn, Ind.	100.0 (Aurora and Lawrenceburg)
Jefferson, Ind.	51.9 (Madison)
Jefferson, Ky.	55.3 (Louisville)
Clark, Ind.	40.2 (Jeffersonville)
Floyd, Ind.	82.8 (New Albany)
Vanderburgh, Ind.	75.0 (Evansville)
McCracken, Ky.	37.1 (Paducah)

Sources: Lucas, *History of Blacks in Kentucky*, xx; Kennedy, *Population of the United States in 1860*, 112–28, 180–83, 182–83, 373–96; Walker,*Compendium of the Ninth Census*, 48–52, 166–77; Census Bureau, Tenth Census, 1880, *Population*, 392–93; Eighth Census, Kentucky Slave Schedules, 1860, rolls 401–6; Bigham, *Towns and Villages of the Lower Ohio*, 255–57.

* Includes only counties with one or more towns of 2,500 or more.

Table 5. Population of the Ohio River counties of Ohio, Indiana, and Illinois in 1860 (east to west)

	Total pop.	White	Black	% Black
Ohio				
Lawrence 1*	23,249	22,564	685	2.9†
Scioto 1	24,297	23,974	323	1.3
Adams 1	20,309	20,204	105	0.5
Brown 2	29,958	28,842	1,116	3.7†
Clermont 2	33,034	32,201	833	2.5†
Hamilton 2	216,410	211,802	4,608	2.1†
Regional total/avg. %	347,257	339,587	7,670	2.2†
State total/avg. %	2,339,511	2,303,838	36,673	1.6
Indiana				
Dearborn 2	24,406	24,332	74	3.0†
Ohio 2	5,462	5,439	23	0.4
Switzerland 2	12,698	12,656	42	0.3
Jefferson 2	25,036	24,524	512	2.0†
Clark 2	20,502	19,982	520	2.5†
Floyd 2	20,183	19,426	757	3.8†
Harrison 3	18,521	18,407	1,744	7.4†
Crawford 3	8,226	8,226	0	0
Perry 3	11,847	11,842	3	0
Spencer 3	14,556	14,554	2	0
Warrick 3	13,261	13,242	19	0.1
Vanderburgh 3	20,552	20,425	128	0.6
Posey 3	16,167	16,031	136	0.8
Regional total/avg. %	211,417	209,086	3,960	1.9†
State total/avg. %	1,350,428	1,383,710	11,719	0.9

(continued)

Table 5 *(continued)*. Population of the Ohio River counties of Ohio, Indiana, and Illinois in 1860 (east to west)

	Total pop.	White	Black	% Black
Illinois				
Gallatin 3	8,055	7,629	426	5.3†
Hardin 3	3,759	3,704	55	1.5†
Pope 3	6,742	6,546	196	2.9†
Massac 3	6,213	6,101	112	1.8†
Pulaski 4	3,943	3,904	39	1.0v
Alexander 4	4,707	4,652	55	1.2†
Regional total/avg. %	33,419	32,536	883	2.6†
State total/avg. %	1,711,951	1,704,291	7,660	0.4

Sources: Kennedy, *Population of the United States in 1860*, 78–85, 102–3, 112–13, 128–30, 373–83. See also Census of 1860, Geospatial and Statistical Data Center, Univ. of Virginia Library, *Historical Census Data Browser,* online, http://fisher.lib. virginia.edu/census (March 30, 2005), cited hereafter as *U.S. Census Browser.*

* Numbers after counties denote region of adjoining Kentucky counties: 1=Appalachian, 2=Bluegrass, 3=Western Kentucky, 4=Jackson Purchase.

† Exceeds average for the state. In Ohio, 21.1% of the state's blacks lived along the Ohio. In Indiana and Illinois, the percentages were, respectively, 33.8 and 11.5.

Table 6. Black population of the Ohio River counties of Ohio, Indiana, and Illinois, 1870–1880 (east to west)

	Black pop. 1860	1870 pop.	Black	% Black	% Increase (decrease)	1880 pop.	Black	% Black	% Increase (decrease)
Ohio									
Lawrence	685	31,361	1,241	4	81	39,068	11,246	3	0
Scioto	323	29,302	1,013	4	214	33,511	1,159	4	14
Adams	105	20,750	373	2	255	24,005	343	1	(8)
Brown	1,116	30,802	2,067	7	85	32,911	2,316	7	12
Clermont	833	34,267	1,829	5	96	36,713	1,817	5	12
Hamilton	4,608	260,366	7,432	3	61	313,374	10,533	3	43
Indiana									
Dearborn	74	24,116	58	0	(22)	26,671	57	0	(2)
Ohio	23	6,537	189	3	722	5,563	205	0	9
Switzerland	42	12,134	121	1	188	13,336	214	2	77
Jefferson	512	29,741	1,105	4	116	25,977	944	4	(15)
Clark	520	24,70	1,970	8	279	28,610	2,536	9	29
Floyd	757	23,300	1,462	6	93	24,590	1,552	6	6
Harrison	114	19,913	349	2	206	21,326	350	2	0

(continued)

Table 6 (continued). Black population of the Ohio River counties of Ohio, Indiana, and Illinois, 1870–1880 (east to west)

	Black pop. 1860	1870 pop.	Black	% Black	% Increase (decrease)	1880 pop.	Black	% Black	% Increase (decrease)
Crawford	0	9,851	3	0	0	12,356	2	0	(33)
Perry	3	14,801	150	1	4,900	16,997	208	1	39
Spencer	2	17,998	949	5	47,350	22,122	1,492	7	57
Warrick	19	17,653	487	3	2,463	20,162	619	3	27
Vanderburgh	128	33,145	2,151	7	1,581	42,193	3,843	9	79
Posey	136	19,185	564	3	315	20,857	955	5	69
Illinois									
Gallatin	426	11,134	612	6	44	12,861	675	5	10
Hardin	55	5,113	89	2	62	6,024	164	3	84
Pope	196	11,426	471	4	140	13,256	570	4	21
Massac	112	9,581	956	10	754	10,443	1,703	16	78
Pulaski	39	8,752	2,394	27	6,039	9,507	3,270	34	37
Alexander	55	10,564	2,296	22	4,075	14,808	4,568	21	99
Total	10,883	685,568	30,131	4	177	827,241	41,341	4	37

Sources: Censuses of 1870 and 1880, at *U.S. Census Browser.*

Table 7. Blacks in Kentucky's Ohio River counties, 1860–1880 (east to west)

	1860	1870			1880		
		No. of Blacks, 1870	% of Total	% Increase (decrease)	No. of Blacks, 1880	% of Total	% Increase (decrease)
1. Appalachian							
Boyd	180	291	4	62	556	5	90
Greenup	410	461	4	12	439	3	(5)
Lewis	264	228	3	(14)	229	2	0
2. Bluegrass							
Mason	4,542	3,582	25	(21)	4,392	21	23
Bracken	833	636	6	(24)	816	6	28
Pendleton	468	641	5	37	780	5	22
Campbell	204	282	1	38	441	12	56
Kenton	652	1,657	5	154	2,528	6	53
Boone	1,841	1,012	11	(45)	1,232	10	22
Gallatin	722	600	13	(17)	647	13	8
Carroll	1,087	540	10	(50)	771	9	42
Trimble	836	456	9	(45)	577	8	22
Oldham	2,468	2,810	31	14	2,211	29	(21)
Jefferson	12,311	19,146	20	56	25,595	18	34

(continued)

Table 7 *(continued)*. Blacks in Kentucky's Ohio River counties, 1860–1880 (east to west)

	1860	1870			1880		
		No. of Blacks, 1870	% of Total	% Increase (decrease)	No. of Blacks, 1880	% of Total	% Increase (decrease)
3. Western							
Hardin	2,563	2,276	17	(11)	3,282	15	44
Meade	1,954	1,294	16	(26)	1,274	12	(2)
Breckinridge	2,357	1,682	14	(29)	2,204	13	90
Hancock	831	729	12	(12)	803	9	10
Daviess	3,591	3,603	12	0	4,854	18	23
Henderson	5,844	5,990	32	5	7,572	31	21
Union	3,125	2,574	23	(18)	3,163	18	23
Crittenden	958	809	9	(16)	1,151	10	33
Livingston	1,258	1,052	15	(16)	1,034	11	(2)
4. Jackson Purchase							
McCracken	1,806	3,289	31	82	4,383	27	33
Ballard	1,742	1,477	13	(15)	1,725	12	17
Total	52,397	57,117			72,659		
% of state total	22.2	25.7			26.8		
Region % increase				8			29

Sources: Censuses of 1860, 1870, and 1880, at U.S. Census Browser.

Table 8. Black populations in the largest Ohio River towns (2,500 or more), 1870 and 1880 (east to west)

	1870			1880		
	Number	% of town pop.	% in county	Number	% of town pop.	% in county
Ohio						
Ironton	306	5	25	769	9	60
Portsmouth	870	5	86	969	9	84
Cincinnati	5,896	3	79	8,131	3	77
Indiana						
Lawrenceburg	25	0	43	19	0	33
Aurora	4	0	7	0	0	0
Madison*	346	3	31	454	5	48
Jeffersonville	802	11	41	1,262	13	50
New Albany	862	6	59	1,331	8	86
Evansville	1,427	7	66	2,712	9	71
Mount Vernon	238	8	42	437	12	46
Illinois						
Metropolis	293	12	31	534	20	31
Cairo	1,849	30	81	3,349	37	73

(continued)

Table 8 (*continued*). Black populations in the largest Ohio River towns (2,500 or more), 1870 and 1880 (east to west)

	1870			1880		
	Number	% of town pop.	% in county	Number	% of town pop.	% in county
Kentucky						
Ashland	46	1	22	170	3	31
Maysville	681	14	19	876	17	20
Newport	122	1	43	313	2	71
Covington	1,075	4	65	1,788	6	71
Louisville	14,956	15	78	20,905	17	82
Owensboro	654	19	18	1,564	25	32
Henderson	1,489	36	25	2,025	38	27
Paducah	2,001	29	61	2,593	32	59

Sources: U.S. Bureau of the Census, Ninth Census, 1870, *The Statistics of the Population of the United States* (Washington, DC: Government Printing Office, 1872), 85–96, 108–30, 147–53, 226–40, 285–96; U.S. Bureau of the Census, Tenth Census, 1880, *Report of the Social Statistics of Cities*, pt. 2, *Southern and Western States* (Washington, DC: Government Printing Office, 1887), 111–34, 344–404, 437; U.S. Bureau of the Census, Tenth Census, 1880, *Statistics of the Population of the United States (June 1, 1880)* (Washington, DC: Government Printing Office, 1883), 130–40, 148–55, 185–96, 285–98, 417.

* Madison totals for 1870 exclude North Madison, which had 1,007 residents, none of whom was black. It became part of Madison in the following decade. In 1870, Kentucky towns accounted for about 66% of African Americans residing in river settlements. Ten years later, the proportion had dropped to 60%.

Notes: Percentages are rounded to the nearest whole number. A percentage < 0.5 is entered as 0.

Totals from the population schedules that I hand-tabulated sometimes differ from those listed in the printed census. I have used the figures from the latter whenever there is a variation.

Table 9. Black population by ward, Ohio River cities, 1870 (east to west)

	Ward with most blacks	Number of blacks	% Black	% of city total
Ironton	3	169	13	55
Portsmouth	4	530	22	61
Cincinnati	13	1,092	15	19
Madison	6	176	9	51
Jeffersonville	1	365	15	46
New Albany	5	322	13	27
Louisville	10	2,225	20	15
Evansville	1	415	15	29

Sources: Census Bureau, Ninth Census, 1870, *Population*, 122–30, 226–40; George C. Wright, *Life behind a Veil: Blacks in Louisville, Kentucky, 1865–1930* (Baton Rouge: Louisiana State Univ. Press, 1985), 111.

Table 10. Distribution of black population along the Ohio, 1870 and 1880

	1870				1880			
	Number	% of state total	County with most blacks	County blacks as a % of state total*	Number	% of state total	County with most blacks	County blacks as % of state total
Ohio	13,755	22	Hamilton (7,452)	12	17,414	22	Hamilton (10,533)	13
Indiana	9,558	39	Vanderburgh (2,151)	9	12,977	33	Vanderburgh (3,843)	10
Illinois	6,818	24	Pulaski** (2,394)	8	10,959	24	Alexander (4,568)	10
Kentucky	57,717	27	Jefferson (19,146)	9	72,659	27	Jefferson (25,595)	9

Sources: Censuses of 1860, 1870, and 1880, at *U.S. Census Browser.*

* The total black population for the fifty counties in 1870 was 84,250, and in 1880 it was 114,000. Hence, Jefferson County had nearly 25% of that population in 1870 and slightly less than 25% ten years later. Hamilton County accounted for about 10% in both censuses.

** Alexander County was a close second in 1870. The two counties constituted 17% of blacks in 1870 and about 20% in 1880.

Notes

Abbreviations

EC   *Evansville Courier*

EDJ   *Evansville Daily Journal*

KE   John E. Kleber, ed., *The Kentucky Encyclopedia* (Lexington:
     University Press of Kentucky, 1992)

JISHS   *Journal of the Illinois State Historical Society*

NAMP   National Archives Microfilm Publications

RKHS   *Register of the Kentucky Historical Society*

Prologue

1. See, for example, Richard C. Wade, *The Urban Frontier, 1790–1830* (Cambridge, MA: Harvard Univ. Press, 1957). My *Towns and Villages of the Lower Ohio* (Lexington: Univ. Press of Kentucky, 1998) does examine many small settlements and focuses on the region downriver, from the Falls to the mouth of the Ohio.

2. See, for example, George C. Wright, *Life behind a Veil: Blacks in Louisville, Kentucky, 1865–1930* (Baton Rouge: Louisiana State Univ. Press, 1985); and Darrel E. Bigham, *We Ask Only a Fair Trial: A History of the Black Community of Evansville, Indiana* (Bloomington: Indiana Univ. Press, 1987). Cincinnati's black history is treated in a number of essays in anthologies dealing with race, ethnicity, and labor. A notable work that focuses on the Queen City is Henry Louis Taylor Jr., ed., *Race and the City: Work, Community, and Protest in Cincinnati, 1820–1970* (Urbana: Univ. of Illinois Press, 1993). Cairo's African American history has been explored by Christopher K. Hays in "The African-American Struggle for Equality and Justice in Cairo, Illinois, 1865–1900," *Illinois Historical Journal* 90 (Winter 1997): 265–84, an article based on his dissertation at the University of Missouri (1996). See also Jacqueline Yvonne Blackmore, "African Americans and Race Relations in Gallatin County, Illinois, from the Eighteenth Century to 1870" (Ph.D. diss., Northern Illinois Univ., 1996). Joe William Trotter Jr., *River Jordan: African American Urban Life in the Ohio Valley* (Lexington: Univ. Press of Kentucky, 1998), examines only Cincinnati, Evansville, Louisville, and Pittsburgh, reflecting in part the fact that little historical analysis of other places has been done. Histories

of Indiana, Kentucky, Ohio, and Illinois also tend to give African Americans short shrift. Notable exceptions are Emma Lou Thornbrough, *Indiana in the Civil War Era, 1850–1880* (Indianapolis: Indiana Historical Bureau and Indiana Historical Society, 1965); James H. Madison, *The Indiana Way* (Bloomington: Indiana Univ. Press, 1986); and Lowell H. Harrison and James C. Klotter, *A New History of Kentucky* (Lexington: Univ. Press of Kentucky, 1997). Andrew R.L. Cayton's recent *Ohio: The History of a People* (Columbus: Ohio State Univ. Press, 2002) is particularly attentive to race, although exploration of the topic in Cincinnati and Ohio River communities is mostly limited to the antebellum era. The paucity of discussion of blacks' history in this region in most written accounts seems to reflect a larger tendency. The significance of the Ohio is generally downplayed after 1850 because of the assumption that the coming of railroads on the north shore turned citizens' eyes inland, making the river an insignificant part of subsequent development. (Cf., for example, my "River of Opportunity: Economic Consequences of the Ohio," in *Always a River: The Ohio River and the American Experience,* ed. Robert L. Reid [Bloomington: Indiana Univ. Press, 1991].) Illinois histories are especially marked by little attention to the river. Kentucky histories are the most attentive to the Ohio, because slightly under one-quarter of its counties border the river, and its largest city is on the Ohio.

3. See tables 1 and 2, in the appendix.

4. See, for example, my "River of Opportunity," 130–79.

5. Ibid., 155, 160.

6. The writings of Charles Dickens, Harriet Martineau, and Alexis de Tocqueville provide some of the most vivid examples of such comments. See ibid., 154. Abraham Lincoln found this kind of difference, going from one side of the river to the other. While visiting Cincinnati in 1855, he pointed out that cross-river Covington had just as fine a location as the Queen City, but it remained a little town because of slavery and nothing else. Comparing his experiences when purchasing rail tickets in both communities as a way of focusing on slavery's effects on white men, he noted how in Covington a lanky fellow was sprawled "across the counter who had to count up quite a while on his fingers how much two and one-half fares would come to." In Cincinnati, by contrast, "when I shove my money through the window, the three tickets and the change would come flying back at me quick." Quoted in Michael Burlingame, *The Inner World of Abraham Lincoln* (Urbana: Univ. of Illinois Press, 1994), 30.

7. There are a number of solid histories of African Americans in three of the four states that do not compare and contrast their accounts with experiences in neighboring states. See David A. Gerber, *Black Ohio and the Color Line, 1860–1915* (Urbana: Univ. of Illinois Press, 1976); Emma Lou Thornbrough, *The Negro in Indiana before 1900: A Study of a Minority,* Indiana Historical Collections, vol. 37 (Indianapolis: Indiana Historical Bureau, 1957); and Marion B. Lucas, *A History of Blacks in Kentucky,* vol. 1, *From Slavery to Segregation, 1760–1891* (Frankfort: Kentucky Historical Society, 1992), hereafter cited as *Kentucky Blacks.* The comparative study is Trotter, *River Jordan.*

8. See, for instance, Harrison and Klotter, *New History,* 22–23.

9. David W. Blight, *Race and Reunion: The Civil War in American Memory* (Cambridge, MA: Belknap Press of Harvard Univ. Press, 2001), offers the best recent examination of

the fate of the emancipationist dream. Various terms have been used for racial identification. Census-takers used *black* or *mulatto*. The latter described persons with one black and one white parent, as well as descendants of those children. Census entries were capricious at best. Some lighter-skinned blacks had mixtures of Indian, black, and white ancestries. The term *colored,* one that whites frequently used, was employed widely by African Americans too in these years in describing themselves and their organizations. Often *colored* appears in the same senses in this text, and I hope that the reader will understand its nineteenth-century context.

1. Uneasy Slavery in Kentucky along the Ohio

1. U.S. Bureau of the Census, Eighth Census, 1860, *Population of the United States in 1860,* vol. 3, *Manufactures* (Washington, DC: Government Printing Office, 1864), 168–93.

2. Eighth Census, 1860, University of Virginia Geospatial and Statistical Data Center, *United States Census Data Browser,* http://fisher.lib.virginia.edu/census (March 30, 2005), hereafter cited as *U.S. Census Browser;* Lucas, *Kentucky Blacks,* xv–xix; Harrison and Klotter, *New History,* 167–68. Lucas's study, often cited in this chapter, is the most thorough account of antebellum African Americans in the commonwealth.

3. Quoted in Lucas, *Kentucky Blacks,* 97.

4. Lucas, *Kentucky Blacks,* 92–93.

5. Victor Howard, *Black Liberation in Kentucky: Emancipation and Freedom, 1862–1884* (Lexington: Univ. Press of Kentucky, 1983), 1.

6. Frank F. Mathias, "Slavery, the Solvent of Kentucky Politics," *RKHS* 70 (Jan. 1972): 15, 92–96, quote on 15.

7. Harrison and Klotter, *New History,* 211–12; William W. Freehling, *The Reinterpretation of American History: Slavery and the Civil War* (New York: Oxford Univ. Press, 1994), 114–15. The Confederacy lost in part, Freehling argues, because it failed to retain the loyalties of border state whites and subsequently those of its millions of blacks (82).

8. Lucas, *Kentucky Blacks,* xix, xxi.

9. For example, see George L. Ridenour, *Early Times in Meade County, Kentucky* (Louisville: Western Recorder, 1929), 93–107. Bigham, *Towns and Villages of the Lower Ohio,* 20.

10. U.S. Bureau of the Census, Eighth Census, 1860, *Population of the United States in 1860,* vol. 1 (Washington, DC: Government Printing Office, 1864), 180–82.

11. Leonard P. Curry, *The Free Black in Urban America, 1800–1850: The Shadow of a Dream* (Chicago: Univ. of Chicago Press, 1981), 244–71. The highest ratio of African Americans working as artisans was .7356 in New Orleans. Among Kentucky counties in 1860, Fayette had the second-largest number of slaves, 10,015. In third place was Christian, with 9,951. Five others had about 6,000 each. See Eighth Census, 1860, *Population,* 183–85.

12. George H. Yater, *Two Hundred Years at the Falls of the Ohio: A History of Louisville and Jefferson County* (Louisville: Heritage Corporation of Louisville and Jefferson County, 1979), 51–79; Martha Kreipke, "The Falls of the Ohio and the Development of the Ohio River Trade, 1810–1860," *Filson Club Quarterly* 54 (April 1980): 197.

13. Yater, *Two Hundred Years,* 42; see also J. Blaine Hudson, "African Americans," in *Encyclopedia of Louisville,* ed. John E. Kleber (Lexington: Univ. Press of Kentucky, 2001), 15.

14. Mary Lawrence Bickett O'Brien, "Slavery in Louisville, 1820–1860," in Kleber, *Encyclopedia of Louisville,* 826; Lynn S. Renan, "African American Jockeys," ibid., 14. The Louisville man is quoted in Yater, *Two Hundred Years,* 43.

15. Ibid., 34–45, 80–81.

16. Hudson, "African Americans," 15; Pen Bogert, "Washington Spradling, Sr.," in Kleber, *Encyclopedia of Louisville,* 845–46.

17. Eighth Census, Kentucky Slave Schedules, 1860, NAMP, no. M653, roll 403, 2:223–57. In this as well as in other cases, I hand-counted the entries in the schedules. My totals are in some cases slightly different from those in the printed census. The latter does not indicate the number of owners, the names of slaves, and the like.

18. Ibid., 2:258–90. Slave schedules did not as a rule identify black people, except by age and gender. Exceptions to the rule were Fannie, who was 100 and the slave of William Craddock in District 1, and William Bullitt, also 100, the slave of William C. Bullitt in District 2. Bullitt owned 36 other African Americans. Of the 10,302 slaves in the county, only these 2 persons were named. See ibid., 2:232, 2:252. Jefferson County Assessors Book for 1860, microfilm reel 199, Willard Library Archives, Evansville, IN, 1–260.

19. Eighth Census, Kentucky Slave Schedules, 1860, roll 401, 1:237–40; roll 404, 2:316–20.

20. Ibid., roll 401, 1:145–46. Jefferson County's slave enumerator, like his Henderson counterpart, identified only centenarians: Phillis Craig, slave of John Cabelle, and Lety Mumford, slave of John J. Holloway. See roll 404, 2:139–76.

21. Ibid., roll 405, 3:4–27. Similar patterns existed in neighboring Bracken County. See roll 401, 1:169–73.

22. Mason County / City of Maysville Assessors Book for 1860, microfilm reel 272, Willard Library Archives, Evansville, bk. 1, 1–25; bk. 2, 1–23; bk. 3, 1–28.

23. Ibid.

24. Eighth Census, Kentucky Slave Schedules, 1860, roll 406, 3:394–400.

25. Eighth Census, 1860, *Population,* 180–81, 183–85. Ranked behind Henderson were Union (24.4), Daviess (23.1), Meade (22.0), and Ballard (20.0). Breckinridge, Livingston, McCracken, and Hardin had 17.8, 17.4, 17.4, and 16.9 percent, respectively.

26. Eighth Census, Kentucky Slave Schedules, 1860, roll 404, 2:89–106, 2:139–76; Edmund L. Starling, *A History of Henderson County, Kentucky* (Henderson, KY: n.p., 1887), 195. The printed census total is lower than that in the Slave Schedules, taken in June, which indicate 5,864. These individual totals do not account for the matrices of power gained through marriage and family. In Division 1, for instance, other people with the surname Dixon owned 63 slaves; four other Powells owned 74; two other Barretts held 38. George, L.A., and John Atkinson had 55 slaves. In Division 2, three persons named Moss owned 67 slaves, and three Elams had 60. This does not measure slaves secured through marriage, and a thorough study of who married whom in the

county would be helpful. Dixon and Powell, former law partners, were political rivals. Powell, a Democrat, defeated Dixon, a Whig, in the 1850 gubernatorial race. Dixon completed Henry Clay's term in the Senate after the Great Compromiser died in 1852.

27. The record for 1863 is the closest extant report to the beginning of the war. See Henderson County Tax Lists, microfilm reel 170, Willard Library Archives, Evansville, 1–50.

28. Ibid.

29. Eighth Census, Kentucky Slave Schedules, 1860, roll 405, 3:400–21.

30. Ibid., roll 402, 1:383–94. For Hancock and Meade counties, see roll 403, 2:83–88; roll 405, 3:28–40. The statistics for these counties generally resemble those for Hardin County.

31. Tax List for Crittenden County, Kentucky, 1862, microfilm reel 86, Willard Library Archives, Evansville, 1–30. This is the closest extant record to the beginning of the war.

32. Eighth Census, Kentucky Slave Schedules, 1860, roll 405, 3:418–29; McCracken County Tax List for 1860, microfilm reel 276, Willard Library Archives, Evansville, 1–41. See also Lucas, *Kentucky Blacks*, xv.

33. Lucas, *Kentucky Blacks*, 2.

34. Ibid., 3, 4–5, quotes on 3.

35. Ibid., 8–9.

36. Ibid., 11–17. The diet of slaves was monotonous, though generally adequate, and often supplemented by growing vegetables and raising chickens and livestock or by hunting wild game and by fishing. Slaves' clothing was homespun, usually distributed by owners at Christmas, although some fortunate slaves were able to obtain hand-me-downs from their owners.

37. See, for example, Betty J. Branson, comp., *Union County Births* (Utica, KY: By the author, 1990), figures for 1852–57, 1859, 1874, 1875, 1877, 1878, and pp. 31–32. These pages comprise records for 1859. Also see Lucas, *Kentucky Blacks*, 17–19, 24, 26–27. For years after the Civil War, older members of Liberty Baptist Church in Evansville demonstrated the "broom drill" in annual ceremonies to remind people in the audience of slave days. See Bigham, *We Ask Only a Fair Trial*, 175.

38. Ibid., 29–30; Starling, *Henderson County*, 296.

39. Lucas, *Kentucky Blacks*, 30–33. See also Alice Allison Dunnigan, comp. and ed., *The Fascinating Story of Black Kentuckians: Their History and Traditions* (Washington, DC: Associated Publishers, 1982), 59. The most thorough and readable study of runaways is John Hope Franklin and Loren Schweninger, *Runaway Slaves: Rebels on the Plantation* (New York: Oxford Univ. Press, 1999).

40. Lucas, *Kentucky Blacks*, 33–39, quote on 33. As to slaves' health care, Lucas notes (39–42) that on the one hand it was in the interest of owners to ensure that adequate medical care was provided. But on the other, some owners were unwilling or unable to pay medical costs, and physicians were few in number. The fact that the state was overwhelmingly rural and its roads were generally primitive added to the problem. Hence the owner's wife's medicine cabinet or the slave's patent medicines and home

remedies provided the first line of defense. State law required owners to provide for the care of infirm or aged slaves, and public officials had the power to enforce it. Owners were also responsible for slaves with disabilities. The number of black women in their childbearing years was disproportionately low, owing to death during childbirth. Hard work, dangerous jobs, mediocre health care, and the Southern slave trade combined to significantly decrease the number of male slaves between ages thirty and thirty-nine. Slavery was inherently cruel. Whippings and other forms of punishment, including branding, were commonplace.

41. Larry Gara, *The Liberty Line: The Legend of the Underground Railroad* (Lexington: Univ. of Kentucky Press, 1961), 40.

42. Ibid., 51–57; Lewis Collins, *History of Kentucky* (Berea, KY: n.p., 1874), 1:9–11.

43. Lucas, *Kentucky Blacks,* 57–59; see also Starling, *Henderson County,* 194–95.

44. Lucas, *Kentucky Blacks,* 59–61.

45. Ibid., 61.

46. Quotes in William W. Freehling, *The South vs. the South: How Anti-Confederate Southerners Shaped the Course of the Civil War* (New York: Oxford Univ. Press, 2001), 25–27; Harrison and Klotter, *New History,* 171; Lucas, *Kentucky Blacks,* 62. See also Wallace B. Turner, "Kentucky Slavery in the Last Ante Bellum Decade," *RKHS* 58 (1960): 301–2.

47. Lucas, *Kentucky Blacks,* 62–64.

48. Ibid., 64–66. Lucas provides a number of other examples of planned escapes, some of which failed because of owners' ability to track fugitives down across the river. Contributing factors were northern whites' assistance and fugitives' ignorance of the lay of the land.

49. Ibid., 66.

50. Ibid., 66–67; Bigham, *We Ask Only a Fair Trial,* 12–13; Gara, *Liberty Line,* 175–78; Levi Coffin, *Reminiscences of Levi Coffin, the Reputed President of the Underground Railroad. . . .* (Cincinnati: Western Tract Society, 1876), 447–48. The most recent study of the Underground Railroad approaches the question in two ways that differ from previous inquiries. Keith P. Griffler, *Front Line of Freedom: African Americans and the Forging of the Underground Railroad in the Ohio Valley* (Lexington: Univ. Press of Kentucky, 2004), xii–xiii, argues that instead of thinking of rail lines, one should contemplate the frontline places on the Ohio and the support networks in the interior. A chronological approach, moreover, appreciates the ebb and flow of the "liberty line."

51. Lucas, *Kentucky Blacks,* 68.

52. Ibid., 68–70. See also Coffin, *Reminiscences,* 107–8, 114, 167, 208, 297–98.

53. Thomas Brown, *Brown's Three Years in Kentucky Prisons . . .* (Indianapolis, 1857), 5–11, 13–15; Lucas, *Kentucky Blacks,* 70–73. Brown's work can be found at Willard Library in Evansville and is cited in Bigham, *We Ask Only a Fair Trial,* 13. Also see Mrs. Avery Boucher, comp., *1860 Census, Meade County, Kentucky. Microfilm Copy 653, Roll 386* (Vine Grove, KY: Ancestral Trails Historical Society, 1978), 7.

54. Coffin, *Reminiscences,* 209–12.

55. Ibid., 318; Lucas, *Kentucky Blacks,* 82–83.

56. Lucas, *Kentucky Blacks,* 101–2.

57. Ibid., 104.

58. Ibid., 117.

59. Boucher, *1860 Census, Meade County,* 76.

60. Robert D. McManaway, comp., *Daviess County, Kentucky 1860 Census* (Utica, KY: McDowell Publications, 1988).

61. *Crittenden County 1860 Federal Census* (Marion, KY: Crittenden County Genealogical Society, 1994), 44, 77, 92.

62. Lucas, *Kentucky Blacks,* 114–16.

63. Ibid., 110.

64. Lucas, *Kentucky Blacks,* 110–11, asserts, unconvincingly, that Kentucky blacks had greater occupational opportunity than their northern brothers and sisters. That does not explain why many left the commonwealth, especially after the war.

65. Ibid., 110–12.

66. Ibid., 119–21.

67. Ibid., 123–26. See also Cornelius Bogert, "Henry Adams," in Kleber, *Encyclopedia of Louisville,* 5; and "Fifth Street Baptist Church," ibid., 287–88.

68. Lucas, *Kentucky Blacks,* 126–27; "Green Street Baptist Church," in Kleber, *Encyclopedia of Louisville,* 358.

69. Lucas, *Kentucky Blacks,* 127–28; Paul E. Stroble, "Methodists," in Kleber, *Encyclopedia of Louisville,* 615.

70. Lucas, *Kentucky Blacks,* 129–30.

71. Ibid., 133.

72. Ibid., 133–34. Central to black worship was congregational singing, and spirituals, "the clearest influence of the slaves' African heritage, and . . . a distinct contribution to American music," were the most important element of the singing (134–35). Inheriting rhythms and tonal patterns from Africa, spirituals were usually unwritten, often improvised, and sung by swaying, clapping, and foot-patting participants. Suffering and sadness, but also joy and victory, were common themes. Sermons, too, reflected African and American elements, especially the challenge-and-response interaction between preacher and congregants. Knowledge of the scripture and the ability to relate stories from the Bible to the needs of listeners were essential elements of a good preacher's craft.

73. Ibid., 135–38.

74. Ibid., 138–39.

75. Ibid., 140.

76. Ibid., 140–42. By 1860 the number of Kentucky freemen in school had declined to about 8 percent, down from 12 percent in 1850 (144–45), but the proportion of literate persons over age nineteen had grown to 56 percent, as compared with 45 percent ten years earlier. Not surprisingly, about half of those attending school lived in Louisville.

77. Ibid., 143–44.

78. Ibid., 145, 181.

2. Incomplete Freedom on the North Shore

1. See, for instance, Kenneth L. Kusmer, *A Ghetto Takes Shape: Black Cleveland, 1870–1930* (Urbana: Univ. of Illinois Press, 1976), 55.

2. Thornbrough, *Indiana in the Civil War Era,* 13. See Frank U. Quillen, *The Color Line in Ohio: A History of Race Prejudice in a Typical Northern State* (Ann Arbor, MI: George Wahr, 1913), 8–9.

3. See, for example, the advertisement in the *Evansville Daily Journal* of March 25, 1851, that promoted what was a quite popular form of entertainment at the time—minstrel shows. The same paper often reported on nighttime disturbances in black neighborhoods using terms like "smutty," "juvenile," and "sable" to describe those involved. See, e.g., the issue of June 3, 1854.

4. William Lee Miller, *Lincoln's Virtues: An Ethical Biography* (New York: Alfred A. Knopf, 2002), 43. Born in Hardin County, Kentucky, which fronted the Ohio, Lincoln moved to a part of Perry County, Indiana, that became Spencer County in 1818. Both Indiana counties lay on the Ohio. In 1843 Larue County was created from that portion of Hardin where he was born and spent his first years. See Ron D. Bryant, "Larue County," in *KE,* 536.

5. Curry, *Free Black,* 239–43, 273, quote on 243. Mortality rates (deaths per 1,000 persons) were lower in 1850 for blacks in Cincinnati than they were for whites. In Louisville they were slightly higher. These were the only cities of the fifteen reported that lay on the lower Ohio.

6. Thornbrough, *Indiana in the Civil War Era,* 541–43; Bruce Bigelow, "The Cultural Geography of African Americans in Antebellum Indiana," *Black History News and Notes* 88 (May 2002): 4.

7. Donald Zimmer, "Madison, Indiana, 1811–1860: A Study in the Process of City Building" (Ph.D. diss., Indiana Univ., 1974), 62; Bigham, *Towns and Villages of the Lower Ohio,* 33–34.

8. Trotter, *River Jordan,* 27; Eighth Census, Population Schedules for Vanderburgh County, 1860, NAMP, M653, roll 302, Indiana, 32:399–926; Blackmore, "Gallatin County," 168.

9. Quote in Trotter, *River Jordan,* 26; Bigham, *We Ask Only a Fair Trial,* 6; Curry, *Free Black,* 52–53. The sex ratio listed in my book, which Trotter cites, is incorrect. There were 63 females and 65 males in the county. See also Wendell P. Dabney, *Cincinnati's Colored Citizens: Historical, Sociological, and Biographical* (New York: Negro Universities Press, 1970; originally published in 1929), 150.

10. Eighth Census, Population Schedules for Vanderburgh County, 1860, 399–926; *Williams's Madison Directory, 1859* (Madison, IN: Williams Directory Co., 1859), 11, 14; *New Albany Daily Register,* Dec. 6, 1856. Not surprisingly, runaways were most frequently hidden (and sought out) in these places.

11. Henry Louis Taylor Jr. and Vicky Dula, "The Black Residential Experience and Community Formation in Antebellum Cincinnati," in Taylor, *Race and the City,* 102.

12. Trotter, *River Jordan,* 31–32, is based on Curry, *Free Black,* 30–51; Eighth Census, *Population 1860,* 381.

13. Taylor and Dula, "The Black Residential Experience," 115. See also Taylor, "Introduction: Race and the City," in Taylor, *Race and the City,* 4.

14. John H. Keiser, "Black Strikebreakers and Racism in Illinois, 1865–1900," *JISHS* 65 (Autumn 1972): 313–14; Elmer Gertz, "The Black Laws of Illinois," *JISHS* 56

(Autumn 1963): 455–64; Dennis Frank Ricke, "Illinois Blacks through the Civil War: A Struggle for Equality" (master's thesis, Southern Illinois Univ., 1972), 8. "Pope County," *JISHS* 42 (1949): 419–22, documents slavery and slave trading in Pope County. Blackmore, "Gallatin County," 20–21, provides data on indentures. Under the terms of the constitution, French residents could keep their slaves, because Virginia law, which governed the region north of the Ohio, had permitted slavery from the 1780s onward. Existing indentures for life were honored. Children of indentured servants were to be freed at ages twenty-one (males) and eighteen (females). See James E. Davis, *Frontier Illinois* (Bloomington: Indiana Univ. Press, 1998), 165.

   15. Arthur Charles Cole, ed., *The Constitutional Debates of 1847,* Collections of the Illinois State Historical Library, 14, Constitution Series, 2 (Springfield: Illinois State Historical Library, 1919), 201, 204, 213, 464, 472. Southern Illinois delegates, who strongly favored Article XIV, wanted to have a single vote on the entire constitution, including Article XIV, because, as one delegate insisted, free blacks were more degraded than slaves. They lost this vote, 97–56, and a separate vote—as in Indiana—was held on Article XIV (863). They also failed to get provisions eliminating civil and political rights, including holding office, for blacks (856, 871). See also Ricke, "Illinois Blacks," 17, 20, 28, 56, 99–100; Blackmore, "Gallatin County," 68–82, 113–17; Rodger D. Bridges, "Equality Deferred: Civil Rights for Illinois Blacks, 1865–1885," *JISHS* 74 (Summer 1981): 83–84. One example of abuse of the law involved a man who had brought a number of slaves across the river and employed them on his property for a period of years, claiming that he could do so because his wagon had not been unpacked.

   16. Thornbrough, *Negro in Indiana,* 64–68; Bigelow, "Cultural Geography," 4–5. Exceptions occurred—for instance, the admission of the black wife of a prominent white man to the state "lunatic asylum." See *Evansville Weekly Journal,* Feb. 5, 1852. See also Thornbrough, *Indiana in the Civil War Era,* 14–18, 20–21. A notice from the county clerk was published in the *Evansville Daily Journal* of June 21, 1853, asking all Negroes and mulattoes who lived in the state on or before November 1, 1851, to appear before him to register. The newspaper also indicated that the law provided that no Negro or mulatto could be compelled to prove his or her right to live in Indiana. Also note Bigham, *We Ask Only a Fair Trial,* 4–5; Zimmer, "Madison, Indiana," 63.

   17. A notable exception was a Mr. Crawford, a respected barber in Evansville, who left the city in May 1851. The Whig editor declared that Crawford "would be more missed from Evansville than almost any white man would be taken from the place." *Evansville Weekly Journal,* May 29, 1851.

   18. Cayton, *Ohio,* 109.

   19. Quillen, *Color Line,* 23–24, 36–37, 42–43; Ernest M. Collins, "The Political Behavior of the Negroes in Cincinnati, Ohio, and Louisville, Kentucky" (Ph.D. diss., Univ. of Kentucky, 1950), 14–15; Walter McKinley Nicholas, "The Educational Development of Blacks in Cincinnati from 1800 to the Present" (Ed.D. diss., Univ. of Cincinnati, 1977), 5–10; and Charles H. Wesley, *Negro-Americans in Ohio, 1803–1953* (Wilberforce, OH: Central State College Press, 1954), 9–10. See also *Minutes of the State Convention, Colored Citizens of Ohio, Convened at Columbus, Jan. 15th, 16th, 17th, and*

18th, 1851 (Columbus, OH: E. Glover, Printer, 1851), 16, http://dbs.ohiohistory.org/africanam/page.cfm?ID=1102&Current=P16&View=Text (July 23, 2002).

20. *Report of the Debates and Proceedings of the Convention for the Revision of the Constitution of the State of Ohio, 1850–1851* (Columbus: S. Medary,1851), 1:12.

21. Quillen, *Color Line,* 60–87. See also map 5, ibid. (no page number), which shows delegates' votes by county. See also *Colored Citizens of Ohio,* 16–23; Thomas Kissen, "Segregation in Cincinnati Public Education:The Nineteenth Century Black Experience" (Ed.D. diss., Univ. of Cincinnati, 1973), 47.

22. Trotter, *River Jordan,* 33.

23. Quoted in Thornbrough, *Negro in Indiana,* 181–82.

24. Thornbrough, *Negro in Indiana,* 161–62. In the census of 1860, about 25 percent of Illinois's school-age youth had attended school the previous year, as compared with 7 percent of black males and 9 percent of black females. See also *Williams' Madison Directory, 1859,* 14.

25. Thornbrough, *Negro in Indiana,* 178–79.

26. Ibid., 179–80. A reliable narrative based on primary sources in Madison and in Indianapolis is found in John Nyberg, "Prospectus: Historical Marker for Eleutherian College," submitted to the Indiana Historical Bureau, Feb. 2002, p. 3.

27. *EDJ,* Feb. 20, 23, 1856; Edward White, *Evansville and Its Men of Mark* (Evansville, IN, 1873), 379–83; Bigham, *We Ask Only a Fair Trial,* 11. A special meeting of black citizens thanked white friends for their help, and the minute books of "our Reform Society" (*EDJ,* Feb. 23, 1856) contained the records of that meeting. The pastor of the white Methodist Episcopal Church was a supporter. Miss Johnson's tenure was brief, and later she became head of the orphan asylum and a home for expectant unwed mothers. Her successors at the school were African Americans.

28. Kissen, "Segregation in Cincinnati," 7–60; Gerber, *Black Ohio,* 14; Quillen, *Color Line,* 45–50; Nicholas, "Educational Development," 63–122; Wesley, *Negro-Americans in Ohio,* 9–12; Shotwell, *History of Schools in Cincinnati,* cited in Dabney, *Cincinnati's Colored Citizens,* 105–8; Samuel Matthews, "John Isom Gaines: The Architect of Black Public Education," *Queen City Heritage* 45 (Spring 1987): 41–45; Cayton, *Ohio,* 63.

29. Trotter, *River Jordan,* 47; quotes from Kissen, "Segregation in Cincinnati," 52–53. See also Matthews, "John Isom Gaines," 41–45, and the reference to the first high school in chapter 12 of this volume.

30. Nicholas, "Educational Development," 65–77.

31. Ibid., 78–97; Kissen, "Segregation in Cincinnati," 47–51.

32. Nicholas, "Educational Development," 93–122; Kissen, "Segregation in Cincinnati," 8, 51–65.

33. *EDJ,* April 15, Aug. 19, 1853. Examples of advertisements for runaways in the *Evansville Daily Journal* are plentiful, as are stories of slave-catchers roaming the city looking for alleged runaways (e.g., *EDJ,* July 18, 1853). See, for instance, an advertisement in the *Evansville Daily Journal,* Aug. 17, 1843, that described a runaway, Toney, as age twenty-one, low and well set, with full eyes and high forehead. "He speaks slow when spoken to." A sure-fire identifier is to take down his pantaloons, and "you will find a scar on his butt caused by a burn when a boy." The reward was fifty dollars, and

the advertiser, Thomas Williams, lived near Harpeth, Tennessee. The advertisements for runaway slaves appeared in the July 18 and Dec. 19, 1853, editions. The editor of this paper declared on May 15, 1854, that the better class of blacks preferred colonization and that there was a striking contrast between conditions of blacks in America and those in Liberia. An example of the portrait of blacks as prone to misbehavior and of the use of derogatory terms like "sable" and "smutty" can be found in the June 3, 1854, edition of *EDJ*.

34. Griffler, *Front Line of Freedom,* 20. This unique study links the development of black communities to the Underground Railroad. It replaces the concept of rail lines with "front line" (Ohio River) and "support operations."

35. Robert P. Sutton, ed., *The Prairie State: A Documentary History of Illinois,* vol. 1, *Colonial Years to 1860* (Grand Rapids, MI: William Eerdmans, 1976), 249–50, 266; Arthur C. Cole, *The Era of the Civil War, 1848–1870,* volume 3 of *Sesquicentennial History of Illinois* (Urbana: Univ. of Illinois Press, 1987; originally published in 1919).

36. Henry Ellis Cheaney, "Attitudes of the Indiana Pulpit and Press toward the Negro, 1860–1880" (Ph.D. diss., Univ. of Chicago, 1961), 28–29; Lawrence M. Lipin, *Producers, Proletarians, and Politicians: Workers and Party Politics in Evansville and New Albany, Indiana, 1850–87* (Urbana: Univ. of Illinois Press, 1994), 57–58. See also Thornbrough, *Negro in Indiana,* 131.

37. *EDJ,* Aug. 7, 10, 19, 25, 1857. The crisis began on July 20 and is described more fully in Bigham, *We Ask Only a Fair Trial,* 14–15. The Record of Leases, vol. 1 (1859–68), 19–20, 48–49, and 94–95, in the Vanderburgh County Recorder's Office indicates that in February and December 1860 Daniel Lyles leased to white farmers two parcels of land totaling 62 acres and including his home and outbuildings. These leases were for five years and would bring him about $150 annual income. In March 1862 Thomas Lyles leased the "Henry Batey place" (Batey was a founder of the black church there in 1850), 57 acres at $2 per acre for five years. A number of residents returned to the region after the Civil War.

38. Gerber, *Black Ohio,* 15. For Cincinnati, see Quillen, *Color Line,* 32; Nicholas, "Educational Development," 5–10; Dabney, *Cincinnati's Colored Citizens,* 34; Curry, *Free Black,* 96, 104–11; Trotter, *River Jordan,* 35. See also Thomas D. Matijasic, "The Foundations of Colonization: The Peculiar Nature of Race Relations in Ohio during the Early Ante-Bellum Period," *Queen City Heritage* 49 (Winter 1991): 23–30, for a more detailed account. He emphasizes the fears of whites, most of whom were from Kentucky and the upper South, that the black population was growing too rapidly. See also Trotter, *River Jordan,* 35–36. Griffler, *Front Line of Freedom,* 54–55, indicates that the alleged violation of the "Black Laws" prompted whites, abetted by large numbers of Kentuckians, to go on an unprecedented rampage. Cayton, *Ohio,* 26–27, stresses whites' fears of economic competition from blacks. The expulsion of all eighty African American residents from Portsmouth in 1830 is described in Nelson A. Evans, *A History of Scioto Co., Ohio, together with a Pioneer Record of Southern Ohio* (Portsmouth, OH: Nelson W. Evans, 1903), 1:613.

39. Curry, *Free Black,* 111. See also Trotter, *River Jordan,* 36.

40. Quoted in Trotter, *River Jordan,* 36.

41. James M. McPherson, *Ordeal by Fire: The Civil War and Reconstruction,* 3rd ed. (New York: McGraw Hill, 2002), 83–89.

42. In late September 1855, Robert King apprehended eight blacks who had sought passage on a north-bound train from Evansville. King locked them up in a freight car and returned them in chains to Evansville, where their owners took them to Henderson. King received $900 for a day's work. It was no wonder that he was paid that much. The *Evansville Daily Journal* reported that at a sale in Henderson an eleven-year-old girl had brought $740, and two men, aged eighteen and twenty, sold for $1,160 and $1,260. See *EDJ,* Sept. 27, Aug. 26, 1855.

43. Pamela R. Peters, comp., "Floyd County Records," *Black History News and Notes* 76 (May 1999): 4–7. One manumission was recorded for the 1820s, in 1827. Two occurred in the 1830s, 44 in the 1840s, and 11 in the 1860s. See also Bigham, *We Ask Only a Fair Trial,* 12. Griffler, *Front Line of Freedom,* 18–20, 84–87, cites many other instances of kidnapping in river towns—persons being taken from Ripley, Ohio, across the river to Mason County, Kentucky; from Madison, Indiana, to Trimble County, Kentucky; or from Cincinnati to Covington and Kenton County, Kentucky.

44. Griffler, *Front Line of Freedom,* 98, 105–6.

45. These cases are described in Eugene H. Roseboom, *The Civil War Era, 1850–1873,* vol. 4 of *The History of the State of Ohio,* ed. Carl Frederick Wittke (Columbus: Ohio Archaeological and Historical Society, 1944), 343–46. See also Stephen Middleton, "The Fugitive Slave Crisis in Cincinnati, 1850–1860: Resistance, Enforcement, and Black Refugees," *Journal of Negro History* 72 (Winter–Spring 1987): 25, also available at http://.www.jstor.org (May 2, 2001); William J. Barnett Manumission Papers, March 2, 1859, at http://dbs.ohiohistory.org/africanam/det.cfm?ID=2978 (January 11, 2000).

46. Middleton, "Fugitive Slave Crisis," 28–29; Roseboom, *Civil War Era,* 345. A fascinating part of the trial is related in Coffin, *Reminiscences,* 569–74. Called "The Hat," it involved the Quaker's being forced by a marshal to remove his hat in the courtroom and Coffin's right to keep it on his head being supported by a Cincinnati policeman, who resented the marshal's presence. The story appeared in a number of Southern newspapers and made Coffin a local hero. Subsequently, non-Quaker antislavery persons attending the trial also refused to remove their hats.

47. Ricke, "Illinois Blacks," 34, 37–38. Table 2-6 on p. 35 of Ricke's thesis indicates that in 1860, 3,545, or 46 percent, lived in southern Illinois and 1,370, about 18 percent, in northern Illinois. The number of the latter nearly doubled in the 1850s. Another 36 percent resided in central Illinois. The numbers of southern and central Illinois blacks increased, respectively, by about 750 and 800. About 69 percent of southern-Illinois blacks in 1860 were natives of Illinois, as compared with 29 percent in central and 3 percent in northern Illinois. See also Bridges, "Equality Deferred," 83–84; Ricke, "Illinois Blacks," 17, 20, 28, 99–100.

48. Middleton, "Fugitive Slave Crisis," 31–32. See also Griffler, *Front Line of Freedom,* 38–39.

49. Griffler, *Front Line of Freedom,* 22, 61–64, 84–87, 94, 115–18. He describes the case of William Casey in Kenton County, who helped a woman and her daughter escape. The owner, father of the young girl, had decided to sell the two of them out of

pique, despite offers by a neighbor to purchase and liberate them. Some ingenious helpers were not part of the "special forces" (97). One woman in Jeffersonville purchased northbound tickets at the Jeffersonville railroad station and handed them over to blacks across the river, who took omnibuses to the ferry, and thence to the railroad station on the north shore and freedom.

50. *Evansville Weekly Journal,* Aug. 21, 1851; *EDJ,* May 15, Aug. 30, 1854. Advertisements can be found, for instance, in *EDJ,* Dec. 19, 1853; June 19, 1856; Aug. 23, 1859.

51. Ray Boomhower, *Destination Indiana: Travels through Hoosier History* (Indianapolis: Indiana Historical Society, 2000), 4–13; Trotter, *River Jordan,* 47.

52. Frank M. Gilbert, *History of the City of Evansville and Vanderburg* [*sic*] *County* (Chicago, 1910), 1:176. Primary citations for Robinson in the Willard Library Biography Index are *EDJ,* Aug. 8, 1850; March 1, 1854; Aug. 6, 31, 1855; Sept. 19, 1856. His obituary is found in *EDJ,* Feb. 27, 1883. Another prominent opponent of slavery and purported agent of the Underground Railroad, Willard Carpenter, died later that year. Like Robinson, he was from Vermont.

53. Gilbert, *History of Evansville,* 1:176; *EDJ,* July 18, 1853.

54. Blight, *Race and Reunion,* 231–37.

55. Larry Gara, "The Underground Railroad in Illinois," *JISHS* 56 (Autumn 1963): 509–14; Gara, "The Underground Railroad: A Re-Evaluation," *Ohio Historical Quarterly* 69 (1960): 223–24; Gara, "The Underground Railroad: Legend and Reality," *Timeline,* Aug.–Sept. 1988, 1831. Griffler, *Front Line of Freedom,* xii–xiii, argues that Gara does not pay sufficient attention to the chronological patterns of the movement, to the linkage between black community-building and the liberty line, and to the connections between white and black operatives on the line. See also Coy D. Robbins, *Reclaiming African Heritage at Salem, Indiana* (n.p.: Heritage Books, 1995), 167.

56. *Caldwell's Illustrated Historical Atlas of Adams County, Ohio, 1797–1880* (Newark, OH: Walter F. Arvis, 1880), 30, 35–36. The only references to blacks are these: the brief listing of two AME churches (23, 101) and the note that there were twenty-three black boys and girls attending school (22, 54). Exactly where they went to school is unexplained. No blacks are named. See also Nelson W. Evans and Emmons B. Stivers, *A History of Adams County, Ohio, from Its Earliest Settlement to the Present* (West Union, OH: E.B. Stivers, 1900), who boast of the county's long opposition to slavery and its citizens' active thwarting of slave-catchers. The one case that is described at length involves a white man who dressed up in a ragged suit and blackened his face and hands, leading would-be catchers on a wild goose chase. Only when he was eventually caught and hauled before local authorities, did he reveal who he really was. The catchers left the county amid jeers and taunts (405–10). See also William M. Cockrum, *History of the Underground Railroad* (Oakland City, IN: n.p., 1915). This work continues to be cited, often by historians who ought to know better. See, for instance, Randy Mills, Mark Coomer, et al., *Report to the Indiana Department of Natural Resources Division of Historic Preservation and Archaeology . . . concerning Underground Railroad Activity in Southwestern Indiana* (n.p., 2001). Cockrum's work, published fifty years after the end of the Civil War, is largely based on oral tradition about the work of his father and others. It reflects the same premises about the working of the "liberty line" as Wilbur Siebert's efforts.

57. Thornbrough, *Negro in Indiana,* 41–43. Her work relies in part on Siebert. The black men she names, though, are also mentioned in a recent history of the line in southeastern Indiana.

58. Bigham, *We Ask Only a Fair Trial,* 12–13.

59. Mills, Coomer, et al., *Report,* 12–13. The principal authors of this study cite works they have written as evidence, and these rely principally on Cockrum. See also Hurley C. Goodall, comp., *Underground Railroad: "The Invisible Road to Freedom through Indiana" as Recorded by the Works Progress Administration Writers Project* (Indianapolis: Indiana Department of National Resources, Division of Historic Preservation and Archaeology, 2000), 274, 276. Willard Carpenter's 1850 mansion a block from the river has often been identified as a haven for fugitives. The evidence for Carpenter's leanings during his lifetime, however, are circumstantial. It was probably not a coincidence that many blacks lived near his mansion. No written statement that Carpenter was an agent, however, appeared until 1915, thirty-two years after his death, and then only via secondhand evidence. In the case of Andrew Robinson, his activities in court in the 1850s strongly suggest a connection with those aiding runaways. See Bigham, *We Ask Only a Fair Trial,* 12–13, 242n33. Also see *EDJ,* Nov. 4, 1850; March 21, 26, 1851. After Thomas Garvin—longtime trustee of Willard Library—died, another trustee indicated in *Willard Library: Statement of the Trustees* (Evansville, 1915), 11, that Garvin had told him about Carpenter's role just before Garvin died. For Robinson, see Gilbert, *History of Evansville,* 1:176; and *EDJ,* Feb. 27, 1883. Gilbert also states that attorney Conrad Baker— Evansville's first governor—alleged that his most satisfying act before the war was managing to liberate "Old Tom," Gilbert's father's longtime slave. When the father died, Gilbert's uncle claimed an indenture on Tom, but Baker—who had migrated to Evansville from south central Pennsylvania in the 1840s—prevented him from succeeding.

60. Mills, Coomer, et al., *Report,* 10–11, 44.

61. Ibid., 18–19. Unfortunately, much of the latter part of this study relies on Siebert.

62. Ibid., 49.

63. Diane Perrine Coon, *Southeastern Indiana's Underground Railroad Routes and Operations* (Indianapolis: Indiana Department of Natural Resources Division of Historic Preservation and Archaeology and the U.S. Department of the Interior, National Park Service, 2001), 26. See also 1, 4–7, 18, 290–91. Coon begins with anecdotes and oral history and attempts to verify them through public records and physical evidence. Records included church minutes, letters, registers of Negroes, memoirs, newspapers, church and family histories, land records, tax lists, plats, and atlases. See also Goodall, *Underground Railroad,* 13, 41. The South Hanover site was important geologically. The large bend of the Ohio that formed the western border of Trimble County across the river caused large, encroaching sandbars. Hence crossing was easier there. Fugitives could also cross to Jefferson and other Indiana counties more easily in summer months, when the water level was low and sometimes slaves could walk across the river. Or they could swim or travel by skiff. See ibid., 29.

64. Elijah Anderson (one of Thornbrough's five) and William Anderson have often been mistakenly identified as brothers. See William J. Anderson, *Life and Narrative of William J. Anderson* (Chicago: Daily Tribune and Job Printing Office, 1857), 1, 35, also

available at http://www.docsouth.unc.edu/neh/andersonw/menu.html (January 30, 2004). For the origin of "Georgetown," see *Madison Courier,* Nov. 6, 1916; *Williams' Madison Directory, 1859,* 11. Coon, *Southeastern Indiana,* 40, declares that there was a major riot in 1846, but no evidence of that exists. A series of violent outrages is more likely. Also see *Madison Courier,* July 5, 1889, Nov. 6, 1916; Oct. 29, 1938.

65. Coon, *Southeastern Indiana,* 178–80, 188–90. Relatively little is known of Underground Railroad activity in the small counties between Jefferson and Dearborn—Switzerland and Ohio. The Andersons are credited with establishing a crossing east of Vevay, the Switzerland County seat, that connected with Carrolton, where nine free black men had been enlisted and trained by Elijah Anderson. In Ohio County, the principal conductor was William Thompson, who was aided by white abolitionist Orthaniel Reed. The chief crossing from Boone County was between Rabbit Hash and the Ohio County seat, Rising Sun. See ibid., 151–68, 224–25.

66. Ibid., 189–91.

67. Griffler, *Front Line of Freedom,* 43–44, 91, 118–19; Cayton, *Ohio,* 108. Parker claimed to have aided 440 runaways between 1845 and 1865.

68. Griffler, *Front Line of Freedom,* 38–39.

69. Middleton, "Fugitive Slave Crisis," 23. See also Henry W. Taylor, "Spatial Organization and the Residential Experience: Black Cincinnati in 1850," *Social Science History* 10 (1986): 10.

70. Boomhower, *Destination Indiana,* 4–13; Trotter, *River Jordan,* 47. Griffler, *Front Line of Freedom,* xii–xiii, 64–66, 84–87, aptly observes that the Underground Railroad was not the smooth-running organization the historians have normally described. Coffin faced much opposition from fellow Quakers. The history of the "liberty line" also had distinctive phases, and certain places—notably Madison, Indiana—were dangerous. Quote in Middleton, "Fugitive Slave Crisis," 24–25.

71. Coffin, *Reminiscences,* 343, 376. See also Griffler, *Front Line of Freedom,* 87–91, 98–102.

72. Ricke, "Illinois Blacks," 99–100, 111, 116.

73. Edgar F. Raines Jr., "The American Missionary Association in Southern Illinois, 1856–1862: A Case History in the Abolition Movement," *JISHS* 65 (Autumn 1972): 247–67.

74. Cayton, *Ohio,* 108–9. The Methodist Church was later named Allen Temple. See B.W. Arnett, ed., *Proceedings of the Semi-Centenary Celebration of the African Methodist Episcopal Church of Cincinnati, Held in Allen Temple, February 8th, 9th, and 10th, 1874 . . .* (Cincinnati: H. Watkin, 1874), 3, also available at http://www.memory.loc.gov (March 31, 2005). Search the African American History Collection. The numbers and dates for churches vary in the histories of this city. Trotter, *River Jordan,* 37–51, identifies three churches before 1860, while Gerber, *Black Ohio,* 20–21, says there were five, and Dabney, *Cincinnati's Colored Citizens,* 363–75, lists three.

75. Quoted in Trotter, *River Jordan,* 38–39. See also Dabney, *Cincinnati's Colored Citizens,* 184.

76. James Oliver Horton and Stacey Flaherty, "Black Leadership in Antebellum Cincinnati," *Race and the City: Work, Community, and Protest in Cincinnati, 1820–1970,*

ed. Henry Louis Taylor Jr. (Urbana: Univ. of Illinois Press, 1993), 83, 91, suggest that about seven in ten community leaders, like educator Peter Clark, were light-skinned. Unlike their Southern counterparts, who distanced themselves from the black masses, Cincinnati's mulattoes led the fight against slavery and racial discrimination. (Cf. Trotter, *River Jordan,* 39–40.) For a discussion of self-help and protest, see Gerber, *Black Ohio,* 22–24; Trotter, *River Jordan,* 44–48; and for occupations and property holding, ibid., 38–40, 42. The pioneering study of black Cincinnati is Carter G. Woodson, "The Negroes in Cincinnati Prior to the Civil War," *Journal of Negro History* 1 (1916): 1–22. See also the work of Henry Taylor noted earlier.

77. Trotter, *River Jordan,* 48–50.

78. Thornbrough, *Negro in Indiana,* 133–35, 139–42.

79. Bigham, *We Ask Only a Fair Trial,* 7–9; *EDJ,* June 17, July 13, 1854.

80. *EDJ,* April 12, 14, 1854; May 15, 1855. The same may have been the fate of the first black physician, who arrived with much fanfare in May 1855 but seems to have left town shortly afterward.

81. Eighth Census, Population Schedules for Vanderburgh County, 1860, 399–926.

82. Thornbrough, *Negro in Indiana,* 151.

83. Ibid., 152–53.

84. Ibid., 153–54.

85. Ibid., 155–56; Bigham, *We Ask Only a Fair Trial,* 9–10. This information is based on records found in the Vanderburgh County Recorder's Office. See also *Evansville Courier and Journal,* Sept. 7, 1930, which also cites the founding as 1843 and recounts its early years and subsequent development. Methodist ministers were rotated every two years. In summer, the Evansville church regularly hosted festivals and suppers to raise money for their pastors. Whites were invited to attend. See, for example, *EDJ,* Aug. 16, 1854; Aug. 1, 1860.

86. Bigham, *We Ask Only a Fair Trial,* 21; Thornbrough, *Negro in Indiana,* 156–60; Coon, *Southeastern Indiana,* 18n6.

87. Thornbrough, *Negro in Indiana,* 143–48.

88. *EDJ,* Feb. 24–25, 1859.

89. Blackmore, "Gallatin County," 89, 117–37, 163–64, 170.

90. Ricke, "Illinois Blacks," 37, 146, 151; Judy Foreman Lee and Carolyn Cromeenes Foss, comp., *Pope County Illinois: 1845, 1855, and 1865 State Census* (n.p., 1991), 25–44.

91. David Dexter, Louise Ogg, and Russell Ogg, transcribers, *Alexander County Illinois Census Records* (Utica, KY: McDowell, 1993), vii–x, 31–67.

92. Blackmore, "Gallatin County," 89, 107, 117–37, 141–42, 163–64, 168, 170. These figures include Hardin and Saline counties, which were carved out of Gallatin before 1860.

93. Ibid., 153–61.

94. Ibid., 180–81, 193–94. Black farmers were relatively successful. The average value of their livestock was slightly lower than that of whites. Their corn and wheat production was nearly that of whites, and in some commodities was higher. See ibid., 195, 202, 282–89.

3. Conflict and Remnants of Slavery on the South Shore

1. Lowell H. Harrison, *The Civil War in Kentucky* (Lexington: Univ. of Kentucky Press, 1975, 1988), 80–106; Freehling, *The South vs. the South,* 131.

2. Harrison and Klotter, *New History,* 211–12. Their chapter on the war, 195–212, offers the most reliable overview of these years. Black Kentuckians' wartime experiences are described ably in Lucas, *Kentucky Blacks,* 146–77; Howard, *Black Liberation,* 3–71. Wright, *Life behind a Veil,* 13–20, offers a brief review of the war's impact in Louisville. The best study of the impact of emancipation remains Leon F. Litwack, *Been in the Storm So Long: The Aftermath of Slavery* (New York: Vintage Books, 1979). Little attention is paid, however, to emancipation in Kentucky. The same can be said for another pioneering work, Herbert G. Gutman, *The Black Family in Slavery and Freedom* (New York: Pantheon Books, 1976).

3. Harrison and Klotter, *New History,* 196–205. Adam Johnson's exploits in capturing Newburgh, Indiana, for a day are documented in Thornbrough, *Indiana in the Civil War Era,* 120.

4. E. Merton Coulter, *The Civil War and Readjustment in Kentucky* (Chapel Hill: Univ. of North Carolina Press, 1926), 451–53, describes the *Louisville Commercial* as the first Republican newspaper in the city, though it opposed the radicals in the party. The *Courier* was pro-secession and the *Journal* pro-Union, though Democratic. The latter two were merged by Henry Watterson in 1868 into a Bourbon Democratic newspaper that promoted reconciliation and economic development of the South. See also James M. McPherson, *Crossroads of Freedom: Antietam* (New York: Oxford Univ. Press, 2002), 61–65, for a succinct discussion of the pragmatic approach to abolition that Lincoln took, which differed from that of the "principled" abolitionists.

5. Harrison and Klotter, *New History,* 206–7.

6. Ibid., 207–8; Harrison, *Civil War in Kentucky,* 80–106; Thomas D. Clark, *History of Kentucky,* 6th ed. (Ashland, KY: Jesse Stuart Foundation, 1992; originally published in 1977), 319–58, 381. See also Kincaid A. Herr, *The Louisville and Nashville Railroad, 1850–1963* (Lexington: Univ. Press of Kentucky, 2000), 29–38.

7. Harrison and Klotter, *New History,* 209–10.

8. Thomas D. Clark, *Kentucky: Land of Contrasts* (New York: Harper and Row, 1968), 121–22, 126–29. For an overview of the commonwealth during this time, see Lowell Harrison, *The Civil War in Kentucky* (1977; repr., Lexington: Univ. of Kentucky Press, 1988), esp. 80–106.

9. Lee Dew, "Hancock County," in *KE,* 419; Stuart S. Sprague, "Civil War," in *KE,* 192–94. See also *The War of the Rebellion: A Compilation of the Official Records of the Union and Confederate Armies,* 128 vols. (Washington, DC: Government Printing Office, 1850–1901), generally known as *Official Records* or *O.R.*

10. "Ballard County," in *KE,* 45; Ron D. Bryant, "Brandenburg," in *KE,* 113; Ron D. Bryant, "Smithland," in *KE,* 832; Livingston County Historical Society, *Livingston County Kentucky* (Paducah, KY: Turner Publishing, 1989), 1:39; Richard Arthur Briggs, *The Early History of West Point, Hardin County, Kentucky* (1955; repr., Utica, KY: McDowell Publications, 1983), 27–33.

11. John E. Burns, "Covington," in *KE,* 236; Ron D. Bryant, "Kenton County," in *KE,* 489; "Campbell County," in *KE,* 155; and "Boyd County," in *KE,* 110.

12. Ron D. Bryant, "Lewis County," in *KE,* 549; and "Boyd County," 110; "Greenup County," in *KE,* 389; James Powers, "Ashland," in *KE,* 36. The Adeline Hotel in Ashland was a Union hospital during the war.

13. Charles A. Clinton, *A Social and Educational History of Hancock County, Kentucky* (Cambridge, MA: Abt Associates, 1974), 37–38; Glenn Hodges, *Fearful Times: A History of the Civil War Years in Hancock County, Kentucky* (Owensboro, KY: Progress Printing, 1986), 3–6, 25–74, 80. Hodges is unsympathetic to the recruitment of blacks in their home region, calling it a slap in the face of the residents that led to anti-Union backlash in the county.

14. Ron D. Bryant, "Breckinridge County," in *KE,* 122; Bill Thompson, *History and Legend of Breckinridge County* (Utica, KY: McDowell Publications, 1976), 78–82; Goodspeed Company, *History of Posey County, Indiana* (Chicago: Goodspeed, 1886), 142–67; Works Progress Administration, Federal Writers Project, *Union County, Past and Present* (1941; repr., Evansville, IN: Unigraphic, 1972), 48–55; Lloyd G. Lee, *A Brief History of Kentucky and Its Counties* (Berea, KY: Kentucke Imprints, 1981), 545; Peyton Heady, *Union County in the Civil War, 1861–1865* (Morganfield, KY: By the author, 1985), 1–39.

15. Starling, *Henderson County,* 193–237.

16. Works Progress Administration, Federal Writers Project, *Henderson: A Guide to Audubon's Home Town in Kentucky* (Northport, NY: Bacon, Percy, and Duggett, 1941), 37–43; Starling, *Henderson County,* 315–28; Maralee Arnett, *The Annals and Scandals of Henderson County, Kentucky* (Corydon, KY: Freeman Publishing, 1976), 41–54.

17. Lee Dew, "Daviess County," in *KE,* 254; Lee A. Dew and Aloma W. Dew, *Owensboro: The City on the Yellow Banks* (Bowling Green, KY: Rivendell Publications, 1988), 42–64; Aloma Williams Dew, "Between the Hawk and the Buzzard: Owensboro during the Civil War," *RKHS* 77 (Winter 1979): 1–14; Hugh O. Potter, ed., *History of Owensboro and Daviess County, Kentucky* (Owensboro, KY: Daviess County Historical Society, 1974), 81–85; *History of Daviess County, Kentucky* (Chicago: Interstate Publishing Co., 1883; repr., Evansville: Unigraphic, 1966), 158–78 (page citations are to the 1966 ed.).

18. John E.L. Robertson, *Paducah, 1830–1980: A Sesquicentennial History* (Paducah, KY: Image Graphics, 1980), 29–65; Robertson, "Battle of Paducah," in *KE,* 76.

19. Ron D. Bryant, "Trimble County," in *KE,* 901; "Gallatin County," in *KE,* 362; and "Boone County," in *KE,* 100; Jean W. Calvert, "Maysville," in *KE,* 622.

20. George H. Yater, "Louisville: A Historical Overview," in *The Encyclopedia of Louisville,* ed. John F. Kleber (Lexington: Univ. Press of Kentucky, 2001), xix–xx; Charles Mitchell Mills, "Civil War," ibid., 194. A more detailed account is Yater, *Two Hundred Years,* 82–94.

21. Yater, "Louisville," xx; Mills, "Civil War," 195.

22. Clark, *History of Kentucky,* 381; Yater, "Louisville," xxi.

23. William C. Davis, *Look Away! A History of the Confederate States of America* (New York: Free Press, 2002), 144–46, 149–54. See also Freehling, *The South vs. the South,* esp. 115–39.

24. Wright, *Life behind a Veil*, 20.

25. Ibid., 21.

26. Lucas, *Kentucky Blacks*, 146.

27. Ibid., 147.

28. Ibid.

29. Davis, *Look Away*, 131–35.

30. Quoted in Litwack, *Been in the Storm*, 51.

31. Ibid., 182.

32. Quoted in Victor B. Howard, "The Civil War in Kentucky: The Slave Claims His Freedom," *Journal of Negro History* 67 (Autumn 1982): 246.

33. Ibid., 247–49.

34. Ibid. See also Howard, *Black Liberation*, 3–11.

35. Howard, *Black Liberation*, 31–44. For an overview of the link between war and emancipation, see Russell F. Weigley, *A Great Civil War: A Military and Political History, 1861–1865* (Bloomington: Indiana Univ. Press, 2000), 168–91, 223. Weigley comments on slave-owners' growing fearfulness of slave restlessness after January 1, 1863.

36. Lucas, *Kentucky Blacks*, 148–49.

37. Ibid., 149. A more complete account of the "Black Brigade" is found in chapter 4. See Peter H. Clark, *The Black Brigade of Cincinnati: Being a Report of Its Labors and a Muster-Roll of Its Members; Together with Various Orders, Speeches, Etc., Relating to It* (Cincinnati: Joseph B. Boyd, 1864), 1–32, also available at http://dbs.ohiohistory.org/africanam/det.cfm?ID=2487 (March 1, 2001).

38. See, for instance, *The Press in the Federal States. Federal Despotism in Kentucky* (Louisville, 1864) http://memory.loc.gov (March 31, 2005). This pamphlet is found in the American Time Capsule collection. The pamphlet railed about the military's "suppression of the *True Presbyterian*, a paper (previously) published in Louisville, Kentucky."

39. Palmer's *Personal Recollections of the Life of John M. Palmer*, published in 1901, is quoted in Wright, *Life behind a Veil*, 18–19. See also Thomas James, *Wonderful Eventful Life of Rev. Thomas James* (Rochester, NY: Post-Express Printing, 1887), 16–20, also available at http://memory.loc.gov (March 31, 2005). This document is found in the African American Perspectives collection.

40. Wright, *Life behind a Veil*, 19–20. Gutman, *Black Family*, 380–81, indicates that exactly what Palmer said is a matter of dispute. A black correspondent said he used the word "substantially" before "free," but the biographer said the audience didn't hear the word and responded as if they were at a revival meeting. A negative picture of these events can be found in Coulter, *Civil War and Readjustment*, 265–70. Coulter asserts that Palmer's actions led to vagrancy, to roads being congested by blacks of all ages and sizes, and to whites' complaints that access to roads and towns was denied because of blacks' presence. He complains that Palmer interfered with state law that denied blacks access to railroads and ferries without passes from their masters and that he enticed slaves to run away, placing himself in frequent conflict with civil authorities. Common carriers were legally liable if they refused service to blacks. And Palmer had the temerity to pronounce slavery dead almost two weeks before the Thirteenth Amendment was declared legally adopted.

41. Dunnigan, *Black Kentuckians,* 73; Starling, *Henderson County,* 193, 195–96, 213. Lucas, *Kentucky Blacks,* 146–77. Federal census records for 1870 show significant increases in the number of African Americans living in Jefferson County—19,146, as compared with 12,311 in 1860. Notable increases were also evident in Boyd, Campbell, Kenton, and McCracken counties. Totals in Daviess and Henderson counties were slightly higher. Dramatic decreases, by contrast, occurred in such slave-rich, rural counties as Ballard, Breckinridge, Carroll, Hancock, Hardin, Livingston, Mason, Meade, Trimble, and Union. See Francis A. Walker, *A Compendium of the Ninth Census (June 1, 1870)* (Washington, DC: Government Printing Office, 1872), 49–53.

42. William Wells Brown, *The Negro in the American Rebellion: His Heroism and His Fidelity* (Boston: Lee and Shepard, 1867), 96.

43. Quoted in Yater, "Louisville," xx.

44. Howard, "Civil War in Kentucky," 252. See also Yater, "Louisville," xxi; Yater, *Two Hundred Years,* 91–92; Lucas, *Kentucky Blacks,* 164–65. There was also a hospital for black soldiers across the river in New Albany.

45. Yater, *Two Hundred Years,* 93–95.

46. The overview of fugitives and Union camps is based on Lucas, *Kentucky Blacks,* 147–52; Howard, *Black Liberation,* 12–28. Initial enlistment reflected the Confiscation Act of 1862: slaves of rebellious owners were liable for confiscation.

47. David Herbert Donald, *Lincoln* (New York: Simon and Schuster, 1995), 15.

48. Howard, *Black Liberation,* 45–54. See also Lowell H. Harrison, *Lincoln of Kentucky* (Lexington: Univ. Press of Kentucky, 2000), 194–246, for an overview of Lincoln's wartime relationship with his native state.

49. Lucas, *Kentucky Blacks,* 152. More detailed accounts are found in Coulter, *Civil War and Readjustment,* 197–206; Howard, *Black Liberation,* 45–70. See also John David Smith, "The Recruitment of Negro Soldiers in Kentucky, 1863–1865," *RKHS* 72 (Oct. 1974): 365–84. Smith also provides a trenchant analysis of Coulter in "E. Merton Coulter, the 'Dunning School,' and *The Civil War and Readjustment in Kentucky,*" *RKHS* 81 (Winter 1988): 52–69.

50. Hudson, "African Americans," 15.

51. Lucas, *Kentucky Blacks,* 154–55; Howard, *Black Liberation,* 56–71.

52. George P. Rawick, ed., *The American Slave: A Composite Autobiography,* ser. 1, vol. 6, *Alabama and Indiana Narratives* (Westport, CT: Greenwood, 1976), 6, 30.

53. Quoted in Lucas, *Kentucky Blacks,* 156.

54. Ibid., 156–57. And not all blacks volunteered readily. Some fled the state to avoid military service, and some free blacks bought substitutes. Many of those who remained on the farm expressed concern for their families' welfare. Those who were deemed unfit for service were returned to their masters.

55. Ibid., 157–58.

56. Smith, "Recruitment," 386–90.

57. Lucas, *Kentucky Blacks,* 153.

58. Ibid. By contrast, Coulter, *Civil War and Readjustment,* insists that agents received $800 to $1,000, of which blacks got a mere $100.

59. Litwack, *Been in the Storm,* 74. See also Lucas, *Kentucky Blacks,* 153; Howard, *Black Liberation,* 56–71.

60. Lucas, *Kentucky Blacks,* 165–66.

61. Ibid., 166–67; *Report of the Adjutant General of the State of Kentucky,* vol. 2, *1861–1866* (Frankfort: Kentucky Yeoman Office, 1867), 1–178. Colored troops from the state are listed in the appendix of the *Report.*

62. Lucas, *Kentucky Blacks,* 167–69.

63. Ibid., 169.

64. Livingston County Historical Society, *Livingston County Kentucky,* 67–70. For a review of black units' service, especially the 12th Artillery, see Lucas, *Kentucky Blacks,* 170–75.

65. Quoted in Arnett, *Annals and Scandals,* 54. See also Starling, *Henderson County,* 201–35; and WPA, *Henderson,* 37–43.

66. Starling, *Henderson County,* 229–30, 235, quote on 229–30.

67. Dew and Dew, *Owensboro,* 42–64; *History of Daviess County,* 170–78.

68. Claims against Union Army damages are found in the Century of Lawmaking collection at the American Memory Web site. See, for instance, *Journal of the Senate of the United States,* Dec. 7, 1864 (38th Cong., 2nd sess.), 17; Jan. 28, 1865 (38th Cong., 2nd sess.), 109; Jan. 24, 1866 (39th Cong., 1st sess.), 102; March 18, 1869 (41st Cong., 1st sess.), 56, 468; *Journal of the House of Representatives,* July 15, 1870 (41st Cong., 2nd sess.), 1225; March 4, 1872 (42nd Cong., 2nd sess.), 443. These are claims filed by senators and representatives on behalf of Paducah residents who alleged army damage to their property, including the Fort Anderson battle. See http://memory.loc.gov/ (March 31, 2005). Enter "Paducah" as the keyword.

69. Lucas, *Kentucky Blacks,* 175–76.

70. Smith, "Recruitment," 384–85.

71. Lucas, *Kentucky Blacks,* 159.

72. Quoted in Coulter, *Civil War and Readjustment,* 269.

73. Ibid., 263. See also Hudson, "African Americans," 15. Coulter, *Civil War and Readjustment,* 385–86, also rues the fact that most owners never received the promised three-hundred-dollar federal payment, since whites' hostility to federal policies led to the suspension of payments in late 1864. The law was repealed in 1867. The state legislature in 1866 requested all owners to certify their claims before county courts, whence records would be sent to the capital—name of slave, where enlisted, when and by whom enlisted, regiment and company, and affidavit of ownership and loyalty.

74. Lucas, *Kentucky Blacks,* 160–61.

75. Richard Sears, "John G. Fee, Camp Nelson, and Kentucky Blacks, 1864–1865," *RKHS 85* (Winter 1987): 29–45. See also Lucas, *Kentucky Blacks,* 162–63; Gutman, *Black Family,* 370–75.

76. Lucas, *Kentucky Blacks,* 163–64.

77. James, *Wonderful Eventful Life,* 20.

78. Lucas, *Kentucky Blacks,* 164–65; James, *Wonderful Eventful Life,* 20.

79. Gutman, *Black Family,* 380–81.

80. Quoted ibid., 381. The events that followed in the summer and fall as well as in 1866 are discussed later.

81. Lucas, *Kentucky Blacks,* 177.

82. Ibid., 128, 139–40, 140–45. The work of William H. Gibson was especially significant, not only for creating elementary and advanced training at Fourth Street Methodist (later Asbury Chapel), but also for establishing branch schools at Quinn Chapel and in two other towns. Gibson left Louisville for Indianapolis in the fall of 1862, as Braxton Bragg's forces threatened the Falls City, but returned in 1866.

83. Litwack, *Been in the Storm,* 221–521, passim.

4. Blacks and Whites Together and Apart on the North Shore

1. Works Progress Administration, Federal Writers Project, *Cincinnati: A Guide to the Queen City and Its Neighbors* (Cincinnati: Wilson-Hart Press, 1943), 66–67; Walter J. Havighurst, *River to the West: Three Centuries of the Ohio* (New York: Putnam, 1970), 247–49; Bigham, *Towns and Villages of the Lower Ohio,* 125–40. Most dramatic of all was Cairo's growth, which nearly tripled in the decade. Mound City grew by 100 percent, as did Rockport. Evansville added 10,000 residents, almost doubling in size. Hamilton County had 260,366 inhabitants in 1870, as compared with 216,410 ten years before. For a fuller study of the economic impact of the war in the North, see Philip Shaw Paludan, *"A People's Contest": The Union and Civil War, 1861–1865* (New York: Harper and Row, 1988), 105–97.

2. Jasper W. Cross, "The Civil War Comes to Egypt," *JISHS* 44 (Summer 1951): 160–69; Cole, *Era of Civil War,* 279, 293, 302; Goodspeed Company, *History of Gallatin, Saline, Hamilton, Franklin, and Williamson Counties, Illinois* (Chicago: Goodspeed, 1887), 78–92; George W. May, *History of Massac County, Illinois* (Galesburg, IL: Wagoner, 1955), 91–101.

3. Works Progress Administration, Federal Writers Project, *Cairo Guide* (Nappanee, IN: Evangel Press, 1938), 34–39; John F. Stover, *History of the Illinois Central Railroad* (New York: Macmillan, 1976), 85–107; John McMurray Lansden, *A History of the City of Cairo* (Chicago: R.R. Donnelly, 1910; repr., Carbondale, IL: Southern Illinois Univ. Press, 1976), 128–37 (page citations are to the 1976 ed.); Cole, *Era of the Civil War,* 331–44; Robert P. Howard, *Illinois: A History of the Prairie State* (Grand Rapids, MI: William Eerdmans, 1972), 302.

4. White, *Evansville Men,* 274–300; on Perry County, see, for instance, Thomas James De La Hunt, *Perry County: A History* (1915; repr., Owensboro, KY: Cook and McDowell, 1980), 212–57; Hodges, *Civil War in Hancock County,* 10, 24.

5. Gerber, *Black Ohio,* 274; Bigham, *We Ask Only a Fair Trial,* 22.

6. Shirley J. Carlson, "Black Migration to Pulaski County, Illinois, 1860–1900," *JISHS* 80 (Spring 1987): 41; Ninth Census, Population Schedules for Vanderburgh County, 1870, NAMP, M593, roll 504, 89–515a, passim. See also Griffler, *Front Line of Freedom,* 125–26.

7. Trotter, *River Jordan,* 55.

8. Ibid., 55–56. See also Joanne Wheeler, "Together in Egypt: A Pattern of Race Relations in Cairo, Illinois, 1865–1915," in *Toward a New South? Studies in Post–Civil War Southern Communities,* ed. Orville Vernon Burton and Robert C. McMath Jr. (Westport, CT: Greenwood Press, 1982), 103–34.

9. Cole, *Era of the Civil War,* 331. The two waves are described in Wheeler, "Together in Egypt," 106–8.

10. Cole, *Era of the Civil War,* 334. Ricke, "Illinois Blacks," 252–53, writes that the Illinois Central was hired by the federal government to carry carloads of black fugitives northward. On October 7, 1862, for instance, 100 were taken to Chicago, and on the previous day two carloads were sent to Chicago and other places to the north. One observer recalled "poor, helpless creatures, black and white . . . dumped under the wood-sheds of the line of the Illinois Central and the Ohio and Mississippi railroads with but a few clothes and little bundles of bedding and articles of household belongings, sick, destitute, powerless, friendless, and among strangers in an inhospitable climate, their condition . . . unalterably sad." It was technically illegal for them to be employed, given the provisions of the state constitution. The federal government required employers to feed and clothe all personnel and keep them busy. Democrats chastised Republicans for promoting the migration, transportation, and employment of contrabands because doing so threatened free white labor. Riots and labor unrest also ensued in Chicago, Quincy, and other northern towns. In August 1862, white ruffians brutally beat a black teamster in Cairo, only because he accepted employment that was perceived as not only competing with whites but also promoting racial integration (276).

11. Ricke, "Illinois Blacks," 214–16; Wheeler, "Together in Egypt," 106–8.

12. Ricke, "Illinois Blacks," 217–22. The quotation is from Griffler, *Front Line of Freedom,* 127. See also Wheeler, "Together in Egypt," 106–8.

13. Gerber, *Black Ohio,* 25–27.

14. Ibid., 27–30.

15. Ibid., 30–32.

16. Ibid., 184–85.

17. Peters, "Floyd County Court Records," 4–7. Seventy-three transactions of this sort are entered in Miscellaneous Court Records, Grantor Book 1, Floyd County Recorder's Office, between 1838 and 1865. Seventy-four slaves are named, and in eleven cases the entry of "&c" or "et al" indicates that at least thirty-eight others were also freed, probably members of the other slaves' families. Most entries occur in the 1850s.

18. Thornbrough, *Negro in Indiana,* 187–91, 194–95; Bigham, *We Ask Only a Fair Trial,* 16–17. On whites' attitudes, see Cheaney, "Indiana Pulpit and Press," 46–47.

19. See, for instance, *EDJ,* Aug. 1, 4, 1863. On June 1 the newspaper reported that another fifty had departed Indianapolis to enlist in the 54th. Henry Butts was named local recruiting officer in late December 1863. Complaints about Indianapolis and other towns getting credit for Evansville men surfaced as early as December 25, 1863. See *EDJ,* Dec. 24–25, 1863. Additional stories about gallantry of black troops can be found in *EDJ,* Oct. 21, 1864; Jan. 19, 1865.

20. Thornbrough, *Negro in Indiana,* 197–99.

21. *EDJ,* Aug. 16, 1864. Blacks were initially enrolled in the 28th Indiana, but six additional regiments of infantry (the 8th, 13th, 14th, 17th, 23rd, and 65th) were organized later, as was the 4th Heavy Artillery Regiment. Unlike white regiments, which

were formed locally, black Hoosier units were created in Indianapolis. See Thornbrough, *Indiana in the Civil War Era,* 137–39. The term *Ethiopian* was commonly used by the Republican newspaper in this era. See Bigham, *We Ask Only a Fair Trial,* 17n53.

22. Bigham, *We Ask Only a Fair Trial,* 17; Thornbrough, *Negro in Indiana,* 199–202. The 28th was assembled and trained in Indianapolis between December 1863 and April 1864. It served in the siege of Petersburg, including the Battle of the Crater, and was discharged at Corpus Christi, Texas.

23. Bigham, *We Ask Only a Fair Trial,* 17. See *EDJ,* Jan. 19, 1865; Sept. 16, Oct. 5, 1864; March 12, 1865.

24. In 1886, 30 blacks (or their widows or orphans) registered with county officials as veterans entitled to a pension. Half had served in Kentucky regiments. William H. Anderson, a prominent Baptist minister, was a veteran of the 13th Indiana. Four years later 67 registered. Most Kentucky veterans had served in the 118th or the 125th regiments. See Bigham, *We Ask Only a Fair Trial,* 18n56. See also Thornbrough, *Negro in Indiana,* 200. William H. Terrell, *Report of the Adjutant General of the State of Indiana,* vol. 7 (Indianapolis: Samuel M. Douglas, State Printer, 1877), offers details about the town and county origins of the various black units from Indiana. The 28th had 53 from Evansville and 58 (most recruits not assigned to a company) from Vanderburgh County. Jeffersonville provided 16 and Clark County another 8. Posey County provided 11, New Albany and Floyd County 4, Madison and Jefferson County 10, and Perry County 3. In all, 163 were from Ohio River counties. The 8th had 131: 32 from Vanderburgh County, 27 from Posey County, 24 from Clark County, and 20 from Jefferson County, the top four represented. Relatively few from Ohio River counties were enrolled in the other Indiana units. Thirty from Ohio River settlements were unassigned recruits, chiefly substitutes enlisted in the fall of 1864 and after. Most were from Posey, Vanderburgh, and Warrick counties. Volume 3 of Terrell's *Report* (1866) includes a list of officers and a history of the 28th.

25. Bigham, *We Ask Only a Fair Trial,* 17–18.

26. *Cairo Gazette,* Dec. 5, 1861, quoted in Ricke, "Illinois Blacks," 288; David Wallace Adams, "Illinois Soldiers and the Emancipation Proclamation," *JISHS* 67 (Sept. 1974): 410–20.

27. Blackmore, "Gallatin County," 227–46. The connection of most of the recruits with slavery is exemplified by the case of William Henry Staples, who, after being mustered out of the 6th U.S. Colored Cavalry in April 1866, returned to Kentucky to retrieve his brother. In the meantime the brother, Robert, had moved to Shawneetown. When William arrived there, Robert was in Virginia looking for their mother. William stayed in Shawneetown, and eventually, fortunately, Robert returned. The two became landowners. They were mustered into service at Quincy, Illinois, mostly in April 1864. All recruits for the 29th enlisted for three years. All were privates. Their ages ranged from 19 to 44, with an average of 30. Three died or were killed in action. See also Victor Hicken, "The Record of Illinois's Negro Soldiers in the Civil War," *JISHS* 56 (Autumn 1963): 529–51.

28. Ricke, "Illinois Blacks," iii–iv, 283–314; Victor Hicken, *Illinois in the Civil War* (Urbana: Univ. of Illinois Press, 1966), 132–41, 334–444; Hicken, "The Record of Illinois's Negro Soldiers, 529–51.

29. *Speech of the Hon. William Allen, of Ohio, on the Enlistment of Negro Soldiers, Delivered in the House of Representatives, February 2, 1863* (pamphlet), http://dbs.ohiohistory.org/africanam/det.cfm?ID=1098 (January 11, 2000); Jacob Bruner to Martha J. Bruner, April 28, 1863, Jacob Bruner Papers, Ohio Historical Society, ibid., (January 11, 2000).

30. "William Dennison, Jr.," http://ohiohistory.org/onlinedoc/ohgovernment/governors/dennison.html (January 12, 2004); Charles J. Wesley, *Ohio Negroes in the Civil War* (Columbus: Ohio State Univ. Press for the Ohio Historical Society, 1962), 13–41; *Official Roster of the Soldiers of the State of Ohio in the War of the Rebellion, 1861–1866* (Akron: Warner Co., 1893), 1:591–92, 625–27, 659–80. See also Cayton, *Ohio,* 137–38.

31. Dabney, *Cincinnati's Colored Citizens,* 25–26.

32. Thornbrough, *Indiana in the Civil War Era,* 628–30.

33. See, for example, Howard Chudacoff's observations in his review of Trotter, *River Jordan,* in *American Historical Review* 99 (April 1999): 565. Also see Wheeler, "Together in Egypt," 112–15.

34. Thornbrough, *Negro in Indiana,* 184.

35. *EDJ,* Aug. 10, 1864.

36. *EDJ,* Jan. 27, 1862; Sept. 30, 1863, for example.

37. Quoted in Litwack, *Been in the Storm,* 223; Brown, *Negro in the Rebellion,* 100. For information on Brown, see John Hope Franklin, *From Slavery to Freedom: A History of Negro Americans,* 5th ed. (New York: Alfred A. Knopf, 1980), 176, 188, 215. Brown was an abolitionist and an agent for antislavery organizations. He wrote about his travels to Europe in behalf of the cause in 1852.

38. Brown, *Negro in the Rebellion,* 103.

39. The most complete account is found in Clark, *Black Brigade,* 1–32. On page 3 he claims it was the first Northern military unit of black men. The Union officer, Colonel William Dickson, ordered the mayor not to arrest any blacks except for crime, thereby opening the prison doors for the hundreds who had been peremptorily arrested and forced to work nonstop for thirty-six hours (18). The next day nearly twice the number that had been impressed freely reported for work. They built fortifications over the following two weeks and earned the laud of Dickson, who on September 20 dismissed them at Fifth and Broadway. Dickson chided local authorities for denying the men the privilege of recognition for their service, which he described as "willing and cheerful. . . . Nor has your seal been dampened by the curl treatment received. . . . Go to your homes with the consciousness of having performed your duty—of deserving, if you do not receive, the protection of the law, and bearing with you the gratitude and respect of all honorable men" (14). In January 1864 Dickson sent a report on the unit to Governor Tod's more sympathetic successor, John Brough, and it was read in the Ohio legislature and placed on the official record. Dickson observed that many in the Black Brigade, denied service in their own state, subsequently joined the army, initially in the 54th Massachusetts (21). The Black Brigade had a total enrollment of 706.

40. Clark, *Black Brigade,* observed that Cincinnati was "a commercial as well as a pro-slavery city." Proceeding to describe how rudely the men were treated, impressed into duty, and supervised by clearly racist policemen, Clark made an exception of the *Cincinnati Gazette,* which on September 4 asked for "our colored fellow-soldiers [to]

be treated civilly. . . . [Only] poor-spirited whites [would] insult a race which they profess as inferior. . . . Since the services of men are from our colored brethren, let them be treated like men" (8). See also Trotter, *River Jordan,* 56–57.

41. Cheaney, "Indiana Pulpit and Press," 67.

42. *New Albany Daily Ledger,* Feb. 14, 21, 1866, quoted in Cheaney, "Indiana Pulpit and Press," 67.

43. Cheaney, "Indiana Pulpit and Press," 82–93.

44. Ibid., 46–47.

45. Ibid., 225–50; Wheeler. "Together in Egypt," 106–208; Gerber, *Black Ohio,* 30–32. The proposed constitutional amendment was rejected by Illinois voters, 141,103 to 125,152. Soldiers voted six to one against it. They also rejected by a similar margin the antiblack amendments, although other voters accepted them. Soldiers' votes undercut Democrats' claims that African American troops were generally detested by white soldiers.

46. Cheaney, "Indiana Press and Pulpit," 188–90.

47. *EDJ,* April 6, 1863.

48. Bigham, *We Ask Only a Fair Trial,* 18. The quotation is from *EDJ,* Nov. 9, 1863.

49. *EDJ,* Jan. 5, 1864, quoted in Bigham, *We Ask Only a Fair Trial,* 15–16.

50. Blackmore, "Gallatin County," 227–46.

51. Steven J. Ross, *Workers on the Edge: Work, Leisure, and Politics in Industrializing Cincinnati, 1788–1890* (New York: Columbia Univ. Press, 1985), 195, 197; Gerber, *Black Ohio,* 27–30. Clark, *Black Brigade,* mentions the attack on Phillips. He places it in the larger context of white Cincinnatians' attitudes—even on the eve of the possible Confederate invasion. A mob drove Wendell Phillips from a gathering, while the "traitor [Robert] Yancey spoke for disunion in a thronged house, and without interruption" (4).

52. According to Cheaney, "Indiana Press and Pulpit," 185n4, authorities later determined that a single black assailant, a barber, was responsible. He fled New Albany on a riverboat and was apprehended in Cairo a week after the shooting.

53. The *Ledger* of July 25 and 29, 1862, is quoted in Cheaney, "Indiana Press and Pulpit," 186. Congressman George Washington Julian's paper in Centerville charged on August 7 that civil authorities had done nothing to check the rioters and that the riots were caused by Democrats who wanted to convince white workers that black newcomers threatened their jobs.

54. Cheaney, "Indiana Press and Pulpit," 187–88.

55. Dabney, *Cincinnati's Colored Citizens,* 58–68. Weigley, *Great Civil War,* 289, states that representatives from freedmen's aid groups in Boston, New York, Philadelphia, and Cincinnati visited President Lincoln in November 1863 to encourage him to create a freedmen's bureau.

56. *EDJ,* Feb. 27, 1883. See also Bigham, *We Ask Only a Fair Trial,* 18. Robinson's appointment occurred in July 1861. His was a recess appointment by President Lincoln. He replaced Charles Denby in that post. See *Senate Executive Journal,* July 10, 1861 (37th Cong., 1st sess.), 387, http://memory.loc.gov (January 19, 2004), Century of Lawmaking collection.

57. *Western Freedmen's Aid Commission, Cincinnati, Ohio, Report* (Cincinnati, July 1864),

at http://dbs.ohiohistory.org/africanam/det.cfm?ID=812&Current=P02&View=Text (March 1, 2001). See also *EDJ,* June 10, 1863.

58. *Western Freedmen's Aid Report,* 1–8.

59. *Western Christian Advocate,* Jan. 22, 1862, quoted in Cheaney, "Indiana Press and Pulpit," 61.

60. E.R. Ames to Abraham Lincoln, Sept. 8, 1862, Abraham Lincoln Papers at the Library of Congress, http://memory.loc.gov (March 31, 2005), Abraham Lincoln collection; *EDJ,* Feb. 24, Oct. 15, 31, 1863; see also *EDJ,* Feb. 17, 1864. On May 11, 1864, *EDJ* reported what it termed the continued barbarism of slavery. In Owensboro, six fugitives were apprehended and each was lashed one hundred times.

61. *EDJ,* Nov. 6, 18, 1862; March 17, 1863; quotes in *EDJ,* March 3, 1864.

62. *EDJ,* Aug. 8, 1863.

63. *EDJ,* Jan. 28, 1862; April 6, July 17, Aug. 15, Sept. 10, 30, 1863; Jan. 5, 1864; quotes in *EDJ,* Aug. 6, 1864.

64. Gerber, *Black Ohio,* 30–32.

65. *EDJ,* Aug. 22, 25, 1863; Feb. 19, 1864.

66. *EDJ,* July 12, Dec. 15, 1864. See also Cheaney, "Indiana Press and Pulpit," 61–64.

67. Frank B. Freidel, ed., *Union Pamphlets of the Civil War, 1861–1865* (Cambridge: Belknap Press of Harvard Univ. Press, 1967), 1:568–70, lists Unionist leaders who attended a massive Union meeting in Indianapolis Feb. 26, 1863. Undoubtedly this event, following the controversial Emancipation Proclamation, evidenced the shift in thinking about slavery that many whites had experienced by then. Eight delegates from Ohio River counties were elected to offices. Three were from Vanderburgh County, two from Harrison, and one each from Clark, Dearborn, and Floyd. Railroad magnate John Ingle Jr. of Evansville was one of the members of the resolutions committee. Editor F.M. Thayer of Evansville was elected as a secretary.

68. Bigham, *We Ask Only a Fair Trial,* 21.

69. Ibid., 16; *EDJ,* Sept. 25, 1863.

70. Ricke, "Illinois Blacks," 326–29.

71. Quoted in Thornbrough, *Negro in Indiana,* 203–4, quotes on 203.

72. *EDJ,* Dec. 31, 1863; Jan. 21, 1864.

73. Bigham, *We Ask Only a Fair Trial,* 17–18; *EDJ,* Aug. 22, 25, 1863; Feb. 19, July 12, Dec. 15, 1864; Cole, *Era of the Civil War,* 336.

74. Blackmore, "Gallatin County," 209–27.

75. *EDJ,* Sept. 14, 1863.

76. *EDJ,* April 26, July 13, 1864; June 14, 1865.

77. *EDJ,* Feb. 20, April 26, 1864. Such campaigns would eventually bear fruit, as shortly after the end of the war the congregation was relocated in a new building on Walnut Street, near Fifth. See Bigham, *We Ask Only a Fair Trial,* 74.

78. Blackmore, "Gallatin County," 209–27.

79. Ibid., 179, 180–81, 184, 195, 198, 208, 291–302.

80. Bigham, *We Ask Only a Fair Trial,* 53–55.

81. Couples who listed their birthplace as the South undoubtedly arrived in the county during and after the war, since so few blacks were enumerated in the county in

1860. Precisely when they came is difficult to pinpoint. But for those with children born in the South and other children born in Indiana, one can identify approximately when they migrated to Indiana. It might be possible to do the same with families in which there are a number of children, all born in the South (mostly Kentucky), whose ages range from, for instance, fifteen to three.

82. Bigham, *We Ask Only a Fair Trial*, 22–23; Ninth Census, Population Schedules for Vanderburgh County, 1870.

83. Parham quoted in Trotter, *River Jordan*, 55; *Indianapolis Sentinel* quoted in Thornbrough, *Negro in Indiana*, 204–5. Republicans chided Democrats for such statements. If God had decreed such racial divisions, he would not have needed men to enforce them (204n46).

84. Ibid., 205.

5. Population and Residential Patterns

1. Wright, *Life behind a Veil*, 46.

2. Indiana's black population doubled in the 1860s and grew another 60 percent in the 1870s. Most of the 1860s growth occurred in the southern part of the state, but by the 1870s the central region accounted for more of the growth than the southern. The Panic of 1873 led to a drop-off in black migration, but in 1879 many blacks came to Indiana, especially from North Carolina as part of a larger pattern of migration to the north and to Kansas. By 1900 eleven counties had 70 percent of the black population. Marion had one-third of the state's total, and Vanderburgh one-sixth. Indianapolis blacks numbered more than all but six Northern cities—even more than Cincinnati—and Evansville's percentage was the highest of all Old Northwest cities. See Thornbrough, *Negro in Indiana*, 206–7, 211–24, 227–30. Cheaney, "Indiana Press and Pulpit," 109–14, notes, though, that blacks never counted for more than 2 percent of any county's population and that three-quarters of the population increase between 1860 and 1880 occurred in one-quarter of the state's counties.

3. Tenth Census, 1880, at *U.S. Census Browser*.

4. Bigham, *We Ask Only a Fair Trial*, 23. In Evansville there were 828 blacks from Kentucky. In 1880 Kentuckians accounted for slightly more than half (52%), while native Hoosiers had risen to 26 percent—a reflection of the number of children born in Indiana. The number of Kentuckians had increased to 1,386; Hoosiers totaled 690. For Floyd County data, see Margaret Lamb Atchley and Sue Pearson Carpenter, abstracters, *1870 Census, Floyd County, Indiana, Ninth Census, Population Schedules for Floyd County, 1870, National Archives Microfilm Publications, No. M593, Roll 313, Indiana* (New Albany: Southern Indiana Genealogical Society, 2000), 1–418, passim. For Jefferson County, see Ninth Census, Population Schedules for Jefferson County, 1870, NAMP, M593, roll 328, Indiana, 194–573a. Ninth Census, Population Schedules for Warrick County, 1870, NAMP, M593, roll 368, Indiana, 40:422–648a. In Madison, 27 of the 49 household heads were Kentuckians, and another 9 were natives of other upper South states. Ten were Hoosiers by birth. See also Kristine Manley and Sharon Patmore, comps., *1870 Perry County Indiana Federal Census* (Evansville: Evansville Bindery, 1998); *Warrick County, Indiana 1870 Federal Census* (Owensboro, KY: Cook-McDowell Publications, 1981).

5. For Massac County, see Ninth Census, Population Schedules for Massac County, 1870, NAMP, M593, roll 255, Illinois, 38:212–332. For Gallatin County, see Blackmore, "Gallatin County," 170. For Pope, see Ricky T. Allen, transcriber, *1870 Federal Census and Mortality Schedule of Pope County, Illinois* (Utica, KY: McDowell Publications, n.d.), 168.

6. For Evansville data, see the previous note. For Madison, see Tenth Census, Population Schedules for Jefferson County, 1880, NAMP, T9, rolls 287–88, Indiana, 1–9294. For Posey County, consult Ilse Horacek, comp., *Tenth Census of the United States: State of Indiana: Posey County, 1880* (Evansville, IN: Evansville Bindery, 1992), 5–378. For Massac County, see Tenth Census, Population Schedules for Massac County, 1880, NAMP, T9, rolls 235–36, Illinois, 1–112b. See also Glenna C. Badgley et al., transcribers, *Pulaski County Illinois: 1880 U.S. Census* (Utica, KY: McDowell Publications, 1986), 1–245; and Carlson, "Black Migration to Pulaski County," 41, who indicates that almost one-fifth of the total number of African Americans were Kentuckians. Tennessee claimed another one-fifth. Another 40 percent were natives of Illinois, most of them children born there after their parents migrated to the state.

7. See, for instance, Gerber, *Black Ohio,* 100–101; Bigham, *We Ask Only a Fair Trial,* 26–30, for more detailed information on settlement patterns. See also Ninth Census, Population Schedules for Massac County, 1870, roll 255, 213–337; and Ninth Census, Population Schedules for Alexander County, 1870, NAMP, M593, roll 188, Illinois, 2:1–252.

8. Wheeler, "Together in Egypt," 111–12.

9. Wright, *Life behind a Veil,* 110–11; U.S. Bureau of the Census, Ninth Census, 1870, *The Statistics of the Population of the United States* (Washington, DC: Government Printing Office, 1872), 1:149; Ninth Census, Population Schedules for Kenton County, 1870, NAMP, M593, roll 478, Kentucky, 18:263–365, 19:1–257.

10. Bigham, *We Ask Only a Fair Trial,* 25; James Lincoln Blue and Donald Hazelwood, comps., *Henderson County, Kentucky, 1880 Census* (Henderson, KY: Henderson County Genealogical and Historical Society, 1995), 41–137; Tenth Census, Population Schedules for Kenton County, 1880, NAMP, T9, rolls 425–26, Kentucky, 17:216–686. For Cincinnati, see Linda Krane Ellwein, "The Negro in Cincinnati: The Black Experience, 1870–1880" (master's thesis, Univ. of Cincinnati, 1970), 51–86.

11. Bigham, *We Ask Only a Fair Trial,* 25; Wright, *Life behind a Veil,* 110–11; Wheeler, "Together in Egypt," 109, 112–15.

12. U.S. Bureau of the Census, Tenth Census, 1880, *Statistics of the Population of the United States* (Washington, DC: Government Printing Office, 1883), 1:122–30, 226–40; Census Bureau, Ninth Census, 1870, *Population,* 1:149; and U.S. Bureau of the Census, *Compendium of the Tenth Census (June 1, 1880)* (Washington, DC: Government Printing Office, 1883), 464–66. Carlson, "Pulaski County Blacks," 41–43, observes that 35 percent of the black population of Pulaski County resided in its towns and villages, and of these Mound City, with 43.2 percent black population, was the leader. In rural precincts of the county, blacks were widely spread, with proportions ranging from 27 to 56 percent. In Cincinnati, the other wards with 300 or more African Americans were Ward 1 (519), Ward 4 (381), Ward 6 (347), Ward 14 (550), Ward 15 (560), and Ward

22 (466). Ward 16 had 299. Seventeen wards and additions had less than 100, and another five had between 121 and 261.

13. Wheeler, "Together in Egypt," 113. See also 114. For Henderson County, see Ninth Census, Population Schedules for Henderson County, 1870, NAMP, M593, roll 478, Kentucky, 14:85–222; and Tenth Census, Population Schedules for Henderson County, 1880, NAMP, T9, roll 419, Kentucky, 12:271–679.

14. Bigham, *We Ask Only a Fair Trial,* 26.

15. Ibid., 27–28.

16. Ibid., 28. The earliest reference to Baptisttown I have found is in *EDJ,* May 4, 1883.

17. Gerber, *Black Ohio,* 100.

18. Ibid., 100–101. See also Dabney, *Cincinnati's Colored Citizens,* 156.

19. Quotation in Trotter, *River Jordan,* 75–76; Henry Louis Taylor Jr., "City Building, Public Policy, the Rise of the Industrial City, and Black Ghetto-Slum Formation in Cincinnati, 1850–1840," in Taylor, *Race and the City,* 163–64.

20. Wright, *Life behind a Veil,* 103.

21. Ibid., 103–4. See also Yater, *Two Hundred Years,* 109–10.

22. Wright, *Life behind a Veil,* 104.

23. Ibid., 110.

24. "California," "Little Africa," and "Neighborhoods," in Kleber, *Encyclopedia of Louisville,* 156, 523, 650.

25. "Smoketown," and "Neighborhoods," ibid., 650 and 830. Lucas, *Kentucky Blacks,* 275–76, offers an overview of Louisville's black neighborhoods.

26. "Brownstown," "Fort Hill," and "Russell," in Kleber, *Encyclopedia of Louisville,* 137, 310, 773. One predominantly black region in rural Jefferson County, originally named Wet Woods, was created in 1851 by a free black couple, Eliza and Henry Tevis, who purchased 40 acres and built a home. The land was subdivided and sold or rented to blacks after the Civil War. When an additional 40 adjoining acres were purchased by Peter Laws in the 1870s, the area became known as Petersburg. The region subsequently was called Newburg and attracted many black families from Smoketown and West Louisville following urban renewal. See "Newburg" and "Wet Woods," ibid., 653, 934.

27. Ninth Census, Population Schedules for Kenton County, 1870, roll 478, 18:263–364, 19:1–257, 228b–229b.

28. Tenth Census, Population Schedules for Kenton County, 1880, rolls 425–26, 17:216–686; *An Atlas of Boone, Kenton, and Campbell Counties, Kentucky* (Philadelphia: D.J. Lake and Co., 1883).

29. Robert D. McManaway, comp., *The 1870 Census of Daviess County, Kentucky* (Owensboro: Cook-McDowell, 1981); and Nancy H. Ford, comp., *Daviess County, Kentucky 1880 Census* (Owensboro: Cook-McDowell, 1980). In 1870, for instance, most blacks in Ward 1 were enumerated on pages 257–62 and 265–76 (22 and 65 residences and 69 and 240 blacks, respectively). In Ward 2, 132 were found in 32 residences on just four pages of the census.

30. Tenth Census, Population Schedules for McCracken County, 1880, NAMP, T9, roll 430, Kentucky, 20:76–245.

31. Tenth Census, Population Schedules for Massac County, 1880, rolls 235–36, 41:19a–45b.

32. Tenth Census, Population Schedules for Jefferson County, 1880, rolls 287–88, 17:1–294. See also Zimmer, "Madison, Indiana," 63–64.

33. Wright, *Life behind a Veil,* 110.

34. Bigham, *We Ask Only a Fair Trial,* 113–14.

35. Ninth Census, Population Schedules for Henderson County, 1870, 85–222; Tenth Census, Population Schedules for Henderson County, 1880, 271–679.

36. Ninth Census, Population Schedules for Vanderburgh County, 1870, roll 264, 38:89–515a; Tenth Census, Population Schedules for Vanderburgh County, 1880, NAMP, T9, rolls 316–17, Indiana, 35:82–542.

37. Ninth Census, Population Schedules for Henderson County, 1870, 94, 138–44, 205, as well as 85–222, passim.

38. James L. Blue, comp., *The Census of the United States in the Year 1870* (Morganfield, KY: Peyton Heady, 1990); Peyton Heady, comp., *The 1880 Census of Union County, Kentucky* (Morganfield, KY: Peyton Heady, 1993).

39. Horacek, *Tenth Census of Posey County,* 5–378.

40. Ninth Census, Population Schedules for Floyd County, 1870, NAMP, M593, roll 313, Indiana, 9:141–437a. See also Wright, *Life behind a Veil,* 123–55, which unfortunately does not include any discussion of families in its section on community life. Nor is the topic included in the chapter on housing (103–22). For Louisville and Jefferson County census records, see Ninth Census, Population Schedules for Jefferson County, Kentucky, 1870, rolls 472–76, vols. 15–17. The first roll (15:245–484a) treats rural Jefferson County. The other four (16:1–642a and 17:1–632) deal with Louisville.

41. Ninth Census, Population Schedules for Trimble County, 1870, NAMP, M593, roll 307, Kentucky, 31:177–240; Tenth Census, Population Schedules for Trimble County, 1880, NAMP, T9, roll 443, Kentucky, 27:434–509. As to surnames and other legacies of slavery, the example of one district in 1870 (pp. 201–10) suffices. Lucy Sibley, age 10 and presumably a "nurse," resided in the home of white farmer John Sibley and his wife and two children. Anthony Peak, also 10, was the sole black inhabitant of Isaac Peak's household. The latter was a farmer who, like John Sibley, was in his twenties and had a wife and young children. Nearby, Philip Sibley, age 72 and a native of Maryland, lived in the household of John Sibley, a wealthy white farmer who was a native Virginian and the same age as Philip. The white man was probably the father of the other white farmer with the same name. Close to the Sibley household was that of another wealthy white farmer, R.J. Morton, 65, whose home included William and Micijah Morton, both teen-age mulattoes. William was a farmhand. The household also contained the family of Daniel and Lucretia Becker. The former, age 50, was a field hand. His wife, 45, was a house servant. The eldest of their three children, John (age 12) was also a house servant.

42. Ninth Census, Population Schedules for Jefferson County, 1870, roll 328, 194–573; Tenth Census, Population Schedules for Jefferson County, 1880, rolls 287–88, 17:1–294.

43. Ninth Census, Population Schedules for Kenton County, 1870, roll 478, 18:263–364, 19:1–257. Dougherty's blacks were named Joe, Bet, Jenny, Clara, Queeny, and Charles.

44. Tenth Census, Population Schedules for Kenton County, 1880, rolls 425–26, 17:216–686.

45. Phyllis Driskill Hunt and Juanita Walker Drennan, comp., *1870 Census Livingston County, Kentucky* (Salem, KY, n.p., 1991), 3–183.

46. Juanita Drennan, comp., *Livingston County, Kentucky 1880 Census* (Ledbetter, KY: n.p., 1992), 1–231.

47. Tenth Census, Population Schedules for McCracken County, 1880, 76–245.

48. Ninth Census, Population Schedules for Gallatin County, 1870, NAMP, M593, roll 224, Illinois, 21:332–476a; Mary N. Douglas, transcriber, *Hardin County Illinois: 1870 United States Census* (Elizabethtown, IL: Nelson, 1985), 3–104; Allen, *1870 Federal Census of Pope County Illinois*, 19–170; Ninth Census, Population Schedules for Massac County, 1870, roll 255, 38:213–337.

49. Joye I. McGrew, compiler, *1880 Census of Gallatin County Illinois* (Herrin, IL: Silkscreen Printing, 1991), 1–309; Tenth Census, Population Schedules for Massac County, 1880, rolls 235–36, 46:1–112; Badgley et al., *Pulaski County Illinois,* 1–246.

50. Wright, *Life behind a Veil,* 112. See also Lucas, *Kentucky Blacks,* 276. Even in tiny, rural Pope County, Illinois, respiratory ailments were the chief cause of death. In 1870, for instance, four of the five blacks who died between June 1, 1869, and May 31, 1870, suffered from consumption, pneumonia, or whooping cough. See Allen, *1870 Federal Census of Pope County,* 175–77. Not until 1908 was a professional study of Louisville tenement conditions made, and its disclosures about the appalling living conditions for poor blacks, whites, and immigrants led to the passage of a new tenement law in 1910, which, like its predecessor, was not enforced. And even reformers generally operated on racist assumptions. Said one, quoted in Wright, *Life behind a Veil,* 115, "Negroes take such conditions with a sort of come-day-go-day, happy-go-lucky philosophy and make merry at their discomforts."

51. Lucas, *Kentucky Blacks,* 274–77.

52. Ibid.

53. Gerber, *Black Ohio,* 101.

54. Ibid., 101–3.

55. Bigham, *We Ask Only a Fair Trial,* 34–35, 40. The *EDJ* of Aug. 31, 1866, and Aug. 17, 1867, had warned city fathers of the abysmal conditions in which "Ethiopians" lived. Twenty-five or thirty were crowded into two rooms in a Second Street tenement, it reported in August 1866, and similar conditions reigned at Fourth and Locust. A year later, in August 1867, an outbreak of cholera struck one black residential cluster, prompting the City Council for the first time to place homeless blacks in the city's pest house or its hospital, rather than adding to crowed conditions and further cases of the dread summertime epidemic.

56. Indiana State Board of Health, *Second Annual Report . . . 1883* (Indianapolis: State Board of Health, 1884), 138–54, 285. Almost 400 died from such "local" causes as digestive ailments. Of these, 91 were respiratory. Another 51 died of "developmental causes" such as stillbirth. Thirty-six died violently, and 162 from "zymotic" causes like typhoid fever. Another 307 were diagnosed with such "constitutional" problems as pneumonia and tuberculosis. For whites, the death rate was 7.3 per 1,000 population,

and for blacks it was 16.5. For persons born in Prussia it was 26.5, and for those born in the German Empire it was 27.

57. Bigham, *We Ask Only a Fair Trial,* 50; Vanderburgh County Coroner, Record of Inquests, Dec. 12, 1888–Dec. 4, 1894, passim. The Massac County Coroner's records, 1869–80, document that 16 of the 36 cases examined involved African Americans.

6. Free and Equal, with Opportunities and Pains

1. Lucas, *Kentucky Blacks,* 209. The most provocative study of the course of race and reunion is Blight, *Race and Reunion,* a work that shares Frederick Douglass's moral outrage. See, for instance, John Hoffman's review of Blight in *Journal of Illinois History* 5 (Winter 2002): 325–27. Eric Foner suggested in 1983 that Reconstruction be viewed not as a specific time period, 1865–77, but as an episode in the lengthy historical process of America's adjustment to the consequences of the Civil War and emancipation. See "The New View of Reconstruction," *American Heritage* 34 (Oct.–Nov. 1983): 10–15.

2. Marion Lucas, "Kentucky Blacks: The Transition from Slavery to Freedom," *RKHS* 91 (1993): 404–6, 407.

3. George P. Rawick, ed., *The American Slave: A Composite Autobiography* (Westport, CT: Greenwood, 1972; vols. 2–19 originally published in 1941), 1:6; 2:16; 5:6–7, 27–35, 50–51, 153–54, 170–72, 176–80, 190–92; 7:69–75. See also Rawick, ed., *The American Slave: A Composite Autobiography: Supplement,* ser. 1 (Westport, CT: Greenwood Press, 1978), 5, 9, 45.

4. "The Biography of a Child Born in Slavery, Samuel Watson: Slave Narratives from the Federal Writers Project," http://memory.loc.gov (March 31, 2005); "Thomas McIntire, Ex-Slave Narrative: Slave Narratives from the Federal Writers Project," http://memory.loc.gov (March 31, 2005). Both are found in the African American Experience collection.

5. Lucas, *Kentucky Blacks,* 184; quotations in Freehling, *The South vs. the South,* 134. There is a rich historiography of the post-Emancipation years, much of which is cited in the notes to this chapter and those to chapters 7–12. Although not cited directly, the pioneering work of W.E.B. Du Bois, as well as more recent studies by Eric Foner and Nell Irvin Painter, have helped to shape my thinking about these years. See W.E.B. Du Bois, *Black Reconstruction in America* (1935; New York: Atheneum, 1992); Eric Foner, *Reconstruction: America's Unfinished Revolution, 1863–1877* (New York: Harper and Row, 1988); and Nell Irvin Painter, *Standing at Armageddon: United States, 1877–1919* (New York: W.W. Norton, 1989). See also Thomas Holt, *Black Over White: Negro Political Leadership in South Carolina during Reconstruction* (Urbana: Univ. of Illinois Press, 1977). My view of these years is eclectic, reflecting a number of interpretations: early revisionism (evidence of cooperation among the races, and the notion that Reconstruction did not go far enough); postrevisionism (the conservatism of Reconstruction); the "splendid failure" argument (blacks' social and cultural achievements, however limited); and the Holt-Painter view (that African Americans' responses were often bourgeois in character).

6. Lucas, *Kentucky Blacks,* 181.

7. Ibid., 178–79.

8. Ibid., 184–85.

9. Ibid., 185–86. See also William S. McFeeley, *Yankee Stepfather: General O. O. Howard and the Freedmen* (1970; repr., New York: W. W. Norton, 1994), esp. 67, 292, 302. Congress changed the law in 1868 to limit bureau activities to unreconstructed states. Education and payment of bounties to veterans were its focus at the end, and these were its chief tasks after the end of 1867.

10. Lucas, *Kentucky Blacks,* 186–87. See also Harrison and Klotter, *New History,* 215–18. An older, fundamentally different view was offered by E. Merton Coulter (1890–1981), a prolific author who was flagrantly antiblack and damned the Freedmen's Bureau as contributing to violence and lawlessness. He did acknowledge the bureau's value in feeding, clothing, and educating blacks. See Smith, "E. Merton Coulter," 52–66.

11. Harrison and Klotter, *New History,* quotations on 237; George C. Wright, *Racial Violence in Kentucky, 1865–1940: Lynchings, Mob Rule, and "Legal Lynchings"* (Baton Rouge: Louisiana State Univ. Press, 1990), 19–25, 66.

12. Lucas, *Kentucky Blacks,* 189. See also Wright, *Racial Violence,* 71, 307–23.

13. Dunnigan, *Black Kentuckians,* 83, 92, 98.

14. Lucas, *Kentucky Blacks,* quotes the historian on 192; the other quote is on 193; see also 192–95.

15. *EDJ,* Nov. 29, 1865. Reports of troops passing by to bring law and order to Henderson, Uniontown, and Smithland appeared in the paper the following day. Reports of the mistreatment of whites and blacks across the river appear in *EDJ,* July 26, 1865.

16. *EDJ,* Feb. 9, 1869. Additional information about Klan activities appeared in *EDJ,* Feb. 17, 1869.

17. Quotation in Lucas, *Kentucky Blacks,* 195; Wright, *Racial Violence,* 26.

18. Lucas, *Kentucky Blacks,* 195–98.

19. Ibid., 199.

20. Ibid.

21. Ibid., 199–200.

22. Ibid., 201.

23. Ibid., 201–4.

24. Ibid., 204–5.

25. Ibid., 205.

26. Ibid., 183, 205–7.

27. Ibid., 207–8.

28. Wheeler, "Together in Egypt," 105, 110–11.

29. Litwack, *Been in the Storm,* 223.

30. Thornbrough, *Negro in Indiana,* 207–11.

31. Bigham, *We Ask Only a Fair Trial,* 39.

32. Ibid., 39–40. In the interim, Morton was appointed to a U.S. Senate seat, and Baker succeeded him as governor.

33. Thornbrough, *Negro in Indiana,* 277–78. The homes of two of the alleged killers

were subsequently burned, and acts of violence against other blacks in the county were reported. See 278n39.

34. Ibid., 40. See also *EDJ*, July 17, 1865.

35. *EDJ*, July 14, 1866. This was the day before John W. Foster, a prominent Republican and veteran of the Union Army, became editor and publisher, succeeding James McNeely, who had edited the paper for about a decade. Foster, who later became Benjamin Harrison's secretary of state, was more sympathetic to blacks, as evidenced by his seeking funds earlier for blacks' education.

36. *EDJ*, July 1, 1865; Dec. 10, 1867; Jan. 1, 1868. There was also intimidation of blacks seeking to establish businesses or professions that whites deemed inappropriate. Such was the case of a physician named Miller. See *EDJ*, May 9, 1867.

37. *EDJ*, Sept. 18–19 (quotation here); Oct. 6, 1868; Edgar F. Raines Jr., "The Ku Klux Klan in Illinois, 1867–1875," *Illinois Historical Journal* 78 (Spring 1985): 17–44.

38. Lois A. Carrier, *Illinois: Crossroads of a Continent* (Urbana: Univ. of Illinois Press, 1993), 128. The label "Ellis Island" is traceable to at least John Lansden's 1910 history of Cairo: Cheaney, "Indiana Pulpit and Press," 98.

39. Quoted in Cheaney, "Indiana Pulpit and Press," 99–101. The white's comment is quoted on 99.

40. *EDJ*, Oct. 12, 1878; *New Harmony Register*, Jan. 11, 1884. The Democratic *Evansville Courier* predictably offered a different perspective on this affair. The fracas began, its editor charged, when seven black men ravished four white women earlier in the week and incensed citizens demanded justice. The five black men who died were portrayed as "brutes in human form" and "bestial villains." The man who was burned alive had a previous conviction of rape and was "a villainous-looking six-footer magnificently built." Though the punishment was "terribly cruel," the culprits' aggravations were substantial. Mount Vernon had been plagued recently by "licentrates [*sic*] and desperados." That was the cause. See *EC*, Oct. 12, 1878.

41. Thornbrough, *Negro in Indiana*, 281. Another lynching occurred in Terre Haute in early 1901. This was the last in which the state failed to take action. A notable instance of the state's intervening occurred in early July 1903, when the militia quelled a nasty race riot in Evansville. See ibid., 282–87; Bigham, *We Ask Only a Fair Trial*, 104–8.

42. I have examined 19 postwar county histories: 7 from Indiana, 6 from Ohio, and 3 each from Illinois and Kentucky. The paucity of histories in the latter two states may reflect relative levels of economic development.

43. Collins, *History of Kentucky*, 1:217, 220. On p. 246 L, for instance, Collins condemned a Klan rally that occurred on September 15, 1873. See also 1:130–47, 162–227.

44. Ibid., 1:139 (Feb. 18–19, 1873), 1:246, delegates quoted on 1:139.

45. Ibid., 2:113, 153, 311, 318, 364, 420, 546; see 1:246 for the comparisons of black and white wealth. Compare Collins with *The Biographical Encyclopedia of Kentucky of the Dead and Living Men of the Nineteenth Century* (Cincinnati: J.M. Armstrong, 1878), which contains no references to black men or even to the slaves owned by such prominent whites as Lazarus Powell and Archibald Dixon. There is one oblique reference—a

glowing portrait of Lincoln that refers to his love of mankind and to abolition as needed to save the Union. See 663, 749, 778.

46. *History of the Ohio Falls Cities and Their Counties, with Illustrations and Biographical Sketches* (Cleveland: L.A. Williams and Co., 1882), 1:414. See also 1:317–53, 359–99, 400–407, 408–26, 571–76.

47. *Atlas of Boone, Kenton, and Campbell Counties*, 54–55.

48. *History of Daviess County*, 367, 376–77, 400–401, 419–22. The reference to education is on 362. It is unclear whether the Third Street Methodist Episcopal Church was African Methodist Episcopal or Colored Methodist Episcopal (now Christian Methodist Episcopal), a branch of the white Methodist Episcopal Church, South.

49. Charles J. O'Malley, *History of Union County, Kentucky* (Evansville: Courier Publishing Co., 1886; repr., Evansville: Unigraphic, 1969), 253 (page citations are to the 1969 ed.).

50. J.H. Battle, *Histories and Biographies of Ballard, Calloway, Fulton, Graves, Hickman, McCracken, and Marshall Counties*, part 2 of J.H. Battle, W.H. Perrin, and C.C. Kniffen, *Kentucky: A History of the State* (Chicago: F.A. Battey Publishing Co., 1885; repr., Murray, KY: Kentucky Reprint Co., 1972), 86–99 (page citations are to the 1972 ed.).

51. Starling, *Henderson County*, 294, 296. See also 99, 171–75, 179–90, 289–96, 476–80.

52. Ibid., 541–65 (these pages cover the war years), 475, 476–80.

53. Ibid., 502.

54. Ibid., 237–38. See also 249.

55. *History of Gallatin, Saline, Hamilton, Franklin, and Williamson Counties, Illinois* (Chicago: Goodspeed Publishing Co., 1887), 31–37.

56. William Henry Perrin, ed., *History of Alexander, Union, and Pulaski Counties, Illinois* (Chicago: O.L. Baskin, 1883), 126–39.

57. Ibid., 560.

58. Ibid., 569, 572, 585.

59. Ibid., 194. This incident refers to the attempt, described in chapter 12 of this volume, to force Cairo officials to provide high school education for black youth.

60. Ibid.

61. Edward White, *Evansville Men*. The first Evansville history to mention black organizations was Brant and Fuller's *History of Vanderburgh County* (Madison, WI: Brant and Fuller, 1889). In format (antiquarian) it resembles the histories of Clark and Floyd counties; Edwin Adams, *History of Warrick County, Indiana* (Evansville: Crescent City Job Office, 1868); Will Fortune, ed., *Warrick and Its Prominent People* (Evansville: Courier Publishing Co., 1881), 172; *History of Warrick, Spencer, and Perry Counties, Indiana* (Chicago: Goodspeed, 1885; repr., Evansville: Unigraphic Publishing Co., 1973), 118–19, 121, 132 (page citations are to the 1973 ed.).

62. *Warrick, Spencer, and Perry Counties*, 705. See also 398–418, 419–36, 710–29.

63. *History of the Falls Cities*, 2:192, 204. See also 2:134–35, 444–46, 509.

64. Ibid., 164, 176–77, 443–44. In the earliest histories of two of the three Indiana counties just downriver from Cincinnati (Dearborn and Switzerland), blacks were totally excluded. The earliest history of Rising Sun and Ohio County, sandwiched be-

tween them, included a brief reference to black churches. Several men from Madison, Lawrenceburg, Rising Sun, and Cincinnati were credited with organizing the Shiloh Baptist Church in Rising Sun in the fall of 1867; the small congregation met in the Universalist Church building. Its first pastor was Elder C. Harris, from Madison, and its original 6 members, 3 of them women, were also identified. The congregation, which grew by the late 1870s to 65 members, subsequently purchased the former Presbyterian edifice on Second Street. Macedonia AME Church, established in 1878 by a Reverend Lee, met in an old hall on Front Street until a new structure was completed in the early 1880s. It had 10 members. See *History of Dearborn, Ohio, and Switzerland Counties, Indiana* (Chicago: F.E. Weakley and Co., 1885; repr., Evansville Bindery, 1999), 382–89 (page citations are to the 1999 ed.).

65. *The History of Clermont County, Ohio, with Illustrations and Biographical Sketches of Its Prominent Men and Pioneers* (Philadelphia: Louis H. Everts, 1880), 134–35.

66. Ibid., 167, 173, 265, 305, 352 and 418, quotation on 167.

67. Ibid., 355, 422.

68. *The History of Brown County, Ohio* (Chicago: W.H. Beers and Co., 1883), 313–16.

69. Ibid., 501. See also 313–16, 400, 403, 422, 463–64, 503. Some blacks resided in other parts of the county. In the northeastern section, Eagle Township appeared to have been a haven for blacks for decades. Most settlers, because of internal bickering, had left before the war, but Baptist and Methodist churches remained. Each had a cemetery. Another interior township, Washington, had eight black pupils. It was unclear where they attended school. Sterling Township, also in the northern part of the county, had a black Baptist church, Todd's Run, organized by an Elder Riley in April 1870. The congregation, originally twenty members, had doubled in size. The township had twenty-six black students and a black teacher in a separate schoolhouse. See ibid., 589–91, 674–78, 691–92.

70. Walter F. Arvis, manager, *Caldwell's Illustrated Historical Atlas of Adams County, Ohio, 1797–1880* (Newark, OH: J.A. Caldwell, 1880), 30. See also 22, 23, 34, 35–36, 40, 54, 101. Information was collected by local managers and provided to a historian and an artist, who compiled the book. Many gaps in coverage exist as a consequence. A later history also focused on white antislavery activities rather than on African Americans. Many early settlers brought slaves across the river with them. Some blacks served practically in bondage, under the guise of free labor—such as Dinah, who served Julia Morrison until her death in 1878 at age 106. We also learn that during the 1840s antislavery sentiment grew, especially in white settlements at Cherry Fork and Brush Creek, and that the Underground Railroad had a number of stations in the county. White men and women heroically sheltered fugitives. The book included the gleefully presented story of the white Dave Dunbar, who dressed in a ragged suit and blackened his face and hands to lead two would-be slave-nabbers on a wild goose chase. See Evans and Stivers, *History of Adams County,* 405–10, 413, 443–44, 479.

71. D.J. Kenny, *Illustrated Cincinnati: A Pictorial Hand-Book of the Queen City* (Cincinnati: Robert Clarke and Co., 1875), 54, 76, 101–9; Henry A. Ford and Kate A. Ford, comps., *History of Hamilton County, Ohio, with Illustrations and Biographical Sketches* (Cleveland: L.A. Williams, 1881), 18–19, 73–74. By contrast, proceedings of the fiftieth anni-

versary of Allen Temple provided great detail of black Cincinnati in 1874 (see chapter 11 of this volume).

72. Evans, *History of Scioto County,* 489–94, quotes on 489.

73. Ibid., 529.

74. Ibid., 612–13.

75. James M. McPherson, *Ordeal by Fire: The Civil War and Reconstruction,* 3rd ed. (New York: McGraw-Hill, 2001), 620–21. The Supreme Court in 1883 ruled the 1875 law (except for juries) unconstitutional on the grounds that the Fourteenth Amendment purportedly applied only to actions by state governments, not by individuals.

76. Quoted in Litwack, *Been in the Storm,* 571.

77. The Kentucky House and Senate voted down the Thirteenth Amendment by 57-28 and 21-12, respectively. They rejected the Fourteenth 67-27 and 24-9, and the Fifteenth 80-5 and 27-6. See Ross A. Webb, "Readjustment," in *KE,* 756–58, for an overview of this period, which is not labeled Reconstruction in the state's histories; quote in Lucas, *Kentucky Blacks,* 292.

78. Lucas, *Kentucky Blacks,* 292–93.

79. Jean Edward Smith, *Grant* (New York: Simon and Schuster, 2001), 522.

80. Gerber, *Black Ohio,* 32–40; Cayton, *Ohio,* 139.

81. Thornbrough, *Negro in Indiana,* 231–32, 233–36, quote on 231–32.

82. Ibid., 248–50, quote on 248–49. See also 236–48.

83. Bridges, "Equality Deferred," 84–86.

84. Ibid., 95.

7. Citizenship and Civil Rights after the Fourteenth Amendment

1. Thornbrough, *Negro in Indiana,* 255, 388–89.

2. Ibid., 256–57. See also Cheaney, "Indiana Pulpit and Press," 281, 293. He provides a number of examples from Evansville and New Albany papers of both parties that rejected the notion that freedom and the vote were linked to social equality.

3. Henderson County Tax List, 1866, microfilm copy, Willard Library Archives, Evansville.

4. Wright, *Life behind a Veil,* 52–54. See also Lucas, *Kentucky Blacks,* 296–98.

5. *EDJ,* March 15, 1875. A similar message was evident in Nicholas's remarks upon being named constable: "We ask only a fair trial." See Thornbrough, *Negro in Indiana,* 258–63, for a fuller account of the impact of the law. The first real test came in 1888.

6. Prominent men before the war were, among others, Carter, James Amos, and Charles Asbury. Green McFarland, Adam Rouse, Willis Green, Robert Nicholas, James Townsend, George Jackson, and others came into prominence after 1865. In most public matters, members of both groups advocated similar strategies. See, for example, *EDJ,* Aug. 1–2, 1872; June 4, 1874.

7. Smith, *Grant,* 562–68; Thornbrough, *Negro in Indiana,* 259.

8. *EDJ,* Oct. 25, 1883.

9. Thornbrough, *Negro in Indiana,* 264. See also 259–63. A significant example of Evansville blacks' formal resistance to second-class citizenship, though beyond the scope of this study, occurred in the spring of 1894, when an Evansville black pastor chal-

lenged a recently passed Kentucky law requiring the separation of races in railway cars. Even though Evansville was a few miles north of the Bluegrass State, the L&N Railroad placed a "Jim Crow" car on its trains leaving the Indiana city. The pastor, W.H. Anderson, rode with his wife in a "whites only" car, only to be expelled when the train crossed the river into Kentucky. Although upheld in a lower court, his protest was eventually muted by high court rulings on "separate but equal" facilities. See Bigham, *We Ask Only a Fair Trial*, 97–98.

10. Quotation in "Indiana and Ohio's Black Laws," *Cleveland Gazette*, Aug. 30, 1884, http:memory.loc.gov (March 31, 2005), material in the African American Experience in Ohio collection; Thornbrough, *Negro in Indiana*, 266. One illustration of the application of the law is found in *EDJ*, Aug. 5, 1867. A lengthy column was devoted to a case in which a man with mixed Negro and Indian blood was charged by the father of a fourteen-year-old white girl with having had sexual relations with his daughter. Two issues were at stake—whether she had acted voluntarily, and whether the man was a Negro. The jury found him not guilty. The editor berated the father and his family as being people of low intelligence and wondered what the girl saw in the alleged assailant.

11. Thornbrough, *Negro in Indiana*, 267.

12. Ibid., 269.

13. Quotations in Bigham, *We Ask Only a Fair Trial*, 50; Thornbrough, *Negro in Indiana*, 269.

14. Ibid., 272. In Evansville, with the highest percentage of blacks in any large city in Indiana, reportedly "a jury commissioner positively refused to summon Negroes" (272).

15. *EC*, Oct. 17, 1870; *EDJ*, Oct. 17, 1870. See also Bigham, *We Ask Only a Fair Trial*, 51. In the 1870 instance, the jury foreman was Alfred Carter, described as a classmate of the son of a prominent German American industrialist and banker, John A. Reitz. That would have meant he had attended a parochial school. See *EDJ*, Oct. 17, 1870.

16. *EDJ*, June 26, 1867.

17. Thornbrough, *Negro in Indiana*, 272–73; *EDJ*, Sept. 18, 1868; April 27, 1871.

18. Bigham, *We Ask Only a Fair Trial*, 51.

19. Ibid., 50–51. See also *EDJ*, Sept. 2, 1872; Jan. 5, Dec. 2, 1875; April 1, 1876.

20. Harris L. Dante, "Western Attitudes and Reconstruction Politics in Illinois, 1865–1872," *JISHS* 49 (Summer 1956): 152–60.

21. *Debates and Proceedings of the Constitutional Convention of the State of Illinois, Convened at the City of Springfield* . . . (Springfield, IL: E.L. Merritt and Brother, 1870), 2:1286–90, 1322, http://www.hti.umich.edu/m/moagrp (March 31, 2005) (search "Constitutional Convention of the State of Illinois"), offers one example of the manner in which the recent ratification of the black suffrage amendment shaped debate. The fact that the vote was guaranteed by the federal government prompted most delegates to argue that similar response in Illinois was required. For an overview of public education for blacks, see Robert McCaul, *The Black Struggle for Public Schooling in Nineteenth Century Illinois* (Carbondale: Southern Illinois Univ. Press, 1987). See also Bridges, "Equality Deferred," 95–97. A more detailed discussion of schooling is found in chapter 12.

22. Bridges, "Equality Deferred," 107–8. See also Irving Dillard, "Civil Liberties of Negroes in Illinois since 1875," *JISHS* 56 (Autumn 1972): 594. The background of this legislation is discussed in chapter 8.

23. Gerber, *Black Ohio,* 170; 44–51, Fox quoted on 170.

24. Quillen, *Color Line,* 102, 105; Roseboom, *Civil War Era,* 449–71.

25. Quillen, *Color Line,* 103, 118, 125–32. The weakness of the law is also discussed in Catron, *Ohio,* 271–73. Quillen reported that about one black was arrested for every two whites, although the black population was just below 5 percent.

26. Wright, *Life behind a Veil,* 15. For an overview of Kentucky politics in this era, see Harrison and Klotter, *New History,* 239–46.

27. Victor B. Howard, "The Kentucky Press and the Negro Testimony Controversy, 1866–1872," *RKHS* 71 (Jan. 1973): 30–48; "The Black Testimony Controversy in Kentucky, 1866–1872," *Journal of Negro History* 58 (April 1973): 140–65. See also Howard, *Black Liberation,* 130–45, 177–79; Lucas, *Kentucky Blacks,* 312–13. Lucas notes that following 1867 black self-help groups were formed in Louisville and other cities because of the disappearance of Freedmen's Bureau courts. These were organized to help freedmen facing complicated court procedures and to assist them in transferring their cases to federal courts. Some white legal organizations also pressured the state for change. In 1871 a federal judge decided to prosecute state judges for violating the Civil Rights Act of 1866 when they denied blacks the right to testify. Black testimony was thus being permitted before the 1872 law, making the latter a fait accompli. See also Harrison and Klotter, *New History,* 247–48.

28. Harrison and Klotter, *New History,* 247–48. Regarding the issue of the origins of Jim Crow racial separation, I am inclined to support the position of Joel Williamson and others (see epilogue), who see it as an outgrowth of antebellum racial proscriptions. The matter is more complicated on the north bank, where the paucity of blacks before the 1860s required little formal decision-making on race. See also Lucas, *Kentucky Blacks,* 292–325.

29. Lucas, *Kentucky Blacks,* 323–24. Cf. Wheeler, "Together in Egypt," 105.

30. *EDJ,* Feb. 17, March 18, 1870. See also *EDJ,* Aug. 10, 1869; February 17–18, March 10–19, 1870; Oct. 6, 1876; Sept. 23, 1880. On the *New Albany Daily Ledger's* view, Cheaney, "Negro Press and Pulpit," 267–77. See also *EDJ,* March 10–19, 1870.

31. Cheaney, "Negro Press and Pulpit," 383–406.

32. Ibid., 409, 411–17, quote on 409.

33. Thornbrough, *Negro in Indiana,* 224–27. The reference to the Democratic paper's boast is found in *EDJ,* July 1, 1883.

34. Bigham, *We Ask Only a Fair Trial,* 26–32, 40, 48; Trotter, *River Jordan,* 75–76.

35. Carlson, "Black Migration to Pulaski County," 41–43; and Wheeler, "Together in Egypt," 109–12.

36. Bigham, *We Ask Only a Fair Trial,* 32–33.

37. Ibid., 34.

38. Quotes ibid., 34–35; on Cairo, see Wheeler, "Together in Egypt," 115–19.

39. *EDJ,* May 13–24, 1872. Similar circumstances existed in Illinois's river counties.

See Edgar F. Raines Jr., "The Ku Klux Klan in Illinois, 1867–1875," *Illinois Historical Journal* 78 (Spring 1985): 19, 44.

40. *EDJ*, Sept. 19–20, 1876. The Republican newspaper seemed amused about the plight of a young black man, Frank Clagett, arrested in early 1875 for allegedly having had premarital relations the previous year with a young woman, Mary Crump, who subsequently had a child. Clagett, who had studied at Fisk College in Nashville, was purportedly en route to Mississippi to take over a black school there. A former slave of William Clagett of Hickman County, Kentucky, he was described as a shrewd person who had boasted that "he'll have no problem proving his innocence." He acknowledged that he was the father and that he intended to marry the girl, a "handsome mulatto" with whom he had a sexual liaison after a ball the previous year. He was nevertheless jailed under a $250 bond for the crime of bastardy. Whites undoubtedly reveled in the fact that even well-educated blacks were inclined to sexual promiscuity. See *EDJ*, Jan. 8, 1875.

41. *EDJ*, Dec. 1, 1879; quotation in the May 4, 1883, issue.

42. The address celebrating the tenth anniversary of the Emancipation Proclamation was published in *EDJ*, Jan. 1, 1875. Whether Robert Nicholas, recently named as the city's first black constable, delivered the address the day before or supplied written comments for publication in the Republican newspaper is unclear. In the years that followed, Evansville's African Americans celebrated the Preliminary Emancipation Proclamation, issued on September 22, 1862.

43. Bigham, *We Ask Only a Fair Trial,* 48–49.

44. Ibid., 49–50.

45. Wheeler, "Together in Egypt," 118–21.

46. William A. Joiner, *A Half Century of Freedom of the Negro in Ohio* (Xenia, OH: Press of Smith Advertising, 1915), 41–45; Quillen, *Color Line,* 105; Roseboom, *Civil War Era,* 403.

47. Quillen, *Color Line,* 105; *Cleveland Gazette,* Jan. 20, 1894, http://dbs.ohiohistory.org/africanam (Jan. 11, 2000).

48. Quillen, *Color Line,* 125–33; Gerber, *Black Ohio,* 56–59.

49. Lucas, *Kentucky Blacks,* 293.

50. *EDJ*, Nov. 29, 30, 1875.

51. Collins, *History of Kentucky,* 1:246a.

52. Ibid., 65–98, 127–29.

53. Wright, *Racial Violence,* 307–23. By region, 44 blacks were lynched in the Purchase, 81 in western Kentucky, and 83 in Central Kentucky. Only 5 lynchings were reported in metropolitan Louisville. Thirty-five occurred in northern Kentucky.

54. *EDJ*, Dec. 28, 1874, to Jan. 6, 1875. See also Lucas, *Kentucky Blacks,* 293–94; Wright, *Racial Violence,* 1–18.

55. Wright, *Racial Violence,* 155–56, 160, 172–76, 215.

56. Lucas, *Kentucky Blacks,* 294.

57. Ibid., 294–95.

58. Ibid., 295–98; Bigham, *We Ask Only a Fair Trial,* 97–98.

59. Wright, *Life behind a Veil,* 63–65. Although the Kentucky law was declared un-

constitutional by a federal court two years later, "separate but equal" rulings of the U.S. Supreme Court later in the decade upheld it. Rev. W.H. Anderson of Evansville, aided by attorney J.H. Lott of Evansville, tested the 1892 law by bringing suit. See Kentucky Commission on Human Rights, *Kentucky's Black Heritage: The Role of the Black People in the History of Kentucky from Pioneer Days to the Present* (Frankfort, KY, 1971), 57.

60. Wright, *Life behind a Veil,* 55.

61. Ibid., 55–56.

62. Ibid., 56.

63. Quoted ibid., 57. William was the son of prominent businessman Washington Spradling.

64. Quoted ibid., 57–58.

65. Ibid., 58.

66. C. Vann Woodward, *The Strange Career of Jim Crow* (New York: Oxford Univ. Press, 1955), quoted in Wright, *Life behind a Veil,* 59.

67. Wright, *Life behind a Veil,* 59. References to hotels and the YMCA are from the *Cleveland Gazette* of Oct. 10, 1885, and July 2, 1887, found in http://memory.loc.gov (March 31, 2005), under African American Experience. The Kentucky legislature, unlike the lawmakers of the three states to the north, did not pass a civil rights law.

68. Wright, *Life behind a Veil,* 60–62, 127–28, quote on 60.

69. Ibid.,.74–75. See also 71–74.

70. Ibid., 76.

71. Ibid., 2–10.

72. Scott Cummings and Michael Price, "Race Relations and Public Policy in Louisville: Historical Development of an Urban Underclass," *Journal of Black Studies* 27 (May 1997): 618–19.

73. William Foster Hayes, *Sixty Years of Owensboro, 1883–1943* (Owensboro, KY, 1944), 370–71, 374–75. See also Howard, *Black Liberation,* 140–41, 145; Wright, *Racial Violence,* 313–16.

74. Wright, *Life behind a Veil,* 158–59, 160.

75. Ibid., 160–63. In the summer of 1890, Simmons surprised State University by resigning and establishing an industrial training institute near Louisville that was funded by L&N executives. He also hoped to open a school to train domestic servants in Louisville. Shortly thereafter, however, Simmons died of a heart attack. State University was subsequently renamed in his honor.

76. Ibid., 163–65.

77. Ibid., 165.

78. Ibid., 168–69. Few advocated the course encouraged by Albert Ernest Meyzeek, educator and civic leader. He was an independent black leader and an outspoken critic of racial discrimination and did not frequently consult with whites. Son of a white Canadian and a black woman, he was born in Ohio in 1862 and reared in Toronto, Canada. His maternal grandfather, John Lott, had once lived in Madison, Indiana, where he helped slaves to escape. Lott had to use the same route northward to Canada when his subterranean activities were discovered. As a teen Meyzeek moved with his family to Terre Haute, Indiana, where he graduated from the largely white high school and

the state normal school. He also received a degree from Indiana University. In the early 1890s he became principal of Central High School as well as several elementary schools in Louisville. See 166–68.

79. Ibid., 169–71. Most newspapers were short-lived, often published before elections. Like the Baptist newspaper that Steward published, they preached the gospel of self-help. See ibid., 171–72.

80. Ibid., 172–75.

81. Bigham, *We Ask Only a Fair Trial*, 88. See *EDJ*, Jan. 1, 1875; quotes in Thornbrough, *Negro in Indiana*, 258; and in Wright, *Life behind a Veil*, 59 (based on Gerber, *Black Ohio*, 48, 189–90). Such men as Carter were able to maintain some influence among white leaders. On June 4, 1874, policemen arrested two black women for violating a city ordinance forbidding two or more "lewd women" to walk city streets. The arrest greatly aroused the black community, because the action was deemed unjustified. A third black woman provided Carter evidence to that effect, and he successfully prevailed upon authorities to release the two women. *EDJ*, June 4, 1874.

82. Bigham, *We Ask Only a Fair Trial*, 99.

83. Ibid., 99–100; Trotter, *River Jordan*, 78–83.

8. The Progress of Blacks and the Ballot Box

1. Blight, *Race and Reunion*, 1–5.

2. *EDJ*, Sept. 23, 1867. References to southern Illinois and Paducah can be found in John W. Allen, *Legends and Lore of Southern Illinois* (Carbondale: Southern Illinois Univ. Press, 1963), 269–71. In some places, especially west of the Mississippi, the celebration was "Juneteenth," the ending of slavery in Texas in 1865. For reference to the 1887 excursion, see *EDJ*, July 27, 1887.

3. See, for instance, Bigham, *We Ask Only a Fair Trial*, 78; Lucas, *Kentucky Blacks*, 299–300.

4. Lucas, *Kentucky Blacks*, 300–301.

5. Thornbrough, *Negro in Indiana*, 231–36; *Journal of the House of Representatives,* November 25, 1867 (40th Cong., 1st sess.), 257, http://memory.loc.gov (March 31, 2005), Century of Lawmaking collection. Black activists faced a variety of challenges from Democrats. Members of the Evansville City Council, for example, sought to deny George Jackson, a prominent black Republican, a liquor license. The sole reason they gave was that he was black. On this occasion, by a 4–3 vote, Republicans overrode Democrats' objections. See *EDJ*, Aug. 8, 1867.

6. Thornbrough, *Negro in Indiana*, 246; for the 1870 event, see *EDJ*, Feb. 23, May 7–27, 1870.

7. Thornbrough, *Negro in Indiana*, 236–54; newspaper quote in Bigham, *We Ask Only a Fair Trial*, 89.

8. *Journal of the House of Representatives,* July 11, 1870 (41st Cong., 2nd sess.), 1210, http://memory.loc.gov (March 31, 2005), Century of Lawmaking collection; quote in *EDJ*, Oct. 3, 1870.

9. Quoted in Bigham, *We Ask Only a Fair Trial*, 88.

10. Thornbrough, *Negro in Indiana*, 288–91; quote on 288; *EDJ*, Feb. 22, Aug. 15, 22, 1872. See also *EDJ*, April 11, Oct. 5, 1871. Alfred Carter reported the previous night on

the Colored Men's' Convention in St. Louis that he had attended. Meeting at the AME Church, black citizens heard him describe the various resolutions adopted there, including one endorsing the present administration. He said blacks should back Grant and the Republicans so long as they supported equal rights.

11. Bigham, *We Ask Only a Fair Trial*, 87–88; *EDJ*, March 18, 1870. Thornbrough, *Negro in Indiana*, 301n24, provides a biographical sketch of Townsend. Born in Ohio and the son of devout AME parents, he continued his studies after leaving Evansville and became a pastor in Terre Haute, Indianapolis, and Richmond. In 1884 he was elected to the Indiana House of Representatives—the first black to achieve that post.

12. *Williams' Evansville Directory for 1872–1873* (Evansville, IN: Williams, 1872).

13. Quote in Thornbrough, *Negro in Indiana*, 293; *EDJ*, Aug. 14, 1872; Oct. 15, 1870. The latter issue chided the Democrats for charging Republicans with using "floaters." It stated that there were five hundred black men in the county who were entitled to vote, and no more than that had voted in the recent election. The Republican paper put Democrats' reluctant conversion this way: "before the war the d———d nigger was a slave; after the war the ignorant negro was free; at the present time our intelligent fellow-citizen is a voter." *EDJ*, July 8, 1867.

14. Cheaney, "Indiana Pulpit and Press," 294–315. *EC*, Oct. 1, 1870. Cf. *EDJ*, April 28, 1871, which criticized Democrats for resurrecting a long-overlooked and unenforced city ordinance requiring voters to have paid city taxes within the twelve months preceding the election. The ordinance existed solely to disenfranchise black voters, although if fairly enforced it would do the same to most whites.

15. Wheeler, "Together in Egypt," 122–26.

16. *EDJ*, April 5–6, 1876.

17. Bigham, *We Ask Only a Fair Trial*, 90. See also *EDJ*, Feb. 7, April 6, 1876; Thornbrough, *Negro in Indiana*, 293–95.

18. *EDJ*, Sept. 30, Oct. 3–9, 1876. Two enthusiastic young Democrats, for instance, challenged an old man, whom they labeled as an "imported voter." According to the Republicans' account, "the old man paused because he was looking down the road to where a half dozen small editions of himself were tumbling over the fence to meet him. 'Well,' he said, 'I's lived here for *nigh onto thirteen years!*'" The newspaper reported that the Democrats left in disgust. "Imported voters don't hang around on trees, waiting to be knocked off." See also Bigham, *We Ask Only a Fair Trial*, 90; *EDJ*, Feb. 7, Nov. 8, 1876.

19. Bigham, *We Ask Only a Fair Trial*, 91. An example of warnings regarding black "repeaters" is found in *EC*, Nov. 4, 1881.

20. Bigham, *We Ask Only a Fair Trial*, 91–92.

21. Ibid., 92. A similar pattern prevailed in 1888. See 92–93. Rev. J.D. Rouse—appointed pastor at Liberty Baptist in 1882 and the son of Adam, a founder of the church and of black Republicanism in the city—was a prominent figure in the campaign. His speeches evoked a familiar refrain: that beneath the surface Democrats still thought of African Americans as "niggers, mokes, or coons."

22. *EDJ*, April 11, 1871; April 6, 1874. On April 3 the paper reported on the Colored Convention, presided over by Carter. Edwin Horn (sometimes spelled Horne) was secretary. See also *EDJ*, Oct. 9, 10, 1874; Bigham, *We Ask Only a Fair Trial*, 92–93.

23. Thornbrough, *Negro in Indiana,* 297–98.

24. *EDJ,* March 13, 1877.

25. *EDJ,* March 14, 19, 1877; *EC,* March 13, 25, 1877.

26. *EDJ,* March 20, 1877.

27. *EDJ,* March 23, 27, 1877.

28. *EDJ,* March 27, 1877.

29. *EDJ,* April 7–9, 1877. The day patrolman was Allston ("Oscar") Shorter, well known for his politeness and good sense as a porter at the city's leading hotel, the Sherwood House. The two night men were Jacob Thompson, a former teacher, and John Miller, a "polite, intelligent young man" who had formerly been porter at a white-owned grocery on First Street. The 1878 election was relatively quiet. In 1878 Democrats again appealed to black voters. Former Republican Bushrod Taylor had a card published in the *Courier* in which he refuted charges of payoffs to him. Democrats took most of the township races and four of the city council seats, and did better in the heavily black First Ward. Taylor and two other men were named to the police force. But blacks also helped elect the district's first German-born congressman, William Heilman, an Evansville industrialist who had been a Republican leader since the 1850s. *EC,* March 31, 1878; Lipin, *Producers, Proletarians, and Politicians,* 162–63.

30. *EDJ,* March 26–28, Aug. 20–22, 1880.

31. *EDJ,* Sept. 12 (quotations here), Oct. 14–16, Nov. 3–9, 1880.

32. *EDJ,* March 21–April 1, Sept. 22, Nov. 9–10, 1882. See also *EDJ,* April 6, 1885. Allston Shorter wrote "An Appeal to Colored People," chiding those blacks who were pledged to the Democratic Party, especially two pastors seen leaving the home of a Democratic city councilman. He asked them what benefits blacks had received in the past three years that Democrats had controlled city government. They had received no work on the streets or otherwise, he insisted. The same theme appears in *EDJ,* Aug. 3, Nov. 5, 1888.

33. Bigham, *We Ask Only a Fair Trial,* 41.

34. *EDJ,* Aug. 9, 1872; Dec. 6, 1875. The column did not appear regularly until the mid-1870s. Horn (or Horne) was an up-and-coming young black man who later got into the newspaper business in Indianapolis. A descendant was the singer Lena Horne.

The first editor of the Democratic "Colored Folks" column was George Washington Buckner, a protégé of John W. Boehne Sr., a staunch Lutheran layman and manufacturer who would dominate the Democratic Party for many years. Buckner's wife was a Fisk University graduate. Their home would become a cultural center for black Evansville and a way station for notable blacks visiting the city. See Bigham, *We Ask Only a Fair Trial,* 94.

35. Thornbrough, *Negro in Indiana,* 302.

36. Ibid., 302–6.

37. Ibid., 307.

38. Ibid., 307–12. It is also worth noting that in 1894 black Republicans, led by a newly arrived attorney, a school teacher, and a longtime loyalist, formed a political club that met with white Republicans after the election and demanded that all of the janitor positions at the courthouse be given to black men in reward for their service. The

appeal fell on deaf ears, and blacks received only one janitorial position and one position at the fire department. Though short-lived, the aggressiveness of this group was
symptomatic of the times and the growing restlessness of black Republicans. See Bigham,
We Ask Only a Fair Trial, 93–94.

39. Bigham, *We Ask Only a Fair Trial,* 94.

40. Quoted in Thornbrough, *Negro in Indiana,* 316. Now seen as being available to
the highest bidder, though, the black voter could not be ignored. The *Evansville Courier*
offered graphic evidence in November 1901 when it stated that 3,100 black voters
resided in the First Congressional District. Of these, well over half (1,800) lived in
Vanderburgh County, and of them, 1,611 resided mostly in the Seventh Ward of Evansville. Vote-buying had become by then the fundamental means by which that part of
the county could be controlled. Democrats were realists, understanding that the black
Republican vote would not disappear through threats of violence. See Bigham, *We Ask
Only a Fair Trial,* 94–96.

41. Bigham, *We Ask Only a Fair Trial,* 96.

42. Arnett, *Proceedings,* 99, 101, 176–86, quotes on 99 and 101. There are 136 pages
in the proceedings. Arnett later became a bishop of his church, a member of the Ohio
legislature, and one of the state's most eminent black men. He spoke at the centennial
celebration in 1903. See Cayton, *Ohio,* 270–72.

43. Trotter, *River Jordan,* 82–83.

44. May, *History of Massac County,* 99–101; Bridges, "Equality Deferred," 97–99.

45. Ibid., 99.

46. Quoted ibid., 99–100.

47. Ibid., 100.

48. Ibid., 101. James Henry MaGee, born in 1839 in Illinois, was educated in Illinois
and Wisconsin. He served as minister and teacher in Ohio, Kentucky, Tennessee, and
Canada before returning to Illinois. In 1885 he was appointed a clerk with the Illinois
Railroad and Warehouse Commission and subsequently held other state government
positions. He died in 1912. See 103.

49. Quoted ibid., 102.

50. Ibid., 104–5, 108, quotes on 104–5.

51. Carlson, "Black Migration to Pulaski County," 44–46. See also Hays, "African-
American Struggle in Cairo," 265–74. Records of elections and appointments are found
in Mound City, Illinois, City Council Minutes, vols. 1 and 2, 1870–1909; and Cairo
City Council Minutes, books G, H, I, O, 1873–1910.

52. Quoted in Gerber, *Black Ohio,* 169. See also Quillen, *Color Line,* 98; Collins,
"Political Behavior," 39–40.

53. Collins, "Political Behavior," 43.

54. Quoted in Gerber, *Black Ohio,* 174.

55. Gerber, *Black Ohio,* 209–10.

56. Ibid., 211–14.

57. Ibid., 214–15. See also Kissen, "Segregation in Cincinnati," 75.

58. Gerber, *Black Ohio,* 215–18.

59. Philip D. Jordan, *Ohio Comes of Age, 1873–1900,* vol. 5, *The History of the State of*

Ohio, ed. Carl F. Wittke (Columbus: Ohio State Archaeological and Historical Society, ca. 1943; repr., 1968), 44–45, 57, 166–68, 172, 194, 199.

60. Gerber, *Black Ohio,* 219–25.

61. Ibid., 225–27. See also Trotter, *River Jordan,* 83–84. Dabney, *Cincinnati's Colored Citizens,* 139, says that the black man was appointed by Democrats who controlled the city just to spite Republicans.

62. For example, an announcement of the formation of a Democratic club at Lime Hall the previous weekend can be found in *Afro-American,* Sept. 19, 1885, http://dbs.ohiohistory.org/africanam/ (January 27, 2000). Jesse Fassett was elected president and Charles Williams secretary. "The roll of membership runs up into the hundreds," declared the *Afro-American. Cleveland Gazette,* May 3, 1884, http://memory.loc.gov (March 31, 2005), African American Experience collection. See also ibid., March 22, May 10, 1884.

63. Quotation in *Cleveland Gazette,* Dec. 19, 1885; Gerber, *Black Ohio,* 228–43. An account of the ending of the "colored schools" can be found in the *Cleveland Gazette* of April 17, 1886; July 2, 1887, http://dbs.ohiohistory.org/africanam/ (January 27, 2000). Clark's dismissal is described in *Cleveland Gazette,* July 7, 1888, http://www.memory.loc.gov (March 31, 2005), African American Experience collection. See ibid., Sept, 3, 1887; Aug. 4, 1888; Dec. 12, 1892; May 5, 1900. In the fall of 1887, for instance, he was hired as principal of the State Normal and Industrial School in Huntsville, Alabama. In 1900 he was living in St. Louis.

64. Wright, *Black Violence,* 21–28.

65. Lucas, *Kentucky Blacks,* 298–99.

66. Ibid., 303.

67. Starling, *Henderson County,* 245; Victor A. Howard, "Negro Politics and the Suffrage Question in Kentucky, 1866–1872," *RKHS* 72 (April 1974): 126–30. Statewide, in 1873 90.2 percent of black men twenty-one and above were considered qualified voters, as compared with 97 percent of whites. Similar percentages were found at the local level. In McCracken County, a significantly larger proportion of whites than blacks who had paid their poll taxes participated in the 1884 election. See Collins, *History of Kentucky,* 1:246; Battle, *Histories and Biographies,* 98.

68. Lucas, *Kentucky Blacks,* 304.

69. Ibid.

70. Wright, *Life behind a Veil,* 170, 176–78.

71. Lucas, *Kentucky Blacks,* 305–7; Howard, "Negro Politics and the Suffrage Question," 132–33; *Louisville Courier-Journal,* July 24, 1877.

72. Lucas, *Kentucky Blacks,* 309–10.

73. Wright, *Life behind a Veil,* 178–79, 181–82. Rev. S.E. South of Owensboro was elected delegate to three consecutive Republican national conventions, 1884–92. See Kentucky Commission on Human Rights, *Kentucky's Black Heritage.*

74. Lucas, *Kentucky Blacks,* 310–11.

75. Wright, *Life behind a Veil,* 176–77, 180.

76. Lucas, *Kentucky Blacks,* 311.

77. Ibid., 311–12.

78. Wright, *Life behind a Veil*, 181–82. See also Trotter, *River Jordan*, 83; Kleber, *Encyclopedia of Louisville*, 547, 567.

79. Wright, *Life behind a Veil*, 181–82.

80. Bigham, *We Ask Only a Fair Trial*, 93. See also Trotter, *River Jordan*, 73–74; May, *History of Massac County*, 99–101.

81. Bigham, *Towns and Villages of the Lower Ohio*, 182, 255.

9. Making a Living

1. See, for example, Nancy Bertaux, "Structural Economic Change and Occupational Decline among Black Workers in Nineteenth-Century Cincinnati," in Taylor, *Race and the City*, 126–28. Also see Ellwein, "Negro in Cincinnati," 30–50.

2. Bertaux, "Economic Change and Occupational Decline," 126–28.

3. Ibid., 130–32. In Cincinnati in 1860, the proportion of nonwhites who worked was 32 percent. In 1890 it was 33 percent. For whites, the percentages were 19 in 1860 and 24 in 1890. See also Thornbrough, *Negro in Indiana*, 347–49; Bigham, *We Ask Only a Fair Trial*, 54, 66; Lipin, *Producers, Proletarians, and Politicians*, 105–6, 201. The first state convention of black men resolved that black youth should be taught trades to become useful members of society. In 1880 Frederick Douglass lamented blacks' exclusion from most respectable lines of work, which led to their crowding the lanes and alleys of cities and living by work that whites would not do. That such work was also occasional, at intervals, exposed them to the "evils of enforced idleness and poverty." Quoted in Thornbrough, *Negro in Indiana*, 349.

4. Trotter, *River Jordan*, 68–69.

5. Thornbrough, *Negro in Indiana*, 349. See also 351, 353–54; Bigham, *We Ask Only a Fair Trial*, 59–60.

6. Thornbrough, *Negro in Indiana*, 355–58; Bigham, *We Ask Only a Fair Trial*, 60, 63. In Evansville there were seven clerks in the 1880s and 1890s. They worked in black-owned businesses.

7. Bigham, *We Ask Only a Fair Trial*, 64, 68; Thornbrough, *Negro in Indiana*, 360–61.

8. Bigham, *We Ask Only a Fair Trial*, 63–64, 74–78, 82–84; Thornbrough, *Negro in Indiana*, 363–66.

9. Gerber, *Black Ohio*, 60, 62, 65–67, 68–69, 76–77, 80–81, 305; Bertaux, "Economic Change and Occupational Decline," 137–38; Bridges, "Equality Deferred," 98–106; Blackmore, "Gallatin County," 180–81. African Americans in several of Illinois's Ohio River counties sustained a small but influential business and professional class. Massac County educator and clergyman James Henry MaGee of Metropolis became one of the state's most eminent black public servants. John J. Bird of Cairo was arguably the most influential black attorney in southern Illinois. His ally was William T. Scott, a saloon-keeper and newspaper publisher. Like their counterparts in Indiana and Ohio, however, nearly all blacks worked in menial positions. Gallatin County was typical. In 1870, 95 percent were enumerated as laborers, farmhands, or servants.

10. Lucas, *Kentucky Blacks*, 268–87. Among other achievements, Fee (1816–1901), an evangelical abolitionist, founded Berea College after the Civil War. See Richard Sears, "John Gregg Fee," in *KE*, 312–13.

11. Howard, *Black Liberation,* 91–98.

12. Ibid., 98–101.

13. Ibid., 105–7.

14. Ninth Census, Population Schedules for Boyd County, 1870, NAMP, M593, roll 448, Kentucky, 3:1–113.

15. Tenth Census, Population Schedules for Boyd County, 1880, NAMP, T9, rolls 403–4, Kentucky, 3:170–286.

16. Ninth Census, Population Schedules for Campbell County, 1870, NAMP, M593, roll 453, Kentucky, 5:123–476; Tenth Census, Population Schedules for Campbell County, 1880, NAMP, T9, rolls 407–8, Kentucky, 5:1–395.

17. Ninth Census, Population Schedules for Kenton County, 1870, roll 478, 18:263–364, 19:1–257.

18. Tenth Census, Population Schedules for Kenton County, 1880, rolls 425–26, 17:216–686.

19. Taylor, *Race and the City,* 3; Dabney, *Cincinnati's Colored Citizens,* 182–85; *Cleveland Gazette,* Aug. 25, 1883, http://dbs.ohiohistory.org/africanam/page.cfm?ID=13950 (May 5, 2003).

20. *Cleveland Gazette,* Sept. 13, 1884, http://dbs.ohiohistory.org/africanam/det.cfm?ID=14328 (May 5, 2003); See also the Dec. 24, 1887, issue, http://memory.loc.gov (March 31, 2005), African American Experience collection; Thornbrough, *Negro in Indiana,* 384–85, 388.

21. *Cleveland Gazette,* Sept. 6, 1890, http://dbs.ohiohistory.org/africanam/page.cfm?ID=16839 (May 5, 2003), and http://dbs.ohiohistory.org/africanam/page.cfm?ID=6388 (May 5, 2003).

22. Ross, *Workers on the Edge,* 6, 72, 74, 212, 256, 262–63.

23. Ibid., 314–15.

24. Ninth Census, Population Schedules for Trimble County, 1870, roll 501, 31:177–240, esp. 177–97, 210, 229–30; Tenth Census, Population Schedules for Trimble County, 1880, roll 443, 27:434–509.

25. Ninth Census, Population Schedules for Jefferson County, 1870, roll 328, 17:194–573, esp. 311–445, for Madison. Tenth Census, Population Schedules for Jefferson County, 1880, rolls 287–88, 17:1–294. The city's most eminent African American was Chapman Harris, 77, a Virginia-born Baptist preacher, who lived with his wife, Patsy, and seven persons aged 20 to 35 who were probably their children. Harris had come to Madison in the 1830s.

26. Wright, *Life behind a Veil,* 43–48.

27. Ibid., 33–34. See also Margaret Merrick, "African American Businesses," in Kleber, *Encyclopedia of Louisville,* 11.

28. Wright, *Life behind a Veil,* 37–38.

29. Ibid., 77–91, quote on 77. See also Yater, *Two Hundred Years,* 109.

30. Wright, *Life behind a Veil,* 96–100; Merrick, "African American Businesses," 11.

31. Wright, *Life behind a Veil,* 79. This discussion of black employment in Louisville is based on Wright, *Life behind a Veil,* 79–100.

32. Ibid., 83.

33. Ibid., 89.

34. Notable newspapers were William H. Steward's *American Baptist* and Henry Fitzbutler's *Ohio Falls Express.*

35. Ibid., 94–97. See also Trotter, *River Jordan,* 81.

36. Lucas, *Kentucky Blacks,* 318–19.

37. Ibid., 101.

38. Ibid.

39. Atchley and Carpenter, *1870 Census, Floyd County Indiana,* 1–483, passim. The federal enumeration schedules are found in NAMP, M593, roll 313, 1–471.

40. Ibid., 7, 199, 429, 483.

41. Thornbrough, *Negro in Indiana,* 225–26. In Indiana, Utica in Clark County and Aurora in Dearborn County forbade black settlement.

42. Robert D. McManaway, comp., *1870 Census of Hancock County, Kentucky* (Utica, KY: McDowell, 1982), 1–68; Claribel Phillips and Dorothy Watkins, comps., *Hancock County Kentucky 1880 Census* (Lewisport, KY: Genealogical Society of Hancock County, 1991), 1–109; Ninth Census, Population Schedules for Perry County, 1870, NAMP, M593, roll 350, Indiana, 30:234–427.

43. McManaway, *1870 Census of Daviess County,* 1–288; Ford, *Daviess County, Kentucky 1880 Census*, 1–571.

44. *Owensboro Messenger and Inquirer,* Sept. 7, 1992.

45. Thornbrough, *Negro in Indiana,* 230.

46. Goodspeed Company, *History of Warrick, Spencer, and Perry Counties, Indiana* (Chicago: Goodspeed Co., 1885; repr., Evansville: Unigraphic, 1973), 293 (page citations are to the 1973 ed.). See also *An Illustrated Historical Atlas of Spencer County, Indiana* (Chicago: D.K. Lake Co., 1879), 4, 10, 13, 41.

47. Ninth Census, Population Schedules for Henderson County, 1870, roll 478, 18:85–222.

48. Ibid., 94, 205, 208.

49. Blue and Hazelwood, *Henderson County, Kentucky, 1880 Census,* 1–220, esp. 84, 95, 99, 103, 111, 112, 120, 125, 217, 219.

50. Ninth Census, Population Schedules for Warrick County, 1870, 40:422–648a. See also Goodspeed, *History of Warrick, Spencer, and Perry Counties.*

51. Bigham, *We Ask Only a Fair Trial,* 22–23; U.S. Bureau of the Census, *Twelfth Census of the United States, Taken in the Year 1900: Census Reports,* vol. 1, *Population,* pt. 1 (Washington, DC: Government Printing Office, 1900), 1:535–36. Significant numbers of farmers lived in northern Union and southern Perry townships. Many of them, including the Lyles family, had lived there before the war and moved elsewhere due to antiblack violence in 1857.

52. Bigham, *We Ask Only a Fair Trial,* 53.

53. Ibid., 53–54, Dreiser quoted on 53.

54. Ibid., 55, 66.

55. Ibid., 54, 63–64.

56. Ibid., 63; *EDJ,* Jan. 25, 1875.

57. Bigham, *We Ask Only a Fair Trial,* 58–60.

58. Lipin, *Producers, Proletarians, and Politicians,* 157, 162–63; Bigham, *We Ask Only a Fair Trial,* 60–61.

59. Ibid., 66–67.

60. Ibid.

61. Peyton Heady, comp., *The Census of the United States in the Year 1870: Union County, Kentucky* (Morganfield, KY: Peyton Heady, 1990); and Heady, *1880 Census of Union County.*

62. Horacek, *Tenth Census of Posey County,* 5–378, passim. See also Blackmore, "Gallatin County," 180–81, 196–97; McGrew, *1880 Census of Gallatin County, Illinois,* 1–309, passim.; Crittenden County Genealogical Society, *The Crittenden County, Kentucky, 1870 Federal Census* (Marion, KY: Crittenden County Genealogical Society, 1996), 1–195; Juanita Walker Drennan, transcriber, *Crittenden County, Kentucky Census of 1880* (Ledbetter, KY: Juanita Walker Drennan, 1992), 1–239. See, for example, Douglas, *Hardin County 1870 Census,* 96–104. Hunt and Drennan, *1870 Census Livingston County,* 3–183, passim. Drennan, *Livingston County 1880 Census,* 1–231, passim. Allen, *1870 Federal Census of Pope County,* 19–170, passim; Rickey T. Allen, transcriber, *1880 Federal Census and Mortality Schedule of Pope County, Illinois* (Evansville: Evansville Bindery, 1996), 1–172, passim.

63. Bigham, *Towns and Villages of the Lower Ohio,* 256. McCracken County's foreign-born population in 1870 was nearly 10 percent, and in 1880 it remained highest among Kentucky counties south of the Falls, though its rate was only about one-fourth that of Evansville in the same year. See also Tenth Census, Population Schedules for McCracken County, 1880, roll 430, 20:76–245. District 123 had 10 artisans: 5 carpenters, 2 plasterers, 2 blacksmiths, 2 coopers, and a brick mason—as well as 5 draymen, 2 ministers, and a saloonkeeper, while District 124 had 2 Baptist ministers, a teacher, and a saloonkeeper. District 126 had 9 draymen or teamsters.

64. J.B. Gardner, comp., *John B. Gaines Paducah City Directory, 1881–1882* (Paducah: Daily Enterprise Steam Print, 1881), 151–57, 209–21; *Olcott and Wilcox Directory, Paducah, Kentucky, 1894–1895* (Paducah: n.p., 1894), 15–19, 206 30.

65. Ninth Census, Population Schedules for Massac County, 1870, roll 255, 38:212–332. See also A. Gilbert Belles, "The Black Press in Illinois," *JISHS* 68 (Sept. 1975): 346. There were two Brooklyns in Illinois at the time. Belles did not distinguish between them. The other was across the river from St. Louis. Hence the reference to the existence of a newspaper in 1880, the *Monitor,* may apply to the Mississippi River village.

66. Bigham, *Towns and Villages of the Lower Ohio,* 255. See also Ninth Census, Population Schedules for Alexander County, 1870, 1–252; and Ninth Census, Population Schedules for Pulaski County, 1870, NAMP, M593, roll 271, Illinois, 47:1–201. By 1900 the proportion of blacks to whites in Pulaski County had risen to about two in five.

67. Bigham, *Towns and Villages of the Lower Ohio,* 254, 257; Ninth Census, Population Schedules for Alexander County, 1870, 1–252; Ninth Census, Population Schedules for Pulaski County, 1870, 1–201; Badgley et al., *Pulaski County Illinois,* 1–244, passim. See esp. 53, 66.

68. Carlson, "Black Migration to Pulaski County," 43–44.

69. Carrier, *Illinois,* 128; Hays, "African-American Struggle in Cairo," 265–69. See also Ninth Census, Population Schedules for Alexander County, 1870, 1–252.

70. Belles, "Black Press in Illinois," 346; Wheeler, "Together in Egypt," 110–11.

71. Hays, "African-American Struggle in Cairo," 270.

72. Ibid., 269–73.

73. Wheeler, "Together in Egypt," 115–21.

74. Mason County Tax Assessors Book, City of Maysville, 1865, books 1–4, microfilm copy, Willard Library Archives, Evansville, IN; Collins, *History of Kentucky,* 1:246; Lucas, *Kentucky Blacks,* 277.

75. Jefferson County Tax List, 1875, books 1–4 and books 1–2 (Southern and Northern Districts), microfilm copy, Willard Library Archives, Evansville, IN. Data for the rural areas are found in books 1–2 for the Southern and Northern Districts. In the Southern District, only 10 men and women owned land. The wealthiest, J. Atchison (book 1, p. 1) owned land worth $4,000. In the Northern District, 25 men and women owned land. The wealthiest 3 had land worth $4,425.

76. Ibid., book 4, pp. 42, 49, 64. Between them, Sidney Page and Marshall Woodson had eight lots valued at nearly $15,000. Also see ibid., book 2, p. 37; book 3, pp. 37, 40. William was the son of Washington Spradling. The others were probably his children as well. Louisa may have been his widow. Louisa also owned four lots in District Two that were valued at $7,300. Lucy Ann Spradling and Willie (William?) Spradling possessed between them eight lots in the vicinity of Eleventh and Walnut streets that were valued at $17,800. William Spradling owned two lots in the First District, on Third between Market and Jefferson and on the northeast corner of Madison and Tenth, valued at $6,200. Ten years later, the city directory identified five Spradlings: Louisa, who resided at 718 Eleventh Street, and four others at 911 West Chestnut Street. William, a barber, lived there, along with his wife and two children. See *Caron's Directory of the City of Louisville* (Louisville: Caron, 1885), 15:719.

77. Breckinridge County Tax List (Commissioners Book), microfilm copy, Willard Library Archives, Evansville, IN. As in other counties, whites and blacks were listed separately, the whites on pp. 1–95, and the blacks on thirteen pages after the whites. See also Hancock County Commissioners Book, 1875, microfilm copy, Willard Library Archives, Evansville, IN. Downstream Crittenden and Ballard counties, thinly populated and rural, were similar. Crittenden had just 97 African Americans on its 1875 tax list, with total assessed property of $9,993. Only 26 owned land (a total of 1,141 acres assessed at $5,755), and most of these lived near Ford's Ferry on the Ohio. The remainder were taxed for their horses, mares, and mules. In 1873 just 7 of the 195 blacks on the Ballard County tax lists owned land: a total of 505 acres, valued at $2,680. Eleven years later, 405 African Americans were entered on the tax list, but most paid no taxes. Some progress was evident, though, as 34 owned land: 2,313 acres assessed at $11,540, or about half of the value of all black-owned property. See Commissioners Book, Crittenden County, 1876, microfilm copy, Willard Library Archives, Evansville, IN. Blacks were listed after page 28, on unpaginated sheets, and also after page 61, in similar form. See also Tax List for Ballard County, 1873; and Tax List for North Ballard County, 1884, microfilm copies, Willard Library Archives, Evansville, IN.

78. See the Henderson County Tax List, 1866, esp. 5, 30, 47, which discloses the huge amount of land owned by former planters like A.B. Barret. See also Assessors Tax Book for Henderson County, 1873, microfilm copy, Willard Library Archives, Evansville, IN, esp. p. 15 of the separate section (pp. 1–38), for blacks.

79. McCracken County Tax List, 1873, microfilm copy, Willard Library Archives, Evansville, IN, pp. 20 and 95; Battle, *Histories and Biographies,* 86–99.

80. Ninth Census, Population Schedules for Boyd County, 1870, 1–113; Ninth Census, Population Schedules for Campbell County, 1870, 123–476; Ninth Census, Population Schedules for Kenton County, 1870, 18:263–364, 19:1–257; Ninth Census, Population Schedules for Trimble County, 1870, 177–240.

81. Heady, *Census of 1870, Union County;* Hunt and Drennan, *1870 Census Livingston County,* 146–47, 166, 177.

82. Ninth Census, Population Schedules for Jefferson County, 1870, 273–361.

83. Atchley and Carpenter, *1870 Census, Floyd County, Indiana,* 7, 185, 289, 335, 386, 391, 410, 429, 483.

84. Ninth Census, Population Schedules for Vanderburgh County, 1870, 89–515a; Bigham, *We Ask Only a Fair Trial,* 68. The number of property owners and the value of their property are slightly different from those provided in my book *We Ask Only a Fair Trial* and reflect a recounting of the population schedules. Joseph Mosely, a Mississippi-born carpenter, and Harmon Cook, an Ohio-born porter, each had real estate valued at $2,500. A widow, Sina McDaniel, had $2,000 in realty, as did Melrose Smith, a laborer. One of those with property worth at least $1,000 was Adam Rouse, forty-two, who was a foreman in a tobacco factory.

85. Bigham, *We Ask Only a Fair Trial,* 68–69.

86. Ninth Census, Population Schedules for Alexander County, 1870, 1–252.

87. Ninth Census, Population Schedules for Pulaski County, 1870, 1–201; and Blackmore, "Gallatin County," 184, 198, 204, 291–304. The pattern in the other Illinois counties resembled that of rural Pulaski County. In Pope County, most families had crossed the river and settled sometime after 1863. Few household heads owned their land, but there were a few exceptions in New Liberty Township, downstream from Golconda. The wealthiest resident there was John Avery, a mulatto age 40 and a native of Virginia, who owned realty worth $4,000 and personal property valued at $1,500. His wife, 38, was a native of Kentucky. They had two children. The family had evidently been living in Pope County since the early to middle 1850s. Some farmers in rural Massac County owned their land. All told, 13 household heads had realty valued at approximately $6,000, an average of $462. About 25 had personal property worth a total of $4,000. In Metropolis, 13 of the 46 heads of household owned realty valued at a combined $3,250, and 6 had personal property worth a total of $950. See Allen, *1870 Federal Census of Pope County,* 168; Ninth Census, Population Schedules for Massac County, 1870, 213–337.

88. Censuses of 1880 and 1890, at *U.S. Census Browser.*

89. George W. Williams, *Centennial: The American Negro from 1776–1876; Oration Delivered at Avondale, Ohio, 1876* (Cincinnati: Robert Clarke and Co., Printers, 1876), 38. See also Franklin, *From Slavery to Freedom,* 291–92, who describes Will-

iams as the first African American scholar whose work was taken seriously by white historians.

10. Families and Community Life

1. Lucas, *Kentucky Blacks*, 325.

2. Of all of the state and community historians of African Americans in the Ohio Valley, only Lucas and I (in *We Ask Only a Fair Trial*) discuss this subject. Lucas devotes a few pages to the topic, focusing on immediate postwar adjustments, and does not do anything with the topic after 1870. Such notable historians as Emma Lou Thornbrough and George Wright do not even mention it. One significant study by a sociologist is Paul J. Lammermeier, "The Urban Black Family of the Nineteenth Century: A Study of Black Family Structure in the Ohio Valley, 1850–1880," *Journal of Marriage and the Family* 35 (August 1973): 440–56. This study does not include any towns downriver from Louisville.

3. Gutman, *Black Family*, 389–431.

4. Ibid., 373–78, 380–82.

5. Quoted ibid., 382–83.

6. Quoted ibid., 384–85.

7. Ibid., 385–86.

8. Lucas, *Kentucky Blacks*, 205–7.

9. Ibid., 207. Unfortunately, Lucas does not explore local and census records to provide examples or a sense of the scale of this phenomenon.

10. Ibid., 207–9. Lucas's discussion of this subject ends here.

11. Wathena Kennedy Miller, comp., *Meade County Marriage Records*, vol. 2, *1824–1884 Marriages* (Vine Grove, KY: Ancestral Trails Historical Society, 1988), 119; Shirley C. Moody, comp., *Marriages in Henderson County, Kentucky, 1858–1900*, vol. 2 (Evansville, IN: n.p., 1990). Perhaps Moody overlooked the special 1866 register for slaves or did not record the race of the couples. Brenda Joyce Jerome, comp., *Crittenden County Marriages* (Newburgh, IN: n.p., 1991), 2:174–75.

12. Jerome, *Crittenden County Marriages*, 2:8–170. Blacks' marriages were not entered in a separate section.

13. Joyce McCandless Woodyard, comp., *Livingston County, Kentucky Marriage Records Including Marriages of Freedmen*, vol. 2, *August 1839–December 1871* (Smithland, KY: By the author, 1994), 185–91.

14. Darrel E. Bigham, "The Black Family in Evansville and Vanderburgh County in 1880," *Indiana Magazine of History* 75 (June 1979): 144. Such inferences are based on the ages and the birthplaces of children.

15. Ninth Census, Population Schedules for Massac County, 1870, 213–75.

16. Ninth Census, Population Schedules for Alexander County, 1870, 1–74, 160–73. Two families had children born elsewhere, and one had only Illinois-born children. In rural Goose Island Precinct, blacks headed 25 households. Of those with children, most (6) included youngsters born elsewhere as well as in Illinois, suggesting migration to Alexander County after 1865.

17. Unfortunately, the records of Adams County, across the river from Appalachian

Lewis County, Kentucky, do not identify persons by race. Clermont County Historical Society, *Clermont County Marriages, 1850–1874* (Batavia, OH: Clermont County Historical Society, 1989), 2–574.

18. Ruth M. Slevin, comp., *Ohio County Marriages,* book 1, *1844–1881* (n.p., 1970), 2–45; Indiana Works Progress Administration, comp., *Index to Marriage Records, Spencer County, Indiana, 1850–1920,* vols. 1–4 (Rockport, [IN?]: Indiana W.P.A., 1940). The first marriage is entered in 1:97.

19. Opal B. Phillips and J. Oscar Phillips, comps., *Marriage Book III of Warrick County, Indiana: July 1860–September 1867* (n.p., n.d.), 3:33. See also Opal B. Phillips, comp., *Marriage Book 4, Warrick County, Indiana: September 1867–May 1873* (n.p., 1965); *Warrick County, Indiana: Marriage Book 5, May 1873–March 1879, and Marriage Book 6, March 1879–January 1880* (n.p., n.d.). See also Indiana Works Progress Administration, comp., *Index to Supplemental Record, Marriage Transcript, Warrick County, Indiana 1880–1906* (Boonville, [IN?]: Indiana W.P.A., 1940), 1:6–232.

20. Indiana Works Progress Administration, comp., *Index of Marriage Records Vanderburgh County 1840–1920,* vols. 1–7 (Evansville: Indiana W.P.A., 1939). The entries noted in the text are found in 1:276; 3:77; 4:9, 252; 5:71, 203; 6:170. See, by contrast, Indiana State Board of Health, *Second Annual Report . . . 1883* (Indianapolis: State Board of Health, 1884), 280, 285, which reported that in Vanderburgh County during the year ending September 30, 1883, there were 45 black and 388 white marriages. This source provides no information on individuals.

21. Indiana Works Progress Administration, *Index to Posey County Marriages, Supplement,* Volumes I-II ([Mount Vernon, IN?]: Indiana W.P.A., 1940); Eloise Hughes and Michele Peters, comps., *Posey County, Indiana Marriage Returns, Dec. 1884–January 1914,* vols. 1–4 (n.p., 1978). See, for instance, 1:96, 108, 201, 235, 261, 349. See also *Posey County Indiana Marriage Affidavits 1868–1876* (n.p., n.d.).

22. Betty Head, transcriber, *Gallatin County Illinois Marriages, 1867–1887* (Harrisburg, IL: Saline County Genealogical Society, 1995). See book B, 1–23; book C, 1–31. In seventeen marriages just one person was identified by the letter *C*. Whether that was a transcription error or an indication of racially mixed marriage is unclear.

23. Carolyn Cromeenes Foss and Judy Foreman Lee, comps., *Pope County Illinois Marriage Books A–E, 1843–1877* (n.p., 1990), 1:24–132. Marriage records of Massac County are also uneven in terms of racial identification, which was not included before 1878, when twenty-two black marriages were recorded. Those records were detailed, giving the age, place of birth, and occupation of man and wife. Most men were farmers. Like their Posey County counterparts, officials identified race idiosyncratically: they used not only the terms *black* and *mulatto* (sometimes entered as *malatta*), but also *brown, yaller, red, dark, light,* and *African.* William Renfro, "brown" and a laborer, a native of Massac County, married Amanda Morris, "yaler" and a native of Tennessee. He was twenty and she twenty-three. In sixteen cases both man and wife were natives of Kentucky or other former slave states. Twenty-three unions occurred the following year and seventeen in 1880. About half of the marriages in 1879–80 involved persons who were natives of Kentucky. Foss and Lee, *Massac County Marriage Register A-I* (n.p., 1991), 2:1–35.

24. Bigham, "Black Family," 124; Lammermeier, "Urban Black Family," 447, 451, 453.

25. Bigham, "Black Family," 128, 137–41; Lammermeier, "Urban Black Family," 447, 451, 453.

26. Ninth Census, Population Schedules for Boyd County, 1870, 3:1–113; Tenth Census, Population Schedules for Boyd County, 1880, 3:170–286. Unfortunately, a number of the pages of the microfilm copy are illegible. In 1880, 83 of the 92 black households in the county had male heads and two parents. Seventy-four families were nuclear, 7 extended, and 11 augmented. Ashland had proportionately more families with boarders and lodgers (one in four) than those in other parts of the county.

27. Bigham, "Black Family," 134.

28. Ninth Census, Population Schedules for Kenton County, 1870, 18:263–364, 19:1–257; Tenth Census, Population Schedules for Kenton County, 1880, 17:216–686. Average family size remained smaller in Covington: 4.5 persons, as compared with 5.3 in rural areas. Ninety of Covington's 301 black households had female heads, as compared with just 5 of the rural 92. Covington's households were far more likely to be extended and augmented than those in adjoining rural areas. Thirty-two contained boarders and lodgers as well as in some cases relatives, and another 25 had relatives other than the immediate family. Abral Broan, age 50, shoveled coal for a living. He had been out of work six months. His wife was 39. His household comprised a total of eleven people: a daughter, two other couples and their children, and two boarders who were laborers. Of the 44 black heads of household in that ward, 25 were common laborers. Sixteen were women, only 6 of whom had an occupation—washerwomen or servants.

29. Ninth Census, Population Schedules for Trimble County, 1870, 31:177–240; Tenth Census, Population Schedules for Trimble County, 1880, 27:434–509.

30. Ninth Census, Population Schedules for Jefferson County, 1870, 17:194–573; Tenth Census, Population Schedules for Jefferson County, 1880, 1–294. In the first postwar census, 56 of the 60 rural households in Floyd County had male heads and two parents. In New Albany, where the largest part of the blacks in the county dwelled, about 40 of the 213 households were extended or augmented or both. Thirty-four, moreover, had female heads. Rozana Common, who lived in Ward 3 and was 55, was identified as keeping house. The son of this mulatto native of Kentucky, Cicero, 22, was a steamboat hand. Daughters Jane and Mary, in their middle to late twenties, were washerwomen. The household also included Lettice, 4, born in Kentucky, and William, 2, born in Indiana. Perhaps these children belonged to one of Rozana's offspring. Ninth Census, Population Schedules for Floyd County, 1870, 141–437a.

31. Ninth Census, Population Schedules for Hancock County, 1870, NAMP, M593, roll 466, Kentucky, 12:1–239; Tenth Census, Population Schedules for Hancock County, 1880, NAMP, T9, roll 417, Kentucky, 11:1–525. In 1880, males headed 135 of 146 black households. As before, most female-headed families were in or near Hawesville. Approximately 27 households, or 18 percent of the total, included relatives or boarders and lodgers. Seven of these were located in Hawesville and 12 in the nearby Hawesville Precinct. In Perry County, only 3 of the 47 enumerated in 1870 resided in white

homes: 2 as domestics in Cannelton and 1 as a farm laborer near Rome, on the Ohio. Few blacks resided in the country. Most lived in the town of Cannelton and a handful in the Swiss-German town of Tell City. In Cannelton, the nine black families averaged four persons in size. Two had female heads—the only ones in Perry County. One was a domestic and the other was a washerwoman. Five households in the county included relatives or boarders. All were located in Cannelton or Tell City. Probably the most well-off was the family of Thomas Smith, 59, who was a servant. The Kentucky native lived next door to Hamilton Smith, president of the American Coal Company, with his wife, 30 (probably his second), and his 17-year-old daughter. Patterns were little changed in the decade that followed. Ninth Census, Population Schedules for Perry County, 1870, 30:234–427; Tenth Census, Population Schedules for Perry County, 1880, NAMP, T9, roll 309, Indiana, 27:1–569.

32. Ninth Census, Population Schedules for Daviess County, 1870, NAMP, M593, Roll 458, Kentucky, Volume 8: 1–371.

33. Tenth Census, Population Schedules for Daviess County, 1880, NAMP, T9, roll 411, Kentucky, 7:151–652. Cross-river Spencer County, like Perry County, differed in its low proportion of blacks living in white households.

34. Ninth Census, Population Schedules for Warrick County, 1870, 40:422–648a.

35. Ninth Census, Population Schedules for Henderson County, 1870, roll 469, 14:1–242a.

36. Ibid.

37. Ibid.

38. Tenth Census, Population Schedules for Henderson County, 1880, 12:271–679.

39. Ninth Census, Population Schedules for Vanderburgh County, 38:89–515; Tenth Census, Population Schedules for Vanderburgh County, 1880, 35:88–542.

40. Ibid.

41. Bigham, We Ask Only a Fair Trial, 66, 71–73; "Black Family Life," 140.

42. Ninth Census, Population Schedules for Vanderburgh County, 1870, 38:89–515.

43. Tenth Census, Population Schedules for Vanderburgh County, 1880, 35:88–542.

44. Ibid.

45. Ninth Census, Population Schedules for Union County, 1870, NAMP, M593, roll 501, Kentucky, 31:1–422; and Tenth Census, Population Schedules for Union County, 1880, NAMP, T9, roll 444, Kentucky, 27:510–701.

46. Ilse Horacek, comp., Tenth Census of Posey County, 15–378. See esp. 77. Valerie Phillips Gilderhaus, comp., 1870 Gallatin County Illinois United States Census (Utica, KY: McDowell, 1991), 1–183. See also McGrew, 1880 Census Gallatin County Illinois, 1–309. The examples are found on 72–73, 239, and 257.

47. Drennan, Livingston County 1880 Census, 1–231. The examples are found on 4. See also 1880 Federal Census and Mortality Schedule of Pope County, Illinois (Evansville, IN: Evansville Bindery, 1996), 1–185.

48. Tenth Census, Population Schedules for McCracken County, 1880, 20:76–245. By contrast, cross-river Massac County was in 1870 a predominantly rural place, and its county seat, Metropolis, had a population of just slightly more than 2,100. Countywide,

the 153 households headed by blacks averaged 5.5 persons each; in Metropolis, they averaged 4.9. Massac County looked a lot like Gallatin and Posey counties. Just 19 blacks in the county resided in white households. Metropolis had most of the families headed by women, although 6 of 7 households were male-headed and nuclear. Slightly over one in four families were augmented or extended. In rural parts of the county, 95 percent of households had male heads, and slightly over 80 percent were nuclear. A representative family in Metropolis was that of Charles Tinsley, 39, who was a spoke factory hand. His wife, Angeline, was 30. Both were Kentuckians. They had children ranging in age from 12 to five months, the youngest of whom had been born in Illinois. It is likely that the Tinsleys moved to Metropolis in the latter part of the 1860s. Metropolis also included such households as that of Nicholas Norrington, 24 and a Tennessean, and his wife, Bell, 23. The family also included Albert Grace, 27, a brickyard hand, and Mary Grace, 17, possibly his wife; Francis Grace, 23, also a brickyard hand, and Pink Grace, 19, possibly his wife; and a child named Mary Grace. See Ninth Census, Population Schedules for Massac County, 1870, 38:212–337a. The census of 1880 revealed few changes. The chief difference was an increase of well over 75 percent in the black population of Massac County and a significant growth in the number of blacks living in Metropolis, which now accounted for 32 percent of the county's black population. Ninety-seven percent of the county's black population resided in households that blacks headed. Tenth Census, Population Schedules for Massac County, 1880, 41:1–110b.

49. Ninth Census, Population Schedules for Pulaski County, 1870, 1–201; Badgley et al., *Pulaski County Illinois,* 1–246. In 1880 nine in ten of the county's 611 black families were male-headed and nuclear. Most of the 71 female-headed families resided in Mound City, Ohio, and Villa Ridge precincts. Even there, however, well over three in four households were male-headed. If one excludes these three precincts, almost all families in Pulaski County were male-headed and contained two parents. Mound City had the largest number of extended or augmented families. The countywide proportion was two in ten. All but 43 household heads and their spouses enumerated in 1880 had been born in slave states.

50. Ibid., 1, 3, 41, 52, 152. The census-taker had great difficulty deciding racial identification. In a number of instances, where at least one parent was defined as a mulatto, children were variously identified as mulatto, black, and sometimes white.

51. Ninth Census, Population Schedules for Alexander County, 1870, 1–252.

11. Black Society

1. Jack S. Blocker Jr., "Building Networks: Cooperation and Communication among African Americans in the Urban Midwest, 1860–1910," *Indiana Magazine of History* 94 (Dec. 2003): 370–86, provides insight into the way in which African American churches, fraternal and benevolent societies, and other organizations in towns and cities on the north shore developed ties that strengthened racial identity and progress.

2. Cheaney, "Black Press and Pulpit," 338–64.

3. Ibid.

4. William E. Montgomery, "Preachers," in *Religion in American History: A Reader,* ed. Jon Butler and Harry S. Stout (New York: Oxford Univ. Press, 1998), 304.

5. Quoted in Bigham, *We Ask Only a Fair Trial,* 76.

6. Ibid., 74–77; *EDJ,* May 15, 1865; Jan. 15, July 8, 1866; Aug. 15, 1867; June 26, 1868; May 3, 1873.

7. Cheaney, "Black Press and Pulpit," 210–11; Trotter, *River Jordan,* 78–80; Thornbrough, *Negro in Indiana,* 368–75; Bigham, *We Ask Only a Fair Trial,* 73–78. Thornbrough notes that the African Methodist Episcopal Church had fifty-one congregations and 4,435 members in Indiana in 1890. As with the Baptists, the second-largest church was in Evansville—Alexander Chapel. The origin of McFarland Baptist Church is described in *EDJ,* Oct. 21, 1882.

8. Wright, *Life behind a Veil,* 127.

9. *Funeral services in respect to the Memory of Rev. William Paul Quinn, late Senior Bishop* . . . (Toledo: Warren Chapel, 1873), 1–52, http://memory.loc.gov (March 31, 2005), African American Experience collection. *EDJ,* Aug. 23–28, 1872; Aug. 26–Sept. 1, 1880. The news accounts of the thirty-third annual state conference, of August 1872, provided reports on annual income of congregations. Bethel in Indianapolis and the Muncie church were tops, with about $3,500. Evansville placed in the top half, with slightly more than $1,600. Near the bottom were the Mount Vernon and Madison churches, each of which raised less than $300. James M. Townsend, formerly of Evansville, was a major presence in each conference. The AME Church in Evansville dedicated the cornerstone of its new edifice in June 1874 and dedicated the new structure itself in July 1879. See *EDJ,* June 11, 1874; July 7, 1879. The AME Zion denomination had churches in Evansville and Jeffersonville. See Thornbrough, *Negro in Indiana,* 369–74.

10. Montgomery, "Preachers," 301–2. Most clergymen fell somewhere between the illiterate country preacher and the college- and seminary-trained clerics. See also Gerber, *Black Ohio,* 150.

11. Bigham, *We Ask Only a Fair Trial,* 77–78; *EDJ,* June 11, 1874; July 7, 1879. See also *Proceedings of the Semi-Centenary Celebration of the African Methodist Episcopal Church of Cincinnati, Held in Allen Temple, February 8th, 9th, and 10th, 1874 . . . ,* ed. Rev. B. W. Arnett (Cincinnati: H. Watkin, Printer, 1874), 55–131, http://memory.loc.gov (March 31, 2005), African American Experience collection. See also *EDJ,* March 9–11, 1870; Nov. 30, 1872.

12. No reference to any black institutions is included, for example, in White, *Evansville Men. History of the Falls Cities,* though, contains some discussion of black schools (1:336, 342, 414). This matter is discussed at length in chapter 6, above. The first history of Methodism in Indiana is virtually silent about black groups as well. When the Indiana Conference was organized at New Albany in 1832, there were 182 colored members (and almost 20,000 whites). See Fernandez C. Holliday, *Indiana Methodism . . . to 1872* (Cincinnati: Hitchcock and Walden, 1872), 75, http://www.hti.umich.edu/m/moagrp (March 31, 2005).

13. See, for instance, Goodspeed, *History of Warrick, Spencer, and Perry Counties,* 721–29. No black churches are listed for Perry County.

14. Gerber, *Black Ohio,* 152–53. Also see Ellwein, "Negro in Cincinnati," 87–132.

15. *Proceedings of the Semi-Centenary,* 1–4, 117. The AME Church was organized

February 4, 1824, by Rev. Moses Freeman at "Father King's House." Gerber, *Black Ohio,* 142–57, indicates that there was one Roman Catholic congregation in Ohio, in Cincinnati. The date and nature of its organization are not provided, but they are undoubtedly similar to what is known of Louisville's. In 1860 there were five black churches in Cincinnati: the AME, two Baptist, one Disciples, and one Methodist Episcopal North. Most were located between Little Bucktown on the west end and the higher-status residential areas on the northwest fringe of the river basin. These were small congregations with comfortable, small, unadorned buildings. AME membership grew from 227 to 325 between 1865 and 1870 and to 2,000 by 1900. Baptist membership grew fastest. As to dates of creation, see *Proceedings of the Semi-Centenary,* 55–62. Brown's Chapel was formed by Allen Temple members in 1862. Union Chapel ME was organized in 1815. The old Deer Creek Church, it was apparently still affiliated with the white Methodists. Union Baptist Church was formed in 1835 and moved to its present site in 1863. Zion Baptist was organized in 1845 by dissident members of Union and was known from the outset as the "Anti-Slavery Baptists." Plum Street Baptist was created as a mission church in July 1867 in Hell's Half Acre. Dates of the founding of Cumminsville Baptist and Walnut Hills Baptist were not provided, but Mount Zion Baptist—created by dissenting members of Zion—was founded in 1873. Cumminsville Baptist; Plum Street Baptist, on Plum near Front; Walnut Hills, on Willow Street; and the Christian Church (Disciples), on Harrison Street east of Broadway had between 40 and 80 members each.

16. Alexander, the oldest Methodist church, was named for pastor J.H. Alexander about 1876. See Bigham, *We Ask Only a Fair Trial* 74.

17. Ibid., 74–77.

18. *EDJ,* Sept. 15, 1868. A separate parish was organized around 1940.

19. Perrin, *History of Alexander, Union, and Pulaski Counties,* 572, 585. See also Hays, "African American Struggle in Cairo," 278–82. Ricks and Thomas Strother were the most influential black pastors in Cairo. See also Wheeler, "Together in Egypt," 118–21.

20. May, *History of Massac County,* 123–25.

21. Lucas, *Kentucky Blacks,* 210–11.

22. Ibid., 212.

23. Ibid., 213–14.

24. Ibid., 217–19.

25. Ibid., 214–17, 219; Wright, *Life behind a Veil,* 127–29. Wright states that the school was renamed after the establishment of the law and medical schools. The school operated during 1890–91 without a president, but secured the services of Rev. J.H. Garrett, an Oberlin graduate and the holder of a B.D. degree from the Baptist seminary in Chicago, in 1891. He strengthened State University's faculty and increased the number and quality of its students.

26. Lucas, *Kentucky Blacks,* 221.

27. Wright, *Life behind a Veil,* 36–37, 129, quote on 130; Lucas, *Kentucky Blacks:* 219–20, 223–24; Kleber, *Encyclopedia of Louisville,* 287–88, 358, 615.

28. Lucas, *Kentucky Blacks,* 224.

29. Kleber, *Encyclopedia of Louisville,* 137; Wright, *Life behind a Veil,* 129.

30. Lucas, *Kentucky Blacks,* 225.

31. Ibid., 225–26.

32. Ibid., 226. See also Dunnigan, *Black Kentuckians,* 133–38; Kleber, *Encyclopedia of Louisville,* 287, 358, 615.

33. Quotes in Lucas, *Kentucky Blacks,* 226, 228; Wright, *Life behind a Veil,* 130.

34. Dunnigan, *Black Kentuckians,* 141; Kleber, *Encyclopedia of Louisville,* 775.

35. Thornbrough, *Negro in Indiana,* 373–75; Du Bois and Cox quotes in Bigham, *We Ask Only a Fair Trial,* 76.

36. Gerber, *Black Ohio,* 152–55.

37. Lucas, *Kentucky Blacks,* 219–20; Wright, *Life behind a Veil,* 126.

38. Quotes in Lucas, *Kentucky Blacks,* 220; Bigham, *We Ask Only a Fair Trial,* 74.

39. Bigham, *We Ask Only a Fair Trial,* 42–43.

40. Gerber, *Black Ohio,* 156–57.

41. Ibid., 157.

42. Lucas, *Kentucky Blacks,* 221–22; Wright, *Life behind a Veil,* 39.

43. *EDJ,* Aug. 28, 1872; *Proceedings of the Semi-Centenary,* 9–29. Biographical sketches of church members follow his comments.

44. *Proceedings of the Semi-Centenary,* 40–41.

45. Ibid., 76.

46. Lucas, *Kentucky Blacks,* 222. For examples of fund-raising events in Evansville, see *EDJ,* Feb. 2, 3, June 7–9, Sept. 17, 1869.

47. *EDJ,* June 8, 1869, Oct. 2–5, 1869. For use of the "Colored Column," see, for example, *EDJ,* Jan. 7–8, Feb. 3, June 7–8, Aug. 17, 1869; May 7, 1870; Sept. 1, 1876.

48. Wright, *Life behind a Veil,* 129–31.

49. Eleanor Bardes and Mary Remler, comps., *Hamilton County, Ohio Burial Records,* vol. 9, *Union Baptist African American Cemetery* (Bowie, MD: Heritage Books, 1997), v, 1–36.

50. Hays, "African American Struggle in Cairo," 273. See also 274–83. The actions of Strother and Ricks are described in chapter 12. Lucas, *Kentucky Blacks,* 222, 224–25; Bridges, "Equality Deferred," 101–6; Bigham, *We Ask Only a Fair Trial,* 78, 97. See also Kleber, *Encyclopedia of Louisville,* 287–88, 358; Lucas, *Kentucky Blacks,* 228.

51. Thornbrough, *Negro in Indiana,* 375.

52. Gerber, *Black Ohio,* 158–65. By 1887 there were 2,615 Masons in Ohio. See also *Proceedings of the Semi-Centenary,* 117–32.

53. *Proceedings of the Semi-Centenary,* 125, 129–31. Records of the purchase of land for the cemetery were found in book 128, p. 374, of the Hamilton County recorder.

54. *Proceedings of the Semi-Centenary,* 119–20. See also U.S. Bureau of the Census, *Tenth Census, 1880, Report of the Social Statistics of Cities,* pt. 2, *Southern and Western States* (Washington, DC: Government Printing Office, 1887), 369.

55. Lucas, *Kentucky Blacks,* 314. Wright, *Life behind a Veil,* 139–55, provides the most detailed account of benevolent and fraternal societies in Louisville and allocates more space to the topic than Lucas does for the entire state. See Lucas, *Kentucky Blacks,* 313–25. Also note Trotter, *River Jordan,* 80. Prisoners were integrated in the state penitentiary. The chief distinctions were twofold: blacks in prison represented more than half

of the prison population, well above their percentage of the state's population; and when convict leasing began, as a means of easing overcrowding, at least 60 percent of those leased were black.

56. Lucas, *Kentucky Blacks,* 314–15.

57. Ibid., 315–16.

58. Ibid., 316–17. Wright, *Life behind a Veil,* 155, argues that whites' financial assistance may have been predicated on the notion that providing separate social services minimized blacks' pressuring whites for access to their social agencies.

59. Lucas, *Kentucky Blacks,* 317–18.

60. Bigham, *We Ask Only a Fair Trial,* 49.

61. Lucas, *Kentucky Blacks,* 322.

62. Ibid., 322–23.

63. Ibid., 323–24.

64. The scarcity of newspaper references and the unevenness of record-keeping in other communities also makes for a much slimmer list.

65. *History of Daviess County* (1883 ed.), 400–401. Henderson had a number of fraternal and benevolent organizations, but records, unfortunately, are sketchy. The oldest was St. John's Masonic Lodge, established in September 1866. A lodge of the UBF was formed in October 1871, and a second one was created about ten years later. Canterbury Lodge number 1642 of the Odd Fellows was organized in 1875. Following these were an organization for women—the Pledies [*sic*] Chamber—as well as Lincoln Lodge number 1, a unit of the Sons and Daughters of Zion formed in 1887, and a black post of the Grand Army of the Republic, established about the same time. Paducah's blacks had four fraternal societies by 1881: two Masons, one Odd Fellows, and the other the Knights of Wise Men. The Masons had a hall on Broadway, between Market and Main streets, and the Odd Fellows had one on the corner of Court and Market streets. The "Worshipful Masters" of these were William Watts, an express wagon driver, and William Hawkins, who worked at Langstaff, Orm and Company's saw and planing mill. A decade later, the number of Masonic and Odd Fellows lodges had expanded to four and six, respectively. The city also had a lodge of the UBF, and a black post of the GAR had been formed in 1888. In addition, it had three women's societies, a "colored juvenile society," and a Union Benefit Society. See Starling, *Henderson County,* 502; *Henderson Directory for 1899* (Evansville: American Directory, 1899[?]), 8–10; Gardner, *John B. Gaines Paducah City Directory, 1881–1882,* 105–6, 148, 200; *Olcott and Wilcox Directory, Paducah 1894–1895,* 13–15.

66. Thornbrough, *Negro in Indiana,* 375–79.

67. *History of the Falls Cities,* 2:164.

68. Bigham, *We Ask Only a Fair Trial,* 78. See also *EDJ,* Feb. 2–3, Sept. 23, 1869; Jan. 4, 1870. The Mutual Aid Society was active through at least September 1876, when Robert Nicholas was its leader. See *EDJ,* Sept. 1, 1876.

69. Bigham, *We Ask Only a Fair Trial,* 78–79.

70. Quoted in ibid., 79.

71. Ibid.

72. Ibid., 79–80.

73. Ibid., 80; *EDJ*, July 5, 1876.

74. Wright, *Life behind a Veil,* 139. See also *EDJ,* Aug. 14, 1869; Aug. 2, 1872; Lucas, *Kentucky Blacks,* 287–90.

75. Kusmer, *Ghetto Takes Shape,* 98.

76. See, for example, Gerber, *Black Ohio,* 100–103, 150.

77. Bigham, *We Ask Only a Fair Trial,* 81. Epitomizing the Evansville elite was Lucy Wilson McFarland, hired as a teacher in the public schools in 1870 and named six years later as principal of the Clark Street School, a position she held until 1897. She married W. Riley McFarland, a stock-keeper. At the time of her death in 1900, she possessed property worth $7,000. She was a member of the auxiliaries of five fraternal orders and state grand matron of the Order of the Eastern Star. She was praised after her death as "one of the most publicly spirited and highly useful women of which the state of Indiana can boast." Thousands paid respects at her funeral. She was described as one "whose life, character and services they deemed worthy of earnest emulation and whose death they deeply mourned" (84).

78. Ibid.; Wright, *Life behind a Veil,* 135.

79. Wright, *Life behind a Veil,* 135–37.

80. Bigham, *We Ask Only a Fair Trial,* 84–85.

81. Ibid., 85–86.

82. Lucas, *Kentucky Blacks,* 325.

12. Schools for Blacks

1. U.S. Bureau of the Census, *Compendium of the Tenth Census (June 1, 1880)* (Washington, DC: Government Printing Office, 1883), 2:1645, 1650–51.

2. Blackmore, "Gallatin County," 244–46.

3. McCaul, *Black Struggle for Public Schooling,* 108–26. See also Charlotte Mason Maine, *The Policy of the Segregation of the Negro in the Public Schools of Ohio, Indiana, and Illinois* (Chicago, 1917).

4. Quoted in Cheaney, "Indiana Pulpit and Press," 238, 252, quote on 238.

5. Quoted in Thornbrough, *Negro in Indiana,* 323.

6. Ibid.

7. Ibid., 324–25.

8. Ibid., 325–34. In 1870, when the state's black population was 24,560, about one in eight attended school. Ten years later, 7,970 in a total black population of 39,228 were attending. See also Cheaney, "Indiana Pulpit and Press," 238–46.

9. Thornbrough, *Negro in Indiana,* 336–37.

10. Ibid., 337–40.

11. Ibid., 340–43; Bigham, *We Ask Only a Fair Trial,* 43–44.

12. Matthews, "John Isom Gaines," 41–48.

13. Gerber, *Black Ohio,* 191–92.

14. Ibid., 192.

15. *Cleveland Gazette,* Nov. 14, 1885; Quillen, *Color Line,* 89–93.

16. Quoted in Kissen, "Segregation in Cincinnati," 121, 122, Parham and Clark quoted on 121.

17. Ibid., 123–24. Kissen describes this period of transition to de facto segregation as one of benign neglect of blacks' education.

18. Ibid., 124–28.

19. Ibid., 128–31.

20. Ibid., 132–33.

21. Ibid., 133–34. Arnett, according to Dabney's *Cincinnati's Colored Citizens,* was the first black legislator elected in a majority white district and the first black foreman of a jury whose other members were white. See 134n22. See also Quillen, *Color Line,* 93.

22. Kissen, "Segregation in Cincinnati," 134–35. Frederick A. McGinnis, *The Education of Negroes in Ohio* (Blanchester, OH: Curless Printing, 1962), 64, declares that this response from black parents reflected the inertia and social weakness of the black community.

23. Gerber, *Black Ohio,* 192–206. See also Nicholas, "Educational Development," ix–x, 63–64. Quillen, *Color Line,* 92–93, states that the state legislature in 1887 repealed the 1853 law and its 1857 amendment on the grounds of expediency. The same legislature also voided the 1861 antimiscegenation law. See also *Cleveland Gazette,* June 25, July 2, 1887, http://memory.loc.gov (March 31, 2005), African American Experience collection.

24. Kissen, "Segregation in Cincinnati," 135–37.

25. Ibid., 137–42.

26. Trotter, *River Jordan,* 86–88. See also Wright, *Life behind a Veil,* 66–69.

27. Lucas, *Kentucky Blacks,* 230.

28. Ibid., 230–32; Howard, *Black Liberation,* 160–69. See also Wright, *Life behind a Veil,* 28–30, 34–36.

29. James D. Anderson, *The Education of Blacks in the South, 1860–1935* (Chapel Hill: Univ. of North Carolina Press, 1988), 13; Harrison and Klotter, *New History,* 237–39; Wright, *Life behind a Veil,* 36; Lucas, *Kentucky Blacks,* 232–34. Blacks' contributions in Kentucky were highest among all southern states except Louisiana.

30. Lucas, *Kentucky Blacks,* 234–36.

31. Wright, *Life behind a Veil,* 35–36. Lucas, *Kentucky Blacks,* 231, estimates that the two major Northern missionary societies contributed a little over $12,000 yearly for the entire state.

32. Lucas, *Kentucky Blacks,* 239, 246, quote on 239.

33. Ibid., 241–44.

34. Ibid., 244–45. See also *History of the Falls Cities,* 1:41, which states that the gathering occurred on July 14, 1869.

35. Lucas, *Kentucky Blacks,* 246.

36. Walker, *Compendium of the Ninth Census,* 468–69.

37. Quoted in Wright, *Life behind a Veil,* 70.

38. Lucas, *Kentucky Blacks,* 246.

39. "Horace Morris," in Kleber, *Encyclopedia of Louisville,* 626–27. Morris was born in Louisville, the son of a Virginia slave, Sheldon Morris, who had moved to Louisville in 1828 after being manumitted. The elder Morris set up a barbershop, ran a bathhouse,

and speculated in real estate. The younger Morris was also a prominent businessman who was active in Republican affairs after the war. He was cashier of the Louisville branch of the Freedmen's Savings Bank, one of the strongest branches in the nation. He helped to found the Colored Orphans' Home in 1878. The first African American to be a steward at the Louisville Marine Hospital, he was active in the Masons and at Quinn Chapel. He launched several ill-fated newspapers.

40. Lucas, *Kentucky Blacks,* 246–47. Eastern's new building was located at the corner of Jackson and Breckinridge, and Western's was on Magazine, between Fifteenth and Sixteenth streets. The address of the new school in Portland was not provided by Lucas.

41. Ibid., 247–48. See also Wright, *Life behind a Veil,* 66.

42. Lucas, *Kentucky Blacks,* 248, 250. Berea Literary Institute, opened by John Fee to all, regardless of race, in the fall of 1865, provided training for a number of teachers who became the backbone of the early black schools. Many studied there for a few months and then taught for the rest of the year to pay school expenses. See 254.

43. Harrison and Klotter, *New History,* 380. See also Lucas, *Kentucky Blacks,* 254–55. See also Ward M. McAfee, *Religion, Race, and Reconstruction: The Public School in the Politics of the 1870s* (Albany: State Univ. of New York Press, 1998), 154–55.

44. Quote in McAfee, *Religion, Race, and Reconstruction,* 103; Lucas, *Kentucky Blacks,* 255–57; Wright, *Life behind a Veil,* 68.

45. Lucas, *Kentucky Blacks,* 257. See also McAfee, *Religion, Race, and Reconstruction,* 155.

46. Lucas, *Kentucky Blacks,* 257–58.

47. *History of the Falls Cities,* 1:414.

48. Wright, *Life behind a Veil,* 68.

49. Ibid., 69.

50. Lucas, *Kentucky Blacks,* 259–61; Howard, *Black Liberation,* 177–79. In addition to leading the drive for equalization, the teachers' association was a major player in the struggle for the creation of a normal school to train black teachers. The school, named the Frankfort Normal School, was created by the legislature in 1886 and opened in the fall of 1887. John H. Jackson became its first president. Students did not have to pay tuition, but they had to agree to teach in the public schools for two years for every year they attended the normal school. One of the by-products of this requirement was the establishment of a variety of teacher enrichment programs, notably institutes for teachers. See Lucas, *Kentucky Blacks,* 262–63.

51. Lucas, *Kentucky Blacks,* 261; Howard, *Black Liberation,* 172–76; Harrison and Klotter, *New History,* 380. The latter work devotes only two pages to the topic of education for Kentucky blacks between 1865 and 1908. See also Wright, *Life behind a Veil,* 66.

52. Lucas, *Kentucky Blacks,* 261–62; Howard, *Black Liberation,* 175–76; "African American Education," in Kleber, *Encyclopedia of Louisville,* 13. The errata section of the *Paducah City Directory* for 1881–82 (no page listed) identified Charles Brooks as the only teacher in the colored school, located at the northwest corner of Tennessee and Poplar streets. In the section on public and private schools (p. 105), there were no listings of black schools. None were listed in the 1894–95 directory, either.

53. Lucas, *Kentucky Blacks,* 256–57.

54. Ibid., 263–64; Wright, *Life behind a Veil,* 139.

55. Wright, *Life behind a Veil,* 139.

56. Lucas, *Kentucky Blacks,* 264–65.

57. Ibid., 266; *History of Daviess County,* 367; "African-American Education," 12–13.

58. Lucas, *Kentucky Blacks,* 267; Crittenden County Historical Society, *History of Crittenden County Schools, 1842–1987* (Utica, KY: Crittenden County Historical Society, 1987), 8, 13, 96, 97. This history does not make it clear whether twenty-four dollars was the amount paid to white or black teachers.

59. Rev. J.R. Slattery, "Facts and Suggestions about the Colored People," *Catholic World* 41 (April 1885): 36; quotes in Lucas, *Kentucky Blacks,* 267; and Wright, *Life behind a Veil,* 70.

60. *History of Clermont County,* 167.

61. Kissen, "Segregation in Cincinnati," 103, 120 (quote on 103); Walker, *Compendium of the Ninth Census,* 464–66; Dabney, *Cincinnati's Colored Citizens,* 29 (May 19, 1866), 2, in http://dbs.ohiohistory.org/africanam (January 27, 2000). Clark signed the article as P.H.C.

62. Kissen, "Segregation in Cincinnati," 107–8.

63. Ibid., 109–10. The Northern Colony School was closed in 1871 and its pupils transferred to an already crowded Western District School. This step was necessary, stated Parham, because the Pleasant Street neighborhood of the Northern Colony School was insalubrious. Samuel W. Clark, principal at Court Street, taught until 1890. Active in the True American Masonic Lodge in Cincinnati, he was elected to a high office in the Ohio Colored Masons. He was also a business partner in the coal supply business.

64. Ibid., 111–16.

65. Ibid., 119.

66. *Proceedings of the Semi-Centenary,* 62–68. Clark was paid $2,220, and four male teachers at Gaines received between $1,200 and $1,500. The two female teachers received $540 and $720. After this portion of the proceedings came Clark's address, which linked educational and material progress to the AME Church, an organization that demonstrated "more fully than any other institution among the colored people of this country" the ability of black people "to organize and manage successfully enterprises of great dimensions." The existence of that church "is a protest against prejudice and an assertion of the equal humanity of the African race, and there is a necessity for it to continue until that prejudice is dead, and that equality acknowledged" (102). See also Kissen, "Segregation in Cincinnati," 89, who indicates that school trustees' policy was to hire male principals whenever possible. There were a total of 23 teachers in the five schools. The 11 who were women were paid considerably less than the men.

67. *Proceedings of the Semi-Centenary,* 104–5. The proceedings contrasted sharply with the "white" history of the city that appeared the following year. All the latter included on black schools was a statement that there were four district and two intermediate schools and one high school in Cincinnati. The district schools enrolled slightly more than 1,000 pupils, while the intermediate and high schools had 70. See Kenny, *Illustrated Cincinnati,* 76.

68. Kissen, "Segregation in Cincinnati," 65–76.

69. Quoted ibid., 90, 93.

70. Ibid., 108–9. In 1891 Parham returned to politics, and was elected to the Ohio House in 1896. He wrote a history of the Masons in Ohio. A school opened in 1970 was named for him.

71. *History of Dearborn, Ohio, and Switzerland Counties,* 274–81, 324–26, 382–89. *History of the Falls Cities,* 2:176–77, 443–44, 509. See also Bigham, "Black Family," 140.

72. "Prospectus, Indiana Historical Marker Program, Division Street School" (Sept. 19, 2003), 5–7, Indiana Historical Bureau, Indianapolis. The sources cited include Carl Arthur Zimmerman, "A History of the School City of New Albany" (master's thesis, Indiana Univ., 1932); and New Albany city directories, 1870–85.

73. *Warrick, Spencer, and Perry Counties,* 398–418; Adams, *History of Warrick County*; Fortune, *Warrick and Its Prominent People*; *Warrick, Spencer, and Perry Counties,* 118–21.

74. Quoted in Bigham, *We Ask Only a Fair Trial,* 40–42, quote on 40.

75. *EDJ,* June 13, Dec. 2, 1865. See also Bigham, *We Ask Only a Fair Trial,* 40–41.

76. *EDJ,* June 30, 1866.

77. *EDJ,* June 29, 1867.

78. Bigham, *We Ask Only a Fair Trial,* 41–42. See also *EDJ,* June 4, 6, 27, 1868.

79. See, for example, *EDJ,* May 12, 1870.

80. Minutes of the Evansville City Council, Sept. 4, 1866; Jan. 3, Aug. 15, 1867; Sept. 22, 1868, Willard Library Archives, Evansville. See also Bigham, *We Ask Only a Fair Trial,* 42.

81. Bigham, *We Ask Only a Fair Trial,* 42.

82. *EDJ,* June 29, Aug. 11, 16, 25, 31, 1869.

83. *EDJ,* Sept. 2, Oct. 12, Nov. 4, 1869; Feb. 8–10, April 28, May 12, 1870; March 1, 1876. The lower school apparently succeeded the AMA school of the 1850s. It was initially housed in an old firehouse on Locust Street, between Seventh and Eighth, before a suitable structure could be erected on Clark Street. It was opened November 4, 1869. Little is known about its dimensions and features, except that it was a one-room school that could accommodate eighty students. It was fitted in a "comfortable style," reported the Republican paper.

84. *EDJ,* Jan. 25, 1875; quote in *EDJ,* Jan. 15, 1875. Much of what Horn wrote—especially about the quality of music—was unflattering. He moved to Indianapolis by the early 1880s.

85. Bigham, *We Ask Only a Fair Trial,* 42, 46. See also *EDJ,* June 10–13, 1870; June 15, 1882.

86. Bigham, *We Ask Only a Fair Trial,* 43–44, quote on 43. As of 1897 Evansville's black schools enrolled 172 students from rural Vanderburgh County.

87. Ibid., 44.

88. Ibid., 45.

89. *EDJ and EC,* Sept. 4–12, 1877.

90. *EDJ,* Sept. 4, 1877.

91. Ibid. Following the report of the exchange, the paper printed the relevant portions of the March 7, 1877, law.

92. *EDJ,* Sept. 5, 1877.

93. *EDJ,* Sept. 6, 7, 1877.

94. *EDJ,* Sept. 8, 1877; *EC,* Sept. 5, 1877. As noted earlier, the Indianapolis High School was integrated in 1879.

95. *EC,* Sept. 6, 1877.

96. Ibid.

97. *EC,* Sept. 9, 11, 1877.

98. *EC,* Sept. 11, 1877. See also *EDJ,* Sept. 11–12, 1877. One writer suggested that the whole issue could have been avoided by giving blacks a more thorough examination, which they could not have passed. The *Journal* editor responded that that was not the problem, as the same exam was provided blacks and whites. If anything, the exam was too easy for both, he added.

99. Bigham, *We Ask Only a Fair Trial,* 43–44. See *EDJ,* Oct. 1, 1879, for an account of troubles in Princeton relating to the same issue. The school trustees enraged citizens by abolishing separate schools. The county school superintendent backed the people and stood in the door to bar entry of a black student, saying he did not like to be near blacks because they smelled bad. The issue was resolved in court. Princeton adopted fully segregated schools, including the high school.

100. Bigham, *We Ask Only a Fair Trial,* 46, 48, 128. John R. Blackburn Jr., a graduate of Dartmouth College, and R.L. Yancey, a Fisk University graduate, were principals between 1897, when the school moved to Clark Street, and 1913, when the school was renamed Frederick Douglass. William E. Best, a graduate of Indiana State Normal College and the holder of a master's degree from Indiana University, was principal from 1913 until well after World War II. Best was a lay leader in the AME Church and a founder of the Evansville chapter of the NAACP in 1915. See also *EDJ,* Sept. 30, 1873, which disclosed that three Evansville black men had been admitted to the state normal school in Terre Haute.

101. Goodspeed, *History of Posey County,* 271–73.

102. Blackmore, "Gallatin County," 209–27. Unfortunately, Blackmore provides Gallatin County school attendance data only as a percentage of the entire population.

103. Ibid., 216–21.

104. Carlson, "Black Migration to Pulaski County," 39; Perrin, *History of Alexander, Union, and Pulaski Counties,* 194. This paragraph and the ones that follow regarding Cairo's early black schools are taken from Hays, "African American Struggle in Cairo," 278–82.

105. Ibid.

106. Ibid., 282–83. Compare the reaction of the first white historian of Cairo, as noted in chapter 6. See also Wheeler, "Together in Egypt," 124–28. This incident soured relations between white and black Republicans and helped accelerate white Republicans' abandonment of black voters.

107. Federal Census Data, 1890, at *U.S. Census Browser.* In Scioto County, Ohio, for instance, there were about 47 black pupils per teacher, as compared with 45 whites. Across the river in Boyd County, Kentucky, the ratios were 68 for blacks and 67 for whites. Henderson County, Kentucky, had 48 black and 46 white students per teacher,

as compared with 46 black and 37 white in cross-river Vanderburgh County. It was not uncommon for black schools in Kentucky to have from 50 to 60 students per teacher.
108. Ibid.

Epilogue

1. George C. Wright, *A History of Blacks in Kentucky,* vol. 2, *In Pursuit of Equality, 1890–1980* (Frankfort: Kentucky Historical Society, 1992), 58–59.

2. See, for example, John David Smith, ed., *When Did Southern Segregation Begin?* (Boston: Bedford / St. Martin's, 2002), 6. See also Raymond Gavins, "Literature on Jim Crow," *OAH Magazine of History* 18 (Jan. 2004): 13–14. Woodward argued fifty years ago that segregation was a product of political battles in the 1890s. Others have asserted it was an extension of antebellum racial customs. Still others insist segregation created a society that included blacks, but on a separate basis. Wheeler, in "Together in Egypt," 105, asserts that all three theories can be supported in the history of Cairo, depending on the phase of the city's history one is describing: before 1910; from 1910 to 1930; and after 1930.

3. Smith, *When Did Southern Segregation Begin,* 5.

4. David W. Blight, *Race and Reunion: The Civil War in American Memory* (Cambridge: Belknap Press of Harvard Univ., 2001), 397.

5. Quoted in Smith, *When Did Southern Segregation Begin,* 7.

6. Otto H. Olsen, quoted ibid., 11.

7. Smith, *When Did Southern Segregation Begin,* 20–21. See also "*Buchanan v. Warley,*" in Kleber, *Encyclopedia of Louisville,* 139. The Court "held that the ordinance denied members of both races the right to own and dispose of property as they saw fit and thus violated the due-process clause of the Constitution as well as the Civil Rights Act of 1866." Unlike the decision in *Plessey v. Ferguson,* this ruling reflected the Court's position that the ordinance "imposed absolute limitations on the disposal of property and thus amounted to an unconstitutional taking." The case could thus be seen as "one of the first judicial steps away from Jim Crow."

8. Smith, *When Did Southern Segregation Begin,* 24. For a discussion of the thesis of C. Vann Woodward, that segregation was a creature of the 1890s, see ibid., 34–35.

9. Leon Litwack, *Trouble in Mind: Black Southerners in the Age of Jim Crow* (New York: Alfred A. Knopf, 1998), 229, 237.

10. Edward L. Ayers, *The Promise of the New South: Life after Reconstruction* (New York: Oxford Univ. Press, 1992), 156, 157.

11. Wright, *Racial Violence,* 1–18, 73, 307–73. His table on 73 shows that 149 lynchings after 1865 occurred in the Jackson Purchase or western Kentucky. In addition to lynchings, 229 persons—131 of them black—were legally executed between 1872 and 1939. Two-fifths of the executions happened in Ohio River counties. The most salacious was the public hanging of Rainey Bethea in Owensboro on August 14, 1936, an event witnessed by a carnival-like crowd of twenty thousand. Bethea had been charged with rape, as fifty other black men were after 1872. See ibid., 227–30, 257–68, 325–31.

12. Bigham, *Towns and Villages of the Lower Ohio,* 234–35. See also Wheeler, "Together in Egypt," 105.

13. Trotter, *River Jordan,* 66, 97; Kusmer, *Ghetto Takes Shape,* 10, 283.

14. Bigham, *We Ask Only a Fair Trial,* 22, 103–9, 114–16, 124. See also Clifton J. Phillips, *Indiana in Transition: The Emergence of an Industrial Commonwealth, 1880–1920* (Indianapolis: Indiana Historical Bureau and Indiana Historical Society, 1968), 370; Thornbrough, *Negro in Indiana,* 230.

15. Wright, *History of Blacks in Kentucky,* 2:1–2; Bigham, *We Ask Only a Fair Trial,* 108; Bigham, *Towns and Villages of the Lower Ohio,* 254–55.

16. Censuses of 1890 and 1900, at *U.S. Census Browser.* Typical of the rural counties that experienced continued decline were Boone (Kentucky), Ohio (Indiana), Gallatin (Illinois), and Clermont (Ohio).

17. Bigham, *Towns and Villages of the Lower Ohio,* 254–59. Also see, for example, the *Chattanooga Daily Times,* Jan. 29, 1901, which described "anti-Negro crusades" in Indiana's river towns that were designed to drive out shiftless blacks.

18. Federal Census of 1900, at *U.S. Census Browser.* Illiteracy rates were also high in the entire black population. The percentage in Illinois's Ohio River counties, for instance, ranged from 51 in Massac County to 72 in Pulaski. Among Indiana's counties below the Falls of the Ohio, Vanderburgh County's rate was the highest, 54.7 percent. See U.S. Bureau of the Census, *Twelfth Census of the United States, Taken in the Year 1900,* vol. 2, *Population,* pt. 2 (Washington, DC: Government Printing Office, 1901), 440–48, 473–76. The percentage of blacks among all illiterates was higher in Kentucky, because the commonwealth had a much lower number of foreign-born residents.

19. Trotter, *River Jordan,* 86–88.

20. Ibid., 89; Bigham, *We Ask Only a Fair Trial,* 172.

21. Trotter, *River Jordan,* 89.

22. Ibid., 90.

23. Bigham, *We Ask Only a Fair Trial,* 133–35.

24. Trotter, *River Jordan,* 90–91.

25. Ibid., 91–92; Bigham, *We Ask Only a Fair Trial,* 123, 126, 139, 147, 149, 176, 186, 187, 188, 219, 223, 224, 231.

26. See, for instance, Joe William Trotter Jr., *The Great Migration in Historical Perspective: New Dimensions of Race, Class, and Gender* (Bloomington: Indiana Univ. Press, 1991).

27. Trotter, *River Jordan,* 95–98, 99–101; Bigham, *We Ask Only a Fair Trial,* esp. 155–61. The occupational index is explained on 161n13. The higher the number, the greater the number of persons occupied in low-level positions.

28. Trotter, *River Jordan,* 103.

29. Bigham, *We Ask Only a Fair Trial,* 125. See also Wright, *Life behind a Veil,* 274–80; Trotter, *River Jordan,* 103–4.

30. Trotter, *River Jordan,* 105–6; Bigham, *We Ask Only a Fair Trial,* 209–11.

31. Taylor, "Introduction: Race and the City," in Taylor, *Race and the City,* 8. See also Trotter, *River Jordan,* 106, 108–9.

32. Bigham, *We Ask Only a Fair Trial,* 32, 113–18.

33. Trotter, *River Jordan,* 106–7.

34. Ibid. See also Bigham, *We Ask Only a Fair Trial,* 219.

35. Trotter, *River Jordan,* 109–11; Wright, *Life behind a Veil,* 199–206.

36. Wright, *Life behind a Veil*, 206–12, 212–20, 229–45. See also Bigham, *We Ask Only a Fair Trial*, 219–21.

37. Bigham, *We Ask Only a Fair Trial*, 165.

38. Trotter, *River Jordan*, 111–12.

39. Ibid., 114–15. In Evansville, prominent blacks—principal William Best and Sallie Stewart, among others—petitioned Democratic mayor Benjamin Bosse, who had been elected in 1913 with the aid of black voters, to prevent the showing of the film. The mayor created a committee of whites to view the film, and they found it inoffensive. A reporter for the progressive Scripps newspaper, the *Evansville Press*, viewed it and in a front page story revealed how virulently racist it was. The Evansville chapter of the NAACP became moribund thereafter. See Bigham, *We Ask Only a Fair Trial*, 121, 219–33.

40. Trotter, *River Jordan*, 115–16. See also Wright, *Life behind a Veil*, 229–45; Bigham, *We Ask Only a Fair Trial*, 121, 221–22.

41. Wright, *Life behind a Veil*, 250–53.

42. Trotter, *River Jordan*, 116–17.

43. Bigham, *We Ask Only a Fair Trial*, 194–214.

44. Wheeler, "Together in Egypt," 122–27.

45. Lansden, *History of Cairo*, 60, 146. See also Wheeler, "Together in Egypt," 125–28.

46. Hays, "African-American Struggle in Cairo," 273–77.

47. Trotter, *River Jordan*, 117–18, quote on 117; Bigham, *We Ask Only a Fair Trial*, 123, 126, 188.

48. Trotter, *River Jordan*, 118–20.

49. Quoted in Bigham, *Towns and Villages of the Lower Ohio*, 175, 177.

50. Wright, *History of Blacks in Kentucky*, 2:6–19.

51. Ibid., 2:54. See also 54–58, 102–3, 106–7; and Robertson, *Paducah*, 129.

52. Wright, *History of Blacks in Kentucky*, 2:107.

53. Ibid., 2:107–8.

54. Ibid., 2:109–11.

55. Ibid., 2:115. See also Frieda Dannheiser, *The History of Henderson County, Kentucky* (Henderson, KY: Henderson County Historical and Genealogical Society, 1980), 245–47.

56. Wright, *History of Blacks in Kentucky*, 2:133–34. Funding problems forced Simmons University to sharply curtail its offerings in the late 1920s. The University of Louisville opened a black junior college, Louisville Municipal College, in 1931. It was closed when the university was desegregated in 1951.

57. Wright, *Life behind a Veil*, 254–57; and Wright, *History of Blacks in Kentucky*, 2:37–42; Trotter, *River Jordan*, 104–5.

58. Bigham, *Towns and Villages of the Lower Ohio*, 235.

59. Bigham, *We Ask Only a Fair Trial*, 222–23; Wright, *History of Blacks in Kentucky*, 2:130, 196–97. The Louisville newspaper, like its Evansville counterparts, began publishing stories in the 1950s designed to provide positive images of black residents. The appellation *Negro* was commonly used instead of *colored*—or worse.

60. Lucas, *Kentucky Blacks*, 327.

Index

DATE DUE

JAN 24 2007		
APR 23 REC'D		